Abbreviated reference:

I.C.J. Pleadings, Legality of the Threat or Use of Nuclear Weapons, Vol. I

Référence abrégée :

C.I.J. Mémoires, Licéité de la menace ou de l'emploi d'armes nucléaires, vol. I

ISSN 0074-4433
ISBN 978-92-1-003845-4

Sales number
N° de vente : 1184

LEGALITY OF THE THREAT OR USE
OF NUCLEAR WEAPONS

LICÉITÉ DE LA MENACE OU DE L'EMPLOI
D'ARMES NUCLÉAIRES

INTERNATIONAL COURT OF JUSTICE

PLEADINGS, ORAL ARGUMENTS, DOCUMENTS

LEGALITY OF THE THREAT OR USE OF NUCLEAR WEAPONS

VOLUME I

COUR INTERNATIONALE DE JUSTICE

MÉMOIRES, PLAIDOIRIES ET DOCUMENTS

LICÉITÉ DE LA MENACE OU DE L'EMPLOI D'ARMES NUCLÉAIRES

VOLUME I

IMPRIMÉ EN FRANCE
PRINTED IN FRANCE

This case, entered on the Court's General List under number 95, was the subject of an Advisory Opinion delivered on 8 July 1996 (*Legality of the Threat or Use of Nuclear Weapons, Advisory Opinion, I.C.J. Reports 1996*, p. 226).

The documents relating to the case are being published in the following order:

Volume I. Request for Advisory Opinion; Written Proceedings.
Volume II. Oral Statements.

*

For the purpose of this edition, the written pleadings have been reproduced in full: the pleadings themselves in hard copy and the other documents in electronic format.

The running heads of the documents reproduced in hard copy contain two sets of page numbers: in addition to the usual continuous pagination, the original pagination of the scanned pleadings appears in brackets; readers should refer to the page numbers in brackets to follow up any references in the body of the text.

The CD-ROM containing the annexes can be found in a sleeve at the end of the paper volume.

The Hague, 2020.

La présente affaire, inscrite au rôle général de la Cour sous le numéro 95, a fait l'objet d'un avis consultatif donné le 8 juillet 1996 (*Licéité de la menace ou de l'emploi d'armes nucléaires, C.I.J. Recueil 1996*, p. 226).

Les documents relatifs à cette affaire sont publiés dans l'ordre suivant :

Volume I. Requête pour avis consultatif ; procédure écrite.
Volume II. Exposés oraux.

*

Aux fins de la présente édition, les pièces de procédure écrite sont reproduites intégralement, en version papier pour la pièce elle-même et en version électronique pour les autres documents.

Les titres courants des documents reproduits en version papier comportent deux genres de folios : outre la pagination continue habituelle, on trouve, entre crochets, la pagination d'origine des pièces scannées, à laquelle il faut se référer en cas de renvoi.

Le CD-ROM des annexes est placé dans une pochette à la fin du volume papier.

La Haye, 2020.

SUMMARY – SOMMAIRE

I. Request for Advisory Opinion 1
Requête pour avis consultatif

II. Written Proceedings 9
Procédure écrite

REQUEST FOR ADVISORY OPINION

REQUÊTE POUR AVIS CONSULTATIF

INTERNATIONAL COURT OF JUSTICE

REQUEST

FOR ADVISORY OPINION

transmitted to the Court under the United Nations General Assembly resolution 49/75 K of 15 December 1994

LEGALITY OF THE THREAT OR USE OF NUCLEAR WEAPONS

COUR INTERNATIONALE DE JUSTICE

REQUÊTE

POUR AVIS CONSULTATIF

transmise à la Cour en vertu de la résolution 49/75 K de l'Assemblée générale des Nations Unies du 15 décembre 1994

LICÉITÉ DE LA MENACE OU DE L'EMPLOI D'ARMES NUCLÉAIRES

1994
General List
No. 95

I. THE SECRETARY-GENERAL OF THE UNITED NATIONS TO THE PRESIDENT OF THE INTERNATIONAL COURT OF JUSTICE

19 December 1994.

I have the honour to inform you that at its 90th meeting held on 15 December 1994, under its agenda item 62 entitled "General and Complete Disarmament: Report of the First Committee" (A/49/699), the General Assembly adopted resolution 49/75 K, "Request for an Advisory Opinion from the International Court of Justice on the Legality of the Threat or Use of Nuclear Weapons". The text of the resolution is attached.

In this resolution, the General Assembly decided, pursuant to Article 96, paragraph 1, of the Charter of the United Nations:

> "to request the International Court of Justice urgently to render its advisory opinion on the following question: 'Is the threat or use of nuclear weapons in any circumstance permitted under international law?'"

Pursuant to Article 65, paragraph 2, of the Statute of the International Court of Justice, the Secretariat is now in the process of preparing a dossier containing "all documents likely to throw light upon the question", which will be transmitted to the Court as soon as possible.

(Signed) Boutros BOUTROS-GHALI.

II. RESOLUTION 49/75 K ADOPTED BY THE GENERAL ASSEMBLY AT ITS 90TH PLENARY MEETING ON 15 DECEMBER 1994

Request for an Advisory Opinion from the International Court of Justice on the Legality of the Threat or Use of Nuclear Weapons

The General Assembly,

Conscious that the continuing existence and development of nuclear weapons pose serious risks to humanity,

Mindful that States have an obligation under the Charter of the United Nations to refrain from the threat or use of force against the territorial integrity or political independence of any State,

Recalling its resolutions 1653 (XVI) of 24 November 1961, 33/71 B of 14 December 1978, 34/83 G of 11 December 1979, 35/152 D of 12 December 1980, 36/92 I of 9 December 1981, 45/59 B of 4 December 1990 and 46/37 D of 6 December 1991, in which it declared that the use of nuclear weapons would be a violation of the Charter and a crime against humanity,

Welcoming the progress made on the prohibition and elimination of weapons of mass destruction, including the Convention on the Prohibition of the Development, Production and Stockpiling of Bacteriological (Biological) and Toxin Weapons and on Their Destruction [1] and the Convention on the Prohibition of the Development, Production, Stockpiling and Use of Chemical Weapons and on Their Destruction [2],

Convinced that the complete elimination of nuclear weapons is the only guarantee against the threat of nuclear war,

Noting the concerns expressed in the Fourth Review Conference of the Parties to the Treaty on the Non-Proliferation of Nuclear Weapons that insufficient progress had been made towards the complete elimination of nuclear weapons at the earliest possible time,

Recalling that, convinced of the need to strengthen the rule of law in international relations, it has declared the period 1990-1999 the United Nations Decade of International Law [3],

Noting that Article 96, paragraph 1, of the Charter empowers the General Assembly to request the International Court of Justice to give an advisory opinion on any legal question,

---

[1] Resolution 2826 (XXVI), annex.

[2] See *Official Records of the General Assembly, Forty-seventh Session, Supplement No. 27* (A/47/27), appendix I.

[3] Resolution 44/23.

Recalling the recommendation of the Secretary-General, made in his report entitled "An Agenda for Peace" [1], that United Nations organs that are authorized to take advantage of the advisory competence of the International Court of Justice turn to the Court more frequently for such opinions,

Welcoming resolution 46/40 of 14 May 1993 of the Assembly of the World Health Organization, in which the organization requested the International Court of Justice to give an advisory opinion on whether the use of nuclear weapons by a State in war or other armed conflict would be a breach of its obligations under international law, including the Constitution of the World Health Organization,

Decides, pursuant to Article 96, paragraph 1, of the Charter of the United Nations, to request the International Court of Justice urgently to render its advisory opinion on the following question: "Is the threat or use of nuclear weapons in any circumstance permitted under international law?".

---

[1] A/47/277-S/24111.

WRITTEN PROCEEDINGS

PROCÉDURE ÉCRITE

CONTENTS

Written Comments of the Government of Egypt 13

Letter dated 18 May from the Permanent Representative of the Democratic People's Republic of Korea to the United Nations 50

Letter dated 13 June 1995 from the Ambassador of Finland, together with Written Statement of the Government of Finland 52

Letter dated 14 June 1995 from Minister at the Embassy of Japan, together with Written Statement of the Government of Japan 56

Letter dated 15 June 1995 from the Permanent Representative of Samoa to the United Nations, together with Written Statement of the Government of Samoa 61

Letter dated 15 June 1995 from counsel appointed by Nauru, together with Written Statement of the Government of Nauru 70

Letter dated 15 June 1995 from Counsel Appointed by Nauru, together with Written Comments of the Government of Nauru 117

Letter dated 16 June 1995 from the Minister for Foreign Affairs a.i. of the Netherlands, together with Written Statement of the Government of the Netherlands 142

Letter dated 16 June 1995 from the Secretary of the Department of Foreign Affairs of Ireland, together with Written Statement of the Government of Ireland 157

Letter dated 16 June 1995 from the Legal Adviser to the Foreign and Commonwealth Office of the United Kingdom of Great Britain and Northern Ireland, together with Written Comments of the United Kingdom 162

Letter dated 16 June 1995 from the Minister for Foreign Affairs of Bosnia and Herzegovina 244

Letter dated 19 June 1995 from the Minister for Foreign Affairs of San Marino 246

Note Verbale dated 19 June 1995 from the Embassy of the Islamic Republic of Iran, together with Written Statement of the Government of the Islamic Republic of Iran 248

Note Verbale dated 19 June 1995 from the Embassy of Malaysia, together with Written Statement of the Government of Malaysia 256

Letter dated 19 June 1995 from the Permanent Representative of Solomon Islands to the United Nations, together with Written Statement of the Government of Solomon Islands 279

Note Verbale dated 19 June 1995 from the Embassy of Italy, together with Written Statement of the Government of Italy 392

Note Verbale dated 19 June 1995 from the Embassy of Mexico, together with Written Statement of the Government of Mexico 399

Letter dated 19 June 1995 from the Ambassador of the Russian Federation, together with Written Comments of the Government of the Russian Federation 418

Note Verbale dated 19 June 1995 from the Permanent Mission of the Burundi to the United Nations 440

Note Verbale dated 20 June 1995 from the Embassy of Sweden, together with Written Statement of the Government of Sweden 442

Note Verbale dated 20 June 1995 from the Embassy of New Zealand, together with Written Statement of the Government of New Zealand 450

Letter dated 20 June 1995 from the Ambassador of India, together with Written Statement of the Government of India 476

Letter dated 20 June 1995 from the Acting Legal Adviser to the Department of State, together with Written Statement of the Government of the United States of America 485

Letter dated 20 June 1995 from the Minister of Foreign Affairs of the French Republic, together with Written Statement of the Government of the French Republic 537

Letter dated 20 June 1995 from the Ambassador of the Federal Republic of Germany, together with Written Statement of the Government of the Federal Republic of Germany 597

Letter dated 20 June 1995 from the Permanent Representative of Lesotho to the United Nations 605

Letter dated 20 June 1995 from the General Director for Multilateral Organizations at the Ministry of Foreign Affairs of Ecuador 607

Communication dated 20 June 1995 from the Ambassador of Egypt, together with Written Statement of the Government of Egypt 611

Letter dated 20 June 1995 from the Ambassador of Qatar, together with Written Statement of the Government of Qatar 634

Letter dated 22 June 1995 from the Permanent Representative of the Marshall Islands to the United Nations, together with Written Statement of the Government of the Marshall Islands 640

Written Comments of the Government of the Solomon Islands 646

WRITTEN COMMENTS
OF THE GOVERNMENT OF EGYPT

LEGALITY OF THE THREAT OR USE OF NUCLEAR WEAPONS

(REQUEST FOR ADVISORY OPINION)

ORDER OF 1 FEBRUARY 1995

WRITTEN COMMENTS OF EGYPT
ON OTHER WRITTEN STATEMENTS
(ARTICLE 66, PARAGRAPH 4, OF THE STATUTE)

September 1995

Table of Contents

INTRODUCTION

I. Should the Court Render its Advisory Opinion on the Present Question?

Arguments against the Court rendering an opinion

1. The abstract character of the question
2. The allegedly political nature of the question
3. Would an advisory opinion on the question put to the Court serve any useful legal purpose?
4. Would an advisory opinion on the question put to the Court have a nefarious effect on the ongoing disarmament efforts?

II. Is there a General Prohibition on the Threat or Use of Nuclear Weapons in General International Law?

III. The Threat or Use of Nuclear Weapons Violates the Laws of Armed Conflict

1. The obligation to distinguish in all circumstances between civilian populations and objects and military personnel and objectives
2. The prohibition against the use of weapons which cause unnecessary suffering
3. The prohibition against causing widespread, long-term and severe damage to the environment, and the obligation not to prejudice the health or survival of the population

IV. The Threat or Use of Nuclear Weapons is Contrary to Numerous other Principles and Rules on Contemporary International Law

A. The International Law of Human Rights

1. The right to life
2. The right to enjoy the highest attainable standard of physical and mental health

B. The prohibition of genocide and crimes against humanity:

C. The International Law of Environment

D. Use of nuclear weapons violates the neutrality and the territorial sovereignty of other States

INTRODUCTION

1. The Government of the Arab Republic of Egypt has the honour to submit to the Court, in accordance with Article 66, paragraph 4 of the Statute, its written comments on other written statements relating to the request for an advisory opinion by the General Assembly in its resolution 49/75K of 15 December 1994.

2. The question contained in resolution 49/75K, for which Egypt has voted, reads as follows:

> "Is the threat or use of nuclear weapons in any circumstance permitted under international law?"

3. The World Health Assembly, in resolution WHA 46/40 of 14 May 1993, had also requested the Court to give an advisory opinion on the following:

> "In view of the health and environmental effects, would the use of nuclear weapons by a State in war or other armed conflict be a breach of its obligations under international law, including the WHO Constitution?"

4. Egypt welcomes the decision of the Court to consolidate the oral hearings on both requests and addresses these comments to statements made in relation to both of them. While the two questions put to the Court are essentially similar, the question of the General Assembly is larger in scope, totally covering that of the World Health Assembly as well. This is the reason why the present comments are mainly addressed to the question of the General Assembly, while referring to the World Health Assembly's question whenever it is deemed necessary.

5. The written statement of Egypt of June 1995, together with the present comments constitute the position of Egypt on the two questions. Egypt believes that the question put to the Court by the General Assembly of the United Nations should be answered in the negative, whereas the answer to the question of the World Health Assembly should be in the affirmative.

6. Egypt notes that a large majority of States who have presented written statements relating to the two questions have adopted the same views as those she has put forward.

I. Should the Court Render its Advisory Opinion on the Present Question?[1]

Arguments against the Court rendering an opinion:

7. Several States have maintained in their statements that the Court should decline to give the requested advisory opinion. It has thus been argued that "[t]he 'propriety' of judicial involvement with [the] question is more than doubtful",[2] and that the Court should not give the requested advisory opinion in the present case because there were several "compelling reasons" for it not to do so,[3] e.g. that "[t]he General Assembly's request ... leads to the question of Court's integrity ... since there is the danger of a pointless procedure."[4]

8. The reasons given for this negative attitude can be synthetically formulated as follows:

- That the question is abstract;
- That it is political;
- That the opinion can have no useful legal effect; or alternatively, and paradoxically
- That it will definitely have a nefarious effect on the ongoing disarmament and arms limitation negotiations.

These arguments are explained and refuted in turn.

[1] The terms "present question", "present request" or "present case" refer to the request made by the General Assembly.

[2] Written statement of Germany, para. 2 at p. 3.

[3] Written statements of France, p. 5; and Germany, *loc. cit.*

[4] Written statement of Germany, para. 2 at p. 5.

1. The abstract character of the question:

9. It has been argued that the wording of the question of the General Assembly was broad, general and abstract, that it was hypothetical because it has not arisen within the context of a concrete legal or factual situation involving a specific use or threat to use nuclear weapons, that it required the Court to make speculative statements going beyond its judicial function, and that the question cannot be answered without reference to the numerous different combinations of circumstances in which the threat or use of nuclear weapons might be contemplated.[5] Therefore, the Court was invited to decline to answer the question posed by the General Assembly,[6] and not to engage in speculations about unknown future situations.[7]

10. That the abstract and general character of the question posed is a reason for the Court to decline to answer it in the exercise of its advisory rather than its contentious function, is a mere affirmation devoid of any justification and an inadmissible confusion between its two functions. The Court has declared that:

> "According to Article 96 of the Charter and Article 65 of the Statute, *the Court may give an opinion on any legal question, abstract or otherwise.*"[8]

---

[5] Written statements of Russia, p. 5; Netherlands, para. 15, at p. 5; United States, pp. 1 and 4; France, para. 5 at pp. 13 f.; United Kingdom, para. 2.38, at p. 16; Germany, para. 2 at p. 5; and Finland, p. 1.

[6] Written statement of the United Kingdom, para. 1.3, at p. 1 and para. 2.23, at p. 9.

[7] Written statement of the United States, p. 4.

[8] Italics added. *Admission of a State to the United Nations (Charter, Art. 4), Advisory Opinion: I.C.J. Reports 1948*, p. 57 at p. 61. See also *Effect of awards of compensation made by the U.N. Administrative Tribunal, Advisory Opinion of July 13, 1954: I.C.J Reports 1954*, p. 47 at p. 51; and *Legal Consequences for States of the Continued Presence of South Africa in Namibia (South West Africa) notwithstanding Security Council Resolution 276 (1970), Advisory Opinion of 21 June 1971, I.C.J. Reports 1971*, p. 16, para. 40 at p. 27.

In fact, in the exercise of its advisory function, the Court has more than once held that it is its "duty ... to envisage the question submitted to it only in the abstract form which has been given to it ..."[9] Moreover, as pointed out by Judge Azevedo, it is quite fitting for the advisory function of the Court to give an answer *in abstracto* which may eventually be applied to several *de facto* situations: *minima circumstantia facti magnam diversitatem juris*.[10]

11. Therefore, to argue that the question cannot be answered without reference to the numerous different combinations of circumstances in which the threat or use of nuclear weapons might be contemplated, and the factual matrix within which a specific use or threat to use nuclear weapons takes place, reveals a fundamental misunderstanding of the advisory function based on a confusion between it and the contentious function of the Court. The purpose of the advisory function is not to settle an actual dispute which cannot be understood without its factual and legal background, but to enlighten the requesting organ on certain legal issues which it has to deal with in discharging its functions.

2. **The allegedly** political nature of the question:

13. It has been suggested that the question posed by the General Assembly was not a legal question but a political one,[11] and that "an opinion by the Court offering advice on what is in many respects essentially a political matter could undermine its authority and effectiveness."[12] It has also been argued that the

[9] *I.C.J. Reports 1948*, p. 57 at p. 61.

[10] *Cf.*, individual opinion of Judge Philadelpho Azevedo, *Admission of a State to the United Nations (Charter, Art. 4), Advisory Opinion: I.C.J. Reports 1948*, p. 57 at p. 74.

[11] Written statements of France, pp. 12 f.; and Germany, para. 2 at p. 2.

[12] Written statement of the United States, p. 6.

use of nuclear weapons "cannot be assessed using the norms of international law without such an assessment turning from a judicial into a political one."[13]

13. The mere fact that the question may have been politically motivated cannot prevent the Court from rendering its advisory opinion. The Court has stated that:

> "It is not concerned with the motives which may have inspired ... [the] request ..."[14]

The Court has also affirmed that:

> "in institutions in which political considerations are prominent it may be particularly necessary for an international organization to obtain an advisory opinion from the Court as to the legal principles applicable with respect to the matter under debate ..."[15]

On another occasion, the Court said:

> "It has been argued that the question put to the Court is intertwined with political questions, and that for this reason the Court should refuse to give an opinion. It is true that most interpretations of the Charter of the United Nations will have political significance, great or small. In the nature of things it could not be otherwise. The Court, however, cannot attribute a political character to a request which invites it to undertake an essentially judicial task ..."[16]

Thus, it is not for the Court to delve into the motivation which leads a duly authorized organ to request an advisory opinion on a legal question obviously falling within the jurisdiction of that organ even when that question relates to an issue which has other important political facets or is itself essentially political. In the two requests before the Court, the legal questions are clear

---

[13] Written statement of Germany, para. 2 at p. 2.

[14] *I.C.J. Reports 1948*, p. 57 at p. 61.

[15] *Interpretation of the Agreement of 25 March 1951 between the WHO and Egypt*, *I.C.J. Reports 1980*, p. 73, para. 33 at p. 87.

[16] *Certain Expenses of the UN, Advisory opinion of 20 July 1962*, *I.C.J. Reports 1962*, p. 151 at p. 155.

and the Court can answer them without enquiring into any apparent or hidden political motives or other political facets of the issue.

14. In the same vein, it was suggested, as a basis for the contention that the Court should decline to give the opinion, that there was very substantial disagreement within the international community as to whether such a request was appropriate.[17] On a previous occasion the Court had clearly indicated that the political controversy at the background of the question was not a reason for it to decline to give the advisory opinion requested.[18] "Differences of views among States on legal issues", explained the Court, "have existed in practically every advisory proceeding; if all were agreed, the need to resort to the Court for advice would not arise."[19]

15. It makes no difference that Resolution 49/75K was adopted amidst political controversy or whether it was adopted by a large majority or not. What matters is that it was properly adopted by the constitutionally required majority. It has thus to be considered as the expression of the legally valid will of the General Assembly.

3. Would an advisory opinion on the question put to the Court serve any useful legal purpose?:

16. It has been argued that an advisory opinion on the question put to the Court would serve no useful legal purpose, and would thus be a futile exercise of the judicial function, which dis-

---

[17] Written statement of the United States, p. 6. Emphasis has been put on the circumstances of adopting resolution 49/75K and on its voting results. It was passed by 78 to 43 votes, with 38 abstentions.

[18] *Legal Consequences for States of the Continued Presence of South Africa in Namibia (South West Africa) notwithstanding Security Council Resolution 276 (1970), Advisory Opinion of 21 June 1971, I.C.J. Reports 1971*, p. 16, para. 40 at p. 27.

[19] *Ibid.*, para. 34 at p. 24.

qualifies the request on grounds of "propriety". The argument goes on to explain that this is because the question does not fall in any of the categories of cases on which the Court has given advisory opinions up to the present.[20] Those categories were enumerated as follows:

> "*(a) Cases where the legal question involved the interpretation of a constitutional provision which has become the subject of dispute in the organ making the request.*"
>
> "*(b) Cases where the legal question involves matters on which the requesting organ or agency seeks guidance in the exercise of its constitutional functions.*"
>
> "*(c) Cases where the legal question involves the interpretation of agreements between the Organization and a Member State.*"
>
> "*(d) Cases where the legal question concerns the obligations of Member States consequential upon decisions or resolutions of the competent organs of the organization.*"[21]

17. This list is obviously a mere academic representation. It is one among many, and of course does not bind the Court nor can it limit the ambit of its advisory jurisdiction in any way. But even if, *arguendo*, it did, one can easily see that the present request falls under (*b*) as shall be apparent from the following point. But what is controlling here is not this list but the Statute. And the Statute is crystal clear when it provides that "[t]he Court may give an advisory opinion on any legal question".[22] The only condition is that the question be of a "legal nature" and falling within the jurisdiction of the requesting organ, which is for the General Assembly coextensive with the Charter.

18. Here again there is an impermissible confusion between the advisory and contentious functions of the Court. There is no need here, as in contentious proceedings, to prove a "legal interest" as a condition of admissibility of a case before the Court. In advisory proceedings, the Charter, including the Statute, leaves

---

[20] Written statement of the United Kingdom, para. 2.27, at p. 11.

[21] *Ibid.*, pp. 12-15.

[22] Article 65 of the Statute of the Court.

it to the discretion of the requesting organ to evaluate the appropriateness and the eventual usefulness of the requested advisory opinion for its current and future work.

19. The Court has on numerous occasions affirmed its duty as "the principal judicial organ of the United Nations",[23] to respond to such requests:

> "The reply of the Court, itself Organ of the United Nations, represents its participation in the activities of the Organization, and in principle should not be refused." 24

Indeed, the Court considered that:

> "no State, ... can prevent the giving of an Advisory Opinion which the United Nations considers to be desirable in order to obtain enlightenment as to the course of action it should take."25

It is not for the Court to decide in place of the General Assembly on the "desirability" or the "opportunity" of the request or to over rule it, when the Assembly had already considered it desirable.

20. It has been argued, nevertheless, that the nature of the case is such that the Court would be unable to give an advisory opinion which would be of positive assistance to the General Assembly and the other organs of United Nations, particularly in the field of disarmament and security.[26] It has also been argued that the Court "would be forced to overstep the bounds of its function as "the principal judicial organ of the United Na-

[23] Article 92, Charter of the United Nations.

[24] *Interpretation of Peace Treaties (first phase), Advisory Opinion, I.C.J. Reports 1950*, p. 65 at p. 71; and *Reservations to the Convention on the Prevention and Punishment of the Crime of Genocide, I.C.J. Reports 1951*, p. 15 at p. 19.

[25] *I.C.J. Reports 1950*, p. 65 at p. 71.

[26] Written statements of the United Kingdom, para. 2.27, at p. 11 and para. 2.37, at p. 16; United States, pp. 1 f.; and France, para. 7 at p. 16.

tions".[27] In this context, it has been stated that "[i]f a response by the Court to a request for an advisory opinion would, in fact, be unlikely to provide any constructive assistance to the other organs of the United Nations but, on the contrary, would be likely to have a detrimental effect on the activities of the United Nations family", it was "both the duty of the Court to protect its own judicial function and the need for it to play its part as an organ of the United Nations call for it to exercise its discretion to decline to respond to the request."[28]

21. It is submitted, however, that the advisory opinion of the Court can be of great practical value. The Court has abundantly reiterated that its advisory activity constitutes its main form of participation in the activities of the United Nations of which it is the principal judicial organ and that a request in principle should not be refused.[29] The present request relates to an issue that lies within the hard core of the first purpose and principal function of the United Nations, namely the maintenance of international peace and security, including disarmament and arms control. The question falls squarely within the ambit of the Assembly's large mandate under Article 10 covering "all matters falling within the Charter". In fact, the General Assembly has been dealing with the legality of nuclear weapons since its first session.[30] The request raises both the *jus ad bellum* question of the threat or use of force (Articles 2(4) and 51 of the Charter), as well as that of the *jus in bello* relating to certain weapons of mass destruction. Answering the request by the Court would enlighten the General Assembly on the legal context in which its activities are carried out. A statement by the Court on the legality of the threat or use of nuclear weapons under international law cannot fail to have a positive effect on the long-standing negotiations in the United Nations and elsewhere,

---

[27] Written statement of Germany, para. 2 at p. 4.

[28] Written statement of the United Kingdom, para. 2.26, at p. 11.

[29] *I.C.J. Reports 1950*, p. 65 at p. 71; and *I.C.J. Reports 1951*, p. 15 at p. 19.

[30] Resolution no. 1(I) of 24 January, 1946.

at least by reducing the scope of a legal controversy.

4. Would an advisory opinion on the question put to the Court have a nefarious effect on the ongoing disarmament efforts?:

22. It has been argued that a judgment on the legality of nuclear weapons might jeopardize the operation of the Non-Proliferation Treaty in particular,[31] and the ongoing negotiations on nuclear disarmament in general.[32] This, it is submitted, is pure conjecture. A pronouncement by the Court on the subject is in no way incompatible with the pursuit of negotiations, especially if they were to be conducted in the light of an authoritative declaration on the issues involved. Confirming the illegality of the threat or use of nuclear weapons by an authoritative statement of the Court would play a major role in clarifying the law and thus, bringing a prolonged debate to a close. Therefore, such a pronouncement cannot harm the ongoing negotiations on nuclear disarmament in general.

23. On the contrary, most probably, a pronouncement by the Court would facilitate the implementation of Article VI of the Non-Proliferation Treaty which provides that the parties should "pursue negotiations in good faith on effective measures relating to cessation of the nuclear arms race ... and to nuclear disarmament, and on a treaty on general and complete disarmament under strict and effective international control."

II. Is there a General Prohibition on the Threat or Use of Nuclear Weapons in General International Law?

24. Moving to the substance of the question, it has been argued

---

[31] Written statement of the Netherlands, para. 11, at p. 4.

[32] Written statements of the United Kingdom, para. 2.27, at p. 11 and paras. 2.41 f., at pp. 18 f.; United States, pp. 5 f; Germany, para. 2 at p. 5 and Finland, p. 1.

that international law does not contain a general prohibition on the use of nuclear weapons *per se*, that no treaty or other binding instrument specifically prohibits the use of nuclear weapons in all circumstances,[33] and that State practice demonstrates that their threat or use is not deemed to be generally unlawful.[34] It was suggested that the existence of several treaties on the prohibition of use in certain geographic regions, non-proliferation, manufacturing or testing of nuclear weapons proves that there is no global prohibition on the acquisition or use of nuclear weapons *per se*, as these treaties are premissed on the lawful existence of nuclear weapons and their possession by States in general.[35]

25. This understanding of the role and the cumulative legal significance of the instruments which prohibit nuclear weapons, each in a certain domain or a certain area, is erroneous for two reasons. In the first place, the existence of numerous treaties each prohibiting a specific aspect or use of nuclear weapons bears witness to the emergence of a comprehensive legal prohibition rather than the reverse.[36]

26. Secondly, the fact that there is no general prohibition on the acquisition or detention of nuclear weapons is a separate

---

[33] Written statements of Russia, p. 5, United Kingdom, para. 1.4, at p. 2 and para. 3.5, at p. 22; United States, pp. 2, 8 and 20; France, paras. 13 at p. 24, 31 at p. 45 and 33 at p. 53; and Italy, p. 1.

[34] Written statement of the United States, pp. 2 and 9.

[35] Written statements of Russia, pp. 6 f.; and United States, pp. 10-14.

[36] They are the Antarctic Treaty of 1959, United Nations, *Treaty Series*, Vol. 402, p. 71; Treaty Banning Nuclear Weapons Tests in the Atmosphere, in Outer Space and under Water of 1963, *op. cit.*, Vol. 480; Treaty on Principles Governing the Activities of States in the Exploration and Use of Outer Space, including the Moon and Other Celestial Bodies of 1967, *op. cit.*, Vol. 601, p. 205; Treaty for the Prohibition of Nuclear Weapons in Latin America of 1967 (Treaty of Tlatelolco), *op. cit.*, Vol. 634, p. 326; Treaty on the Prohibition of the Emplacement of Nuclear Weapons and Other Weapons of Mass Destruction on the Sea-Bed and Ocean Floor and the Subsoil Thereof of 1971, *op. cit.*, Vol. 955, p. 115; South Pacific Nuclear Free Zone Treaty of 1985 (Treaty of Rarotonga), 24 *I.L.M.*, 1440 (1985); and the African Nuclear-Weapon-Free Zone Treaty of 1995.

question from, and without prejudice to, the question of their use or threat thereof.

27. The general significance of these partial efforts to ban or outlaw different aspects of nuclear weapons has to be assessed in the light of the relevant resolutions of the General Assembly of the United Nations which are the clearest indications of the *opinio juris* of the international community on the subject.

28. General Assembly resolution no. 1653 (XVI) of 24 November, 1961 entitled "Declaration on the Prohibition of the Use of Nuclear and Thermo-nuclear Weapons" reads as a prohibition *de lege lata* of nuclear weapons.[37] It states that "[t]he use of nuclear ... weapons is contrary to the spirit, letter and aims of the United Nations and, as such, a direct violation of the Charter of the United Nations".[38] The resolution goes on to add that "[a]ny State using nuclear ... weapons is to be considered as ... acting contrary to the laws of humanity and as committing a crime against mankind and civilization."[39]

29. Equally, resolution 2936 (XXVII) of 29 November, 1972 on the Non-Use of Force in International Relations and Permanent Prohibition of the Use of Nuclear Weapons, enunciates "the permanent prohibition of the use of nuclear weapons".[40]

30. These two resolutions have been followed, almost annually,

---

[37] Its preamble states that:

"the use of weapons of mass destruction, causing unnecessary human suffering, was in the past prohibited, as being contrary to the laws of humanity and to the principles of international law, by international declarations and binding agreements, such as the Declaration of St. Petersburg of 1868, the Declaration of the Brussels Conference of 1874, the Conventions of the Hague Peace Conferences of 1899 and 1907, and the Geneva Protocol of 1925, to which the majority of nations are still parties".

[38] Paragraph 1 (*a*).

[39] Paragraph 1 (*d*).

[40] Paragraph 1.

by others reiterating the illegality of nuclear weapons, e.g. resolutions 33/71 B, 35/152 D, 36/92 I, 45/59 B, 46/37 D, 47/56 C and 48/76 B.

31. It has been argued, however, that the link between the assertion of the illegality of nuclear weapons in paragraph 1 of resolution 1653 (XVI), and the request in the same resolution addressed to the Secretary-General of the United Nations to consult with Member States about the conclusion of a convention to prohibit the use of nuclear weapons, raises the question whether those States which voted in favour of the resolution regarded the use of nuclear weapons as unlawful in the absence of such a convention. This, it was suggested, casted doubts on the extent to which those States, which voted in favour of the resolutions, saw them as containing statements *de lege lata* about the legality of the use of nuclear weapons.[41]

32. The vote on a resolution calling, *inter alia,* for the conclusion of a convention prohibiting the use of nuclear weapons cannot be construed as a negation of the existence of such a prohibition under general international law. Otherwise, the conclusion of any codification convention would bear the negation of the prior existence of the rules it codifies. Such a convention is useful in spite of the prior existence of the rules, because it purports to eliminate or reduce the controversies over their existence and exact interpretation as rules of general international law.

33. In addition, the States which have voted in favour of resolution 1653 (XVI) calling, *inter alia,* for the conclusion of the convention are largely those who have voted for resolutions declaring that nuclear war "[r]esolutely, unconditionally and for all time condemn[ed] ... as being contrary to human conscience and reason, as the most monstrous crime against peoples and as a violation of the foremost human right - the right to life",[42]

---

[41] Written statement of the United Kingdom, para. 3.28, p. 34.

[42] General Assembly resolution no. 38/75 B of 15 December, 1983.

that the use of nuclear weapons would be a violation of the Charter of the United Nations and a crime against humanity,[43] and that nuclear weapons pose the greatest danger to mankind and to the survival of civilization.[44]

34. It has been argued that General Assembly resolutions on nuclear weapons were not binding in themselves[45] and did not offer binding interpretations of the United Nations Charter.[46] It was held that the resolutions were not accepted by a majority of the nuclear weapon States. It was also claimed that such resolutions would only be declaratory of the existence of principles of customary international law to the extent that such principles had been recognized by the international community, including the States "most directly affected".[47] The question of the voting results is raised in order to prove that the resolutions were not binding and to minimize their value.[48]

35. The resolutions of the General Assembly are an important component in the thickening legal network on the prohibition of nuclear weapons *per se*. It is important, therefore, to address the issue of their legal significance. Though formally most General Assembly resolutions addressed to Member States are mere recommendations, depending on their contents and the circumstances of their adoption, they can bear greater legal significance. Thus, the Court in its advisory opinion on *Namibia* declared that:

"it would not be correct to assume that, because the General Assembly is

---

[43] Resolutions nos. 1653 (XVI), 33/71 B, 34/83 G, 35/152 D and 36/92 I 45/59 B, 46/37 D, 47/56 C and 48/76 B.

[44] Paragraph 47 of the Final Document of the First Special Session on Disarmament of the General Assembly of 1978.

[45] Written statements of the United Kingdom, para. 3.27, at p. 33; United States, pp. 18 f.; and France, para. 22 at p. 34.

[46] Written statement of Russia, p. 8.

[47] Written statement of the United States, pp. 18 f. See also written statement of the United Kingdom, para. 3.27, at p. 33.

[48] Written statement of Italy, pp. 1 f.

> in principle vested with recommendatory powers, it is debarred from adopting, in specific cases within the framework of its competence, resolutions which make determinations or have operative design."[49]

They can also interact with the rules of general international law by having a declaratory, crystallizing or generating effect on them.[50]

36. As for General Assembly resolutions on nuclear weapons, they should be considered as declaratory of norms of general international law because they reveal the illegality of nuclear weapons in the light of the Charter and other rules of general international law. There are a number of factors which enhance their legal significance. The resolutions are drafted in precise legal language, and mostly make determinations of fact and law.[51] The voting patterns of those resolutions demonstrate a high and consistent support from the membership of the United Nations. Such an accumulation of resolutions can generate and result in the formation of a rule of customary international law.[52] It demonstrates continuity and distinguishes those resolutions as having stable support. It equally impresses the importance which States attach to them.[53] Repetition of the resolutions also answers the objection that a resolution may have only been

---

[49] *I.C.J. Reports 1971*, p. 16, para. 105 at p. 50.

[50] See ABI-SAAB, Georges: La coutume dans tous ses états ou le dilemme du développment du droit international général dans un monde éclaté, in *Essays in Honour of Roberto Ago*, Dott. A. Giuffrè Editore, Milano, 1987, p. 56:

> "il est possible de dire qu'à l'heure actuelle la très grande majorité de la doctrine est d'avis que les resolutions normatives de l'Assemblée générale peuvent susciter les mêmes modes d'interaction avec la coutume que ceux que la Cour a identifié par rapport aux traités de codification, c'est-à-dire qu'elles peuvent produire les mêmes effets potentiels que ceux-ci, déclaratoires, cristallisants ou générateurs de règles coutumières."

[51] For example see the language of General Assembly resolution no. 38/75 B of 15 December, 1983 quoted above, *supra*, para. 33 at p. 13.

[52] Judge Tanaka, dissenting opinion, *South West Africa, Second Phase, Judgment, I.C.J. Reports 1966*, p. 6 at p. 291.

[53] *Cf.*, SLOAN, Blaine: General Assembly Resolutions Revisited (Forty Years Later), 58 *B.Y.I.L.*, p. 132 (1987).

adopted to please a temporary majority in a certain situation.[54] There is also a strong moral element in the resolutions which renders contrary practice increasingly of doubtful legality.

37. As for the claim that General Assembly resolutions on nuclear weapons were not declaratory of an existing custom because the nuclear-powers, being "the most directly affected States" have voted against them, it is obviously an argument worthy of consideration, based on some truth, but not the whole truth. For not only nuclear powers but all States of the world are "most directly affected", as potential recipients of nuclear wrath, by the issue of threat or use of nuclear weapons under international law.

38. The nuclear States can perhaps delay, but cannot definitely set obstacle to the emergence and consolidation of an *opinio juris* underlying a general rule of international law to the effect of the illegality of the threat or use of nuclear weapons *per se*, in any circumstance.

But even if the Court comes to the conclusion that such a rule has not yet reached the ultimate stage of consolidation, and that the threat or use of nuclear weapons is not prohibited *per se*; their use would still be prohibited in any circumstance , *by their effects*, under the general rules of the law of armed conflict.

III. The Threat or Use of Nuclear Weapons in any Circumstance is Contrary to the Laws of Armed Conflict

39. All threat or use of force, including by nuclear weapons, is prohibited under Article 2(4) of the Charter, which provides only two exceptions to this general prohibition of the threat or use of force, namely self-defence in accordance with Article 51 of

[54] *Cf., loc. cit.*

the Charter and enforcement actions under Article 42 of the Charter.

40. As for enforcement action, in such cases where it deems it necessary to apply military force to "maintain or restore international peace and security", it is unimaginable that the Security Council would resort to or authorize the use of nuclear weapons with their wide ranging disastrous effects; that which would surely immensely aggravate any threat to or breach of peace, rather than restore international peace and security.

41. As to the other and more important exception to the prohibition of the use of force, as it is not subject to a prior decision by the Security Council, it has been argued that the questions put to the Court by the General Assembly and the World Health Assembly do not "draw a distinction between the use of nuclear weapons by the aggressor and the use of such weapons in self-defence",[55] and that general international law does not specifically prohibit the threat or use of nuclear weapons in self-defence.[56] It was also claimed that it would be entirely arbitrary to exclude *ex hypothesi* the right of a State to rely on nuclear weapons as a means of defence against a conventional attack, and that there can be no easy assumption that the use of nuclear weapons can never be justified in response to a conventional attack on the basis of the "disproportion" between the two, because what mattered was the result to be achieved by the "defensive" action and not the forms, substance and strength of the action itself. It was, thus, suggested that the question to be posed was whether, in the actual circumstances of an attack, the use of a particular nuclear weapon was necessary in order to defend the victim State?[57] It was finally claimed that the possibility of using nuclear weapons in self-defence found

---

[55] Written statement of Russia, p. 5.

[56] Written statement of France, para. 18 at p. 30.

[57] Written statement of the United Kingdom, para. 3.36, at p. 37 and para. 3.40, at p. 38; see also written statement of France, para. 17 at pp. 28 f.

confirmation in Security Council resolution no. 984 (1995), and particularly in its preamble which refers *only* to "any aggression" with the use of nuclear weapons as "endangering international peace and security" "in accordance with the relevant provisions of the Charter of the United Nations".

42. By contesting the legality of the threat or use of nuclear weapons, even in self-defence, it is not suggested that the nuclear powers cannot use force in self-defence. It is simply submitted that the use of force, even in self-defence, has to conform with the rules of the *jus in bello*, and that nuclear weapons by their very nature and inevitable effects fall fowl with these rules, which are of absolute nature and do not permit their setting aside even in retaliation in the form of belligerent reprisals. Thus, even if the State or States exercising self-defence were attacked by nuclear weapons this does not mean that they may respond by nuclear weapons.

43. Reprisals are prohibited against protected persons and objects according to the Geneva Conventions of 1949 and their additional Protocols. This prohibition of reprisal is absolute and applies to the use of all weapons. In consequence, the protected persons and objects can never become targets of any attack, including nuclear attacks. The provisions of the Conventions and the Protocols carrying this prohibition of reprisals against protected persons and objects are considered declaratory of customary law.[58]

44. Moreover, paragraph 5 of Article 60 of the Vienna Conventions on the Law of Treaties of 1969[59] and 1986[60] provides

---

[58] *Cf.*, RONZITTI, Natalino: *The Law of Naval Warfare*, ed. by N. Ronzitti, Martinus Nijhoff Publishers, 1988, p. 47.

[59] Vienna Convention on the Law of Treaties. Concluded at Vienna on 23 May 1969. Entered into force on 27 January 1980. United Nations, *Treaty Series*, Vol. 1155, p. 331.

[60] Vienna Convention on the Law of Treaties Between States and International Organizations or Between International Organizations. Concluded at Vienna on 21 March 1986. Not yet in force. A/CONF.129/15.

that the rights open to an injured party, in terms of suspension or termination of a treaty in cases of material breach, shall not apply to treaties of "humanitarian character"; thus, excluding the application of the maxim *inadimplenti non est adimplendum*.[81] Hence, if a treaty of such a character was violated by another party, the injured party or parties may not proceed toward terminating the treaty or suspending its operation in whole or in part, or retaliate in kind against the breaching party. Consequently, even on the hypothesis that the use of nuclear weapons is at all permitted, they cannot be used in reprisals because breached treaties of "humanitarian character" applicable in this case, notably the Geneva Conventions and their Protocols, will still apply between the parties *durante bello* according to their own terms and by the application of the rules of the law of treaties. And in any case regardless of the treaties, the relevant principles and rules of humanitarian law expressed in these treaties are part of general international law. They are of a *jus cogens* character and thus cannot be waived.

45. It has been argued, however, that nothing in international humanitarian law indicates that nuclear weapons were prohibited *per se*.[82] More particularly, it was claimed that nuclear weapons were not prohibited by the Protocols of 1977[83] as the Diplomatic Conference which adopted the Protocols[84] had decided not to treat that issue.

---

[81] Article 60, paragraph 5 provides that:

> "Paragraphs 1 to 3 do not apply to provisions relating to the protection of the human person contained in treaties of a humanitarian character, in particular to provisions prohibiting any form of reprisals against persons protected by such treaties."

[82] Written statement of the United States, pp. 2, 7 and 21.

[83] Protocols Additional to the Geneva Conventions of 12 August 1949, and Relating to the protection of Victims of International Armed Conflicts of 1977.

[84] The Diplomatic Conference on Reaffirmation and Development of International Humanitarian Law Applicable in Armed Conflicts, Geneva, 1974-77.

46. Indeed the United States, the United Kingdom and France made declarations at the time of signature and ratification (by those among them who ratified) to the effect that their understanding, which was generally accepted by the Conference according to them, was to consider the negotiations as well as the ensuing instruments as not covering nuclear weapons. This was made in the form of an interpretative declaration (revealing their own understanding of what happened) and not as a reservation subject to objections by other parties to the instruments; though several of the latter did append differing interpretative declarations on this point to their own signature or ratification. In fact, the American, British and French declarations have unreasonably stretched the significance of the decision of the Conference not to deal specifically with weapons and particularly with weapons of mass destruction and more particularly nuclear arms, leaving it to other fora where negotiations on their prohibition *per se* were in process or about to start. The general understanding was that these weapons will not be addressed specifically. But this was without prejudice to the applicability to such weapons of the general rules of humanitarian law which were in process of reaffirmation and development in the Conference. What was excluded from the ambit of the Conference and the ensuing Protocols was specific treatment of the nuclear weapons, and not the applicability of general rules to them as to all other weapons whether existing or non-existing yet. This comes clearly from the Commentary of the International Committee of the Red Cross on the Protocols which reads:

> "delegations agreed not to discuss nuclear weapons. But it cannot be inferred from that that the rules of Protocol I do not apply to nuclear weapons. On the contrary, if the rules of Protocol I do not prohibit the use of nuclear weapons, they nevertheless seriously restrict such use.[65]

47. Thus, whether the Conference did or did not specifically discuss nuclear weapons is a matter that has no bearing on the applicability of the provisions of Protocol I to nuclear weapons, as long as the effects of these weapons violate the rules and

---

[65] Para. 1851 at p. 603.

principles expressed therein. The mere fact that the Protocol, or any other instrument, does not *specifically* prohibit the use of nuclear weapons, does not imply that their use is permissible if such use falls within the patterns of conduct prohibited by the provisions of these instruments.

48. Indeed the use of nuclear weapons violates several fundamental principles and rules of the international law of armed conflicts, prominent among them are the following:

49. *1. The obligation to distinguish in all circumstances between civilian populations and objects and military personnel and objectives:* One of the most fundamental rules of humanitarian international law is that "[t]he civilian population ... as well as individual civilians, shall not be the object of attack."[86]

50. It is especially forbidden "[t]o destroy ... the enemy's property, unless such destruction ... be imperatively demanded by the necessities of war".[87] The attack or bombardment, by whatever means, of towns, villages, dwellings, or buildings which are undefended is prohibited.[88] Equally, in "bombardments" all necessary precautions must be taken to spare buildings dedicated to religion, art, science, or charitable purposes, historic monuments, hospitals, and places where the sick and wounded are collected.[89] Furthermore, it is also prohibited to attack civilian hospitals, convoys of vehicles, hospital trains, hospital ships, aircraft exclusively employed for the removal of wounded and sick civilians, or the transport of medical personnel and

[86] Article 52(2) of the First Protocol.

[87] Article 23 (g) of the Hague Regulations Respecting the Laws of and Customs of War on Land annexed to Convention No. IV of 1907.

[88] *Ibid.*, Article 25.

[89] Article 27 of the First Protocol of 1977.

equipment.[70]

51. In order to ensure compliance with this prohibition the parties to the conflict are required *at all times* to "distinguish between the civilian population and combatants and between civilian objects and military objectives and accordingly ... direct their operations only against military objectives."[71] In other words, indiscriminate attacks are absolutely prohibited.[72]

52. This fundamental principle of the laws of armed conflict, most recently reiterated in the First Protocol of 1977, is a well established and uncontested rule of general international law. It applies to the use of any weapon old or new, existing or to come, conventional or non-conventional. It is not the nature of the weapon as such but the effect of its use which makes it fall under the prohibition. Thus, the most precise weapons can be used in an indiscriminate manner. But some weapons, by their massive and uncontrollable effects in terms of destruction, killing and

---

[70] Articles 18, 21 and 22 of the Geneva Convention Relative to the Protection of Civilian Persons in Time of War, of 12 August 1949. United Nations, *Treaty Series,* Vol. 75, p. 386. Also, Articles 12, 22 and 23 of the First Protocol of 1977.

[71] *Ibid.*, Articles 48 and 51(2).

[72] *Ibid.*, Article 51. According to this article indiscriminate attacks are:

"4. ...

c) those which employ a method or means of combat the effects of which cannot be limited as required by this Protocol;

and consequently ... are of a nature to strike military objectives and civilians or civilian objects without distinction.

5. Among others, the following types of attacks are to be considered as indiscriminate:

a) an attack by bombardment by any methods or means which treats as a single military objective a number of clearly separated and distinct military objectives located in a city, town, village or other area containing a similar concentration of civilians or civilian objects; and

b) an attack which may be expected to cause incidental loss of civilian life, injury to civilians, damage to civilian objects, or a combination thereof, which would be excessive in relation to the concrete and direct military advantage anticipated."

pollution, are not amenable to discriminate use, directed only against military personnel and objectives; they are constitutionally (*i.e.* by their physical nature) "indiscriminate" in their effects.

53. This is the case of nuclear weapons. By their inherent qualitative and quantitative characteristics, the effects of nuclear weapons are necessarily and inescapably cataclysmic and indiscriminate. They cannot distinguish, it is submitted, between combatants and non-combatants and between protected and unprotected objects. They are expected to cause immense incidental loss of civilian life, injury to civilians, damage to civilian objects and to the environment, or a combination thereof, excessive in relation to any concrete and direct military advantage.

54. It has been contended, without being proven, that like any other weapons, nuclear ones can target military objectives, particularly when they are situated in isolated areas away from civilian concentrations, and that incidental damage to civilian population and objects, is collateral damage which is tolerated in humanitarian law as long as the military advantage outweigh the risks.[73] Thus, it cannot be said before hand and in general that the use of nuclear weapons is prohibited in all cases, as it will depend on the circumstances of each case.

55. It has been argued, furthermore, that modern nuclear weapons were capable of precise targeting and can be, therefore, directed against specific military objectives without indiscriminate effect on the civilian population,[74] and that modern weapon-designers were able to tailor the effects of a nuclear weapon to deal with various types of military objectives.[75] However, these arguments ignore, *inter alia,* the surrounding natural environment of the objective, and the risk-factor of error which can be extremely costly in cases of use of nuclear weapons, as

[73] Written statement of the United States, p. 22.

[74] Written statement of the United Kingdom, para. 3.68, at p. 52.

[75] Written statement of the United States, p. 23.

well as the incalculable effects as to the general environment and the future generations, as certain effects cannot be locally contained and can be vehicled by the natural elements such as water and air.

56. One should thus not be misled by the concept of the so-called "low yield nuclear weapon", which remains a nuclear weapon with all the inherent effects and dangers of such weapons.[76]

57. Apart from the fundamental principle of discrimination at all times between military personnel and objectives and civilian populations and objects, several other principles and rules of the law of armed conflict also render the use of nuclear weapons illegal in any circumstance.

Prominent among them is the general principle enunciated in the Preamble of the Declaration of St. Petersburg of 1868[77] that:

> "the *only legitimate object* which States should endeavour to accomplish during war is to *weaken the military forces* of the enemy".78

Similarly, the principle expressed in Article 22 of the Hague Regulations of 1907 states that:

> "the right of the belligerent to adopt means of injuring the enemy is not unlimited."

These are, however, general injunctions, specified further *inter alia* in the following principles.

58. *2. The prohibition against the use of weapons which cause unnecessary suffering:* It has been argued that the use of nuclear

---

[76] For more details see the thorough examination of the question of "micro-nukes", "mini-nukes" and "tiny-nukes" in *Memorial of the Government of the Republic of Nauru*, September 1994, made in connection with the request for and advisory opinion made by the World Health Assembly, at pp. 53-8.

[77] Signed at St. Petersburg 29 November - 11 December 1868.

[78] Italics added.

weapons would not necessarily lead to a violation of the rule laid down in Article 23(e) of the Hague Regulations of 1907 which forbids belligerents "to employ arms, projectiles, or materials calculated to cause unnecessary suffering". It was suggested that suffering may be called "unnecessary" only when its infliction is not necessary to attain a lawful military advantage or greatly exceeds what could reasonably have been considered necessary to attain that military advantage,[79] that the question of whether a specific use is in contravention of the said obligation cannot, therefore, be answered until the exact implications, both as to the military advantage gained and to the injury caused, are known.[80]

59. It was argued, furthermore, that the prohibition was intended for weapons designed to increase the injury or suffering of the persons attacked beyond what is necessary to put them "*hors combat*";[81] for example weapons which would unnecessarily inflame wounds.[82]

60. Since the nineteenth century, this principle has been embodied in two rules: one forbids the use of poisons, while the other prohibits the use of weapons capable of causing superfluous injuries. Nuclear weapons fall in the latter category by reason, of their enormous blast waves, air blasts, fires, residual nuclear radiation or radioactive fallout, electromagnetic impulses and thermal radiation which cause extensive "unnecessary suffering".[83] By their poisonous effect, the use of nuclear weapons also violates the other rules as well as the 1925 Geneva Protocol.

---

79 Written statement of the Netherlands, para. 20. at p. 7. On a similar opinion see written statement of the United Kingdom, paras. 3.64 and 3.66, at pp. 50-52.

80 Written statement of the Netherlands, para. 22, at p. 8.

81 Written statement of the United States, p. 28.

82 Written statement of the United States, f.n. 65 at p. 28.

83 *Cf.* General Assembly resolution no. 1653 (XVI) of 24 November, 1961.

61. *3. The prohibition against causing widespread, long-term and severe damage to the environment, and the obligation not to prejudice the health or survival of the population:* It has been argued that the prohibition to use "methods or means of warfare which are intended, or may be expected, to cause widespread, long-term and severe damage to the natural environment" in the First Protocol of 1977[84] did not apply to nuclear weapons on the basis that the Protocol did not apply to such weapons.[85]

62. However, as it has been demonstrated, the Protocol governs the use and the effects of nuclear weapons. Thus, these prohibitions apply to them.[86] Even, if it were not used with the intent to attack the environment, the use of nuclear weapons becomes unlawful because its use will inevitably and on a wider scale harm the environment,[87] and would thereby prejudice the health or the survival of the population.[88]

IV. The Threat or Use of Nuclear Weapons is Contrary to Numerous other Principles and Rules of Contemporary International Law

The following are but a sample of some important principles of contemporary international law which would be violated by the threat or use of nuclear weapons in any circumstance.

---

[84] Articles 35 (3) and 55 (2).

[85] Written statement of the United States, pp. 29 f.

[86] It is equally prohibited to carry out "[a]ttacks against the natural environment by way of reprisals". Article 55 (2) of the First Protocol of 1977.

[87] The violation by nuclear weapons of rules regulating the environment will be dealt with later, *infra*, paras. 70-73 at pp. ...

[88] Article 55 of the First Protocol of 1977.

A. The International Law of Human Rights:

63. *1. The right to life:* It has been argued that the right to life did not mean that it was not possible to deprive a person of his life through legitimate use of force.[88] Attention was drawn to Articles 2, paragraph 2, and 15, paragraph 2, of the European Convention on the Protection of Human Rights and Fundamental Freedoms of 1950 which respectively provide that:

> "Deprivation of life shall not be regarded as inflicted in contravention of this article when it results from the use of force which ... is absolutely necessary ... in defence of any person from unlawful violence ..."

and that:

> "No derogation from Article 2, except in respect of deaths resulting from lawful acts of war ... shall be made under this provision."

Moreover, it has been argued that according to the International Covenant on Civil and Political Rights,[90] the "deliberate taking of life" is prohibited only if it is done "arbitrarily".[91] It was also argued that death resulting from the use of nuclear weapons in self-defence would thus not fall under these prohibitions.

64. Article 6(1) of the International Covenant on Civil and Political Rights[92] provides that "Every human being has the inherent right to life."[93] Although it is expected that in

---

[88] Written statements of Russia, p. 9; and the Netherlands, para. 27, at p. 10.

[90] Article 6(1). United Nations, *Treaty Series*, Vol. 999, p. 171.

[91] Written statements of the United Kingdom, para. 3.101, at pp. 65 f.; and United States, p. 43.

[92] United Nations, *Treaty Series*, Vol. 999, p. 171.

[93] See also article 3 of the Universal Declaration of Human Rights of 1948.

times of war human beings, whether military or civilians, might perish, the killing of human beings should not exceed the limits of lawful acts of war. It should be recalled, however, that Article 40 of the Fourth Geneva Convention stipulates that "[i]t is prohibited to order that there shall be no survivors". Although an order to use nuclear weapons may not intend that "there shall be no survivors", it is an indirect order to do so by virtue of the immense lethal capabilities of such weapons. The use of nuclear weapons necessarily causes wide-scale deaths, thus "arbitrarily" depriving human beings of the right to life.

65. *2. The right to enjoy the highest attainable standard of physical and mental health:* Everyone has a right to "the enjoyment of the highest attainable standard of physical and mental health."[84] It is needless to say that the adverse effects of nuclear explosions on the human health are immeasurable and irreparable. Two generations continue to suffer from the Hiroshima and Nagasaki bombs. It is noteworthy that existing modern nuclear weapons may be hundreds of times more powerful and damaging than those thrown over Japan in 1945. The use of nuclear weapons is an absolute impediment to the "enjoyment of the highest attainable standard of physical and mental health" by human beings.

B. The prohibition of genocide and crimes against humanity:

66. It has been argued that the mere use of nuclear weapons does not constitute genocide if it was not "committed with the intent to destroy, in whole or in part, a national, ethnical, racial or religious group" on the grounds that genocide was a crime of intent.[85] It was, further, claimed that the prohibition of genocide was clearly not directed at collateral casualties resulting from attack on military objectives.

---

[84] Article 12 of the International Covenant on Economic, Social and Cultural Rights. United Nations, *Treaty Series*, Vol. 999, p. 3.

[85] Written statements of Russia, p. 9; the Netherlands, para. 26, at p. 10; United Kingdom, para. 3.73, p. 54; and United States, pp. 33 f.

67. According to Article II of the Convention on the Prevention and Punishment of the Crime of Genocide of 1949[86] any acts "committed with the intent to destroy, in whole or in part, a national, ethnical, racial or religious group" is considered genocide. It has already been demonstrated that by the inherent qualitative and quantitative characteristics of their effects, collateral damage of the use of nuclear weapons necessarily results in cataclysmic and indiscriminate effects, and is expected to cause immense incidental loss of civilian life inevitably excessive in relation to any concrete and direct military advantage anticipated. Therefore, their use cannot at all be justified by stating that extensive losses in life are simply collateral damage.

68. This is of special relevance to the argument that genocide is a crime of intent. For as long as it was unambiguously clear and known before hand to the user of nuclear weapons that their use would result in immense incidental loss of life, how can it still be argued that nuclear weapons can be lawfully used on the basis that there was no intention to cause such wide killing, or that the primary objective was something else? The question of intent applies to cases where the result was unexpected and the user could not have predicted its occurrence. Hence, the use of nuclear weapons necessarily implies an intent to destroy, or at least not to mind destroying, in whole or in part, the groups within which the target is situated.

C. The International Law of Environment:

69. It has been argued that no international environmental instrument is expressly applicable in armed conflict, or expressly prohibits or regulates the use of nuclear weapons.[87] It was mentioned that out of the some 300 multilateral treaties, 900

---

[86] United Nations, *Treaty Series*, Vol. 78, p. 278.

[87] Written statements of the United States, p. 34; and France, para. 26 at p. 38.

bilateral treaties and 200 other instruments on the protection of the environment scarcely any of them makes any references to the use of nuclear weapons.[98]

70. Every State has, in accordance with the Charter of the United Nations and the principles of international law, the responsibility to ensure that activities within its jurisdiction or under its control do not cause damage to the environment of other States or areas beyond the limits of national jurisdiction.[99] This general rule, which figures in Principle 21 of the Stockholm Declaration, is further specified in numerous other instruments. For example the Convention for the Protection of the World Cultural and Natural Heritage of 1972,[100] and the Vienna Convention for the Protection of the Ozone Layer of 1985[101] provide that States Parties shall not take deliberate measures which might damage the cultural or natural heritage and that they shall take appropriate measures to protect the environment against adverse effects resulting from human activities which modify or are likely to modify the ozone layer.[102] More emphatically, Principle 26 of the Stockholm Declaration of 1972 states, *inter alia,* that:

> "Man and his environment must be spared the effects of nuclear weapons and all other means of mass destruction."

It has been argued that this text as well as the Rio Declaration have no binding legal effect.[103] It is submitted, however, that those Declarations must be seen as declaratory of the

---

[98] United Kingdom, paras. 3.109 f.

[99] Principle 21 of the Stockholm Declaration of the United Nations Conference on the Human Environment of 1972. 11 *I.L.M.*, 1416 (1972); and Principle 2 of the Rio Declaration. 31 *I.L.M.*, 851 (1992).

[100] 11 *I.L.M.*, 1358 (1972).

[101] 12 *I.L.M.*, 1529 (1987).

[102] Articles 6(3) and 2(1) of the Convention on Cultural and Natural Heritage, and the Ozone Layer Vienna Convention respectively.

[103] Written statement of France, para. 26 at p. 39.

evolving normative regulation for the protection of the environment, including from the effects of the use of nuclear weapons.

71. It has been argued, more concretely, that the Convention on the Prohibition of Military or Any Other Hostile Use of Environmental Modification Techniques (ENMOD) of 1977[104] was not applicable to most cases in which nuclear weapons might be used. It was argued that the Convention was designed to deal with the "deliberate manipulation" of the environment as a method of war.[105]

72. Article I of the ENMOD Convention provides that it is prohibited "to engage in military or any other hostile use of environmental modification techniques having widespread, long-lasting or severe effects as the means of destruction, damage or injury to any other State Party." It also prohibits States from assisting, encouraging or inducing any State, group of States or international organization to engage in activities contrary to the provisions of paragraph 1 of Article I. Obviously, the use of nuclear weapons has such "widespread, long-lasting or severe effects" on the environment, as to fall under the prohibition of the Convention.

D. Use of nuclear weapons violates the neutrality and the territorial sovereignty of other States:

73. It has been argued that the principle of neutrality was not a broad guarantee to neutral States of immunity from the effects of war. It was equally maintained that no belligerent was held responsible for collateral damage to such States for acts of war committed outside their territories.[106] In addition, it has

[104] United Nations, *Treaty Series*, Vol. 1108, p. 151.

[105] Written statements of the United Kingdom, para. 3.75, at p. 56; and United States, p. 29.

[106] Written statement of the United States, pp. 31 f.

been argued that the Court could not find that such damage would occur without knowing the precise circumstances of a particular use.[107]

74. Such arguments would render the principle of neutrality devoid of all meaning and legal value. But in international law, on the contrary, if a belligerent carries out a policy which infringes the rights of neutrals, the latter can not only protest but also take measures aimed at ending the illegal policy of the belligerent.[108]

75. Moreover, as was just mentioned in relation to environmental law, States have, in accordance with the Charter of the United Nations and the principles of international law, the responsibility to ensure that activities within their jurisdiction or control do not cause damage to the environment of the *other States or of areas beyond the limits of national jurisdiction.*[108] However, electromagnetic impulses resulting from a nuclear explosion at an altitude of 100 k.m. may travel to up to 1100 k.m.[110] Radioactive contamination may also reach the neighbouring countries of the State in which the explosion occurred.

76. In consequence, the use of nuclear weapons would necessarily violate the territorial sovereignty of other States, where the impact is bound to be felt, which is a fundamental principle of international law, and the principle of good neighbourliness provided for in Article 74 of the Charter of the United Nations.

---

[107] Written statement of the United States, p. 32.

[108] RONZITTI, Natalino: *The Law of Naval Warfare*, ed. by N. Ronzitti, Martinus Nijhoff Publishers, 1988, p. 50.

[108] Principle 21 of the Stockholm Declaration of 1972 and Principle 2 of the Rio Declaration of 1992.

[110] 1987 WHO Report, para. 13 at p. 11 (French).

* * *

77. In the light of the foregoing, Egypt maintains its submissions concluding its statement of 20 June, 1995.

78. As some States have reserved the right to make further submissions with regard to the request of the General Assembly should the Court decide to respond to it, Egypt reserves the right to respond to such submissions should the Court decide to receive them and in the manner which the Court will prescribe.

LETTER DATED 18 MAY 1995 FROM THE PERMANENT REPRESENTATIVE OF THE DEMOCRATIC PEOPLE'S REPUBLIC OF KOREA TO THE UNITED NATIONS

Democratic People's Republic of Korea
Permanent Mission to the United Nations
515 East 72nd Street, 38F, New York, N.Y. 10021
Tel. (212) 772-0712 (0725) FAX (212) 772-0735

18 May 1995

Your Honour,

With regard to the UN General Assembly resolution 49/75 K adopted on 15 December 1994, I have the honour, upon authorization of H.E. Foreign Minister of the Democratic People's Republic of Korea, to refer to the position of the Government of the Democratic People's Republic of Korea on the legality of the threat or use of nuclear weapons.

The Government of the Democratic People's Republic of Korea takes it that the threat or use of nuclear weapons in any case is violation of the UN Charter and the existing international laws, and therefore should not be allowed on any account.

It is deplorable that the legality of the threat or use of nuclear weapons is debated when complete elimination of nuclear weapons is under serious discussion on the international arena.

I would like to remind you of the letter of H.E. Foreign Minister of the DPRK addressed to Registrar of the International Court of Justice in January 1994 pursuant to the resolution of the 46th World Health Assembly, which has clearly stated the position of my Government against the threat or use of nuclear weapons.

Please accept, Your Honour, the assurances of my highest considerations.

Pak Gil Yon
Ambassador
Permanent Representative

His E. Mohammed Bedjaoui
President
International Court of Justice

LETTER DATED 13 JUNE 1995
FROM THE AMBASSADOR OF FINLAND,
TOGETHER WITH WRITTEN STATEMENT
OF THE GOVERNMENT OF FINLAND

EMBASSY OF FINLAND

Groot Hertoginnelaan 16
2517 EG THE HAGUE

The Hague, 13 June 1995

No. 1185

Dear Sir,

Referring to your letter of 8 February 1995 please find enclosed the answer of the Ministry for Foreign Affairs of Finland.

Accept, Sir, the assurances of my highest consideration.

Erkki Mäentakanen
Ambassador of Finland

Encls.

H.E. Mr. M. Bedjaoui
President of the International
Court of Justice
T h e H a g u e

AE 22
27/543L

MINISTRY FOR FOREIGN AFFAIRS
OF FINLAND

In response to the letter of 8 February 1995 from the Registrar of the International Court of Justice to the Minister for Foreign Affairs of Finland regarding the request for an advisory opinion made by the United Nations General Assembly, the Government of Finland has the honour to refer to its response submitted to the Court on 10 June 1994 concerning a similar request made by the World Health Assembly, and to state the following:

The request made by the General Assembly seeks to attain an *in abstracto* determination of the legality, or otherwise, of the use of nuclear arms in war or other armed conflict. It ignores the complexity of the technical, strategic and moral aspects of the problem posed by the existence of nuclear weapons. It fails to recognize the fact that effective security arrangements can only be attained through agreements which take into account all relevant circumstances including the specific security interests of each State. During the years, Finland has actively promoted the conclusion of such agreements and will do so in the future.

It would thus be improper for the Court to give the opinion requested by the General Assembly. In view of the Court's long-standing practice in the matter of advisory opinions, such impropriety would seem to be constituted by two factors:

1. Answering the request the Court could not remain faithful to its character as a judicial organ

This factor has to do with the hypothetical, future-oriented character of the request. In the absence of a concrete factual situation, the Court would itself be required to analyze different types of nuclear weapons and to entertain various hypotheses about situations in which they might conceivably be used and the factual consequences of their use. This would require analyzing extremely complex and controversial pieces of technical, strategic and scientific information. The counter-factual character of such speculation would make any hypothesis uncertain. Entering such speculation, the Court would not be able to remain faithful to the requirements of its character as a judicial organ.

2. No reply to the substance of the request would constitute a useful service to the United Nations of which the Court is the principal judicial organ

A statement *in abstracto* on the legal status of the use of nuclear weapons would seriously intervene in the diplomatic negotiations being conducted on various bilateral and multilateral fora to limit and reduce the threat posed by nuclear weapons. It would create blanket support for one or another disputed position and fail to respect the comprehensive give-and-take character of such negotiations - even make them seem altogether superfluous. During recent years, a number of important agreements on the limitation, prohibition or control of specific types of armaments have been attained, among them the 1993 Convention on Chemical Weapons, and the 1995 decision on the indefinite extension of the Treaty on the Non-Proliferation of Nuclear Weapons. To undermine such negotiations by a judicial *fiat* would not constitute a useful service by the Court to the efforts of the United Nations in this field.

LETTER DATED 14 JUNE 1995 FROM MINISTER AT THE EMBASSY OF JAPAN, TOGETHER WITH WRITTEN STATEMENT OF THE GOVERNMENT OF JAPAN

EMBASSY OF JAPAN
THE NETHERLANDS

The Hague
June 14, 1995

Mr. Eduardo Valencia-Ospina
Registrar
International Court of Justice
Peace Palace
2517 KJ The Hague

Dear Mr. Valencia-Ospina,

Upon instructions of my Government, I have the honor to transmit herewith the written statement of the Government of Japan in response to the International Court of Justice's letter dated February 8, 1995, addressed to H.E. the Minister for Foreign Affairs of Japan, in accordance with Article 66, paragraph 2, of the Statute of the Court.

Yours sincerely,

Yukio Sugano
Minister

enclosure

WRITTEN STATEMENT OF THE GOVERNMENT OF JAPAN

The Government of Japan herewith submits the written statement of the Government, in pursuance of the Court's Order of February 1, 1995, and the letter of the Registrar of the Court addressed to the Minister for Foreign Affairs of Japan, dated February 8, 1995, in accordance with Article 66, paragraph 2, of the Statute of the International Court of Justice.

I. The question on which an advisory opinion is asked

On 15 December, 1994, the Forty-Ninth United Nations General Assembly, by its Resolution A49/75K, decided to request the International Court of Justice to give an advisory opinion on the following subject:

"Is the threat or use of nuclear weapons in any circumstance permitted under international law?"

II. The view of the Government of Japan with respect to international law on the use of nuclear weapons in war or other armed conflict

The Government submits its view on the subject in question, namely, the use of nuclear weapons in war or other armed conflict, as follows:

The Government believes that, because of their immense power to cause destruction, the death of and injury to human beings, the use of nuclear weapons is clearly contrary to the spirit of humanity that gives international law its philosophical foundation.

III. The position of the Government of Japan on the elimination of nuclear weapons

Japan, the only nation that has suffered nuclear attack, taking advantage of the opportunity offered by its submission of this written statement, desires to state also the following view, on the importance of eliminating nuclear weapons, in addition to stating its assessment regarding the use of nuclear weapons in international law.

(1) With their devastating power, nuclear weapons can in an instant take a tremendous toll in human life and deprive people of their local community structures; they can also cause the victims who survive an attack itself indescribable and lasting suffering due to atomic radiation and other lingering effects. Japan, based on its tragic nuclear suffering of Hiroshima and Nagasaki, considers that nuclear weapons must never be used. The Government of Japan firmly maintains the "three non-nuclear principles" of not possessing nuclear weapons, not producing them and not introducing them into its territory, and will always strive to promote nuclear disarmament and nuclear non-proliferation, with a view to achieving the ultimate elimination of nuclear weapons.

(2) Nuclear disarmament, non-proliferation of nuclear weapons and the ultimate elimination of nuclear weapons are crucial for preventing nuclear war and the use of nuclear weapons. To this end, it is imperative that concrete and realistic measures be taken, one by one. Convinced of this, Japan strives constantly to strengthen the nuclear non-proliferation regime, the central pillar of which is the Treaty on the Non-Proliferation of Nuclear Weapons (NPT). Japan makes every possible effort to enhance the Treaty's effectiveness and universality. At the NPT Review and Extension Conference in May this year, decisions had been made on "strengthening the review process for the Treaty" and on "principles and objectives for nuclear non-proliferation and disarmament," together with the decision to indefinitely extend the NPT. These decisions indicate a future path regarding nuclear disarmament, nuclear non-proliferation, and other issues. It is extremely important that the international community strives along this path. Japan, while welcoming the recent significant progress in nuclear disarmament made by the United States and the former Soviet Union such as the signing of START I and START II and the entry into force of START I since the end of Cold War, urges all nuclear weapon States, which have a special responsibility for

nuclear disarmament, to make yet greater efforts for nuclear disarmament, with the goal of achieving the ultimate elimination of nuclear weapons, in accordance with Article 6 of the Treaty. Last year in the United Nations General Assembly, Japan sponsored the resolution, "Nuclear disarmament with a view to the ultimate elimination of nuclear weapons," which was adopted by an overwhelming majority. Japan believes that the adoption reflects the wide appreciation by the international community of Japan's such fundamental view.

(3) Japan welcomes the developments in the negotiations on a Comprehensive Nuclear Test Ban Treaty (CTBT) at the Conference on Disarmament and will do everything possible to contribute to early conclusion of those negotiations. Japan will also contribute to the early commencement and development of negotiations on a convention banning the production of fissile material for nuclear weapons or other nuclear explosive devices. Japan will, moreover, work actively to contribute to the actual reduction of nuclear weapons through assistance for dismantling of nuclear weapons of the former Soviet Union.

LETTER DATED 15 JUNE 1995
FROM THE PERMANENT REPRESENTATIVE OF SAMOA
TO THE UNITED NATIONS,
TOGETHER WITH WRITTEN STATEMENT
OF THE GOVERNMENT OF SAMOA

PERMANENT MISSION OF SAMOA
TO THE UNITED NATIONS
820 Second Avenue • New York, N.Y. 10017
Tel.: (212) 599-6196 • Fax: (212) 599-0797

15 June 1995

The Registrar
International Court of Justice
Peace Palace
2517 The Hague
Netherlands

Dear Sir,

I have the honour to attach the submission of Samoa in respect of the General Assembly request for an Advisory Opinion on the legality of the threat or use of nuclear weapons.

Yours sincerely,

Tuiloma Neroni Slade
Ambassador and Permanent Representative

PERMANENT MISSION OF SAMOA
TO THE UNITED NATIONS
820 Second Avenue • New York, N.Y. 10017
Tel.: (212) 599-6196 • Fax: (212) 599-0797

Legality of the Threat or Use of Nuclear Weapons (Request for Advisory Opinion)

Submission by Samoa

The Government of the Independent State of Western Samoa (Samoa) refers to the request from the General Assembly of the United Nations for an advisory opinion of the International Court of Justice (the Court) on the following question:

> "Is the threat or use of nuclear weapons in any circumstance permitted under international law?"

Samoa believes that the question should be answered "No."

Samoa is a small island state located in the Pacific Ocean. The Pacific was the scene of the only hostile use of nuclear weaponry and the scene of much nuclear explosions for testing purposes. Such nuclear testing has had significant and long term effects on the health of Pacific people and the environment. Samoa is not a member of any military grouping. It has no military forces and it has no enemies. The danger to it from nuclear weaponry is that of fallout from someone else's war. Samoa has a large stake in safeguarding its environment, and in the survival of the planet.

Samoa became independent in 1962. It joined the World Health Organization the same year, and the United Nations in 1976. Before joining the United

Nations, it became a party to the Treaty Banning Nuclear Weapons Tests in the Atmosphere, in Outer Space and Under Water in 1965, and to the Treaty on the Non-Proliferation of Nuclear Weapons in 1975. It is a party to and strong supporter of the South Pacific Nuclear Free Zone Treaty (Treaty of Rarotonga) which prohibits the stationing of nuclear weapons on the territories of the parties to the Treaty. It has voted for many General Assembly resolutions on nuclear disarmament issues.

Samoa believes that there is a continuing threat of use of nuclear weapons which must be addressed by the international community. Notwithstanding the end of the cold war, nuclear states have yet to relinquish their policies of first use, use and threat of use of nuclear weapons: not all have signed Protocols 1, 2 or 3 to the Treaty of Rarotonga under which they would refrain from using or threatening to use any nuclear explosive devices and from testing or stationing any nuclear devices in the area defined by the Treaty.

Samoa shares the view which it believes to be generally accepted among nations that the threat or use of nuclear weapons is illegal.

Samoa places considerable importance on the role of international law in governing the practice of States. It believes that an opinion from the Court would clarify the legal situation and would be of assistance to small states in their efforts to protect themselves from the threat or use of nuclear weapons. Samoa believes that an advisory opinion from the Court would also be an important step towards a universally accepted and legally binding prohibition on the threat or use of nuclear weapons, and would also be an important step towards the elimination of nuclear weapons.

On 16 September 1994, Samoa submitted to the Court that it believes that the use of nuclear weapons is illegal. This was in response to the question asked by the World Health Organisation whether the use of nuclear weapons by a State in war or other armed conflict would be a breach of its obligations under international law. Samoa will continue to work towards the complete elimination of such weapons, including the destruction of all existing stockpiles.

Samoa believes that the prohibition of the use or threat of use of nuclear weapons has been achieved under general international law. It has occurred by the cumulative effect of a series of multilateral treaties and of a series of resolutions of the General Assembly. In particular, Samoa relies on the:

- Declaration Renouncing the Use, in Time of War, of Explosive Projectiles Under 400 Grammes Weight (St. Petersburg Declaration) (1868);
- Convention (No. IV) Respecting the Laws and Customs of War on Land, done at The Hague, 1907;
- Protocol for the Prohibition of the Use in War of Asphyxiating, Poisonous or Other Gases, and of Bacteriological Methods of Warfare (1925);
- Charter of the United Nations (1945);
- Constitution of the World Health Organisation (1946);
- Geneva Conventions of 12 August 1949;
- Nuremberg Principles as codified by the International Law Commission (1950);
- Geneva Protocol I (1977);
- Declaration on the Prohibition of the Use of Nuclear and Thermo-Nuclear Weapons, G.A. Res. 1653 (XVI) (1961);
- Non-use of Nuclear Weapons and Prevention of Nuclear War, G.A. Res. 33/71B (1978);
- Non-use of Nuclear Weapons and Prevention of Nuclear War, G.A. Res. 35/152D (1980);
- Non-use of Nuclear Weapons and Prevention of Nuclear War, G.A. Res. 36/92I (1981);
- Convention on the Prohibition of the Use of Nuclear Weapons, G.A. Res. 45/59B (1990);
- Convention on the Prohibition of the Use of Nuclear Weapons, G.A. Res. 46/37D (1991).

Samoa further believes that the combined weight of these instruments is so overwhelming that the fundamental principles contained therein bind all states.

The General Assembly resolutions and treaties noted above have already been discussed in many of the statements presented to the Court concerning the advisory opinion requested by the World Health Organization on the use of nuclear weapons. They will no doubt be canvassed by others in the present proceedings. Samoa does not propose to repeat those arguments, but it does believe that it will be helpful for the Court to be apprised of some deeply-felt views of a small-state member of the international community.
Samoa believes that the General Assembly is well within its powers in requesting the advisory opinion, and that, in so far as the Court has a discretion whether to respond to the question, it should exercise that discretion in favour of answering.

Article 96, paragraph 1 of the Charter empowers the General Assembly to request the Court "to give an advisory opinion on <u>any</u> legal question." (Samoa's emphasis.) To the extent that organisations such as the World Health Organization are under any limits on the subjects about which they may ask for advisory opinions by virtue of the words "on legal questions <u>arising within the scope of their activities</u>" (Samoa's emphasis) contained in Article 96, paragraph 2, there is no such restriction on the right of the General Assembly. (Samoa does not doubt the power of the World Health Organization to make its request; the point is simply that the General Assembly's power is even clearer.) The question asked by the General Assembly is one which can only be answered by an analysis of sources of law such as those contained in Article 38 of the Statute of this Court. Samoa is of the view that "international custom, as evidence of a general practice accepted as law" (in the words of Article 38, paragraph 1.b of the Statute) is broad enough to encompass widely ratified multilateral treaties (even so far as non-ratifying states are concerned) and certain resolutions of international organisations.

The question which the General Assembly has asked is, moreover, a question which concerns quite fundamental interests of the General Assembly and its members. The General Assembly has a very broad mandate under the Charter to consider matters affecting war and peace and the survival of the planet. Article 11, for example, empowers the Assembly to "consider the general principles of co-operation in the maintenance of international peace and security, including the principles governing disarmament and the regulation of armaments, and may make recommendations with regard to such principles to the Members or to the Security Council or to both."

Acting pursuant to such mandate, the General Assembly has, beginning in its very first session in 1946, given careful consideration to the issue of disarmament, including nuclear disarmament. It has done so at its regular sessions, at three special sessions, and through the Disarmament Commission which it created and which reports to it. The Assembly follows carefully the work of the Conference on Disarmament which meets in Geneva. Both on the basis of the language of the Charter and the subsequent practice of the General Assembly, the question of the legality of the threat or use of nuclear weapons is of abiding concern to the General Assembly.

Samoa is a faithful member of the United Nations and follows closely the work of the General Assembly. Its ultimate strength, like that of other small states, lies in the rule of law. It thus believes that it is very important to the General Assembly - and to states like Samoa - that the Court answer the question referred to it by the General Assembly.

Samoa does not believe that any pronouncement by the Court will harm the ongoing negotiations on nuclear disarmament. On the contrary, Samoa believes that advice from the Court confirming the illegality of the threat or use of nuclear weapons will be a necessary force towards the conclusion of current negotiations on a comprehensive test ban treaty and a fissile-material cut-off, and will also be a stimulus to the commencement of negotiations on a convention prohibiting and eliminating nuclear weapons.

It is important in this connection to bear in mind the function of the First Committee of the United Nations General Assembly and its role in the introduction of and adoption of the question now before this Court. The First Committee is responsible for recommending to the Conference on Disarmament disarmament measures which should be negotiated. The Committee would not have agreed to the request for an advisory opinion from this Court if it believed that such a request would undermine in any way the negotiations on nuclear disarmament. And neither would the General Assembly.

Samoa also believes that an opinion from the Court would assist in the implementation of Article VI of the Treaty on Non-Proliferation of Nuclear Weapons, according to which parties to the Treaty pledge themselves to "pursue negotiations in good faith on effective measures relating to cessation of the nuclear arms race at an early date and to nuclear disarmament, and on a treaty on general and complete disarmament under strict and effective international control." A pronouncement of illegality from this Court would, Samoa believes, enhance that negotiation process by emphasising the illegality of the use or threat of use of nuclear weaponry, and will help to bring home to public opinion - especially in nuclear states - the ultimate need for nuclear disarmament under suitable control arrangements.

The argument against the legality of nuclear weapons relies in part, as we have suggested, on the General Assembly's pronouncements on the subject. It is noted that there are resolutions of the General Assembly, such as Res. 1653 (XVI), which declare the illegality of the use of nuclear and thermo-nuclear weapons, and then go on to contemplate the possibility of "convening a special conference for signing a convention on the prohibition of the use of nuclear and thermo-nuclear weapons for war purposes." Samoa submits that the requirement for such a convention does not detract from the normative effect of the declaratory part of the resolution.

Samoa believes that the practice of the General Assembly, from the first days of the organisation supports such a submission. For example, one of the early resolutions adopted by the GA was Resolution 96(I) on the Crime of Genocide. That resolution affirmed that "genocide is a crime under international law which the civilised world condemns." It went on to request the Economic and Social Council "to undertake the necessary studies, with a view to drawing up a draft convention on the crime of genocide." In its advisory opinion on Reservations to the Convention on the Punishment of the Crime of Genocide, 1951 I.C.J. 4, 23, this Court noted that "the principles underlying the Convention are principles which are recognised by civilised nations as binding on States, even without any conventional obligation." The same is true here.

Samoa understands that there may be many reasons for following up a determination by a political organ of the illegality of an action or situation by treaty commitments. This may be for such reasons as to focus the attention of domestic legislative bodies where they have a role in ratifying treaties, to clarify the concrete details of what may have been stated only at the level of principle, or to provide for a regime to deal with dismantling or preventing that which is illegal. That was what happened with genocide. The definition was made more concrete. A regime was created for its suppression. In the present instance, a treaty regime is still needed for the destruction of nuclear weapons. The law develops step by step. An affirmative answer to the General Assembly's question will, however, contribute towards nudging the negotiations in the right direction.

To the extent that the Court may consider hearing oral statements Samoa would wish to avail itself of the opportunity to make such a statement or to be part of a joint presentation in that respect.

15 June 1995

LETTER DATED 15 JUNE 1995
FROM COUNSEL APPOINTED BY NAURU,
TOGETHER WITH WRITTEN STATEMENT
OF THE GOVERNMENT OF NAURU

15 June 1995

Registrar
International Court of Justice
Peace Palace
2517 KJ The Hague
The Netherlands

Dear Registrar,

Enclosed please find two Responses to Submissions of Other States by the Republic of Nauru in the case concerning *The Legal;ity of the Use of Nuclear Weapons by States in Armed Conflict* and one Memorial in the case concerning the *Legality of the Use and Threat of Use of Nuclear Weapons.*

I understand that the Court has set the date of 30 October as the date for the beginnig of oral hearings in the two cases. I would like permission to use a number of witnesses. In the case concernng *The Legal;ity of the Use of Nuclear Weapons by a State in Armed Conflict* I would like to put on the stand a Dr. Frank Barnaby who is a nuclear physicist of repute. I would also like to put on the stand the Mayors of Hiroshima and Nagasaki. In the case concerning the *Legality of the Use and Threat of Use of Nuclear Weapons* I would like to place on the stand Ms. Hilda Lini, former Minster of Health of Vanuatu, Ms. Ligon Eknilang who has experienced the effects of U. S. nuclear tests during Operation Bravo or some other woman from the Pacific who has experienced those effects and Ms. Claudia Peterson who has experienced the effects of nuclear tsets in the UnitedStates.

Sincerely,

Jerome B. Elkind

INTERNATIONAL COURT OF JUSTICE

LEGALITY OF THE USE OR THREAT OF USE OF NUCLEAR WEAPONS (REQUEST FOR AN ADVISORY OPINION)

MEMORIAL OF THE GOVERNMENT OF THE REPUBLIC OF NAURU

MEMORIAL OF THE GOVERNMENT OF THE REPUBLIC OF NAURU

Introduction

Nauru is a small island state in the Pacific Ocean. Nauru believes that peace and freedom from the threat of war is necessary for the social, cultural and economic development of people, both in the Pacific and world wide.

Nauru believes that the threat or use of force is contrary to international law and the development of positive international relations. Nauru has no armed forces, and as such threatens no state with the use of force.

The threat of nuclear weapons

Nauru believes that there is a continuing threat of use of nuclear weapons which must be addressed by the international community.

Despite the end of the cold war the nuclear states have yet to relinquish their policies of first use, use and threat of use of nuclear weapons. In addition, some of the nuclear states have not signed Protocols 1, 2 and 3 of the Treaty of Rarotonga under which they would refrain from using or threatening to use any nuclear devices and from testing or stationing any nuclear devices in the area defined by the Treaty.

The Pacific was the scene of the only hostile use of nuclear weapons and the scene of over 250 nuclear explosions for testing purposes. The nuclear tests have significantly affected the health of Pacific people, wildlife and the environment, and will continue to do so for generations.

The testing of nuclear weapons in the Pacific from 1946 until 1992 has contaminated numerous islands and large areas of ocean with radiation that has severely affected health and the environment. The U.S. Atomic Energy Commission has called the Marshall Islands "by far one of the most contaminated areas in the world". [1] Miscarriages, still births, cancers, birth deformities and other radiogenic diseases have increased by up to 10 times pre-testing levels in areas closest to the testing. [2]

A description of some of these effects is given by Lijon Eknilang from the Marshall Islands:

> I was seven years old at the time of the Bravo tests on Bikini. I remember that it was early in the morning that I woke up with a bright light in my eyes. I thought someone was burning the house. Soon after we heard a big loud noise, just like thunder and the earth started to move... . Then came the fallout. It was white and to us kids we thought it was white soap powder. The kids were playing in the powder and having fun, but later on everyone was sick and we couldn't do anything... . My cousin died of tumour cancer in 1960. In 1972 I had another cousin die of leukaemia. Two of my sisters have had thyroid surgery... .
>
> And I have had seven miscarriages and still births. Altogether there are eight other women on the island

---

[1] U.S. Atomic Energy Commission, 54th Meeting of the Advisory Committee on Biology and Medicine, New York, 1956.

[2] "Radioactive Heaven and Earth; The health and environmental effects of nuclear weapons testing in, on and above the earth." IPPNW, Apex Press, N.Y. 1991.

Independent Survey of Marshallese Women and reproduction, unpublished field report. Statement by Glenn Alcalay before the Presidential Advisory Committee on Human Radiation Experiments, March 15, 1995.

> nothing. Other children are born who will never recognise this world or their own parents. They just lie there with crooked arms and legs and never speak. Already we have seven such children.... [3]

The leakage of radiation from nuclear testing sites and waste dumps, the continued human ingesting of radiation released into the environment and the radiation already ingested by Pacific peoples threatens them with radiation induced diseases and death for generations to come. In addition, the coral reefs damaged by nuclear testing has caused considerable ciguatera poisoning and will continue to threaten such poisoning.

There is also a very real threat that nuclear testing may resume in the Pacific.

<u>The need for a Court opinion</u>

Nauru shares the view which it believes to be generally accepted among nations that the threat or use of nuclear weapons is illegal. Nauru is concerned however that some nations, including some of the declared nuclear states, do not share this view.

Nauru places considerable importance on the role of international law and the role of the International Court of Justice in governing the practice of states and in the development of peace and security among states. In this light, Nauru accepts the compulsory jurisdiction of the I.C.J. for contentious cases, and has utilised the contentious case procedure in seeking peaceful resolution of one of its conflicts with a neighbouring state.

---

[3] "Pacific Women Speak", Green Line, Oxford 1987, pp.15-17.

Nauru believes that an opinion from the Court would clarify the legal situation and would be of assistance to small states in their efforts to protect themselves from the threat or use of nuclear weapons. It believes that an advisory opinion from the Court would also be an important step towards a universally accepted and legally binding prohibition on the threat or use of nuclear weapons, and would be an important step towards the elimination of nuclear weapons.

Nauru does not believe that any pronouncement by the Court will harm the ongoing negotiations on nuclear disarmament. On the contrary, Nauru believes that a Court pronouncement confirming the illegality of the threat or use of nuclear weapons will be a stimulant to the conclusion of current negotiations on a Comprehensive Test Ban Treaty and a fissile material cut off, and will also be a stimulus to the commencement of negotiations on a convention prohibiting and eliminating nuclear weapons.

This opinion is supported by the fact that the question was introduced in and adopted by the first Committee of the United Nations General Assembly. This committee is responsible for recommending to the Conference on Disarmament measures which should be negotiated. The First Committee would not have requested such An advisory opinion if it believed that such a request would harm the negotiations on disarmament measures which the Committee has initiated in the Conference on Disarmament.

Nauru also believes that an opinion from the Court would assist in the implementation of Article VI of the Non Proliferation Treaty, according to which parties to the NPT pledged themselves " ...to pursue negotiations in good faith on effective measures relating to cessation of the nuclear arms race at an early date and to nuclear disarmament, and on a Treaty on general and complete disarmament under strict and effective international control."

The threat or use of nuclear weapons is illegal

On 20 September 1994, Nauru submitted to the Court that it believes that the use of nuclear weapons in armed conflict is illegal. This was in response to the question asked by the World Health Organisation on whether the use of nuclear weapons by a State in war or other armed conflict would be a breach of its obligations under international law.

Nauru would like the Court to consider this submission in connection with the present case as support for our belief that any use of nuclear weapons is a violation of international law. In addition, Nauru supports the submissions made in that case by Azerbaijan, Colombia, Costa Rica, Democratic Peoples' Republic of Korea, India, Iran, Kazakhstan, Lithuania, Malaysia, Mexico, Moldova, Papua New Guinea, Philippines, Rwanda, Samoa, Saudi Arabia, Solomon Islands, Sri Lanka, Sweden, Uganda, Ukraine, which argue that the use of nuclear weapons is a violation of international law.

In adddition Nauru wishes to respectfully submit to the Court the following statement to support our belief that the threat or use of nuclear weapons is illegal.

Questions presented........ 1

Background........ 1

Summary........ 2

I. Introduction........ 2

II. The Law of Peace and Security (*Jus ad Bellum*)........ 3

A. United Nations Charter........ 3

B. United Nations Resolutions and Declarations........ 7

C. Collective Security Treaties........ 9

D. The Nuremberg Principles........ 10

E. *Opinio Juris*........ 11

F. Threats of Aggression........ 14

III. Specific Law Regarding the Threat of use of Nuclear Weapons........ 16

A. Treaties........ 17

B. Security Council Resolutions........ 18

C. Unitrd Nations General Assembly, Conference on Disarmament and Disarmament Commission........ 18

D. The Non-Derogable Right to Life........ 20

IV. The Threat of Use of Nuclear Weapons is Prohibited in any Circumstances........ 22

A. The Correlation Between Threat and Use of Force: Threat is Use........ 22

B. The Conditional Threat of force is Prohibited in any Circumstances........ 23

C. A Retaliatory Threat to Use Nuclear Weapons is Illegal in Any Circumstances........ 24

1. **The Threat of First Use** 24

2. **The Threat of Second Use** 25

3. **Implicit Threats of Use** 26

4. **Deterrence** 29

V. **The Illegality of the Threat to Commit an Illegal Act** 31

A. **International Legal Instruments** 31

B. **General Principles of Law Recognized by Civilized Nations** 32

Conclusion 37

Appendix A General Assembly Resolutions Which Conclude that the Use of Nuclear Weapons is a Crime Against Humanity

Appendix B General Assembly Resolutions Stating the Elimination of Nuclear Weapons as a Goal

Appendix C Nuclear Threats in History; Excerpts from "To Win a Nuclear War", and "Nuclear Targeting of the Third World"

Question Presented

Is the threat or use of nuclear weapons in any circumstance permitted under international law?

Background

On 14 May 1993, the World Health Assembly adopted Resolution WHA 46.40, requesting the International Court of Justice to give an advisory opinion on the following question:

> In view of the health and environmental effects, would the use of nuclear weapons by a State in war or other armed conflict be a breach of its obligations under international law including the WHO Constitution?

Following receipt of this request from the Director-General of WHO, the Court set a term of June 20, 1994, subsequently extended to September 20, 1994 for the submission of statements by member governments. Thirty five countries submitted statements, the majority arguing for an affirmative answer to the question presented. A number of states challenged the question's admissibility, arguing that WHO lacked the competence to submit it. Some states argued for the proposition that, while humanitarian law applies to nuclear weapons as it does to all other weapons, the legality *vel non* of their use must be determined by the specific facts of each case. A few states reserved their position on the merits, should the Court decide to give an opinion. In accordance with the Court's Rules, all submissions were transmitted to all states which made submissions. The Court has set a term of June 20, 1995 for states to comment on each other's submissions.

On December 15, 1994, the General Assembly of the United Nations, by Resolution 49/75/K, requested the Court to give an advisory opinion on the following question:

> Is the threat or use of nuclear weapons in any circumstance permitted under international law?

The Court has set a term of June 20, 1995, for the submission of statements relative to the question posed by the General Assembly, and September 20, 1995, as the timeline for responses to these statements.

It is expected that the Court will eventually consolidate the two questions, but it has not yet done so.

Summary

This Statement endorses the arguments already before the Court supporting the thesis that any use of nuclear weapons is illegal under international law. Focusing on the question of threat, this Statement will argue that the threat of use of nuclear weapons is illegal because the law of peace and security, as it has evolved since the adoption of the United Nations Charter, treats "threat or use" as a single, indivisible concept and because it is a general principle of law that the illegality of a particularly serious offense entails as well the illegality of the threat to commit such an offense.

I. Introduction

The possession of nuclear weapons by some states but not others, and the horrendous nature of these weapons, has created an unprecedented disparity of power between these two groups of states. So long as the nuclear "haves" do not take seriously their solemn obligation under Article VI of the Nuclear Non-Proliferation Treaty to move in good faith and with all deliberate speed toward the complete elimination of nuclear weapons, this disparity will continue to exist and will, in and of itself, constitute a threat to the survival of the "have nots" and of the "haves" as well.

This threat is further enhanced by the announced intention of the nuclear weapon states to reserve to themselves the right to use nuclear weapons in response to a perceived or actual threat of an attack or, more generally, in defense of their national interest or security. In a speech at l'Ecole Militaire on November 3, 1959, General Charles de Gaulle said, "...it is evidently necessary that we be able to provide ourselves in the coming years with a force that can act on our account, with what is customarily called a 'force de frappe,' able to be deployed anywhere at any time. It goes without saying that the basis for this force will be a nuclear armament--whether we make it or buy it--which must belong to us. And, since eventually France can be destroyed from any point in the world, our force must be designed to act anywhere on earth."[1]

Nor is this threat diminished by the position of the nuclear weapon states that the only purpose of their nuclear arsenals is to deter the use of force by others. Indeed, the very concept of deterrence is meaningless without a credible willingness to use; hence "deterrence" equals "threat to use."

---

[1] Quoted in M. Bundy, DANGER AND SURVIVAL: CHOICES ABOUT THE BOMB IN THE FIRST FIFTY YEARS 480 (1988).

Thus, the question posed by the General Assembly goes beyond the **jus in bello** query of the World Health Assembly and ventures forth into the area of **jus ad bellum**. But the doctrine of **jus ad bellum**, as elaborated since the enactment of Article 2(4) of the United Nations Charter, leaves no room for the legality of the threat of force under international law. Article 2(4) categorically prohibits the threat or use of force by one state against another. The only exception to this prohibition is Article 51, which preserves "the inherent right of individual or collective self-defense if an armed attack occurs against a Member of the United Nations." But nothing in Article 51 sanctions a standing threat - a threat **in futuro** - by one state against another, named or unnamed. It sanctions only the use of retaliatory force once an armed attack occurs. Its application is limited to the very brief time span following an attack; it cannot, therefore, sanction the threat of the use of force as a hypothetical matter inherent in the military doctrine of this or that state.

Furthermore, the use of force in self-defense is subject to the rules of **jus in bello**. Hence, if use of nuclear weapons is prohibited under the rubric of **jus in bello**, the threat to use nuclear weapons can never be sanctioned under the rubric of **jus ad bellum**.

II. The Law of Peace and Security (*Jus ad Bellum*)

All States must avoid the threat or use of force in their relations with one another.

A. United Nations Charter

The United Nations Charter specifically prohibits the threat or use of force. Under the U.N. Charter, Article 2(4):

> All Members shall refrain in their international relations from the threat or use of force against the territorial integrity or political independence of any state, or in any other manner inconsistent with the Purposes of the United Nations.[2]

The prohibition on the threat or use of force under Article 2(4) has the status of *jus*

---

[2] U.N. Charter art. 2, para. 4.

cogens, a peremptory rule of international law.[3] Moreover, this prohibition extends to non-member States.[4]

The United Nations Charter permits the threat or use of force only in individual or collective self-defense, including Security Council enforcement measures. Under Article 51:

> Nothing in the present Charter shall impair the inherent right of individual or collective self-defence if an armed attack occurs against a Member of the United Nations, until the Security Council has taken measures necessary to maintain international peace and security....[5]

The Charter's prohibition on the threat or use of force, with the limited exception of self-defense, reflects a change in the development of international law. Historically, ***Jus ad Bellum***, or the law of "just war", recognized the right of a state to resort to war for "just" reasons. In 1919, the Covenant of the League of Nations further limited a State's right to "resort to war".[6]

---

[3] According to the International Law Commission, "the great majority of international lawyers today unhesitatingly holds that [Article 2(4)] together with other provisions of the U.N. Charter, authoritatively declares the modern customary law regarding the threat or use of force." ILC Yearbook, 1966, vol. 2, p.247. The International Court of Justice affirmed this position in Military and Paramilitary Activities in and Against Nicaragua (Nicaragua v. United States), Merits, 1986 ICJ Rep. 14, 98-101 (Judgment of June 27). In addition, the Restatement (Third) of Foreign Relations Law includes "the principles of the United Nations Charter prohibiting the use of force" among peremptory norms. § 102 comment k.

[4] U.N. Charter art. 2, para. 6 provides:

> The Organization shall ensure that states which are not Members of the United Nations act in accordance with these Principles so far as may be necessary for the maintenance of international peace and security.

See also Josef Mrazek, *Prohibition of the Use and Threat of Force: Self-Defence and Self-Help in International Law,* 1989 CANADIAN Y.B. OF INT'L L. 81, 85.

[5] U.N. Charter art. 51. The Security Council, acting within the interests of collective security, has the authority to determine "the existence of any threat to the peace, breach of the peace, or act of aggression", U.N. Charter, art. 39. The Security Council is further authorized to determine and employ enforcement measures under Article 41 (not involving the use of armed force) and Article 42 (action involving the use of armed force).

[6] League of Nations Covenant, art. 12, para. 1, states:

> The Members of the League agree that if there should arise between them any dispute likely to lead to a rupture, they will submit the matter either to

In 1928, the General Treaty for the Renunciation of War (Kellogg-Briand Pact, also known as the Paris Peace Pact of 27 August 1928) prohibited aggressive war "as an instrument of national policy" and "for the solution of international controversies".[7]

The language of the Charter prohibits the "threat or use of force" rather than "resort to war", as the Covenant of the League of Nations did. The change in terminology reflects the recognition that a State might resort to the threat or use of force which does not rise to the level of war or resort to armed conflict without an open declaration of war.[8]

The League of Nations Covenant did, nevertheless, recognize the danger of threats in international relations. The Covenant declared "any war or threat of war" a matter of concern to the entire League and grounds for the League to take action to "safeguard the peace of nations."[9]

The principles behind the Kellogg-Briand Pact and the League of Nations Covenant provided a foundation for the United Nations Charter.[10] The *travaux preparatoires* that preceded the adoption of the Charter further indicate a general understanding that a state of peace "could not be regarded merely as maintenance of the status quo but that it should imply active co-operation between Member States in order to promote the purposes of the Organization."[11] Thus, Article 2(3), which requires States to settle disputes peacefully, complements the prohibition on the threat or use of force.[12] Moreover, the Charter's preamble calls on States "to practice

---

> arbitration or judicial settlement or to inquiry by the Council, and they agree in no case to resort to war until three months after the award by the arbitrators or the judicial decision or the report by the Council.

[7] 46 Stat. 2343, T.S. No. 796, 2 Bevans 732, 99 L.N.T.S. 57

[8] N. Bentwich and A. Martin, A COMMENTARY ON THE CHARTER OF THE UNITED NATIONS 13 (1950).

[9] League of Nations Covenant art. 11, para. 1.

[10] J. Keegan, A HISTORY OF WARFARE 383 (1993); G. Herczegh, *The Prohibition of the Threat and Use of Force in Contemporary International Law*, in QUESTIONS OF INTERNATIONAL LAW 70 (1964).

[11] Herczegh, *Id.* at 78.

[12] U.N. Charter, art. 2, para. 3, provides:

> All Members shall settle their international disputes by peaceful means in such a manner that international peace and security, and justice, are not endangered.

tolerance and live together in peace with one another as good neighbours". These affirmative obligations to cooperate peacefully would clearly be inconsistent with a legal regime that tolerates threats between States.

The Opening Statement by Mr. Hans Corell, Under-Secretary-General for Legal Affairs at the United Nations, during the Congress on Public International Law in March, 1995, reaffirmed the principles that law should govern the relations between States and that disputes should be resolved peacefully:

> [L]et this Congress also be a resounding appeal to those who ultimately make the decisions that affect our destiny. To them, our message should be:
>
> -Yours is the responsibility to ensure that international law is applied and that legal advice is sought before important decisions are made in foreign policy matters. . . .
>
> -And, if disputes occur, yours is the responsibility to refrain from the use of force and to make sure that these disputes are resolved by peaceful means.[13]

The preparatory work of the United States in anticipation of the creation of the United Nations reflects a concern with threats of force. A Memorandum containing "basic ideas which might be embodied in a constitution of an international organization for the maintenance of peace and security" listed as the first among the functions and purposes of the organization "to prevent the use of force or of threats to use force".[14] As the first of the principal obligations of a member state, the Memorandum listed "To refrain from use of force or threat to use force. . . ."[15]

The proposals which emerged from the Dumbarton Oaks Conference, in preparation for the United Nations Conference in San Francisco, formed the basis of the U.N. Charter. At Dumbarton Oaks, the United States proposals were accepted as the basis for discussion and the structure they established was generally accepted.[16] The Dumbarton Oaks draft of the principle

---

[13] H. Corell, Opening Statement, United Nations Congress on Public International Law, New York, 13-17 March, 1995.

[14] Memorandum for the President, Dec. 29, 1943, in U.S. Department of State, *Postwar Foreign Policy Preparation, 1939-1945,* Publication 3580 (February 195), Appendix 33, pp. 376-81 (reproduced in R. Russel, A HISTORY OF THE UNITED NATIONS CHARTER, App. F (1958)).

[15] *Id.*

[16] E. Luard, A HISTORY OF THE UNITED NATIONS, Vol. 1, 27 (1982). *See also* L. Goodrich & E. Hambro, CHARTER OF THE UNITED NATIONS: COMMENTARY AND DOCUMENTS 6 (2nd ed. 1949).

which became Article 2(4) read:

> All members of the Organization shall refrain in their international relations from the threat or use of force in any manner inconsistent with the purpose of the Organization.[17]

Australia's amendment added the prohibition on threats or use of force "against the territorial integrity or political independence of any member or State."[18]

B. United Nations Resolutions and Declarations

Numerous United Nations resolutions and declarations have confirmed the principle that States shall refrain from the threat or use of force in their international relations.

The Declaration on Principles of International Law Concerning Friendly Relations and Co-operation Among States in Accordance with the Charter of the United Nations[19] reiterates the language of Article 2(4) and adds:

> Such a threat or use of force constitutes a violation of international law and the Charter of the United Nations and shall never be employed as a means of settling international issues.[20]

The Declaration on the Inadmissibility of Intervention in the Domestic Affairs of States and the Protection of Their Independence and Sovereignty[21] states: "No state has the right to intervene . . . in the internal or external affairs of any other state. Consequently, armed intervention and all other forms of interference or attempted threats . . . are condemned." The Declaration notes that intervention is not admissible "for any reason whatever."

The 1987 Declaration on the Enhancement of the Effectiveness of the Principle of Refraining from the Threat or Use of Force in International Relations affirms the principle of Article 2(4) and of the Declaration on Principles of International Law Concerning Friendly Relations, and adds:

---

[17] Doc. 1 (English) G/1. UNCIO Documents, Vol. III, p. 3.

[18] Doc. 2 (English) G/14 (1), May 5, 1945. UNCIO Documents, Vol. III, p. 543.

[19] G.A. Res. 2625 (XXXV 1970).

[20] *Id.*, para.1.

[21] G.A. Res. 2131 (XX) (1965).

> The principle of refraining from the threat or use of force in international relations is universal in character and is binding, regardless of each State's political, economic, social or cultural system or relations of alliance.[22]

This Declaration provides further that "States have the duty to abstain from armed intervention and all other forms of interference or attempted threats against the personality of the State or against its political, economic and cultural elements."[23] In addition, neither acquisition nor occupation of territory resulting from the threat or use of force will be recognized as legal,[24] and a treaty procured by the threat or use of force is void.[25]

The Final Document of the First Special Session of the United Nations General Assembly on Disarmament stated that "[State members] stress the special importance of refraining from the threat or use of force against the sovereignty, territorial integrity or political independence of any State, or against peoples under colonial or foreign domination. . . ."[26]

Additional Declarations, which reaffirm the principle of refraining from the threat or use of force include: Essentials of Peace,[27] Declaration on the Strengthening of International Security,[28] Declaration on the Inadmissibility of Intervention and Interference in the Internal Affairs of States,[29] and Declaration on the Prevention and Removal of Disputes and Situations

---

[22] G.A. Res. 42/22 (XLII), para. 2.

[23] *Id.* para. 7.

[24] *Id.* para. 10.

[25] *Id.* para. 11.

[26] First Special Session of the General Assembly on Disarmament 1978, Final Document, para. 26.

[27] G.A. Res. 290 (IV). Paragraph 3 calls upon every nation "To refrain from any threats or acts, direct or indirect, aimed at impairing the freedom, independence or integrity of any State...."

[28] G.A. Res. 2734 (XXV). Paragraph 5 provides that the General Assembly:

> Solemnly reaffirms that every State has the duty to refrain from the threat or use of force against the territorial integrity and political independence of any other State . . . and that every State has the duty to refrain from organizing, instigating, assisting or participating in acts of civil strife or terrorist acts in another State.

[29] G.A. Res. 36/103. Paragraph 2 provides that: "The principle of non-intervention and non-interference in the internal and external affairs of States comprehends the following rights and

Which May Threaten International Peace and Security and on the Role of the United Nations in This Field.[30]

C. Collective Security Treaties

A number of collective security treaties confirm the symbolic nature of threat and use of force. The North Atlantic Treaty (the NATO Treaty)[31] requires State Parties "to refrain in their international relations from the threat or use of force in any manner inconsistent with the purposes of the United Nations." Similarly, the now-lapsed Treaty of Friendship, Cooperation and Mutual Assistance (the Warsaw Pact)[32] requires Contracting Parties "to refrain in their international relations from the threat or use of force".

The Final Act of the Conference on Security and Co-operation in Europe[33] requires States participating to refrain from the threat or use of force, repeating the language of the Charter. Moreover, "[n]o consideration may be invoked to serve to warrant resort to the threat or use of force in contravention of this principle" and "[n]o such threat or use of force will be employed as a means of settling disputes, or questions likely to give rise to disputes. . . ."

The American Treaty on Pacific Settlement[34] requires the contracting parties to ". . .refrain

---

duties . . . [including, under II(a)] the duty of States to refrain in their international relations from the threat or use of force in any form whatsoever . . . to disrupt the political, social or economic order of other States. . . ."

[30] G.A. Res. 43/51, Preamble:

> Reaffirming the Declaration on Principles of International Law Concerning Friendly Relations and Co-operation Among States in Accordance with the Charter of the United Nations . . . and the Declaration on the Enhancement of the Effectiveness of the Principle of Refraining from the Threat or Use of Force in International Relations,
>
> Recalling that it is the duty of States to refrain in their international relations from military, political, economic or any other form of coercion against the political independence or territorial integrity of any State . . . .

[31] 63 Stat. 2241, T.I.A.S. No. 1964, 4 Bevans. 828, 34 V.A.T.S. 243 (1949) art. 1.

[32] 219 U.N.T.S. 3 (1955) art. 1.

[33] 14 I.L.M. 1292 (1975), also knows as "the Helsinki Final Act", Section II, Refraining from the Threat or Use of Force.

[34] Also known as the "Treaty of Bogota", 30 U.N.T.S. 55 (1948), chapter one, art. I.

from the threat or the use of force, or from any other means of coercion for the settlement of their controversies. . . ."

The Convention on the Rights and Duties of States[35] holds that "No state has the right to intervene in the internal or external affairs of another."

In addition, the Charter of the Organization of American States[36] provides:

> No State or group of States has the right to intervene, directly or indirectly, for any reason whatever, in the internal or external affairs of any other States. The foregoing principle prohibits not only armed force but also any other form of interference or attempted threat against the personality of the State or against its political, economic and cultural elements.

D. The Nuremberg Principles

The General Assembly unanimously affirmed "the principles of international law recognized by the Charter of the Nuremberg Tribunal and the judgment of the Tribunal."[37] The principles "have since been universally considered to constitute an authoritative statement of the rules of customary international law."[38] The Nuremberg offenses "correspond largely to the obligations imposed by certain rules of jus cogens".[39]

The principles as codified by the International Law Commission[40] define crimes against peace as:

i. Planning, preparation, initiation or waging of a war of aggression or a

---

[35] Also known as the "Treaty of Montevideo", 49 Stat. 3097, T.S. No. 881, Bevans 145, 165 L.N.T.S. 19 (1933) art. 8.

[36] 2 U.S.T. 2394, T.I.A.S. 2361, 119 U.N.T.S. 3 (1948) art. 15.

[37] G.A. Res. 95(I), 188 U.N. Doc. A/64/Add.1 (1946).

[38] F. Boyle, *The Relevance of International Law to the "Paradox" of Nuclear Deterrence*, 80 Nw. U.L. Rev. 1407, 1416 (1986) (citing I. Brownlie, INTERNATIONAL LAW AND THE USE OF FORCE BY STATES 154-213 (1963)).

[39] *Report of the International Law Commission*, 28th Session, 31 U.N. GAOR Supp. (No. 10) at 246, (1976) 2 Y.B. Int'l L. Comm'n (Pt. 2) at 104.

[40] *Report of the International Law Commission*, 2d Session, 5 U.N. GAOR Supp. (No. 12) 11, U.N. Doc. A/1316 (1950), 2 Y.B. Int'l L. Comm'n 374, U.N. Doc. A/Cn.4/SERA/1950/Add.1

war in violation of international treaties, agreements or assurances

ii. Participation in a common plan or conspiracy for the accomplishment of any of the acts mentioned under (i).

A crime against peace is "a culpable violation of the *jus ad bellum*".[41]

Planning and preparing for aggression thus is clearly proscribed. In addition, while not so applied by the Nuremberg tribunals, the Nuremberg principles support the proscription of planning and preparation for war crimes and crimes against humanity. A war involving such crimes would be a "war in violation of international treaties, agreements or assurances". Also, the Charter of the International Military Tribunal[42] and Control Council Law No. 10[43] provided for individual responsibility for participation in a "plan" to commit all three Nuremberg offenses (crimes against peace, war crimes, and crimes against humanity). Similarly, the Statute of the International Tribunal for the Prosecution of Persons Responsible for Serious Violations of International Humanitarian Law Committed in the Territory of the Former Yugoslavia provides for individual responsibility for the planning and preparation or execution of any crime referred to in the Statute.[44]

The discussion regarding crimes against peace turns on the concept and definition of aggression. Section II.F *infra* examines threats of aggression.

E. Opinio Juris

The United Nations Charter and the treaties and resolutions cited above do not distinguish between the legal status of the threat to use force and that of the use of force itself. Both are equally prohibited. Indeed, "[i]f the promise is to resort to force in conditions in which no justification for the use of force exists, the threat itself is illegal."[45]

---

[41] H. McCoubrey and N. White, INTERNATIONAL LAW AND ARMED CONFLICT 334 (1992).

[42] Art. 6, 59 U.S. Stat. 546 (1945).

[43] Art. I(2), 3 Official Gazette Control Council for Germany 50 (1946), (reprinted in 2 L. Friedman, THE LAW OF WAR 908 (1972)) Law No. 10 governed the 12 subsequent trials of major war criminals.

[44] Art 7(1), Annex to Report of the Secretary-General Pursuant to Paragraph 2 of Security Council Resolution 808 (1993), S/25704, 2 May 1993.

[45] Brownlie, INTERNATIONAL LAW AND THE USE OF FORCE BY STATES (1963), p. 364 (citing L. Oppenheim, INTERNATIONAL LAW: A TREATISE, Vol. II, 7th Ed. (Ed. H. Lauterpacht, 1952); U.K. MANUAL OF MILITARY LAW, part iii (1958), para. 11).

The significance of the prohibition on threats of force becomes apparent when one considers the implications for previously accepted legal norms. Oppenheim's discussion of threats of force in relation to the obligation to issue an ultimatum before resorting to war suggests that the prohibition on the threat of force overrides previously accepted and codified legal standards:

> In so far as the Charter of the United Nations prohibits not only acts of force but also threats of force, the question arises as to the operation, as between the Members of the United Nations, of the provisions of the Hague Convention in the matter of ultimatum and, to some extent, of declaration of war. If it is unlawful for Members of the United Nations to threaten another State with the use of force, how can they properly be in a position to comply with the obligation to issue an ultimatum prior to resorting to war? The correct answer is probably that as between Members of the United Nations these provisions of the Hague Convention, although not directly conflicting with the Charter, are substantially obsolete.[46]

The prohibition of the threat of force applies even where the threat is not carried out. As Professor Oscar Schachter notes,

> The preponderance of military strength in some states and their political relations with potential target states may justifiably lead to an inference of a threat of force against the political independence of the target state. . . . [and] the applicability of article 2(4) in principle can hardly be denied.[47]

However, even though relative military strength and political relations can create situations of threat, "[c]uriously [Article 2(4)] has not been invoked much as an explicit prohibition of such implied threats."[48] According to Schachter, this may be due to the "difficulty of demonstrating coercive intent" or to the widespread, though not unlimited, tolerance for disparities of power.[49]

---

[46] L. Oppenheim, INTERNATIONAL LAW: A TREATISE, Vol. II, 297 (7th ed., H. Lauterpacht, ed. 1952).

[47] O. Schachter, *The Right of States to Use Armed Force*, 82 MICH. L. REV. 1620, 1625 (1984).

[48] Id.

[49] *Id.* Schachter notes further that:

> A blatant and direct threat of force, used to compel another state to yield territory or make substantial political concessions (not required by law), would have to be seen as illegal under article 2(4) if the words "threat of force" are to have any meaning.

An alternative explanation for the underuse of the prohibition on threat in Article 2(4) is the difficulty of invoking it effectively. Since the authority to do so lies with the Security Council, the failure of the non-permanent members to exercise that authority does not so much indicate their tolerance of implied or actual threats by the permanent members - who are also the declared nuclear weapon states - but rather their recognition of power disparities and the veto power of the permanent members.

International legal scholars differ somewhat in their analyses of what constitutes a threat of force and what the role of threats in international law is. According to Ian Brownlie, a threat "consists in an express or implied promise by a government of a resort to force conditional on non-acceptance of certain demands of that government."[50] Romana Sadurska regards a threat in the international arena as "a message, explicit or implicit, formulated by a decision maker and directed to the target audience, indicating that force will be used if a rule or demand is not complied with."[51] Both experts suggest that use of force is conditional on the target's response to the threat and that the threat might be "implicit" or "implied", as well as "explicit" or "express".

In the *Corfu Channel Case*[52] the International Court of Justice concluded that the passage of British warships through the North Corfu Strait did not violate Albanian sovereignty. In that case, Albania had earlier fired on British ships, and the British "'mission' was designed to affirm a right which had been unjustly denied,"[53] i.e., the right of passage. The Court also held that Albania's obligation to notify international shipping of the mining of her waters stemmed from "certain general and well-recognized principles, namely: elementary considerations of humanity, even more exacting in peace than in war; and every state's obligation not to allow knowingly its territory to be used for acts contrary to the rights of other states."[54] A concurring opinion by Judge Alvarez drew "special attention" to "acts contrary to international law, which are related to the present dispute: *intervention, pressure* or *threat of force, demonstration of force,* with a view to intimidation, *violation of sovereignty,* and *misuse of right. . . .*"[55]

---

[50] Brownlie, *supra* note 45, at 364.

[51] R. Sadurska, *Threats of Force*, 82 AM. J. INT'L L. 239, 242 (1988). Sadurska argues that threats "may not be detrimental, indeed may even be beneficial, to the preservation of international order" but admits that "this is a precarious game" and that "an environment in which threats of force are regularly used is likely to be very unstable." *Id.*, at 239-240, 247, 250, n. 54.

[52] United Kingdom v. Albania, 1949 ICJ Rep. 4 (Merits), (Judgment of April 9).

[53] *Id.* at 30.

[54] *Id.* at 22.

[55] *Id.* 39 (Individual Opinion by Judge Alvarez) at 46 (emphasis in the original).

In the *Fisheries Jurisdiction Case,*[56] a dissenting opinion by Judge Padilla Nervo notes the following regarding threats:

> A big power can use force and pressure against a small nation in many ways, even by the very fact of diplomatically insisting in having its view recognized and accepted. The Royal Navy did not need to use armed force, its mere presence on the seas inside the fishery limits of the coastal State could be enough pressure. It is well known by professors, jurists and diplomats acquainted with international relations and foreign policies, that certain "Notes" delivered by the government of a strong power to the government of a small nations, may have the same purpose and the same effect as the use or threat of force.[57]

F. Threats of Aggression

A threat of force alone does not constitute an "act of aggression" under the U.N. "Definition of Aggression" Resolution.[58] In fact, the Definition suggests that not all uses of force constitute acts of aggression, noting in the Preamble that "aggression is the most serious and dangerous form of the illegal use of force."[59]

The International Law Commission incorporated the General Assembly's definition of aggression in the Draft Code of Crimes Against Peace and Security of Mankind.[60] Significantly, the Draft Code includes a separate article for the crime of the Threat of Aggression:[61]

> 1. An individual who as leader or organizer commits or orders the commission of a threat of aggression shall, on conviction thereof, be sentenced . . . .

---

[56] United Kingdom v. Iceland, 1973 ICJ Rep. 3 (Judgment of February 2).

[57] *Id.* at 47.

[58] G.A. Res. 3314 (XXIX 1974). Article 1 of the Definition states that:

> Aggression is the use of armed force by a State against the sovereignty, territorial integrity or political independence of another State, or in any other manner inconsistent with the Charter of the United Nations. . . .

[59] *Id.*

[60] *Draft Code of Crimes Against the Peace and Security of Mankind, Report of the Commission to the General Assembly on the work of its forty-third session,* 1991 Y.B. Int'l L. Comm'n vol. II, part two, art. 15, U.N. Doc. A/CN/4/SER.A/1991/Add.1 (part 2).

[61] Id. art. 16.

> 2. Threat of aggression consists of declarations, communications, demonstrations of force or any other measures which would give good reason to the Government of a State to believe that aggression is being seriously contemplated against that State.

The International Law Commission Report on the Draft Code to the General Assembly notes that in the context of this article, "the word 'threat' denotes acts undertaken with a view to making a State believe that force will be used against it if certain demands are not met by that State."[62] A threat might take the form of declarations ("expressions made public in writing or orally"), communications ("messages sent by the authorities of one Government to the authorities of another Government, by no matter what means of transmission") and demonstrations of force (eg., "concentrations of troops near the frontier").[63] Moreover, the Commission emphasized that the threat of aggression does not justify a threatened State resorting to force in self-defence.[64]

The Commission was careful to link the acts of an individual who commits a crime against peace and security with the State. Only individuals "vested with the authority of the State" have the potential to commit this offense.[65] However, the State is not exempted from its responsibility for the crime. Thus, although the Draft Code places the liability directly on the individual[66], it also provides that:

> Prosecution of an individual for a crime against the peace and security of mankind does not relieve a State of any responsibility under international law for an act or omission attributable to it.[67]

The Commission also noted the importance of defining a crime of threat of aggression, particularly since powerful states have the potential to achieve improper objectives without committing an actual act of aggression.[68] Indeed, the Sixth Committee of the General Assembly, in its review of the Commission Report, noted that "there had been many cases of States that had

---

[62] 1989 Y.B. Int'l L. Comm'n, vol. 2, part 2, U.N. Doc. A/CN.4/SER.A/1989/Add.1 (part 2), p.68.

[63] *Id.*

[64] Id.

[65] 1989 Y.B. Int'l L. Comm'n, vol. 1, U.N. Doc. A/CN.4/SER.A/1989, p. 296.

[66] Article 3, Responsibility and punishment.

[67] Article 5.

[68] 1989 Y.B. Int'l L. Comm'n vol. 1, *supra* note 60, at 294, para. 11 (statement of Mr. Beesley).

lost their independence through threats and ultimatums."[69] The record went on to note:

> Contemporary international law prohibited not only the use of force, but also the threat of the use of force, and thus its inclusion in the code would reaffirm the position of the international community in that regard.[70]

The Draft Code of Crimes Against the Peace and Security of Mankind reflects the recent development of the concept of crimes against peace.

III. Specific Law Regarding the Threat of Use of Nuclear Weapons

The Charter of the United Nations was adopted in San Francisco on June 26, 1945, six weeks before the first use of the atom bomb on August 6, 1945.[71] Had this time sequence been reversed, the Charter might well have contained a specific prohibition on the threat and use of nuclear weapons and other weapons of mass destruction. "The fact, however, that the existence of atomic weapons means an unprecedented source of danger for mankind, and that it may be one of the gravest forms of the threat of force, was immediately recognized by the United Nations, which then tried to solve this problem."[72] The concern of the world community with this new, startling development was evidenced by the fact that the first resolution adopted by the United Nations dealt with the subject of atomic energy and called, *inter alia*, "for the elimination from national armaments of atomic weapons and of all other major weapons adaptable to mass destruction. . . ."[73]

---

[69] U.N. GAOR Sixth Committee (31st mtg.) at 15, U.N. Doc. A/C.6/44/SR.31 (1989) (statement of Mr. Gondra).

[70] *Id.*

[71] Herczegh, *supra* note 10, at 88.

[72] *Id.* Former United States Secretary of State John Foster Dulles also stressed that if the drafters of the Charter had known of the role nuclear weapons were to play, they would have adopted more "emphatic and realistic" provisions to deal with disarmament and regulation. *U.S. Constitution and U.N. Charter: An Appraisal*, Address by the Secretary of State John Foster Dulles before the American Bar Association at Boston on Aug. 26, 1953, Dept. of State Publication 5194.

[73] G.A. Res. 0101, Establishment of a Commission to Deal with the Problems Raised by the Discovery of Atomic Energy, adopted unanimously, para. 5(c) (1946).

A. Treaties

The preamble of the Treaty on the Non-Proliferation of Nuclear Weapons[74] calls for "the cessation of the manufacture of nuclear weapons, the liquidation of all their existing stockpiles, and the elimination from national arsenals of nuclear weapons and their means of delivery...." Specifically, the Treaty prohibits the manufacture or acquisition of nuclear weapons by non-nuclear weapon States,[75] and it requires nuclear weapon States to "pursue negotiations in good faith on effective measures relating to cessation of the nuclear arms race at an early date and to nuclear disarmament."[76] The threat of use of nuclear weapons is inconsistent with the general purpose and goal of the treaty as well as the specific requirements of State parties.

The South Pacific Nuclear Free Zone Treaty prohibits the manufacture, acquisition, possession or control of nuclear weapons.[77] The Treaty for the Prohibition of Nuclear Weapons in Latin America prohibits the testing, use manufacture, production or acquisition of nuclear weapons, directly or indirectly, by parties to the treaty or within the region defined by the treaty.[78]

The pattern in international law regarding weapons of mass destruction is to prohibit not only the use but also the manufacture and acquisition of these weapons. The treaties discussed above seek to eliminate both the use and the threat to use nuclear weapons; in no instance do they prohibit use but tolerate possession. Similarly, treaties regarding other weapons of mass destruction, namely biological weapons[79] and chemical weapons[80], link threat and use. The

---

[74] 21 U.S.T. 483, T.I.A.S. No. 6839, 729 U.N.T.S. 161, 7 I.L.M. 811 (1968).

[75] *Id.* art. II.

[76] *Id.* art. VI.

[77] Also known as the Treaty of Rarotonga, 24 I.L.M. 1440, (1985), art. 3.

[78] Also known as the Treaty of Tlatelolco, 22 U.S.T. 762, T.I.A.S. No. 7137, 6 I.L.M. 521 (1967), art. 1.

[79] Convention on the Prohibition of the Development, Production, and Stockpiling of Bacteriological (Biological) and Toxin Weapons and on Their Destruction, U.N. Res. 2826 (XXVI 1972), 26 U.S.T. 583, T.I.A.S. No. 8062, 11 I.L.M. 309 (1972). Article I provides: "Each State Party to this Convention undertakes never in any circumstances to develop, produce, stockpile or otherwise acquire or retain" biological weapons.

[80] Convention on the Prohibition of the Development, Production, Stockpiling and Use of Chemical Weapons and on Their Destruction, opened for signature in Paris on 13 January 1993. A United Nations *Treaty Series* registration number will be assigned once it enters into force. Article I.1 provides: "Each State Party to this Convention undertakes never under any

illegality of the threat to use these weapons is underscored by provisions calling for their destruction.[81]

B. Security Council Resolutions

Resolution 984 (April 11, 1995) gives non-nuclear States assurances from the nuclear States that nuclear weapons will not be threatened or used against them. All of the declared nuclear States supported this resolution.

Resolution 255 of the Security Council provides that aggression or the threat of aggression with nuclear weapons against a non-nuclear weapon State would require the Security Council to act immediately.[82]

Resolutions 984 and 255 therefore implicitly recognize the illegality of the threat and use of nuclear weapons against a non-nuclear weapon state. A legal act would not require assurances against use nor require Security Council response.[83]

C. United Nations General Assembly, Conference on Disarmament and Disarmament Commission

As discussed above, the framers of the Charter could not be aware of the threat of nuclear weapons, but the first United Nations resolution addressed elimination of these weapons.[84]

---

circumstances (a) To develop, produce, otherwise acquire, stockpile or retain chemical weapons . . . (b) To use chemical weapons. . . ."

[81] Article II of the Biological Weapons Convention and Article I.2 of the Chemical Weapons Convention.

[82] S.C. Res. 255 (1968). The relevant text reads as follows:

> The Security Council . . . [r]ecognizes that aggression with nuclear weapons of the threat of such aggression against a non-nuclear weapon State would create a situation in which the Security Council, and above all its nuclear-weapon State permanent members, would have to act immediately in accordance with their obligations under the United Nations Charter.

[83] *Supra* note 5.

[84] *See supra* notes 71-73 and accompanying text.

Another early resolution of the General Assembly[85] reaffirms the prohibition on the threat or use of force and, in this context, calls on the Disarmament Commission to develop comprehensive plans providing for the "elimination and prohibition of all major weapons . . . adaptable to mass destruction"[86] and, specifically, the "effective international control of atomic energy to ensure the prohibition of atomic weapons . . . ."[87]

The issue of assurances for non-nuclear weapon States against the use or threat of use of nuclear weapons has received overwhelming support from the international community. The General Assembly has passed numerous resolutions affirming the urgency of reaching an early agreement on effective international arrangements to assure non-nuclear weapon States against the use or threat of use of nuclear weapons.[88] Significantly, no state has opposed the conclusion of these assurances. Most recently, for example, 168 States voted in favor of this resolution and only three countries abstained (France, the United Kingdom, and the United States). Even the three States generally considered to have secret nuclear weapons arsenals (India, Israel and Pakistan) voted in favor of these assurances.

The conclusion of effective international arrangements to assure non-nuclear-weapons States against the use or threat of use of nuclear weapons has been a key agenda item of the U.N. Conference on Disarmament, and the Ad Hoc Committee established to review this item has consistently been re-established at the start of each annual session. Most recently, the Committee's report, adopted by the Conference on Disarmament, noted as follows:

> All delegations reiterated that they attach particular importance to the question of international arrangements to assure non-nuclear-weapon States against the use or threat of use of nuclear weapons and expressed their readiness to engage in a search for a mutually acceptable solution of the issue.[89]

Additionally, the report of the Conference "stressed the necessity to recognize the right

---

[85] G.A. Res. 704 (VII) (1953).

[86] *Id.* para. 2(a).

[87] *Id.* para. 2(c).

[88] *E.g.* G.A. Res. 49/73 (1994), G.A. Res. 48/73 (1993), G.A. Res. 47/50 (1992), G.A. Res. 46/32 (1991), G.A. Res. 45/54 (1990), G.A. Res. 44/111 (1989), G.A. Res. 43/69 (1988), G.A. Res. 42/32 (1987), G.A. Res. 41/52 (1986), G.A. Res. 40/86 (1985), G.A. Res. 39/58, G.A. Res. 38/68 (1983) et al. All of these resolutions bear the name "Conclusion of effective international arrangements to assure non-nuclear-weapon States against the use or threat of use of nuclear weapons."

[89] Report of the Conference on Disarmament, 49 U.N. GAOR Supp. (No. 27) (Agenda Item 33) at 130-131, U.N. Doc. A/49/27 (1994).

of non-nuclear-weapon States not to be attacked nor threatened with these weapons."[90] It is significant that, in referring to this right, the Report called for its recognition rather than its creation.

The complete elimination of nuclear weapons has been a constant and recurring objective of the Disarmament Commission and the Conference on Disarmament.[91]

In addition, the General Assembly has passed over 100 resolutions stating nuclear disarmament or the elimination of nuclear weapons as a goal.[92] Thus, the majority of states do not accept the necessity argument for deterrence. A growing number of states have specifically prohibited nuclear weapons in their territory and have established, or are in the process of establishing, nuclear weapons free zones.

D. The Non-Derogable Right to Life

The United Nations Human Rights Committee, which supervises the implementation of the International Covenant on Civil and Political Rights[93] [ICCPR], has determined that nuclear weapons threaten the non-derogable right to life:

> [T]he designing, testing, manufacture, possession and deployment of nuclear weapons are among the greatest threats to the right to life which confront mankind today. This threat is compounded by the danger that the actual use of nuclear weapons may be brought about, not only in the event of war, but even through human or mechanical error or failure. Furthermore, the very existence and gravity of this threat generates a climate of suspicion and fear between States, which is in itself antagonistic to the promotion of universal respect for and observance of human rights and fundamental freedoms in accordance with the Charter of the

---

[90] *Id.*

[91] *E.g.* Report of the Disarmament Commission, 49 U.N. GAOR Supp. (No. 42) (Agenda Item 4) at 4, U.N. Doc. A/49/42; Report of the Disarmament Commission, 48 U.N. GAOR Supp. (No. 42) (Agenda Item 4) at 4, U.N. Doc. A/48/42; Report of the Conference on Disarmament, *supra* note 41, (Agenda Item 2) at 1; Report of the Conference on Disarmament, 48 U.N. GAOR Supp. (No. 27) (Agenda Item 2) at 1, U.N. Doc. A/48/27; Report of the Conference on Disarmament, 47 U.N. GAOR Supp. (No. 27) (Agenda Item 2) at 2, U.N. Doc. A/47/27.

[92] *See* Appendix B.

[93] 999 U.N.T.S. 171, 6 I.L.M. 368 (1967). Entered into force on March 23, 1976. Article 6, para. 1 reads: "Every human being has the inherent right to life. This right shall be protected by law. No one shall be arbitrarily deprived of his life."

United Nations and the International Covenants on Human Rights.[94]

In other words, nuclear weapons both threaten the right to life and contribute to the spirit of mistrust among States which compounds the likelihood of threats being carried out. In addition, the threat to use nuclear weapons conflicts with the commitment to provide children with the protection of society and the State[95] and to protect families.[96]

The right to life is confirmed as well in the European Convention for the Protection of Human Rights and Fundamental Freedoms[97] [ECHR], and the American Convention on Human Rights[98] [ACHR]. Under the ICCPR, the ECHR, and the ACHR, a derogation clause may be invoked in exceptional situations that threaten the life of the nation. However, the right to life is one of the four non-derogable rights which constitute the "irreducible core"[99] of human rights. A non-derogable right is one which cannot be suspended by the State even in times of public emergency.

Moreover, according to Judge Schwebel of the International Court of Justice, matters affecting international human rights obligations cannot be regarded as exclusively within domestic jurisdiction of a particular State:

> Once a state has undertaken obligations toward another state, or toward the international community, in a specified sphere of human rights, it may no longer maintain, vis-a-vis the other state or the international community, that matters in that sphere are exclusively or essentially within its domestic jurisdiction and

---

[94] Report of the Human Rights Committee, General Comment 14(23) on Article 6 of the Covenant, 2 November 1984: U.N. GAOR (40th Session) Supp. (No.40), Annex VI, 162, U.N. Doc. A/40/40.

[95] ICCPR, art. 24.

[96] ICCPR, art. 23.

[97] 213 U.N.T.S. 221, E.T.S. 5 (1950), art. 2.

[98] O.A.S. Official Records OEA/SER. K/XVI/1.1 Doc. 65, Rev. 1, Corr. 1, 9 ILM 101 (1970), 65 A.J.I.L. 679 (1971), art. 4.

[99] J. Oraa, HUMAN RIGHTS IN STATES OF EMERGENCY IN INTERNATIONAL LAW 96 (1992). The other non-derogable rights are: the right to be free from torture and other inhuman or degrading treatment or punishment (ICCPR, art. 7; ECHR, art.3; ACHR, art. 5), the right to be free from slavery or servitude (ICCPR, art. 8; ECHR, art. 4, ACHR, art. 6), and the principle of non-retroactivity of penal laws (ICCPR, art. 15, ECHR, art. 7, ACHR, art. 9).

outside the range of international concern.[100]

Thus the manufacture and possession of nuclear weapons, which violate the right to life, cannot be defended by nuclear weapon States either as essential for defense in times of public emergency or as matters of domestic jurisdiction.

IV. The Threat of Use of Nuclear Weapons is Prohibited in Any Circumstance

A. The Correlation Between Threat and Use of Force: Threat Is Use

For purposes of the following analysis, it will be useful to examine briefly the meanings of the terms "threat" and "force", both generically and within the context of the legal instruments relevant to this discussion.

The common meaning of "force" is "strength, energy, power". The normal meaning of "the use of force", within the context of Article 2(4) of the Charter, is the application of physical force of a military nature by one member state against another, as in the invasion of Kuwait by Iraq.

Upon closer examination, however, it becomes apparent that more is involved here than a transborder launch of tanks, troops or missiles. Art. 2(4) forbids not only the use of force against the territorial integrity of a state, but also against its political independence, or "in any other manner inconsistent with the purposes of the United Nations." If Art. 2(4) had been aimed only at cross-border military action, it would not have been necessary to add this further language.

What kind of force, then, other than military force in action, can be used by one state against the political independence of another, without affecting its territorial integrity? Non-military force, to be sure, as for instance the erection of tariff barriers or other economic measures, but also the open or veiled promise of the use of force, including armed force, if certain demands are not met. This interpretation is consistent with the definitions of "force" as "power to influence, affect or control", "persuasive power, power to convince."[101]

"Threat", on the other hand, is defined as "a declaration of an intention or determination to inflict punishment, injury, death, or loss on someone **in retaliation for, or conditionally upon**, some action or course; an indication of probable evil, loss or violence to come; ...

---

[100] S. Schwebel, *Human Rights in the World Court*, 24 VAND. J. TRANSNAT'L L. 945 (1991).

[101] Random House Dictionary of the English Language, Third Unabridged Edition.

warning."[102]

Even more relevant, for present purposes, is the definition of "threat" in Black's Law Dictionary: "In criminal law, ... any menace of such a nature as to unsettle the mind of the person on whom it operates, and to take away from his acts that free and voluntary action which alone constitutes consent."

The United Nations Secretary General, in considering what constitutes a threat to use force, noted that, "[t]he person who utters the threat may not intend to carry it out, and the threat is then only a form of intimidation and 'blackmail'."[103]

As one philosopher has noted:

> Nuclear weapons are being used today and can be expected to be used in the future. Not that they are being detonated . . . [b]ut that is not a requirement of their being used. A man uses a gun when he sticks it in your ribs and demands your money. He does not need to fire the gun. And a country uses nuclear weapons when it makes it known that it may launch them unless certain conditions are met, as the United States did against the Soviets in the Cuban Missile Crisis, against China during the Korean War, and against North Vietnam during the Vietnam War. And the very threat of retaliation that is at the heart of nuclear deterrence is a use of nuclear weapons, even if it is not the actual exploding of them.[104]

Thus, the concepts of "threat" and "use" in Article 2(4) merge into each other in most circumstances: The threat of use is itself a kind of use.

B. The Conditional Threat of Force is Prohibited in Any Circumstance

As has been shown in Section II, **supra**, the prohibition on the threat of force for the purpose of affecting another state's political independence, or in any manner inconsistent with the purposes of the United Nations, - what we may call a conditional threat - runs like a mantra through the entire post-World War II law of peace and security. Whether stated in terms of threat, attempted threat, planning or preparation, coercion, interference in the internal or external

---

[102] *Id.*, emphasis added.

[103] Secretary General of the United Nations, *Report on the Question of Defining Aggression*, U.N. Doc. A/2211 at 51 (Oct. 3, 1952) para. 368. (Reprinted in Henkin, Pugh et al., INTERNATIONAL LAW: CASES AND MATERIALS 894-896 (Third ed., 1993).

[104] R.L. Holmes, ON WAR AND MORALITY 8 (1989).

affairs of states or "all other forms of interference"[105], it is clear that all "threats" of this kind are unequivocally outlawed by the United Nations Charter, many other international instruments and, indeed, the customary law of peace and security.

This being so, and considering that nuclear weapons represent the greatest conceivable instrument of threat available to any nation, the conditional threat to use nuclear weapons is, a fortiori, a gross violation of the law of peace and security.

C. A Retaliatory Threat to Use Nuclear Weapons is Illegal in Any Circumstance

What of threat in the retaliatory sense, i.e. "if you do such and such to me, I will do such and such to you"? Surely no person, nor any state, can be deprived of the right to threaten harm as a means of self-defense. But this right is not unlimited: There is no right to threaten to commit a crime or other illegal act. Hence, if, as has been argued elsewhere,[106] the use of nuclear weapons is illegal in any circumstance, i.e. even by way of self-defense or reprisal, the threat to use nuclear weapons must also be illegal in any circumstance.[107]

Although this general proposition is dispositive of the question of the legality of retaliatory threats of nuclear weapons,it may be useful to examine somewhat more closely the forms which such threats may take.

1. The Threat of First Use

A threat of first use could include a threatened preemptive nuclear strike against a perceived nuclear or conventional attack or a threatened nuclear response to an actual conventional attack. Moreover, a threat of first use could be directed against developments falling short of the perception of an immediate attack: The essence of the current doctrine of "counterproliferation" is that the nuclear weapon states reserve to themselves the right to use nuclear weapons to discourage "rogue states" from developing--not necessarily using--weapons of mass destruction, whether nuclear, chemical, biological or other. Of the declared nuclear

---

[105] *See supra* Sections II.B and II.C.

[106] P. Weiss, B. Weston, R. Falk, S. Mendlovitz, *Draft Memorial in Support of the Application by the World Health Organization for an Advisory Opinion by the International Court of Justice on the Legality of the Use of Nuclear Weapons Under International Law, Including the W.H.O. Constitution*, 4 TRANSNAT'L L. & CONTEMP. PROBS. 721, 753-757 (1994). *See also* Statements submitted by Malaysia, Mexico, Nauru, Solomon Islands, and Sweden in support of the request by the World Health Organization for an advisory opinion on the legality of use of nuclear weapons in armed conflict.

[107] Brownlie, *supra* note 45; Oppenheim, *supra* note 46.

powers, only China has an official no-first-use policy.[108] The nuclear weapon States, specifically the United States and the United Kingdom, have repeatedly used threats of first use of nuclear weapons against both nuclear and non-nuclear weapon States.[109]

A threat of first use of nuclear weapons is a direct violation of *jus ad bellum*. The prohibition on the threat of force under the United Nations Charter[110] covers threats of both conventional and nuclear weapons. The threat of first use is inherently a threat against the political independence and territorial integrity of another State. This is true not only when the threat is imminent and aimed at exacting specific changes but also, because of the unique nature of the weapons, when it is a longstanding posture not directly linked to specific demands. Any State in actual or potential conflict with a nuclear State that has a first-use policy, recognizes that the nuclear State has the weapons and the will to use these weapons should it be deemed necessary by the nuclear State. This inevitably influences the decision making of that State.

The unique nature of nuclear weapons, as weapons of mass destruction, makes the threat of their use a tool of unequalled intimidation, undermining the political independence of the threatened State.

Any nuclear threat or use and especially first use and its threat is contrary to the purposes of the United Nations, which include the maintenance of international peace and security and prevention of "threat to the peace" and suppression of "breaches of the peace" (Art. 1(1)) and the achievement of cooperation in promoting and respecting human rights (Art. 1(3)).

Furthermore, the threat of first use of nuclear weapons can never satisfy the principle of proportionality, one of the foundation stones of the laws of war, since the magnitude of the event to which a preemptive response is being made is necessarily a matter of speculation.

2. The Threat of Second Use

The second use of nuclear weapons, and therefore the threat of such use, are not permitted under the law of reprisals. Reprisals "must conform in all cases to the laws of humanity and morality."[111] "Civilian populations ... should not be the object of reprisals ...."[112] "Attacks against

---

[108] NUCLEAR WEAPONS: A COMPREHENSIVE STUDY Appendix I, U.N. Sales No. E.91.IX.10 (1990).

[109] *See* Appendix C.

[110] *See supra* notes 2-5 and accompanying text.

[111] Art. 86, Manual Published by the Institute of International Law (Oxford Manual), 1880. Schindler and Toman, The Laws of Armed Conflict, p.48 (hereafter Schindler).

the civilian population or civilians by way of reprisals are prohibited."[113] "Reprisals may be justified, but they too must be in accordance with customary law."[114]

It is common ground that the laws of war apply equally to all weapons and tactics, including those used in self-defense.[115] The use of genocide, torture or terrorist attacks by one state against another does not justify the use of genocide, torture or terrorist attacks in response. Hence self-defense cannot justify the threat of use of nuclear weapons in self-defense.

3. Implicit Threats of Use

Threats need not be expressly communicated to be effective.[116] While it is true that the bully on the block threatens the safety of his peaceful neighbors by his very presence and his past behavior, it is also true that not every disparity of power between persons or economic or political units constitutes a threat actionable at law. Nevertheless, most systems of law recognize that mere size can and frequently does lead to abuses of power.

---

[112] Par. 7, GA Res. 2675 (XXV), 1970, Basic Principles for the Protection of Civilian Populations in Armed Conflicts, adopted by 109 votes to none. with 18 states abstaining or absent.

[113] Art. 51(6), Protocol I Additional to the Geneva Conventions, 1977. The Protocol also prohibits reprisals against civilian objects (Art. 52[1]), cultural objects and places of worship (Art.53[c]), objects indispensable to the survival of the civilian population (Art.54[4]), the natural environment (Art.55[2]) and works and installations containing dangerous forces, namely dams, dykes and nuclear generating stations (Art.56[4]).

[114] N. Singh & E. McWhinney, NUCLEAR WEAPONS AND CONTEMPORARY LAW 167 (2d ed., 1989).

[115] "Whatever may be the cause of a war that has broken out, and whether or no the cause may be a so-called just cause, the same rules of international law are valid as to what must not be done, may be done, and must be done by the belligerents themselves in making war against each other." U.S. v. Wilhelm List et al. (Hostage Case), 11 Trials of War Criminals 1247 (1950). The quoted statement was made by international lawyer L. Oppenheim and adopted by the tribunal.

[116] For example, Farrands, *The Regional Use of Force*, in THE USE OF FORCE IN INTERNATIONAL RELATIONS 70, 84-85 (F. Northedge, ed., 1974) notes:

> The best example of . . . "concealed threat" was the first Sputnik of October 1957; this great scientific achievement would have been nothing more if the implication that for the first time the USSR could destroy American cities had not been evident.

The field of competition law, for instance, is replete with examples of statutes and treaties intended to compensate for inequalities of size and power in the market place in order to create that "level playing field" which alone can guarantee the functioning of the free market. Many countries and regional groupings have laws forbidding the abuse of a dominant position.[117] However, as the European Court of Justice observed:

> The concept of abuse is an objective concept relating to the behaviour of an undertaking in a dominant position which is such as to influence the structure of a market where, *as a result of the very presence of the undertaking in question*, the degree of competition is weakened and which, through recourse to methods different from those which condition normal competition . . ., has the effect of hindering the maintenance of the degree of competition still existing in the market.[118]

Substitute "country possessing nuclear weapons" for "undertaking in a dominant position" and you have a description of the distortion of "normal" international relations resulting from the "very presence" of such weapons.

Similarly, the rationale of antitrust laws providing for state control of mergers and acquisitions is to prevent mere size from distorting normal market relations, which is another way of saying that mere size poses a threat to their operation. Countries and regional arrangements having such laws include the European Union, Austria, Belgium, Brazil, Colombia, the Czech Republic, Finland, France, Germany, Hungary, Ireland, Italy, Norway, Poland, Portugal, Russia, Spain, Sweden, the United Kingdom, Australia, India, Israel, Japan, Kenya, Korea, New Zealand, South Africa, Taiwan, Canada, the United States, and Venezuela.[119]

The possession of nuclear weapons, i.e., weapons capable of wreaking complete destruction on an enemy, represents a unique case of power disparity. By its very existence, a nuclear arsenal in the hands of one State constitutes a threat of the greatest magnitude to the safety, indeed the survival, of every other state.[120]

---

[117] *E.g.*, Art. 86, Treaty of Rome (EEC), Art. 22, German Competition Law.

[118] Hoffmann-La Roche v. Commission, 1979 E.C.R. 461, par. 6 (emphasis added).

[119] B.E. Hawk, UNITED STATES, COMMON MARKET AND INTERNATIONAL ANTITRUST, 1031, n.1, (2d ed., 1994 supplement).

[120] Herczegh, *supra* note 10, observes:

> In our days the major form of the threat of force is concomitant with the armament race, the manufacture of thermonuclear and other weapons of mass destruction and with the tests conducted with them.

It may be argued, in rebuttal, that the actual policy of the nuclear weapon states is to maintain their arsenals for the sole purpose of insuring their own security, i.e., for deterrence. But nations are not famous for observing their solemn promises when they perceive their vital interest to be at risk. If they were, the world would not have seen numerous cross-border wars[121] break out since the enactment of the U.N. Charter.

What is known in current political science parlance as "vital interest" or "national interest" or "national security" used to be referred to as "reasons of state" and was then, as now, understood to take priority over law or morality. One might say, in a variant on Pascal's well-known aphorism, "the state has its reasons which reason knows nothing of."

A recent example of this attitude is the statement by Gen. Vladimir Semyonov, commander of Russian ground forces, that the violation of the Conventional Armed Forces Treaty in Europe[122] by the deployment of a new Russian army in Chechnya is justified because "the interests of Russia's security and integrity must come above the provisions set in this treaty."[123] An earlier example is the statement by Jeane Kirkpatrick, U.S. Ambassador to the United Nations, that the Charter "is not a suicide pact."[124]

The point here is not to chastise this or that nation for placing its perceived vital interest above the commands of the law, since all nations are guilty of this offense, but to submit that, in assessing the threat posed by overwhelming power, one must look at what nations do, not what they say.

Starting from Lord Acton's famous aphorism that "power tends to corrupt and absolute

---

As early as 1939, before serious work had started anywhere on developing a nuclear weapons plant, Lord Cherwell, Winston Churchill's advisor on science, is said to have held the view that "[w]hoever possessed such a plant would be able to dictate terms to the rest of the world." Bundy, *supra* note 1, at 27.

[121] *See generally* BORDER AND TERRITORIAL DISPUTES (A.J. Day, ed., 2nd ed., 1987). Examples include Iran-Iraq (pp. 238-241), Iraq-Kuwait (pp.244-247), Argentina-United Kingdom (Falklands) (pp. 391-92), Ecuador-Peru (pp. 424-425). *See also* Comment, *International Intervention: The United States' Invasion of Panama*, 31 HARV. INT'L L.J. 633 (1990); R. Beck, *International Law and the Decision to Invade Grenada: A Ten Year Retrospective*, 33 VA. J. INT'L L. 765 (1993).

[122] Treaty on Conventional Armed Forces in Europe, 30 I.L.M. 1 (1990)

[123] New York Times, April 27, 1995, p. A6.

[124] J. Kirkpatrick *The Limits of International Law*, address before the American Society of International Law, New York, NY April 12, 1984. (Reprinted in LEGITIMACY AND FORCE, vol. II (1988) pp. 241-252, at 251.)

power corrupts absolutely", Norman Cousins, adjunct professor of Medical Humanities at the University of California, gives the following summary of "the tendencies that emerge from the pages of historians":

-The tendency of power to drive intelligence underground;

-The tendency of power to become a theology, admitting no gods before it;

-The tendency of power to distort and damage the traditions and institutions it was designed to protect;

-The tendency of power to create a language of its own, making other forms of communication incoherent and irrelevant;

-The tendency of power to spawn imitators, leading to volatile competition;

-The tendency of power to set the stage for its own use.[125]

It is not difficult to see how all of these "tendencies" apply to the enormous power flowing from the possession of nuclear weapons, nor how this power is bound to be used as an instrument of national policy by those who possess it.

4. Deterrence

Deterrence cuts across the three categories of threat discussed above. Because it is generally claimed to be the principal purpose of nuclear weapons, it merits special consideration.

According to the U.S. Joint Chiefs of Staff:

> "[T]he fundamental purpose of US nuclear forces is to deter the use of weapons of mass destruction, particularly nuclear weapons, and to serve as a hedge against the emergence of an overwhelming conventional threat."[126]

Note the use of the adjective "fundamental" rather than "sole", suggesting that U.S. nuclear forces may have purposes other than deterrence. The Joint Chiefs go on to say that:

> Deterrence is founded in real force capabilities and the national determination to

---

[125] N. Cousins, THE PATHOLOGY OF POWER 23 (1987).

[126] Joint Chiefs of Staff, DOCTRINE FOR JOINT NUCLEAR OPERATIONS, Joint Pub 3-12, 29 April 1993, p. I-1.

> use those forces if necessary[127]

and that deterrence is:

> a defense posture that makes possible war outcomes so uncertain and dangerous, as calculated by potential enemies, as to remove all incentive for initiating attack under any circumstance.[128]

The Joint Chiefs of Staff state further that:

> U.S. forces and command and control systems [must] be viewed by enemy leadership as capable of inflicting such damage upon their military forces and means of support, or *upon their country*, as to deny them the military option.[129]

Thus, the doctrine of deterrence implies a readiness and willingness (1) to use nuclear weapons, (2) to inflict great damage on the enemy, and (3) if necessary, to inflict such damage on the enemy's country, not simply his military forces and means of support.

Nor should deterrence be seen as a purely defensive doctrine. As one analyst has noted:

> The development of modern nuclear weapons and the systems needed to deliver them cannot be explained if one insists on defining deterrence in an essentially defensive and reactive form. Instead, the modern concept of deterrence has evolved into something much closer to the traditional understanding of the role of military force in the pursuit of national objectives. Deterrence is now seen as "flexible" or "extended", and a "second-strike counterforce" capability is defended as part of a deterrent on the grounds that a credible (i.e., non-suicidal) response must be available if deterrence fails.[130]

Another makes the following comment:

> [T]he theory of nuclear deterrence, far from being one of the great advances of our time . . . is so little understood in its conceptual foundations and so thoroughly confused in its implementation as to be practically useless from the standpoint of the rational, not to mention moral, guidance of policy. It may, in

---

[127] *Id.*

[128] *Id.*

[129] *Id.* (emphasis supplied).

[130] A. Krass, *Deterrence and Its Contradictions*, in TOWARD NUCLEAR DISARMAMENT AND GLOBAL SECURITY 219 (B. Weston, ed., 1984).

fact, ultimately prove disastrous.[131]

A recent United States Congressional study on the proliferation of weapons of mass destruction discussed the "potentially conflicting objectives" of nuclear non-proliferation and the nuclear powers' reliance on nuclear deterrence.[132] The study admits that:

> One way to reduce the appeal of nuclear weapons is to deemphasize the role that play in international relations. But to do so would mean that the nuclear powers must rely on them less, weakening the credibility and utility of U.S. nuclear deterrent threats. . . ."[133]

V. The Illegality of the Threat to Commit an Illegal Act

Support for the principle that the threat to commit an illegal act is also illegal can be found in international legal instruments and opinio juris[134] as well as the general principles of law recognized by civilized nations.

A. International Legal Instruments

We have already seen that treaties regarding weapons of mass destruction prohibit possession and manufacture of these weapons in addition to their use.[135] Similarly, the Nuremberg Principles define as Crimes Against Peace the "planning" and "preparation" of war in addition to the "initiation" or "waging" of war.[136]

---

[131] Holmes, *supra* note 104, at 259.

[132] U.S. Congress, Office of Technology Assessment, *Proliferation of Weapons of Mass Destruction: Assessing the Risks*, OTA-ISC-559 (Washington, DC: U.S. Government Printing Office, August 1993) pp. 25-29.

[133] *Id.* at 28.

[134] *Supra* notes 45-46 and accompanying text.

[135] *Supra* Section III.A.

[136] *Supra* Section II.D.

Additional examples include Protocol I of the Geneva Convention[137], which lists, in Article 75, paragraph 2, a number of prohibited acts, namely, murder, torture, corporal punishment, mutilation, outrages upon personal dignity, taking of hostages, collective punishments, and *"threats to commit any of the foregoing acts"* (emphasis added).

In addition, the Convention on the Prevention and Punishment of the Crime of Genocide[138] renders punishable not only genocide,[139] but also conspiracy to commit genocide,[140] direct and public incitement to commit genocide,[141] attempt to commit genocide,[142] and complicity in genocide,[143] all of which might be perceived by the target as the threat of genocide.

B. General Principles of Law Recognized by Civilized Nations

Given the paucity of discussions in the legal literature concerning the meaning of "threat" in Article 2(4) of the Charter, it may be useful to consider the treatment of "threat" in ordinary civil and criminal law.

The principle of criminalizing threat, either in itself or for the purpose of achieving some unlawful end, is well established in the legal systems of many countries, as will be shown by the following examples:

Argentina:

Article 211, Penal Code:

> Anybody who, in order to spread general fear or to produce a riot or disorder, makes any sign, voices any alarm, **threatens the commission of any crime of common danger**, or uses any other physical means which would normally produce any such result, shall be punished by jailing from one month to

---

[137] Protocol Additional to the Geneva Conventions of 12 August 1949, and Relating to the Protection of Victims of International Armed Conflicts (Protocol I), 16 I.L.M. 1391 (1977).

[138] 78 U.N.T.S. 277 (1948).

[139] *Id.*, art. III(a).

[140] *Id.*, art. III(b)

[141] *Id.*, art. III(c).

[142] *Id.*, art. III(d).

[143] *Id.*, art. III(e).

three years. . . .

Brazil:

Article 147 of the Criminal Code provides for a penalty of imprisonment of one to six months, or a fine, for "threatening anyone through words, writing or gesture, or any other symbolic means of causing any unjust or serious harm."

Chile:

Article 494 (16) of the Penal Code penalizes anyone who threatens a violent act of physical force as a form of intimidation to cause fear among the general public.

Article 296 penalizes anyone who threatens another with a harm that constitutes a criminal offense, regardless of whether the harm occurs.

France:

Article 305 of the Penal Code renders punishable by imprisonment from two to five years and by a fine of 50,000 to 450,000 francs any person, who by anonymous or signed writing, picture, symbol or emblem, threatens the assassination, poisoning or any other attempt against the life of a person which is punishable by a death sentence, hard labor for life or deportation whenever the threat is accompanied by an order to deposit an amount of money in cash at a designated place, or to fulfill any other requirement.

Article 306 of the Penal Code provides for imprisonment of no less than one nor more than three years and a fine of 50,000 to 450,000 francs, when the threat is not accompanied by any order or condition.

Germany:

Section 126, Penal Code:

> Anybody who endangers the public peace by threatening to commit felonies entailing common danger, shall be punished by imprisonment for a term not to exceed one year.

India:

Section 503, Penal Code:

> Whoever threatens another with any injury to his person, reputation or property, or to the person or reputation of anyone in whom that person is interested, with intent to cause alarm to that person, or to cause that person to do

any act which he is not legally bound to do, or to omit to do any act which that person is legally entitled to do, as the means of avoiding the execution of such threat, commits criminal intimidation.

Italy:

Article 421, Penal Code:

Whoever threatens to commit crimes against public safety, or acts of devastation or pillage, in a manner which arouses public fear, shall be punished by imprisonment for up to one year.

Article 612, Penal Code:

Whoever threatens another with any wrongful harm shall be punished, on complaint of the victim, by a fine of up to 20,000 lire.

Korea:

Article 283, Penal Code penalizes a person who intimidates another.

Article 284 penalizes "a person who commits a crime under . . . the preceding Article by the threat of collective force or while carrying a dangerous weapon".

Nigeria:

Section 252, Penal Code:

A person who . . . attempts or threatens to apply force of any kind to the person of another without his consent . . . is said to assault that person.

Philippines:

Art. 282, Penal Code, defines as "Acts punishable as grave threats":

1. By threatening another with the infliction upon his person, honor or property or that of his family of any wrong amounting to a crime and demanding money or imposing any other condition . . . .

3. By threatening another with the infliction upon his person, honor or property or that of his family of any wrong amounting to a crime which is not subject to a condition.

Spain:

Article 263, Penal Code, penalizes anyone who threatens to commit certain terrorist acts with the intent of disrupting the security of the State or of altering the public order, even though the threat is not dependent on the fulfillment of some condition.

Article 493, Penal Code, penalizes anyone who threatens another with harm to his person or honor or that of his family or to harm the property of either with an injury that constitutes a criminal offense.

Thailand:

Title XI, Section 309, penalizes "[w]hoever compels any person to do, or not to do, or to suffer any act by putting him in fear of injury to life, body, liberty or reputation or property of him or of another person . . . ."

Uganda:

Section 76, Penal Code, penalizes anyone who "with intent to intimidate or annoy any person . . . threatens to injure, assault, shoot or kill any person, or to burn, break or injure any property."

United States of America:

The distinction between assault and battery, in the crime of "assault and battery", lies in the fact that the threat of unlawful force suffices to constitute the crime of assault, while battery requires physical contact.[144]

Robbery is frequently defined as the commission of theft by means of the use or threat of physical force or intimidation, whether property is actually taken from the victim or not.[145]

"Threatening" or "Menacing" is defined as a separate crime in some criminal codes.[146]

---

[144] U.S. Model Penal Code § 211.1 (1)(c), Official Draft and Revised Comments 1982. The code prohibits an attempt "by physical menace to put another in fear of imminent serious bodily injury."

[145] Model Penal Code § 222.1

[146] Examples include: N.Y. Penal Law §§ 120.13, 120.14, and 120.15 (Menacing in the first, second, and third degrees, respectively); N.Y. Penal Law § 240.20 (Disorderly Conduct by Threatening Behavior); Cal. Penal Code § 519 (Threats); Ohio Rev. Code Ann. § 2903.21 (Aggravated Menacing), §2903.211 (Menacing by Stalking), § 2903.22 (Menacing).

Extortion and blackmail are normally defined as "the extraction of money or other value by means of an unlawful threat".[147]

"Terroristic threat" statutes are entering the vocabulary of criminal statutes.[148]

Zambia:

Section 77, Penal Code, penalizes a person who "threatens another with any injury to his person or property. . . ."

---

[147] Model Penal Code § 212.5; N.Y. Penal Law § 155.05(e) (Larceny by Extortion, defined as obtaining property by instilling in another a "fear that, if the property is not delivered, the actor . . . will cause physical injury . . . or cause damage to property.)

[148] *See, e.g.*, Model Penal Code, § 211.3. "A person is guilty of a felony of the third degree if he threatens to commit any crime of violence with purpose to terrorize another. . . ."

Conclusion

The 1995 Review and Extension Conference of the Parties to the Treaty on the Non-Proliferation of Nuclear Weapons has ended with two results significant for the consideration of the question before the Court:

> The nuclear arsenals of both declared and undeclared nuclear weapon states remain intact, at a level variously estimated at 41,000 to 45,000 warheads.[149]
>
> There is no unambiguous, binding commitment by the declared nuclear weapon states, much less the undeclared ones, to the ultimate abolition of all nuclear weapons, even in the distant future.

Thus, the subjective threat of use of nuclear weapons remains as an objective threat to the survival of all or part of the world's present population and of generations to come. If this threat were regarded as an epidemic of potentially incalculable proportions, like polio in bygone days and AIDS in the present, the medical and scientific resources of humanity would be mobilized to combat it. The only weapons available to combat the potential of a nuclear epidemic are common sense, and the rule of law.

In light of the arguments presented here and in other Statements filed with the Court in support of both the World Health Organization and General Assembly Advisory Opinion cases, this Court is respectfully requested to advise that the threat and use of nuclear weapons is not permitted under international law in any circumstance.

---

[149] The Center for Defense Information, *Nuclear Weapon Facts*, 1995. If the Treaty on the Reduction and Limitation of Strategic Offensive Arms II (START II) is fully carried out, the estimated number of warheads in the year 2003 would be 20,000 to 22,000.

LETTER DATED 15 JUNE 1995 FROM COUNSEL APPOINTED BY NAURU, TOGETHER WITH WRITTEN COMMENTS OF THE GOVERNMENT OF NAURU

15 June 1995

Registrar
International Court of Justice
Peace Palace
2517 KJ The Hague
The Netherlands

Dear Registrar,

Enclosed please find two Responses to Submissions of Other States by the Republic of Nauru in the case concerning *The Legal;ity of the Use of Nuclear Weapons by States in Armed Conflict* and one Memorial in the case concerning the *Legality of the Use and Threat of Use of Nuclear Weapons.*

I understand that the Court has set the date of 30 October as the date for the beginnig of oral hearings in the two cases. I would like permission to use a number of witnesses. In the case concernng *The Legal;ity of the Use of Nuclear Weapons by a State in Armed Conflict* I would like to put on the stand a Dr. Frank Barnaby who is a nuclear physicist of repute. I would also like to put on the stand the Mayors of Hiroshima and Nagasaki. In the case concerning the *Legality of the Use and Threat of Use of Nuclear Weapons* I would like to place on the stand Ms. Hilda Lini, former Minster of Health of Vanuatu, Ms. Ligon Ekniiang who has experienced the effects of U. S. nuclear tests during Operation Bravo or some other woman from the Pacific who has experienced those effects and Ms. Claudia Peterson who has experienced the effects of nuclear tsets in the UnitedStates.

Sincerely,

Jerome B. Elkind

REPUBLIC OF NAURU RESPONSE TO SUBMISSIONS OF OTHER STATES

Very few of the submissions presented by States in the case concerning the *Use of Nuclear Weapons by a State in Armed Conflict* address the legal arguments that we have offered to show that the use of nuclear weapons is unlawful but the submissions make other points. One point made about the legality of the use of nuclear weapons is that the issue is abstract and theoretical. It is difficult to see how the question can be considered abstract. It is really quite simple. The General Assembly has asked the question "is the use or threat of use of nuclear weapons in any circumstances unlawful"? The World Health Assembly has asked "is the use of nuclear weapons by a State in armed conflict unlawful"? Even assuming that the question is abstract, in the Reply of the Court to the Request for an Advisory Opinion in the *Status of Eastern Carelia* Case,[1] the Permanent Court of International Justice said:

> The question put to the Court is not one of abstract law, but concerns directly the main point of the controversy between Finland and Russia,... .

As a result the Court refused to give an advisory opinion in that case. Clearly if the Court refused to give an advisory opinion because the question was not sufficiently abstract, then it is appropriate to give advisory opinions when an abstract question of law is asked. Perhaps one reason for feeling that the question is abstract is the difficulty of determining who has standing to request the opinion. But this is a request for an advisory opinion and questions of standing are irrelevant. Perhaps the argument can best be

---

[1] [[1923] P.C.I.J. Rep. Ser. B, No.5, p.7 at pp. 28-29.

understood by looking at the written statement of the Government of Finland: [2]

> ...the legality of the use of nuclear weapons can only be determined in respect of the circumstances of the case,...it follows that in the absence of a concrete factual situation, the court would itself be required to entertain various hypotheses about situations in which nuclear arms might conceivably be used. That is to say, the Court would be required to speculate with a very large number of potential situations, including, for example, situations of first use and counter-use, various types of limited use and practices of targeting, the Court would be required to analyze different types of nuclear weapons and entertain hypotheses about the factual consequences of their use. All this would require analyzing extremely complex and controversial pieces of technical, strategic and scientific information.

It should be pointed out that the difficulty foreseen by the Government of Finland can arise only if the Court decides that not all uses of nuclear weapons are unlawful. We submit that *all* uses and threats of use are unlawful and that the Court is not required to distinguish among them.

Secondly, the nuclear weapons owning States imagine that the majority of States have consented to the legality of the use of nuclear weapons because of their participation in such treaties as the Non-Proliferation Treaty[3]. It should be pointed out that the Non-Proliferation Treaty is not really relevant to this case. The Non-Proliferation Treaty appears to validate the possession of nuclear weapons. Even thugh we believe that the possession of nuclear weapons is a relevant issue, it is not a relevant issue in this case. This case is about the legality of the *use* of such weapons. Secondly it is wrong to imagine that the majority of states support the legality of the use and threat of use of

---

[2] Page 4.

[3] 729 U.N.T.S. 161 (1968).

nuclear weapons. States are aware that the existence of nuclear weapons is a fact of life. Given that they are a fact of life, whether they are lawful or not, it is essential that their use, manufacture, possession and testing be regulated and controlled. Therefore States have participated in negotiations and agreements to regulate and control their use, manufacture, possession and testing. But the position of most States can be gleaned by the fact that a majority of States have voted in the United Nations General Assembly and the World Health Assembly to request these advisory opinions and a review of the submissions made to this Court in this case will show that the majority of States oppose the legality of the use of nuclear weapons.

A number of States have expressed a fear that a decision in this case will somehow hinder negotiations on the extension of the Non-Proliferation Treaty, on disarmament and on a test ban treaty. It is difficulty to see how negotiations will be hindered if this Court decides that the use and threat of use of nuclear weapons is unlawful. Negotiations can only be enhanced if they are carried out in the knowledge that the use and threat of use of these weapons is unlawful. It is a short logical step from a finding that the use and threat of use of these weapons is unlawful to a belief that possession, manufacture and testing of these weapons is therefore pointless.

The only argument that we made that has been addressed is the argument that the use of nuclear weapons contravenes customary and treaty prohibitions against the use of poisonous weapons. The argument seems to be that nuclear weapons are not specifically poisonous weapons. They kill by other means as well. In the view of the United States: [4]

> This prohibition was established with specific reference to projectiles that carry poison into the body of the victim. It was

[4] Written Statement of the Government of the United States of America, p. 27.

> not intended to apply, and has not been applied, to weapons that are designed to injure or cause destruction by other means, even though they may also create toxic byproducts. For example, the prohibition on poison weapons does not prohibit conventional explosives or incendiaries, even though they may produce dangerous fumes. By the same token, it does not prohibit nuclear weapons, which are designed to injure or cause destruction by means other than poisoning of the victim, even though nuclear explosions may also create toxic radioactive byproducts.

The fundamental flaw in this reasoning is that it equates radiation with the purely incidental toxic fumes of incendiaries and explosives. Nuclear weapons kill in three ways, blast, heat and radiation [5] . Of these three ways, radiation is the most persistent killer. Victims of blast and heat are usually killed in the first seconds of the explosion. Victims of radiation may take days, months, years, even decades to die. The radiation effects of nuclear weapons which consist of the transmission of gamma rays, neutrons, beta particles and some alpha particles, are very similar to the effects produced by chemical weapons as opposed to conventional high explosive weapons. In 1979-80, thirty-five years after the bombing, 2,279 names were added to the list of deaths *officially* attributed to the delayed radiation effects on victims of the "little boy" bomb that was dropped on Hiroshima. In 1983 the list of deaths from radiation in Hiroshima totalled 97,964.

A study prepared by the United States Department of Defense and the United States Department of Energy had this to say about nuclear weapons:

> ...there are several basic differences between nuclear and high explosive weapons. ... Fourth, the nuclear explosion is accompanied by highly penetrating and

---

[5] Rumble, *The Politics of Nuclear Defence* (1985) pp. 130-7; *Effects of Nuclear Weapons on Health and Health Services* (World Health Organisation 2d ed. 1987) pp. 9, 15: Tone (ed.) , *The Effects of Nuuclear Weapons* (3d ed. Prepared and published by the United States Defence Department 1977).

> harmful invisible rays called the "initial nuclear radiation."Finally, the substances remaining after a nuclear explosion are radioactive, emitting similar radiation over an extended period of time. This is known as the "residual nuclear radiation" or "residual radioactivity".

Figure 1.02 is labelled "Effects of a nuclear explosion". The effects listed are "blast and shock", "thermal radiation", "initial nuclear radiation" and "residual nuclear radiation". [6]

Concerning the harmful effects of radiation, the book says : [7]

> The harmful effects of nuclear radiation appear to be caused by the ionization (and excitation) produced in the cells composing living tissue. As a result of ionization, some of the constituents, which are essential to the normal functioning of the cells, are altered or destroyed. In addition, the products formed *may act as poisons*.. Among the observed consequences of the action of ionizing radiations on cells are breaking of the chromosomes, swelling of the nucleus and of the entire cell, increase in viscosity of the cell fluid, increased permeability of the cell membrane, and destruction of cells. (Emphasis added)

In total the book devotes 136 pages to "initial nuclear radiation" and "residual radiation and fallout", evidence that at least two Departments of the United States Government consider the radiation effects of nuclear explosions to be more than incidental effects.

---

[6] Glasstone and Dolan (eds.), *The Effects of Nuclear Weapons* (3d ed. United States Dapartment of Defense and the United States Department of Energy 1977) pp.1-3.

[7] Ibid. at p. 575.

The fact is that most nuclear weapons are deployed in part to utilise the destructive effects of radiation and fallout. [8] The neutron bomb is a weapon specifically designed to kill by radiation so that human beings are killed while buildings and other structures are left standing.

There are five main arguments supporting the legality of the use of nuclear weapons. The submissions do not make all those arguments. But they may be made subsequently. The arguments are:

(a) There is no specific treaty making the use of nuclear weapons unlawful.

(b) Nuclear weapons are justified by military necessity.

(c) Nuclear weapons may lawfully be used in retaliation.

(d) Nuclear weapons may lawfully be used in self-defence.

(e) It is possible to invent a scenario where the use of nuclear weapons would be lawful.

We will consider these arguments one at a time.

(a)There is no treaty specifically banning the use of nuclear weapons

The answer to the argument that there is no specific treaty banning the use of nuclear weapons and that therefore they must be legal is found in the

[8] Brownlie, "Some Legal Aspects of the Use of Nuclear Weapons" (1965) 14 ICLQ 437, 445.

Martens clause of the Preamble to the IVth Hague Convention of 1907 Concerning the Laws and Customs of War on Land. Martens was a leading member of the Russian delegation to the Hague Peace conference. The clause says:

> Until a more suitable code of the laws of war can be drawn up, the high contracting parties deem it expedient to declare that, in cases not covered by the rules adopted by them, the inhabitants and the belligerents remain under the protection and governance of the general principles of the law of nations, derived from the usages established among civilised peoples, from the laws of humanity, and from the dictates of the public conscience.

This tells us that a complete answer to the legality of nuclear weapons cannot be had by a study of treaty law alone. A specific treaty rule is not required. If a weapon or its use violates the dictates of the public conscience and the laws of humanity, then it is certainly a violation of the Hague Convention.

We might say that the United Nations General Assembly Resolution is redundant when it asks the Court to consider whether the use and threat to use nuclear weapons is unlawful. Threatening is an active and destructive use of nuclear weapons. If I hold a gun to someone's head and say "if you don't give me all your money I will blow your brains out", is there any doubt that I am using that gun even if I do not actually pull the trigger?

There is a more sophisticated version of the argument that there is no specific treaty banning nuclear weapons and that version is that there is neither a specific treaty nor a specific rule of customary international law. International law recognises that legal effect stems from more than treaties. Article 38 (1) of the Statute of the International Court of Justice is frequently recognised as an authoritative statement of the sources of international law. It says:

> The Court, whose function is to decide in accordance with international law such disputes as are submitted to it shall apply:
>
> a. international conventions, whether general or particular, establishing rules expressly recognised by the contesting states;
>
> b. international custom, as evidence of a general practice accepted as law;
>
> c. the general principles of law recognised by civilised nations;
>
> d. subject to the provisions of Article 59, judicial decisions and the teachings of the most highly qualified publicists of the various nations, as subsidiary means for the determination of rules of law.

The Article contains three specific sources of law as outlined in (a)-(c). It also mentions in (d) two "subsidiary" law determining agencies. The three prime sources of law are treaty, custom and general principles of law. Therefore if we can say that there are rules emanating from any of those sources which outlaw nuclear weapons, then we can say that the use of nuclear weapons is unlawful.

Let us look at the first source, treaties. In the first place we do not need a specific treaty outlawing nuclear weapons to make these weapons unlawful. If we find that they violate the terms of any existing treaty, then we may say that they are unlawful under that treaty. At the outset I think it is necessary to reject the notion that nuclear weapons are banned by implication. If these weapons are the type of weapons that do what the treaties do not allow weapons to do, then we must say that the weapons are outlawed by the treaty. If the use of such weapons amounts to conduct that is prohibited by a treaty then we must say that the use of those weapons directly contravenes the treaty. In the course of our argument we have cited many existing international treaties that outlaw the use of certain weapons in warfare. If nuclear weapons are the sort of weapon that offends the terms of the treaty then we may say that nuclear weapons are outlawed by that treaty. In the first place the use of nuclear weapons violates the United Nations Charter. It violates the International Covenant on Civil and Political Rights and it violates the International Covenant on Economic, Social and Cultural Rights. Nuclear weapons are also offensive to the Declaration of St. Petersburg of 1868, The Hague Declaration on Asphyxiating Gases of July 29, 1899, the Geneva Gas Protocol of 1925, [9] the Hague Regulations on Land Warfare of 1907, [10] the Geneva Convention for the Amelioration of the Condition of the Wounded and Sick in Armed Forces in the Field of August 12, 1949 (the First Geneva convention), the Geneva Convention for the Amelioration of the Wounded, Sick and Shipwrecked Members of the Armed Forces at Sea of August 12, 1940 (the second Geneva Convention), the Geneva Convention Relative to the Treatment of Prisoners of War of August 12, 1949 (the third Geneva Convention), the Geneva Convention Relative to the Protection of Civilian Persons in Times of War of August 12, 1949 (the fourth Geneva Convention) and Geneva Protocol I (1977). [11] Arguably the use of nuclear weapons is criminal. Article 6 of the Agreement for the Prosecution and

---

[9] Cmnd. 3604 (1930); 94 LNTS 65 (1927),

[10] Supra note 11.

[11] Protocol Additional to the Geneva Conventions of 12 August 1949, and Relating to the protection of Victims of International Armed Conflicts adopted at Geneva, June 8, 1977, U.N. Doc. A/32/144 August 12, 1977; 16 ILM 1391 (1977); Misc, No. 19;(Cmnd. 6927) p.23.

Punishment of the Major War Criminals of the European Axis [12] (The Nuremberg Charter) provides:

> ...The following acts, or any of them, are crimes coming within the jurisdiction of the [Nuremberg] Tribunal for which there shall be individual responsibility:
>
> (b) War crimes. Namely, violation of the laws and customs of war. Such violations shall include, but not be limited to, murder, ill treatment...wanton destruction of cities, towns or villages, or devastation not justified by military necessity.
>
> (c) Crimes against humanity. Namely murder, extermination...and other inhumane acts committed against any civilian population...whether or not in violation of the domestic law of the country where perpetrated.

On May 25, 1993, the United Nations Security Council established an international tribunal to punish persons responsible for violation of international law in the former Yugoslavia. Article 3 establishes jurisdiction over the violation of the "laws and customs of war" which the article describes as including " but not limited to":

> (a) employment of poisonous weapons or other weapons calculated to cause unnecessary suffering;
>
> (b) wanton destruction of cities, towns or villages or devastation not justified by military necessity;
>
> (c) attack, or bombardment, by whatever means, of undefended towns, villages, dwellings or buildings;

* * *

Nuclear weapons are poisonous and they are capable of causing unnecessary suffering.They are capable of destroying cities, towns and

---

[12] Signed August 8, 1945. 39 A.J.I.L. Supp. 259 (1945).

villages including undefended towns, villages, dwellings or buildings. So we can see that the use of nuclear weapons violates many principles of treaty law and may is not only a war crime but also a crime against humanity.

As to customary international law, again we may say that there is no specific rule of customary law banning nuclear weapons as such. But this does not mean that nuclear weapons do not offend principles of customary international law. We have already demonstrated the inconsistency of the use of nuclear weapons with the Universal Declaration of Human Rights. If we accept the idea that the Universal Declaration has found its way into the corpus of customary international law then here is one important set of customs that the use of nuclear weapons violates. But we have shown that there are other rules of customary law which the use of nuclear weapons offends. Clearly it is a violation of customary international law to use poisons or other analogous substances. Thus even where a State is not a party to the Geneva Gas Protocol it is nonetheless bound under customary international law to refrain from using poisonous weapons and this would seem to include weapons that emit radiation. It is also a violation of customary international law to use weapons that cause unnecessary suffering and to use weapons that cause severe damage to the environment. Furthermore it is probably a violation of customary international law to use weapons that cause injury to neutral territory.

Secondly, although Resolutions of the United Nations General Assembly are not binding, as such, upon the Members of the United Nations, some Resolutions, if they are passed with substantial majorities may be taken to reflect the views of States as to what the law is; in other words they may be taken as reflections of the *opinio juris* of States. Hence they can assist us in ascertaining the nature of customary international law. There are quite a few

Resolutions of the General Assembly which hold that the use of nuclear weapons is unlawful. One example is G.A. Res. 2936 XXVIII, Nov. 29, 1970; G.A.Res. 1653 (XVI) , 16 GAOR Supp. (No. 17) (1961) which is also called the Declaration on the Prohibition of the Use of Nuclear and Thermonuclear Weapons of November 24, 1961. See also Resolution on the Non-use of Force in International Relations and Permanent Prohibition of the Use of Nuclear Weapons, G.A.Res. 2936, U.N. GAOR 20th Sess., Supp. No. 31, at 5, U.N. Doc. A/8730 (1972); Resolution on the Non-use of Nuclear Weapons and the Prevention of Nuclear Weapons, G.A. Res. 33/71B, 33 U.N. GAOR, Supp. No. 45, at 48, U.N. Doc. A/33/45 (1978); Resolution on the Non-use of Nuclear Weapons and Prevention of Nuclear War, G.A.Res. 34/83G, 34 U.N. GAOR, Supp. No. 46, at 56, U.N. Doc.A/34/46 (1979); Resolution on the Non-use of Nuclear Weapons and Prevention of Nuclear War, G.A. Res.35/152D, 35 U.N. GAOR, Supp. No. 48, at 69, U.N. Doc. A/35/48 (1980); Resolution on the Non-use of Nuclear Weapons and Prevention of Nuclear War, G.A. Res. 36/921, 36 U.N. GAOR, Supp. No. 51, at 64, U.N. Doc. A/36/51 (1981); Resolution 37/100C Convention on the Prohibition of the Use of Nuclear Weapons, U.N. GAOR Supp. No. 51 at 83 (1982); Resolution 38/75, Condemnation of Nuclear War, U.N. GAOR, Supp. No. 47 at 69 (1983); Resolution 39/63H, Convention on the Prohibition of the Use of Nuclear Weapons, U.N. GAOR, Supp. 57 at 70 (1984); Resolution 40/51F, Convention on the Prohibition of the Use of Nuclear Weapons, U.N. GAOR, 40th Sess., Supp. 53 at 90 (1985); Resolution 41/60F, Convention on the Prohibition of the Use of Nuclear Weapons, U.N. GAOR, 41st Sess., Supp. 53 at 85 (1986); Resolution 42/39C, Convention on the Prohibition of the Use of Nuclear Weapons, U.N. GAOR, 42nd Sess., Supp. No. 49 at 81 (1987); Resolution 43/76E, Convention on the Prohibition of the Use of Nuclear Weapons, U.N. GAOR, 43rd Sess., Supp. No.49 at 90 (1988); Resolution 44/117C, Convention of the Prohibition of the Use of Nuclear Weapons, U.N. GAOR 44th Sess., Supp. No. 49 at 80 (1989); Resolution

45/59B, Convention on the Prohibition of the Use of Nuclear Weapons, U.N. GAOR 45th Sess., Supp. No. 49 at 71 (1990); Resolution 46/37D, Convention on the Prohibition of the Use of Nuclear Weapons (1991), U.N. Doc. GA/8307 at 217;Resolution 47/53C, Convention on the Prohibition of the Use of Nuclear Weapons (1992) U.N. Doc. GA/8470 at 112 (1993); Resolution 48/76B, Convention on the prohibition of the Use of Nuclear Weapons (1993), U.N. Doc. GA/8637 at 124 (1994). See Appendix B of Memorial 1.

The Martens clause seems to require the application of general principles of law. It speaks of the laws of humanity and the dictates of public conscience. General principles of law recognised by civilised nations would therefore seem to embody the principles of humanity and the public conscience. Inhumane weapons and weapons which offend the public conscience are therefore prohibited.

Now we come to the two law-determining agencies. As for judicial decisions, there are certainly no international decisions yet that are relevant to our discussion. There is one important municipal case that requires discussion. That case is the *Shimoda* case. The case was begun in May of 1955 when five individuals instituted legal action against the Japanese Government to recover damages for injuries allegedly sustained as a consequence of the atomic bombings of Hiroshima and Nagasaki. On December 7, 1963 the District Court of Tokyo delivered a lengthy decision.[13] The case is important both for its third party decision-making genre, and for the fact that it appears to be the only attempt by any court of law anywhere to wrestle with the legal implications of nuclear warfare. The Court accepted the plaintiffs' argument that the dropping of atomic bombs on Hiroshima and Nagasaki constituted a

---

[13] The decision has been translated into English and printed in the Japanese annual; of International Law for 1964. It is digested in 58 A.J.I.L. 1016 (1964).

violation of international law on the ground that the dropping of said bombs not only constituted an indiscriminate bombardment of undefended cities far beyond the requirements of destroying military objectives within those cities, but also violated the general principle of international law (which it derived from the specific treaty limitations on the use of poisonous gas) that weapons which give rise to "unnecessary ailments" to enemy personnel must not be used. However the Court recognised that individuals have no standing under international law. Consequently, there was no liability to the plaintiffs on the part of the Government of Japan.

With regard to publicists-There are many publicists who would argue that the use of nuclear weapons is unlawful for the reasons cited above and in Nauru's Memorials nos. 1 and 3. The attitude of publicists is summarised by Meyrowitz in his article "The Opinions of Legal Scholars on the Legal Status of Nuclear Weapons" [14] Many legal scholars take the view that the use of nuclear weapons is unlawful. A fairly complete list of them appears in Memorial 1 at p. 66. Others are seduced by the argument that nuclear weapons must be lawful in the absence of any treaty banning them specifically. We have already demonstrated why we believe this argument to be fallacious.

(b) Nuclear weapons are justified by military necessity

When we speak of military necessity we must ask two questions. The first question is what is military necessity? The second question is, what is justified by it? The object of war is to hurt the enemy, to kill as many enemy soldiers as possible and to convince the enemy that it is not worthwhile to continue their campaign. But international humanitarian law tells us that the

[14] 24 Stanford J.I.L. 111 (1987-88).

means of hurting the enemy are not unrestricted. Article 22 of the Hague Rules says:

> The right of belligerents to adopt means of injuring the enemy is not unlimited.

In a trial before a United States Military Tribunal called the *Hostages Trial*, the Tribunal said:

> Military necessity or expediency do not justify a violation of positive rules. International Law is prohibitive law. [15]

The right to adopt measures to injure the enemy is subject to very definite limitations and these limitations are spelled out by the principles of international humanitarian law. Said a former President of the International Court of Justice:

> ...it is submitted that if the mere fact of defeat were accepted as a legal justification for ignoring the rules of warfare, the entire *raison d'etre* of the laws of war would disappear, since the object of every war is the achievement of victory or success. Thus. if, for the attainment of that objective, no rules whether customary or conventional can be accepted, all wars would degenerate into wild savagery and cruelty and the society of nations would revert to the law of the jungle. Such a concept of the doctrine of success would wipe out the achievements of humanity as enshrined in the Hague and Geneva Conventions and usher in the worst experiences of the Middle Ages. [16]

One thing which the military is not permitted to do is to attempt to convince the enemy to surrender by terrorising the civilian population. Article 22 of the Hague rules provides that:

[15] *Law Reports of Trials of War Criminals*, vol. 8, p. 34 at p. 66.
[16] Singh, N., *Nuclear Weapons and International Law* (1959) p. 82.

> Aerial bombardment for the purpose of terrorising the civilian population, of destroying or damaging private property not of a military character, or of injuring non-combatants is prohibited.

Strategic nuclear weapons are instruments of terror against the civilian population. So we can say that military necessity does not permit this use of nuclear weapons.

The 1863 Lieber Code [17] spells out the restrictions on the principle of military necessity:

> Article 14. Military necessity, as understood by modern civilized nations, consists of the necessity of those measures which are indispensable for securing the ends of war, and which are lawful according to the modern law and usages of war.
>
> Article 15. Military necessity admits of all direct destruction of life or limb of armed enemies, and other persons whose destruction is incidentally unavoidable.
>
> Article 16. Military necessity does not admit of cruelty-that is, the infliction of suffering for the sake of suffering or for revenge, nor of maiming or wounding except in fight, nor of torture to exact confessions. It does not admit of the use of poison in any way, [18] nor of the wanton devastation of a district...and, in general military necessity does not include any act of hostility which makes the return to peace unnecessarily difficult.

---

[17] For the text see Friedman, L., THE LAW OF WAR: A DOCUMENTARY HISTORY (1971) p.158.

[18] Note that this prohibition predates the 1925 Geneva Gas Protocol.

Military necessity consists in all measures immediately indispensable and proportionate to military objectives when taken on the decision of a responsible commander.

A weapon, any weapon must be justified according to four basic limitations regarding the purpose, nature and scope of permissible violence. The first limitation concerns the *purpose* of permissible violence. Inflicting injury on the enemy as an end in itself is not permitted. Violence must have a legitimate purpose if it is to be described as violence having "military necessity". The second limitation is concerned with the *nature* of permissible violence, and is particularly though not exclusively addressed to the weapons of warfare. Use of weapons which cause cruel suffering or unavoidable death may or may not be helpful to the party who would use them for the achievement of an otherwise legitimate military end. Their use is, however, forbidden under any circumstances. The third limitation relates to the scope of permissible violence. The rule here is that of proportionality. Only such amount of violence is permissible as is reasonably proportionate to the legitimate military objective sought to be achieved in the given military operation. The fourth limitation concerns the *objectives* of permissible violence. This limitation is particularly though not exclusively concerned with the protection of civilian lives and property.

The measures taken must not be contrary to the laws of war. There are certain weapons and conduct which are prohibited even though they may lead to military advantage. Among the weapons which are prohibited are those which cause unnecessary or aggravated suffering, those which are poisonous and those which are harmful to the environment. Resort to such weapons is not permitted by military necessity. Prohibited conduct includes the use of such weapons. It has been the thrust of our argument that nuclear weapons cause unnecessary and aggravated suffering, create radiation which can be seen to have poisonous effects and are devastating to the environment. Therefore the use of such weapons cannot be justified by military necessity.

(c) Nuclear weapons may lawfully be used in retaliation

There is a heavy emotional content to this argument. It is the argument that was most strongly used to justify the use of atomic weapons against Japan. Because the Japanese military was contemptuous of the laws of war, the argument goes, the use of the atomic bomb was a justified punishment. A string of Japanese atrocities, including the rape of Nanking, the treatment of allied prisoners of war and even the treachery of the attack on Pearl Harbour are cited as justification for the use of the atomic bomb. But the fact is that hundreds of thousands of people; men, women and children were killed by the atomic bomb and most of the victims had nothing to do with the treacherous and brutal actions of their government. Why did they deserve to die because of the actions of someone else? The fact is that the Emperor Hirohito and the Prime Minister Tojo were not even in Hiroshima and Nagasaki when the Atomic bomb was dropped. They survived. Perhaps their punishment was the defeat of Japan. But they did not suffer the grusome injuries and deaths that thousands of ordinary, innocent people suffered.

Secondly, it is a fundamental principle of international humanitarian law that a violation does not justify a counterviolation. Article 46 of the Geneva Convention for the Amelioration of the Condition of the Wounded and Sick in Armed Forces in the Field of August 12, 1949 (the First Geneva convention) says:

> Reprisals against the wounded, sick, personnel, buildings

or equipment protected by the Convention are prohibited.

The same prohibition of reprisals appears in Article 47 of the Geneva Convention for the Amelioration of the Wounded, Sick and Shipwrecked Members of the Armed Forces at Sea of August 12, 1940 (the second Geneva Convention), Article13 and Article 33 of the Geneva Convention Relative to the Protection of Civilian Persons in Times of War of August 12, 1949 (the fourth Geneva Convention). The prohibition against reprisals also appears in Article 20 of Protocol I to the Geneva Conventions. Articles 51-56 of that Protocol also have provisions prohibiting reprisals. So it is clear that retaliation or reprisal with nuclear weapons is prohibited by the laws of war.

(d) Nuclear weapons may lawfully be used in self-defence

Article 51 of the United Nations Charters says:

> Nothing in the present Charter shall impair the inherent right of individual or collective self-defence if an armed attack occurs against a Member of the United Nations... .

Given this approval of self-defence expressed in the Charter many States will attempt to claim that the use of nuclear weapons is lawful if they are used in self-defence. But a slightly more careful reading is required. It says "nothing in the present Charter". This means that the Charter prohibitions against the use of force do not apply where the Member is exercising the right of self-defence. It does not and cannot mean that no rules of international law shall apply. Defensive military action is subject to the laws of war to the same extent as offensive military action. None of the rules which we have cited in our submission make any exception for a 'defensive' use of nuclear weapons. Therefore where we have rules of international law that prohibit (a) the use of poisonous weapons or (b) weapons that cause unnecessary or aggravated suffering or (c) harm the environment or (d) destroy medical facilities or (e) damage or pollute neutral territory or (f) cannot distinguish between civilian objects and military objectives, then their use is unlawful.

In fact it is hard to see how one might use nuclear weapons in self-defence. If one has been attacked with nuclear weapons, then the use of nuclear weapons against the attacker will do nothing to defend the attacked State. It has already been hit. Its cities have been devastated. There is no way for it to defend itself against a result which has already occurred. So its use of nuclear weapons in that situation will, of necessity, be retaliation and we have already shown why it is not lawful to use nuclear weapons in retaliation. One might argue that a State may threaten to use nuclear weapons in self-defence. But this is acceptable only if one accepts the validity of the deterrence theory of international affairs. There are serious flaws in deterrence theory.

(e) It is possible to invent a scenario where the use of Nuclear Weapons would be Lawful

Some state representatives will attempt to argue that nuclear weapons are lawful in certain circumstances. In attempting to so argue they will present scenarios in which the use of nuclear weapons are free of the legal defects which the use of nuclear weapons possess. On the general question of scenarios Ian Brownlie has commented [19]:

> It is rather ridiculous to allow refined examples of putatively lawful use to dominate the legal regime [thus ignoring] the general context of conflict and the risk of escalation.

---

[19] Brownlie, supra note 2 at 450.

Certainly, the risk of escalation must not be ignored, but as we will show, it is doubtful that any scenarios invented can meet the test of lawfulness.

It is submitted that, in any scenario designed to meet the criterion of lawfulness, six conditions would have to be met:

1. The nuclear weapons would have to be radiation free. We submit that there is no such thing as a nuclear weapon which is entirely radiation free. We venture to predict that all scenarios will talk about "substantially" radiation free nuclear weapons. But just a little probing will reveal that none of the so-called "clean" weapons are entirely free of radiation.

2. The nuclear weapons for which the status of legality is claimed should not cause unnecessary or aggravated suffering.

3. The nuclear weapons for which the status of legality is claimed should not be harmful to the environment.

4 The nuclear weapons for which the status of legality is claimed should not be likely to destroy medical facilities.

5 Nuclear weapons for which the status of legality is claimed should not damage or pollute neutral territory. (This was not dealt with in Nauru's submissions. But the point was made quite effectively in other submissions.)

5. The nuclear weapons for which the status of legality is claimed should be capable of distinguishing between miliary objectives and civilian objects .

6. At any rate it must be unlikely that conventional weapons could accomplish the desired military result.

The scenario most commonly invented is the use of low yield tactical nuclear weapons on a military base isolated in the dessert. The scenario attempts to eliminate some of the illegal consequences of the use of nuclear weapons. By calling the weapons low-yield the argument theoretically eliminates the poison argument because the weapons would not contain as much radiation. It is my intention to call to the stand a nuclear scientist who will testify that there is no such thing as a completely clean nuclear weapon. So we can see that it is not possible to completely do away with radiation and the harmful effects of radiation.

Another matter which this scenario is intended to deal with is the desirability of eliminating the failure to distinguish between civilian and military targets. This may be true. But even in this case.

1. A nuclear weapon would still cause unnecessary and aggravated suffering.

2. As I have shown it would still be poisonous.

3. It would still damage the environment, and

4. It would still destroy any medical facility that might exist on the base. So it would still be unlawful.

Conclusion

We have shown that the use of nuclear weapons violates a number of important rules of international law. There may be no specific treaty barring the use of nuclear weapons but we have shown that these are weapons which do things which many rules of treaty and customary law prohibit weapons from doing. We have also shown that international humanitarian law does not cease to have effect just to satisfy claims of miliary necessity. Furthermore the rules of international humanitarian law apply whatever the nature of the conflict. They apply when a State is acting in self-defence and when a State is acting in retaliation.

LETTER DATED 16 JUNE 1995
FROM THE MINISTER FOR FOREIGN AFFAIRS A.I.
OF THE NETHERLANDS, TOGETHER WITH WRITTEN STATEMENT
OF THE GOVERNMENT OF THE NETHERLANDS

MINISTER FOR FOREIGN AFFAIRS

JURA-107713

The Hague, 16 June 1995

In response to your invitation, on the basis of the articles of the Charter of the United Nations and of the Statute of the Court, I enclose the observations of the Government of the Kingdom of the Netherlands with regard to the advisory opinion requested by the General Assembly of the United Nations.

The Minister for Foreign Affairs a.i.
of the Kingdom of the Netherlands

H.F. Dijkstal

The Registrar of the
International Court of Justice
Peacepalace
Carnegieplein 2
2517 KJ The Hague

Ministry of Foreign Affairs

The Hague

THE NETHERLANDS GOVERNMENT,

Having regard to Resolution 49-75K adopted on 15 December 1994 by the General Assembly of the United Nations, whereby the General Assembly decided to request the International Court of Justice urgently to give an advisory opinion on the following question:

> "Is the threat or use of nuclear weapons in any circumstance permitted under international law?";

Having regard to the Order of the Court of 1 February 1995, by which the Court designated 20 June 1995 as the time-limit within which written statements might be submitted to the Court by the United Nations and by States which are entitled to appear before the Court, in accordance with Article 66(2) of the Statute of the Court;

Having regard to the fact that the Netherlands is a member State of the United Nations and by virtue of Article 92 of the Charter of the United Nations also a party to the Statute of the Court;

Wishing to avail itself of the opportunity given by the Court's Order of 1 February 1995 to States entitled to appear before the Court to make a written statement on the above-mentioned request by the General Assembly of the United Nations for an advisory opinion from the Court;

Has the honour to present the following statement:

I OBSERVATIONS ON THE COMPETENCE OF THE GENERAL ASSEMBLY OF THE UNITED NATIONS TO REQUEST, AND ON THE COMPETENCE AND DISCRETION OF THE COURT TO GIVE, THE ADVISORY OPINION

1. According to Article 96 of the Charter of the United Nations

> "(1) The General Assembly or the Security Council may request the International Court of Justice to give an advisory opinion on any legal question.
> (2) ...." (Emphasis added)

2. According to Article 65 of the Statute of the International Court of Justice which forms an integral part of the UN Charter:

> "(1) The court may give an advisory opinion on any legal question at the request of whatever body may be authorized by or in accordance with the Charter of the United Nations to make such a request.
> (2) ...." (emphasis added)

3. While Article 96 of the UN Charter determines who is competent to request an advisory opinion from the Court, Article 65(1) of the Court's Statute determines the competence of the Court to give an advisory opinion. According to Article 96(1) of the UN Charter only the UN General Assembly or Security Council may request the Court to give an advisory opinion on any legal question.

4. The question submitted to the Court for an advisory opinion concerns the permissibility of the threat or use of nuclear weapons in any circumstance under international law, and therefore constitutes a legal question.

5. In the opinion of the Netherlands Government, the General Assembly of the United Nations must be deemed competent to request an advisory opinion on the question submitted to the Court.

6. If the Court considers the General Assembly of the United Nations competent to request, and itself competent to give, the advisory opinion concerned, the Netherlands Government would nevertheless draw attention to the fact that the Court's power to give advisory opinions is a discretionary one, As stated by the Court itself in the Peace Treaties case (ICJ Rep. 1950, p. 71):

> "Article 65 of the Statute is permissive. It gives the Court the power to examine whether the circumstances of the case are of such a character as should lead it to decline to answer the Request".

7. Although the Netherlands Government is in general very much in favour of the exercise by the Court of its competence to give advisory opinions, it believes that there are good policy reasons why, in this particular case, the Court should decide to abstain from giving the advisory opinion requested.

8. The Netherlands Government attaches great value to the Non-Proliferation Treaty (NPT), the operation of which has been indefinitely extended by the NPT conference on May 11 1995 in New York. By their decision to extend this treaty indefinitely, the parties to the treaty reaffirmed the importance of this treaty as the international instrument for preventing the proliferation of nuclear weapons.

9. The universal application of the norm provided by the NPT has recently been enhanced by the accession to the treaty of a number of states, making the NPT one of the treaties with the most universal adherence.

10. As is well known, the Non-Proliferation Treaty acknowledges the legality of the possession of nuclear weapons by certain States, i.e. the five recognized nuclear weapon States, while other States parties to the treaty have undertaken not to develop or otherwise acquire nuclear weapons (Article II of the NPT).

11. A judgment of the Court declaring the threat or use of nuclear weapons illegal might jeopardize the operation of the Non-Proliferation Treaty. On the other hand, a judgment of the Court declaring the threat or use of nuclear weapons legal might induce a number of States to withdraw their support for the treaty or encourage other States to refrain from acceding to the treaty, thereby undermining its universal application.

12. Another important provision of the NPT regards disarmament. In Article VI of the NPT each of the NPT parties undertakes to pursue negotiations in good faith on effective measures relating to cessation of the nuclear arms race at an early date and to nuclear disarmament. This undertaking has guided the international community in its disarmament efforts, and was reconfirmed during the recently held NPT conference.

13. The Netherlands Government believes that the risks involved in the threat or use of nuclear weapons will be more effectively countered by further negotiations in the field of disarmament and non-proliferation of nuclear weapons, in line with the provisions of the NPT. Any judgment of the Court in reply to the request submitted by the General Assembly would create a real danger of undermining the ongoing process of nuclear non-proliferation and disarmament.

II OBSERVATIONS ON THE MERITS OF THE LEGAL QUESTION SUBMITTED TO THE COURT FOR AN ADVISORY OPINION

14. Should the Court decide to consider admissible the request of the General

Assembly of the United Nations for an advisory opinion contained in UNGA Res. 49/75K of 15 December 1994 and should the Court be willing to examine the merits of the legal question submitted by the General Assembly, the Netherlands Government would like to make the following observations.

15. The legal question submitted by the General Assembly is couched in extremely general terms, i.e. "Is the threat or use of nuclear weapons in any circumstance permitted under international law?" Theoretically this question could be answered either in the negative or in the affirmative. An answer in the negative would mean that the threat or use of nuclear weapons would under no circumstances be permitted under international law and hence be unlawful per se under international law. An answer in the affirmative would mean that there would be at least certain circumstances under which the threat or use of nuclear weapons would be permitted and hence not unlawful under international law. It is clear that a rejection of the first answer necessarily implies the acceptance of the second answer. Moreover, it should be kept in mind that the request for the advisory opinion submitted by the General Assembly to the Court does not compel the Court to give an answer to the question of under what circumstances, if any, the threat or use of nuclear weapons would be permitted under international law.

16. As already observed in the statement made by the Netherlands Government in connection with the request for an advisory opinion submitted to the Court by the Forty-sixth World Health Assembly of the WHO in its resolution WHA 46.40 of 14 May 1993, the question of the illegality of the use of nuclear weapons put in general terms - i.e. the question of whether the use of nuclear weapons would in all circumstances be unlawful - can only be answered in the negative. As already indicated above such a negative answer to the request for an advisory opinion submitted by the WHA implies necessarily a positive

answer to the request for an advisory opinion submitted by the General Assembly of the United Nations. Henceforth the legal reasoning set forth by the Netherlands Government in respect of the WHA request for an advisory opinion can be followed likewise in respect of the request for an advisory opinion submitted by the General Assembly of the United Nations.

The fact that the WHA request referred merely to "the use of nuclear weapons by a State in war or other armed conflict" while the UNGA request refers to "the threat or use of nuclear weapons in any circumstance" does not lead to a different reply. It may be recalled in this connection that in setting limits on the use of force by member States of the UN - of which the use of nuclear weapons is only one form - Article 2(4) of the UN Charter also sets limits on the threat of such force. Indeed where the use of force is deemed unlawful, the threat of such use of force must, in principle, be deemed equally unlawful.

17. As stated by the Netherlands Government on other occasions - e.g. during the debate in the Netherlands Parliament on the approval of the 1985 Agreement between the Netherlands and the United States on the Stationing of Ground-launched Cruise Missiles in the Netherlands (Treaty Series of the Kingdom of the Netherlands 1985 No. 145) - with regard to the question of the legality or otherwise under international law of the possession or even use of cruise missiles, such possession or even use does not inevitably constitute a violation of the rules or principles of international humanitarian law in armed conflict or of other rules or principles of the jus in bello which more particularly concern the permissibility of certain types of weapons in war or other armed conflict.

18. Thus, according to the Netherlands Government, Article 23(a) of the Hague Regulations respecting the Laws and Customs of War on Land annexed to Convention IV concluded at the 1907 Hague Peace Conference (2 AJIL 1908 Suppl. p. 90), which prohibits the employment

of "poison" or "poisoned weapons" and/or the 1925 Geneva Protocol for the Prohibition of the Use in War of Asphyxiating, Poisonous and other Gases, and of Bacteriological Methods of Warfare (94 LNTS p. 65), which condemns the (first) use of "asphyxiating, poisonous or other gases, and of all analogous liquids, materials or devices" do not entail a prohibition per se of the use of nuclear weapons. Indeed, the use of poison and poisonous gas is generally categorized under chemical warfare and nuclear weapons are usually distinguished from chemical or biological weapons which are the concern of the provisions referred to here. Article 23(a) of the Hague Regulations and the 1925 Geneva Protocol were intended to apply only to weapons whose principal effect was poisonous and not to those where poison was only a secondary effect. It should be noted that the primary effects of the use of nuclear weapons are the enormous blast wave and thermal radiation they produce, effects which are not covered by the said provisions.

19. The Netherlands Government rejects the view that the use of nuclear weapons would be unlawful per se on the grounds that such use would necessarily lead to a violation of the rule laid down in Article 23(e) of the 1907 Hague Regulations which forbids belligerents "to employ arms, projectiles, or material calculated to cause unnecessary suffering " (emphasis added). The question to be raised here is when suffering caused by a certain weapon can reasonably be called "unnecessary".

20. It seems that suffering may be called "unnecessary" when its infliction was not necessary to attain a lawful military advantage or greatly exceeds what could reasonably have been considered necessary to attain that military advantage.

21. The availability of considerably less harmful means to attain the military advantage or the causing of suffering out of proportion to the military advantage to be gained therefore appear to be the essential yardstick for

determining whether the use of certain weapons must be deemed to cause "unnecessary" suffering. This approach has governed the development of rules with regard to means and methods of warfare since 1868.

22. Hence, in the view of the Netherlands, the use of nuclear weapons cannot in abstracto be deemed unlawful. The question of whether a specific use is in contravention of the said obligation cannot therefore be weighed until the exact implications, both at the level of military advantage gained and with regard to the injury caused, are known.

23. The Netherlands Government further wishes to emphasize that the drafting history of the 1977 Additional Protocol I (Int. Com. Red Cross, Protocols Additional to the Geneva Conventions of 12 August 1949, Geneva 1977, p. 3) to the 1949 Geneva Conventions (75 UNTS pp. 33, 85, 135 and 287) makes clear the intention of the negotiating States that the rules introduced by that protocol, in so far as they relate to the use of weapons, should not cover warfare with weapons of mass destruction such as nuclear weapons. As the restriction to conventional weapons was not explicitly laid down in that protocol, the Netherlands - like several other parties to the protocol - made a declaration on the occasion of its ratification that it was the understanding of the Netherlands Government that the rules introduced by Protocol I relating to the use of weapons were intended to apply and consequently would apply solely to conventional weapons without prejudice to any other rules of international law applicable to other types of weapons.

24. The drafting history of Additional Protocol I to the 1949 Geneva Conventions, moreover, indicates that in any event the majority of States acknowledged, explicitly or tacitly, that the use of nuclear weapons is not already unlawful per se under international humanitarian law.

25. In this connection the Netherlands Government also wishes to note that a general prohibition of the use of nuclear weapons de lege lata cannot be deduced from UNGA Resolution no. 1653 (XVI) entitled "Declaration on the Prohibition of the Use of Nuclear and Thermo-nuclear Weapons" which was adopted by the General Assembly of the United Nations on 24 November 1961. This resolution which, it is true, declared the use of nuclear weapons illegal, as it would be contrary to the Charter of the United Nations, the rules of international law and the laws of humanity, cannot in the view of the Netherlands Government be considered as embodying an already existing rule or principle of general international law. The very fact that the resolution was adopted with 55 votes for, 20 against (including the nuclear weapon States the United States, Great Britain and France) and 26 abstentions proved the absence of a general opinio iuris on the part of States that the use of nuclear weapons is unlawful per se.

UNGA Resolution 2936 (XXVII) on the Non-Use of Force in International Relations and Permanent Prohibition of the Use of Nuclear Weapons, which was adopted by the General Assembly on 29 November 1972 - this time with 73 votes for, 4 against (including China) and 46 abstentions (including France, the United Kingdom and the United States) - inter alia again solemnly declared "the permanent prohibition of the use of nuclear weapons".

Considering the special weight to be attached to the position of the nuclear weapon States among the States voting against or abstaining and the very high number of States which abstained, it would, the Netherlands Government believes, still be very difficult to conclude that the resolution codified or gave rise to a generally recognized rule or principle of international law.

It is also relevant in this connection that the UNGA Resolution 1653 (XVI) of 1961 referred to above invited the Secretary-General of the United Nations to examine the possibility of a conference being convened where participating States would sign a convention on the prohibition of nuclear weapons, but that this attempt, as well as many later attempts to promote the conclusion of such a convention, remained without success due to disagreement on the matter among States.

26. According to the Netherlands Government the use of nuclear weapons need not - as is sometimes alleged - necessarily amount to genocide in terms of the 1948 Convention on the Prevention and Punishment of the Crime of Genocide (45 AJIL 1951 Suppl. p. 7). Indeed, as long as the use of nuclear weapons, or for that matter of any weapons, remains directed at the combatants of the other belligerent and is not directed at the population (which may be considered as a national group) as such, with the intent to destroy that population in whole or in part as such, i.e. whether having the status of combatant or not, there can be no question of genocide within the meaning of the 1948 Genocide Convention.

27. The Netherlands Government is, moreover, of the opinion that the use of nuclear weapons cannot be considered in itself to be in violation of the right to life, as enshrined inter alia in Article 6 of the 1966 International Covenant on Civil and Political Rights (Annex to UNGA Res. 2200 (XXI) of 16 December 1966) or in Article 2 of the 1950 European Convention for the Protection of Human Rights and Fundamental Freedoms (Eur. Treaty Series. No. 5). According to the Netherlands Government, these articles do not create an absolute right to life. Thus, the travaux préparatoires of Article 6 of the International Covenant make clear that, instead of listing the circumstances in which the deprivation of life would not be considered contrary to the right to life, the drafters decided to agree on the formulation that "No one shall be arbitrarily deprived of his life" (emphasis added). One of the instances mentioned in this connection by the drafters as an example of a deprivation of life which is not

arbitrary was "the performance of lawful acts of war". Explicit support for such an exception, as far as Article 2 of the European Convention is concerned, can also be found in Article 15(2) of the European Convention, which provides that "No derogation from Article 2, except in respect of deaths resulting from lawful acts of war ... shall be made under this provision." (emphasis added).

28. The Netherlands Government is aware of the existence of certain treaties which prohibit the deployment of nuclear weapons in Antarctica (1959 Antarctic Treaty, 402 UNTS p. 71), outer space or on celestial bodies (1967 Outer Space Treaty, 610 UNTS p. 205), or on the deep seabed (1971 Treaty on the Prohibition of the Emplacement of Nuclear Weapons and other Weapons of Mass Destruction on the Sea-Bed and the Ocean Floor and in the Subsoil thereof, 995 UNTS p. 115) or most of Latin America and certain adjacent waters and islands (1967 Treaty of Tlatelolco, 634 UNTS p. 326, or its First Protocol, idem p. 360), or in certain parts of the South Pacific (1985 Treaty of Rarotonga, 24 ILM 1985 p. 1440, or its First Protocol, 28 ILM 1989 p. 1600), but such treaties impose such obligation only on parties to those treaties and, moreover, - except of the Rarotonga Treaty - only in respect of certain areas. The existence of a general prohibition under general international law on the use of such weapons anywhere cannot be concluded from such treaties. Indeed the contrary conclusion can more readily be deduced from them. The same applies to the 1963 Partial Test Ban Treaty which prohibits the parties from conducting nuclear tests in certain areas (i.e. in the atmosphere, under water or in outer space) but does not purport to restrict their use of nuclear weapons in the course of hostilities.

The Netherlands Government believes that the unlikelihood of a general prohibition of the use of nuclear weapons under existing international law would, also follow from the fact that there are certain treaties which regulate the possession of nuclear weapons, such as the 1968 Non-Proliferation Treaty referred to above. Indeed, the fact that certain States are permitted, subject to certain conditions at least, to possess nuclear weapons also would seem to be difficult to reconcile with the idea that the use of those weapons is unlawful in itself.

29. The Netherlands Government further believes that even if it were to be assumed that the (first) use of nuclear weapons by a State were unlawful per se under present international law - quod non -, this would not necessarily exclude the permissibility of the use of nuclear weapons by way of belligerent reprisal against an unlawful use of (nuclear) weapons, provided of course the retaliating State observed the conditions set by international law for the taking of lawful reprisals, i.e. satisfies, inter alia, the requirement that the retaliation is proportionate and serves as an ultimum remedium.

30. The view held by the Netherlands Government that existing international law does not in itself prohibit the use of nuclear weapons does not, of course, mean that in the opinion of the Netherlands Government every use of nuclear weapons would necessarily always be lawful.

31. Thus the use of weapons, and hence of nuclear weapons, is permissible only in the case of the lawful exercise of the right of self-defence or under a mandate conferred by the UN Security Council in the exercise of its powers under Chapter VII of the Charter. In this connection it should also be pointed out that the presently existing variety of nuclear weapons creates, in principle, a possibility for States to take necessary and proportionate action with such weapons in self-defence against an armed attack with or without nuclear weapons.

32. Moreover, according to the Netherlands Government, the general principles of international humanitarian law in armed conflict also apply to

the use of nuclear weapons. Two principles, in particular, which form part of that law are the prohibition on making the civilian population as such the target of an attack and the prohibition on attacking military targets if this would cause disproportionate harm to the civilian population. The applicability of general principles of international humanitarian law in armed conflict - among which must also be counted the principle laid down in Article 22 of the 1907 Hague Regulations that the right of a belligerent to adopt means of injuring the enemy is not unlimited - to the use of nuclear weapons was also confirmed as long ago as 1965 in Resolution XXVIII of the 20th International Conference of the Red Cross (Vienna) which was passed unanimously. Consensus on this point was also reached at the diplomatic conference on Additional Protocol I to the 1949 Geneva Conventions.

The Hague, 16 June 1995

LETTER DATED 16 JUNE 1995
FROM THE SECRETARY OF THE DEPARTMENT
OF FOREIGN AFFAIRS OF IRELAND,
TOGETHER WITH WRITTEN STATEMENT
OF THE GOVERNMENT OF IRELAND

OIFIG AN TÁNAISTE AGUS AN AIRE GNÓTHAÍ EACHTRACHA
OFFICE OF THE TÁNAISTE AND MINISTER FOR FOREIGN AFFAIRS

BAILE ÁTHA CLIATH 2
DUBLIN 2

16 June, 1995

C8/2

H.E. Eduardo Valencia-Ospina,
Registrar,
International Court of Justice,
Peace Palace 2517 KJ,
The Hague,
Netherlands.

Your Excellency,

I refer to your letter of 8 February 1995 informing me that the Secretary General of the United Nations had notified the Court of the adoption of Resolution 49/75K whereby the General Assembly of the United Nations decided to request the Court to render an advisory opinion on the question of the threat or use of nuclear weapons.

The Tanaiste and Minister for Foreign of Ireland considers that it may be helpful to the International Court of Justice, in its deliberations, to be informed of the policy of the Government of Ireland on the question of nuclear weapons. I have been asked, therefore, to transmit the enclosed statement which Ireland wishes to submit to the Court.

Yours sincerely,

Noel Dorr
Secretary

Statement by Ireland to the International Court of Justice

1. Ireland is strongly committed to the achievement of general and complete disarmament under strict and effective international control, including the prohibition and elimination of all types of weapons of mass destruction. Ireland has consistently promoted and supported concrete steps towards this end.

2. It has been the long-standing position of successive Irish Governments that the use of strategic nuclear weapons would have incalculable consequences on mankind and on the environment. Though small-scale tactical nuclear weapons are less indiscriminate in their effects, there is a very serious danger that the use of such weapons could escalate and lead quickly to the use of strategic nuclear weapons and other weapons of mass destruction and indiscriminate effect. For these reasons Ireland has urged that every effort should be made to achieve the complete abolition of this whole category of weapons and it has worked for, and given its support to, proposals to this end.

3. The Irish Government recognise that a number of States already possess such weapons, and that those States which do so have seen the deployment of these weapons, and their use as a deterrent to attack, as a crucial factor in their security policies. The Irish Government appreciate that the steps which they advocate towards reductions in the levels of nuclear warheads and their ultimate elimination should not have destabilising consequences for the States concerned and thus for the international community as a whole. In this context, it is important to ensure that the dismantling of nuclear weapons should not lead inadvertently to the spread of these weapons to countries or groups which do not yet possess them. It is also important that the process of nuclear disarmament be conducted in accordance with the highest standards of environmental protection and nuclear safety.

4. In keeping with its broad approach to the issue, Ireland has welcomed agreements reached through negotiation between two of the nuclear powers, which have resulted in significant reductions in the levels of the nuclear weapons which they hold. It has seen these agreements as both valuable in themselves and important as steps towards the larger goal of the complete abolition of nuclear weapons throughout the world.

5. While the possession and deployment of nuclear weapons by a certain number of States already gives rise to grave dangers, it is self evident that the spread of these weapons to other States would compound the threat, adding greatly to the risk that these weapons will eventually be used. The further spread of such weapons would exacerbate distrust between neighbouring States in regions of tension and give rise to local arms races. It could tempt weaker States which may not have the ability or the means to acquire nuclear weapons, to seek to acquire other weapons of mass destruction as a deterrent against attack or threat from a dominant local power armed with nuclear weapons. In all of these ways, the spread of nuclear weapons would add greatly to global instability.

6. For these reasons, Ireland has always worked to halt the proliferation of nuclear weapons on the one hand and, simultaneously, to promote nuclear disarmament on the other. As early as 1958, Ireland took the initiative at the United Nations in putting forward a resolution calling for the negotiation of a treaty on the non-proliferation of nuclear weapons. Since its entry into force in 1970, the Treaty on the Non-Proliferation of Nuclear Weapons has served as the foundation of international efforts for nuclear non-proliferation and nuclear disarmament. Ireland was the first State to ratify the Treaty.

7. The Irish Government believe that the Treaty on the Non-Proliferation of Nuclear Weapons is still of central importance; and that universal accession to the Treaty and full compliance with its obligations would be a major contribution to the maintenance and promotion of international peace and security. They welcome the decision of the 1995 Review and Extension Conference of the Parties to the Treaty on the Non-Proliferation of Nuclear Weapons that the Treaty shall continue in force indefinitely.

8. The Conference also agreed a set of principles and objectives for nuclear non-proliferation and disarmament and arrangements for strenthening the review process for the Treaty on the Non-Proliferation of Nuclear Weapons. The Irish Government attach importance to these decisions. In particular, they will seek to ensure that the programme of action contained therein for the full realization and effective implementation of Article VI of the Treaty is implemented.

9. In this context, the completion by the Conference on Disarmament, no later than 1996, of negotiations for a

Comprehensive Test Ban Treaty would constitute a major step in limiting the further development of nuclear weapons, as well as ensuring an end to the unacceptable health and environmental effects of nuclear weapons tests themselves. Similarly, the commencement without further delay and early conclusion of negotiations for a convention banning the production of fissile material for nuclear weapons would contribute significantly to nuclear disarmament by halting the build-up of such materials. The problem of excess stockpiles also needs urgent attention.

10. The approach of the Irish Government as outlined above has been to work politically, by every means open to it, towards the aim of the ultimate abolition by agreement of nuclear weapons. As steps towards this end, and because of the importance of such measures in themselves, the Irish Government has worked for, and supported, international agreements which would end all nuclear testing, end the production of fissile material for nuclear weapons and stop the further spread of nuclear weapons.

11. The approach which Ireland has taken in promoting and supporting efforts to bring about the ultimate elimination of nuclear weapons has been political in character. The referral to the International Court of Justice by the United Nations General Assembly requests an advisory opinion on whether the threat or use of nuclear weapons in any circumstances is permitted under international law. The earlier referral by the World Health Assembly requested an advisory opinion on whether the use of nuclear weapons by a State in war or other armed conflict would be a breach of its obligations under international law including the WHO Constitution. The Irish Government do not see the approach reflected in these referrals, which seeks to situate the issues within the framework of obligations under international law, as in any way incompatible with their own efforts in the political field to secure the abolition of nuclear weapons. The Irish Government, therefore, await with interest the advisory opinion(s) of the Court which may clarify the legal issues which arise for States in relation to this most dangerous category of weapons.

16 June, 1995

LETTER DATED 16 JUNE 1995 FROM THE LEGAL ADVISER TO THE FOREIGN AND COMMONWEALTH OFFICE OF THE UNITED KINGDOM OF GREAT BRITAIN AND NORTHERN IRELAND, TOGETHER WITH WRITTEN COMMENTS OF THE UNITED KINGDOM

Foreign &
Commonwealth
Office

London SW1A 2AH

From The Legal Adviser

16 June 1995

The Registrar
International Court of Justice
Peace Palace
The Hague
THE NETHERLANDS

Sir,

I have the honour to refer to my separate letter of today's date under cover of which was enclosed the written statement of the United Kingdom in response to the Court's Order of 1 February 1995 in connection with a request from the General Assembly of the United Nations for an Advisory Opinion on the Legality of the Threat or Use of Nuclear Weapons.

I have the honour to indicate that the said statement should also be taken, so far as relevant, as the response by the United Kingdom to the written statements submitted by other States in the separate proceedings on a request from the World Health Organisation for an Advisory Opinion on the Legality of the Use by a State of Nuclear Weapons in Armed Conflict. The United Kingdom is accordingly willing that the text of that statement be made available to all States which have submitted written statements in those proceedings.

I have the honour, however, to state that, having considered the written statements submitted by other States in those proceedings, the United Kingdom wishes to maintain in their entirety the conclusions in its own written statement, including (but not limited to) that the Request is not within the competence of the World Health Organisation.

Accept, Sir, the assurances of my highest consideration.

(Sir Franklin Berman)

International Court of Justice

Legality of the Threat or Use of Nuclear Weapons (Request for an Advisory Opinion by the United Nations General Assembly)

Statement of the Government of the United Kingdom

JUNE 1995

CONTENTS

		Page
I	**Introduction**	1
II	**The Background to the Request and the Propriety of Response**	3
	1. The Background to United Nations General Assembly Resolution 49/75K	3
	2. Nuclear Disarmament and Non-Proliferation	6
	3. Whether the Court should answer the Question posed	9
III	**The Principles of Law Raised by the Question**	21
	1. The meaning of the Question	21
	2. Provisions specifically referring to Nuclear Weapons	23
	3. The United Nations Charter and the Right of Self-Defence	36
	4. The Laws of Armed Conflict	40
	5. International Law on Human Rights and the Environment	61
	6. Threats to use Nuclear Weapons	72
IV	**Conclusion**	74

1

I INTRODUCTION

1.1 The terms of the request made by the General Assembly of the United Nations in Resolution 49/75K, adopted on 15 December 1994, are as follows:

> *The General Assembly* ....
>
> *Decides*, pursuant to Article 96, paragraph 1, of the Charter of the United Nations, to request the International Court of Justice urgently to render its advisory opinion on the following question:
>
> "Is the threat or use of nuclear weapons in any circumstance permitted under international law ?"'

1.2 This request, which overlaps to a large extent with one made in 1993 by the World Health Organization and still before the Court, is the result of a sustained campaign by a group of non-governmental organizations ('NGO's') which have long been active in promoting what they have termed 'The World Court Project', namely an attempt to obtain from the Court an advisory opinion to the effect that the use of nuclear weapons is unlawful in all circumstances.[1] To that end, these NGO's campaigned to obtain both the WHO and General Assembly requests and claim to have prepared the written statements submitted by a number of States in connection with the WHO request.

1.3 The United Kingdom submits that the present case is one in which the Court should exercise its discretion under Article 65, paragraph 1, of its Statute to decline to answer the question posed. That question is couched in vague, abstract terms and cannot be answered without reference to the numerous different combinations of circumstances in which the threat or use of nuclear weapons might be contemplated. The Court does not, and could not, have before it sufficient material to enable it to consider all the combinations of circumstances which might arise. Moreover, an answer to the question posed would not assist the General Assembly in the exercise of its functions under the Charter and might have a harmful effect on the work of the United Nations as a whole and on the different sets of negotiations which are taking place regarding disarmament and other aspects of the control of nuclear weapons. These issues are addressed in Part II of this Statement, which also examines the background to the present request and the progress of the disarmament negotiations.

---

1 See *The World Court Project on Nuclear Weapons and International Law* (2nd edition, 1993).

1.4 If, however, the Court should decide to answer the question which has been put to it, the United Kingdom submits that that question does not admit of a simple answer in terms as abstract as those of the question itself. There is no treaty or other binding instrument which specifically prohibits the use of nuclear weapons in all circumstances. The legality of using nuclear weapons can therefore be determined only by reference to the circumstances in which that use occurs. In particular, it would be necessary to examine whether the State resorting to nuclear weapons was entitled to take action by way of individual or collective self-defence and whether the action thus taken met all the requirements of the right of self-defence. It would also be necessary to consider whether, in such circumstances, the use of a nuclear weapon was lawful under the laws of armed conflict. In Part III of this Statement the United Kingdom sets out the principles of law relevant to such an inquiry and again submits that the application of these principles is not an abstract matter but depends upon the factual circumstances of each case.

1.5 In view of the complexity of these questions, the United Kingdom reserves the right to make further submissions with regard to the request, should the Court decide to respond to it.

2

II THE BACKGROUND TO THE REQUEST AND THE PROPRIETY OF RESPONSE

1 The Background to United Nations General Assembly Resolution 49/75K

2.1 The present section examines the background to the adoption by the General Assembly of Resolution 49/75K which contains the request for an advisory opinion from the Court.

2.2 In August 1987 an international conference of NGO's on nuclear weapons and international law was held in New York, sponsored by the Lawyers' Committee on Nuclear Policy (USA) and the Association of Soviet Lawyers. This conference decided to found a world-wide organization of lawyers opposed to nuclear weapons. This organization, the International Association of Lawyers against Nuclear Arms ('IALANA'), was founded in April 1988 at another meeting in Stockholm. In September 1989, at the Hague, the IALANA adopted its 'Hague Declaration on the Illegality of Nuclear Weapons'. It also appealed to all member States of the United Nations 'to take immediate steps towards obtaining a resolution by the United Nations General Assembly under Article 96 of the United Nations Charter, requesting the International Court of Justice to render an advisory opinion on the illegality of the use of nuclear weapons.' [2]

2.3 Subsequently, in January 1992, IALANA, with two other NGO's, the International Peace Bureau and International Physicians for the Prevention of Nuclear War, established the 'World Court Project'. In May 1992 the International Peace Bureau organized a meeting in Geneva to promulgate the project's ideas. The NGO's involved in the World Court Project lobbied States in order to persuade them to submit a draft resolution to the World Health Organization and the UN General Assembly requesting an advisory opinion on the illegality of the threat or use of nuclear weapons. On 14 May 1993, the World Health Assembly adopted resolution 46.40, which forms the subject of a separate request to the Court.

2.4 A meeting of the Non-Aligned Movement Co-ordinating Bureau in New York discussed in October 1993 tabling a draft resolution in the First Committee of the

---

[2] *The World Court Project on Nuclear Weapons and International Law* (2nd edition, 1993), p. xiii and Appendix I.

General Assembly. The item had not been on the agenda of the Co-ordinating Bureau but was raised under 'Other Matters'.

2.5 At the 48th session of the United Nations General Assembly the representative of Indonesia introduced in the First Committee, at its 23rd meeting on 9 November, a draft resolution entitled 'Request for an Advisory Opinion from the International Court of Justice on the Legality of the Threat or Use of Nuclear Weapons.' [3] The draft resolution was stated to be introduced on behalf of the States members of the United Nations that are members of the movement of Non-Aligned Countries. The single operative paragraph of the draft resolution read:

> '*Decides*, pursuant to Article 96(1) of the Charter, to request the International Court of Justice to urgently render its advisory opinion on the following question, "Is the threat or use of nuclear weapons in any circumstance permitted under international law ?" '

2.6 However, at the 30th Meeting of the First Committee, on 19 November 1993, the sponsors announced that they had decided not to press for action on the draft resolution. The representative of Indonesia, speaking on behalf of the Non-Aligned Countries, said that the fact that the legal implications of nuclear weapons had yet to be addressed had prompted the Non-Aligned Countries to submit the draft resolution.

> 'However, they recognized that recent developments in the sphere of disarmament made the attainment of the complete elimination of nuclear weapons a more likely prospect. The progress achieved under the auspices of the Amendment Conference and the Conference on Disarmament had, moreover, facilitated the adoption by the Committee of consensus resolutions on a comprehensive test-ban and a ban on the production of fissionable materials which might lead to renunciation of the use of nuclear weapons. To preserve the momentum of the progress being made, the Non-Aligned Countries had therefore decided not to press for final action on draft resolution A/C.1/48/L.25 but would continue instead to monitor developments in different forums, with particular interest in the early conclusion of a comprehensive test ban treaty (CTBT).' [4]

2.7 From 31 May to 3 June 1994 the Eleventh Ministerial Conference of the Non-Aligned Countries was held in Cairo, at which the decision was taken to re-table the draft resolution and to put it to the vote at the next session of the UN General Assembly. On 9 November 1994 at the 15th Meeting of the First Committee at the 49th Session of the UN General Assembly, Resolution A/C.1/49/L.36 was introduced

---

3 A/C.1/48/L.25.

4 A/C.1/48/SR.30, page 2.

by the delegation of Indonesia on behalf of the Non-Aligned Countries. The single operative paragraph of that draft resolution contained the request set out in the introduction to this Statement. No indication was given as to why the situation was thought to have changed since the previous year.

2.8 At the 24th Meeting of the First Committee on 18 November 1994, the delegation of Morocco proposed, in accordance with Rule 116 of the Rules of Procedure of the General Assembly, that no action be taken on the request contained in the draft resolution. The delegations of Germany and Hungary spoke in support of the Moroccan proposal. The delegations of Indonesia and Colombia opposed the motion. In addition, the delegation of Senegal deplored the submission of the resolution on behalf of the Movement of Non-Aligned Countries and stated that they could not in any way support the draft resolution.

2.9 The motion that no action be taken on the draft resolution was rejected by 67 votes to 45, with 15 abstentions. The First Committee then took a decision on the draft resolution, which was adopted by 77 votes to 33, with 21 abstentions.

2.10 The draft resolution was then submitted to the General Assembly as resolution K in paragraph 60 of the First Committee's Report.[5] At the 90th meeting of the General Assembly on 15 December 1994 the delegation of France moved that no action be taken on the draft resolution, in accordance with Rule 74 of the General Assembly's Rules of Procedure. The motion was supported by the delegations of Germany and Hungary and opposed by the delegations of Malaysia and Indonesia. The motion was then put to a vote and rejected by 68 votes to 58, with 26 abstentions.

2.11 The delegation of France then noted the profound division within the Assembly on the appropriateness of the draft resolution and emphasised their concern that the Court should not be in the situation of being pressurised by a specific group. The French delegation proposed an amendment to the draft resolution to delete the word 'urgently' in the operative paragraph, in order to ensure the freedom of a juridical body to make its own assessment. The representative of Indonesia moved, in accordance with Rule 74 of the Rules of Procedure, that no action be taken on the amendment. This motion was adopted by 61 votes to 56, with 30 abstentions. The draft resolution was then adopted by 78 votes to 43, with 38 abstentions, as Resolution 49/75K.

---

5 A/49/699.

2 Nuclear Disarmament and Non-Proliferation

2.12 This section will deal with recent efforts by the international community in the field of nuclear disarmament and non-proliferation, which constitute an important part of the context within which the present Request must be seen.

2.13 The Treaty on the Non-Proliferation of Nuclear Weapons ('the NPT') was opened for signature at London, Moscow and Washington on 1 July 1968 and entered into force on 5 March 1970. The NPT sets out in detail the obligations of nuclear-weapon States (those which manufactured and exploded a nuclear weapon or other nuclear explosive device before 1 January 1967) and those of non-nuclear-weapon States, in particular in respect of: the transfer and manufacture of nuclear weapons; the application of safeguards, administered by the International Atomic Energy Agency, to nuclear materials; the use of nuclear energy for peaceful purposes; and general disarmament, including nuclear disarmament.

2.14 Article VIII(3) of the NPT provides for a conference to be held, five years after the entry into force of the Treaty, to review the operation of the Treaty, and for further such conferences to be held at five-yearly intervals thereafter. Such conferences have been held every five years since the Treaty's entry into force in 1970. Article X(2) of the NPT provides that twenty-five years after the entry into force of the Treaty, a conference shall be convened to decide whether the Treaty shall continue in force indefinitely, or shall be extended for an additional fixed period or periods, and that this decision shall be taken by a majority of parties to the Treaty.

2.15 From 17 April to 12 May 1995 the 1995 Review and Extension Conference of the Parties to the Treaty on the Non-Proliferation of Nuclear Weapons was held at United Nations Headquarters in New York. The Conference was attended by 175 of the 178 States Parties. On 11 May the Conference decided without a vote that, as a majority existed among States Parties for the indefinite extension of the Treaty, in accordance with Article X(2), the Treaty should continue in force indefinitely.[6]

---

6 A draft copy of that decision is attached at Annex A.

2.16 On 11 May the Conference also adopted without a vote a Decision on Principles and Objectives for Nuclear Non-Proliferation and Disarmament. [7] This decision contained the following paragraphs relating to nuclear disarmament:

> '3. Nuclear disarmament is substantially facilitated by the easing of international tension and the strengthening of trust between States which have prevailed following the end of the cold war. The undertakings with regard to nuclear disarmament as set out in the Treaty on the Non-Proliferation of Nuclear Weapons should thus be fulfilled with determination. In this regard, the nuclear-weapon States reaffirm their commitment, as stated in Article VI, to pursue in good faith negotiations on effective measures relating to nuclear disarmament.
>
> 4. The achievement of the following measures is important in the full realization and effective implementation of Article VI, including the programme of action as reflected below:
>
> (a) The completion by the Conference on Disarmament of the negotiations on a universal and internationally and effectively verifiable Comprehensive Nuclear-Test-Ban Treaty no later than 1996. Pending the entry into force of a Comprehensive Test-Ban Treaty, the nuclear-weapon States should exercise utmost restraint;
>
> (b) The immediate commencement and early conclusion of negotiations on a non-discriminatory and universally applicable convention banning the production of fissile material for nuclear weapons or other nuclear explosive devices, in accordance with the statement of the Special Coordinator of the Conference on Disarmament and the mandate contained therein;
>
> (c) The determined pursuit by the nuclear-weapon States of systematic and progressive efforts to reduce nuclear weapons globally, with the ultimate goal of eliminating those weapons, and by all States of general and complete disarmament under strict and effective international control.'

2.17 Sub-paragraphs 4 (a) to (c) reflect disarmament negotiations currently under way in other forums. The United Nations Conference on Disarmament in Geneva is currently engaged in the negotiation of a universal and internationally and effectively verifiable comprehensive test-ban treaty, and is due to begin negotiations on a non-discriminatory and universally applicable convention banning the production of fissile material for nuclear weapons or other nuclear explosive devices. Further efforts towards the reduction of nuclear weapons are also being made, particularly in the context of the United States-Russia Strategic Arms Reduction Treaty II ('START II'), of which those two States are committed to seek ratification in 1995. At their September 1994 meeting in Washington, the Presidents of the United States and Russia instructed their experts to intensify their dialogue on, *inter alia*, the possibility

---

7 A draft copy of that decision is attached at Annex B.

after ratification of START II of further reductions on, and limitations of, remaining nuclear forces.

2.18 Paragraph 8 of the Decision on Principles and Objectives for Nuclear Non-Proliferation and Disarmament contained the following provisions on security assurances:-

> '8. Noting United Nations Security Council resolution 984 (1995), which was adopted unanimously on 11 April 1995, as well as the declarations by the nuclear-weapon States concerning both negative and positive security assurances, further steps should be considered to assure non-nuclear-weapon States party to the Treaty against the use or threat of use of nuclear weapons. These steps could take the form of an internationally legally binding instrument.'

2.19 This paragraph reflected the fact that on 5-6 April 1995 the five nuclear-weapon States had made statements containing both positive security assurances (statements of the steps they would take in the event of aggression with nuclear weapons, or the threat of such aggression) and negative security assurances (statements of the circumstances in which they undertook not to use nuclear weapons against non-nuclear-weapon States).[8] The negative security assurances given by the United Kingdom, France, Russia and the United States are in similar terms. The 1995 security assurances replaced earlier positive assurances given by the United Kingdom, the United States and the Soviet Union in 1968, and negative security assurances given by the nuclear-weapon States at various times since 1978.

2.20 On 11 April 1995 the United Nations Security Council unanimously adopted resolution 984, in which it welcomed the statements which had been made.[9]

2.21 The third decision adopted without a vote by the Conference of Parties to the NPT was a Decision on Strengthening the Review Process for the Treaty.[10] Paragraph 2 of that decision provides that Review Conferences of the NPT should continue to be held every five years, and that the next such conference should be held in the year 2000. Paragraph 3 provides for the holding of a Preparatory Committee in each of the three years prior to the Review Conference. Paragraph 4 provides that:

---

8 Copies of these assurances are attached at Annex C.

9 The text of resolution 984 is attached at Annex D.

10 A copy of this decision is attached at Annex E.

> '4. The purposes of the Preparatory Committee meetings would be to consider principles, objectives and ways in order to promote the full implementation of the Treaty, as well as its universality, and to make recommendations thereon to the Review Conference. These include those identified in the Decision on Principles and Objectives for Nuclear Non-Proliferation and Disarmament adopted on 11 May 1995. These meetings should also make the procedural preparations for the next Review Conference.'

2.22 None of the above decisions, statements and resolutions - which represent the most recent combined efforts of the international community to address nuclear disarmament and non-proliferation issues - refer to, or address the need for, an opinion on the legality or otherwise of the use or threat of use of nuclear weapons. Intensive negotiations were required by the States concerned to conclude those texts. In the course of those negotiations, and of the proceedings at the Conference, the issue of whether or not the use or threat of use of nuclear weapons would or would not be lawful was not a factor.

3 Whether the Court should Answer the Question Posed

2.23 In the view of the United Kingdom, the Court should decline to answer the question posed by the General Assembly.

2.24 It is clear that the Court has a discretion in deciding whether it should respond to a request for an advisory opinion. The language of Article 65 of the Statute is permissive, not mandatory. As the Court said, in the *Interpretation of Peace Treaties* case:

> 'Article 65 of the Statute is permissive. It gives the Court the power to examine whether the circumstances of the case are of such a character as should lead it to decline to answer the Request.... the Court possesses a large amount of discretion in the matter.' [11]

---

11 Advisory Opinion of 30 March 1950, ICJ Reports, 1950, pp. 71-2. See also the advisory opinions on *Reservations to the Genocide Convention* , ICJ Reports, 1951, at p. 19, and *Certain Expenses of the United Nations*, ICJ Reports, 1962, at p. 155.

Similarly, in the *Western Sahara* case, the Court said:

> 'In exercising this discretion, the International Court of Justice, like the Permanent Court of International Justice, has always been guided by the principle that, as a judicial body, it is bound to remain faithful to the requirements of its judicial character even in giving advisory opinions. If the question is a legal one which the Court is undoubtedly competent to answer, it may none the less decline to do so. As this Court has said in previous Opinions, the permissive character of Article 65, paragraph 1, gives it the power to examine whether the circumstances of the case are of such a character as should lead it to decline to answer the request.' [12]

2.25 It is within that margin of discretion that the question of propriety falls to be considered. The Court has repeatedly emphasised that there are inherent limitations on the judicial function [13] and these limitations apply particularly to issues raised with the Court which jeopardise its judicial propriety. Judgments which are 'devoid of object or purpose',[14] or 'remote from reality' [15] or incapable of effective application have been found to fall into this category. As the Court held in the *Northern Cameroons* case:

> 'If the Court were to proceed and were to hold that the Applicant's contentions were all sound on the merits, it would still be impossible for the Court to render a judgment capable of effective application...' [16]

And in the same judgment the Court stressed that all the considerations of judicial propriety apply equally to the exercise of its advisory jurisdiction.[17]

2.26 The Court has nevertheless indicated that, as the principal judicial organ of the United Nations, it should normally give its opinion on a legal question when requested to do so by a competent organ (or specialized agency) of the United Nations. As the Court said, in the *Peace Treaties* case.

---

12 ICJ Reports, 1975, at p. 21.

13 See e.g. *Free Zones Case of Upper Savoy and Gex*, PCIJ, Ser. A/B, No. 46, 1932, p. 161; *Status of Eastern Carelia*, PCIJ, Ser. B, No. 5, 1923, p. 29; *Nuclear Tests Case*, ICJ Reports 1974, p. 271; *Northern Cameroons Case*, ICJ Reports 1963, p. 30.

14 *Western Sahara Case*, ICJ Reports 1975 at p. 37.

15 ICJ Reports 1963, p. 33.

16 *Ibid.*, p. 33.

17 *Ibid.*, pp. 30-31. See also the passage from the *Western Sahara* case, above.

> 'the reply of the Court, itself an "organ of the United Nations", represents its participation in the activities of the Organization, and, in principle, should not be refused.' [18]

It is, of course, highly desirable that the Court should play a constructive role in assisting the other organs of the United Nations. The emphasis should, however, be on the constructive role which an opinion from the Court can play in a particular case. If a response by the Court to a request for an advisory opinion would, in fact, be unlikely to provide any constructive assistance to the other organs of the United Nations but, on the contrary, would be likely to have a detrimental effect on the activities of the United Nations family, the position would be very different. In such a case, both the duty of the Court to protect its own judicial function and the need for it to play its part as an organ of the United Nations call for it to exercise its discretion to decline to respond to the request.

2.27 It is the view of the United Kingdom that that is the case here and that the Court should accordingly decline to give an answer to the question posed by the General Assembly. First, an examination of the categories of cases in which the Court has held that an opinion should, as a matter of propriety, be given demonstrates that the present case falls outside those categories. Secondly, the nature of the case is such that the Court would be unable to give an advisory opinion which would be of positive assistance to the other organs of the United Nations. Thirdly, the rendering of an advisory opinion in this case could well have a harmful effect upon important and complex negotiations in the field of disarmament. Each of these considerations will be examined in turn.

(1) The Present request does not fall within any of the Categories of Cases in which, as a matter of propriety, an Opinion ought to be given

2.28 All the categories examined below show a common characteristic. They are all cases in which the opinion of the Court was likely to make a positive contribution to the work of the requesting organ and to the well-being of the United Nations as a whole. That is to say, whilst there were groups of States who might have had difficulties with the opinion (and the matter must be assumed to have generated some disagreement to merit reference to the Court), the likelihood that these difficulties would have had effects detrimental to the work of the United Nations was small; and, conversely, the benefits of settling a disputed legal question were considerable. In

---

18 ICJ Reports, 1950, at p. 71.

short, the positive advantages to the United Nations clearly outweighed the possible negative consequences.

(a) Cases where the legal question involved the interpretation of a constitutional provision which had become the subject of dispute in the organ making the request

2.29 Many of the cases fall into this category. For example, in the *Conditions of Admission* [19] and *Competence* [20] cases the essential question raised was the proper interpretation of Article 4 of the Charter, specifically whether a member State in voting on an application for admission could take into account conditions not expressly provided for in Article 4(1) and, in the second opinion, whether the general Assembly might proceed to a vote on an application in the absence of a recommendation from the Security Council. The Court dealt with both questions in abstract terms and, although it was well aware of the highly political and acutely controversial nature of the disputes in the United Nations which had led to those requests,[21] its opinions proved most constructive. The impasse over the admission of new members was broken and the Organization moved rapidly towards the goal of universality. Similarly, in the *IMCO (Composition of the Maritime Safety Committee)* case, [22] the Court's opinion on the proper interpretation of Article 28 of the Constitution of IMCO made a highly positive contribution to the future well-being of IMCO.

2.30 The present case is entirely different. Although the question posed by the General Assembly would require the interpretation and application of certain provisions of the Charter, especially Articles 2(4) and 51, the case is not a constitutional one (in the sense in which the cases surveyed in the previous paragraph were constitutional), because the Charter provisions concerned deal not with the powers of the Organization or its internal workings but establish or codify rules of international law of general application. Moreover, to answer the question posed by

---

19 Advisory Opinion of 28 May 1948: ICJ Reports, 1948, p. 57.

20 Advisory Opinion of 3 March 1950: ICJ Reports, 1950, p. 54.

21 See Higgins 'Policy Considerations and the International Judicial Process' 17 ICLQ (1968) 58, at p. 78, who supports the Court (*contra* Greig, 'The Advisory Jurisdiction of the ICJ and the Settlement of Disputes between States' 15 ICLQ (1966) 325) in the view that most issues raised in requests for opinions will have given rise to disputes within the UN but that this should not *per se* prevent the Court from responding.

22 Advisory Opinion of 8 June 1960: ICJ Reports, 1960, p. 150.

the Assembly would involve more than an examination of those provisions of the Charter, for the Court would be obliged also to consider the whole body of international law applicable to the use of weapons in armed conflicts.

(b) Cases where the legal question involves matters on which the requesting organ or agency seeks guidance in the exercise of its constitutional functions

2.31 There is a broad range of cases in which the question posed related not directly to the interpretation of a constitutional provision but rather to the manner in which an organ should carry out its functions, or to a question of law which needed to be clarified in order that an organ should be able to carry out its functions. Thus, in the *Reparations* case [23] the United Nations sought to know whether it might bring a claim against a State in respect of injuries suffered by an agent of the Organization. In the *Peace Treaties* case [24] the General Assembly asked whether disputes under the Peace Treaties existed and, if so, whether under the provisions of those treaties the Secretary-General was empowered to nominate the third member of the Treaty Commissions, notwithstanding that the government concerned had failed to appoint a representative. In effect, it was the Secretary-General who required legal guidance about the extent of his powers. The *Reservations* case [25] was similar, in that the Secretary-General needed to know how to deal with reservations to the Genocide Convention in order to carry out his duties as depositary under that Convention. In cases such as the *Effect of Awards of the UN Administrative Tribunal* [26] or the series of cases dealing with South-West Africa [27] it was the Assembly which sought guidance regarding the exercise of its functions.

---

[23] *Reparations for Injuries suffered in the Service of the UN*, Advisory Opinion of 11 April 1949, ICJ Reports, 1949, p. 174.

[24] *Interpretation of Peace Treaties with Bulgaria, Hungary and Romania*, Advisory Opinion of 18 July 1950, ICJ Reports, 1950, p. 221.

[25] *Reservations to the Genocide Convention*, Advisory Opinion of 28 May 1951, ICJ Reports, 1951, p. 15.

[26] Advisory Opinion of 13 July 1954, ICJ Reports, 1954, p. 47.

[27] *International Status of South-West Africa*, Advisory Opinion of 11 July 1950, ICJ Reports, 1950, p. 128; *Voting Procedure on Questions relating to the Reports and Petitions concerning the Territory of SW Africa*, Advisory Opinion of 7 June 1955, ICJ Reports, 1955, p. 67; *Admissibility of Hearings of Petitioners by the Committee on SW Africa*, Advisory Opinion of 1 June 1956, ICJ Reports, 1956, p. 23.

2.32 It is certainly true that in the South-West Africa cases, or the *Western Sahara* case [28] the opinion sought by the Assembly also had a bearing on the legal obligations of Member States. Nevertheless, as the Court emphasised in *Western Sahara*, the primary motivation for the opinion was to give guidance to the Assembly.

> '...The opinion is sought for a practical and contemporary purpose, namely, in order that the General Assembly should be in a better position to decide at its thirtieth session on the policy to be followed for the decolonisation of Western Sahara.
>
> ...
>
> 'the object of the request is ... to obtain from the Court an opinion which the General Assembly deems of assistance to it for the proper exercise of its functions concerning the decolonisation of the territory.' [29]

2.33 In the present case, however, the General Assembly is not seeking guidance on the performance of its functions. As Part II.2 of this Written Statement has demonstrated, it is not in the Assembly but in other fora, notably the Security Council and the Conference on Disarmament, that the issue of nuclear disarmament is being addressed and action taken. The question on which the Court's opinion has been sought concerns not the powers of the Assembly but rather the rights and obligations of States and, in particular, the extent of their inherent right of self-defence. Moreover, there is nothing to suggest that some new problem has arisen in the recent period so that the General Assembly is now hampered in carrying out its functions by the lack of an answer to the question posed to the Court. Indeed, taking into account the progress made in the nuclear non-proliferation and disarmament fields (referred to in Part II.2, above), the remarks of the delegate of Indonesia at the United Nations First Committee (when announcing that no action would be taken on a previous draft request) are now even more pertinent than they were then.[30]

(c) Cases where the legal question involves the interpretation of agreements between the Organization and a Member State

2.34 Cases of this kind have long been regarded as appropriate for the use of the Court's advisory jurisdiction. As early as 1946, Section 30 of the UN Convention on Privileges and Immunities provided for reference of disputes to the Court by way of a

---

28 Advisory Opinion of 16 October 1975, ICJ Reports, 1975, p. 12.

29 *Ibid.*, at pp. 20 and 27. So too in *Certain Expenses of the UN (Article 17(2) of the Charter)*, ICJ Reports, 1962, p. 151, although giving guidance to the Assembly on its budgetary functions, the Opinion carried necessary implications for the legal obligations of Member States.

30 See paragraph 2.6, above.

request for an advisory opinion. The *WHO Regional Office* case [31] and the *Applicability of the Obligation to Arbitrate arising under Section 21 of the United Nations Headquarters Agreement of 26 June 1947* case [32] both fell into this category. The present case, however, does not concern any agreement between the United Nations and a Member State. No such agreement concerning the use of nuclear weapons has ever been concluded.

(d) Cases where the legal question concerns the obligations of Member States consequential upon decisions or resolutions of the competent organs of the organization

2.35 In the *Namibia* case [33] the question put to the Court did involve the legal obligations of Member States but, of course, in the specific context of action by both the General Assembly and the Security Council with regard to the territory, in respect of which both organs had special responsibilities as a result of its mandated status. The Assembly, by Resolution 2145 (XXI), had terminated the Mandate under which South Africa held the territory, and the Security Council, by Resolution 276 (1970), had endorsed that decision, confirmed the illegality of further acts by South Africa in the territory and called upon Member States to refrain from dealing with South Africa contrary to paragraph 2 of the resolution. It was these decisions which created the legal obligations on which the Court was asked to advise.

2.36 In the present case the matter is entirely different. Although the General Assembly has adopted numerous resolutions regarding nuclear weapons since 1961, the Assembly has no power to create legal obligations for Member States with respect to the possession or use of nuclear weapons - or, indeed, with regard to any aspect of Member States' exercise of the right of self-defence - in the circumstances in which Resolution 49/75 K was adopted.

---

31 Advisory Opinion of 20 December 1980, ICJ Reports, 1980, p. 73.

32 Advisory Opinion of 26 April 1988, ICJ Reports, 1988, p. 12.

33 *Legal Consequences for States of the Continued Presence of South Africa in Namibia (SW Africa) notwithstanding Security Council resolution 276 (1970)*, Advisory Opinion of 21 June 1971, ICJ Reports, 1971, p. 16.

(2) An opinion from the Court in the present case would have no positive effect for the United Nations as a whole

2.37 The case law of the Court regarding the advisory jurisdiction emphasises the importance of this jurisdiction as a means by which the Court, as the principal judicial organ of the United Nations, can 'participate in the activities of the Organization'.[34] As the survey of the case law in the preceding paragraphs demonstrates, however, the Court has naturally been concerned that its participation should take the form of making a *positive* contribution to the activities of the United Nations. Moreover, the very fact that the Court is a principal organ of the United Nations means, it is submitted, that it must be concerned with the effect of an advisory opinion on the activities of the Organization as a whole and not just on the requesting organ. The United Kingdom considers that if the Court were to give an opinion in the present case, that opinion could not have a positive effect, either on the work of the General Assembly or in the context of the activities of the United Nations as a whole in the field of disarmament and security issues. First, the question posed by the General Assembly is a hypothetical one to which a proper judicial answer cannot be given, since the legality of the use, or threat of use, of nuclear weapons depends upon an analysis of the circumstances of the particular use or threat. Secondly, although it is the General Assembly which has sought the Court's opinion regarding the legality of the use of nuclear weapons, the dangers posed by such weapons are currently being addressed elsewhere in the United Nations in a manner which would not be helped (and, as will be demonstrated, may indeed be harmed) by a pronouncement on the legality of the use of such weapons.

(a) The question posed is hypothetical

2.38 As the preceding section has shown, the question put to the Court in the present case does not relate to the extent of the powers of the General Assembly or the exercise by the Assembly of its functions. Nor has it arisen in the context of a concrete factual situation involving a specific use or threat to use nuclear weapons. It is a purely hypothetical question which is removed from any factual or legal context which alone could provide the Court with a manageable framework within which it could set about answering the question. Although the Court has said, on a number of occasions, that the advisory jurisdiction may be used to answer an abstract question,[35]

---

34 *Peace Treaties* case, ICJ Reports, 1950, at p. 71.

35 See, e.g., the *Admissions* case, ICJ Reports, 1948, at p. 61 and the discussion by Fitzmaurice in *The Law and Procedure of the International Court of Justice* (1986), vol. I at p. 117.

it must nevertheless be possible to analyse the question in some particular factual matrix and not merely in the context of purely speculative or hypothetical facts.

2.39 The essence of the judicial function is the application of principles of law to specific factual situations. As Judge Hudson said of the Permanent Court of International Justice,

> 'The Court has not been made the school-master of the Council [of the League]. It has not been asked to propound the law, but to apply it. It has not been confronted with legal problems of the future, but of the present. It is not asked to work in vacuo, but as part of a live, active and functioning international system.' [36]

In the present case, however, the Court is being asked to work 'in vacuo'. It is asked to pronounce on whether the threat or use of nuclear weapons is permitted 'in any circumstance'. As the United Kingdom will demonstrate in Part III of this Written Statement, there is no legally binding instrument which directly and specifically prohibits the threat or use of nuclear weapons. In the absence of such an instrument, the question posed by the General Assembly can be answered only by reference to rules and principles of international law of more general application. Yet the application of such rules and principles to a specific weapon will necessarily depend upon the precise circumstances in which that weapon is used, or its use is threatened. No indication of what those circumstances might be is given in the question and it is difficult to see how the Court could have before it sufficient material to enable it to consider all of the combinations of circumstances which might arise. The combinations of circumstances are virtually unlimited. The Court would be constrained to consider such variable factors as: the location, scale and nature of the attack, whether actual or imminent; the means of defence available to the State under attack or threat of attack; the presumed objectives of the attacker; the particular type of nuclear weapon used in response to the attack, and its effects in the particular locality in which it is employed, including its likely effects on non-military targets and long-term environmental effects. The factors, and their permutations, are endless.

---

36 Hudson, 'The Advisory Opinions of the Permanent Court of International Justice', *International Conciliation* (November 1925), No. 214, p. 374.

(b) Nuclear weapons are being addressed in other contexts in the United Nations

2.40 Although the General Assembly has discussed nuclear weapons for over thirty years, it has not had sole, or even primary, responsibility for this matter within the United Nations. The possibility of a use of nuclear weapons is pre-eminently a question of international peace and security, primary responsibility for which is vested in the Security Council by virtue of Article 24(1) of the Charter. In addition, the Conference on Disarmament has long been the focus of efforts to achieve measures of nuclear disarmament. The Conference on Disarmament has consistently approached the question of reducing and eliminating the threat posed by nuclear weapons by means of negotiating specific measures, such as limitations on their proliferation and the achievement of limitations on nuclear testing, rather than by debating whether the use of a particular nuclear weapon would or would not be lawful in general or in some hypothetical combination of circumstances. This approach has recently been endorsed by the Security Council in resolution 984 (1995) [37] which expressly welcomes the assurances given by nuclear-weapon States to the non-nuclear-weapon States which are parties to the Non-Proliferation Treaty. [38] There is no indication that an opinion on the legality of the use of nuclear weapons would make any positive contribution to this process.

2.41 In Judge Hudson's words, the Court has to operate as part of a 'live, active and functioning international system'. In the present case, that international system must be seen as extending beyond the General Assembly to include the United Nations as a whole. It must also entail recognition of the fact that, so far as nuclear weapons are concerned, the most important parts of that system are to be found in the Conference on Disarmament and the Security Council, as well as in the recent Review and Extension Conference of the Non-Proliferation Treaty. If the Court's answer to the question posed by the General Assembly will make no positive contribution to the work of those parts of the international system then that is a good reason for the Court to decline to answer that question.

---

37 See Annex D.

38 See paragraphs 2.19 to 2.22, above.

(3) An advisory opinion on this question could have a harmful effect on important disarmament negotiations

2.42 It has already been shown, in Part II.2 of this Statement, that the present case comes before the Court at a time when the parties have just decided, without the need for a vote, to extend indefinitely the Non-Proliferation Treaty, when new negative and positive security assurances have been unanimously welcomed by the Security Council, and when a number of other measures to reduce the threat posed by nuclear weapons are under the most active consideration. These negotiations form part of a disarmament process which it has taken many years to construct and which now offers the prospect of additional very considerable achievements. However, as paragraph 4(c) of the Decision on the Principles and Objectives for Nuclear Non-Proliferation and Disarmament makes clear, efforts to reduce nuclear weapons globally, with the ultimate goal of eliminating those weapons, are linked to the pursuit by all States of general and complete disarmament under strict and effective international control. That necessarily involves the consideration not only of nuclear weapons but also of conventional arms. Moreover, it would be unrealistic to imagine that that ultimate objective could be achieved within a short time-frame. In the meantime, therefore, the disarmament process has sought to achieve interim protection of international peace and security through a stable system of deterrence which includes both positive and negative security assurances from the nuclear-weapon States to the non-nuclear-weapon States.

2.43 The existing treaties and other texts which refer to nuclear weapons have been concluded after lengthy and complicated negotiations among States with widely differing views about the utility and even morality of possessing such weapons. The success achieved so far in these negotiations has been based on striking a balance between those views; and because States have, in fact, concentrated not upon the differences between them but on points where their interests coincide, with the result that specific steps towards goals of nuclear non-proliferation and disarmament have been achieved. These achievements have been welcomed within the United Nations. If, however, the Court were to give an opinion on the principles of law raised by this request (and in particular if in doing so it were to cast doubt on the basis for existing agreements) the continued participation of States concerned in these activities might be called into question. For example, an opinion of the Court that the possession of nuclear weapons, and their use in self-defence, could never be lawful might lead some States to conclude that they should no longer participate in existing regimes concerning nuclear weapons which did not amount to measures of complete disarmament. Alternatively, an opinion of the Court recognising that the use of nuclear weapons could be lawful in appropriate circumstances might diminish the incentive for those States not parties to applicable treaty regimes to renounce the possession of nuclear weapons. In these circumstances, the viability of existing achievements in the field of nuclear disarmament and non-proliferation would be undermined.

2.44 Similar considerations apply as regards current disarmament negotiations. An advisory opinion by the Court on the principles of law raised by this request is not a necessary pre-condition for the successful conclusion of the disarmament negotiations referred to in paragraphs 2.16 to 2.21 above. Moreover, there is again a risk that such an opinion would actually play a divisive role. It might lead the States participating in those negotiations to become side-tracked into a debate on the implications of the Court's opinions, rather than concentrating on the complex and detailed matters before them. There would also be the risk, in the case of an opinion casting doubt on the legality of the use or threat of use of nuclear weapons in any circumstances, that some States might feel unable to continue their participation in nuclear disarmament and non-proliferation negotiations which build upon the existing position and which seek to bring about further reductions and controls, rather than total disarmament. Whatever the view the Court were to come to on the merits, it is in any case unlikely to have any significant effect in assisting progress in these negotiations.

2.45 The United Kingdom therefore submits that, in view of the considerations set out in this Part of the Statement, there are compelling reasons why the Court should exercise its discretion to decline to answer the question put to it.

III THE PRINCIPLES OF LAW RAISED BY THE QUESTION

1 The Meaning of the Question

3.1 The question posed by the General Assembly is wider than that posed by the World Health Assembly in that it refers to 'the threat or use of nuclear weapons' as compared with 'the use of' such weapons. This broader phase in the General Assembly's question is closer to the wording of Article 2, paragraph 4 of the U.N. Charter, which refers to 'the threat or use of force'. Neither question touches possession of nuclear weapons as such.

3.2 In so far as the General Assembly's question reflects the wording of Article 2, paragraph 4 of the U.N. Charter, this represents, in the view of the United Kingdom, the correct approach. For it essentially equates nuclear weapons with 'force'. They are one form, an extreme form, of 'force' and as such their use is subject to the same prohibitions - and the same exceptions - as the use of 'force' is in general under the U.N. Charter.

3.3 The question addressed to the Court is whether the threat or use of nuclear weapons is in any circumstance *permitted* under international law. It is, however, axiomatic that, in the absence of a prohibitive rule opposable to a particular State, the conduct of the State in question must be permissible.[39] Properly, therefore, the question should be whether the threat or use of nuclear weapons is *prohibited* by any rule of international law. In contrast, the question as formulated is implicitly cast in

---

[39] This principle was recently given specific application and endorsed by the Court in the *Nicaragua* case in the following terms:

> '... in international law there are no rules, other than such rules as may be accepted by the State concerned, by treaty or otherwise, whereby the level of armaments of a sovereign State can be limited, and this principle is valid for all States without exception.' (*Military and Paramilitary Activities in and Against Nicaragua* (Merits), ICJ Reports, 1986, p. 14, at paragraph 269.)

The principle stated in the text flows in some measure from the often quoted statement of the Permanent Court in the *Lotus* case that international law leaves to States 'a wide measure of discretion which is only limited in certain cases by prohibitive rules' (PCIJ Reports, Series. A, No. 10, at p. 19). The principle does not, however, rely thereon but draws its support from the more general proposition that the basis of international law is 'the express or tacit consent of States to the body of rules comprising international law as a whole at any particular time' (Jennings and Watts, *Oppenheim's International Law* (9th ed., 1992), vol. I, paragraph 5).

terms of a presumption of illegality, rebuttable on proof that the conduct in question is permitted.

3.4 Flowing from this presumption of illegality is an almost imperceptible shifting in the burden of proof from those seeking to show that the conduct in qustion is prohibited to those seeking to show that it is permitted. In other words, contrary to accepted principles of international law, the formulation of the question places the burden on those seeking to show that the threat or use of nuclear weapons may in some circumstances be permissible to prove this to be the case. In the United Kingdom's view, it is for those contending for a prohibitive rule to prove that it exists and that it is opposable to other States. In the event that the Court decides to respond to the request for an advisory opinion, the correct interpretation of the question would therefore be whether the threat or use of nuclear weapons is in any circumstance *prohibited* by any rule of international law. In the absence of proof that this is so, it would follow that the conduct in question is lawful.

3.5 Whichever way the question is framed, it does not admit of a simple answer. There is no foundation for the view that the use of nuclear weapons would automatically contravene international law. The international community has never adopted in binding form any general prohibition on the use of nuclear weapons. On the contrary, those treaties which have been adopted regarding nuclear weapons presuppose that there are circumstances in which such weapons might lawfully be used. Moreover, an examination of the principles of international law regarding the threat and use of force and the conduct of hostilities reveals that, while nuclear weapons (like all methods and means of warfare) are subject to limitations on their use, those limitations are not such as to render the use of nuclear weapons unlawful *per se*.

3.6 This part of the United Kingdom's statement addresses these issues in the following way. Section 2 examines those treaties and other instruments which specifically refer to nuclear weapons. Section 3 considers the legality of the use of force in self-defence under the terms of the United Nations Charter. Section 4 looks at the application of the laws of armed conflict to the use of nuclear weapons. Section 5 considers the possible effect on the use of nuclear weapons of human rights treaties and treaties and customary law relating to the protection of the environment. Finally, Section 6 examines the legal issues raised by a threat to use nuclear weapons.

2 Provisions specifically referring to nuclear weapons

3.7 Since the middle of the nineteenth century, the international community has adopted a long list of treaties banning - or severely restricting - the use of specific weapons. Prominent on this list are:

(1) the St Petersburg Declaration, 1868, which prohibits the use of projectiles under 400 grammes in weight which are explosive or charged with fulminating or inflammable substances;[40]

(2) Hague Declaration No. 2, 1899, banning the use of projectiles the sole object of which is the diffusion of asphyxiating or deleterious gases;[41]

(3) Hague Declaration No. 3, 1899, prohibiting the use of bullets which expand or flatten easily in the body;[42]

(4) the Hague Regulations on Land Warfare annexed to Hague Convention No. IV, 1907, Article 23 (a) of which prohibits the use of poison and poisoned weapons;[43]

(5) Hague Convention No. VIII, 1907, restricting the use of automatic submarine contact mines;[44]

(6) the Geneva Protocol, 1925, prohibiting the use of asphyxiating, poisonous or other gases, all analogous liquids, materials or devices, and bacteriological methods of warfare;[45]

(7) the Convention on the Prohibition of Development, Production and Stockpiling of Bacteriological and Toxin Weapons, 1972, which prohibits the

---

40 138 CTS (1868-69) 297; LXIV UKPP (1869) 659.

41 187 CTS (1898-99) 453; UKTS 32 (1907), Cd. 3751.

42 187 CTS (1898-99) 459; UKTS 32 (1907), Cd.3751.

43 205 CTS (1907) 227; UKTS 9 (1910), Cd. 5030.

44 205 CTS (1907) 331; UKTS 12 (1910), Cd. 5116.

45 XCIV LNTS (1929) 65; UKTS 24 (1930), Cmd. 3604.

possession of bacteriological and toxin weapons and reinforces the prohibition on their use;[46]

(8) the United Nations Convention on the Prohibition of Military or any other Hostile Use of Environmental Modification Techniques, 1977, prohibiting the use of weapons intended to change the environment through the deliberate manipulation of natural processes;[47]

(9) the United Nations Convention on Prohibitions or Restrictions on the Use of Certain Conventional Weapons, 1981, the Protocols to which prohibit the use of weapons the primary effect of which is to injure by non-detectable fragments, and impose certain restrictions on the use of mines, booby-traps and incendiary weapons;[48]

(10) the Chemical Weapons Convention, 1993, which prohibits all use of chemical weapons and requires the destruction of existing stocks.[49]

3.8 In marked contrast, no treaty has been adopted specifically prohibiting the use of nuclear weapons. Nor is the use of nuclear weapons outlawed by a provision in a treaty of more general application. The Charter of the United Nations makes no reference to nuclear weapons. Nor do the Principles of the Charter elaborated in the Declaration of Friendly Relations and Co-operation among States in accordance with the Charter of the United Nations (UNGA Resolution 2625 (XXV)), the Resolution on the Definition of Aggression (UNGA Resolution 3314 (XXIX)) or the Declaration on the Enhancement of the Effectiveness of the Principle of refraining from the Threat or Use of Force in International Relations (UNGA Resolution 42/22) expressly prohibit or regulate the use of nuclear weapons.[50]

3.9 On the contrary, the international community has consistently declined to address the question of the lawfulness or unlawfulness of nuclear weapons *per se*.

---

46 1015 UNTS 164.

47 1108 UNTS 151.

48 19 ILM (1980) 1523; 1342 UNTS 7.

49 32 ILM (1993) 800.

50 Resolution 42/22 refers to nuclear weapons only in the context of statements about the importance of avoiding armed conflict and contains no statement about whether the use of such weapons would be lawful.

Although in 1961 and in subsequent years the United Nations General Assembly proposed the conclusion of a treaty prohibiting the use of nuclear weapons,[51] that proposal has not been followed up and no conference to consider such a treaty has been convened. In another context, the Diplomatic Conference which adopted the four Geneva Conventions of 1949 rejected a proposal that it adopt a resolution on the illegality of using nuclear weapons as being outside the terms of reference of the Conference.[52]

3.10 The Diplomatic Conference on the Development of Humanitarian Law, 1974 to 1977, which adopted the two Additional Protocols to the Geneva Conventions of 1949 and which had broader terms of reference than the 1949 Conference, also did not discuss the legality of nuclear weapons. In submitting draft protocols to the Diplomatic Conference, the International Committee of the Red Cross stated:

> 'Problems relating to atomic, bacteriological and chemical warfare are subjects of international agreements or negotiations by governments, and in submitting these draft Additional Protocols the ICRC does not intend to broach those problems. It should be borne in mind that the Red Cross as a whole, at several International Red Cross Conferences, has clearly made known its condemnation of weapons of mass destruction and has urged governments to reach agreements for the banning of their use.'[53]

During the four sessions of the Conference, the United Kingdom and a number of other States made statements to the effect that the subject of nuclear weapons should not be discussed by the Conference.[54] A number of other States, while not expressly referring to nuclear weapons, made clear that they shared the view of the ICRC that this question was better dealt with in the context of disarmament negotiations and that the Conference should do nothing to prejudice such talks. For example, the Representative of Brazil said that:

---

51 Resolution 1653 (XVI). This resolution and subsequent resolutions on the same subject are discussed below, paragraphs 3.25 to 3.32.

52 *Final Record of the Diplomatic Conference of Geneva*, vol. IIA, pp. 802-5.

53 ICRC, *Draft Additional Protocols to the Geneva Conventions of August 12, 1949* (Geneva June 1973), p. 2.

54 *Official Records*, vol. V, pp. 134 (UK), 121 (USSR), 145-6 (Sweden), 179 (Argentina), vol VII, pp. 192 (France), 295 (USA).

'...other international bodies which were trying to bring about the reduction of armaments and to achieve general and complete disarmament were in a better position than the Conference to deal with certain weapons.'[55]

3.11 Although some States maintained that the Conference should consider a ban on some or all uses of nuclear weapons,[56] it is clear from the records of the Conference that this was not done. No formal proposal to deal with nuclear weapons was put before the Conference and discussion of specific weapons was confined to certain conventional weapons considered by the Conference's *Ad Hoc* Committee, the terms of reference of which were expressly confined to conventional weapons.[57] In its Report to the Conference, the *Ad Hoc* Committee stated that:

> 'There was general agreement that a consideration of certain modern *conventional* weapons in the light of such factors as the degree of suffering caused or their indiscriminateness had by now become an urgent necessity. Tremendous technological developments had led to ever more sophisticated weapons, in many cases with increasingly destructive power. Nuclear weapons and other weapons of mass destruction were, of course, the most destructive. In that connexion, some delegations rejected the view that the debate on those weapons and their possible prohibition should be left to the disarmament discussions, and they urged that the Conference include them in its programme of work. Another delegation expressed its regret at the decision not to consider these weapons. Many other delegations, however, accepted the limitation of the work of this Conference to conventional weapons. As it was pointed out by some, nuclear weapons in particular had a special function in that they act as deterrents preventing the outbreak of a major armed conflict between certain nuclear powers.'[58]

The Conference formally recorded the Report without a vote.[59] The Conference also adopted a resolution recommending that a Conference of Governments be convened with a view to reaching 'agreements on prohibitions or restrictions on the use of specific *conventional* weapons including those which may be deemed to be

---

55 *Official Records*, vol. V, p. 98. See also the statements by Ukraine (p. 113), Byelorussia (p. 150) and Mongolia (p. 192).

56 *Official Records*, vol. V, pp. 97 (Ghana), 103 (Romania), 105 (Yugoslavia), 120 (China), 123 (Iraq) and 195 (Zaire); vol. XIV p. 70 (Albania) and p. 241 (North Korea).

57 Pilloud et al. *Commentary on the Additional Protocols of 8 June 1977* (ICRC, 1987), p. 591 (the 'ICRC Commentary'). A proposal to remove the word 'conventional' from the title of the *Ad Hoc* Committee was rejected. For the debate on the establishment and terms of reference of this committee, see *Official Records*, vol. V, pp. 82-90.

58 *Official Records*, vol XVI, p. 454 (emphasis added).

59 *Official Records*, vol. V, pp. 219-221.

excessively injurious or have indiscriminate effects'. [60] Subsequently, a number of States made declarations, on signature or ratification, to the effect that the new rules contained in Protocol I did not apply to nuclear weapons. [61]

3.12 It is not surprising, therefore, that the Commentary on the Protocols published under the auspices of the ICRC (the 'ICRC Commentary') concludes that 'there is no doubt that during the four sessions of the Conference agreement was reached not to discuss nuclear weapons,' [62] or that the Protocols contain no references to nuclear weapons.[63]

3.13 Those treaties which have dealt expressly with the subject of nuclear weapons have not addressed the question whether such weapons are unlawful *per se* but have concentrated, for the most part, upon issues regarding possession, deployment and testing. The effect of these treaties may be summarised as follows:-

Possession

3.14 By becoming parties to the Non-Proliferation Treaty, 1968,[64] or to a regional treaty, such as the Treaty of Tlatelolco,[65] most non-nuclear-weapon States have now undertaken not to manufacture or acquire nuclear weapons. The Peace Treaties concluded at the end of the Second World War also bind a number of States not to possess nuclear weapons.[66] In the case of Germany, this obligation was reaffirmed in the Treaty on the Final Settlement with Respect to Germany, 1990.[67] The disarmament treaties concluded between some of the nuclear powers limit by

---

60 Resolution 22: *Official Records*, vol. I, p. 215 (emphasis added).

61 See below, paras. 3.45 to 3.55.

62 *ICRC Commentary*, p. 593.

63 The possible effect on the use of nuclear weapons of the more general provisions of Additional Protocol I is considered below, paragraphs 3.45 to 3.55.

64 729 UNTS 161.

65 634 UNTS 281.

66 Treaties of Peace with Bulgaria, Finland, Hungary, Italy and Romania.

67 29 ILM (1990) 1186, Article 3.

agreement the number and types of nuclear weapons delivery-systems which those States may possess.[68]

Deployment

3.15 The deployment of nuclear weapons is prohibited in Antarctica,[69] in outer space or on celestial bodies [70] and on the deep seabed.[71] For those States which have become parties to the Treaty of Tlatelolco or its 1st Protocol, the deployment of nuclear weapons is prohibited within the areas covered by that agreement.[72] Similarly, those States which are parties to the Treaty of Rarotonga or its 1st Protocol have undertaken not to deploy nuclear weapons within the areas covered by that agreement.[73]

Testing

3.16 Those States parties to the Partial Test Ban Treaty, 1963, [74] have agreed not to carry out atmospheric nuclear tests. Bilateral agreements also restrict underground nuclear testing by some of the nuclear powers. In addition, testing in certain parts of the world is restricted by agreements such as the Antarctic Treaty. Negotiations currently taking place with a view to the adoption of a comprehensive test ban treaty are described in Part II.2, above.

---

68 See, e.g., the Anti-Ballistic Missiles Systems Treaty, 1972 (944 UNTS 13), and the Intermediate-Range Nuclear Forces Treaty, 1987 (27 ILM (1988) 84), between the Soviet Union and the United States.

69 Antarctic Treaty, 1959, Article I (402 UNTS 71).

70 Outer Space Treaty, 1967, Article IV (610 UNTS 205).

71 Sea-Bed Treaty, 1971, Article I (955 UNTS 115).

72 The areas covered by the Treaty of Tlatelolco comprise most of Latin America and certain adjacent waters and islands. The United Kingdom is a party to Protocols I and II to the Treaty.

73 The Treaty of Rarotonga applies to parts of the South Pacific. The United Kingdom has not become a party to the protocols to that treaty but the United Kingdom Government have stated that they are ready, as a matter of policy, to respect the intentions of the regional States and that they have no intention of testing nuclear weapons in the South Pacific or of basing nuclear weapons on British territories in the South Pacific (statement by the Minister of State, Foreign and Commonwealth Office in the House of Commons, 20 March 1987; HC Debs, vol. 112, Written Answers, col. 639; 58 BYIL (1987) 635).

74 480 UNTS 43.

3.17 The treaties, however, say little about the possible use of nuclear weapons by those States which have no obligation not to possess them. The Partial Test Ban Treaty, for example, while prohibiting the parties from conducting atmospheric nuclear tests, does not purport to restrict their use of nuclear weapons in the course of hostilities.[75] Similarly, the Sea Bed Treaty prohibits the emplacement of nuclear weapons on the sea bed but does not restrict the use of nuclear weapons fired from other locations.

3.18 The Treaty of Tlatelolco is an exception. Article 3 of Protocol II to the Treaty contains an undertaking by those nuclear States which are parties to the Protocol not to use or threaten to use nuclear weapons against the States party to the Treaty of Tlatelolco. All five permanent members of the Security Council are now parties to this Protocol and have thus accepted this obligation, although each made a declaration on becoming party in which it indicated the circumstances in which it would regard itself as free to take military action involving the use of nuclear weapons. Thus, the United Kingdom declared that:

> 'the Government of the United Kingdom would, in the event of any act of aggression by a Contracting Party to the Treaty in which that Party was supported by a nuclear-weapon State, be free to reconsider the extent to which they could be regarded as committed by the provisions of Additional Protocol II.'[76]

---

75 That the Partial Test Ban Treaty was not intended to apply to the use of nuclear weapons in an armed conflict was made clear by the United States Secretary of State in his report of 8 August 1963 to the President, in which he said:

> 'The article [Article I] does not prohibit the use of nuclear weapons in the event of war nor restrict the exercise of the right of self-defense recognized in Article 51 of the Charter of the United Nations.' (*Documents on Disarmament*, 1963, p. 297.)

See also the advice of the State Department Legal Adviser, *op. cit.* pp. 343-4. The Government of the Soviet Union took a similar approach in a statement on 21 August 1963, in which it said:

> 'the treaty also does not prohibit the Soviet Union, if need be, from holding underground nuclear tests, from increasing the stockpiles of nuclear arms, and even from using these weapons against the imperialist aggressors if they unleash a war in a fit of insanity.' (*Op. cit.*, p. 456.)

76 28 ILM (1989) p. 1400 at 1422. The United States made a similar statement on ratification (*loc. cit.* p. 1423). On signature of the Protocol, China repeated its general undertaking that it would not be the first State to resort to the use of nuclear weapons (p. 1414); France stated that:

> 'The French Government interprets the undertakings set forth in Article 3 of the Protocol as not presenting an obstacle to the full exercise of the right of self-defence confirmed by Article 51 of the United Nations Charter.' (p. 1415)

The Soviet Union stated that:

3.19 Although the Non-Proliferation Treaty contains no comparable provision,[77] China, France, Russia, the United Kingdom and the United States have each given security assurances to non-nuclear-weapon States in connection with the Treaty. These assurances are described in Part II, above.[78] In resolution 984 [79] the Security Council has welcomed the fact that these assurances had been given.

3.20 In addition, some of the treaties discussed in Part II prohibit any use of force (whether with nuclear or conventional weapons) within a defined area.[80]

3.21 The treaties reviewed here, together with the absence of a general treaty prohibition on the use of nuclear weapons, show that the international community has addressed the question of nuclear weapons through the medium of practical measures of disarmament and non-proliferation by agreement, rather than through an attempt to outlaw nuclear weapons or their use. The preambles, substantive provisions and drafting histories of the various treaties which have dealt with the question of nuclear weapons clearly place those treaties in the context of disarmament, as steps on the road to the goal of a more general disarmament by agreement between the States specially concerned, or between all States. Neither expressly nor impliedly do they attempt to outlaw all uses of nuclear weapons in any circumstances.

3.22 Nor do these treaties support the inference that the use of nuclear weapons is regarded as unlawful under existing international law.[81] On the contrary, many of

---

'Any action carried out by a State or States party to the Tlatelolco Treaty that are incompatible with its statute of denuclearization as well as the perpetration by one or several States party to the Treaty of an act of aggression with the support of a State possessing nuclear weapons or together with such State, shall be considered by the Soviet Union to be incompatible with the obligations of those countries under the Treaty. In such cases the Soviet Union reserves the right to review its obligations under Additional Protocol II.' (p. 1418)

77 The Preamble to the Treaty makes clear that the Treaty was designed to contribute to the prevention of nuclear war by preventing the dissemination of nuclear weapons, that in doing so it was a response to the calls from the United Nations General Assembly for the adoption of an agreement on the spread of nuclear weapons and that it was a critical step in the process of concluding disarmament agreements.

78 See paragraph 2.19 and Annex C.

79 Annex D.

80 Eg the Antarctic Treaty, 1959, and the Moon Treaty (1363 UNTS 3).

81 Attempts to draw such an inference are made by, for example, Sri Lanka in its statement to the Court regarding the request by the WHO for an advisory opinion (Written Statement of the Government of Sri Lanka, p. 2).

the provisions of those treaties are only explicable on the assumption that the use of nuclear weapons was not regarded by the negotiating States as unlawful *per se*. The commitment made by the nuclear-weapon States in Protocol II to the Treaty of Tlatelolco would be entirely unnecessary if the use of nuclear weapons was in all circumstances prohibited by general international law. Moreover, the declarations made by the nuclear-weapon States at the time of signing or ratifying the Protocol, which were not challenged by the parties to the Treaty of Tlatelolco, indicate that those States consider that there are circumstances in which resort to nuclear weapons would be lawful.

3.23 The Non-Proliferation Treaty and the security assurances offered by the nuclear-weapon States rest on the same assumption. Although the Non-Proliferation Treaty is concerned with possession, rather than use, of nuclear weapons, it is based upon a balance of responsibilities between nuclear-weapon and non-nuclear-weapon States, which the agreement treats as two distinct categories. Thus, nuclear-weapon States parties are subject to clearly differentiated obligations under the Treaty from those parties which do not possess such weapons and undertake not to acquire them. To treat the nuclear-weapon States in this way is incompatible with any assumption that the possible use of nuclear weapons is totally prohibited. The entire structure of the Non-Proliferation Treaty (which on 11 May 1995 was extended indefinitely by the Conference of States Parties without the need for a vote) presupposes that the parties did not regard the use of nuclear weapons as being proscribed in all circumstances. Moreover, the security assurances given by the nuclear-weapon States can only be regarded as possessing any significance on the assumption that there are conditions in which nuclear weapons could and might lawfully be used. Similarly, Security Council resolution 984 (which was unanimously adopted on 11 April 1995) is based upon the assumption that there are circumstances in which the use of nuclear weapons in response to aggression might be a lawful measure of individual or collective self-defence.

3.24 The absence of any challenge to the declarations made in connection with the Treaty of Tlatelolco, together with the response to the security assurances made in connection with the Non-Proliferation Treaty, is highly pertinent to the matter under consideration. Since it is clear that there is no treaty provision which imposes a general prohibition on the threat or use of nuclear weapons, any such prohibition must be derived from customary law. For the Court to find, however, that a rule of customary international law embodying such a prohibition exists, it would need to be provided with clear evidence that that rule enjoys the support of the generality of States. The existence of the nuclear-weapon States already weakens the argument that there is a sufficient 'generality' in support of a prohibitive rule. To this number must be added the number of States failing to make any challenge to the declarations and assurances considered in the preceding paragraphs. The attitude of those States can only be consistent with the view that no prohibitive rule exists. It is clear, therefore, that the 'generality' of States needed to support a prohibitive rule can be shown categorically *not* to exist. That this is the position becomes even clearer when one considers other evidence of State attitudes towards the question.

3.25 The only documents which claim to treat nuclear weapons as unlawful *per se* are certain resolutions of the United Nations General Assembly, starting with Resolution 1653 (XVI) in 1961, paragraph 1 of which declared that:

> '(a) The use of nuclear and thermonuclear weapons is contrary to the spirit, letter and aims of the United Nations and, as such, a direct violation of the Charter of the United Nations;
> (b) The use of nuclear and thermonuclear weapons would exceed even the scope of war and cause indiscriminate suffering and destruction to mankind and civilization and, as such, is contrary to the rules of international law and to the laws of humanity;
> (c) The use of nuclear and thermonuclear weapons is a war directed not against an enemy or enemies alone but also against mankind in general, since the peoples of the world not involved in such a war will be subjected to all the evils generated by the use of such weapons;
> (d) Any State using nuclear and thermonuclear weapons is to be considered as violating the Charter of the United Nations, as acting contrary to the laws of humanity and as committing a crime against mankind and civilization.'

However, the resolution went on to request the Secretary-General to consult States about the possibility of convening a conference to discuss *the adoption of a convention* in order to prohibit the use of nuclear weapons.

3.26 This resolution was followed in 1972 by Resolution 2936 (XXVII), paragraph 1 of which solemnly declared

> 'on behalf of the States members of the Organization, their renunciation of the use or threat of force in all its forms and manifestations in international relations in accordance with the Charter of the United Nations, and the permanent prohibition of the use of nuclear weapons.'

A series of subsequent resolutions [82] declared that the use of nuclear weapons would be unlawful and called upon States *to adopt a convention* prohibiting their use and the threat of their use.

---

82 Resolutions 33/71 B, 35/152 D, 36/92 I, 45/59 B, 46/37 D, 47/53 C and 48/76 B.

3.27 These resolutions are not, of course, legally binding instruments.[83] Moreover, there are several reasons for rejecting the suggestion that they are declaratory of a rule of customary international law forbidding all use of nuclear weapons. First, an analysis of the voting figures reveals that the resolutions were controversial. Resolution 1653 (XVI) was adopted by 55 votes to 20, with 26 abstentions. Of the nuclear powers, France, the United Kingdom and the United States voted against the resolution, while the Soviet Union voted in favour. It is evident, therefore, that, as an authoritative United Nations Report stated, this resolution demonstrated not a consensus but rather the sharp conflict of views on this issue.[84] Resolution 2936 (XXVII) was adopted by 73 votes to 4, with 46 abstentions. The Soviet Union was one of the sponsors of the resolution and voted in its favour; France, the United Kingdom and the United States abstained. The later resolutions [85] also failed to command the general support which has characterised those resolutions which have been widely regarded as declaratory of customary international law. [86]

3.28 Secondly, it is evident that many of those States which voted for the resolutions concerned did not regard them as stating such a customary law principle. In the case of Resolution 1653, the link between the assertion of the illegality of

---

83 The General Assembly has no power under the Charter to impose binding obligations upon Member States except in respect of certain internal matters. This is in contrast to the position of the Security Council, the resolutions of which are, in certain circumstances, binding by virtue of Article 25 of the Charter. The criteria identified by the Court in the *Namibia* Opinion (ICJ Reports, 1971, p. 15 at p. 53) for determining whether or not such a resolution is a binding one concerned only resolutions of the Security Council and did not, contrary to what is suggested by the Solomon Islands in its submissions regarding the WHO request for an Advisory Opinion (Written Statement of the Government of the Solomon Islands, p. 38, paragraph 3.26), suggest that resolutions of the General Assembly possess a binding character merely because they are couched in language similar to that of a Security Council resolution. The Court in the *Namibia* Opinion considered General Assembly resolutions to have a determinative effect only in certain exceptional matters, none of which are relevant in the present case.

84 UN Secretary-General's Report on *Existing Rules of International Law concerning the Prohibition or Restriction of Use of Specific Weapons* (UN Doc. A/9215), vol. I, p. 147.

85 Adopted by votes of 103-18-18; 112-19-14; 121-19-6; 125-17-10; 122-16-22; 126-21-21 and 120-23-24 respectively.

86 For example Resolution 2625 (XXV) (Declaration on Principles of International Law) and Resolution 3314 (XXIX) (Definition of Aggression), which were treated by the Court in the *Case Concerning Military and Paramilitary Activities in and against Nicaragua*, ICJ Reports, 1986, p. 3 at paragraphs 188 and 195, as reflecting the content of customary international law, were both adopted without a vote, as was Resolution 3452 (XXX) (Declaration on Torture), which was regarded as declaratory of customary international law by a United States court in *Filartiga* v. *Pena-Irala* 630 F 2d 876 (1980); 77 ILR 169. The requirement that a General Assembly resolution must command wide support, including support from all the various groups of States most closely affected, if it is to be treated as declaratory of customary international law was also emphasised by Professor Dupuy as Sole Arbitrator in *Texaco/Calasiatic* v. *Libya* 53 ILR 389.

nuclear weapons in paragraph 1 and the request that the Secretary-General consult States about the conclusion of a convention to prohibit the use of nuclear weapons raises the question whether those States which voted for the resolution regarded the use of nuclear weapons as unlawful in the absence of such a convention.[87] Statements by a number of States, including some of the sponsors of the resolution, suggest that they did not take such a position. [88] The later resolutions also refer to the adoption of a convention prohibiting the use of nuclear weapons, again casting doubt on the extent to which those States which voted for them saw the resolutions as containing statements *de lege lata* about the legality of the use of nuclear weapons.

3.29 Thirdly, in Resolution 2936 the prohibition of nuclear weapons was expressly linked to the renunciation of the use of force 'in accordance with the Charter of the United Nations'. The resolution thus leaves open the possibility of the lawful use of nuclear weapons, since the renunciation of the use of force was evidently not intended to preclude the exercise of that right.[89] That was made clear by the Soviet Union, one of the sponsors of the resolution, [90] whose subsequent security assurances given to the Conference on Disarmament also showed that it regarded the use of nuclear weapons as lawful where that was a necessary measure of self-defence.

3.30 Finally, the significance of the General Assembly resolutions has to be seen in the light of State practice as a whole, including the conclusion of the agreements discussed above, the failure to adopt a convention of the kind called for in the resolutions themselves, the decision not to discuss nuclear weapons at the Diplomatic Conference on the Development of Humanitarian Law and the statements and security assurances made by the nuclear powers in the context of the Non-Proliferation Treaty and the Treaty of Tlatelolco, all of which indicate that there is no consistent State practice from which a customary law prohibition of nuclear weapons might have developed. Thus, there is no real evidence of an *opinio juris* shared by the generality of States.

---

87 See Kalshoven, 'Arms, Armaments and International Law' 191 *Recueil des cours* (1985-II) 183 at pp. 276-7.

88 See, e.g., the statement by Ceylon GAOR, 17th Sess., Ist Ctee., 1288th Mtg, para. 8. See also the discussion in UN Doc A/9215, vol. I, pp. 147-54.

89 See Part III.3, below.

90 See the statement by the Soviet Union at A/PV. 2040, pp. 26-33.

3.31 Indeed, the practice of the General Assembly itself reinforces this conclusion. The resolutions on the use of nuclear weapons are by no means the only resolutions adopted by the General Assembly with regard to the question of nuclear arms. The Assembly has supported (or in some cases launched) the various initiatives which led to the adoption of the treaties considered above. In particular, it has expressed its support for the principle of 'an acceptable balance of mutual responsibilities and obligations between nuclear-weapon States and those which do not possess nuclear weapons', [91] and for the notion of embodying the security assurances given by the nuclear-weapon States in connection with the Non-Proliferation Treaty [92] in an international agreement.[93] For the reasons already given, such an approach cannot be reconciled with the view that international law already prohibits all use of nuclear weapons.

3.32 The position is, therefore, as recently summarized by the Federal Republic of Germany, that:

> '...international law in force...does not contain any explicit provisions definitely prohibiting the use of nuclear weapons, nor can any such prohibition be derived from current contractual and customary law.'[94]

In the absence of a rule of international law specifically prohibiting the use of nuclear weapons, the legality of their use has to be assessed by reference to the principles of law which are applicable to any use of armed force. According to these principles, the use of force is lawful only if it is in circumstances in which resort to force is permissible under the principles enshrined in the United Nations Charter and if it meets the requirements of the law of armed conflict regarding the conduct of hostilities.

---

91 Resolution 2028 (XX). See also Resolution 49/83.

92 See Part II.2. above, and Annex C.

93 Resolution 49/73.

94 Federal Ministry of Defence, *Humanitarian Law in Armed Conflicts Manual* (1992), paragraph 428. Other military and naval manuals have taken the same position. See Switzerland, *Gesetze und Gebrauche des Krieges* (1987), Section 3, Art. 24; United States, *Naval Commander's Handbook*, NWP-9 (1989), paragraph 10.2.1; Canada, *Draft Manual of the Law of Armed Conflict* , para. 511; United Kingdom, *Manual of Military Law, Part III* (1958), paragraph 113; Australian Defence Force, *Law of Armed Conflict: Commander's Guide* (1994) paragraph 313. Although the New Zealand Defence Force manual contains no express statement about the legality of nuclear weapons, they are not included in the list of prohibited weapons at paragraph 511.

3 The United Nations Charter and the Right of Self-Defence

3.33 The use of force is not prohibited by Article 2(4) of the United Nations Charter if it is duly authorized by the competent organ of the United Nations, or if it is in the exercise of the right of self-defence. Although for Member States of the United Nations Article 51 of the Charter recognizes their right to self-defence, Article 51 is not the source of that right. Indeed, the use of the word 'inherent' in Article 51 was intended to mark the pre-existence of this right, based on customary international law.[95] There had been no reference to self-defence in the Dumbarton Oaks Proposals and the view of Committee I at the San Francisco Conference was that the prohibition of the use of force, contemplated as a core provision of the new UN Charter, would leave the use of arms in self-defence unimpaired. [96] The same view had been taken earlier in relation to the Covenant of the League and the 1928 Pact of Paris. The decision to make express reference to the right of individual or collective self-defence came largely as a response to the demand of regional organizations, such as the Organization of American States and the Arab League, that the legitimacy of their arrangements for collective self-defence should be expressly recognized.

(1) The Terms and Effects of Article 51

3.34 The terms of Article 51 are well known:

> 'Nothing in the present Charter shall impair the inherent right of individual or collective self-defence if an armed attack occurs...'

On its face, therefore, the effect of this provision is to safeguard the right of Member States to take such action as would be permissible in self-defence independently of the United Nations Charter. In other words, if action by a State meets all the requirements of legitimate self-defence under traditional, customary international law, such action is not impaired or prohibited by anything contained in the Charter. Such measures must, however, be reported to the Security Council.

3.35 The elaboration of this provision at San Francisco in 1945 did not in fact turn on a discussion of different types of weapons, and certainly there is nothing in the *travaux préparatoires* to suggest that any particular type of weapon was, *per se*,

---

95 See *Case Concerning Military and Paramilitary Activities in and Against Nicaragua*, Judgment of 27 June 1986, ICJ Reports 1986, paragraph 176.

96 See Bowett, *Self-defence in International Law* (1958), pp. 182-184.

incapable of use in self-defence. It follows, therefore, that discussion of the legality of the use or threat of use of nuclear weapons in the exercise of the right of self-defence must centre on whether such use of nuclear weapons would meet the traditional criteria for lawful self-defence.

(2) The Conditions of Lawful Self-defence

3.36 As an inherent, customary law right of States, recognized by Article 51 of the Charter, self-defence is permitted under certain conditions. These conditions are, in particular, that it is necessary to act in self-defence and that the steps taken by way of self-defence are proportionate. These principles are equally applicable to the use of nuclear weapons in self-defence as to the use of any other type of weapon in self-defence. Moreover, it would be entirely arbitrary to exclude *ex hypothesi* the right of a State to rely on nuclear weapons as a means of defence against a conventional attack.

(a) The necessity to react in self-defence

3.37 The notion has long been accepted that States should only use force in self-defence as a matter of last resort. This is inherent in the concept of self-defence. The burden of showing necessity would exist whether the weapons used are nuclear or conventional.

3.38 In this context the theory of nuclear 'deterrence' falls to be considered. For the past forty or so years States have relied upon their possession of nuclear weapons, or on alliance with nuclear-weapon States, and even their targeting of another nuclear-weapon State, as a necessary means of deterring an attack by the latter. Whatever the theoretical criticisms voiced of the idea of deterrence, the fact is, first, that it has worked and, second, that for many years a number of States have based their self-defence upon that idea, in the belief that the possession of nuclear weapons, and the threat to use them in self-defence, is legitimate.

(b) The Proportionality of the Reaction

3.39 It has always been accepted that self-defence must be proportionate. The controversy has been over the question of what the measures of self-defence have to be proportionate to: to the scale of the attack or to the extent to which the target State is jeopardised ?

3.40 The former view has its adherents,[97] but, as Ago wrote as Rapporteur of the I.L.C. on State responsibility:

> 'It would be mistaken ... to think that there must be proportionality between the conduct constituting the armed attack and the opposing conduct. The action needed to halt and repulse the attack may well have to assume dimensions disproportionate to those of the attack suffered. What matters in this respect is the result to be achieved by the "defensive" action, and not the forms, substance and strength of the action itself.' [98]

Thus, on this argument, there can be no easy assumption that the use of nuclear weapons can never be justified in response to a conventional attack, because there is 'disproportion' between the two. The question to be posed is whether, in the actual circumstances of the attack, the use of the particular nuclear weapon was necessary in order to defend the victim State.[99]

3.41 The answer to that question may depend upon a host of factors: the nature, scale and location of the attack, the means of defence available to the victim State; the extent to which the defensive means chosen (nuclear or non-nuclear) will minimise the danger to non-military targets; whether the damage is caused on the territory of the aggressor or the victim State, and so on.

(3) Conclusion

3.42 The notion that the use of nuclear weapons in response to an armed attack should not be regarded as necessarily unlawful but is capable of falling within the scope of the right of self-defence finds confirmation in Security Council resolution 984 (1995).[100] The preamble of that resolution contains the following statement:

> '*The Security Council*,
>
> ...
>
> *Considering further* that, in accordance with the relevant provisions of the Charter of the United Nations, any aggression with the use of nuclear weapons would endanger international peace and security...'

---

97 See, for example, Singh, 'The right of self-defence in relation to the use of nuclear weapons' 5 *Indian Yearbook of International Affairs* (1956), vol. 3, pp. 32-34.

98 Ago, 'Addendum to Eighth Report on State Responsibility' 1980 II (i) I.L.C.Y.B., 13 at p. 69.

99 For a discussion of this question, see Dinstein, *War, Aggression and Self-Defence* (2nd ed., 1994) pp. 230-236.

100 See Annex D.

The Council did not, therefore, characterise every use of nuclear weapons as incompatible with the Charter but only acts of *aggression* with the use of such weapons. Indeed, the resolution clearly envisages that such aggression might give rise to a lawful use of nuclear weapons against the aggressor.

3.43 It follows, therefore, that not only have States not accepted the view that nuclear weapons are *per se* incompatible with self-defence but, equally, that no absolute, all-embracing postulate, either directed to their legality or illegality, can be made. In short, the question posed to the Court by the General Assembly is impossible to answer properly in the abstract. Any court, facing that same question in a concrete case, would be bound to take account of all the factors of place, type of threat, type of nuclear weapon used, immediacy of the threat and so on. It would be incompatible with the judicial function to apply broad sweeping generalisations, as opposed to close and careful scrutiny of all the relevant facts.

4 The Laws of Armed Conflict

3.44 Assuming that a State's use of nuclear weapons meets the requirements of self-defence, it must then be considered whether it conforms to the fundamental principles of the law of armed conflict regulating the conduct of hostilities.

(1) The Additional Protocols to the Geneva Conventions

3.45 It has already been shown that the Diplomatic Conference on the Development of Humanitarian Law which adopted Protocol I proceeded from the outset on the basis that it would not discuss the use of nuclear weapons as such.[101] It was on that basis that the ICRC submitted the draft protocols to the Conference.[102] The implications of this decision not to broach the subject of nuclear weapons were made clear by the Representative of the United Kingdom speaking in the plenary session shortly after the opening of the Conference, when he stated that:

> 'His delegation also endorsed the ICRC's view, expressed in the Introduction to the draft Protocols, that they were not intended to broach problems concerned with atomic, bacteriological or chemical warfare, which were the subject of existing international agreements and current delicate negotiations by Governments elsewhere. It was on the assumption that the draft Protocols would not affect those problems that the United Kingdom Government had worked and would continue to work towards final agreement on the Protocols.'[103]

The result of this understanding about the work of the Conference was that any new rules introduced by Protocol I were applicable only to the use of conventional weapons, without prejudice to those rules of customary international law which were codified in the Protocol and which were already applicable to the use of nuclear weapons.

---

101 See above, paragraphs 3.9 to 3.11

102 Professor Kalshoven, who attended the Conference as a member of the Netherlands delegation, has described the ICRC's position in these terms: '...the ICRC had consciously discarded not only the question of a categorical prohibition on use of nuclear weapons but all questions specifically relating to possible restrictions on such use.' ('Arms, Armaments and International Law' 191 *Recueil des cours* (1985-II) 183 at pp. 281-2.)

103 *Official Records*, vol. V, p. 134.

3.46 The United Kingdom, United States and France again put on record this understanding about the scope of the Protocol at the final session of the Conference. On that occasion, the United Kingdom Representative stated that:

> 'At the first session of the Diplomatic Conference, his delegation had expressed in plenary its concurrence in the view that the draft Protocols were not intended to broach problems concerned with atomic, bacteriological or chemical warfare. Nothing in the four years' work of the Conference or in the texts themselves had caused it to depart from that view. It therefore continued to be his government's understanding that the new rules were not intended to have any effect on and did not regulate or prohibit the use of nuclear or other non-conventional weapons. Such questions were rightly the subject of agreements and negotiations elsewhere.'[104]

Similarly, the United States Representative stated that:

> 'From the outset of the Conference it had been his understanding that the rules to be developed had been designed with a view to conventional weapons. During the course of the Conference, there had been no discussion of the use of nuclear weapons in warfare. He recognized that nuclear weapons were the subject of separate negotiations and agreements and, further, that their use in warfare was governed by the present principles of international law. It was his government's understanding that the rules established by the Protocol were not intended to have any effect on, and did not regulate or prohibit the use of, nuclear weapons. It further believed that the problem of the regulation of nuclear weapons remained an urgent challenge to all nations which would have to be dealt with in other forums and by other agreements.'[105]

The Representative of France commented that:

> 'Already in 1973, the French Government noted that the ICRC did not include any regulations on nuclear weapons in its drafts. In participating in the preparation of the Additional Protocols, therefore, the French Government has taken into consideration only conflicts using conventional weapons. It accordingly wishes to stress that in its view the rules of the Protocols do not apply to the use of nuclear weapons. On numerous occasions the French Government has indicated its willingness to study the problems of nuclear weapons with the Powers directly concerned, in an attempt to achieve general disarmament with suitable controls.'[106]

3.47 It has occasionally been suggested that these statements do not reflect a common understanding about the scope of the Protocol, on the grounds that they are not consistent with one another and that contrary statements were made by other

---

104 *Official Records*, vol. VII, p. 303.

105 *Official Records*, vol. VII, p. 295.

106 *Official Records*, vol. VII, p. 193.

States.[107] This suggestion is without foundation. The statements by the United Kingdom and the United States, though couched in different terms, were identical in substance. Both States maintained that the new rules laid down in the Protocol were not applicable to nuclear weapons, while recognizing that the use of such weapons was subject to the rules of customary international law, including those codified in the Protocol. That the term 'rules established by the Protocol' was intended to refer only to new rules is shown by the report of the United States Delegation to the Secretary of State, which stated that:

> '...it was the understanding of the United States Delegation throughout the Conference that the rules to be developed were designed with a view to conventional weapons and their effects and that the new rules established by the Protocol were not intended to have any effects on, and do not regulate or prohibit the use of nuclear weapons.'[108]

The French statement is also clear in rejecting the application to nuclear weapons of the new rules contained in the Protocol, although its language is broad enough to suggest that it might go further than the statements by the United Kingdom and the United States. The three States were therefore in complete agreement about the inapplicability to nuclear weapons of the new rules contained in the Protocol.

3.48 It is true that, as explained above,[109] a number of States made statements at the first session of the Conference urging that the Conference discuss the question of nuclear weapons. Closer examination of those statements, however, shows that the States concerned sought the adoption of a specific prohibition on the use of nuclear weapons and, in some cases, their goals could have been met only by the conclusion of a full disarmament treaty. Thus, the representative of Romania stated that:

> 'Nuclear, chemical and biological weapons as well as all weapons of mass destruction should be banned. A universal agreement on general disarmament and, in particular, nuclear disarmament, was an urgent necessity.'[110]

Similarly, the Representative of the People's Republic of China said that:

---

107 See paras. 3.11 to 3.24 of the Written Statement of the Government of the Solomon Islands submitted in connection with the WHO's request for an Advisory Opinion.

108 *Digest of United States Practice in International Law*, 1977, p. 917 at 919.

109 See paragraphs 3.9 to 3.11.

110 *Official Records*, vol. V, p. 103.

> 'The new Protocols should unequivocally provide for the prohibition and destruction of nuclear weapons ...'[111]

and the Representative of the Democratic People's Republic of Korea maintained that:

> '...the production, testing and use of such weapons should be prohibited and existing stocks should be destroyed.' [112]

3.49 These statements urged (though without any formal proposal to that effect) that the Conference should expressly proscribe the use of nuclear weapons, which the Conference not only did not do but did not even discuss doing. They have no bearing on the entirely different question of whether general rules introduced by the Protocol are applicable to nuclear weapons.

3.50 Of the States which had initially wanted to discuss nuclear weapons, only Romania repeated its views at the final session of the Conference and its statement is seen, on closer examination, to be ambiguous:

> 'The delegation of Romania was convinced that humanitarian law must develop within the framework of modern international law, which prohibited aggression and interference in the internal affairs of States and supported the right of peoples to self-determination and to self-defence by every possible means against aggression.
>
> 'In present conditions, humanitarian law must make a clear distinction between the victim of aggression and the aggressor, unreservedly protecting the former. Humanitarian law must also prohibit the use of weapons of massive destruction and methods of warfare which struck indiscriminately at combatants and civilians alike. The latter must be protected against the dangers of military operations. Many of those aims were covered by the provisions of Protocol I, including the case of peoples struggling for their independence, the status of prisoners of war, and the prohibition or restriction of the use of certain conventional weapons and weapons of massive destruction.'[113]

It is unclear to which provisions of the Protocol the delegate of Romania was referring or in what respect he considered that nuclear weapons were regulated *de lege lata,* as opposed to expressing a view that they should be prohibited. The only other statement which appears to contradict those of the nuclear powers is one made

---

111 *Official Records*, vol. V, p. 120

112 *Official Records*, vol. XIV, pp. 241-2.

113 *Official Records*, vol. VII, pp. 289-90.

by India following the adoption by consensus of Article 33 of the draft protocol (Article 35 of the final text), in which India said that it had joined the consensus.

> 'with the understanding that the basic rules contained in this article will apply to all categories of weapons, namely nuclear, bacteriological, chemical or conventional weapons or any other category of weapons.'[114]

This statement has also been described as ambiguous, since it may have referred only to paragraphs 1 and 2 of Article 35, which both state rules which have long been part of customary international law.[115]

3.51 However, no State challenged then, or has challenged since, the statements made by the United Kingdom, United States and France. Moreover, several non-nuclear States made similar statements regarding the applicability of the new rules contained in the Protocol when depositing their instruments of ratification. Italy, for example, stated that:

> 'It is the understanding of the Government of Italy that the rules relating to the use of weapons introduced by Additional Protocol I were intended to apply exclusively to conventional weapons. They do not prejudice any other rule of international law applicable to other types of weapons.'

Similar statements of understanding were made on ratification by Belgium, Canada, the Federal Republic of Germany, the Netherlands and Spain and on signature by the United Kingdom and the United States.[116] No other signatory or contracting party to Protocol I challenged these statements then, or has done so since. In addition, the bills submitted to the Parliaments of Norway, Sweden and Switzerland to provide for ratification of the Protocols by those States made reference to the non-applicability of parts of Protocol I to nuclear weapons.[117]

---

114 *Official Records*, vol. VI, p. 115.

115 Bothe, Partsch and Solf, *New Rules for Victims of Armed Conflicts* (1982), p. 192.

116 The United Kingdom statement recorded its understanding that 'the new rules introduced by the Protocol are not intended to have any effect on and do not regulate or prohibit the use of nuclear weapons' (UK Misc. 19 (1977), Cmnd. 6927).

117 Bring and Reimann, 'Redressing a Wrong Question: the 1977 Protocols Additional to the 1949 Geneva Conventions and the Issue of Nuclear Weapons', 33 Netherlands International Law Review (1986), p. 99 at p. 103. The authors were respectively members of the Swedish and Swiss delegations to the Diplomatic Conference. See also the statement of the *Conseil d'Etat* to the Belgian Parliament cited at pages 27-8 of the Written Statement of the Government of the Solomon Islands in the WHO case.

3.52 This history has led two commentators, who were members of the delegations of neutral States at the Conference, to conclude that:

> 'A study of the context of the Additional Protocol accordingly shows that the intentions of the parties were, during the negotiations and at the time of signature, that the rules in the Protocol should not specifically appertain to the question of weapons of mass destruction.'[118]

Similarly, Professor Kalshoven, who was also present at the Conference, has commented that:

> 'Additional Protocol I does not purport to prohibit the use of nuclear weapons, and neither does it lay down any further restrictions on such use than already result from pre-existent rules and principles of the law of armed conflict (and which were reaffirmed in the Protocol). Without any attempt at completeness, the following items may be listed among the "new law" which on account of its novelty remains inapplicable to the use of nuclear weapons: the "ecological principle" ... which protects the natural environment from "widespread, long-term and severe damage"; the sophisticated rules in Article 57 of the Protocol, elaborating the customary principle of proportionality in the protection of the civilian population; and last but not least, the prohibition of reprisals against the civilian population and civilian objects, as now laid down in various paragraphs of Articles 51 to 56 of the Protocol.
>
> 'To those who, like the Romanian delegate, would have wished to see the question of use of nuclear weapons dealt with in Additional Protocol I, it should be pointed out that the choice has been clear throughout the proceedings of the Diplomatic Conference: it was either a Protocol not bearing on the use of nuclear weapons, or no Protocol at all.'[119]

3.53 The treatment of this question in the military manuals of a number of States confirms that the new rules in Additional Protocol I do not apply to the use of nuclear weapons. Thus, the Manual published by the Federal Republic of Germany states that:

> 'The new rules introduced by Additional Protocol I have been established with the intention of being applied to conventional weapons irrespective of other rules of international law applicable to other types of weapons. They do not influence, regulate or prohibit the use of nuclear weapons.' [120]

Similarly, a manual published by the Swedish Ministry of Defence states that:

---

118 Bring and Reimann, *loc cit.*.

119 *Loc cit.*, p. 283.

120 Federal Ministry of Defence, *Humanitarian Law in Armed Conflicts Manual* (1992), paragraph 430.

> '...it was assumed that the rules of Additional Protocol I concerning the protection of civil populations and property during military operations had been negotiated with the tacit reservation that they should only apply during conventional warfare.' [121]

The Swiss Manual also refers to the nuclear understanding and concludes that the use of nuclear weapons is not prohibited by, for example, the prohibition on the use of indiscriminate weapons in Protocol I.[122] Manuals published by the United States and Canada contain similar statements.[123]

3.54 The ICRC Commentary comes to the same conclusion:

> 'Clearly the hypothesis that States acceding to the Protocol bind themselves without wishing to - or even without knowing - with regard to such an important question as the use of nuclear weapons is not acceptable. The desire not to broach it during the [Diplomatic Conference] is a determining factor in this respect.' [124]

Other authoritative commentaries take the same view.[125]

3.55 It follows that the law of armed conflict by which the legality of any given use of nuclear weapons falls to be judged includes all the provisions of customary international law (including those which have been codified in Additional Protocol I) and, where appropriate, of conventional law but excludes those provisions of Protocol I which introduced new rules into the law. It has sometimes been argued that the use (or, at least, some uses) of nuclear weapons would violate various principles of the law of armed conflict. These arguments will now be considered in turn.

---

121 *International Humanitarian Law in Armed Conflict, with reference to the Swedish Total Defence System* (1991), pp. 25-6.

122 *Gesetze und Gebrauche des Krieges* (1987), Section 3, Art. 24.

123 See footnote 94, above.

124 Pilloud, et al. *Commentary on the Additional Protocols of 1977* (1987), paragraph 1858 .

125 Bothe, Partsch and Solf, *New Rules for Victims of Armed Conflicts* (1982), p. 191, Rauschning, 'Nuclear Warfare and Weapons, in Bernhardt (ed), *Encyclopaedia of Public International Law* , vol. IV, (1982), p. 49.

(2) The Principle that the parties to a conflict do not have an unlimited choice of the methods and means of warfare

3.56 It has been suggested [126] that the use of nuclear weapons would violate the principle that the parties to an armed conflict do not have an unlimited choice of the methods and means of warfare, a principle stated in Article 22 of the Hague Regulations, 1907,[127] and reaffirmed in Article 35(1) of Additional Protocol I. While that principle is undoubtedly well established as part of customary international law, however, it cannot stand alone as a prohibition of a particular category of weapons. In any event, there is no incompatibility between the two propositions (i) that States do not have an unlimited choice of the methods and means of warfare and (ii) that States may use nuclear weapons where this is consistent with their right of self-defence. There is no suggestion that self-defence is "unlimited". On the contrary, self-defence is always limited to the necessities of the case.[128]

3.57 It is necessary, therefore, to look outside the principle in Article 22 of the Hague Regulations in order to determine what limitations are imposed by customary or conventional law upon the choice of methods and means of warfare. The argument thus begs the question whether there exists some other principle of international law which limits the right to choose nuclear weapons as a means of warfare.

3.58 The same is true of the argument based upon the 'Martens Clause' which appeared in the preamble to Hague Convention No. IV respecting the Laws and Customs of War on Land, 1907. The most recent version of this clause appears in Article 1(2) of Additional Protocol I, 1977, which provides that:

> 'In cases not covered by this Protocol or by other international agreements, civilians and combatants remain under the protection and authority of the principles of international law derived from established custom, from the principles of humanity and from the dictates of public conscience.'

---

126 Singh and McWhinney, *Nuclear Weapons and Contemporary International Law* (1989), p. 115.

127 Regulations annexed to Hague Convention No. IV, Respecting the Laws and Customs of War on Land, 1907, UKTS 9 (1910), Cd. 5030.

128 See Part III.3, above.

While the Martens Clause makes clear that the absence of a specific treaty provision on the use of nuclear weapons is not, in itself, sufficient to establish that such weapons are capable of lawful use, the Clause does not, on its own, establish their illegality. The terms of the Martens Clause themselves make it necessary to point to a rule of customary international law which might outlaw the use of nuclear weapons. Since it is the existence of such a rule which is in question, reference to the Martens Clause adds little.

(3) The Prohibition of Poison, Chemical Weapons and Analogous Liquids and Materials

3.59 The use of nuclear weapons has been said to violate the long established prohibition on the use of poison and poisoned weapons, [129] because the effects of radiation are described as a form of poisoning. [130] In addition, some commentators have invoked the provisions of the Geneva Protocol for the Prohibition of the Use in War of Asphyxiating, Poisonous or Other Gases and of Bacteriological Methods of Warfare, 1925, which applies to 'the use in war of asphyxiating, poisonous or other gases, and of all analogous liquids, materials or devices, on the ground that the effects of radiation are said to make nuclear weapons analogous to asphyxiating or poisonous gases.

3.60 The prohibitions in both Article 23(a) of the Hague Regulations and the 1925 Protocol were, however, intended to apply to weapons whose primary effect was poisonous and not to those where poison was a secondary or incidental effect. As one leading commentator says of the 1925 Protocol, its drafting history makes clear that 'the scope *ratione materiae* of the Protocol is restricted to weapons the primary effect of which is to asphyxiate or poison the adversary.' [131] In the case of almost all nuclear weapons, the primary effects are blast and heat and it is these which give the weapon its main military advantages.

3.61 In addition, State practice does not support the argument that nuclear weapons fall within the prohibition in the 1925 Protocol. That argument has never been seriously advanced by any of the States party to the 1925 Protocol. Moreover, when

---

129 Article 23(a) Hague Regulations, 1907.

130 Singh and McWhinney, *op. cit.*, p. 127. Schwarzenberger, *The Legality of Nuclear Weapons* (1958).

131 Kalshoven, *loc. cit.*, p. 284.

the United States became party to the 1925 Protocol in 1975, thirty years after becoming the world's leading nuclear power, it made no reservation of its right to use nuclear weapons. It is inconceivable that a major nuclear power would inadvertently assume a treaty obligation which prohibited it from using one of the most important weapons in its armoury. None of the other parties to the 1925 Protocol suggested, at the time of United States ratification, that the United States had assumed new obligations regarding the use of its nuclear weapons. It would appear, therefore, that the subsequent practice of the parties to the 1925 Protocol does not sustain the interpretation placed upon its terms by those who argue that it applies to the use of nuclear weapons.

3.62 Although a number of commentators have argued that nuclear weapons fall within the scope of the 1925 Protocol, there is a considerable division of opinion on this point. Thus, Bailey maintains that,

> '...it might be thought by the non-expert that nuclear weapons were encompassed by the Geneva Protocol's ban on using liquids, materials and devices analogous to chemical weapons but this has never been seriously advanced.'[132]

Kalshoven,[133] Hearn,[134] McDougal and Feliciano,[135] and Rauschning[136] also reject the argument that the use of nuclear weapons would necessarily violate the ban on poisoned weapons or the provisions of the 1925 Protocol.

---

132 *War and Conscience in the Nuclear Age* (1988), p. 117.

133 *Loc. cit.*

134 'Nuclear Deterrence and Warfare' 61 British Year Book of International Law (1990), p. 199 at pp 230-2.

135 *The International Law of War* (1994), pp 664-5.

136 'Nuclear Warfare and Weapons', in Bernhardt (ed) *Encyclopaedia of Public International Law*, vol. IV, p. 44 at p. 47.

(4) The unnecessary suffering principle

3.63 It has also been argued that the use of nuclear weapons would violate the prohibition on weapons which cause unnecessary suffering. [137] The most recent statement of this principle is contained in Article 35(2) of Additional Protocol I, 1977, which provides:

> 'It is prohibited to employ weapons, projectiles and material and methods of warfare of a nature to cause superfluous injury or unnecessary suffering.'

The principle is, however, a long established one. [138]

3.64 The principle prohibits only the use of weapons which cause *unnecessary* suffering or *superfluous* injury. It thus requires that a balance be struck between the military advantage which may be derived from the use of a particular weapon and the degree of suffering which the use of that weapon may cause. [139] The more effective the weapon is from the military point of view, the less likely that the suffering which its use causes will be characterized as unnecessary. [140] In particular, it has to be asked whether the same military advantage can be gained by using alternative means of warfare which will cause a lesser degree of suffering. The use of a nuclear weapon may be the only way in which a State can concentrate sufficient military force to achieve a legitimate military objective, such as the defeat of an invader. In those circumstances, it cannot be said that the use of such a weapon causes *unnecessary* suffering, however great the casualties which it produces among enemy combatants. [141]

---

137 See, e.g., Brownlie, 'Some Legal Aspects of the Use of Nuclear Weapons' 14 ICLQ (1965) p. 437 at 450 and paras. 3.42 to 3.44 of the Written Statement of the Government of the Solomon Islands in the WHO case.

138 See, e.g., Article 23(e) Hague Regulations, 1907.

139 ICRC, *Weapons that may Cause Unnecessary Suffering or have Indiscriminate Effects* (1973): Report of a Conference of Experts, p. 13.

140 This point is conceded even in the decision of the Tokyo District Court which held that the bombings of Hiroshima and Nagasaki were unlawful, *Shimoda* v. *The State* 32 ILR 626 (1963), at p.634: 'the use of a certain weapon, great as its inhuman result may be, need not be prohibited by international law if it has a great military effect.'

141 Kalshoven, *loc. cit.*, p. 284; Hearn, *loc. cit.* p. 235. Even Singh and McWhinney, who maintain that the use of nuclear weapons would violate this principle, concede that State practice suggests otherwise, *op. cit.*, p. 117.

3.65 A variation on the unnecessary suffering argument is the contention that the use of nuclear weapons would be unlawful because any use of such a weapon would render death inevitable for those in the immediate area of the explosion. [142] The basis for this argument is the preamble to the St Petersburg Declaration, 1868, which stated:

> 'That the only legitimate object which States should endeavour to accomplish during war is to weaken the military forces of the enemy;
>
> 'That for this purpose it is sufficient to disable the greatest possible number of men;
>
> 'That this object would be exceeded by the employment of arms which uselessly aggravate the sufferings of disabled men, or render their death inevitable.
>
> 'That the employment of such arms would, therefore, be contrary to the laws of humanity.'

The reference to weapons which render death inevitable must, however, be seen in context. The declaration prohibited only the use of projectiles of a weight below 400 grammes which were explosive or were charged with fulminating or inflammable substances. The use of such a weapon against personnel was considered to be gratuitously cruel, because it caused horrific and almost invariably fatal injuries, while offering little or no military advantage over the use of ordinary ammunition, since a soldier hit by either type of bullet would normally be disabled and rendered incapable of further participation in the battle. The Declaration did not prohibit the use of explosive artillery shells, even though they can cause horrific injuries and are usually fatal to those in the immediate area of the explosion, because the military utility of explosive artillery shells was so great that it was considered to justify the human costs.

3.66 The Declaration was, therefore, no more than a specific application of the unnecessary suffering principle, the suffering caused by the exploding bullet being seen as unnecessary, while that caused by the exploding shell was not so characterized, because of the effectiveness of that weapon. Although the preamble to the Declaration is widely regarded as having played an influential role in the development of customary international law, subsequent statements of the customary principle have referred only to weapons causing unnecessary suffering or superfluous

---

[142] Written Statement of the Government of the Solomon Islands in the WHO case, paras 3.42 to 3.44.

injury and have omitted references to rendering death inevitable.[143] Since all weapons are capable of being used in a way which renders death inevitable, this is not surprising.[144] The use of a nuclear weapon must, therefore, be judged by reference to whether the suffering which it causes should be regarded as unnecessary when balanced against the military effectiveness of the weapon in the circumstances in which it is used, rather than by concentrating on whether it will inevitably cause death. This is not a judgement which can be made in the abstract. It can be made only on the basis of a careful appraisal of the circumstances of a particular case.

(5) The principle that the civilian population as such must not be made the object of attack

3.67 A further argument which has been raised is that the use of any nuclear weapon would necessarily have such terrible effects upon civilians that it would violate those rules of the law of armed conflict which exist for their protection. There are two principles of particular relevance in this respect. First, it is a well established principle of customary international law that the civilian population and individual civilians are not a legitimate target in their own right. The parties to an armed conflict are required to discriminate between civilians and civilian objects on the one hand and combatants and military objectives on the other and to direct their attacks only against the latter. Secondly, the principle of proportionality requires that even a military objective should not be attacked if to do so would cause collateral civilian casualties or damage to civilian objects which would be excessive in relation to the concrete and direct military advantage anticipated from the attack.

3.68 Those who argue that nuclear weapons are inherently indiscriminate and cannot be used without causing excessive civilian casualties frequently fail to differentiate between these two rules.[145] That reflects the fact that much of the writing on nuclear weapons on which these arguments rely dates from the 1950's and early 1960's. Modern nuclear weapons are capable of far more precise targeting and can therefore be directed against specific military objectives without the indiscriminate effect on the civilian population which the older literature assumed to be inevitable. Moreover, the United Kingdom's and NATO's current doctrine

---

143 See, e.g., Article 23(e) Hague Regulations, 1907, and Article 35(2) of Additional Protocol I.

144 McDougal and Feliciano, *op. cit.*, p. 661.

145 See, e.g., the argument at paragraph 3.48 *et seq*. of the Written Statement of the Government of the Solomon Islands in the WHO case.

emphasizes that nuclear weapons would only ever be used in a defensive role and that the threat posed by an aggressor which would invite a nuclear response would be of a scale which would make that nuclear response proportionate.

3.69 All weapons, nuclear weapons included, are capable of being used against centres of civilian population or in an indiscriminate way. Subject to what is said below about reprisals, such use would be illegal. What is not true is that nuclear weapons cannot be used in any other way. The use of nuclear weapons against specific military objectives would undoubtedly not be contrary to the first of the two principles set out in paragraph 3.67, above.

3.70 So far as the principle of proportionality is concerned, it is often assumed both that any use of nuclear weapons would cause extensive civilian losses and that such losses would necessarily be excessive in relation to any military advantage which might result. [146] These assumptions tend to be based on assessments of the likely effects of a nuclear attack on or near a city. The reality, however, is that nuclear weapons might be used in a wide variety of circumstances with very different results in terms of likely civilian casualties. In some cases, such as the use of a low yield nuclear weapon against warships on the High Seas or troops in sparsely populated areas, it is possible to envisage a nuclear attack which caused comparatively few civilian casualties. It is by no means the case that every use of nuclear weapons against a military objective would inevitably cause very great collateral civilian casualties.

3.71 Moreover, the principle of proportionality prohibits an attack upon a military objective only if the likely civilian casualties and damage to civilian objects would be excessive in relation to the expected military advantage. Like the unnecessary suffering principle, this principle requires a balance to be struck between the military advantage resulting from an attack and the effect on the civilian population. Only if the latter is wholly disproportionate to the former will the attack violate the principle. Since no nuclear-weapon State is likely lightly to resort to the use of nuclear weapons, [147] it is unlikely that a nuclear weapon would be used unless its use was expected to produce a very substantial military advantage. That expected advantage

---

[146] See, e.g., paragraph 3.50 of the Written Statement of the Government of the Solomon Islands in the WHO case. Proportionality as a requirement of the law of self-defence is considered in Part III.3, above.

[147] See, e.g., the security assurances given in connection with the Non-Proliferation Treaty and the statements made in connection with the Treaty of Tlatelolco; paragraphs 2.19 and 3.18 to 3.19, above.

would have to be weighed against the likely civilian losses to determine whether the use of the weapon would violate the principle of proportionality. It cannot, however, be right to assume, as an abstract proposition, that those losses would always outweigh that advantage especially where the destruction of a particular military objective was essential to the survival of a State which was under attack (and, perhaps, to the lives of millions of members of that State's civilian population) and the use of a nuclear weapon offered the only means of destroying that objective.[148] As with the unnecessary suffering principle, the question whether the use of a nuclear weapon would be contrary to the principle of proportionality is not one which can be answered in the abstract but only by reference to the circumstances of each individual case.[149]

3.72 A similar answer has to be made to two related arguments. First, it has sometimes been said that the use of nuclear weapons would be unlawful because it would make it impossible for a State to discharge its obligations towards persons and objects protected under the Geneva Conventions, 1949, such as the sick, wounded and prisoners of war or hospitals, as such persons and objects would inevitably be amongst the casualties of any nuclear exchange. The deliberate targeting of protected persons and objects would be unlawful, irrespective of the weapons used, but the Geneva Conventions do not require the suspension of large scale hostilities merely because of the proximity of protected persons or objects. Moreover, the argument overlooks the drafting history of the Conventions and, in particular, the rejection of proposals to discuss the legality of nuclear weapons at the 1949 Conference. As one commentator has put it, 'to argue like this is to lay a heavier burden on the Geneva Conventions than they were ever meant to sustain.'[150]

3.73 Secondly, it has been argued that the use of nuclear weapons would inevitably cause so many civilian casualties that it would amount to the commission of

---

148 Kalshoven, *loc. cit.*, pp. 286-7; Hearn, p. 236; McDougal and Feliciano, *op. cit.*, p. 666; Green, in Cohen and Gouin (eds) *Lawyers and the Nuclear Debate* (1988), p. 102; Dinstein, *ibid.*, p. 61.

149 The same approach has to be taken with regard to the argument that the use of nuclear weapons would cause wanton or unnecessary destruction of property. While the wanton destruction of property has long been recognized as contrary to the laws of armed conflict, destruction of property is legitimate where it is required by military necessity. The question would therefore be whether the destruction caused by a particular instance of the use of a nuclear weapon could be regarded as necessary. That question can be answered only by reference to the military goal which the use of the weapon was designed to achieve and the efficacy of other methods which might have achieved that goal at a lower cost.

150 Kalshoven, *loc. cit.*, p. 285.

genocide.[151] The Court has stressed that genocide is a crime which 'shocks the conscience of mankind, results in losses to humanity...and is contrary to moral law and to the spirit and aims of the United Nations.' [152] It has been demonstrated above, however, that it is by no means the case that the use of a nuclear weapon, targeted upon a military objective, would necessarily entail massive civilian casualties. Moreover, genocide is a crime of intent. Article II of the Genocide Convention, 1948, requires 'intent to destroy, in whole or in part, a national, ethnical, racial or religious group, as such.' The prohibition of genocide is clearly not directed at collateral casualties resulting from an attack upon a military objective.[153]

(6) The Laws of Armed Conflict and the Protection of the Environment [154]

3.74 A more recent argument is that the use of nuclear weapons is prohibited because of the effect that it would have upon the natural environment. [155] This argument rests on two sets of treaty provisions. Article I of the United Nations Convention on the Prohibition of Military or any other Hostile Environmental Modification Techniques, 1977, prohibits 'military or other hostile use of environmental modification techniques having widespread, long-lasting or severe effects as the means of destruction , damage or injury' to another State. Article 35(3) of Additional Protocol I prohibits the employment of 'methods or means of warfare which are intended, or may be expected, to cause widespread, long-term and severe damage to the natural environment.' [156]

---

151 Paragraph 3.50 of the Written Statement of the Government of the Solomon Islands in the WHO case.

152 *Case concerning the Application of the Convention on the Prevention and Punishment of the Crime of Genocide*, Order of 13 September 1993, paragraph 51; ICJ Reports, 1993, p. 348.

153 Kalshoven, *loc. cit.* p. 285, comments as follows on the argument that the use of nuclear weapons would necessarily contravene the Genocide Convention:

'It follows, moreover, from the *travaux préparatoires* of the Convention that the notion of genocide was expressly defined in such a manner as to prevent a mixing up with the law of war....the argument based on the Genocide Convention must be rejected as disingenuous and manifestly ill-founded.'

154 This section deals only with those parts of the law of armed conflict which concern the protection of the environment. The general environmental agreements are considered in Part III.5, below.

155 See, e.g., Written Statement of the Government of the Solomon Islands, Section IIB and Written Statement of the Government of Nauru, pp. 36-47, in the WHO case.

156 See also Article 55.

3.75 The Environmental Modification Convention, however, is not really applicable to most cases in which nuclear weapons might be used. That Convention was designed to deal with the deliberate manipulation of the environment as a method of war. Thus, Article II of the Convention defines the term 'environmental modification technique' as

> 'any technique for changing - through the *deliberate* manipulation of natural processes - the dynamics, composition, or structure of the Earth, including its biota, lithosphere, hydrosphere and atmosphere, or of outer space' (emphasis added).

While the use of a nuclear weapon may have considerable effects on the environment,[157] it is unlikely that it would be used for the deliberate manipulation of natural processes. The effect on the environment would normally be a side-effect of the use of a nuclear weapon, just as it would in the case of use of other weapons.

3.76 Moreover, the *travaux préparatoires* of the Environmental Modification Convention indicate that the intention of the parties was to 'limit the potential danger to mankind from possible *new* means of warfare'.[158] The environmental modification techniques in contemplation were techniques which had not yet been developed. As the United States Secretary of State said at the ceremony to mark the signature of the Convention:

> 'While the intentional modification of the environment at present can be done only on a local and small scale at best, we scarcely need remind ourselves that in our era technology can advance to make possible actions which would cause hitherto inconceivable environmental consequences. So we believe it would be wise to outlaw what is commonly called "environmental warfare" before it has a real chance to develop significantly for military purposes, with potentially disastrous consequences.'[159]

This emphasis on new methods of warfare and the anticipatory nature of the Convention are further evidence that the parties did not intend that it should apply to the collateral environmental effects of nuclear (or, indeed, other battlefield) weapons, which were far from new in 1977.

---

157 Though, once again, how substantial those effects would be is likely to vary depending on the type of weapon and the circumstances in which it is used.

158 Joint statement by the United States and the Soviet Union, 3 July 1974; 1974 *Digest of United States Practice in International Law* 744.

159 1977 *Digest of United States Practice in International Law* 966-7.

3.77 Articles 35(3) and 55 of Additional Protocol I are broader in scope than the Environmental Modification Convention, in that they are applicable to the incidental effects on the environment of the use of weapons. They were, however, innovative provisions when included in Additional Protocol I, as was made clear in a statement by the Federal Republic of Germany on the adoption of what became Article 35 of the Protocol:

> 'The delegation of the Federal Republic of Germany joined in the consensus on Article 33 [subsequently renumbered Article 35] with the understanding that paragraphs 1 and 2 reaffirm customary international law, while paragraph 3 of this article is an important new contribution to the protection of the natural environment in times of international armed conflict.'[160]

As new rules, the provisions of Articles 35(3) and 55 are subject to the understanding, which was discussed above, that the new provisions created by Additional Protocol I do not apply to the use of nuclear weapons.[161] The view that the environmental provisions of Protocol I are new rules and thus inapplicable to the use of nuclear weapons is confirmed by a number of commentators.[162]

---

160 *Official Records*, vol. VI, p. 115.

161 See above, paragraphs 3.9 to 3.11 and 3.45 to 3.55.

162 Kalshoven, *loc. cit.*, p. 283, quoted in paragraph 3.52, above; Hearn, *loc. cit.*, pp. 244-6. The ICRC Commentary does not include Articles 35(3) and 55 in the list of provisions which it regards as declaratory of custom and hence as applicable to nuclear weapons; ICRC Commentary, paras. 1857-59. It is interesting to note that the Government of Nauru, in its written submissions in the WHO case, notwithstanding its strongly expressed view that the use of nuclear weapons would be unlawful, concedes that Article 35(3) lays down new rules (Written Statement of the Government of Nauru, p. 22.)

(7) The effect on neutral States

3.78 It has been suggested [163] that the use of nuclear weapons would inevitably have such catastrophic effects on the territory of neutral States and States not party to a conflict that it would violate the principle laid down in Article 1 of Hague Convention No V, Respecting the Rights and Duties of Neutral Powers and Persons in case of War on Land, 1907, which provides that 'the territory of neutral Powers is inviolable.' Whether the use of nuclear weapons would deposit radioactive fall-out on the territory of neutral States would, however, depend upon the type of weapon used and the location at which it was used. The assumption that any use of nuclear weapons would inevitably have such an effect is unfounded. Moreover, Hague Convention No V was designed to protect the territory of neutral States against incursions by belligerent forces or the deliberate bombardment of targets located in that territory, not to guarantee neutral States against the incidental effects of hostilities.

(8) Belligerent Reprisals

3.79 Even if a particular use of nuclear weapons might be contrary to the laws of armed conflict, it remains necessary to consider whether that use might nevertheless be justified as a belligerent reprisal. A belligerent reprisal is an action, taken by a party to an armed conflict, which would normally constitute a violation of the laws of armed conflict but which is lawful because it is taken in response to a prior violation of that law by an adversary. Since such a reprisal takes place in the context of a continuing armed conflict, it raises legal questions entirely distinct from those concerning the taking of armed reprisals in a normal peacetime environment (a matter which is not considered in these submissions). To be lawful, a belligerent reprisal must meet two conditions. First, it must not be directed against persons or objects against which the taking of reprisals is specifically prohibited. Secondly, it must meet the criteria for the regulation of reprisals, namely that it is taken in response to a prior wrong, is proportionate, is undertaken for the purpose of putting an end to the enemy's unlawful conduct and for preventing future illegalities, and is a means of last resort.

---

163 Written Statement of the Government of Nauru, p. 35.

3.80 The Geneva Conventions of 1949 prohibit the taking of reprisals against persons or objects protected by the Conventions. [164] That, however, would have little relevance here, since it is difficult to conceive of the use of nuclear weapons against such persons or objects. [165] The Conventions do not preclude the taking of reprisals against the enemy's civilian population or civilian objects in enemy territory.

3.81 Additional Protocol I prohibits the taking of reprisals against the civilian population (Article 51(6)), civilian objects (Article 52(1)), historic monuments (Article 53(c)), objects indispensable to the survival of the civilian population (Article 54(4)), the natural environment (Article 55(2)) and works and installations containing natural forces (Article 56(4)). The application of these provisions would have a greater effect on the retaliatory use of nuclear weapons. Again, however, these provisions are correctly regarded as innovative and thus as inapplicable to the use of nuclear weapons. [166]

3.82 So far as the second condition for the conduct of lawful reprisals is concerned, it has been argued that the use of nuclear weapons could never satisfy the requirements of proportionality and preventiveness. [167] This argument, however, suffers from the same flaws as the argument that the use of nuclear weapons could never satisfy the requirements of self-defence. Whether the use of nuclear weapons would meet the requirements of proportionality cannot be answered in the abstract: it would depend upon the nature and circumstances of the wrong which prompted the

---

164 Convention No. I, Article 46, prohibits reprisals against the wounded, sick and those medical personnel, buildings and equipment covered by the Convention.

Convention No. II, Article 47, prohibits reprisals against the wounded, sick, shipwrecked and those medical personnel, vessels and equipment protected by the Convention.

Convention No. III, Article 13, prohibits reprisals against prisoners of war.

Convention No. IV, Article 33, prohibits reprisals against those civilians protected by the Convention (principally civilians detained in the territory of an adverse party and the civilian population of occupied territory) and their property.

165 See paragraph 3.72, above.

166 Sir Hersch Lauterpacht, *Oppenheim's International Law*, (7th ed 1952), vol. II, p. 351; Kalshoven, *loc. cit.*, p. 283; Hearn, *loc. cit.*, p. 217. The ICRC Commentary, does not include the reprisals provisions in the list of provisions which it expressly regards as applicable to nuclear weapons, paragraphs 1857-9.

167 Brownlie, *loc. cit.*, p. 445 goes further and contends that:

> 'it is hardly legitimate to extend a doctrine related to the minutiae of the conventional theatre of war to an exchange of power which, in the case of the strategic and deterrent uses of nuclear weapons, is equivalent to the total war effort and is the essence of the war aims.'

But the same reasoning would lead to the conclusion that it is hardly legitimate to extend any of the doctrines of the laws of war designed for the non-nuclear age to the use of nuclear weapons.

taking of reprisal action. Nor can it be ruled out that the retaliatory use of a nuclear weapons might have the effect of putting a stop to a series of violations of the law by an adversary. Indeed, military doctrine for fifty years has been based on the belief that it is the threat of retaliation in kind which is the principal factor deterring the use of nuclear weapons.

(9) Conclusion

3.83 It follows that, while some uses of nuclear weapons would violate the laws of armed conflict, the argument that their use would invariably be contrary to this part of international law is unfounded. Whether the use of a nuclear weapon in a particular case is lawful will depend upon the circumstances of that case. Moreover, the scope for variation in those circumstances is so great and the effect of those variations so important that any abstract statement about the legality of using nuclear weapons would be either unhelpful in its generality or misleading.

5 International Law on Human Rights and the Environment

3.84 This section will address the question of whether the use, or threat of use, of nuclear weapons is prohibited *per se* by the law of human rights or any rule of international law requiring the protection of the environment.

3.85 Although the scope of the enquiry is broad, the conclusion which results from a review of these issues is essentially clear. As the law stands, the threat or use of nuclear weapons is not prohibited *per se* by provisions of international law on human rights or the protection of the environment. *De lege lata*, the threat or use of nuclear weapons is lawful, subject to such rules of the *jus ad bellum* or *jus in bello* as may be applicable. Those rules have been considered in the preceding sections of this Written Statement. Given that States actively disagree on the development of a rule of law regulating the threat or use of nuclear weapons as such, and in view also of the sensitivity of the disarmament process, this matter is one in which, in the view of the United Kingdom, an opinion *de lege ferenda* would be fundamentally inappropriate.

3.86 There are also cogent reasons, relative to a consideration of the matter from the perspective of human rights and environmental protection why the Court should, on grounds of propriety, exercise its discretion and decline to respond to the request for an advisory opinion.

3.87 International law on human rights and the protection of the environment is largely treaty-based. It is therefore important that the interpretation and application of such agreements is properly located within the law of treaties. Some preliminary observations are thus warranted.

(1) General Considerations

3.88 First, it is a fundamental principle of the law of treaties that a prohibitive rule, purporting to exclude a particular activity from the scope of permissible State practice, must be clearly stated. Referring to 'the need of express terms to alter an existing rule of law', Lord McNair quotes, 'in spite of its antiquity' the principle stated by Sir Leoline Jenkins that

> '...Treaties ... are not to be understood as altering or restraining the Practice generally received, unless the Words do fully and necessarily infer an Alteration or Restriction.' [168]

3.89 As a basic proposition, one cannot, therefore, infer from general words, or a treaty of general application, a prohibitive rule of specific content that would have the effect of limiting the scope of otherwise permissible State conduct. It would be neither sound practice nor sufficient to rely upon general provisions of international law on human rights or the environment for the purpose of conjuring up a rule prohibiting the threat or use of nuclear weapons by way of legitimate self-defence. Indeed, such an approach would pose considerable dangers for the wider integrity and effectiveness of the provisions of law in question.

3.90 Secondly, both the performance and interpretation of treaties are subject to the overriding obligation of good faith. One aspect of this is that:

> '... it would be a breach of this obligation for a party to make use of an ambiguity in order to put forward an interpretation which it was known to the negotiators of the treaty not to be the intention of the parties.' [169]

3.91 In the words of the Permanent Court of International Justice, the text of a treaty cannot

> '... be enlarged by reading into it stipulations which are said to result from the proclaimed intentions of the authors of the Treaty, but for which no provision is made in the text itself.' [170]

3.92 Considering this obligation in the light of the principle of effectiveness, Sir Hersch Lauterpacht noted that:

> '... good faith requires no more than that effect be given, in a fair and reasonable manner, to the intention of the parties. This means that on occasions, if such was the intention of the parties, good faith may require that the effectiveness of the instrument should fall short of its apparent and desirable scope. The principle of effectiveness cannot transform a mere declaration of lofty purpose - such as the Universal Declaration of Human Rights - into a source of legal rights and obligations. ... Equally, although a recommendation, which is not binding, by an organ of the League of Nations or the United Nations is of less potency than a binding decision, this does not

---

168 McNair, *The Law of Treaties* (1961), p. 463.

169 *Ibid.*, p. 465.

170 *Polish War Vessels in Danzig*, PCIJ Reports, Series A/B, No. 43, p. 142.

> mean that it is open to a judicial tribunal to endow with binding character an expression, however politically or morally weighty, of collective opinion.' [171]

3.93 Thus, the fact that a treaty *could* be construed to achieve a particular result does not mean that it *should* be so construed. Particularly in the context of a case such as that presently in issue, the construction of a treaty to achieve a purpose not within the contemplation of its authors would be inappropriate. In the context of treaties having as their express object the protection of specific aspects of the eco-system, there is also a danger that such an approach could undermine the integrity of these conventions and impugn their normative quality more generally. It would also do great disservice to the cause of environmental protection if the prospect of judicial creativity in the interpretation and application of such treaties translated into caution on the part of States when it came to participating in such agreements in the future.

3.94 Thirdly, 'treaties must be applied and interpreted against the background of general principles of international law.' [172] This rule now finds partial expression in Article 31(3)(c) of the Vienna Convention on the Law of Treaties, 1969, which permits 'any relevant rules of international law applicable in the relations between the parties' to be taken into account for the purposes of the interpretation of treaties. On this principle, one commentator has noted that 'every treaty provision must be read not only in its own context, but also in the wider context of general international law, whether conventional or customary'. [173] A treaty cannot, therefore, be construed in a vacuum, or in the abstract, without reference to other rules of international law with which it may interact.

3.95 One aspect of this rule which is of particular importance in the present context is that, save to the extent expressly provided, a treaty must be construed against the background of the inherent right of self-defence. In other words, save to the extent expressly provided, a treaty cannot be construed so as to restrict the inherent right of States to act by way of legitimate self-defence.

---

171 *The Development of International Law by the International Court of Justice* (1958), pp. 292-3.

172 McNair, *op. cit.*, p. 466.

173 Sinclair, *The Vienna Convention on the Law of Treaties* (2nd ed., 1984), p. 139.

3.96 As stated, this proposition merely reflects the fundamental and overriding character of self-defence in general international law. In the words of Judges Anzilotti and Huber in the *Wimbledon* case:

> 'The right of a State to adopt the course which it considers best suited to the exigencies of its security and to the maintenance of its integrity, is so essential a right that, in case of doubt, treaty stipulations cannot be interpreted as limiting it, even though those stipulations do not conflict with such an interpretation.' [174]

3.97 Although these comments were made in the context of a joint dissenting opinion, the text of Article 380 of the Treaty of Versailles in issue in the proceedings, and the judgment of the Court, implied that Germany would have been entitled, in the event of a war in which it was involved, to restrict access to the Kiel Canal, notwithstanding the terms of the Treaty. The dissent was therefore on the issue of Germany's rights in the case of a war in which it was not involved. In so far as is material to the present case, therefore, the proposition stated by Judges Anzilotti and Huber is not at variance with the judgment of the Court and may be regarded as of general application.

3.98 In the light of these observations, the issue before the Court in respect of the law of human rights and the law on protection of the environment is not whether the use or threat of use of nuclear weapons is, in the abstract, compatible with those laws. Rather, it is whether any of the rules of the law of human rights or the law on environmental protection can be construed, in accordance with the general principles stated above, as prohibiting the use or threat of use of nuclear weapons *when carried out by way of legitimate self-defence.*

(2) The Law of Human Rights

3.99 In the written statements submitted to the Court in the WHO case, it was argued by two States that the use of nuclear weapons would be contrary to the law of human rights and, in particular, to the right to life. [175] This right is protected by all

---

174 *Case of the SS Wimbledon*, PCIJ Reports, Series A, No. 1, p. 37.

175 Written Statement of the Government of the Solomon Islands, Part IIB; Written Statement of the Government of Nauru, vol. I, pp. 48-51.

the international agreements for the protection of human rights. Thus, Article 6(1) of the International Covenant on Civil and Political Rights, 1966, provides that:

> 'Every human being has the inherent right to life. This right shall be protected by law. No one shall be arbitrarily deprived of his life.'

The right to life is also expressly guaranteed by Article 2 of the European Convention for the Protection of Human Rights and Fundamental Freedoms, Article 4 of the American Convention on Human Rights and Article 4 of the African Charter on Human and People's Rights.

3.100 Although the right to life is the most fundamental of all human rights, it is not unqualified, otherwise its application in time of armed conflict would invariably render the use of any weapon unlawful. This issue is expressly addressed in the European Convention on Human Rights, Article 15 of which provides for parties to derogate from their obligations under the Convention in times of 'war or other public emergency threatening the life of the nation'. Article 15(2) stipulates that no derogation is permitted from Article 2, which guarantees the right to life, 'except in respect of deaths resulting from lawful acts of war.' The European Convention thus expressly refers to the law of armed conflict to determine whether deaths resulting from the conduct of hostilities involve a violation of the right to life. Deaths caused by the use of nuclear (or conventional) weapons would violate the right to life only if the particular use of the weapons was contrary to the laws of armed conflict. As the United Kingdom has sought to demonstrate (in Part III.4, above), there are circumstances in which the use of nuclear weapons is not prohibited *per se* by the laws of armed conflict.

3.101 Although the International Covenant on Civil and Political Rights contains no provision equivalent to Article 15(2) of the European Convention, Article 6(1) prohibits only the 'arbitrary' deprivation of life. [176] If the Covenant is applicable at all to the taking of life in the context of an armed conflict, it is necessary to determine what the term 'arbitrary' means in that context. Since the taking of life is an inescapable feature of the conduct of armed conflict and since it has never seriously been suggested that the Covenant outlaws the use of force by way of national self-defence, the reference to 'arbitrary' deprivation of life must contain the means for distinguishing between those acts of taking life in armed conflict which are compatible with Article 6 of the Covenant and those which are not. The only sensible

---

176 The same is true of Article 4 of the American Convention on Human Rights and Article 4 of the African Charter on Human and People's Rights.

construction which can be placed on the term 'arbitrary' in this context is that it refers to whether or not the deliberate taking of life is unlawful under that part of international law which was specifically designed to regulate the conduct of hostilities, that is the laws of armed conflict. On that basis, the use of a weapon to take life in armed conflict could only amount to an arbitrary deprivation of life, for the purposes of Article 6 of the Covenant, if it was contrary to the laws of armed conflict but not otherwise.

3.102 This interpretation is confirmed by the *travaux préparatoires* of the Covenant. In drafting Article 6, it was decided not to attempt to list those circumstances in which the deprivation of life might be lawful but, instead, to rely upon the concept of arbitrariness to exclude such cases from the scope of the prohibition. One of the examples given of a taking of life that would not be arbitrary was killing in the course of a 'lawful act of war'.

3.103 Whether the use of nuclear weapons in an armed conflict entails a violation of the right to life under Article 6 of the Covenant would thus depend on whether that use was contrary to the laws of armed conflict discussed in Part III.4 of this Statement.

3.104 It is in this context that the references to nuclear weapons by the United Nations Human Rights Committee, in their two General Comments on Article 6, must be seen. The Committee is empowered, under Article 40(4) of the Covenant, as part of the procedure for considering the reports submitted by the States parties, to transmit to them such general comments as it may consider appropriate. [177]

3.105 The first such Comment, adopted in 1982, contains the following passage:

> 'The Committee observes that war and other acts of mass violence continue to be a scourge of humanity and to take the lives of thousands of human beings every year. Under the Charter of the United Nations the threat or use of force by any State against another State, except in the case of the inherent right of self-defence, is already prohibited. The Committee considers that States have the supreme duty to prevent wars, acts of genocide and other acts of mass violence causing arbitrary loss of life. Every effort they make to avert the danger of war, especially thermo-nuclear war, and to strengthen international peace and security would constitute the most important condition and guarantee for the safeguarding of the right to life.' [178]

---

177 These general comments are, by definition, not binding.

178 General Comment 6(16): UN Doc. A/37/40, p. 93, paragraph 2.

This comment does not suggest that all acts of war or all uses of nuclear weapons are a violation of the right to life. On the contrary, it expressly recognizes that the use of force in self-defence is lawful under international law.

3.106 The General Comment adopted by the Committee in 1984 goes further. After recalling the 1982 General Comment, the Committee noted the expressions of concern in the General Assembly at the proliferation of weapons of mass destruction and continued:

> '4. ... It is evident that the designing, testing, manufacture, possession and deployment of nuclear weapons are amongst the greatest threats to the right to life which confront mankind today. This threat is compounded by the danger that the actual use of such weapons may be brought about, not only in the event of war, but even through human or mechanical error or failure.
>
> ...
>
> '6. The production, testing, possession, deployment and use of nuclear weapons should be prohibited and recognized as crimes against humanity.' [179]

3.107 This General Comment was highly controversial, not least because the Committee had made very little of the threat to the right to life created by nuclear weapons in the questions which it had posed to States in connection with their reports to the Committee. Moreover, the Committee did not consider whether any particular use of a nuclear weapon would or would not violate the laws of armed conflict. The General Comment does not, however, assert that the use (let alone the testing, possession or deployment) of nuclear weapons would inevitably contravene Article 6 of the Covenant. The statement in paragraph 6 of the Comment is clearly framed as a proposal for the adoption of a new prohibition and not as a statement *de lege lata*. In the words of one leading commentary:

> 'It is difficult to accept that the term "should" suggests anything other than a desirable goal to be achieved rather than a statement of immediate legal obligation derived from Article 6 of the [Covenant].' [180]

3.108 The protection given by the law of human rights does not, therefore, lead to a different conclusion regarding the legality of the use of nuclear weapons from that

---

179 General Comment 14 (23), UN Doc. A/40/40, p. 162, paragraphs 4 and 6.

180 McGoldrick, *The Human Rights Committee* (1994), p. 336.

provided by the law of armed conflict. Since the law of human rights is concerned primarily with the protection of human rights in peacetime, whereas the law of armed conflict is a *lex specialis* designed to regulate the conduct of hostilities, it is entirely appropriate that the human rights agreements should, in effect, refer to the law of armed conflict in order to determine whether or not any particular instance of the deprivation of life in wartime is arbitrary. The same principle applies, *a fortiori*, in respect of the protection of other human rights.

(3) International Law requiring the Protection of the Environment

3.109 The very considerable number of treaties concluded over the past century providing for the protection of some or other aspect of the eco-system - by one count over 300 multilateral treaties, 900 bilateral treaties and 200 other instruments [181] - have addressed matters ranging from pollution of one sort or another to the protection of the cultural and national heritage, wetlands, tropical forests and endangered and migratory species. Amongst these agreements are a number which, it has sometimes been argued, should be construed as prohibiting the threat or use of nuclear weapons. There are also various resolutions, declarations and statements, which are not legally binding, but which have sometimes been relied upon as evidence of a general rule of international law prohibiting the threat or use of nuclear weapons *per se*.

3.110 Scarcely any of these texts, however, make any reference to the use of nuclear weapons. There was, for example, virtually no discussion of the environmental consequences of nuclear weapons during the Stockholm Conference on the Human Environment in 1972 or the Rio Conference on Environment and Development in 1992. Nor do the resolutions of the United Nations General Assembly dealing with the environment refer to nuclear weapons. [182] Conversely, the General Assembly resolutions on the use of nuclear weapons do not refer to the environment.

---

181 See Prieur, 'Protection of the Environment' in Bedjaoui (ed.), *International Law: Achievements and Prospects* (1991), p. 1017, at p. 1018.

182 See, e.g., resolution 47/37, which addresses the protection of the environment in times of armed conflict but makes no mention of nuclear weapons.

(a) Environmental Agreements and the Threat or Use of Nuclear Weapons

3.111 With the exception of certain treaties, discussed in Part III.2 of this Statement,[183] which prohibit any use of force within a defined area, international treaties having as their object the protection of the environment have not in terms addressed the use or threat of use of nuclear weapons. The question is, therefore, whether agreements of a general nature[184] are to be construed as prohibiting the threat or use of nuclear weapons as a matter of necessary implication. Examples of such treaties might be said to include the Convention for the Protection of the World Cultural and Natural Heritage, 1972,[185] and the Vienna Convention for the Protection of the Ozone Layer, 1985.[186]

3.112 However, the nature and scope of these agreements is such that they cannot be construed as containing an implied prohibition on the threat or use of nuclear weapons. Such an approach would run contrary to the principles discussed in paragraphs 3.88 to 3.98, above, that a prohibitive rule must be clearly stated, that the interpretation and performance of treaties are subject to the obligation of good faith and that treaties must be construed against the background of the inherent right of individual and collective self-defence. To read into environmental agreements of a general nature a prohibition on the use or threat of use of nuclear weapons could have absurd effects. If the Convention for the Protection of the World Cultural and Natural Heritage may be construed, in the absence of an express clause to this effect, as prohibiting the threat or use of nuclear weapons, so could the European Convention for the Protection of Pet Animals, 1987,[187] Article 3(1) of which provides that

---

183 See, e.g., the Antarctic Treaty, 1959, and the other treaties considered in paragraphs 3.13 to 3.23, above.

184 Treaties dealing specifically with the protection of the environment in time of armed conflict are discussed in paragraphs 3.74 to 3.77, above.

185 11 ILM (1972) 1358; UKTS 2 (1985). Article 6(3) of this Convention provides that:

> 'Each State Party to this Convention undertakes not to take any deliberate measures which might damage directly or indirectly the cultural or natural heritage referred to in Articles 1 and 2 situated on the territory of other States Parties to this Convention.'

186 26 ILM (1987) 1529; UKTS 1 (1990). Article 2(1) of this Convention provides that:

> 'The Parties shall take appropriate measures in accordance with the provisions of the Convention and of those protocols in force to which they are party to protect human health and the environment against adverse effects resulting from or likely to result from human activities which modify or are likely to modify the ozone layer.'

187 ETS 125.

'nobody shall cause a pet animal unnecessary suffering or distress.' In the United Kingdom's view, the relevant principle of law is that stated by the Permanent Court of International Justice in the *Polish War Vessels in Danzig* case - the text of a treaty cannot be enlarged by reading into it stipulations for which no provision is made in the text itself. [188]

(b) Customary International Law on the Environment and the Threat or Use of Nuclear Weapons

3.113 It has also been suggested that customary international law on the environment has developed a prohibition on the use of nuclear weapons. This prohibition is said to be derived from international agreements and other texts, such as resolutions of the General Assembly and other bodies. The Court has, however, made it clear that the existence of a rule of customary law will not lightly be presumed:

> 'It is, of course, axiomatic that the material of customary international law is to be looked for primarily in the actual practice and *opinio juris* of States, even though multilateral conventions may have an important role to play in recording and defining rules deriving from custom, or indeed in developing them. [189]

3.114 In the present case, the practice of States in environmental matters gives no hint of a rule regarding the use, or threat of use, of nuclear weapons. Treaties on the environment which contain no reference to such weapons and in which no prohibition on their use can reasonably be implied clearly cannot be relied upon as evidence of a customary rule prohibiting the threat or use of nuclear weapons. Resolutions of the General Assembly and other bodies may be relied upon as evidence of customary international law only if they command widespread and representative support, are regarded by the States voting for them as articulating a principle of customary law and are capable of normative application. Hortatory provisions with only partial support among States cannot give rise to, or change the content of, a rule of customary law.

---

188 See paragraph 3.91, above.

189 *Continental Shelf (Libyan Arab Jamahiriya/Malta)*, ICJ Reports, 1985, p. 13, at paragraph 27.

3.115 Two instruments are sometimes said to be particularly relevant to the use or threat of use of nuclear weapons. Principle 26 of the Stockholm Declaration on the Human Environment, 1972, provides that:

> 'Man and his environment must be spared the effects of nuclear weapons and all other means of mass destruction. States must strive to reach prompt agreement, in the relevant international organs, on the elimination and complete destruction of such weapons.'

Principle 24 of the Rio Declaration on Environment and Development, 1992, provides that:

> 'Warfare is inherently destructive of sustainable development. States shall therefore respect international law providing protection for the environment in times of armed conflict and cooperate in its further development, as necessary.'

Quite apart from the non-binding character of these declarations as a matter of form, an examination of the detail leaves no room for doubt that they cannot be considered a basis for a rule of customary international law prohibiting the threat or use of nuclear weapons. For example, the language of Principle 26 of the Stockholm Declaration is clearly hortatory in nature. Equally, while Principle 24 of the Rio Declaration provides that States shall respect international law providing protection for the environment in times of armed conflict, it gives no indication of what that law entails. An authoritative proscription of the threat or use of nuclear weapons cannot be inferred from such a statement.

3.116 The fact that there is no evidence of 'widespread and representative' support for the existence of a rule of custom prohibiting *per se* the threat or use of nuclear weapons, as well as the absence of *opinio juris* on the part of States concerning the existence of such a rule, has effectively precluded the emergence of a rule of customary international law to this effect.[190]

---

[190] See, in this regard, the comment by Birnie and Boyle that the rule of customary international law that has now developed prohibiting atmospheric nuclear testing

> 'does not extend beyond deliberate nuclear tests or peaceful explosions ... nor does it imply that the actual use of nuclear weapons is forbidden by international law. ... Explicit treaty limitations on the conduct of military operations place some constraints on methods of warfare which cause widespread, long-lasting and severe damage to the natural environment, but the use of nuclear weapons is prohibited entirely only in Latin America and the Pacific.' (Birnie and Boyle, *International Law and the Environment* (1992), pp. 360-61; footnotes omitted).

6 Threats to Use Nuclear Weapons

3.117 Unlike the earlier request from the World Health Organization, the question submitted to the Court by the United Nations General Assembly asks the Court whether the threat to use nuclear weapons is in any circumstances permitted by international law. Whereas the use of force is regulated by a large body of detailed rules under both the *jus ad bellum* and the *jus in bello*, the only express regulation of the threat of force is contained in Article 2(4) of the United Nations Charter, which provides that:

> 'All Members shall refrain in their international relations from the threat or use of force against the territorial integrity or political independence of any State, or in any other manner inconsistent with the Purposes of the United Nations.'

3.118 The question what constitutes a threat of force within the meaning of Article 2(4) has received very little attention. A widely accepted definition, however, appears to be that of Professor Brownlie, who states that:

> 'A threat of force consists in an express or implied promise by a government of a resort to force conditional on non-acceptance of certain demands of that government. If the promise is to resort to force in conditions in which no justification for the use of force exists, the threat itself is illegal.' [191]

A threat to use nuclear weapons thus involves much more than merely the possession of such weapons. In the absence of a specific commitment by a State not to possess such weapons, [192] their possession cannot, in itself, be contrary to international law. As the Court held in the *Case Concerning Military and Paramilitary Activities in and Against Nicaragua*,

> 'in international law there are no rules, other than such rules as may be accepted by the State concerned, by treaty or otherwise, whereby the level of armaments of a sovereign State can be limited, and this principle is valid for all State without exception.' [193]

---

191 Brownlie, *International Law and the Use of Force by States* (1963), p. 364. See also the similar approach adopted by Sadurska 'Threat of Force', 82 AJIL (1988) 239 at p. 242, Schachter, *International Law in Theory and Practice* (1991) at p. 111 and Randelzhofer in Simma (ed), *The Charter of the United Nations - A Commentary* (1994) at p. 118.

192 Such commitments are considered in Part III.2

193 ICJ Reports, 1986, p. 3 at p. 135.

Nor does the deployment of nuclear weapons amount to a threat of their use unless the surrounding circumstances make clear that such a threat is implicit in the fact of their deployment, something which is not lightly to be presumed, since all States have a right to possess and deploy weapons for their own self-defence unless they have agreed to forego or curtail this right.

3.119 In circumstances where the actual use of force would be lawful, it follows that the threat to use force would also be lawful. Thus, for one State to make clear (whether by words or deeds) to another State that, if attacked, it will use force to defend itself is not an unlawful threat of force, if, indeed, it can be described as a threat at all. In the *Corfu Channel* case, the Court held that the action of the United Kingdom in sending four warships through the Corfu Channel with their crews at action stations after a previous occasion on which coastal artillery had fired on British warships was not an unlawful action. Having held that United Kingdom warships had a right of passage through the Corfu Channel, the Court accepted that even though

> 'the intention must have been, not only to test Albania's attitude, but at the same time to demonstrate such force that she would abstain from firing on passing ships' [194]

there was no violation of Albania's sovereignty. Similarly, for a State to make clear that, if attacked, it will resort to nuclear weapons would involve no threat of force in violation of Article 2(4) of the Charter or of any other rule of international law, since the first State is not attempting to coerce the second into complying with a demand which it has no right to make and there is no danger that it will use nuclear weapons unless it is itself the victim of an unlawful armed attack.

3.120 Moreover, in assessing this aspect of the question posed by the General Assembly, it is important to bear in mind that the deterrent effect of nuclear weapons has played an essential part in maintaining the self-defence of a number of States without recourse to force proving necessary.[195] In that respect, it cannot be regarded as contrary to the policy underlying Article 2(4) and Article 51 of the Charter.

---

194 ICJ Reports, 1949, p. 3 at p. 31.

195 See paragraphs 2.18 to 2.21 and 3.11, above.

IV CONCLUSION

4.1 On the basis of the arguments set out above, the United Kingdom submits that the Court should, in the exercise of its discretion, decline to give an answer to the question posed by the General Assembly because:-

(1) the case is not one in which the opinion of the Court would be capable of providing any constructive assistance to the General Assembly in the exercise of its functions under the United Nations Charter;

(2) the request for an opinion should be considered in the context of the effects which such an opinion might have upon the United Nations as a whole and, in particular, upon the disarmament process where an opinion on the legality of nuclear weapons would be unlikely to have any beneficial effects and would be likely to be detrimental to further progress at a time when the prospects for such progress are otherwise promising;

(3) the question put to the Court is in vague and abstract terms, whereas an answer would require detailed examination of the circumstances of any possible use of nuclear weapons, or the threat thereof, and the necessary material regarding such circumstances could not be brought before the Court.

4.2 As regards the principles of law raised by the question, the United Kingdom submits that:

(1) there is no rule contained in either treaty or customary international law which expressly prohibits the use of nuclear weapons *per se*, nor can such a rule be inferred from more general treaty provisions;

(2) State practice regarding the possession of nuclear weapons necessarily implies that the use of nuclear weapons would be lawful in proper circumstances. This practice has received recent confirmation in the unanimous adoption of Security Council resolution 984 and the decision of the Conference on the renewal of the Non-Proliferation Treaty to extend the Treaty indefinitely;

(3) the legality of the use of nuclear weapons must therefore be assessed in the light of the applicable principles of international law regarding the use of force and the conduct of hostilities, as is the case with other methods and means of warfare;

(4) the threat or use of nuclear weapons will not be contrary to the Charter of the United Nations if it meets the criteria for the exercise of the right of self-defence. Whether the use of nuclear weapons meets those criteria will depend upon the circumstances of each individual case;

(5) nuclear weapons are not prohibited *per se* by the law of armed conflict. Their use will be lawful provided that it complies with the applicable rules of that law. Their use in circumstances which would otherwise be illegal may, moreover, be lawful if it constitutes a legitimate belligerent reprisal:

(6) the threat or use of nuclear weapons is not prohibited *per se* by any rule of international law for the protection of human rights or the environment.

LETTER DATED 16 JUNE 1995
FROM THE MINISTER FOR FOREIGN AFFAIRS
OF BOSNIA AND HERZEGOVINA

The Republic of Bosnia and Herzegovina
MINISTRY OF FOREIGN AFFAIRS

To the Registrar of the
International Court of Justice
Mr. E. Valencia - Ospina
Peace Palace
2517 KJ DEN HAAG

16 June, 1995

ahj / gs

Re.: Advisory Opinion on threat or use of nuclear weapons (Res. 49 - 75K, General Assembly, 15 December 1994

Dear Sir.

This is to inform the Court that the Government of the Republic of Bosnia and Herzegovina is of the opinion that an Advisory Opinion of the Court on the issue of the legality or the illegality of the threat or use of nuclear weapons would serve as an authoritative and indeed very important guidance for any international efforts to come to a more peaceful world.

For obvious reasons the Government of the Republic of Bosnia and Herzegovina is at this very moment not in the position to serve the Court with any lenghty observations regarding these issues.

The Government of the Republic of Bosnia and Herzegovina would, however, like to reserve its right to comment on any Submisions sent to the Court by other States, before the next time - limit (20 September 1995).

Accept, Sir, the assurances of my highest consideration,

Muhamed Sacirbey
Foreign Minister of the Republic of Bosnia and Herzegovina

LETTER DATED 19 JUNE 1995 FROM THE MINISTER FOR FOREIGN AFFAIRS OF SAN MARINO

REPUBBLICA DI SAN MARINO
SEGRETERIA DI STATO PER GLI AFFARI ESTERI

San Marino, 19th June 1995

n° 7296/AA/1/10

Mister Registar,

With reference to your letter n. 95586 dated 8th February 1995, please take note of the following:

The Republic of San Marino affirms that the existence of nuclear weapons and their proliferation represents a serious threat to peace and reaffirms the need for the International Court of Justice to express an advisory opinion on "Legality of the threat or use of nuclear weapons". The Republic of San Marino in fact considers it as a violation of the United Nations Charter and of any national and international rule protecting human rights, as stated by the Resolution 49/75 K., adopted by the General Assembly in its 90th plenary session of December 15th, 1994.

The Ministry of Foreign Affairs of San Marino wishes to know any decision that the International Court of Justice will adopt on this matter.

I shall be grateful if you could give instructions on the above-mentioned position of San Marino and I avail myself of this opportunity to renew to you, Mister Registar, the assurance of my highest consideration.

Gabriele Gatti
Minister of Foreign Affairs

Mr. Eduardo Valencia-Ospina
Registar of the International Court of Justice
THE HAGUE

MAB/cf

NOTE VERBALE DATED 19 JUNE 1995
FROM THE EMBASSY OF THE ISLAMIC REPUBLIC OF IRAN,
TOGETHER WITH WRITTEN STATEMENT
OF THE GOVERNMENT OF THE ISLAMIC REPUBLIC OF IRAN

Embassy of the Islamic Republic of Iran
Duinweg 24, The Hague

IN THE NAME OF GOD

No. 1270-01-1368

The Embassy of the Islamic Republic of Iran presents its compliments to the International Court of Justice and has the honour to enclose herewith the written statement of the Islamic Republic of Iran in regard with "Legality of the threat or use of Nuclear Weapons (request for advisory opinion).

The Embassy of the Islamic Republic of Iran avails itself of this opportunity to renew to the International Court of Justice the assurances of its highest consideration.

The Hague, 1[illegible] June 19[illegible]

Encl. written statement

International Court of Justice
Peace Palace
The Hague

The Government of the Islamic Republic of Iran is pleased to see that the International Court of Justice is requested by the General Assembly Resolution 49/57(K) of 15 December 1994 to render its advisory opinion on the following question: "Is the threat or use of nuclear weapons in any circumstance permitted under international law?"

This request has been made as General Assembly has competence under Article 96(1) of the Charter of the United Nations to ask the Court for its advisory opinion on any legal question, and, in accordance with Article 11(1), it has the capacity to "... consider the general principles of cooperation in the maintenance of international peace and security including the principles governing disarmament and the regulation of armaments ...." Our preliminary observations on this question are as follow:

A) Article 2(4) of the Charter stipulates that "All Members shall refrain in their international relations from the threat or use of force against the territorial integrity or political independence of any State ...." It is therefore concluded, in accordance with paragraph 1(a) of General Assembly resolution 1653(XVI) of 24 Nov. 1961 that "the use of nuclear and thermo-nuclear weapons is contrary to the spirit, letter and aims of United Nations and, as such, a direct violation of the Charter of the United Nations."

B) Notwithstanding that the prohibition of threat or use of force is a fundamental principle and a preemptory norm of international law, the humanitarian international law imposes certain restrictions on the conduct of States in times of conflict, for the purpose of alleviating the sufferings of human beings in times of armed conflict. Some of these restrictions are clearly stipulated in humanitarian international instruments. In accordance with the Hague Regulations annexed to Convention No. IV respecting the Laws and Customs of War on Land (1907) "the right of belligerents to adopt means of injuring the enemy is not unlimited." Article 35(1) of the Protocol I of

1977 additional to the Four Geneva Conventions (1949) states that "in any armed conflict, the right of the parties to the conflict to choose methods or means of warfare is not unlimited."

It is therefore plausible to conclude that the non-existence of a legally binding instrument on the prohibition of certain types of weapons does not mean that States have an absolute right to use them. It could also be argued that norms rules and general principles adopted in the field of humanitarian international law with a view to prohibiting and limiting the use of some special conventional weapons, is also effectively extended to nuclear weapons, due to the destructive nature of this kind of weapons. Some of the principles of humanitarian international law from which one can deduce the illegitimacy of the use of nuclear weapons are, _inter alia_, as follow:

- Prohibition of means and methods of war that cause unnecessary suffering to human societies and environment [1];
- Distinguishing between military and civilian targets [2];
- The existence of proportionality between military advantages gained and the weapons and methods used [3];
- Prohibition of the use of instruments that cause indiscriminate effects, including means and methods that are used suddenly and equally against both civilian and military targets.

As a result of global efforts, a number of legally binding instruments have been adopted which imposes certain limits on the emplacement, testing and

---

[1]) The Declaration of St. Petersburg of 1866 and Article 23(e) of the Hague Regulations annexed to the 1907 Hague Convention No. IV

[2]) Article 51, paras. 4 & 5 and Article 52 of Protocol I of 1977

[3]) Article 57 (2b) of Protocol I of 1977

proliferation of nuclear weapons These include, *inter alia*;

- The Antarctic Treaty of 1959 which prohibits nuclear weapons explosion and testing in the Antarctica;
- Treaty Banning Nuclear Weapons Tests in the Atmosphere, in Outer Space and under Water (1963);
- Treaty on Principles Governing the Activities of States in the Exploration and Use of Outer Space, including the Moon and Other Celestial Bodies (1967);
- Treaty for the Prohibition of Nuclear Weapons in Latin America (Treaty of Tlatelolco) (1967);
- Treaty on the Non-Proliferation of Nuclear Weapons (1968);
- Treaty on the Prohibition of the Emplacement of Nuclear Weapons and Other Weapons of Mass Destruction on the Sea-Bed and the Ocean Floor and in the Subsoil Thereof (1971);
- South Pacific Nuclear-Free Zone Treaty (1985).

In addition to treaties directly relating to nuclear weapons, certain legal instruments were also concluded in order to eliminate other types of weapons of mass destruction, like:

- Convention on the Prohibition of the Development, Production and Stockpiling of Bacteriological (Biological) and Toxin Weapons and on their Destruction (1972);
- Convention on the Prohibition of Military or Any Other Hostile Use of Environmental Modification Techniques (1977);
- Convention on the Prohibition of the Development, Production, Stockpiling and Use of Chemical Weapons and their Destruction, (1993)

It would not be logical to conclude that the threat or use of nuclear weapons is permitted, when the international community has prohibited other weapons of mass destruction with much less effects on human life.

C) Prohibition of the use of nuclear weapons, due to their huge destructive and modifying effects, could also be understood from the rules of international law relating to the environment. First of all reference can be made to Principle 21 of 1972 Stockholm Declaration on Human Environment which, as a customary rule, stipulates that States are responsible for any acts in their territory having adverse effects on the environment of other States. The same idea is also reflected in Principle 1 of Rio Declaration of 1992. It can be argued that, while States are prevented from such conducts in their own territory, they are duly bound to refrain from any such acts against other States.

Article 35 of Protocol I of 1977 should be particularly mentioned which prohibits the use of methods and means of warfare that are indeed, or may be expected to cause widespread, long term and severe damage to the natural environment. No doubt, this prohibition applies to nuclear weapons for their enormous destructive and long term effect on the environment. In this regard mention can also be made of Article 23 of the Fourth Hague Convention of 1907 and Article 52 of the Fourth Geneva Convention (1949).

The progressive development of international environmental law in recent years has resulted in the adoption of a series of treaties, such as:

- Vienna Convention for the Protection of the Ozone Layer (1985)
- United Nations Framework Convention on Climate Change (1992)
- Convention on Biological Diversity (1992)

which is indicative of the awareness of international community and the emergence of an <u>opinio juris</u> concerning the preservation of the environment.

Therefore the use of nuclear weapons, having the most destructive effects on environment, is a great concern of international society.

D) Furthermore, Article 1 of the Fifth Hague Convention of 1907 Respecting the Rights and Duties of Neutral Powers and Persons in Case of War on Land states that "the territory of the neutral powers is inviolable." In accordance with Article 1 of the Hague Convention No. XIII concerning the Rights and Duties of Neutral Powers in Naval War, the belligerents are bound to respect the sovereign rights of neutral Powers and to abstain, in neutral territory of neutral waters, from any act which would constitute a violation of neutrality. The belligerent States have an obligation not only to abstain from directly attacking neutral States, but also to refrain from using methods and instruments that threaten indirectly the life and environment of third States. It is clear that the effects of the use of nuclear weapons are not confined to the national boundaries of belligerent States and have far-reaching consequences _vis-a-vis_ the rights of third States.

E) There exists an _opinio juris_ on the right of every person to life and security, which has been confirmed on numerous occasions by the United Nations General Assembly. In this regard, the General Assembly, exercising its functions under Article 11 of the Charter with the ultimate goal of achieving complete nuclear disarmament, has adopted a number of resolutions on the illegality of the threat or use of nuclear weapons, some of which are as follow:

- "The Declaration of the Prohibition of the Use of Nuclear and Thermonuclear Weapons", Resolution 1653 (XVI) of 24 Nov. 1961;
- Resolution 2936 (XXVII) of 29 Nov. 1972 concerning Non-Use of Force in International Relations and Permanent Prohibition of Nuclear Weapons;
- Resolution 33/71 of 14 Dec. 1978 on Non-Use of

Nuclear Weapons and Prevention of Nuclear Weapons;

- Resolution 34/83 of 11 Dec. 1979 on Non-Use of Nuclear Weapons and Prevention of Nuclear War;
- Resolution 35/152 of 12 Dec. 1980 on Non-Use of Nuclear Weapons and Prevention of Nuclear War;
- Resolution 36/92 of 9 Dec. 1981 on Non-Use of Nuclear Weapons and Prevention of Nuclear War;

This <u>opinio juris</u> can also be deduced from the 1995 Review and Extension Conference of the Parties to the Treaty on the Non-Proliferation of Nuclear Weapons in which States reiterated their belief in "the ultimate goals of complete elimination of nuclear weapons and a treaty of general and complete disarmament . . . ."

Taking into consideration the end of the Cold War and the new developments in the international relations, the Islamic Republic of Iran believes that the International Court of Justice is now in a better position to respond to the international public conscience and render its advisory opinion on the illegality of the threat or use of nuclear weapons.

NOTE VERBALE DATED 19 JUNE 1995 FROM THE EMBASSY OF MALAYSIA, TOGETHER WITH WRITTEN STATEMENT OF THE GOVERNMENT OF MALAYSIA

BOE 30/95

The Embassy of Malaysia presents its compliments to the Registry of the International Court of Justice and with reference to the United Nations General Assembly (UNGA) Resolution 49/75K requesting the International Court of Justice to provide an advisory opinion on the question of the legality of the use of threat of use of nuclear weapons, has the honour to submit the faxed statement by the Government of Malaysia in support of the application by the UNGA.

The Embassy has further the honour to inform that it will be submitting the original copy to the Registry in due course.

The Embassy of Malaysia avails itself of this opportunity to renew to the Registry of the International Court of Justice the assurances of its highest consideration.

EMBASSY OF MALAYSIA
THE HAGUE

The Hague,

19th June, 1995

Office of the Registrar
International Court of Justice
Peace Palace
2517 KJ THE HAGUE.

STATEMENT

by

THE GOVERNMENT OF MALAYSIA

in support of the

APPLICATION BY THE UNITED NATIONS GENERAL ASSEMBLY

for an

ADVISORY OPINION BY THE INTERNATIONAL COURT OF JUSTICE

on

THE LEGALITY OF THE THREAT OR USE OF NUCLEAR WEAPONS

QUESTION PRESENTED TO THE INTERNATIONAL COURT OF JUSTICE

Is the threat or use of nuclear weapons in any circumstance permitted under international law?

BACKGROUND

On 14 May 1993, the World Health Assembly adopted Resolution WHA 46.40, requesting the International Court of Justice to give an advisory opinion on the following question:

In view of the health and environmental effects, would the use of nuclear weapons by a State in war or other armed conflict be a breach of its obligations under international law including the WHO Constitution?

Upon receipt of this request from the Director-General of WHO, the Court set a term of 20 June 1994, later extended to 20 September 1994, for the submission of statements by member governments. Thirty-five states submitted statements, the majority arguing for an affirmative answer to the question asked. In accordance with the Court's Rules, all submissions were transmitted to all states which made submissions. The Court has set a term of 20 June 1995 for states to comment on each other's submissions.

On 15 December 1994, the General Assembly of the United Nations (UNGA), by resolution 49/75/K, requested the Court to give an advisory opinion on the following question:

Is the threat or use of nuclear weapons in any circumstance permitted under international law?

The Court has set a term of 20 June 1995 for the submission of statements relative to the question posed by the General Assembly, and 20 September 1995 as the deadline for responses to these statements.

It is expected that the Court will eventually consolidate the two questions, but it has not yet done so.

SUMMARY

This Statement endorses the arguments already before the Court supporting the thesis that any use of nuclear weapons is illegal under international law. In focusing on the question of threat, this Statement will argue that the threat of use of nuclear weapons is illegal because the law of peace and security, as it has evolved since the adopton of the

United Nations Charter , treats "threat or use" as a single, indivisible concept and because it is a general principle of law that the illegality of a particularly serious offence encompasses as well the illegality of the threat to commit such an offence.

I. INTRODUCTION

The possession of nuclear weapons by some states and not others, and the genocidal nature of these weapons, has created an unprecedented disparity of power between the nuclear "haves" and the nuclear "have-nots". As long as the nuclear weapon powers do not fulfil their solemn obligation under Article VI of the Nuclear Non-Prolferation Treaty "to pursue negotiations in good faith on effective measures relating to cessation of the nuclear arms race at an early date", this disparity will continue to exist and to lead eventually to the spread of nuclear weapons and nuclear war, which will constitute a threat to the survival of civilisation.

This threat is reinforced by the declared intention of the nuclear weapon states to base their security and national interest on nuclear deterrence and to reserve to themselves the right to use nuclear weapons in response to a perceived or actual threat of an attack. The very concept of deterrence is meaningless without a credible willingness to use nuclear weapons - hence, "deterrence" equals "threat to use".

Thus, the question posed by the General Assembly goes beyond the jus in bello query of the World Health Assembly and impinges on the area of jus ad bellum. But the doctrine of jus ad bellum, as elaborated since the enactment of Article 2(4) of the United Nations Charter, leaves no room for the legality of the threat of force under international law. Article 2(4) categorically prohibits the threat or use of force by one state against another. The only exception to this prohibition is Article 51, which preserves "the inherent right of individual or collective self-defence if an armed attack occurs against a Member of the United Nations". But nothing in Article 51 sanctions a standing threat - a threat in futuro - by one state against another, named or unnamed. It sanctions only the use of retaliatory force once an armed attack occurs. Its application is limited to the very brief time span following an attack. It cannot therefore sanction the threat of the use of force as a hypothetical matter inherent in the military doctrine of any state.

Furthermore, the use of force in self-defence is subject to the rules of jus in bello. Hence, if the use of nuclear weapons is prohibited under the rubric of jus in bello, the threat to use nuclear weapons can never be sanctioned under the rubric of jus ad bellum.

II. THE LAW OF PEACE AND SECURITY (JUS AD BELLUM)

All States must avoid the threat or use of force in their relations with one another.

A. UNITED NATIONS CHARTER

The United Nations Charter specifically prohibits the threat or use of force. Under the UN Charter, Article 2(4):

All members shall refrain in their international relations from the threat or use of force against the territorial integrity or political independence of any state, or in any other manner inconsistent with the Purposes of the United Nations.(1)

The prohibition on the threat or use of force under Article 2(4) has the status of jus cogens, a peremptory rule of international law.(2) Moreover, this prohibition extends to non-member States.(3)

The United Nations Charter permits the threat or use of force only in individual or collective self-defence, including Security Council enforcement measures. Under Article 51:

Nothing in the present Charter shall impair the inherent right of individual or collective self-defence if an armed attack occurs against a Member of the United Nations, until the Security Council has taken measures necessary to maintain international peace and security....(4)

The Charter's prohibition on the threat or use of force, with the limited exception of self-defence, reflects a change in the development of international law. Historically, Jus ad Bellum, or the law of "just war", recognised the right of a state to resort to war for "just" reasons. In 1919, the Covenant of the League of Nations further limited a State's right to "resort to war".(5)

In 1928, the General Treaty for the Renunciation of War (Kellog-Briand Pact, also known as the Paris Peace Pact of 27 August 1928) prohibited aggressive war "as an instrument of national policy" and "for the solutuion of international controversies".(6)

The language of the Charter prohibits the "threat or use of

force" rather than "resort to war", as the Covenant of the League of Nations did. The change in terminology reflects the recognition that a State might resort to the threat or use of force which does not rise to the level of war or resort to armed conflict without an open declaration of war.(7)

The League of Nations Covenant did, nevertheless, recognise the danger of threats in international relations. The Covenant declared "any war or threat of war" a matter of concern to the entire League and grounds for the League to take action to "safeguard the peace of nations'.(8)

The principles behind the Kellogg-Briand Pact and the League of Nations Covenant provided a foundation for the United Nations Charter.(9) Thus, Article 2(3), which requires States to settle disputes peacefully, complements the prohibition on the threat or use of force.(10) Moreover, the Charter's preamble calls on States "to practise tolerance and live together in peace with one another as good neighbours". These affirmative obligations to cooperate peacefully would clearly be inconsistent with a legal regime that tolerates threats between States.

The Opening Statement by Mr Hans Corell, Under-Secretary-General for Legal Affairs at the United Nations, during the Congress on Public International Law in March 1995, reaffirmed the principles that law should govern the relations between States and that disputes should be resolved peacefully:

..let this Congress also be a resounding appeal to those who ultimately make the decisions that affect our destiny. To them, our message should be:

Yours is the responsibility to ensure that international law is applied and that legal advice is sought before important decisions are made in foreign policy matters...

And, if disputes occur, yours is the responsibility to refrain from the use of force and to make sure that these disputes are resolved by peaceful means.(11)

The preparatory work of the United States in anticipation of the creation of the United Nations reflects a concern with threats of force. A Memorandum containing "basic ideas which might be embodied in a constitution of an international organisation for the maintenance of peace and security" listed as the first among the functions and purposes of the organisation "to prevent the use of force or of threats to use force".(12) As the first of the principal obligations of a member state, the Memorandum listed "To refrain from the use of force or threat to use force..."(13)

The proposals which emerged from the Dumbarton Oaks Conference, in preparation for the United Nations Conference in San Francisco, formed the basis of the UN Charter. At Dumbarton Oaks, the United States proposals were accepted as the basis for discussion and the structure they established was generally accepted.(14) The Dumbarton Oaks draft of the principle which became Article 2(4) read:

All members of the Organisation shall refrain in their international relations from the threat or use of force in any manner inconsistent with the purpose of the Organisation.(15)

Australia's amendment added the prohibition on threats or use of force "against the territorial integrity or political independence of any member or State."(16)

B. UNITED NATIONS RESOLUTIONS AND DECLARATIONS

Numerous United Nations resolutions and declarations have confirmed the principle that States shall refrain from the threat or use of force in their international relations.

The Declaration on Principles of International Law Concerning Friendly Relations and Cooperation Among States in Accordance with the Charter of the United Nations(17) reiterates the language of Article 2(4) and adds:

Such a threat or use of force constitutes a violation of international law and the Charter of the United Nations and shall never be employed as a means of settling international issues.(18)

THe Declaration of the Inadmissibility of Intervention in the Domestic Affairs of States and the Protection of Their Independence and Sovereignty(19) states: "No state has the right to intervene ... in the internal or external affairs of any other . Consequently, armed intervention and all other forms of interference or attempted threats ... are condemned." The Declaration notes that intervention is not admissible "for any reason whatever."

THe 1987 Declaration on the Enhancement of the Effectiveness of the Principle of Refraining from the Threat or Use of Force in International Relations affirms the principle of Article 2(4) and of the Declaration on Principles of International Law Concerning Friendly Relations, and adds:

The principle of refraining from the threat or use of force in international relations is universal in character and is binding, regardless of each State's political, economic, social or cultural system or relations of alliances.(20)

This Declaration provides further that "States have the duty to abstain from armed intervention and all other forms of interference or attempted threats against the personality of the State or against its political, economic and cultural elements."(21) In addition, neither acquisition nor occupation of territory resulting from the threat or use of force will be recognised as legal,(22) and a treaty procured by the threat or use of force is void.(23)

The Final Document of the First Special Session of the United Nations General Assembly on Disarmament stated that "[State members] stress the special importance of refraining from the threat or use of force against the sovereignty, territorial integrity or political independence of any State, or against peoples under colonial or foreign domination..."(24)

Additional Declarations, which affirm the principle of refraining from threat or use of force include: Essentials of Peace,(25) Declaration on the Strengthening of International Security,(26) Declaration on the Inadmissibility of Intervention and Interference in the Internal Affairs of States,(27) and Declaration on the Prevention and Removal of Disputes and Situations Which May Threaten International Peace and Security and on the Role of the United Nations in This Field.(28)

C. COLLECTIVE SECURITY TREATIES

A number of collective security treaties confirm the symbolic nature of threat or use of force. The North Atlantic Treaty (the NATO Treaty)(29) requires State Parties "to refrain in their international relations from the threat or use of force in any manner inconsistent with the purposes of the United Nations." Similarly, the now-lapsed Treaty of Friendship , Cooperation and Mutual Assistance (the Warsaw Pact)(30) requires Contracting Parties "to refrain in their international relations from the threat or use of force."

The Final Act of the Conference on Security and Cooperation in Europe(31) requires States participating to refrain from the threat or use of force , repeating the language of the Charter. Moreover, "no consideration may be invoked to serve to warrant resort to the threat or use of force in contravetion of this principle" and "no such threat or use of force will be employed as a means of settling disputes, or questions likely to give rise to disputes...."

The American Treaty on Pacific Settlement(32) requires the contracting parties to "...refrain from the threat or the use of force, or from any other means of coercion for the settlement of their controversies..."

The Convention on the Rights and Duties of States(33) holds that "No state has the right to intervene in the internal or external affairs of another."

In addition,the Charter of the Organisation of American States(34) provides:

No State or group of States has the right to intervene, directly or indirectly, for any reason whatever, in the internal or external affairs of any other States. The foregoing principle prohibits not only armed forces but also any other form of interference or attempted threat against the personality of the State or against its political, economic and cultural elements.

D. THE NUREMBERG PRINCIPLES

THe General Assembly unanimously affirmed "the principles of international law recognised by the Charter of the Nuremberg Tribunal and the judgement of the Tribunal."(35) The principles "have since been universally considered to constitute an authoritative statement of the rules of customary international law."(36) The Nuremberg offences "correspond largely to the obligations imposed by certain rules of jus cogens".(37)

The principles as codified by the International Law Commission(38) define crimes against peace as:

(i) Planning, preparation, initiation or waging of a war of aggression or a war in violation of international treaties, agreements or assurances.

(ii) Participation in a common plan or conspiracy for the accomplishment of any of the acts mentioned under (i).

A crime against peace is "a culpable violation of the jus ad bellum".(39)

Planning and preparing for aggression are thus clearly proscribed. In addition, the Nuremberg principles support the proscription of planning and preparation for war crimes and crimes against humanity. A war involving such crimes would be a "war in violation of international treaties, agreements or assurances".

E. OPINIO JURIS

The United Nations Charter and the treaties and resolutions cited above do not distinguish between the legal status of the threat to use force and that of the use of force itself. Both are equally prohibited. Indeed, "if the promise is to resort to force in conditions in which no justification for the use of force exists, the threat itsef is illegal."(40)

The significance of the prohibition on threats of force becomes apparent when one considers the implications for previously accepted legal norms. Oppenheim's discussion of threats of force in relation to the obligation to issue an ultimatum before resorting to war suggests that the prohibition on the threat of force overrides previously accepted and codified legal standards:

In so far as the Charter of the United Nations prohibits not only acts of force but also threats of force, the question arises as to the operation, as between the Members of the United Nations, of the provisions of the Hague Convention in the matter of ultimatum and, to some extent, of declaration of war. If it is unlawful for Members of the United Nations to threaten another State with the use of force, how can they properly be in a position to comply with the obligation to issue an ultimatum prior to resorting to war? The correct answer is probably that, as between Members of the United Nations, these provisions of the Hague Convention, although not directly conflicting with the Charter, are substantially obsolete.(41)

The prohibition of the threat of force applies even where the threat is not carried out. As Professor Oscar Schachter notes:

The preponderance of military strength in some states and their political relations with potential target states may justifiably lead to an inference of a threat of force against the political independence of the target state....and the applicability of Article 2(4) in principle can hardly be denied.(42)

However, even though relative military strength and political relations can create situations of threat, "curiously Article 2(4) has not been invoked much as an explicit prohibition of such implied threats."(43) According to Schachter, this may be due to the "difficulty of demonstrating coercive intent" or to the widespread, though not unlimited, tolerance for disparities of power.(44)

An alternative explanation for the underuse of the prohibition on threat in Article 2(4) is the difficulty of invoking it effectively. Since the authority to do so lies with the Security Council, the failure of the non-permanent members to exercise that authority does not so much indicate their tolerance of implied or actual threats by the permanent members (who are also the declared nuclear weapon states) but rather their recognition of the realities of power disparities and the veto power of the permanent members.

International legal scholars differ somewhat in their analyses of what constitutes a threat of force and what the role of threats is in international law. According to Ian Brownlie, a threat "consists in an express or implied promise by a government of a resort to force conditional on non-acceptance of certain demands of that government."(45) Romana Sadurska regards a threat in the international arena as "a message, explicit or implicit, formulated by a decision-maker and directed to the target audience, indicating that force will be used if a rule or demand is not complied with."(46) Both experts suggest that use of force is conditional on the target's response to the threat and that the threat might be "implicit" or "implied", as well as "explicit" or "express".

In the Fisheries Jurisdiction Case(47), a dissenting opinion by Judge Padilla Nervo examines the nature of threats:

A big power can use force and pressure against a small nation in many ways, even by the very fact of diplomatically insisting in having its views recognised and accepted. The Royal Navy did not need to use armed force, its mere presence on the seas inside the fishery limits of the coastal State could be enough pressure. It is well known by proferssors, jurists and diplomats acquainted with international relations and foregn policies that certain "Notes" delivered by the government of a strong power to the goverment of a small nation, may have the same purpose and the same effect as the threat or use of force.(48)

F. THREATS OF AGGRESSION

A threat of force alone does not constitute an "act of aggression" under the UN "Definition of Aggression" Resolution.(49) In fact, the Definition suggests that not all uses of force constitutes acts of aggression, noting in the Preamble that "aggression is the most serious and dangerous form of the illegal use of force."(50)

The International Law Commission incorporated the General Assembly's definition of aggression in the Draft Code of Crimes Against Peace and Security of Mankind.(51) Significantly, the Draft Code includes a separate article for the crime of the Threat of Aggression:(52)

1. An individual who, as leader or organiser, commits or orders the commission of a threat of aggression shall, on conviction thereof, be sentenced.....

2. Threat of aggression consists of declarations, communications, demonstrations of force or any other measures which would give good reason to the Government of a State to believe that aggression is being seriously contemplated against that State.

The International Law Commission Report on the Draft Code to the General Assembly notes that in the context of this article, "the word 'threat' denotes acts undertaken with a view to making a State believe that force will be used against it if certain demands are not met by that State."(53)

The Commission was careful to link the acts of an individual, who commits a crime against peace and security, with the State. Only individuals "vested with the authority of the State" have the potential to commit this offence.(54) However, the State is not exempted from responsibility for the crime. Thus, although the Draft Code places the liability directly on the individual,(55) it also provides that:

Prosecution of an individual for a crime against the peace and security of mankind does not relieve a State of any responsibility under international law for an act or ommission attributable to it.(56)

The Commission also noted the importance of defining a crime of threat of aggression, particularly since powerful states have the potential to achieve improper objectives without committing an actual act of aggression.(57) Indeed, the Sixth Committee of the General Assembly, in its review of the Commission Report, noted that "there had been many cases of States that had lost their independence through threats and ultimatums."(58) The record went on to note:

Contemporary international law prohibited not only the use of force, but also the threat of use of force, and thus its inclusion in the code would affirm the position of the international community in that regard.(59)

The Draft Code of Crimes Against the Peace and Security of Mankind reflects the recent development of the concept of crimes against peace.

III. SPECIFIC LAW REGARDING THE THREAT OF USE OF NUCLEAR WEAPONS

The Charter of the United Nations was adopted in San Francisco on 26 June 1945, six weeks before the first use of the atom bomb on 6 August 1945.(60) Had this time sequence been reversed, the Charter might well have contained a specific prohibition on the threat and use of nuclear weapons and other weapons of mass destruction.

The concern of the world community with the awesome, destructive power of the atom bomb was evidenced by the fact that the first resolution adopted by the United Nations dealt with the subject of atomic energy and called, inter alia, "for the elimination from national armaments of atomic weapons and all other weapons adaptable to mass destruction..."(61)

A. TREATIES

The preamble of the Treaty on the Non-Proliferation of Nuclear Weapons(62) calls for "the cessation of the manufacture of nuclear weapons, the liquidation of all their existing stockpiles, and the elimination from national arsenals of nuclear weapons and their means of delivery..." Specifically, the Treaty prohibits the manufacture or acquisition of nuclear weapons by non-nuclear weapon states,(63) and it requires nuclear weapon states to "pursue negotiations in good faith on effective measures relating to cessation of the nuclear arms race at an early date and to nuclear disarmament."(64) The threat of use of nuclear weapons is inconsistent with the general purpose and goal of the Treaty as well as the specific requirements of State parties.

The South Pacific Nuclear Free Zone Treaty prohibits the manufacture, acquisition, possession or control of nuclear weapons.(65) The Treaty for the Prohibition of Nuclear Weapons in Latin America prohibits the testing, use, manufacture or acquisition of nuclear weapons, directly or indirectly, by parties to the treaty or within the region defined by the treaty. (66)

The pattern in international law regarding weapons of mass destruction is to prohibit not only the use but also the manufacture and acquisition of these weapons. The treaties discussed above seek to eliminate both the use and the threat to use nuclear weapons, but in no instance do they prohibit the use of nuclear weapons. Similarly, treaties on other weapons of mass destruction, namely biological weapons(67) and chemical weapons(68), also link threat and use. The illegality of the threat to use these weapons is underscored by provisions calling for their destruction.(69)

B. SECURITY COUNCIL RESOLUTIONS

Resolution 984 (11 April 1995) gives non-nuclear states assurances from the nuclear states that nuclear weapons will not be threatened or used against them. All of the declared nuclear weapon states supported this resolution.

Resolution 225 of the Security Council provides that aggression or the threat of aggression with nuclear weapons against a non-nuclear weapon state would require the Security Council to act immediately.(70)

Resolutions 984 and 225 therefore implicitly recognise the illegality of the threat and use of nuclear weapons against a non-nuclear weapon state. A legal act would not require assurances against use nor require a Security Council response.(71)

C. UNITED NATIONS GENERAL ASSEMBLY, CONFERENCE ON DISARMAMENT, AND DISARMAMENT COMMISSION

As discussed above, the framers of the UN Charter could not be aware of the threat of nuclear weapons, but the first United Nations resolution addressed the elimination of these weapons.(72)

Another early resolution of the General Assembly(73) reaffirms the prohibition on the threat or use of force and, in this context, calls on the Disarmament Commission to develop comprehensive plans providing for the "elimination and prohibition of all major weapons...adaptable to mass destruction"(74) and, specifically, the "effective international control of atomic energy to ensure the prohibition of atomic weapons...."(75)

The issue of assurances for non-nuclear weapon states against the use or threat of use of nuclear weapons has received overwhelming support from the international community. THe General Assembly has passed numerous resolutions affirming the urgency of reaching an early agreement on effective international measures to assure non-nuclear weapon states against the use or threat of use of nuclear weapons.(76)

Significantly, no state has opposed the conclusion of these assurances.

The conclusion of effective international arrangements to assure non-nuclear weapon states against the use or threat of use of nuclear weapons has been a key agenda item of the UN Conference on Disarmament, and the Ad Hoc Committee established to review this item has consistently been re-established at the start of each annual session. Most recently, the Committee's report, adopted by the Conference on Disarmament, noted as follows:

All delegations reiterated that they attach particular importance to the question of international arrangements to assure non-nuclear weapon states against the use or threat of use of nuclear weapons and expressed their readiness to engage in a search for a mutually acceptable solution of the issue.(77)

In addition, the Report of the Conference "stressed the necessity to recognise the right of non-nuclear weapon states not to be attacked nor threatened with these weapons."(78) It is significant that, in referring to this right, the Report called for its recognition rather than its creation.

The complete elimination of nuclear weapons has been a constant and recurring objective of the Disarmament Commission and the Conference on Disarmament.(79)

In addition, the General Assembly has passed over 100 resolutions stating nuclear disarmament or the elimination of nuclear weapons as a goal.(80) Thus, the majority of states do not accept the necessity argument for deterrence. A growing number of states have specifically prohibited nuclear weapons in their territory and have established, or are in the process of establishing, nuclear weapon-free zones.

D. THE NON-DEROGABLE RIGHT TO LIFE

The United Nations Human Rights Committee, which supervises the implementation of the International Covenant on Civil and Political Rights(81), has determined that nuclear weapons threaten the non-derogable right to life:

The designing, testing, manufacture, possession and deployment of nuclear weapons are among the greatest threats to the right to life which confront mankind today. THe threat is compounded by the danger that the actual use of nuclear weapons may be brought about, not only in the event of a war, but even through human or mechanical error or failure.

Furthermore, the very existence and gravity of this threat generates a climate of fear and suspicion between states, which undermines the promotion of universal respect for and observance of human rights and fundamental freedoms in accordance with the Charter of the United Nations and the International Covenant of Human Rights.(82)

In other words, nuclear weapons both threaten the right to life and contribute to the spirit of mistrust among nations, compounding the likelihood of threats being carried out. Moreover, the threat to use nuclear weapons conflicts with the commitment to provide children and families with the protection of society and the state(83,84)

The right to life is confirmed as well in the European Convention for the Protection of Human Rights and Fundamental Freedoms (85), and the American Convention on Human Rights(86). Under these Conventions, a derogation clause may be invoked in exceptional situations that threaten the life of the nation. However, the right to life is one of the four non-derogable rights which constitute the "irreducible core" of human rights(87). A non-derogable right is one that cannot be suspended by the State, even in times of public emergency.

Moreover, according to Judge Schwebel of the International Court of Justice, matters affecting international human rights obligations cannot be regarded as exclusively within the domestic jurisdiction of a particular state:

Once a state has undertaken obligations toward another state, or toward the international community, in a specified sphere of human rights, it may no longer maintain, vis-a-vis the other state or the international community, that matters in that sphere are exclusively or essentially within its domestic jurisdiction and outside the range of international concern.(88)

Therefore, the manufacture, possession, deployment and threat of use of nuclear weapons, which violate the right to life, cannot be defended by nuclear weapon states on grounds that they are essential for defence in times of public emergency or as matters of domestic jurisdiction.

IV. THE THREAT OF USE OF NUCLEAR WEAPONS IS PROHIBITED IN ANY CIRCUMSTANCE

A. CORRELATION BETWEEN THREAT AND USE OF FORCE: THREAT IS USE

For purposes of the following analysis, it will be useful to examine briefly the meanings of the terms "threat" and "force", both generically and within the context of the legal instruments relevant to this discussion.

The common meaning of "force" is "strength, energy, power". The normal meaning of "the use of force", within the context of Article 2(4) of the UN Charter, is the application of physical force of a military nature by one member state against another, as in the invasion of Kuwait by Iraq.

Upon closer examination, however, it becomes apparent that more is involved here than a trans-border launch of troops, tanks and missiles. Article 2(4) forbids the use of force not only against the territorial integrity of a state, but also against its political independence, or "in any other manner inconsistent with the purposes of the United Nations." If Article 2(4) had been aimed only at cross-border military action, it would not have been necessary to add this further clause.

What kind of force, then, other than military force in action, can be used by one state against the political independence of another, without affecting its territorial integrity? Non-military force, to be sure, as for instance the erection of tariff barriers or other economic measures, but also the open or veiled promise of the use of force, including armed force, if certain demands are not met. This interpretation is consistent with the definitions of "force" as "power to influence, affect or control", "persuasive power, power to convince".(89)

"Threat", on the other hand, is defined as "a declaration of an intention or determination to inflict punishment, injury, death, or loss on some one in retaliation for, or conditionally upon, some action or course...".(90)

Even more relevant, for present purposes, is the definition of "threat" in Black's Law Dictionary: "In criminal law...any menace of such a nature as to unsettle the mind of the person on whom it operates, and to take away from his acts that free and voluntary action which alone constitutes consent."

THe United Nations Secretary General, in considering what constitutes a threat to use force, noted that "the person who utters the threat may not intend to carry it out, and the threat is then only a form of intimidation and blackmail."(91)

As one philosopher has noted:

Nuclear weapons are being used today and can be expected to

be used in the future. Not that they are being detonated... but that it is not a requirement of their being used. A man uses a gun when he sticks it in your ribs and demands your money. He does not need to fire the gun. And a country uses nuclear weapons when it makes known that it may launch them unless certain conditions are met, as the United States did against the Soviet Union in the Cuban Missile Crisis, against China during the Korean War, and against North Vietnam during the Vietnam War. And the very threat of retaliation that is at the heart of nuclear deterrence is a use of nuclear weapons, even if it is not the actual exploding of them.(92)

Thus, the concepts of "threat" and "use" in Article 2(4) merge into each other in most circumstances. The threat of use is itself a kind of use.

B. THE CONDITIONAL THREAT OF FORCE IS PROHIBITED IN ANY CIRCUMSTANCE

As has been shown above in Section II, the prohibition on the threat of force for the purpose of altering another state's political independence runs like a mantra through the entire post-World War II laws and treaties of peace and security. Whatever the form of these conditional threats, it is clear that they are unequivocally outlawed by the United Nations Charter, many other international instruments and, indeed, the customary law of peace and security.

This being so, and considering that nuclear weapons represent the greatest conceivable instrument of threat available to any nation, the conditional threat to use nuclear weapons is, a fortiori, a gross violation of the law of peace and security.

C. A RETALIATORY THREAT TO USE NUCLEAR WEAPONS IS ILLEGAL IN ANY CIRCUMSTANCE

Although no person or state may be deprived of the right to retaliate as a means of self-defence, this right is not unlimited. In exercising this right, no person or state may commit or threaten to commit a crime or illegal act. Hence, if, as has already been argued, the use of nuclear weapons is illegal in any circumstance, even by way of self-defence or reprisal, the use or threat to use nuclear weapons must also be illegal in any circumstance.(93)

Although this general proposition is dispositive of the question of the legality of retaliatory threats of nuclear weapons, it may be useful to examine somewhat more closely the forms which such threats may take.

1. THE THREAT OF FIRST USE

A threat of first use could include a threatened preemptive nuclear strike against a perceived nuclear or conventional attack or a threatened nuclear response to an actual conventional attack. Moreover, a threat of first use could be directed against developments falling short of the perception of an immediate attack. The essence of the current doctrine of "counter-proliferation" is that the nuclear weapon states reserve to themselves the right to use nuclear weapons to discourage "rogue states" from developing, not necessarily using, weapons of mass destruction, whether nuclear, chemical biological or other. Of the declared nuclear powers, only China has an official no-first-use policy.(94) The United States and the United KIngdom have repeatedly used threats of first use of nuclear weapons against both nuclear and non-nuclear weapon states.(95)

A threat of first use of nuclear weapons is a direct violation of jus ad bellum. The prohibition on the threat of force under the United Nations Charter covers threats of both conventional and nuclear weapons. The threat of first use is inherently a threat against the political independence and territorial integrity of another state. This is true not only when the threat is imminent and aimed at exacting specific changes but also, because of the unique nature of the weapons, when it is a longstanding posture not directly linked to specific demands. Any state, in actual or potential conflict with a nuclear state that has a first-use policy, recognises that the nuclear state has the weapons and the will to use these weapons, should it be deemed necessary by the nuclear state. This inevitably influences the decision-making of that state.

Furthermore, as a tool of unequalled intimidation and destruction, the first use of nuclear weapons can never satisfy the principle of proportionality, one of the foundations of the laws of war, since the magnitude of the event to which a preemptive strike is being made is necessarily a matter of speculation.

2. THE THREAT OF SECOND USE

The second use of nuclear weapons and therefore the threat of such use are not permitted under the law of reprisals, in which reprisals " must conform in all cases to the laws of humanity and morality".(96) "civilian populations...should not be the object of reprisals..."(97) Attacks against the civilian population or civilians by way of reprisals are prohibited".(98)

It is common ground that the laws of war apply equally to all weapons and tactics, including those of self-defence.(99) THe use of genocide, torture or terrorist attacks by one state against another does not justify the use of genocide, torture or terrorist attacks in response. Hence, self-defence cannot justify the threat of use of nuclear weapons in self-defence.

3. DETERRENCE

The following statements appear in the US Joint Chiefs of Staff's 'Doctrine for Joint Nuclear Operations', published on 29 April 1993:

"The fundamental purpose of US nuclear forces is to deter the use of weapons of mass destruction, particularly nuclear weapons, and to serve as a hedge against the emergence of an overwhelming conventional threat."

"Deterrence is founded in real force capabilities and the national determination to use those forces if necessary."

"Deterrence is a defence posture that makes possible war outcomes so uncertain and dangerous, as calculated by potential enemies, as to remove all incentive for initiating attack under any circumstance."

"US forces and command and control systems must be viewed by enemy leadership as capable of inflicting such damage upon their military forces and means of support, or upon their country, as to deny them the military option."

Thus, the doctrine of deterrence implies a readiness and willingness:

- to use nuclear weapons;
- to inflict great damage on the enemy;
- if necessary, to inflict such damage on the enemy's country, not simply his military forces and means of support.

It is of the utmost importance to understand that the doctrine of deterrence cannot be seen as a purely defensive doctrine. As one analyst has noted:

The development of modern nuclear weapons and the systems needed to deliver them cannot be explained, if one insists on defining deterrence in an essentially defensive and reactive form. Instead, the modern concept of deterrence has evolved into something much closer to the traditional understanding of the role of military force in the pursuit of national objectives. Deterrence is now seen as "flexible" or "extended", and a "second-strike counterforce" capability is defended as part of a deterrent on the grounds that a credible (i.2. non-suicidal) response must be available if deterrence fails.(100)

Another analyst makes the following comment:

The theory of nuclear deterrence, far from being one of the great advances of our time....is so little understood in its conceptual foundations and so thoroughly confused in its implementation as to be practically useless from the standpoint of the rational, not to mention moral, guidance of policy. It may, in fact, ultimately prove disastrous.(101)

A recent United States Congressional study on the proliferation of weapons of mass destruction discussed the "potentially conflicting objectives" of nuclear non-proliferation and the nuclear powers' reliance on nuclear deterrence.(102) The study admits that "one way to reduce the appeal of nuclear weapons is to deemphasise the role that they play in international relations. But to do so would mean that the nuclear powers must rely on them less, weakening the credibility and utility of US nuclear deterrent threats.."(103).

V. THE ILLEGALITY OF THE THREAT TO COMMIT AN ILLEGAL ACT

International legal instruments, opinio juris and the general principles of law have recognised the principle that the threat to commit an illegal act is also illegal.

A. INTERNATIONAL LEGAL INSTRUMENTS

We have already seen that treaties on weapons of mass destruction prohibit possession, manufacture and use of these weapons.(104) Similarly, the Nuremberg Principles define as Crimes Against Peace the "planning" and "preparation" of war and the "initiation" or "waging of war".(105)

In addition, the Convention on the Prevention and Punishment of the Crime of Genocide(106) renders punishable not only genocide, but also conspiracy to commit genocide, direct and public incitement to commit genocide, attempt to commit genocide, and complicity in genocide, all of which might be perceived as the threat of genocide by the human targets of nuclear weapons.

CONCLUSION

The 1995 Review and Extension Conference of the Parties to the Treaty on Non-Proliferation of Nuclear Weapons has ended with two results which are significant for the consideration of the question before the Court:

1. The nuclear arsenals of both declared and undeclared nuclear weapon states remain intact, at a level variously estimated at 41,000 to 45,000 warheads.(107)

2. There is no unambiguous, binding commitment by the declared nuclear weapon states, much less the undeclared ones, to the ultimate abolition of all nuclear weapons, even in the distant future.

Thus, the subjective threat of use of nuclear weapons remains as an objective threat to the survival of all or part of the world's present population and of generations to come. If this threat were regarded as an epidemic of potentially incalculable proportions, like polio or small pox in bygone days and AIDS in the present, there would be no hestitation to mobilise all the medical and scientific resources of humanity to combat it. The only weapons available to combat the potential of a nuclear epidemic are common sense, our common code of morality, and the rule of law.

In the light of the arguments presented here and in the other Statements filed with the Court in support of both the World Health Organisation and UN General Assembly Advisory Opinion cases, this Court is respectfully requested to advise that the threat and use of nuclear weapons are not permitted under international law in any circumstance.

LETTER DATED 19 JUNE 1995
FROM THE PERMANENT REPRESENTATIVE
OF SOLOMON ISLANDSTO THE UNITED NATIONS,
TOGETHER WITH WRITTEN STATEMENT
OF THE GOVERNMENT OF SOLOMON ISLANDS

SOLOMON ISLANDS MISSION TO THE UNITED NATIONS
Suite 800B, 820 Second Avenue, New York, N.Y. 10017
TEL: (212) 599-6193 • FAX: (212) 661-8925

19 June 1995

His Excellency Eduardo Valencia Ospina
Registrar,
International Court of Justice
Peace Palace
The Hague
THE NETHERLANDS

Your Excellency,

GENERAL ASSEMBLY - ADVISORY OPINION

By the direction of the Minister for Foreign Affairs, Solomon Islands, I have the pleasure in sending you herewith, on behalf of the Government of Solomon Islands', Solomon Islands Written Observation in respect of the request by the General Assembly for an Advisory Opinion from the International Court of Justice.

Solomon Islands avails itself of the right to submit these Written Observations as a member of the United Nations according to which it is, ipso facto a party to the Statute of the Court of Justice.

In view of the importance of the request made by the General Assembly and the nature of the international legal questions arising thereunder, Solomon Islands considers that it would be appropriate for an oral hearing to be held in this matter.

I would be grateful if correspondence could be addressed to me at the above address, with copies to the Minister of Foreign Affairs at: P.O. Box G-10, Honiara, Solomon Islands.

Please, Your Excellency, accept the assurances of my highest consideration.

Rex S. Horoi
Ambassador Extraordinary and Plenipotentiary
Permanent Representative of Solomon Islands
to the United Nations
NEW YORK

SOLOMON ISLANDS MISSION UNITED NATIONS

REQUEST BY THE UNITED NATIONS GENERAL ASSEMBLY FOR AN ADVISORY OPINION ON THE LEGALITY OF THE THREAT OR USE OF NUCLEAR WEAPONS

WRITTEN OBSERVATIONS SUBMITTED BY THE GOVERNMENT OF SOLOMON ISLANDS TO THE INTERNATIONAL COURT OF JUSTICE

Government of Solomon Islands

20 JUNE 1995

Table of Contents

INTRODUCTION . . . . (1.1-1.15)

(A) Background . . . . (1.1-1.6)

(B) Solomon Island's interest in the question . . . . (1.7-1.15)

PART I THE GENERAL ASSEMBLY IS COMPETENT TO REQUEST AN ADVISORY OPINION FROM THE INTERNATIONAL COURT OF JUSTICE ON THIS QUESTION AND THE COURT IS COMPETENT TO GIVE AN ADVISORY OPINION ON THE QUESTION SUBMITTED . . . . (2.1-2.49)

(A) The General Assembly's request fulfils the conditions of Article 96 of the UN Charter . . . . (2.5-2.8)

(B) The General Assembly is acting in accordance with the UN Charter . . (2.9-2.11)

(C) The practice of the General Assembly confirms its competence over matters relating to the legality of the threat or use of nuclear weapons . . . . (2.12-2.28)

(a) General Assembly Resolutions on the legality of the use of nuclear weapons and related issues . . . . (2.14-2.23)

(b) General Assembly Special Sessions on nuclear weapons under the aegis of disarmament . . . . (2.24-2.25)

(c) General Assembly studies on nuclear weapons . . . . (2.26-2.28)

(D) The Court should give the Advisory Opinion requested by the General Assembly . . . . (2.29-2.48)

(a) The reasons of principle which have led the Court to decide to give an Advisory Opinion . . . . (2.31-2.35)

(b) Criteria which need to be satisfied in order for the Court to reply to a request for an Advisory Opinion . . . . (2.36-2.46)

(c) The WHO request does not prevent the Court from giving the Advisory Opinion requested by the General Assembly . . . . (2.47)

(E) Conclusion . . . . (2.49)

PART II THE LEGALITY OF THE THREAT OR USE OF NUCLEAR WEAPONS

SECTION A THE THREAT OR USE OF NUCLEAR WEAPONS AND THE INTERNATIONAL LAW OF ARMED CONFLICTS . . . . (3.2-3.104)

(A) The meaning of threat . . . . (3.3-3.11)

(B) The use of nuclear weapons is subject to international law, including the rules relating to armed conflicts . . . . (3.12-3.42)

(a) The use of nuclear weapons is subject to general international law . . . . (3.14-3.16)

(b) The use of nuclear weapons is subject to international law of armed conflicts . . . . (3.17-3.21)

(c) The use of nuclear weapons is subject to the 1977 Geneva Protocol I . . . . (3.22-3.35)

(d) The use of nuclear weapons is subject to the rules of international law specifically prohibiting the use of nuclear weapons . . . . (3.36-3.42)

(C) The use of nuclear weapons is contrary to international law of armed conflicts . . . . (3.43-3.89)

(a) The use of nuclear weapons violates international law by reason of the quantitative effects of such weapons . . . . (3.44-3.63)

(i) Nuclear weapons render death inevitable . . . . (3.51-3.53)
(ii) The use of even a single nuclear weapon could result in total nuclear war . . . . (3.54-3.56)
(iii) Nuclear weapons have indiscriminate effects . . . . (3.57-3.63)

(b) The use of nuclear weapons violates international law by reason of the qualitative effects of such weapons . . . . . (3.64-3.79)

(i) The specific consequences of the disintegration of the atom . . . . (3.65-3.74)

(ii) The effects of radioactive fallout . . . . (3.75-3.79)

(c) The use of nuclear weapons violates international law irrespective of the circumstances in which they are used . . . . (3.80)

(d) The use of nuclear weapons cannot be justified by international law in any circumstances . . . . (3.81-3.89)

(i) Self-defence does not justify the use of nuclear weapons . . . . (3.82)
(ii) Reprisals do not justify the use of nuclear weapons . . . . (3.83-3.88)
(iii) Necessity does not justify the use of nuclear weapons . . . . (3.89)

(D) The relevant rules of international law prohibiting the use of nuclear weapons apply to all States . . . . (3.90-3.100)

(E) Conclusions . . . . (3.101-3.104)

SECTION B THE THREAT OR USE OF NUCLEAR WEAPONS VIOLATES APPLICABLE RULES OF INTERNATIONAL LAW FOR THE PROTECTION OF HUMAN HEALTH, THE ENVIRONMENT AND FUNDAMENTAL HUMAN RIGHTS . . . . (4.1-4.49)

(A) The use of nuclear weapons is subject to international law for the protection of human health and the environment, and fundamental human rights . . . . (4.1-4.7)

(B) The use of nuclear weapons violates international law for the protection of human health and the environment . . . . (4.8)

(a) Sovereignty and territorial integrity . . . . (4.9-4.15)

(b) The general obligation of each State not to cause damage to human health and the environment outside its territory or other areas subject to its jurisdiction or control . . . . (4.16-4.20)

(c) The specific obligations not to cause damage to human health and the environment . . . . (4.21-4.28)

(d) The obligation not to cause massive damage to human health or the environment anywhere . . . . (4.29-4.30)

(e) Conclusion . . . . (4.31)

(C) The use of nuclear weapons violates international law for the protection of fundamental human rights . . . . (4.32-4.35)

(D) International obligations for the protection of human health, the environment an human rights apply during armed conflict . . . . . (4.36-4.49)

(a) The operation of treaties during armed conflict . . . . (4.37-4.47)
(b) Customary law . . . . (4.48)
(c) Conclusion . . . . (4.49)

SECTION C ANY VIOLATION BY A STATE OF THESE OBLIGATIONS UNDER INTERNATIONAL LAW GIVES RISE TO ITS INTERNATIONAL RESPONSIBILITY AND LIABILITY . . . . (5.1-5.4)

PART III SUMMARY OF CONCLUSIONS . . . . (6.1-6.2)

INTRODUCTION

(A) Background

1.1 On 15 December 1995 the United Nations General Assembly adopted Resolution 49-75 K, which requested the International Court of Justice ("the Court") to "urgently render an Advisory Opinion on the following question:

> 'Is the threat or use of nuclear weapons in any circumstance permitted under international law?'"

1.2 The request was made by the General Assembly under Article 96(1) of the United Nations Charter. Under Article 65(1) of its Statute

> "the Court may give an advisory opinion on any legal question at the request of whatever body may be authorized by or in accordance with the Charter of the United Nations to make such a request."

1.3 By an Order of 1 February 1995, the Court fixed 20 June 1995 as the time limit within which written statements relating to the question may be submitted to the Court. As a member of the United Nations and a party to the Statute of the Court, Solomon Islands is entitled to appear before the Court in this matter and to submit these Written Observations.

1.4 These Observations are divided into two Parts. Part I addresses the competence of the General Assembly to request the Advisory Opinion and the competence of the Court to render an Advisory Opinion. Part II, which is divided into three Sections, addresses: the legality of the threat or use of nuclear weapons by reference to the rules of international law relating to armed conflicts (A); the rules of international law relating to the protection of human health and the environment and the protection of fundamental human rights (B); and the responsibility of States under international law for violation of these obligations (C). Part III summarises the Conclusions.

1.5 These Written Observations generally follow those submitted by Solomon Islands in respect of the request submitted by the World Health Organization in 1993. The differences relate to the discussion of the General Assembly's competence (*infra* paras. 2.1-2.49), the question of the "threat" of use of nuclear weapons (*infra* paras. 3.1-3.11), and the application of human rights rules to the question (*infra* paras. 4.12-4.35). Solomon Islands reserves the right to take advantage of the opportunity granted by the Court to make Further Written Observations to elaborate on the differences between this request of the General Assembly and that posed by the WHO.

1.6 In summary, for the reasons set out in these Written Observations the Government of Solomon Islands submits that the Court should give an Advisory Opinion that:

(A) the General Assembly is competent to request an Advisory Opinion from the

International Court of Justice on this question, and that the Court is competent to give an Advisory Opinion on the question submitted (paras. 2.1 to 2.49);

(B) any use of a nuclear weapon by a State would violate its obligations under international law as reflected in the rules of international law concerning methods and means of warfare (*jus in bello*) and neutrality, ALTERNATIVELY that the use of nuclear weapons must not violate applicable rules of international law concerning methods and means of warfare (*jus in bello*) and neutrality (paras. 3.1 to 3.104);

(C) any use of a nuclear weapon by a State would violate its obligations under international law as reflected in the rules of international law for the protection of human health and the environment and fundamental human rights, ALTERNATIVELY the use of nuclear weapons must not violate applicable rules of international law for the protection of human health and the environment and fundamental human rights (paras. 4.1 to 4.49);

(D) any use of a nuclear weapon by a State would constitute a crime against humanity, ALTERNATIVELY the use of nuclear weapons in violation of international law constitutes a crime against humanity (para. 3.49); and

(E) any use by a State of a nuclear weapon gives rise to its international responsibility ALTERNATIVELY the violation by a State of these obligations under international law gives rise to its international responsibility (paras. 5.1 to 5.4); and

(F) any threat of use by a State of a nuclear weapon would, by consequence of the illegality of actual use, be prohibited under international law.

(B) Solomon Islands' interest in the question

1.7 Solomon Islands is a non-nuclear State which does not propose to engage in nuclear warfare or other nuclear activity. Nor does Solomon Islands anticipate being a primary target of such activity. It nevertheless has a great interest in the General Assembly's request for an Advisory Opinion from the Court, perceiving as an "innocent bystander" the serious danger to the safety and health of its people, its economy and its fragile environment from the effects of increases of radioactive material in the environment.

1.8 Solomon Islands is a widespread archipelago of mountainous islands and low-lying coral atolls in the south-west Pacific between latitudes 5 and 12 degrees South and longitudes 155 to 177 degrees East (see map after page 5). The island chain is some 1,500 kilometres (900 miles) long, running in a northwesterly/southeasterly direction. The total land area is estimated at 27,556 square kilometres, comprising over 800 islands. They range from the largest (Guadalcanal on which the capital, Honiara, is located) to the very small. The population is about 325,000. The Solomon Islands became an independent State within the Commonwealth on 7 July 1978. It is a member of, *inter alia*, the United Nations, the World Health Organization, and the South Pacific Forum. The Head of State, Queen Elizabeth II, is represented in Solomon Islands by a Governor General. Solomon Islands is a parliamentary democracy and respects fundamental human rights.

1.9 Solomon Islands depends heavily on subsistence agriculture, forestry and fishing. The formal cash economy also depends largely on agriculture, forestry and marine primary production. The tourist industry is developing and makes a significant contribution to the cash economy. One of the major attractions of Solomon Islands and its produce is the relative freedom of its land and sea environment from pollution.

1.10 The impact of any increases in radioactive material in or around the territory of Solomon Islands would have grave consequences for the health of its citizens, for the environment, and for the economy. The fisheries, agricultural and tourism sectors which are the mainstay of the economy would be significantly damaged, if not wiped out by any radiation effects resulting from the use of nuclear weapons which affected the territories. As the Permanent Representative of the Solomon Islands to the United Nations explained on 24th April 1995 at the 1995 Extension and Review Conference of the States Parties to the Treaty on the Non-Proliferation of Nuclear Weapons:

> "Most of the population of the Solomon Islands lives in small coastal villages, and we are reliant on a healthy and flourishing environment for our very survival as a nation. Therefore we are acutely aware of the need to protect and preserve our fragile environment both for now and for future generations.
>
> Eighty per cent of our population use seawater to flavour their food. They drink water from rivers and wells. Our major industry and food source is fishing. If our rain is poisoned by radioactive fallout, we cannot drink the water and our crops will make us sick. If our seas are poisoned, gone is our most bountiful source of food and the salt which we use to flavour our food.
>
> Therefore we must be concerned about ... the very possibility of nuclear war or explosions anywhere in the world."

For these reasons, Solomon Islands takes an active interest in the Advisory Opinion requested by the General Assembly from the International Court.

1.11 As a member of the United Nations, Solomon Islands has consistently supported those General Assembly resolutions (*infra* para. 3.36) which condemn the use of nuclear weapons in any circumstance and restate international law as prohibiting any use of such weapons. As a member of the United Nations Solomon Islands supported the request for an Advisory Opinion by the General Assembly in 1994.

1.12 Solomon Islands' long-standing commitment towards minimising the risks posed by radioactive substances is reflected in its participation in numerous treaties, including the 1968 Treaty on Non-Proliferation of Nuclear Weapons. Earlier this year it strongly supported the indefinite extension of that Treaty in international negotiations and now welcomes that indefinite extension (NPT/CONF.1995/L.6, 9 May 1995), together with the Principles and Objectives for Nuclear Non-Proliferation and Disarmament which were adopted contemporaneously (NPT/CONF.1995/L.5, 9 May 1995). Its commitment towards international humanitarian law is reflected in the fact that it is a party to, *inter alia*, the 1925 Protocol for the Prohibition of the Use in War of Asphyxiating, Poisonous or Other Gases, and of Bacteriological Methods of Warfare; the four 1949 Geneva Conventions for the Protection of War Victims; the 1976 Convention on the Prohibition of Military or Any Other Hostile Use of Environmental Modification Techniques; and the 1966 International Covenant on Economic and Social Rights.

1.13 Solomon Islands' long-standing commitments towards the protection of human health and the environment is also reflected in its active participation in the UN Conference on Environment and Development and the fact that it is a party to many treaties intended to protect the environment. In particular, it is a party, *inter alia*, to the 1958 Convention on the High Seas, the 1972 London Convention on the Prevention of Marine Pollution by Dumping of Wastes and Other Matter, and the 1992 UN Framework Convention on Climate Change.

1.14 Finally, by way of more general observation, Solomon Islands believes that the threat or use of nuclear weapons, especially for hostile purposes, is a matter of global concern which affects all people and all States. This reason alone justifies the submission of these written observations.

***

1.15 On 13th June 1995 France announced a unilateral decision to resume nuclear testing in the Pacific region, on Mururoa Atoll, far from its own metropolitan territory but close to that of Solomon Islands and more than a dozen other Pacific nations. Mururoa Atoll (French Polynesia) is within the nuclear-free zone area established by the South Pacific Nuclear Free Zone Treaty (Rarotonga, 6 August 1985). Solomon Islands has already indicated to France that it considers such tests would be unacceptable and would violate her substantive and procedural obligations under international law, including the obligation to cooperate and consult in decisions which are likely to affect shared natural resources within the Pacific region. Coming shortly after the Parties to the NPT agreed by consensus on a unanimous extension of the 1968 Treaty on the Non-Proliferation of Nuclear Weapons, this unwelcome and surprisingly ill-timed development provides the clearest possible evidence of the reasons for Solomon Islands' strong interest in the Advisory Opinion sought by the General Assembly. It also confirms the importance of the question, the reasons for Solomon Islands' concern, and the need for the Court to affirm the rule of law in international relations. Although this Advisory Opinion does not relate to the testing of nuclear weapons, it does have important implications for the conduct by nuclear-weapon States of nuclear activities very far from their own home territories and populations. The French action shows the casual and arrogant attitude of some nuclear-weapon States with respect to other States. If one State is able to act thus in time of peace, Solomon Islands feels all the more concerned about what could happen in time of war or armed conflict. Solomon Islands hopes that the tests announced last week will not take place either before or after the Court gives this Advisory Opinion.

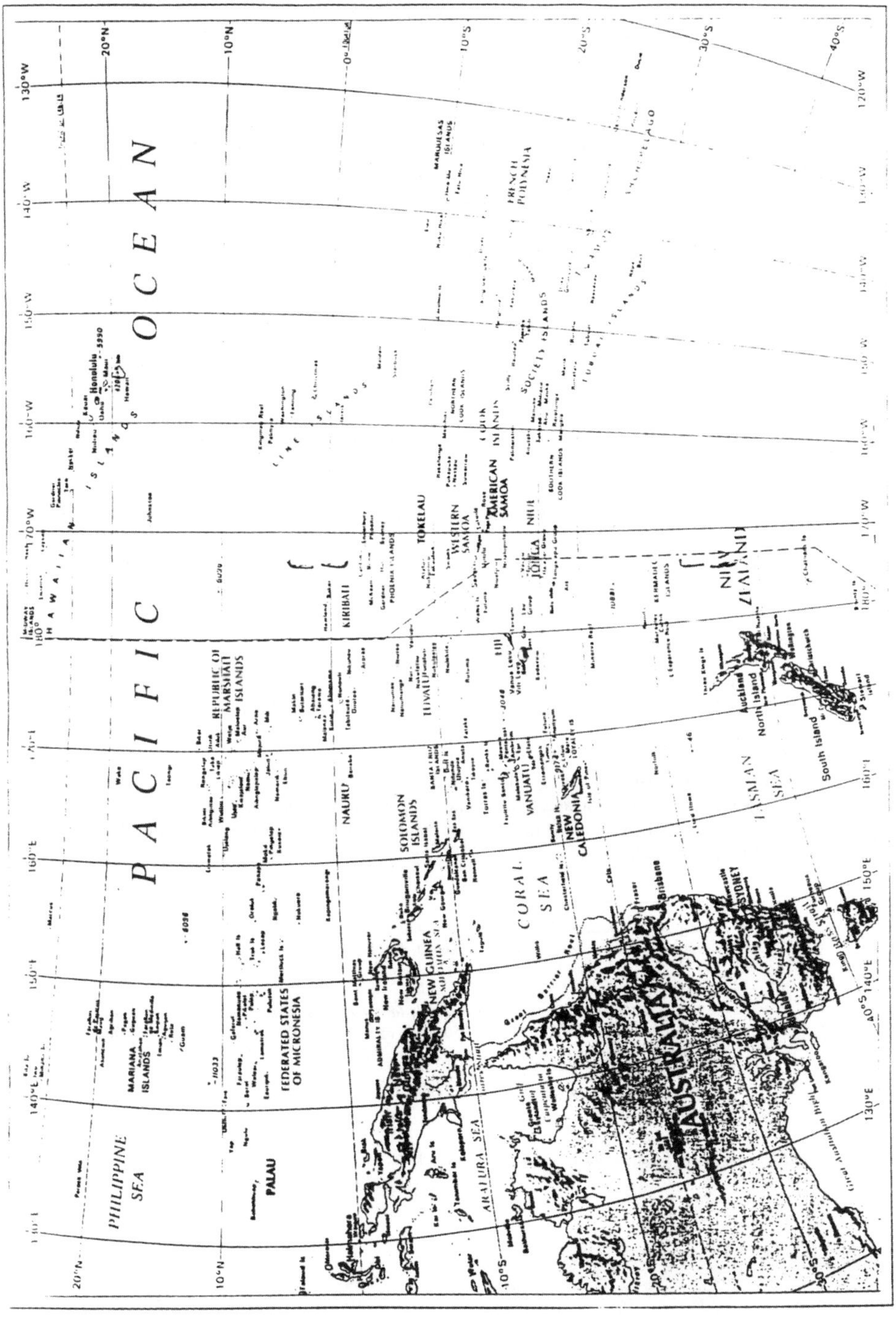
PACIFIC OCEAN
PHILIPPINE SEA
PALAU
MARIANA ISLANDS
FEDERATED STATES OF MICRONESIA
REPUBLIC OF MARSHALL ISLANDS
NAURU
KIRIBATI
SOLOMON ISLANDS
TUVALU
TOKELAU
WESTERN SAMOA
AMERICAN SAMOA
FIJI
TONGA
NIUE
VANUATU
NEW CALEDONIA
CORAL SEA
ARAFURA SEA
TASMAN SEA
AUSTRALIA
NEW GUINEA
NEW ZEALAND
North Island
South Island
Auckland
SYDNEY
Brisbane
COOK ISLANDS
FRENCH POLYNESIA
MARQUESAS ISLANDS
SOCIETY ISLANDS
Honolulu

PART I

THE GENERAL ASSEMBLY IS COMPETENT TO REQUEST AN ADVISORY OPINION FROM THE INTERNATIONAL COURT OF JUSTICE ON THIS QUESTION, AND THE COURT IS COMPETENT TO GIVE AN ADVISORY OPINION ON THE QUESTION SUBMITTED

2.1 Under Article 96(1) of the United Nations Charter the General Assembly may request an Advisory Opinion from the International Court of Justice (ICJ) on any legal question. In accordance with Article 65(1) of the Statute of the ICJ, the Court may give an Advisory Opinion on any legal question at the request of any body authorised by the Charter. The General Assembly has asked the Court for Advisory Opinions on many previous occasions and on a variety of issues. Some of these requests relate to specific disputes or situations,[1] others have involved more general issues.[2] This Court has never refused to give an Advisory Opinion which has been requested by the General Assembly.

2.2 In making the request the General Assembly is acting in the spirit of the recommendation set forth in its resolution 171A (II) of 14 November 1947 on the "Need for greater use by the United Nations and its organs of the International Court of Justice",[3] and in the context of the call by the Secretary-General Boutros-Ghali in 'Agenda for Peace' that "United Nations organs turn to the Court more frequently for advisory opinions".[4]

2.3 Solomon Islands considers that this request by the General Assembly gives the Court an opportunity to clarify an important question of international law, to contribute to the work of the General Assembly (in particular in its efforts to contribute to "systematic and progressive efforts to reduce nuclear weapons globally, with the ultimate goal of eliminating these weapons", NPT/CONF.1995/L.5, para. 4(c)), to emphasize the relevance of international law, and to underscore the international community's commitment to the development and application of the rule of law in international relations.

---

1 See e.g., *Consequences for States of the Continued Presence of South Africa in Namibia (South West Africa) notwithstanding Security Council Resolution 276*, Adv. Op., 21 June 1971, *ICJ Rep. 1971*.

2 See e.g., *Competence of the General Assembly for the Admission of a State to the United Nations*, Adv. Op., 3 March 1950, *ICJ Rep. 1950*; *Reservations to the Convention on the Prevention and Punishment of the crime of Genocide*, Adv. Op., 30 March 1951, *ICJ Rep. 1951*.

3 A/RES/171A (II), UN, *Repertory of the United Nations Organs*, vol. V, Articles 92-111 of the Charter.

4 Boutros Boutros-Ghali, *Agenda for Peace*, 1992, p. 22.

2.4 The General Assembly's request for an Advisory Opinion from the Court relates to a matter which clearly lies within the scope of its activities, and on which it has devoted considerable effort. The Court's Opinion would assist it in the future conduct of its activities.

(A) The General Assembly's request fulfils the conditions of Article 96 of the UN Charter

2.5 Aside from the requirement that the request must relate to a legal question, Article 96 is otherwise unqualified. The General Assembly's power under Article 96 is unlimited as to subject matter. Further, the power is a discretionary one (the General Assembly "may request"). Having decided to make the request the presumption must be that the General Assembly has validly exercised its power in this particular case.

2.6 The Opinion requested is clearly a "legal question".[5] It concerns international legal aspects of the use and threatened use of nuclear weapons. Further, the subject matter of the request is one that the General Assembly has previously addressed and acted upon in the course of its activities (see *infra* Part (B)). Any political character which the question might also have cannot prevent the Court from giving an Opinion.[6] Whilst Article 65 refers to "any legal question", the Court has consistently affirmed that it "cannot attribute a political character to a request which invites it to undertake an essentially judicial task, namely the interpretation of a treaty provision."[7] The concrete legal questions which the Court has been asked falls within the normal exercise of the Court's jurisdiction, and the Court need not consider the motives which inspired the request. On the contrary, the Court has affirmed that:

> "in situations in which political considerations are prominent it may be particularly necessary for an international organization to obtain an advisory opinion from the Court as to the legal principles applicable with respect to the matter under debate, especially when these may include the interpretation of its constitution".[8]

2.6 The General Assembly's request has been made to the Court as the principal judicial organ of the United Nations. The request invites the Court to contribute, through the

---

5 *Conditions of Admission of a State to Membership in the United Nations*, Adv. Op., 28th May 1948, *ICJ Rep.* 1947-1948, p.61.

6 D.W. Bowett, *The Law of International Institutions*, (4th ed., 1982), at p.278.

7 *Certain Expenses of the United Nations*, Adv. Op., 20 July 1962, *ICJ Rep. 1962*, p.155; *Condition of Admission*, Adv. Op., 20 May 1948, *ICJ Rep. 1947-1948*, p.61; *Competence of the General Assembly for the Admission of a State to the United Nations*, Adv. Op., 3 March 1950, *ICJ Rep 1950*, pp.6-7; *Interpretation of the Agreement of 25 March 1951 between the WHO and Egypt*, Adv. Op., 20 December 1980, *ICJ Rep. 1980*, p.87, para. 33.

8 *Interpretation of the Agreement of 25 March 1951 between the WHO and Egypt*, Adv. Op., 20th December 1980, *ICJ Rep. 1980*, p.87, para. 33.

exercise of its advisory role, to the effective functioning of the United Nations system, and in particular that of the General Assembly within that system. In fulfilling its judicial role, including the advisory function, the Court has always adopted an approach which is "*volontairement très libérale*",[9] taking the view that "the reply of the Court, itself an 'organ of the United Nations', represents its participation in the activities of the Organization, and, in principle, should not be refused".[10]

2.7 According to the Court the objective of the General Assembly's request for an Advisory Opinion should be to "enlighten" it on the proper conduct of "its own activities".[11] The Opinion requested is of real importance for the General Assembly in the conduct of its activities relating to the effects of the use of nuclear materials and weapons. The General Assembly takes a similar view to that of the World Health Assembly, which has stated that the "primary prevention of the health hazards of nuclear weapons requires clarity about the status in international law of their use" since "over the last 48 years marked differences of opinion have been expressed by Member States about the lawfulness of the use of nuclear weapons".[12] The General Assembly request seeks to clarify the international legal context in which its activities are conducted, and to provide a proper legal basis for the conduct of its future activities.

2.8 The fact that the question addressed to the International Court arises within the scope of the General Assembly's activities is clear from the United Nations Charter and the Assembly's practice thereunder. Accordingly, the General Assembly is within its rights and entitled to request an Opinion on this particular question from the Court.

---

9 Nguyen Quoc Dinh, Patrick Dailler, Alain Pellet, *Droit international public* (4th ed., 1992), p. 837. See also L. Goodrich, E. Hambro, A. Simons, *Charter of the United Nations, Commentary and Documents* (3rd. ed., rev., 1969) p. 567.

10 *Interpretation of Peace Treaties with Bulgaria, Hungary and Rumania*, interim phase, Adv. Op., 30th March 1950, *ICJ Rep.* 1950, p.71; *Reservations to the Convention for the Prevention and Punishment of the Crime of Genocide*, Adv. Op., 28th May 1951, *ICJ Rep.* 1951, p.19.

11 *Reservations to the Convention on the Prevention and Punishment of the Crime of Genocide*, Adv. Op., 28th May 1951, *ICJ Rep.* 1951 p.19; *Legal Consequences for States of the Continued Presence of South Africa in Namibia (South West Africa) notwithstanding Security Council Resolution 276* (1970), Adv. Op., 21st June 1971, *ICJ Rep.* 1971 p.24, para. 32; *Western Sahara*, Adv. Op., 16th October 1975, *ICJ Rep.* 1975 p.24, para. 31; *Applicability of Article VI, Section 22, of the Convention on the Privileges and Immunities of the United Nations*, Adv. Op., 15th December 1989, *ICJ Rep.* 1989, p.189, para. 31.

12 Resolution of the World Health Assembly (WHA) 46.40 of 14 May 1993.

(B) The General Assembly is acting in accordance with the UN Charter.

2.9 The question posed by the General Assembly clearly falls within the objective and functions of the Charter of the United Nations, which embraces a broad scope of activities relating to international peace and security, including the legality of the use or threatened use of force.

2.10 The Preamble to the Charter of the United Nations expresses the determination "to save succeeding generations from the scourge of war". Article 2(4) states that "all Members shall refrain in their international relations from the threat or use of force against the territorial integrity or political independence of any state, or in any other manner inconsistent with the Purposes of the United Nations". Those purposes are clearly expressed in the Charter. Article 26 refers to the "establishment and maintenance of international peace and security with the least diversion for armaments of the world's human and economic resources". Article 55 calls for the promotion *inter alia* of "higher standards of living, full employment, and conditions of economic and social progress and development" with a view to "the creation of conditions of stability and well-being". Proposals relating to nuclear arms control and disarmament have been made and discussed within the framework of the United Nations since its establishment. Consequently, the role and involvement of the General Assembly, one of the main political organs of the United Nations, in addressing legal aspects of the use of nuclear weapons, including nuclear disarmament issues, can be traced back to the very first decade of the existence of the United Nations.[13]

2.11 The specific powers of the General Assembly are broadly stated in Chapter IV of the Charter and include the power to "discuss any questions or any matter within the scope of the present Charter..." (Article 10). In addition, Article 11 of the Charter authorises the General Assembly to:

> (a) consider general principles of co-operation in the maintenance of international peace and security, including the principles governing disarmament (Article 11 (1)); and
>
> (b) to discuss any questions relating to the maintenance of international peace and security brought before it by any Member of the United Nations (Article 11 (2)).

Consequently, issues pertaining to the legality of the use of nuclear weapons falls squarely within the General Assembly's express powers as provided by its constituent document.

---

13 In 1950, the General Assembly adopted resolution 380 (V) determining, inter alia, to "reduce to a minimum the diversion for armaments of its human resources for the general welfare, with due regard to the needs of the underdeveloped areas of the world"

(C) The practice of the General Assembly confirms its competence over matters relating to the legality of the use of nuclear weapons

2.12 Consideration of the practice of the General Assembly since its establishment confirms that issues relating to the use of nuclear weapons, including legality, lie within its scope of activity and that the General Assembly is competent to request an Opinion from the Court on the legality of the use of nuclear weapons.

2.13 The practice of the General Assembly has long been concerned with the legality of the use of nuclear weapons. The extent to which the General Assembly is involved with the subject of nuclear weapons, their effects and legal status is illustrated *inter alia* by reference to the adoption by the General Assembly of resolutions on the legality of the use of nuclear weapons (a), as well as the General Assembly's Special Sessions devoted to the issue of disarmament (b) and the commissioning of various studies on the effects of the use of nuclear weapons (c).

(a) General Assembly Resolutions on the legality of the use of nuclear weapons and related issues

2.14 In its activities since the late 1950's the General Assembly has been consistently concerned with legal aspects of nuclear weapons. It has addressed *inter alia* the legality of their use, treaty arrangements for nuclear disarmament, the legality of testing, and the creation of nuclear-free zones in international law. In the context of these and other activities the General Assembly's competence over the subject matter of the question it has sent to the Court for an Advisory Opinion cannot reasonably be challenged.

2.15 The General Assembly has specifically addressed the issue of the legality of the use of nuclear weapons since at least 1961, adopting many resolutions which have affirmed that any use of nuclear weapons would be a violation of the Charter of the United Nations, a crime against humanity and contrary to the principles of international law. General Assembly resolution 1653 (XVI) of 24 November 1961 was the first among many other General Assembly resolutions which declared:

> "(a) The use of nuclear and thermo-nuclear weapons is contrary to the spirit, letter and aims of the United Nations and, as such, a direct violation of the Charter of the United Nations;
>
> (b) The use of nuclear and thermo-nuclear weapons would exceed even the scope of war and cause indiscriminate suffering and destruction to mankind and civilization and, as such, is contrary to the rules of international law and to the laws of humanity;
>
> (c) The use of nuclear and thermo-nuclear weapons is a war directed not against an enemy or enemies alone but also against mankind in general, since the peoples of the world not involved in such a war will be subjected to all evils generated by the use of such weapons;
>
> (d) Any State using nuclear and thermo-nuclear weapons is to be considered as violating the Charter of the United Nations, as acting contrary to the laws of humanity and as committing a crime against

mankind and civilization;"[14]

Since 1961 the General Assembly has addressed the issue almost annually.

2.16 Since 1978 the General Assembly has *annually* requested the Conference on Disarmament to commence negotiations on a complete ban on the use of nuclear weapons, providing a four Article draft convention prohibiting the "use or threat of use of nuclear weapons under any circumstances" (Article 1, draft General Assembly convention on the prohibition of the use of nuclear weapons).[15]

2.17 In 1981 the General Assembly proclaimed that :

> "1. States and statesmen that resort first to the use of nuclear weapons will be committing the gravest crime against humanity."[16]

And in 1983 it "*Resolutely, unconditionally and for all time condemns* nuclear war as being contrary to human conscience and reason, as the most monstrous crime against peoples and as a violation of the most foremost human right- the right to life".[17]

2.18 The General Assembly has long sought to adopt special legal measures to protect non-nuclear-weapon States from the threat or use of nuclear weapons. It has consistently recommended that the Conference on Disarmament "should actively continue intensive negotiations with a view to reaching early agreement and concluding effective international arrangements to assure non-nuclear-weapon States against the use or threat of use of nuclear weapons".[18]

2.19 The General Assembly has also addressed legal aspects of nuclear weapons by laying the groundwork for nuclear arms control agreements. As early as 1959 the General Assembly proposed that the Ten-Nation Disarmament Committee consider the feasibility of an international agreement by which the nuclear Powers would not hand over control of those weapons to other Powers, and non-nuclear weapons would not

---

14 A/RES/1653 (XVI) of 24 November 1961. See also GA resolutions: 2936 (XXVII) of 29 November 1972, 33/71 B of 14 December 1978, 34/83 G of 11 December 1979, 35/152 D of 12 December 1980, 36/92 I of 9 December 1981, 44/117 C of 15 December 1989, 45/59 B of 4 December 1990 and 46/37 of 6 December 1991.

15 A/RES/37/100 C of 13 December 1982 (annex of draft convention on the Prohibition of the Use of Nuclear Weapons).

16 A/RES/36/100 of 9 December 1981 (Declaration on the Prevention of Nuclear Catastrophe).

17 A/RES/38/75, Condemnation of nuclear war, of 15 December 1983.

18 A/RES/49/73 of 15 December 1994.

manufacture such weapons.[19] This was the first in a series of General Assembly resolutions which led to the adoption in 1968 of the Treaty on the Non-Proliferation of Nuclear Weapons (NPT).[20] The Treaty itself incorporates the five principles enunciated in General Assembly resolution 2028 (XX).[21] General Assembly resolutions also note the establishment of Preparatory Committees for each Conference of the Parties to the NPT.[22]

2.20 Other international treaties on nuclear weapons have been negotiated as a result of General Assembly resolution initiatives.[23] By way of example, the Treaty Banning Nuclear Weapon Tests in the Atmosphere, in Outer Space and under Water (Partial Test-Ban Treaty)[24] was preceded by many General Assembly resolutions on the subject.[25] The Partial Test-Ban Treaty closely followed the principles laid down in the Declaration of Legal Principles Governing the Activities of States in the Exploration and Use of Outer Space, in Assembly Resolution 1962 (XVIII),[26] together with the associated principles laid down in resolution 1884 (XVIII).[27] In

---

19 A/RES/1380 (XIV) of 20 November 1959.

20 See A/RES/1576 (XV) of 20 December 1960, A/RES/1664 (XVI) of 4 December 1961, A/RES/1665 (XVI) of 4 December 1961, A/RES/2149 (XXI) of 4 November 1966, A/RES/2153 A (XXI) of 17 November 1966, A/RES/2346 A (XXII) of 19 December 1967 and A/RES/2373 (XXII) of 12 June 1968 (with text of Treaty annexed)

21 General Assembly resolution calling upon the Conference of the Eighteen-Nation Committee on Disarmament to give urgent consideration to the negotiation of an international treaty to prevent proliferation of nuclear weapons, based on five main principles. A/RES/2028 (XX), 19 November 1965.

22 A/RES/3184 B (XXVIII) of 18 December 1973, A/RES/33/57 of 14 December 1978, A/RES/38/74 of 15 December 1983, A/RES/43/82 of 7 December 1988, A/RES/47/52 A of 9 December 1992.

23 1967 Treaty on Principles Governing the Activities of States in the Exploration and use of Outer Space, including the Moon and other Celestial Bodies, in force 10 October 1967, A/RES/2222(XXI) of 19 December 1966, annex; 1979 Agreement Governing the Activities of States on the Moon and other Celestial Bodies, in force 11 July 1984, A/RES/34/68 of 1979, annex.

24 The Treaty Banning Nuclear Weapon Tests in the Atmosphere, in Outer Space and under Water, also known as the Partial Test Ban Treaty was signed on 5 August 1963 and entered into force on 10 October 1963; UN Treaty Series vol. 480, No. I-6964.

25 See e.g. GA/RES/1649 (XVI) of 8 November 1961 on "The urgent need for a treaty to ban nuclear weapons tests under effective international control" and GA/RES/1762 (XVII) of 6 November 1962 on "The urgent need for suspension of nuclear and thermonuclear tests".

26 A/RES/1962 (XVIII) of 13 December 1963.

27 A/RES/1884 (XVIII) of 17 October 1963.

1993, the Conference on Disarmament gave its Ad Hoc Committee on a Nuclear Test Ban a mandate to negotiate a comprehensive test-ban treaty. The General Assembly has adopted numerous resolutions commending the efforts of the Conference on Disarmament on its negotiations on a Comprehensive Test-Ban Treaty and urged it to "proceed intensively" in its negotiation of a "universal and internationally and effectively verifiable treaty".[28] The General Assembly has stressed that pending the conclusion of such a ban, nuclear weapons States should "suspend all nuclear-test explosions through an agreed moratorium or unilateral moratorium".[29]

2.21 The General Assembly has also long sought to promote nuclear-weapon-free zones, defining the concept in resolution 3472 B (XXX) of 11 December 1975. Two regional groups have already concluded treaties: The Treaty for the Prohibition of Nuclear Weapons in Latin America and the Caribbean (Treaty of Tlatelolco)[30] and the South Pacific Nuclear Free Zone Treaty (Treaty of Rarotonga), to which Solomon Islands is a party.[31] African States are in the process of finalizing a draft treaty,[32] and proposals have been made by the General Assembly for such zones in South Asia[33] and in the Middle East.[34]

2.22 The General Assembly's request for an Advisory Opinion follows on from other recent efforts aimed at addressing legal aspects of nuclear weapons. In 1993 it adopted a unanimous resolution recommending the negotiation of a non-discriminatory, multilateral and effectively verifiable treaty banning the production of fissile material for nuclear weapons or other nuclear explosive devices.[35]

---

28 A/RES/48/70 of 16 December 1993. See also GA resolutions: A/RES/44/106 of 15 December 1989, 45/50 of 4 December 1990, A/RES/46/28 of 6 December 1991, A/RES/47/46 of 9 December 1992, A/RES/48/69 of 16 December 1993 and A/RES/49/69 of 9 January 1995.

29 A/RES/48/69 of 16 December 1993 and A/RES/49/69 of 9 January 1995.

30 The Treaty for the Prohibition of Nuclear Weapons in Latin America and the Caribbean, also known as the Treaty of Tlatelolco, was signed at Mexico City on 14 February 1967 and entered into force on 22 April 1968; UN Treaty Series, vol. 634, No. 9068.

31 The South Pacific Nuclear Free Zone Treaty, Rarotonga, Cook Islands, 6 August 1985, in force 11 December 1986; CD/633 and Corr.1.

32 Under the terms of General Assembly resolution 47/76 of 15 December 1992 the Secretary General convened a Group of Experts to draw up a draft treaty on the denuclearization of Africa. Most recently, at its forty-ninth session, the General Assembly adopted a resolution (49/138) that encouraged African States to continue their efforts towards finalizing the draft and requested that the text of the treaty be submitted to the General Assembly at its next session.

33 A/RES/48/72 of 16 December 1993.

34 A/RES/48/71 of 16 December 1993.

35 Resolution 48/75 L of 16 December 1993.

2.23 The above examples illustrate non-exhaustively the General Assembly's practice in relation to international legal aspects of nuclear weapons, including their use or threatened use. In the context of this practice there can be no doubts as to the General Assembly's competence to ask for the Advisory Opinion it has requested from the Court.

(b) General Assembly Special Sessions on nuclear weapons under the aegis of disarmament

2.24 In addition to consideration of legal issues the General Assembly has addressed political aspects, convening four special sessions on disarmament. The Programme of Action of the first such special session, held in 1978,[36] noted inter alia that:-

> 47.Nuclear weapons pose the greatest threat to mankind and to the survival of civilization. It is essential to halt and reverse the nuclear arms race in all its aspects in order to avert the danger of war involving nuclear weapons. The ultimate goal in this context is the complete elimination of nuclear weapons.
>
> ....
>
> 57.Pending the achievement of this goal, for which negotiations should be vigorously pursued, and bearing in mind the devastating results which nuclear war would have on belligerents and non-belligerents alike, the nuclear-weapon States have special responsibilities to undertake measures aimed at preventing the outbreak of nuclear war.
>
> 58....All States should actively participate in efforts to bring about conditions in international relations among States in which a code of peaceful conduct of nations in international affairs could be agreed and which preclude the use or threat of use of nuclear weapons."

2.25 In 1982, the General Assembly convened its second special session devoted to disarmament, and in 1988 its third. At its 90th plenary meeting on 15 December 1994, the General Assembly decided to convene, possibly in 1997, the fourth special session devoted to disarmament.[37]

(c) General Assembly studies on nuclear weapons

2.26 Finally, the General Assembly's competence is reflected in its efforts to pursue further knowledge and understanding of the effects of the use of nuclear weapons. On the recommendation of General Assembly resolutions a number of United Nations studies on nuclear weapons have been undertaken by Groups of Experts under the direction of the Secretary-General. By its resolution 33/91 D of 16 December 1978, the General Assembly requested the carrying out of the first Comprehensive Study on nuclear weapons. That study was published by the Secretary-General in September

[36] The General Assembly's Tenth Special Session devoted to Disarmament was held at New York from 23 May to 1 July 1978: GA Res. S-10/2 of 30 June 1978.

[37] A/RES/49/75.I of 15 December 1994.

1980.[38]

2.27 By its resolution 43/75 N of 7 December 1988, the General Assembly requested the Secretary-General to conduct an update of the Comprehensive Study on Nuclear Weapons that would "provide factual and up-to-date information on and would pay regard to the political, legal and security aspects of: (a) nuclear arsenals and pertinent technological developments; (b) doctrines concerning nuclear weapons; (c) efforts to reduce nuclear weapons; (d) physical, environmental, medical and other effects of use of nuclear weapons and nuclear testing; (e) efforts to achieve a comprehensive nuclear-test ban; (f) efforts to prevent the use of nuclear weapons and their horizontal and vertical proliferation; (g) the question of verification of compliance with nuclear-arms limitation agreements." That study was published in September 1990.[39]

2.28 Other United Nations Expert studies on nuclear weapons include, a Comprehensive Nuclear Test Ban study (May 1980) which was based on General Assembly resolution 34/422 of December 1979. Its contents included a section on the negotiations leading to the partial test ban treaty, on the Nuclear Non-Proliferation Treaty and on negotiations on a comprehensive test ban.[40] A study was also conducted on the Implementation of the Declaration on the Denuclearization of Africa, based on General Assembly resolution 34/76 B of December 1979. Amongst other matters it considered South Africa's nuclear weapon capability.[41]

(D) The Court should give the Advisory Opinion requested by the General Assembly

2.29 As is clear from the preceding discussion the General Assembly is entitled to request an Advisory Opinion from the Court. In conformity with Article 65 of its Statute, however, the Court is not required to reply to the question asked. The Court has frequently in the past invoked the "permissive" formulation of Article 65 to conclude that "compelling reasons" could lead it to refuse to give an Advisory Opinion (see. *infra* para. 2.34) In fact, the Court has only relied on its right to refuse a request on one occasion. This was in 1923 in the *Eastern Carelia* case where the Council of the League of Nations had asked the Court if the Treaty between Finland and Russia of 1920 and its Annex relating to the recognition of the autonomy of Eastern Carelia, a Russian region, was binding on Russia. The Permanent Court of International

---

38 Comprehensive Study on Nuclear Weapons: Report of the UN Secretary-General, *UN Doc. A/45/392*, 12 September 1980.

39 Comprehensive Study on Nuclear Weapons: Report of the UN Secretary-General, *UN Doc. A/45/373*, 18 September 1990.

40 A/35/257 of May 1980.

41 A/35/402 of September 1980.

Justice replied that the request encompassed a dispute between Finland and Russia, that Russia was not a member of the League of Nations, that it had not recognised the competence of the Court and that it refused to participate in the Court's procedure. According to the Court, these were "peremptory reasons" justifying its refusal to give an Advisory Opinion.[42]

2.30 That was the only occasion on which the Court relied upon the exception, despite the frequent requests by States, since 1949, that it should not on a particular matter give an Advisory Opinion. Subsequently, in accordance with a well-established jurisprudence, the Court has **never refused** to give an Advisory Opinion on the question posed. This has occurred (a) for reasons of principle, and (b) on the basis of certain criteria which have been fulfilled. Additionally, the fact that the WHO has made a similar request should not prevent the Court from giving an Advisory Opinion to the General Assembly (c).

(a) *The reasons of principle which have led the Court to decide to give an Advisory Opinion*

2.31 The reasons of principle which have led the Court to agree to give an Advisory Opinion are the following:

(i) the Opinion is not binding; and

(ii) the Court has adopted a principle of not refusing to give an Advisory Opinion

(i) *The Opinion is not binding*

2.32 In a case concerning the *Interpretation of Peace Treaties* (1950) the Court emphasised that given the non-binding character of the Opinion which it was giving - which flowed from "the scope attributed by the Charter and by the Statute of the Court to an Advisory Opinion"[43]- no State can oppose the giving of the Opinion:

> "The Court's reply is only of an advisory character: as such, it has no binding force. It follows that no State, whether a member of the United Nations or not, can prevent the giving of an Advisory Opinion which the United Nations considers to be desirable in order to obtain enlightenment as to the course of action it should take."[44]

---

42 PCIJ, opinion of 23 July 1928, *Series B No. 5*, pp.27-28.

43 *Judgment of the Administrative Tribunal of the I.L.O upon Complaints made against the UNESCO*, Adv. Op., 23 October 1956, *ICJ Rep. 1956*, p.84.

44 *Interpretation of Peace Treaties*, Adv. Op., 30 March 1950, *ICJ Rep. 1950*, p.71; *Applicability of Art. VI, Sect. 22 of the Convention on the Privileges and Immunities of the UN (Mazilu Case)*, Adv. Op., 15 December 1989, *ICJ Rep. 1989*, pp.188-189.

2.33 The same principle governs the present request by the General Assembly. Any Opinion granted by the Court would be merely advisory in nature and will not be binding on State Members of the United Nations. Accordingly, the giving of the Opinion does not depend on the consent of any particular State or group of States.[45]

(ii) *In principle the Court does not refuse to give Advisory Opinions*

2.34 If the "permissive" provisions in Article 65 implies that the Court is entitled in theory to refuse to give an Advisory Opinion, it has in practice adopted an approach of replying positively to all requests for Advisory Opinions which are addressed to it where its response is intended to, and will, enlighten in legal terms the organ which has made the request. As the Court stated in the *Interpretation of Peace Treaties* case (1950):

> "The Court's Opinion is given not to the States, but to the organ which is entitled to request it; the reply of the Court, itself an 'organ of the United Nations', represents its participation in the activities of the Organization, and, in principle, should not be refused"[46]

2.35 *Mutatis mutandis*, this principle applies to the General Assembly's request. The General Assembly has considered the issue of the legality of the use of nuclear weapons almost from its creation (see *supra* paras 2.14-2.28). It is therefore indispensable for the conduct of its activities now and in the future in this field for the General Assembly to be enlightened on the question of the legality of the use or threat of use of nuclear weapons (see *infra* para. 2.42-2.45).

(b) *Criteria which need to be satisfied in order for the Court to reply to a request for an Advisory Opinion*

2.36 In order for the Court to give an Advisory Opinion, it is necessary that the request fulfils the following criteria:

(i) the Opinion should not relate to a dispute in which one of the parties is a total stranger to the Court;

(ii) the Court is acting within its judicial function;

---

45 *Id.*

46 *Interpretation of Peace Treaties (First Phase)*, Adv. Op., 30 March 1950, *ICJ Rep. 1950*, p.71-72; see also *Reservations to the Convention on the Prevention and Punishment of the Crime of Genocide, ICJ Rep. 1950, p.19; Judgements of the Adm. Trib. of ILO upon Complaints made against the UNESCO*, Adv. Op., 23 October 1956, *ICJ Rep. 1956*, p.86; *Certain Expenses of the UN*, Adv. Op. 20 July 1962, *ICJ Rep. 1962*, p.155.; *Applicability of Art. VI, Sec. 22 of the Convention on the Privileges and Immunities of the UN*, Adv. Op., 15 December 1989, *ICJ Rep. 1989*, pp.188-189.

(iii) the Opinion has a practical significance.

As will be shown, the present request on the legality of the use or threatened use of nuclear weapons by the General Assembly fulfils these criteria. The Court should not refuse to reply to the General Assembly's request for an Advisory Opinion.

(i) *The Opinion does not relate to a dispute in which one of the parties is a total stranger to the Court*

2.37 In the *Eastern Carelia* case (1923), the Court said that it could not, in the guise of an Advisory Opinion, deal with a dispute between two States where one had not recognised its competence, had refused to participate in the procedure and was not even a member of the organisation which had asked the Opinion.[47] Since then, the Court has on numerous occasions declared that only "compelling reasons" would lead it to refuse to reply to a request for an Opinion.[48] The "compelling reasons" envisaged by the Court have always been limited to the situation that the Court has been called upon to address a dispute in respect of which one of the parties thereto had not accepted the competence of the Court. In the *Western Sahara* case (1975), the Court said:

> "In certain circumstances, therefore, the lack of consent of an interested State may render the giving of an advisory opinion incompatible with the Court's judicial character. An instance of this would be when the circumstances disclose that to give a reply would have the effect of circumventing the principle that a State is not obliged to allow its disputes to be submitted to judicial settlement without its consent. If such a situation should arise, the powers of the Court under the discretion given to it by Art. 65, para. 1, of the Statute would afford sufficient legal means to ensure respect for the fundamental principle of consent to jurisdiction."[49]

2.38 Admittedly, in the present case, the question asked by the General Assembly does relate to an important controversy between States. However, the Court itself has recognised that underlying each request for an Advisory Opinion there will always be a controversy which has led the organisation to make the request:

> "Differences of view amongst States on legal issues have existed in practically every advisory proceeding; if all were agreed, the need to resort to the Court for advice would not arise."[50]

---

47 *Eastern Carelia* case, *PCIJ*, Opinion of 23 July 1928, Series B, No. 5, pp.27-28.

48 *Interpretation of Peace Treaties case*, Adv. Op., 30 March 1950, *ICJ Rep. 1950*; p.72; *Judgment of the Administrative Tribunal of the ILO upon Complaints made against the UNESCO*, Adv. Op., 23 October 1956, *ICJ Rep. 1956*, p.86; *Certain Expenses of the UN*, Adv. Op., 20 July 1962, *ICJ Rep. 1962*, p.155; *Legal Consequences for States of the Continued Presence of South Africa in Namibia (South West Africa) notwithstanding Security Council Resolution 276*, Adv. Op., 21 June 1971, *ICJ Rep. 1971*, p.27.

49 *Western Sahara*, Adv. Op., 16 October 1975, *ICJ Rep. 1975*, p.25.

50 *Namibia Case*, Adv. Op., 16 October 1975, *ICJ Rep. 1975*, p.25.

The mere existence of the controversy does not mean that a contentious dispute exists between the parties. In giving the Opinion on the legality of the use or threat of use of nuclear weapons, the Court would not in any event be addressing any dispute within the meaning of Article 36 of the Statute of the Court, but it would be helping to resolve a controversy.

(ii) *The Court, in giving its opinion, will remain within its judicial function*

2.39 The Court has frequently emphasised that as "the principal judicial organ"[51] it should remain faithful to its character:

> "There are certain limits, however, to the Court's duty to reply to a Request for an Advisory Opinion. It is not merely an 'organ of the United Nations', it is essentially the 'principal judicial organ' of the Organization (Art.92 of the Charter and Art. 1 of the Statute)"[52]

By lending its assistance in the solution of a problem confronting the General Assembly, the Court would be discharging its functions as the principal judicial organ of the United Nations. Moreover, as frequently recalled the Advisory Opinion requested of the Court must relate to a **legal** question:

> "[..] in accordance with Art. 65 of its Statute, the Court can give an advisory opinion only on a legal question. If a question is not a legal one, the Court has no discretion in the matter; it must decline to give the opinion requested."[53]

2.40 The fact that the question has political implications is not in itself an obstacle to the giving of an Advisory Opinion: where the Court has been asked to characterise a particular form of behaviour with respect to the provisions of treaty and customary law, the Court is performing a task which is essentially legal:

> "It has been argued that the question put to the Court is intertwined with political questions, and that for this reason the Court should refuse to give an opinion. It is true that most interpretations of the Charter of the United Nations will have political significance, great or small. In the nature of things it could not be otherwise. The Court, however, cannot attribute a political character to a request which invites it to undertake an essentially judicial task, namely, the interpretation of a treaty provision."[54]

In the present case, the question asked relates to the compatibility of the use or threat

---

51 *Interpretation of Peace Treaties*, Adv. Op., 30 March 1950, *ICJ Rep.* 1950, p.71.

52 *Id.*, *Judgments of the Adm. Trib. of ILO upon Complaints made against the UNESCO*, Adv. Op., 23 October 1956, *ICJ Rep.* 1956, p.84.

53 *Certain Expenses of the UN*, Adv. Op., 20 July 1962, *ICJ Rep.* 1962, p.155.

54 *Certain Expenses of the UN*, Adv. Op., 20 July 1962, *ICJ Rep.* 1962, p.155.

of use of nuclear weapons with international law. In asking the Court to characterise the behaviour (the use or threat of use of nuclear weapons) in the context of rules of positive law, the General Assembly is inviting the Court, in effect, to carry out a task which falls within the normal exercise of its judicial powers, namely "an interpretative function which falls within the normal exercise of its judicial powers".[55]

(iii) *The Opinion will have a practical effect*

2.41 The Court does not give Advisory Opinions as an end in themselves: its opinions must have practical consequences, for example by helping a requesting organisation to take decisions which will affect its activities on the basis of the answers given to the question posed to the Court. In the *Western Sahara* case (1975), the Court said:

> "In general, an opinion given by the Court in the present proceedings will furnish the General Assembly with elements of a legal character relevant to its further treatment of the decolonization of Western Sahara.
> 73. In any event, to what extent or degree its opinion will have an impact on the action of the General Assembly is not for the Court to decide. The function of the Court is to give an opinion based on law, once it had come to the conclusion that the questions put to it are relevant and have a practical and contemporary effect and, consequently, are not devoid of object or purpose."[56]

2.42 In sum, the choices made and the acts taken by the General Assembly will depend directly on its knowing whether the use of nuclear weapons is legal or illegal. Even if this has considerable political implications, it is nevertheless fundamentally a legal matter, and the Court's reply would, in concrete terms, enlighten the General Assembly in the conduct of its activities. In the light of the Court's prior jurisprudence, there are no legal grounds for the Court to decline to give an Advisory Opinion on the question submitted by the General Assembly. Moreover, world public opinion would find it difficult to understand why the Court should refuse to answer an important legal question which has dominated international relations for more than half a century, particularly where the question has such profound implications for the future of humanity.

2.43 Assuming that the Court was of the opinion that under certain conditions the use of nuclear weapons could be compatible with international law - *quod non* (see *infra* paras. 3.43 *et seq.*) - the General Assembly would then be entitled to take specific *a priori* measures to seek to prevent and reduce the chances of a nuclear conflict from arising. It could aim to further strengthen existing international arrangements relating to *inter alia* nuclear-free zones and the guarantees given to non-nuclear-weapon

[55] *Condition of Admission of a State to Membership in the United Nations (Art. 4 of the Charter)*, Adv. Op., 20 July 1948, *ICJ Rep. 1947-1948*, p.61; *Certain Expenses of the UN*, Adv. Op., 20 July 1962, *ICJ Rep.* 1962, p.156.

[56] *Western Sahara*, Adv. Op., 16 October 1975, *ICJ Rep.* 1975, p.37.

States. It might also decide to strengthen its efforts in relation to *a posteriori* measures to attend to the needs of the victims of any such conflict. Even if, since 1961, a great majority of States have taken the view that any use of nuclear weapons would be illegal under international law (*infra* paras. 3.36 *et seq.*), there remains a minority which takes the opposite view. It is clearly necessary to limit the number of victims and to limit the suffering of those who are injured as a result. In conjunction with the Specialised Agencies of the United Nations such as the WHO and other international organisations, the General Assembly would need to redouble its efforts to determine what level of result radiation in foodstuffs, if any, would be safe for human consumption, and what level of radiation in a given environment, if any, could be safe enough to allow human access to such areas.

2.44 Specifically in regard to preventive measures, the General Assembly working alongside its Specialised Agencies, in particular the WHO would, for example, be justified in recommending the development of a programme for the construction of shelters, including basic standards for their construction and the availability of foodstuffs for survivors and necessary survival equipment. The General Assembly would be entitled to recommend also that the WHO develop special programmes of preparation and education for nuclear war which might be made available in schools and for the public at large. It could equally recommend the training of appropriate health services and civil protection and with regard to assistance to the injured, to give serious study to the specific needs of hospitals, and to consider the means of making appropriate treatment available to large numbers of victims of burns of radiation. Either way there will be need to take into account the particular conditions of each State, including its health and economic conditions. These new aid programmes might be studied or established with a view to providing developing countries with the necessary means of protecting itself against the consequences of a nuclear conflict. For a small island country with a limited territory and financial resources the active role of the General Assembly and its Specialised Agencies, in both a preventive and curative capacity, would be indispensable to its survival.

2.45 If, on the other hand, the Court decides that there are no circumstances in which the threat or use of nuclear weapons would be legal under international law, as Solomon Islands believes is the case, then the General Assembly would be entitled to limit its policy to actions taken to prevent not the effects of a nuclear war but the very use or threatened use of nuclear weapons. In particular, the General Assembly would be assisted in its efforts to contribute to the recent decision of the Review and Extension Conference of the Parties to the NPT to eliminate all nuclear weapons and define the terms of "effective international control" pertaining to that objective (see NPT/CONF.1995/L.5, para. 4(c)).

2.46 Whether legal or illegal, the Opinion of the Court, and the conclusion it reaches, will determine the direction which the General Assembly takes in action and in policy in the coming years in this area.

(c) *The WHO request does not prevent the Court from giving the Advisory Opinion requested by the General Assembly*

2.47 The WHO has made a similar, but not identical, request to that made by the General Assembly. Solomon Islands considers that it would be appropriate for the Court to give both organizations the Advisory Opinions they have requested, since this is an area in which there are clearly overlapping competences. Although the competence of the WHO is narrower, the General Assembly does not have exclusive competence. This is confirmed by the fact that the General Assembly has not expressed to the WHO or to the Court any disagreement with the WHO request, whether in its terms or in the fact of its having been made.

2.48 The fact that the WHO has made its own request does not in any way prejudice the General Assembly's request. If the Court decides to proceed to give an Opinion to the WHO then its additional consideration of the General Assembly request would, presumably, build on that earlier Opinion. If, on the other hand, the Court decides not to give an Opinion to the WHO (some States submitting Written Observations in respect of the WHO request have argued that the question should have been requested by the General Assembly) then it would still be free to address the General Assembly's request. Either way, Solomon Islands does not see any incompatibility between the two requests.

(E) **Conclusion**

2.49 For the reasons set out above it is submitted that the Court should give an Opinion on the basis that the General Assembly is competent to request an Advisory Opinion from the Court on this subject, and the Court is competent to give, and should give, an Advisory Opinion on the question submitted.

PART II

THE LEGALITY OF THE THREAT OR USE OF NUCLEAR WEAPONS

3.1 Part II of these Written Observations of Law is divided into three Sections. Section A addresses the legality of the threat or use of nuclear weapons by reference to the applicable rules of international law of armed conflict (paras. 3.2-3.104). Section B addresses the legality of the threat or use of nuclear weapons by reference to the rules of international law for the protection of human health and the environment and of fundamental human rights (paras. 4.1-4.49). Section C briefly addresses the responsibility of a State for the consequences of a violation of its obligations as set forth in Sections A and B (paras. 5.1-5.4).

SECTION A

The threat or use of nuclear weapons and the international law of armed conflict

3.2 Before addressing the substantive law it is appropriate to consider the meaning of the term "threat" as used in the General Assembly's request. The circumstances in which the "use" of a nuclear weapons will have occurred are self-evident.

(A) The meaning of threat

3.3 The General Assembly's request asks "Is the *threat* or use of nuclear weapons in any circumstances permitted under international law?". In raising the issue of threat two further questions need to be addressed:

— at what point has a "threat" been made? and

— when would such a "threat" be unlawful?

3.4 There is no generally accepted definition of "threat" in international law. It has been defined as a "communicated intent to inflict physical or other harm on any person or on properties".[57] If States manufacture or possess nuclear weapons it is presumably in the expectation that they could, in certain circumstances, be used. Since the use of nuclear weapons is intended to "harm" rather than to do some good, it might therefore be said that mere possession constitutes a form of "threat". State practice indicates that this is not the case. For half a century a small group of States have possessed nuclear weapons, and such possession has never been considered by the rest

[57] Le Petit Robert, Dictionnaire alphabétique et analogique de la langue française, Paris, Robert, 1973.

of the international community to be a "threat" which is contrary to international law. When the USSR sought to deploy nuclear weapons in 1962 in Cuba, the United States considered this to be a "threat" of the use of force within the meaning of Article 2(4) of the United Nations Charter. But the Security Council did not endorse this view and did not vote on a draft resolution proposed by the United States which would have characterized the Soviet action as a threat to international peace and security.[58]

3.5 The use of the term "threat" by the General Assembly in its request for an Advisory Opinion must therefore be considered to be limited to the situation where one or more States clearly express an intention to use nuclear weapons against one or more specifically designated States or populations in precise circumstances. It is the illegality of this type of "threat" — real and specific rather than theoretical and general — which should be considered by the Court in addressing this request for an Advisory Opinion.

3.6 With this understanding, Solomon Islands considers that international law prohibits the following "threats":

- to act in such a way as to threaten international peace and security (this prohibition is implicit in Articles 1(1) and 39 of the UN Charter);
- to threaten the use of force in violation of Article 2(4) of the UN Charter;
- to make other threats prohibited by the UN General Assembly Declaration on the Principles of International Law Governing Friendly relations between States (resolution 2625(XXV), 24 October 1970), including prohibitions relating to:
  - threat or use of force (Principle 1, paras. 1, 4, 5 and 10); and
  - prohibition on intervention (Principle 3, para. 1).

As these different types of threat would be illegal, any stated intention to use nuclear weapons in support of such threats would also be *a fortiori* unlawful.

3.7 Are there other circumstances in which a threat to use nuclear weapons might be made? In particular, would it be lawful to threaten the use of nuclear weapons, for example, to respond to an unlawful act of aggression? As set forth below, Solomon Islands considers that any use of nuclear weapons would *prima facie* violate international law. Although the threat of use is less serious, and would not of itself give rise to a violation of those rules of international law which proscribe the use of nuclear weapons by reference to their effects, Solomon Islands considers that the threat of use of nuclear weapons would violate general rules of international law (a) and specific rules of international law (b).

[58] See Security Council debates, 22-25 October 1962, 1022nd-1025th sessions.

(a) General rules of international law

3.8 Given that the international community would treat with exceptional gravity any use of nuclear weapons, any threat of use might lead to an actual use and should also be considered to be exceptionally dangerous. A State which threatens such use would threaten international peace and security. It would also violate the general rules of international law such as the obligation to fulfil in good faith its obligations under the United Nations Charter and the commitment to cooperate with other States consistently with the Charter. Both these principles are elaborated in the General Assembly's Declaration of Principles Governing Friendly Relations between States (resolution 2625 (XXV), 24 October 1970, 4th and 7th principles). Their formulation in this instrument are applicable to the threat of use of nuclear weapons, namely:

— in relation to the duty of cooperation:

> "a. States shall co-operate with other States in the maintenance of international peace and security;
> b. States shall co-operate in the promotion of universal respect for and observance of human rights [...]"
> (Principle 4, para. 2)

— in relation to good faith:

> "Every State has the duty to fulfil in good faith the obligations assumed by it in accordance with the Charter of the U.N.
> Every State has the duty to fulfil in good faith its obligations under the generally recognized principles and rules of international law.
> Every State has the duty to fulfil in good faith its obligations under international agreements valid under the generally recognized principles and rules of international law."
> (Principle 7)

3.9 In this context it seems reasonable to conclude that threatening the use of nuclear weapons against the territory of another State can hardly be considered as cooperation to maintain international peace and security or to ensure universal respect for human rights, or to fulfil in good faith obligations arising under the UN Charter (particularly the principles of humanity set forth in the Martens Clause) and other international agreements (especially those relating to international humanitarian and environmental law).

(b) Specific rules of international law

3.10 In Solomon Islands view any use of nuclear weapons would *prima facie* violate international humanitarian law. The threat of their use must be considered as totally incompatible with the solemn obligation undertaken by States under common Article 1 of the four Geneva Conventions of 1949 and Article 1(1) of the 1st 1977 Additional Protocol "to respect and ensure respect" of the four Conventions and the Protocol. Given the inevitability of the lethal effects of nuclear weapons, threatening their use must surely also violate the rights of potential victims as set forth in Article 40 of the

1st Additional Protocol, which provides that

> "It is prohibited to order that there shall be no survivors, to threaten an adversary therewith or to conduct hostilities on that basis."

3.11 In summary, the threat of the use of nuclear weapons is clearly unlawful when it is accompanied by a threat prohibited by international law or when it appears in relation to the use of force or intervention also prohibited by international law. Even if the threat to use nuclear weapons might be used for apparently lawful purposes, such threat is unlawful by operation of general rules of international law and specific rules requiring respect for humanitarian and environmental objectives. Accordingly, in the discussion which follows references to the use of force should be construed to include also the threat of use of force where appropriate.

(B) The use of nuclear weapons is subject to international law, including the rules relating to armed conflict

3.12 The legality of the threat or use of nuclear weapons raises three issues in relation to the rules governing the methods and means of warfare:

(a) what is the law applicable to the use of nuclear weapons?
(b) what are the applicable substantive rules of that law? and
(c) to whom do those rules apply?

The submissions made in this part of the Written Observations are that:

— the use of nuclear weapons is subject to international law, including the rules relating to armed conflicts (A);
— that any use of nuclear weapons is illegal under general international law (B); and
— that the relevant rules of international law apply to all States (C).

3.13 Specifically, Part A of Section II argues that the rules of law of armed conflict and law governing friendly relations prohibit the use of nuclear weapons in any circumstances, since any such use would violate:

- the limitation on the choice of means of attacking the enemy;
- the permanent obligation to distinguish between combatants and non combatants;
- the prohibition against attacking civilian targets;
- the prohibition against attacking health services;

- the prohibition against the use of chemical weapons or poisons or weapons which have indiscriminate effects;
- the prohibition against the use of weapons which render death inevitable or cause unnecessary suffering;
- the prohibition against violating the territorial integrity and neutrality of third States;
- the prohibition against causing widespread, long-term and severe damage to the environment;
- the obligation to respect the principles of proportionality and humanity; and
- the prohibition against genocide or crimes against humanity.

These rules are well-established, finding their source in many of the classical instruments governing *jus in bello*, including the 1868 St Petersburg Declaration, the 1874 Brussels Declaration, 1899 Hague Declaration IV, Regulation annexed to 1907 Hague Convention IV, 1925 Geneva Protocol, 1948 Genocide Convention, 1949 Geneva Conventions

(a) The use of nuclear weapons is subject to general international law

3.14 It has been suggested that in the nuclear age the normal rules of international law have been suspended, or perhaps set aside altogether, for all matters relating to nuclear weapons.[59] There are no principled grounds in law or policy to support this view. The use of nuclear weapons like any other activity carried out or authorised by States, is subject to the general and the specific rules of international law.

3.15 The use of nuclear weapons is subject to the rule of law. The development of new forms of behaviour, including methods and means of armed conflict, does not bring into question the law applicable to it. The arrival of a new *modus operandi* does not modify the application or effect of the rule of law. As the first Advocate General of the Belgium Military Court stated:

> "Ce n'est pas à des pénalistes qu'il faut rappeler que la découverte d'un nouveau modus operandi en vue de commettre une infraction ne pourrait avoir l'effet de rendre caduque la législation qui définit

59 See E. David, "A propos de certaines justifications théoriques à l'emploi des armes nucléaires," *Melange Pictet* (1984), p.349; Part IIA of the written observations is largely based on that study.

cette infraction, ni qu'aucune forme nouvelle de criminalité n'a d'effet abrogatoire du droit positif".[60]

Accordingly, the invention of the machine gun or the tank has not forced States to adopt specific rules to determine the legality or the illegality of their use.[61] The law of armed conflicts applies to **all** forms of weaponry. Any other view would undermine the international rule of law. It is the arms that man invents which ought to adapt to existing rules, not the other way round. Any other approach would permit the invention of new weapons to circumvent the operation of legal rules under international law.

3.16 As set out hereafter, the use of nuclear weapons is subject to the general international law of armed conflict and to the more specific rules, including those reflected in the 1977 Geneva I Additional to the Geneva Conventions of 12 August 1949, and Relating to the Protection of Victims of International Armed Conflict ("1977 Geneva Protocol I").

(b) The use of nuclear weapons is subject to international law of armed conflicts

3.17 The practice of States reflects the overwhelming view that nuclear weapons are subject to the international law of armed conflict. UN General Assembly resolution 1653 (XVI), which specifically addresses nuclear weapons, states in its preamble that:

> "the use of weapons of mass destruction, causing unnecessary human suffering, was in the past prohibited, as being contrary to the laws of humanity and to the principles of international law, by international declarations and binding agreements, such as the Declaration of St. Petersburg of 1868, the Declaration of the Brussels Conference of 1874, the Conventions of the Hague Peace Conferences of 1899 and 1907, and the Geneva Protocol of 1925, to which the majority of nations are still parties".

The paragraph was adopted by 63 votes in favour, one vote against, and 31 abstentions. Since then, the General Assembly has consistently endorsed the approach taken by the vast majority of States in resolution 1653(XVI).[62] Other organisations

[60] Cited in A. Andries, "Pour une prise en considération de la compétence des juridictions pénales nationales a l'égard des emplois d'armes nucléaires," *RDPC* 1984, p.34 ("Andries").

[61] *Cf.* J. Fried, "International Law Prohibits the First Use of Nuclear Weapons", *RBDI* 1981-1982, p.37.

[62] A/Res. 2936 (XXVII), 29 November 1972 (73-4-46), Preamble; 35/152 D, 12 December 1980 (112-19-14), Preamble; 36/92 I, 9 December 1981 (121-19-6), Preamble; 37/100, 13 December 1982 (117-17-8), Preamble; 38/73 G, 15 December 1983 (126-17-6), Preamble; 39/63 H, 12 December 1984 (128-17-5), Preamble; 40/151 F, 16 December 1985 (126-17-6), Preamble; 41/60 F, 3 December 1986 (132-17-4), Preamble; 42/39 C, 30 November 1987 (135-17-4), Preamble; 43/76 E, 7 December 1988 (133-17-4), Preamble; 44/117 C, 15 December 1989,

have taken the same approach. The Xxth International Conference of the Red Cross (Vienna, October 1965) adopted a resolution by 128 votes in favour and three abstentions (with no votes against) solemnly declaring that "the general principles of the law of armed conflict apply to nuclear weapons and other similar weapons" (translation). The resolution reflects State practice, as it was supported notably by non-governmental organisations (national organisations of the Red Cross, League of Red Cross Societies, International Committee of the Red Cross) and also by States (State Parties to the Geneva Conventions of 12 August 1949 ("1949 Geneva Conventions"), which participated in the International Conferences of the Red Cross in accordance with the Statute of the International Red Cross (Article 1(2)).

3.18 Military manuals addressing this issue also stipulate that the use of nuclear weapons is subject to the rules of international humanitarian law applicable to the methods and means of warfare.[63] For example, the military instructional manual of the United States of America states that the use of nuclear weapons is subject to "three basic principles of the law of war - military necessity, humanity and chivalry - that limit the discretion of belligerents in all circumstances".[64] At the signing of the Final Act adopting the 1977 Geneva Protocols the US representative declared, moreover, that even if the 1977 Geneva Protocol I does not regulate or prohibit the use of nuclear weapons (on this point, see *infra* para. 3.28) it is nevertheless the case that: "their use in time of hostilities is governed by existing principles of international law."[65] The British military manual adopts a similar approach:

> "[t]here is no rule of international law dealing specifically with the use of nuclear weapons. Their use, therefore, is governed by the general principles laid down in this Chapter".[66]

3.19 In Belgium, during the preparatory work for Parliamentary approval of the 1977 Geneva Protocol I the *Conseil d'Etat* (legislative section) implicitly recognised that if the new rules of the Protocol did not apply to nuclear weapons, these were nonetheless subject to the classical rules of the international law of armed conflict:

Preamble (134-17-4); 45/59 B, 4 December 1990 (125-17-10), Preamble; 47/53 C (126-21-21), Preamble; 48/76 B, 16 December 1993 (120-23-24), Preamble.

63 See UN Doc. A/9215, Vol. 1, pp.172-73 (French).

64 Cited in R. Falk and E. Meyrowitz, *The Status of Nuclear Weapons under International Law* (roneo), p.84, n.114.

65 9 June 1977, CDDH/SR.58, para. 82; in *Actes de la Conférence diplomatique sur la réaffirmation et le développement du droit international humanitaire applicables dans les conflits armés* (Genève, 1974-77) ("Actes"), Berne, 1978, I, 3e partie, p.301.

66 Manual of Military Law, 1958, Part III, sec.113 cited in *Commentaires des Protocoles additionels du 7 juin 1977 aux Conventions de Genève du 12 août 1949* ed. by Y. Sandoz, C. Swinarski, B. Zimmerman, ICRC - Martinus Nijhoff (1986) ("*Commentaires*"), p.604, n.33.

> "The consensus which was established on this point [the fact that the negotiations were not concerned with the regulation of the use or non-use of nuclear weapons] between the great nuclear powers and which has frequently been qualified as the placing 'between brackets' of nuclear weapons, must be interpreted as relating **exclusively to the new rules** in Protocol I. The rules contained in other international instruments, such as the Hague Conventions of 1899 and 1907 and the Geneva humanitarian conventions of 1949 are not affected and retain their value".[67] (authors' translation; emphasis added)

3.20 The jurisprudence of courts on the applicability of international law to nuclear weapon is limited. A noteworthy exception is the 1963 decision of the Tokyo District Court, which rejected the view that international law did not regulate the use of a nuclear weapon on Hiroshima because of its novelty:

> "the prohibition in this case is understood to include not only the case where there is an express provision of direct prohibition, but also the case where it is necessarily regarded that the use of a new weapon is prohibited from the interpretation and analogical application of existing international laws and regulations (international customary laws and treaties). Further, we must understand that the prohibition includes also the case where, in the light of principles of international law which are the basis of the above mentioned positive international laws and regulations, the case of a new weapon is admitted to be contrary to the principles [...] Therefore, we cannot regard a new weapon as legal only because it is a new weapon, and it is still right that a new weapon must be exposed to the examination of positive international law."[68]

At various points in the judgment the Tokyo District Court recognised the applicability of the classical rules of international law of armed conflict to the bombardment of Hiroshima and Nagasaki by nuclear weapons.[69]

3.21 For the great majority of international jurists there is no doubt that the use of nuclear weapons is subject to international law, and the examples cited below are merely illustrative.[70] The amount written on this subject reflects the strongly held views of

---

67 J. Salmon and R. Ergec, "La pratique du pouvoir exécutif et le contrôle des chambres législatives en matière de droit international" (1984-1986) *RBDI*, 1987, p.391, note E-D.

68 Tokyo District Court, Judgment of 7 December 1963, *Jap.Ann.I.L.*, 1964, pp. 235-36.

69 *Id.*, pp.234, 236, 241.

70 See E. Castren, *The Present Law of War and Neutrality*, (1954), pp.206-07; Spaight, *Air Power and War Rights*, (1947), p.276; H. Lauterpacht, *Oppenheim's International Law*, 1952, 7th ed. p.347, s116; J. Greenspan, *The Modern Law of Land Warfare*, (1959), p.371 cited in M. Whiteman, *Digest of International Law*, Washington US GPO 1968, pp.482-83; R.E. Charlier, "Questions juridiques soulevées par l'évolution de la science atomique", *RCADI*, (1957), vol 91, p.354; G. Schwarzenberger, *The Legality of Nuclear Weapons*, (1958), pp.43-44; N. Singh; *Nuclear Weapons and International Law*, 1959 pp.147 *et seq*; H. Meyrowitz, "Les juristes devant l'arme nucléaire", *RGDIP* 1963 pp.844-848; Fried *loc.cit.* pp.34 *et seq*; A. Andries "L'emploie de l'arme nucléaire est un crime de guerre" *La Revue Nouvelle* (Brussels), March 1983, p.320, *id.*, Andries *loc.cit.*, pp.33 *et seq.*; J. Verhaegen, "Le problème pénal de la dissuasion nucléaire", *RDPC*, 1984, pp.20-21; *Statement on the Illegality of Nuclear Warfare*, The Lawyers

many jurists on the subject of the use of nuclear weapons and international law, including Judges of the International Court and other illustrious jurists.

Thus, the Institut de Droit International adopted at its 1969 Edinburgh session a resolution on "La distinction entre les objectifs militaires et non militaires en général et notamment les problèmes que pose l'existence des armes de destruction massive". The resolution recalled

> "les conséquences que la conduite indiscriminée des hostilités, et particulièrement l'emploi des armes nucléaires, [...] peut entraîner pour les populations civiles et pour l'humanité tout entière"

and noted the existence of rules "à observer lors de conflits armés par tout gouvernment", notably the prohibition against attacking civilians, the use of weapons having indiscriminate effects, and

> "notamment l'emploi des armes dont l'effet destructeur est trop grand pour avoir être limité à des objectifs militaires déterminés ou dont l'effet est incontrôlable (armes 'autogénératrices' ainsi que des armes aveugles".[71]

In other words, the Institut has implicitly recognised the applicability of the law of armed conflicts to the use of nuclear weapons.

(c) The use of nuclear weapons is subject to the 1977 Geneva Protocol I

3.22 The use of nuclear weapons is also subject to the relevant provisions of the 1977 Geneva Protocol I. It is important to expressly demonstrate this, since the Protocol does not expressly mention nuclear weapons, and further:

(i) during the presentation of the draft text to serve as a base for the discussions of the diplomatic conference the ICRC had declared its unwillingness to broach the question of nuclear weapons;[72] and

(ii) declarations made by the United Kingdom, the United States and France, (at the beginning and/or at the end of the Conference), stated that all or part of the 1977

Committee on Nuclear Policy, New York 1984; *Appel des juristes contre la guerre nucléaire*, petition by the Bureau International de la Paix (1987).

71 *Ann.I.D.I.*, 1969, Vol.53, II, p.360.

72 "Problems relating to atomic, bacteriological and chemical warfare as subjects of international arguments or negotiations by governments, and in submitting these draft Additional Protocols the ICRC does not intend to broach those problems" (translation), in ICRC, *Projets de Protocoles additionels aux Convention de Genève du 12 août 1949*, Geneva, 1973, p.2, in *Actes*.

Geneva Protocol I did not apply to nuclear weapons.[73]

(i) No consensus exists on whether nuclear weapons are covered by Protocol I

3.23 When the law prohibits certain conduct without specifying all the ways in which such conduct might occur, such silence does not imply that the conduct is authorised under another guise. The silence of Protocol I does not therefore signify that it is permissible to use nuclear weapons to carry out activities prohibited by the Protocol. It may be possible to go further in adopting the view that the Protocol does prohibit the use of nuclear weapons in a *quasi*-explicit way, since it prohibits attacks on nuclear power plants (Art. 56). As A. Andries has written:

> "Il y'aurait en effet contradiction dans les termes à interdire la destruction des centrales nucléaires à cause des forces dangereuses qu'elles peuvent libérer (art. 56.1) tout en n'interdisant pas la libération directe de ces forces par l'explosion d'une arme nucléaire."[74]

3.24 Some writers have concluded that a consensus existed at the Diplomatic Conference on the Reaffirmation and Development of International Humanitarian Law Applicable in Armed Conflicts (Geneva, 1974-1977), that Protocol I did not apply to the use of nuclear weapons.[75] Solomon Islands does not share this view. Many States put forward the opposite view, both during the Conference and afterwards. Indeed, the proliferation of views is so contradictory that it is impossible to identify a consensus on the inapplicability of Protocol I to the use of nuclear weapons.

3.25 During the early sessions of the Conference, the UK, relying on the ICRC Declaration, declared that the Protocols

> "must not broach problems concerned with atomic, bacteriological or chemical warfare, which were the subject of existing international agreements and current delicate negotiations by Governments elsewhere. It was on the assumption that the draft Protocols would not affect those problems that the United Kingdom Government had worked and would continue to work towards final agreement on the Protocols."[76]

Similarly, Sweden wanted to address certain conventional weapons, but emphasised that "[t]he proposals did not cover atomic, bacteriological and chemical weapons

---

73 UK, 6th March 1974, CDDH/SR 13 para. 36, *Actes* V, p.130; 9th June 1977, CDDH, SR.58 para.119, *Actes* VII p.310; US, 9th June 1977, CDDH/SR.58, para. 82, *Actes* VII, p.301; France 8th June 1977, *CDDH/SR* 56, para. 3, *Actes* VII p.199.

74 A. Andries, *loc. cit.* pp. 35-6.

75 H. Meyrowitz: "La stratégie nucléaire et le Protocole additionnel I aux Conventions de Genève de 1949", *RGDIP*, 1979 pp.915-17, 928-29, Andries *loc.cit.*, pp.35-36.

76 6th March 1974, CDDH/SR.13 para. 36, *Actes* V, p.130.

[and] that discussion should be confined to conventional types of warfare [...]."[77]

3.26 During the same session, however, many other States took an alternative view. The following are illustrative examples. Ghana stated that

> "The use of new types of weapons appeared on the agenda of two important conferences currently meeting in Geneva and in Vienna. The main purpose of at least one of them was to limit the use of strategic arms which could result in the destruction of all mankind. Consistently with the contemporary trend of political thought, the Conference should declare the complete prohibition of the use of new weapons in all conflicts. Experience had shown that the use of such weapons could affect innocent civilians some distance from the area directly attacked. Surely, prevention was better than cure".[78]

According to Rumania:

> "Nuclear, bacteriological, chemical and biological weapons as well as all weapons of mass destruction should be banned".[79]

A similar view was proposed by the People's Republic of China:

> "The new Protocols should unequivocally provide for the prohibition and destruction of nuclear weapon; [...]".[80]

According to Iraq:

> "The principles that had to be stressed were the protection of the civilian population in armed conflicts; the prohibition of nuclear, biological and chemical weapons and of certain conventional weapons of mass destruction; [...]".[81]

For Zaire, the Conference should

> "Give particular attention to the following points [...] prohibition of the use of weapons liable to inflict unnecessary suffering on civilians, especially bacteriological, chemical and nuclear weapons; [...]".[82]

---

77 7th March 1974, CDDH/SR.14 para. 21, *Actes* V, p.141.

78 5th March 1974, CDDH/SR.10 para. 36, *Actes* V, p.92.

79 5th March 1974, CDDH/SR.11 para. 13, *Actes* V, p.99.

80 6th March 1974, CDDH/SR.12 para. 18, *Actes* V, p.116.

81 6th March 1974, CDDH/SR.12 para. 32, *Actes* V, p.119.

82 11th March 1974, CDDH/SR.19 para. 5, *Actes* V, p.189.

For Albania,

> "Methods of warfare indiscriminately affecting the civilian population, such as atomic weapons, bombardment of civilian population and deportation, must be specifically prohibited".[83]

It is therefore clear that during the early stages of the Conference no consensus existed.

3.27 The nuclear weapons issue was hardly debated again during the Conference, although in 1975, the People's Democratic Republic of Korea complained about the installation of nuclear weapons in South Korea and stated that:

> "the production, testing and use of such weapons should be prohibited [...]".[84]

In response, the US made it clear that it did not wish to address nuclear weapons, recalling the ICRC draft had not included any rules on nuclear weapons.[85]

3.28 The question of nuclear weapons reappeared at the end of the Conference, during the final declarations. France, the US, and the UK declared that 1977 Geneva Protocol I did not apply to nuclear weapons. The declarations differ in tone and content. France, which proposed a most extreme approach:

> "wishes to make it quite clear that its Government could not under any circumstances permit the provisions of Protocol I to [...] prohibit the use of any specific weapon which it considers necessary for its defence. [...] It accordingly wishes to stress that in its view the rules of the Protocols do not apply to the use of nuclear weapons".[86]

The US representative, whilst admitting that the use of nuclear weapons "is regulated by existing principles of international law", stated

> "It was his Government's understanding that the rules established by the Protocol were not intended to have any effect on, and did not regulate or prohibit the use of, nuclear weapons."[87]

The UK took the view that **only** "the <u>new</u> rules" established by Protocol I would not apply to nuclear weapons. For the UK representative

---

[83] 19th March 1974, CDDH/III.SR.8, para. 87, *Actes* XIV, p.76.

[84] 27th February 1975, CDDH/III/SR.26 para. 31, *Actes* XIV, p.260.

[85] 14th April 1975, CDDH/III/SR.40, para. 123, *Actes*, XIV, p.466.

[86] 8th June 1977, CDDH/SR.56 para. 3, *Actes* VII, p.199.

[87] 8 June 1977, CDDH/SR.58, para. 82, *Actes* VII, p.301.

> "the new rules introduced by the Protocols were not intended to have any effect on and did not regulate or prohibit the use of nuclear or other non-conventional weapons. Such questions were rightly the subject of agreements and negotiations elsewhere".[88]

In other words, as commentators have emphasized,

> "The British declaration refers expressly to ***new*** rules and therefore implicitly confirms that the rules ***reaffirmed*** in the Protocol apply to all arms;"[89] (translation - emphasis added)

Accordingly, the only consensus between the three States is confined to the inapplicability of the new rules of the Protocol to the use of nuclear weapons. As between the US and France, one could identify a consensus on the inapplicability of the whole of Protocol I to nuclear weapons (despite the fact that the US recognises that their use is subject to the general rules of the law of armed conflicts: *supra* para. 3.18). But this view is taken only by these two States and not by the other Parties to Protocol I.

3.29 It is significant that other States have affirmed that Protocol I applies to nuclear weapons, and except for the three above-mentioned States, they have not been contradicted on this point. Accordingly, in referring to Article 33 of the draft text (Article 35 in the final text) which stipulates that Parties do not have an unlimited right as to the choice of weapons and that they cannot use weapons causing excessive harm or widespread, long lasting and serious damage to the natural environment, India declared:

> "that the basic rules contained in this article will apply to all categories of weapons, namely **nuclear**, bacteriological, chemical or conventional weapons or any other category of weapons".[90] (emphasis added)

In more general terms, according to Rumania,

> "Humanitarian law must also prohibit the use of weapons of massive destruction and methods of warfare which struck indiscriminately at combatants and civilians alike [...] **Many of those aims were covered by the provisions of Protocol I,** including... the prohibition or restriction of the use of certain conventional weapons and weapons of massive destruction".[91] (emphasis added)

3.30 Other States do not specifically refer to nuclear weapons, although certain declarations suggest that Protocol I is applicable to their use. According to Yugoslavia, for example, it would be dangerous to permit, as certain States have

---

[88] 9 June 1977, CDDH/SR.58, para. 119, *Actes*, p. 310 (emphasis added).

[89] *Commentaires*, p.604, para. 1853.

[90] 25th May 1977, CDDH/SR.39. *Actes* VI, p.114.

[91] 9th June 1977, CDDH/SR.58, para. 61, *Actes* VII, p.296.

suggested, that:

> "certain methods and means of combat permissable in "exceptional" circumstances. In Protocol I, as also in other texts codifying the laws of armed conflict, and in accordance with the principle confirmed by the Nürnberg Tribunal, there had been due regard for military necessity, but the new rules were also based on humanitarian requirements [...] If the use of weapons that might cause superfluous injury or have indiscriminate effects was not renounced, or restricted in practice, the rules that the Conference had so carefully drafted would in fact be impossible to apply."[92]

According to the German Democratic Republic,

> "The unambiguous rule prohibiting the civilian population being made the object of attack, the prohibition of indiscriminate attacks, the protection of civilian objects and of the natural environment form [...] the core of the Protocol. In view of the terrible experience the civilian population had to endure during the Second World War and afterwards, each rule in this field - even if it only reaffirms existing law - is a real progress."[93]

According to Mozambique,

> "The destructive power of present-day weapons strikes mainly at the civilian population, so we congratulate the Conference on its adoption of the articles relating to the protection of the unarmed population."[94]

3.31 It is therefore clear that no consensus existed in Geneva as to the applicability of Protocol I to nuclear weapons. The various declarations identified above are inconclusive. As against the unchallenged declarations, of differing content and value, of the UK, US and France (*supra* paras. 3.25 and 3.28) one can rely on the express declarations of India and Rumania, which were also uncontested, as well as the implicit rejection of weapons of mass destruction reflected in declarations of other States.

3.32 Practice following the adoption of Protocol I confirms the lack of a consensus to exclude the use of nuclear weapons from its field of application. Such practice is reflected in the following:

(i) One of the States the most adamantly opposed to the application of Protocol I to nuclear weapons — France — itself recognised in 1984 that there was no consensus that the Protocol was inapplicable to nuclear weapons. At the time of depositing its instrument of ratification to Protocol II, France justified her refusal to adhere to Protocol I by referring to

---

92 8th June 1977, CDDH/SR.56, para. 70-71, *Actes* VII, p.214.

93 8th June 1977, CDDH/SR.56, Acts. VII, p.247.

94 9th June 1977, CDDH/SR.58, Acts, VII, p.332.

"the **absence of consensus** between the signatory States of the first Protocol in what concerns the exact obligations assumed by them in respect to dissuasion" [95](authors' translation - emphasis added).

(ii) If there had usually been a consensus on the "setting aside" of nuclear weapons, it would not have been necessary for certain States, in accepting Protocol I, to adopt reservations on its applicability to nuclear weapons. However, various member States of NATO declared in a broadly uniform manner upon ratification of Protocol I that it applied "exclusively to classical weapons" and that it did not

"préjudice à aucune autre règle de droit international applicable à d'autres types d'armes."[96]

Significantly, no other State, including some member States of NATO such as Greece, Portugal and Iceland,[97] made this kind of declaration upon ratifying Protocol I. It is thus clear that there is no consensus on the matter.

3.33 The jurists at the ICRC also take the view that there has never been a consensus to exclude the use of nuclear weapons from the field of application of Protocol I "puisqu'aucune décision n'a été prise".[98] Only "une entente s'est réalisée pour ne pas discuter des armes nucléaires".[99] This does not mean that the rules of the Protocol do not apply to such weapons. The jurists at the ICRC have concluded, on the contrary, that if

"les principes raffirmés dans le Protocole n'interdisent pas l'usage des armes nucléaires lors d'un conflit armé, ils restreignent donc très sérieusement cet usage."[100]

We will see that the characteristically prudential approach of the ICRC on the legality of the use of nuclear weapons is unsupported by the positive law. It is submitted that the "principles reaffirmed in the Protocol" do prohibit the use of nuclear weapons,

---

95 *RICR*, 1984 p.239.

96 Italy in *RICR*, 1986 p.114; for the same idea and similar wording, see Belgium, the Netherlands, Spain, Federal German Republic in *RICR* 1986 p.178; 1987 p.444; 1989 p.389; 1991, pp.250-51. With regard to Canada: "the rules introduced by Protocol I are adopted in order to apply exclusively to conventional weapons" and "have no effect whatsoever on nuclear weapons, which they neither apply to nor prohibit", *RICR*, 1991, p.82: (this statement is ambiguous: by referring to "rules introduced" is Canada referring to all the provisions of the Protocol or only those which establish new rules?)

97 *RICR*, 1989, p.267; 1992, p.416.

98 *Commentaires*, p.603, para. 1851; *RICR* , 1987 p.352; 1989, p.267; 1992, p.416.

99 *Id.*, para. 1852.

100 *Id.*, p.605, para. 1859.

in view of their nature and the extent of their destructive effects.

3.34 In conclusion, the lack of any consensus on the express exclusion of nuclear weapons from the field of application of Protocol I suggests that the Protocol, and in particular the principles of general international law reaffirmed therein, are applicable to nuclear weapons together with all other types of weapons.

3.35 It remains necessary to determine whether the declarations "setting aside nuclear weapons" which have been made by certain States to prevent or limit the applicability of Protocol I to the use of nuclear weapons in treaty relations (as opposed to customary law relations) of these States, as between themselves or as between themselves and the other Parties to the Protocol. This is considered at paragraphs 3.99 and 3.100.

(d) The use of nuclear weapons is subject to the rules of international law specifically prohibiting the use of nuclear weapons

3.36 Certain rules of international law specifically expressly prohibit the use of nuclear weapons. These are reflected in UN General Assembly resolutions, which have been consistently supported by the vast majority of the members of the UN. The practice of that body began in 1961 with the Declaration on the Prohibition of the Use of Nuclear and Thermo-Nuclear Weapons,[101] which declares that any use of nuclear weapons would:

- be contrary to the spirit, letter and aims of the UN and, as such, "a direct violation of the Charter of the United Nations";[102]

- be contrary to the "rules of international law and to the laws of humanity", since it would exceed the scope of war and cause indiscriminate destruction to mankind and civilization;[103] and

- constitute the commission of a "crime against mankind and civilization".[104]

Resolution 1653 was recalled by the General Assembly in 1972 and has subsequently been recalled at each Session of the General Assembly since 1980.[105] In 1972, the

---

101 A.Res.1653 (XVI), 24 November 1961 (55-20-26).

102 *Id.*, para. 1(a) and (d).

103 *Id.*, para. 1(b).

104 *Id.*, para. 1(d).

105 *Supra*, note 101.

General Assembly "solemnly declared, on behalf of the States Members of the Organization, [...] the permanent prohibition on the use of nuclear weapons."[106] In 1978, the special Commission of the 10th Extraordinary Session of the UN General Assembly declared in its final document that

> "Les armes nucléaires sont celles qui menacent le plus gravement l'humanité et la survie de la civilisation"[107]

The General Assembly has frequently invoked this provision or the idea contained in it.[108] Also in 1978, the General Assembly

> "declared that the use of nuclear weapons will be a violation of the UN Charter and a crime against humanity".[109]

From 1980 (35th Session)[110] to the present day (48th Session), the General Assembly has repeated, year after year, its condemnation of the use of nuclear weapons by characterising such use as a "violation of the Charter" and "a crime against humanity".[111]

Furthermore, in 1981 the General Assembly solemnly declared that

> "States and statesmen that resort first to the use of nuclear weapons will be committing the gravest crime against humanity"[112]

In 1983, the General Assembly

> "Resolutely, unconditionally and for all time condemns nuclear war as being contrary to human conscience and reason, as the most monstrous crime against peoples and as a violation of the foremost

---

106 A/Res. 2936 (XXVII), 29 Nov.1972 (73-4-46), para.1.

107 A/Res. 5. 10/2, 30th June 1978 (adopted without a vote), para.47.

108 See e.g. A/Res. 38/183M, 20th Dec.1983 (133-1-14), preamble; 39/148 P, 17th Dec.1984 (128-6-12), preamble; 40/152 P, 16th Dec.1985 (131-16-6), preamble; 41/60 I, 3rd Dec.1986 (139-12-4), preamble; 42/42 D., 30th Nov.1987 (140-3-14) preamble; 43/78 F, 7th Dec.1988 (136-3-14), preamble.

109 A/Res. 33/71 B, 14th Dec. 1978 (103-18-18), para.1.

110 A/Res. 35/152, 12th Dec.1980 (112-19-14) para.1.

111 *Supra*, note 103.

112 See e.g. A/Res. 36/100, 9th Dec.1981 (82-19-41), para.1; 37/78 J, 9th Dec. 1982 (112-19-15), preamble, and para. 1; 38/183 B, 20th Dec.1983 (110-19-15), preamble, and para.1.

human right - the right to life".[113]

These resolutions raise two questions: do they constitute rules, and if so, do they bind all States?

3.37 Resolutions of the UN General Assembly can be a source of law to the extent that they relate to questions which are within the competence of the General Assembly and are elaborated in a normative mode. The power of the General Assembly to adopt resolutions on nuclear weapons is based on Article 11(1) of the Charter which states that:

> "The General Assembly may consider the general principles of co-operation in the maintenance of international peace and security, including the principles governing disarmament and the regulation of armaments, and may make recommendations with regard to such principles to the Members or to the Security Council or to both."

Although this provision gives the General Assembly only a power of "recommendation", this does not preclude the Assembly from exercising other powers of a normative character. Practice confirms[114] this and the ICJ had affirmed this in the *Namibia Case* (1971):

> "For it would not be correct to assume that, because the General Assembly is in principle vested with recommendatory powers, it is debarred from adopting, in specific cases within the framework of its compliance, resolutions which make determinations or have operative design."[115]

The normative character of resolutions flows from their formulation. As the International Court has stated with respect to the Security Council resolutions:

> "The language of a resolution of the Security Council should be carefully analyzed before a conclusion can be made as to its binding effect. In view of the nature of the powers under Article 25, the question whether they have been in fact exercised is to be determined in each case, having regard to **the terms of the resolution** to be interpreted, the discussion leading to it, the Charter provisions invoked and in general, all circumstances that might assist in determining the legal consequences of the resolution of the Security Council"[116] (emphasis added)

Similarly, the 13th Commission of the Institut de Droit International, during the 1987 session in Cairo, proposed with regards to resolutions of the UN General Assembly

113 A/Res. 38/75 B, 15th Dec.1983 (95-19-30), para.1.

114 For examples of the legal effect of UN General Assembly resolutions see *Texaco-Calasiatic v. Libya*, Arbitral award of 19 January 1988, *JDI* 1977, pp.378-79; *Military and Paramilitary Activities in and against Nicaragua*, *ICJ Rep.* 1986, pp.100 and 103, paras. 188 and 195.

115 Adv. Op. 21st June 1971, *ICJ Rep.* 1971, p.50, para. 105.

116 *Namibia Case*, *loc.cit.* p.53, para. 114.

that

> "Le libellé et le texte d'une résolution aident à déterminer la portée normative. La présence de références au droit international ou de formules équivalentes, ou l'omission délibérée de telles références ou formules sont des indices utiles mais non décisifs en soi" (Conclusion 10)

In casu, the General Assembly resolutions identified above are drafted in the present tense and utilise verbs in an affirmative manner according to which the Assembly, "declares" or "imposes" principles enunciated in legal terms which are based upon sources of positive law: nuclear weapons **are** "weapons of massive destruction causing unnecessary harm and human suffering"; in this context their use is "prohibited" by reason of the Declaration of St Petersburg, Brussels, etc. (*infra* paras. 3.47 and 3.51); moreover, their usage is a "violation of the Charter" and a "crime against humanity".

In **referring** to the existence of an obligation of customary and treaty law imposed on States not to use nuclear weapons, an obligation the violation of which would constitute an **international crime**, these resolutions of the General Assembly are of a normative character.

3.38 Advocates for the legality of the use of nuclear weapons would perhaps take the view that these resolutions are contradictory, since they declare that the use of nuclear weapons is illegal but also demand the conclusion of a treaty prohibiting the use of nuclear weapons.[117] Alternatively, they argue that if the use of those nuclear weapons was already illegal it would be pointless to conclude another treaty on the subject. Other resolutions condemn the first use of nuclear weapons,[118] which seems to suggest that a second, or retaliatory, use would be lawful, etc.[119] These arguments might be invoked in support of the view that the use of nuclear weapons is not yet contrary to international law.

3.39 The inclusion of an international legal obligation in a treaty does not imply that the obligation did not pre-date the treaty, perhaps as a rule of customary law or alternatively in another treaty. Many treaty rules (for example those relating to the law of diplomatic relations, law of treaties, law of the sea, etc) codify pre-existing customary rules. It is quite normal in international law for the most common and the most fundamental rules to be reaffirmed and repeatedly incorporated into treaties; examples include the prohibition on the use of force, the obligation to settle disputes

---

117 See A/Res. 33/71 B, 14th Dec. 1978, para. 2 and resolutions cited in note 62.

118 A/Res. 36/100, 9th Dec. 1981 (82-19-41), para.1. *Ann.I.D.I.* 1987, Vol.62, T.II. p.73.

119 For a more detailed analysis see E. David *Examen de certaines justifications théoriques a l'emploi des armes nucléaires* (Part II), in *Les conséquences juridiques de l'installation éventuelle de missiles cruise et pershing en Europe, Brussels*, ed. of the University of Brussels and Bruylant, 1984 pp.15 *et seq* ("Examen") are largely inspired by this study.

peacefully. The formal re-affirmation of these rules in a treaty clearly does not imply their prior non-existence as binding obligations. To read into the fact that certain States call for the elaboration of a treaty to expressly prohibit the use of nuclear weapons as proof that their use is not yet prohibited illustrates the dangers of an *a contrario* approach to treaty interpretation. Used in a way which is too general, this approach to interpretation introduces in effect a character of reversibility, that is to say that it could just as easily result in one conclusion as another. As has been written:

> "Seules les règles dont la vocation est d'être particulière, ainsi les exceptions, les énumérations limitives, les dispositions onéreuses se prêtent-elles à une interprétation a contrario"[120]

In these circumstances the will of the United Nations, as expressed in General Assembly resolutions, to adopt a convention prohibiting the use of nuclear weapons is an objective far too general to lend itself to an *a contrario* form of interpretation. The United Nation's desire to adopt such a convention could either be because the use of nuclear weapons has not yet been prohibited in international law or because it is only prohibited in a generic manner - *quod est*: a treaty would emphasise or reinforce an existing prohibition.

The context of these resolutions proves that only the second conclusion is compatible with the text of the preambular paragraphs and the substantive commitments set forth in the resolutions, which proclaim categorically and in a peremptory manner the illegality of any use of nuclear weapons.

3.40 As for the fact that the General Assembly has generally focused on the first use of nuclear weapons, this again might simply provide evidence of a narrow, juridical approach, rather than one which justifies the conclusion that anything other than first use might be permitted. It is noteworthy that when the General Assembly commends those States which have undertaken never to resort first to the use of a nuclear weapon, it stipulates that this constitutes an important **first step** towards a reduction of the threat of a nuclear war.[121] In other words, the Assembly welcomes all actions which can diminish the risk of a nuclear war, but evidently this does not imply that it accepts *a contrario* anything which might increase such risks. It would therefore be incorrect to find in these resolutions implicit acceptance of the right of recourse to nuclear weapons in any circumstances.

3.41 If the UN General Assembly resolutions reflect a source of international law applicable to the use of nuclear weapons, as an expression of the *opinio juris* of States

---

120 F. Ost, "L'intépretation logique et systématique et le postulat de rationnalité du légilateur," in *L'intépretation en droit* (1978), p.124.

121 See e.g. A/Res. 37/78 J, 9th Dec.1982 (112-19-15), para. 1; 38/183 B, 20th Dec.1983 (110-19-15), para. 1.

it is of little importance that they have only been supported by a majority of States. Insofar as they reflect customary international law applicable to the entire international community they reflect obligations imposed on all States. As was said by the 13th Commission of the Institut de Droit International in its conclusion 17 *in fine*:

> "Si une résolution énonce le droit existant, un état ne peut se libérer de la force obligatoire de ce droit en emèttant une réserve".[122]

Whether any State has entered such a reservation is considered at paragraphs 3.99 and 3.100.

3.42 In conclusion, there therefore exists in the law of the UN a corpus of rules specifically prohibiting - and characterising as a "crime against humanity" - the use of nuclear weapons. These rules, which are reflected in the Declaration adopted by resolution 1653,[123] do not, however, create new law since the texts which endorse them are based upon the classical prohibitions embodied in the law of armed conflicts.

The UN General Assembly resolutions are therefore an expression and application of a pre-existing and positive law to nuclear weapons, rather than a source of new rules. Even if they did constitute new rules — *quod non* — the Court is still entitled to take account of the resolutions as the General Assembly had already invited it to do so:

> "the development of international law may be affected by declarations and resolutions of the General Assembly, which may to that extent be taken into consideration by the International Court of Justice"[124]

(C) The use of nuclear weapons is contrary to international law of armed conflicts

3.43 Just as the use of certain conventional weapons is specifically prohibited by international law because of their inherent characteristics (such as "dum-dum" bullets,[125] chemical weapons,[126] etc.), it is the very characteristics of the consequences of nuclear weapons which provides the basis for the inherent illegality of their use. These inherent characteristics relate to their effect on human health and

---

122 Ann.I.D.I., 1987 Vol.62 II, p.75.

123 24 November 1961 (55-20-26).

124 *Examen du rôle de la C.I.J.*, A/Res. 3232 (XXIX), 12th Nov.1974 (consensus) preamble.

125 Declaration IV of the Hague, 28 July 1899.

126 *Id.*, IV, 2; Geneva Protocol of 17th June 1925; Paris Convention of 13th January 1993, Art I.

the environment, namely their quantitative effects (a) and their qualitative effects (b). It is by reason of both these effects that the use of nuclear weapons, in any context, violates the most fundamental rules of international law in relation to both international and non-international armed conflict (c). Under international law there are no circumstances justifying the use of a nuclear weapon (d).

Nuclear weapons are characterised by their effects on human health and the environment, which are both quantitative and qualitative.

(a) The use of nuclear weapons violates international law by reason of the quantitative effects of such weapons

3.44 There are three types of nuclear weapons: atom bombs, hydrogen bombs and neutron bombs. Without entering into the specific details of how each of these weapons works, it is worth noting that the power of each of these bombs varies between:

— 1 to 75 kilotonnes (1 kilotonne = 1,000 tonnes of dynamite) for atomic bombs; the minimum level of one kilotonne corresponds to the minimum critical mass of fissile material necessary to unleash a nuclear reaction (the bombardment of uranium-235 atoms or plutonium-239 atoms by neutrons — when bursting (fission) these atoms free other neutrons and a great amount of energy). It is now possible to go below the level of 1 kilotonne through the use of certain "compression" techniques of fissile material, and it has been suggested that nuclear weapons with a power equivalent to 10 or 100 tonnes of TNT might be constructed;

— between several kilotonnes and several megatonnes (1 megatonne = 1,000 kilotonnes) for hydrogen bombs (thermonuclear weapons) which comprise two bombs: a thermonuclear bomb with virtually unlimited power and an atomic explosive which allows the necessary temperature of several million degrees to be reached to unleash a nuclear reaction where isotopes of heavy hydrogen (tritium and deuterium) unite (fusion) to create a helium core, thereby unleashing a vast quantity of energy; the atomic explosive which triggers the fusion is approximately 1 kilotonne, the amount of fissile material necessary for a nuclear reaction; these materials are generally then encased in a mass of uranium-238 which is more stable than uranium-235, but which as a result of the fusion and the intense bombardment of neutrons itself enters the reaction (fission). The whole process thereby comprises one of fission-fusion-fission. The maximum power of such a weapon is limited only by limitations relating to packaging and transportation, and certain attempts have been made to create larger weapons, although it seems that at present the majority of nuclear weapons arsenals comprise bombs of between ½ and 1 megatonne (some 38 to 76 times more powerful than the bomb used at Hiroshima);

- neutron bombs from 1 to several kilotonnes: these are actually thermonuclear bombs of limited power which are not surrounded by a belt of uranium-238; the effect of the shockwaves is less significant than other nuclear weapons. Although neutron bombs have less of an effect on solid objects (buildings, vehicles) they produce proportionately more radiation and hence create greater damage to victims and the environment in relation to their actual size.[127]

3.45 The destructive effect of these weapons results from the following phenomena:

- shock waves or air blasts;
- thermic waves or radiation;
- fires;
- initial nuclear radiation (emitting neutron or gamma rays);
- residual nuclear radiation or radioactive fallout; and
- electro-magnetic impulses.[128]

These effects vary according to a range of factors, including the nature and power of the bomb used, the population density of the bombarded area, the topography of that area, the availability of protection for the population, the foreseeability or otherwise of the attack, local weather conditions, and the height at which the explosion occurs. Forecasts have been prepared as to the damage which would result from the use of a nuclear weapon under different scenarios, and the precise effect will obviously vary from one situation to the next.

3.46 Without identifying all possible situations, it is worth recalling that at Hiroshima a small bomb of only 13 kilotonnes was used. This exposed some 320,000 people to the effects of the explosion, of whom 70,000 thousand civilians died within one month. In 1950 it was estimated that 200,000 people had died as a direct result of the use of the bombing.[129] In Nagasaki, out of some 280,000 people exposed to the effects of the 22 kilotonnes bomb, 100,000 people had died by 1950.[130] The

---

127 *L'Encyclopaedia Universalis*, v° "Nucléaire (armement)"; *Etude d'ensemble des armes nucléaires*, Rapport du Secrétaire général, doc. ONU A/35/392, 12 septembre 1980 ("*1980 UN Report*"), Appendix 1, p. 180, para. 23; *Etude d'ensemble des armes nucléaires*, Rapport du Secrétaire général, doc. ONU A/45/373, 18 septembre 1990 ("*1990 UN Report*"); A. Resibois and A. Joffroy, *Armes nucléaires : les médecins désarmés*, Bruxelles, Assoc. Méd pour la Prév. de la Guerre Nucl., 1981, pp.12-13 ("Resibois and Joffroy"); H. Firket, "Effets biologiques et médicaux des explosions nucléaires", in *Vivre ensemble ou mourir : le dilemme nucléaire*, Bruxelles, Assoc. Méd. pour la Prév. de la Guerre Nucl., 1986, pp.17-18.

128 *1980 UN Report*, Appendix 1, paras. 1-35; *1983 WHO Report*, p. 8; *1987 WHO Report*, p. 9.

129 *1980 UN Report*, paras. 162-63.

130 *Id.*, para. 163.

difference in the figures results from the different topographies of the two cities: Hiroshima is a town situated on flat land close to the sea, whereas different parts of Nagasaki are separated by several small hills, diminishing the shock wave and blowing effects of the explosion.[131]

Other than the effects on civilians, virtually all health services were affected or destroyed. In Hiroshima only three out of 45 hospitals and dispensaries remained intact; out of 1,780 nurses, 1,654 were killed or too seriously injured to allow them to work; 65 of the 150 doctors were killed and most of the others injured.[132]

3.47 Under international law it is clear beyond any doubt that the use of a nuclear weapon against civilians, whatever the nature or size and destructive power of the weapon, will be rendered illegal by virtue of the application of the customary rule which states that belligerents must always distinguish between combatants and non-combatants and limit their attack only to the former. This is an old and well-established rule which has achieved universal acceptance. The first multilateral instrument to state it was the St. Petersburg Declaration of 1868, the second paragraph of which declares that:

> "the only legitimate object which States should endeavour to accomplish during war is to weakening the military forces of the enemy".

This obligation is repeated and further elaborated in different forms in many instruments, including :

- Article 25 of the Regulation annexed to the 1907 Hague Convention IV Respecting the Laws and Customs of War on Land, and Article 1 of the 1907 Hague Convention IX Concerning Bombardment by Naval Forces in Times of War, to the extent that these provisions prohibit attacks on undefended areas and undefended buildings;

- the resolution of 30 September 1928, whereby the Assembly of the League of Nations forbade the civilian population from being considered a military objective;

- the 1949 Geneva Conventions prohibiting attacks on military establishments and health transports (Art 19 *et seq.* of Convention I; Article 22 *et seq.* of Convention II; Articles 14, 15, 18, 21, 22 of Convention IV);

---

131 *Id.*, para. 162; *1983 WHO Report*, p.88: British Medical Association, *The Medical Effects of Nuclear War*, Chichester, J. Wiley, 1983, pp.3-4.

132 Resibois and Joffroy, *loc.cit.*, p.9; for slightly different figures see also T. Okihita, in *1983 WHO Report*, p.95 (French). For estimates of damage to medical and hospital staff following an attack on London or Boston see A. Leaf, in *1987 WHO Report.*, Annex 6, pp. 169-70 (French).

- UN General Assembly resolutions 2444 (XXIII) of 19 December 1968 and 2675 (XXV) of 9 December 1970;[133]

- the 1977 Geneva Protocol I, Articles 12 and 21 (which prohibit attacks against sanitary units and health transports), Article 48 (which restates the St. Petersburg rule), and Article 51 (which states and develops the prohibition against attacking the civilian population).

The illegality of the Hiroshima bombings, on these grounds, was recognized by the Tokyo District Court in the Shimoda case in 1963.[134] It is therefore unnecessary to dwell on the use of nuclear weapons against civilians and health units: the use of a nuclear weapon against civilian targets, or of a weapon having incidental effects on civilians in any circumstance is rendered illegal by virtue of the most elementary rules of the international law of armed conflict.

3.48 Further, it is clear that the use of a nuclear weapon against civilians would not only constitute a "simple" violation of international humanitarian law; it would also constitute a war crime under Article 85 of 1977 Geneva Protocol I, since it would constitute an intentional attack on sanitary units and transportation (Art. 85(2)), on the civilian population or individual civilians (Art. 85(3a)), or the launching of an indiscriminate attack affecting the civilian population or civilian objects in the knowledge that such an attack would cause excessive loss of life or injury to civilians (Art. 85(3b)).

3.49 Moreover, the use of a nuclear weapon against a civilian target would constitute a crime against humanity, as defined by Article 6(c) of the Statute of the Nuremberg Military International Tribunal (which defines crimes against humanity as all "acte inhumain commis contre toute population civile avant ou pendant la guerre [...]" and Article 2 of the 1948 Convention for the Prevention and Punishment of the Crime of Genocide (78 *U.N.T.S.* 277). The UN General Assembly has characterised as "crimes against humanity and civilisation" **any** use by a State of a nuclear or thermonuclear weapons (*supra* para. 3.36), irrespective of whether they are even used against civilians. This view is shared by many distinguished jurists (a non-exhaustive list is set out *supra* para. 3.21 at note 70).

---

133 Resolution 2444 provides, *inter alia*:

"b) Qu'il est interdit de lancer des attaques contre les populations civiles en tant que telles;
"c) Qu'il faut en tous temps faire la distinction entre les personnes qui prennent part aux hostilités et les membres de la population civile afin que ces derniers soient épargnés dans toute la mesure possible;"

Resolution 2675 further develops those principles.

134 32 *ILR* 627-634.

3.50 Further use of a nuclear weapon against a military target will also be illegal. This arises from the following considerations:-

— even the use of a limited nuclear weapon with reduced power (such as a battlefield nuclear weapon) renders death inevitable for those within the range of its effects (i);

— the use of a limited nuclear weapon with reduced power could lead to total nuclear war (ii);

— the use of nuclear weapon with enhanced power increases the effects identified above and adds indiscriminate effects which cannot be limited to any "permitted" military objectives (iii).

(i) Nuclear weapons render death inevitable

3.51 Even if the power of a nuclear weapon could be reduced to a fraction of one kilotonne[135] (equivalent perhaps to the size of the *blockbusters* used during the Second World War, which contained approximately 10 tonnes of TNT)[136] it would nevertheless be the case that such a bomb would not leave those within the immediate vicinity of the explosion with any reasonable chance of survival.[137] In addition to the shock waves or blowing effect, there would also be thermic waves which, for those in the vicinity, would leave no chance of survival; with a power of 10 to 20 kilotonnes (the size of the Hiroshima and Nagasaki bombs) the fireball alone would be felt in a radius of some 200 metres:[138]

> "Dans la boule de feu et a proximité immédiate, tout se volatiserait ou fonderait".[139]
>
> "A Hiroshima et a Nagasaki, la température a atteint 3000-4000 OC a proximité du point zéro; elle a dépassé 570° OC meme a une distance de 1100-1600 m.".[140]

The "eclair thermique" of a one kilotonne bomb will cause 3rd degree burns to a

135 *1990 UN Report*, paras. 39 *et seq*. (French).

136 *1983 WHO Report*, p. 9, para. 9 (French); *1987 WHO Report*, p. 10, para. 10.

137 *1990 UN Report*, para. 295 (French).

138 *1990 UN Report*, para. 293, n. 2 (French).

139 *1990 UN Report*, para. 294.

140 T. Okhita, in *1983 WHO Report*, p.88 (French); A. Leaf, *1987 WHO Report*, p.163 and notes (French).

person at 600 metres distant from the explosion,[141] and can also ignite secondary fires which, if occurring simultaneously, could lead to fireballs of the type which occurred at Hiroshima,[142] or occurred as a result of the Allied bombings of Hamburg, Dresden and Tokyo.[143] Many survivors of the shock waves would be killed by these incendiaries. Such a consequence violates the prohibition on the use of weapons which render death inevitable. According to the 1868 Declaration of St Petersburg, the "legitimate objective" of war

> "would be exceeded by the employment of arms which uselessly aggravate the sufferings of disabled men, or **render their death inevitable**".[144] (emphasis added)

3.52 The obligation reflected in the preamble to the St. Petersburg Declaration remains in force and applicable today. It has been neither abolished nor superseded. Nuclear weapons are far more lethal than any other weapon, including chemical weapons (which do not necessarily render death inevitable since appropriate shelter would provide protection) and which have been universally condemned. According to a group of UN experts,

> "There is therefore no target strong enough to resist the intense effects of nuclear weapons [...]"[145]

Death is inevitable for all those in the vicinity of a nuclear explosion.

3.53 The prohibition on the use of weapons which render death inevitable reflects an even more fundamental principle of the law of armed conflict: the obligation to minimise harm to combatants. Accordingly in its use of force a State must not injure its enemy when it can capture him, nor cause serious injury when it can cause only slight injury, and not kill the enemy if he can be injured.[146]

---

141 Resibois and Joffroy, *op. cit.*, p.20.

142 *1990 UN Report*, para. 294 (French).

143 Resibois and Joffrey, *op. cit.*, p.24; A. Leaf, in *1987 WHO Report* Annex VI, pp.163-64 (French); T. A. Postol, "Possible Fatalities from Superfires Following Nuclear Attacks in or Near Urban Areas," in F. Solomon and R.Q. Marston (eds.), *The Medical Implications of Nuclear War*, Institute of Medicine and National Academy of Sciences, Washington DC, National Academy Press (1986), pp.15 *et seq*.

144 On this text see E. David, *Principes de droit des conflits armés* (1994), pp.266 *et seq* ("Principes").

145 1980 UN Report, para. 142.

146 Examen, *supra*. note 119, pp. 206-07, 279, 332 and 336.

The principle is reflected in a number of rules: the limitation on the choice of methods or means of warfare (Regulation annexed to the 1907 Hague Convention IV Art. 22; 1977 Geneva Protocol I, Art. 35(1)); the prohibition on declaring that no quarter will be given (1907 Hague Convention IV, Art. 23; 1977 Geneva Protocol I, Art. 40); the prohibition of the use of weapons which cause unnecessary suffering (*infra* para. 3.74); the obligation to take necessary precautions during attacks to avoid the civilians and their property (1977 Geneva Protocol I, Art. 57; 1907 Hague Convention IV, Art. 26). This list is merely illustrative, and many more examples could be given.

As a result of the scale of the devastation which the use of a nuclear weapon will cause, and the unavoidable lethal effects within a certain perimeter, the use of a nuclear weapon would certainly violate these widely accepted principles and rules of international law.

(ii) The use of even a single nuclear weapon could result in total nuclear war

3.54 Proponents of the use of nuclear weapons probably consider it inappropriate to contemplate catastrophic scenarios and maintain that a limited nuclear conflict is possible. This view is only realistic, if it could ever be called realistic, in the context of the use of a nuclear weapon against a State which did not possess nuclear weapons, or which did not have allies which both possessed nuclear weapons and were willing to use them. In a conflict between two or more States possessing nuclear weapons the likelihood of an escalation is great, and would probably lead to total nuclear war and the devastation of a substantial part of the international community. This view has been endorsed by UN experts,[147] by independent academics,[148] and by political figures.[149]

3.55 In other words, there is a good chance that a State which made first-use of a nuclear weapon, even in a limited manner, would provoke a global nuclear conflagration. It is difficult to see how such behaviour, with the mere possibility of such consequences, can be compatible with international law. It would violate the obligation "to respect and make others respect" international humanitarian law,[150] further enhancing the inherent illegality of the use of nuclear weapons. Even if a

147 1980 UN Report, para. 199.

148 1987 WHO Report, Annex 4(c), p.127.

149 See e.g. the views of Lord Mountbatten: "in warfare without triggering an all-out nuclear exchange leading to the final holocaust . . . is more and incredible . . . In all sincerity, as a military man I can see no use for any nuclear weapons which would not end in escalation with consequences that no one can conceive"; cited in British Medical Association, *op.cit.* pp.26-27.

150 Art. 1 common to the four 1949 Geneva Conventions, and Art. 1(1) of the 1977 Geneva Protocol I.

State could not have known that its act would result in such consequences, it would be regarded as "an encouragement [...] to commit acts contrary to general principles of international humanitarian law reflected in treaties" the view taken by the Court in the *Case concerning certain military and paramilitary activities against Nicaragua.*[151]

3.56 The first use of a nuclear weapon, even of limited power and targeted only against military objectives, would therefore be illegal independently of any of its unavoidable lethal effects. This arises simply by reason of the possibility that it might lead to the massive use of nuclear weapons and the violation of most of the rules of the law of armed conflict.

It is no doubt for this reason that the UN General Assembly has solemnly proclaimed that

> "1.States and Statesmen that resort *first* to the use of nuclear weapons will be committing the *gravest* crime against humanity;
>
> 2.There will never be any justification or pardon for Statesmen who take the decision to be the first to use nuclear weapons";[152] (emphasis added).

(iii) Nuclear weapons have indiscriminate effects

3.57 In the case of a strategic nuclear war it is conceivable that nuclear weapons might be used against combatants with limited side effects against civilians: for example, an attack against enemy forces in the desert or on the high seas or outside an inhabited zone. The surgical precision of a nuclear attack of this kind is entirely theoretical, notwithstanding that even in such a circumstance, violations of general international law for the protection of human health and the environment would occur (*infra* paras. 3.61-3.62, 4.21-4.28). As reflected in the reports of the UN referred to frequently in these Written Observations (cited *supra* at note 127), such a scenario is, historically, speculative and beyond the realms of possibility. Experience with the use of nuclear weapons (Nagasaki, Hiroshima) and major nuclear accidents (Chernobyl) indicates clearly that the effects of radiation, once released, are uncontrollable.

3.58 The limited use of nuclear weapons would, however, most likely lead to an escalation into an all out nuclear war. According to the SIPRI figures adopted by the 1990 UN Report, the majority of Russian and American arsenals comprise nuclear weapons with a power of 100 kilotonnes or more.[153] Accordingly a first use or an escalation

---

151 *ICJ Rep.* 1986, p.130, para. 256.

152 A/RES 36/100, 9 December 1981 (82 in favour, 19 against, 41 abstentions).

153 *1990 UN Report*, Appendix II (French).

involving either or both of these States would probably result in the use of nuclear weapons having eight times the power of that used in Hiroshima. The greater the power of the weapon, the greater the collateral damage caused to civilians, their property and the environment.

It has been estimated that to halt a classical attack led by four divisions (80,000 troops) supported by 100 planes operating out of ten airbases, it will be necessary to have:

> "some tens of weapons of 1 to 10 kt. yield against important elements of the ground forces and up to 10 weapons of 20 to 100 kt. yield to reduce the opponent's air force."[154]

The number of civilian victims resulting from a limited action of this type, even if it had only military objectives, would undoubtedly vary considerably according to the density of the population in the regions attacked. On the basis of median figures it is not inconceivable that the total number killed or seriously injured could be 180,000 civilians (150,000 as a result of direct effect of the explosions and 30,000 as a result of radioactive fallout) and 35,000 military personnel (30,000 and 5,000 respectively).[155] These figures could be reduced if certain protective measures were taken (alerts, evacuation, shelter),

> "[h]owever, this does not invalidate the most conspicuous conclusion that can be drawn from the table: even when only military targets are selected, and even if protection is provided, the civilian casualties may far outnumber the military ones."[156]

Other simulations confirm this prognosis. It has been calculated that in the case of a nuclear conflict in Western and Eastern Europe in which less than 1% of the total available nuclear weaponry were used[157] against 470 exclusively military targets (in which 379 targets were the subject of a single attack of 150 kilotonnes each, and the other 91 targets were the subject of three attacks of 150 kilotonnes each), the total number of dead and injured resulting from the shock waves, blowing effect and heat alone would exceed 15.6 million. If you add to this figure the foreseeable victims resulting in the short term from radioactive fallout, a figure of more than 100 million dead and injured would be reached.[158] According to other studies which concern limited nuclear attacks, targeting only military objectives in the United States or in the former USSR, figures suggest that the number of victims, depending upon

---

154 *1980 UN Report*, para. 186.

155 *Id.*, para. 189.

156 *Id.*, para. 190.

157 A. Ottolenghi, in *1987 WHO Report*, Annex 4.C, p.130 (French).

158 *Id.*

geographical circumstances, winds and the theoretical models used, would vary between 23 million and 45 million in the United States, and 54 million in the former USSR.[159]

3.59 In the context of the likelihood of escalation, the use of small nuclear weapons become incrementally more significant (see *supra* paras. 3.54-3.56). Where the use of nuclear weapons in the above-mentioned cases affects a large number of non-combatants, it will be seen that their use necessarily has indiscriminate effects even where belligerents have sought to limit their actions to military targets. Legally, any such use would violate the obligation to distinguish between combatants and non-combatants by limiting any attacks to the former (*supra* para. 3.47) and not using weapons with indiscriminate effects (see 1977 Geneva Protocol I, Art. 51(4)-(5)).[160] With a large number of victims it is impossible to argue that the collateral damage was not "excessive in relation to the concrete and direct military advantage anticipated" within the meaning of Art. 51(5)(b) *in fine* of the 1977 Geneva Protocol I. Losses of the scale indicated above would not only be "excessive", they would constitute a war crime, a crime against humanity, and possibly even genocide if it could be shown that the person using the nuclear weapon had the requisite element of intent (see 1948 Convention on the Prevention of the Crime of Genocide, Art. 2). The element of intent for genocide could be inferred from the mere failure of the person using the nuclear weapons to take account of its full effects: in such conditions it is impossible to say that they were ignorant as to the consequences of use and that therefore they did not intend to exterminate the victim population.

These observations become all the more pertinent when one considers the possibility of **any** use of **any** nuclear weapon against a small island state, which would have the effect of wiping out the entire population and rendering its environment uninhabitable.

3.60 Another consequence of a "limited" nuclear attack would be the impossibility for health services, assuming they remained intact, to assure the care required for those victims who had not been killed. The burden placed on medical facilities and staff would be overwhelming. According to one expert:

> "Le nombre de victimes que provoquerait ne serait-ce que l'utilisation d'une petite partie des arsenaux nucléaires d'aujourd'hui montre bien qu'il est vain d'envisager qu'un quelconque système de santé puisse offrir des soins médicaux adaptés à la situation."[161]

> "Dégager les blessés des décombres, leur prodiguer les premiers soins, puis les transporter hors de la zone de destruction dans des établissements médicaux appropriés serait une tâche extrêmement difficile, même en l'absence de retombées radioactives, d'incendies violents et d'obstruction des rues

---

[159] B. Levi and F. von Hippel, in *id.*, Annex 4.B, pp. 105 *et seq.* (French).

[160] *Cfr. Principes, op. cit.*, pp.281 et 331 (French).

[161] A. Leaf, in *id.*, Annex 6, p.167 (French).

par les décombres des bâtiments effondrés. [...] Il s'agit là d'une situation exigeant une contribution maximale de la part des services médicaux dans de nombreux domaines: sang, plasma, autre liquides administrables par voie parentérale, actes chirurgicaux, antibiotiques, soins infirmiers, soins médicaux, chambres stériles, de même que toutes les autres ressources sophistiquées de la médecine moderne. Il s'agit en outre de blessures dont chacune exige des journées entières de soins intensifs et des semaines ou des mois de soins hospitaliers. En fait, il n'existe aucun moyen de soigner un aussi grand nombre de victimes."[162]

These conclusions, which address the consequences of the use of nuclear weapons in industrialised countries, are *a fortiori* valid in respect of any developing country which might be subject to a nuclear attack.

3.61 The use of a nuclear weapon which affects a large number of non-combatants will necessarily have indiscriminate effects, even if the action was intended to be limited to military targets. Such use violates the obligation to distinguish between combatants and non-combatants, to limit attacks to combatants (*supra* para. 3.47), and not to use weapons with indiscriminate effects (1977 Geneva Protocol I, Art 51(4-5)). The large number of victims resulting from the use of any nuclear weapon, as evidenced by the Reports cited above, would be indiscriminate in causing incidental loss to civilian life or objects and would be excessive in relation to any military advantage anticipated (see 1977 Geneva Protocol I, Art. 51(5)(b)). Such damage to human health and the environment would constitute a war crime and a crime against humanity and, to the extent that the necessary intentional element could be proved (whether such intention is express or could be implied), genocide (*supra* para. 3.49, 1948 Genocide Convention, Art. II).

3.62 Another consequence of a "strategic" nuclear at tack would be the overwhelming burden imposed upon a country's health services to respond to the needs of victims. In countries with less highly developed health services the burden would be even greater. The use of a weapon which prevents health services from functioning or which renders any possibility of helping the injured violates international humanitarian law. Thus, the 1949 Geneva Convention IV provides that "the wounded and sick **shall** be cared for" (Art. 3(2), emphasis added). As the International Court has recognised, this provision applies *a fortiori* in an international armed conflict.[163] The obligation is further developed in various provisions of the Geneva Conventions (1949 Geneva Convention I, Art. 12 *et seq.*; 1949 Geneva Convention II, Art. 12; 1949 Geneva Convention IV, Arts. 16 *et seq.* and 55 *et seq.*), as well as the 1977 Geneva Protocols (Protocol I, Arts. 8, 61, 68; Protocol II, Art. 7 *et seq.*). Article 10 of the 1977 Geneva Protocol I provides:

"1.All the wounded, sick and shipwrecked, to whichever Party they belong, shall be respected and protected.

---

162 *Id.*, p. 168 (French).

163 *Military and Paramilitary Activities in and Against Nicaragua*, *ICJ Rep.* 1986, p.114, para. 218.

2.In all the circumstances they shall be treated humanely and shall receive, to the fullest extent practicable and with least possible delay, the medical care and attention required by their condition."

This obligation will be violated even where it is impossible to save the victims of a "limited" nuclear conflict.[164]

3.63 In conclusion, the extraordinary power of nuclear weapons and the enormity of their effects on human health and the environment necessarily means that their use violates, directly or indirectly, those rules of the international law of armed conflict which prohibits:

- the use of weapons that render death inevitable;
- the use of weapons which have indiscriminate effects;
- any behaviour which might violate this law.

(b) The use of nuclear weapons violates international law by reason of the qualitative effects of such weapons

3.64 The qualitative effects of nuclear weapons which distinguish them from conventional weapons are those which result (i) from the disintegration of the atom and (ii) from radioactive fallout. The disintegration of the atom has two consequences: the emission of electromagnetic impulses and initial nuclear radiation.

(i) The specific consequences of the disintegration of the atom

3.65 The disintegration of the atom has two effects:

— electromagnetic impulses (a); and
— initial nuclear radiation (b).

(a) Electromagnetic impulses and their consequences

3.66 The explosion of a nuclear weapon produces high energy gamma rays which remove electrons from surrounding matter and leave electrically charged atoms (ions). It is the removal of electrons which produces an extremely short and high intensity electromagnetic impulse.[165] Without going into the technical details of the phenomenon,[166] it should be remembered that if the electro-magnetic impulse does not seem to cause direct physical damage to the human body, it has serious indirect consequences insofar as it can damage all the electrical and electronic equipment of

---

164 Singh, *op. cit.*, pp.200-01.

165 *1980 UN Report*, Appendix I, p. 179, para. 18 (French).

166 *Id.*

an area affected by an explosion. The electro-magnetic impulse might destroy computers, transistors, and integrated circuits to which it is transmitted through electromagnetic energy captors such as antennae, telephone wires, railway lines, the aluminium fuselage of planes etc. Many systems which are essential for the life and health of civilian populations, as well as civil society in general, would be rendered unworkable, including electronic devices for medical purposes, telecommunications for civil use, and water, gas and electricity supplies.[167] The effect of cutting communications links between military personnel might also precipitate a further escalation in the use of nuclear weapons.[168]

It should nevertheless be noted that the effects of electromagnetic impulses are relatively negligible in contrast to the other effects of nuclear weapons described above, so long as the explosion takes place at an altitude of less than 10 or 15 kilometres. On the other hand, if the explosion takes place at a higher altitude, the blowing, thermic and radioactive effects have more limited consequences for the population on the ground, but the electromagnetic impulse effects are greater since they will reach "une vaste zone dont les limites coincident avec la ligne d'horizon par rapport au point d'explosion".[169] It has been calculated that:

> "L'explosion d'une bombe à une altitude de 100 km., par exemple, produirait un effet électromagnétique sensible dans un rayon de 1100 km. Une explosion unique à 350 km. d'altitude produirait une impulsion qui toucherait pratqiuement la totalité de l'Europe ou des E.-U., ainsi qu'une partie du Canada et du Mexique."[170]

3.67 Electromagnetic impulses have effects which cannot be directed or limited, and they affect indiscriminately:

- combatants and civilians;
- medical safety, health and assistance units; and
- third States and areas beyond national jurisdiction.

It follows that the use of the nuclear weapons will violate those rules of the law of armed conflicts which prohibit the use of weapons of indiscriminate effects (*supra* paras. 3.57-3.63). It also violates the rules of international law governing friendly relations between States which prohibit the effects of a conflict being felt by third Party States, namely:

---

167 *1987 WHO Report*, p.11, para. 12, *et seq.* (French).

168 *Id.* p.12, para. 14.

169 *1980 UN Report*, Appendix I, p.179, para. 20 (French).

170 *1987 WHO Report*, p.11, para. 13 (French).

- the rule prohibiting States from damaging human health or the environment in the territory of other States (*infra*, paras. 4.9-4.20);

- the laws of neutrality — to the extent that they apply — according to which "[t]he territory of neutral Powers is inviolable" (1907 Convention (V) Respecting the Rights and Duties of Neutral Powers and Persons in Case of War on Land, Article 1)

- the rules prohibiting aggression, to the extent that the UN General Assembly has defined aggression as "the use of all weapons by a State" acting first "against the territory of another State",[171] which amounts to a violation of Art. 2(4) of the UN Charter.

(b) The initial nuclear radiation

3.68 "Initial nuclear radiation" lasts just one or two seconds, during which time it has very grave consequences for those who are exposed to it, involving both short and medium term consequences. The effect on living organisms is similar to that of a genotoxic poison (as opposed to the neurotoxic poison unleashed by a chemical weapon).[172] The effects are even more extensive in the case of neutron bombs. Initial nuclear radiation only affects living matter; acts as a poison; complicates or precludes the possibility of treating the sick or wounded; causes unnecessary suffering and superfluous injury; and poses long-term genetic risks for those who are not directly involved in the conflict, including the children of those who are directly exposed. Moreover, it is an inherent characteristic of the use of nuclear weapons and would occur in any use.

3.69 In the short term, the principal effects of radiation on the human body have been commonly referred to as radiation sickness and have been described as follows:

> "The severity of these syndromes depends on the radiation dose received. In the lethal range of doses three degrees of severity can be recognized: (1) the central nervous system syndrome, characterized by alternating states of stupor and hyperexcitability, with unavoidable death within a few days (this is the effect aimed at by the use of neutron bombs); (2) the gastrointestinal syndrome, characterised by nausea, persistent vomiting, and haemorrhagic diarrhoea, with death occurring within a week or two; and (3) the haematopoietic syndrome, characterized by nausea, vomiting, cytopenia, anaemia, and immunity disturbances. When the whole body is exposed over a short period to doses less than 6 Gy (600 rad) the prognosis is directly related to the doses received by the bone marrow. It the same dose is received over a longer period of time the chances of survival increases. The risk of death is greatly reduced if some bone marrow, even as little as a tenth, is shielded from the radiation. In the range of whole-body irradiation of 2-6Gy (200-600 rad) survival depends largely on the

---

171 A/RES 3314 (XXIX), 14 December 1974, Art. 3(b) and 2 (adopted by consensus).

172 See reference in Andries, *supra*, note 60, at 21.

therapeutic measures taken."[173]

According to their proximity to the place of the explosion and the power of the weapon, victims can either die in hours, days or weeks following their exposure to radiation:

> "For an explosion similar to those over Hiroshima or Nagasaki, the radiation is strong enough to render human beings in the open unconscious within minutes at distances up to 700 or 800 m from ground-zero. The exposed persons, if they survive the blast and heat, would die in less than one or two days from the radiation injury. The radiation received at a distance of 1,300-1,400 m from such an explosion would also be fatal but death may be delayed up to about a month. At 1,800 m or more from ground-zero few if any acute radiation injuries would be expected to occur. However, late radiation injuries may be induced by lower radiation levels."[174]

Shelters specifically constructed to deal with nuclear conflict might provide certain protection against initial nuclear radiation:

> "En demeurant dans un local ou dans un abri spécialement conçu, on réduirait considérablement la dose d'irradiation. Un bon abri diviserait cette dose par 1000 ou davantage [...]. La protection assurée par une maison ordinaire dépendrait de son type de construction et d'autres caractéristiques."[175]

This type of protection is going to have a limited efficacy with regard to neutron bombs:

> "qui sont précisément conçues pour tuer sous l'effet des rayonnements sans infliger par ailleurs trop de dégâts d'origine mécanique ou thermique."[176]

If these reduced doses of radiation are not themselves lethal, combined with other traumatic effects felt by victims, they become fatal. Radiation reduces the defence system of the human organism by attacking the immune system and consequently increasing the risk of exposure to diseases and illnesses which might not otherwise prove to be fatal:

> "En raison de l'effet combiné des blessures et de l'immunosuppression, beaucoup de victimes succomberaient immédiatement après une explosion nucléaire à des blessures ou à des infections qui auraient été bénignes dans des circonstances normales."[177]

---

173 *1983 WHO Report*, p. 12, para. 28.

174 *1990 UN Report*, p.81, para. 297; Leaf, *1987 WHO Report*, p.165 (French).

175 *1983 WHO Report*, p.12, para. 25 (French).

176 Rotblat, J., *ibid.*, p.36, para. 48 (French).

177 *1987 WHO Report*, p.32, para. 76; Leaf, *ibid.*, p.180 (French).

The health needs of victims who have been exposed to nuclear radiation require a high level of technical, medical and hospital infrastructure. The 200 who were injured by the accident at the Chernobyl nuclear power plant, and the 135,000 people who had to be evacuated from a 30km exclusion zone, mobilised "le personnel et the matériel des services de santé de l'ensemble du pays".[178] In the case of a nuclear war, even if it was limited, (see the figures cited *supra* at paras. 3.46 and 3.58) "les services de santé, même à l'échelle mondiale, ne pourraient en aucun cas faire face à cette situation". Developing countries would be more adversely affected than developed countries.

3.70 In the medium and long term, epidemiological studies carried out on large numbers of people exposed to the bombings of Hiroshima and Nagasaki, as well as experiments carried out on animals, have shown a relationship between exposure to radiation (and/or to radioactive fallout) and the accrued subsequent consequences: malignant tumours (leukaemias, thyroid cancers and tumours of the breast, the lung and stomach, and multiple myelomas), cataracts, chromosomal abnormalities, including for those who are exposed *in utero*.[179] Moreover, it is likely the use of nuclear weapons would lead to a significant increase in genetic consequences resulting from any children born from people exposed to radiation.[180]

3.71 Experts are in agreement in recognising that nuclear radiation acts on organisms in the same way as a poison. According to Professor M. Errera of the laboratory of biophysics and radiology at the Université libre de Bruxelles,

> "Il y a deux sortes de poisons: les neurotoxiques et les génotoxiques. Les premiers sont particulièrement le fait des armes chimiques, les seconds celui des armes nucléaires."[181]

According to Professor M.F. Lechat, of the epidemiology unit of the Catholic University of Louvain, and adviser to the Comité internationale d'experts en sciences médicales et santé publique created by the WHO pursuant to Assembly resolution WHA 34.38.[182]

> "On peut considérer l'arme nucléaire comme un 'poison' surtout du fait des effects écologiques: passage dans la chaîne alimentaire avec concentration et dépôt d'isotopes radioactifs dont l'élimination

---

178 *Id.*, p.30 (French).

179 Kato, H and Shigematsu, I.; Land, Ch., Oftedal, P. *1983 WHO Report*, pp. 103-48.

180 Oftedal, P., *id.*, p.154.

181 Cited in Andries, *supra*. note 60, at 21.

182 *1983 WHO Report*, p. 5.

est lente, pouvant s'étager pour certains des isotopes les plus communs sur des années."[183]

Finally, according to annex II of Protocol III of the Paris Accords of 23 October 1954 relating to the control of armaments:

"L'arme nucléaire est définie comme toute arme qui contient ou est conçue pour contenir ou utiliser un combustible nucléaire ou des isotopes radioactifs et qui, par explosion ou autre transformation nucléaire non contrôlée ou par radioactivité du combustible nucléaire ou des isotopes radioactifs, est capable de destruction massive, dommages généralisés ou **empoisonnements** massifs." (emphasis added)[184]

3.72 It should be noted that the lethal synergy of effects (blowing and heat combined with radiation) do not occur in the explosion of nuclear devices with a power of more than 100 kilotonnes

"car la zone mortelle créée par l'effet de souffle et l'effet thermique est bien supérieure à celle qui résulte du rayonnement."[185]

On the other hand, in the case of a neutron bomb

"la zone mortelle où s'exercent les effets des neutrons et des rayons gamma est beaucoup plus étendue que celle de l'onde de choc et de l'onde thermique."[186]

3.73 These qualitative consequences bring nuclear weapons within the scope of those international rules prohibiting the use of weapons which have analogous consequences. Nuclear weapons can thereby be characterised as, or have consequences analogous to, chemical weapons, the use of which is prohibited by international law, notably by:

- 1899 Hague Declaration 2 Concerning Asphyxiating Gases;
- 1925 Geneva Protocol for the Prohibition of the Use in War of Asphyxiating, Poisonous or Other Gases, and of Bacteriological Methods of Warfare;
- 1993 Convention on the Prohibition of the Production, Storage and use of Chemical Weapons and their Destruction.

---

183 *Supra*. note 179.

184 Cited id.; text in *RGDIP*, 1963, p. 825 (French); OTAN Documents fondamentaux Bruxelles, 1981, p. 59.

185 *1987 WHO Report*, p. 16 (French).

186 *Id*. (French).

The 1925 Geneva Protocol is noteworthy because it addresses "asphyxiating, poisonous or other gases, and [..] **all analogous liquids materials** or devices" (emphasis added), reflects the Parties' intention not to limit the category of weapons in a restrictive manner. Moreover, a restrictive approach to interpretation is not the rule in international humanitarian law, which should always be interpreted to give the benefit of any doubt in favour of the protection of the victim. This is particularly reflected in the Martens clause, which provides that:

> "Until a more complete code of the laws of war has been issued, the high contracting Parties deem it expedient to declare that, in cases not included in the Regulations adopted by them, the inhabitants and the belligerants remain under the protection and the rule of the principles of the law of nations, as they result from the usages established among civilized peoples, from the laws of humanity, and the dictates of the public conscience."[187]

3.74 Nuclear weapons have other characteristics which render their use unlawful. They have poisonous consequences and their use is therefore prohibited by the 1899 Hague Convention 2 (Article 23) and the Regulations annexed to the 1907 Hague Convention (IV). They "uselessly aggravate the sufferings of disabled men" in violation of the principle enunciated by the 1868 St Petersburg Declaration, and they cause "superfluous injury" in violation of, *inter alia*, 1907 Hague Convention IV Regulations (Art. 23(e)), 1977 Geneva Protocol I (Art. 35(2)). Moreover, their use would violate the principles of proportionality which regulate the law of armed conflict.

(ii) The effects of radioactive fallout

3.75 Apart from the energy generated by the initial nuclear radiation, nuclear fission produces radioactive substances which attach themselves to particles of the debris of the nuclear weapon as well as to matter dispersed by the explosion (if it takes place at ground level or at a low altitude). These particles produce a "residual" radiation with a life ranging from a fraction of a second to several years. Thus,

> "Two important elements, strontium 90 and caesium 137, for instance, will retain half of their radioactivity after about 30 years, and hence cause long term health hazards. Carbon 14, which is formed from nitrogen in the atmosphere when irradiated with neutron, has a half life of about 5,800 years and will thus continue to give small radiation doses to many generations."[188]

The fallout of radioactive particles will vary according to their weight, the altitude at which the explosion occurred, the prevailing atmospheric conditions, the nature and

---

187 See e.g. 1907 Hague Convention IV, preamble; 1977 Geneva Protocol I, Art. 1(2); 1981 UN Convention on Prohibitions or Restrictions on the Use of Certain Conventional Weapons Which May be Deemed to be Excessively Injurious or to Have Indiscriminate Effects, preamble.

188 *1980 UN Report*, p.169, Appendix 1, para. 31.

size of the weapon used, etc. The heavier and denser particles may be subject to fallout within a few minutes, although lighter particles may remain in the stratosphere for months or years before falling to earth.[189]

3.76 The biological effects of radioactive fallout are analogous to those of the initial nuclear radiation, except that they can cover infinitely greater areas and consequently affect far more people. It has been estimated that for a ground-level explosion of a one megatonne bomb

> "les personnes restant à découvert pendant une longue période recevront des doses mortelles sur une supeficie de près de 2000km^2 et des doses engendrant des lésions sur une superficie d'environ 10000 km^2."[190]

It should also be noted that radioactive particles affect persons both "par irradiation externe de l'ensemble ou d'une partie du corps" and by "irradiation interne (Inhalation ou ingestion d'éléments radioactifs)".[191]

3.77 Given the analogous effects of the initial nuclear radiation and the residual nuclear radiation resulting from radioactive fallout, the rules of international law applicable to the former (*supra* paras. 3.73-3.74) are evidently applicable also to the latter. Accordingly, the use of nuclear weapons doubly violates six capital rules of the international law of armed conflicts as a result of their qualitative effects. International law prohibits the use of weapons which:

- are chemical;
- are poisonous;
- render death inevitable;
- cause unnecessary suffering;
- have indiscriminate effects; and
- violate the principles of proportionality and humanity.

To these six prohibitions there must be added a seventh. As radioactive fallout does not respect national frontiers, third States will certainly be affected by fallout and by the residual nuclear radiation.[192] This fallout would violate the rules of international law governing friendly relations between States and prohibiting any interference with third States (*infra* paras. 4.9-4.20).

---

189 *Id.*; see also *1980 UN Report*, pp.81-83 (French); J. Rotblat, in *1983 WHO Report*, pp.36-39.

190 *1983 WHO Report*, p. 12, para. 23 (French).

191 *Id.*

192 See e.g. the radioactive fallout anticipated in a hypothetical attack against strategic Soviet targets in February, *1987 WHO Report*, Annex 4.B, p.122, fig. 3. (French).

3.78 Additionally, international law now also regulates the methods and means of warfare with the aim of ensuring appropriate protection for the environment. It establishes, in particular, an absolute prohibition on the use of weapons which will cause "widespread, long-term and severe damage to the environment". Article 35(3) of the 1977 Geneva Protocol provides that:

> "It is prohibited to employ methods or means of warfare which are intended, or may be expected, to cause widespread, long-term and severe damage to the natural environment."

Article 55 of Protocol I, which relates to the protection of the civilian population, provides, *inter alia*, that:

> "1.Care shall be taken in warfare to protect the natural environment against widespread, long-term and severe damage. Thus protection includes a prohibition of the use of methods or means of warfare which are intended or may be expected to cause such damage to the natural environment and thereby to prejudice the health or survival of the population."

There can be little doubt that **any** use of nuclear weapons would cause "widespread, long-term and severe damage" to the environment, engendering a violation of Articles 35(3) and 55 of Protocol I and the customary obligation reflected therein. As described in the following Section (*infra* para. 4.3), the Chernobyl accident illustrated the gravity for the environment of a release into the atmosphere of significant quantities of radioactive material, with potential damage to the natural environment lasting several decades.

3.79 The approach in the 1977 Protocol I follows, in general terms, the language used in the 1977 Convention on the Prohibition of Military or other Hostile Use of Environmental Techniques (ENMOD). The basic obligation of Parties, under Article I(i) is:

> "not to engage in military or any other hostile use of environmental modification techniques having widespread, long-lasting or severe effects as the means of destruction, damage or injury to any other State party".

In the context of the definition of "environmental modification technique", (Art. II) this obligation leaves open the question of whether the use of a nuclear weapon could constitute the "deliberate manipulation of natural processes" and lead to the violation of the obligation under ENMOD. Nevertheless, the Convention signals widespread recognition of the need to limit the use of the environment as a weapon of war, without diminishing in any way the customary and treaty obligations establishing clear norms for the protection of the environment which must be followed in times of war and armed conflict (*infra* paras. 4.21-4.28). As supplemented by the more detailed and emphatic obligations of the 1977 Geneva Protocol I, it is submitted that ENMOD now reflects the customary obligation not to cause "widespread, long-lasting or severe" harm to the environment.

(C) The use of nuclear weapons violates international law irrespective of the circumstances in which they are used

3.80 The majority of the rules cited in the preceding discussion apply essentially to international armed conflicts. Although the possibility remains remote, the use of nuclear weapons would also be unlawful in the case of a non-international armed conflict. The fundamental rules which invalidate the use of nuclear weapons — notably the limitation on the methods and means to threaten the enemy and the obligation not to attack civilians — are applicable to **all** armed conflicts. This is reflected in UN General Assembly resolution 2444 (XXIII) which provides:

> "Recognizing the necessity of applying basic humanitarian principles **in all armed conflicts**,
>
> — Affirms resolution XXVIII of the Xxth International Conference of the Red Cross held at Vienna in 1965, which laid down, *inter alia*, the following principles for observance **by all governmental and other authorities** responsible for action in armed conflicts:
>
> (a) that the right of the parties to a conflict to adopt means of injuring the enemy is not unlimited;
>
> (b) that it is prohibited to launch attacks against the civilian populations as such;
>
> (c) that distinction must be made **at all times** between persons taking part in the hostilities and members of the civilian population to the effect that the latter be spared as much as possible"[193] (emphasis added)

The 1977 Geneva Protocol II confirms and extends the principles reflected in resolution 2444, notably by prohibiting attacks against non-combatants, the commission of acts of terrorism, and orders against giving quarter (Arts. 4(1) and (2)(d), 7, 9, 11, and 13). Like Protocol I, Protocol II prohibits attacks against nuclear plants (Art. 15) thus confirming the applicability *a fortiori* of the prohibition on the use of nuclear weapons (*supra* para. 3.23).

It is significant that the General Assembly generally condemns the use of nuclear weapons without distinguishing between international and non-international armed conflicts and qualifies any use as "a crime against humanity" (*supra* para. 3.26). Thus the field of application of crimes against humanity is not limited to international armed conflicts. This is further reflected in the Statute of the International War Tribunal for Crimes committed in the territory of the former Yugoslavia, which recognises the competence of the Tribunal to judge the crimes "committed during an armed conflict, whether international or internal" (Art 5).[194]

---

193 19 December 1968, adopted unanimously (111 votes).

194 Text in Doc. UN S/25704, 3rd May 1993, p.40 on the field of application *ratione contexti* of the crime against humanity; E. David, *Principes, op.cit.* p.604.

(d) The use of nuclear weapons cannot be justified by international law in any circumstances

3.81 Proponents of the legality of the use of nuclear weapons might attempt to justify their use under the principles of (i) legitimate defence; (ii) reprisal; and (iii) necessity. None of these justifications survive a careful scrutiny of the applicable rules of international law.[195]

(i) Self-defence does not justify the use of nuclear weapons

3.82 Self-defence is an exception to the prohibition against the use of force when a State is subject to an armed attack (UN Charter, Art. 51). Accordingly, the self-defence rule is subject to the rules governing *jus ad* (or *contra) bellum*, whereas the rules relating to the use of nuclear weapons arise in relation to *jus in bello*. Moreover, the application of *jus in bello* does not depend on the legality of the defended causes; whether aggressor or victim, each party is equally subject to the law of armed conflict in conformity with the customary principle of the equality of belligerents in the law of war, a principle reflected in the fifth preambular paragraph of the 1977 Geneva Protocol I. Recourse to nuclear weapons, prohibited by the rules of the law of armed conflicts, cannot be justified according to the inherent right of self-defence.

(ii) Reprisals do not justify the use of nuclear weapons

3.83 Recourse to nuclear weapons by way of reprisal must be considered with regard to targets:

(a) which cannot be the object of reprisals: non-combatants and non-military targets;

(b) against which recourse to reprisals is not categorically prohibited: the combatants and military targets.

(a) Reprisals with regard to non-combatants and non-military targets

3.84 During hostilities it is forbidden to resort to reprisals against medical installations, transportation and units; the injured; the infirm; civilian populations, property and various categories of civilian property which are subject to special protection (1977 Geneva Protocol I, Arts. 20, 51(6), 52(1), 53, 54(4), 55(2), 56(4)). The prohibition applies in respect of all weapons, including nuclear weapons. This rule had previously been established in a general manner by Art. 60(5) of the 1969 Vienna Convention on the Law of Treaties (1969 Vienna Convention) which provides that the right to suspend, or denounce a treaty for substantial violation of the latter does not apply

> "to provisions relating to the protection of the human person contained in treaties of a humanitarian

---

[195] The following paragraphs are again largely inspired by *Examen* (2 ed.) *loc. cit.*, pp. 23 *et seq.*

> character, in particular to provisions prohibiting any form of reprisals against persons protected by such treaties."

A similar provision is set forth in paragraph 7 of UN General Assembly resolution 2675 (XXV) of 9 December 1977 on "the fundamental principles [...] concerning the protection of the civilian population during an armed conflict", which declares that

> "Civilian populations, or individual members thereof, **should not be the object of reprisals**, forcible transfers or other assaults on their integrity" (emphasis added)

The prohibition on reprisals in these situations appears also in Principle 1, paragraph 6 of UN General Assembly resolution 2625 (XXV) on friendly relations. Even if, in that case, it relates to *jus ad* (or *contra*) *bellum* rather than *jus in bello*, it is nonetheless applicable to the second. It follows from the above that reprisals can, in no circumstances, be lawful against this category of targets.

(b) Reprisals with regard to combatants and military targets

3.85 The prohibition of reprisals against combatants and military targets is not expressly provided for in legal instruments, but the prohibition of the use of nuclear weapons against the former or the latter is nonetheless certain. Combatants fall under the same title as non-combatants as "protected people" by virtue of the law of armed conflicts and benefit from specific protection against the use of certain forms of weaponry. Thus Art 60(5) of the 1969 Vienna Convention on the law of treaties prohibits the use of *exceptio non adimpleti contractus* in the case of "provisions relative to the protection of human beings". In the case of treaties of a humanitarian character this takes into account combatants as well as non-combatants, with all "human beings" entitled to the minimum standards of humanitarian protection guaranteed by international law. The fact that Art. 60(5) refers "**in particular** to provisions prohibiting any form of reprisals" (emphasis added) does not imply that the other humanitarian provisions — those in which the prohibition of reprisals is not expressly mentioned — fall outside its field of application, since the adverb "notably" shows that the reference to those provisions prohibiting reprisals is not intended to be exhaustive. In this perspective, the use of nuclear weapons by way of reprisal, even if exclusively directed against combatants and military targets, would violate Art. 60(5) and the general provisions of the law of armed conflicts prohibiting this use.

3.86 In a similar manner, the International Law Commission, in its Draft Articles on the Responsibility of States, stresses about Art. 30, on counter-measures, that:

> "even where the internationally wrongful act in question would justify a reaction involving the use of force [...], action taken in this guise certainly cannot include, for instance, a breach of obligations of international humanitarian law. Such a step could never be 'legitimate' and such conduct would

remain wrongful."[196]

3.87 Art. 1 common to the four 1949 Geneva Conventions and Art. 1(1) of 1977 Geneva Protocol I states that:

> "The High Contracting Parties undertake to respect and to ensure respect for the present Convention in all circumstances."

Moreover, as set out in the *Commentaire* to the Geneva Conventions:

> "Les mots 'en toutes circonstances' signifient qu' [. . .] une Partie contractante ne peut se donner aucun prétexte valable, d'ordre juridique ou autre, à ne pas respecter la Convention dans son ensemble [. . .] L'art. 1er, loin d'être une clause de style, a été volontairement revêtu d'un caractère impératif. Il doit être pris à la lettre."[197]

In other words, the absence of an expressed prohibition on reprisals in the rules of Protocol I relating to methods and means of combat does not imply any right to use them: independently of this *a contrario* approach to interpretation,[198] the obligation to respect the Protocol in "all circumstances" necessarily excludes the right of recourse to reprisals.

Moreover, the rule elaborated in Art. 1 also indicates that reciprocity has no place in the law of armed conflicts. As indicated in the *Commentaire* to the Geneva Conventions:

> "En prenant d'emblée cet engagement, les Parties contractantes soulignent que la Convention n'est pas seulement un contrat de réciprocité liant un Etat avec son ou ses co-contractants dans la seule mesure où ceux-ci respectent leurs propres engagements, mais plutôt une série d'obligations unilatérales, solennellement assumées à la face du monde représenté par les autres Parties contractantes. Chaque Etat s'engage aussi bien vis-à-vis de lui-même que vis-à-vis des autres."[199]

The principle of non-reciprocity excludes *a fortiori* recourse to reprisals in relation to the use of nuclear weapons, even against combatants.

---

196 *Ybk ILC*, 1979, Vol. II, Part 2, p. 116, para. 5.

197 *Les Conventions de Genève du 12 août 1949, Commentaire*, Genève, CICR, 1956 vol IV, pp.21-22. ("Commentaire des Conventions").

198 The *a contrario* argument would only be acceptable if a text could be found in humanitarian law which said "reprisals are only prohibited against the following objectives ... ". It would only be in that case that the *a contrario* argument could be upheld with respect to the legality of reprisals against all objectives not appearing in this list.

199 *Commentaire des Conventions*, III, p.24; see also *Commentaires*, pp.37-38; *Principes loc. cit.* pp.473-74.

3.88 The draft article of the ICRC on the regulation of reservations to 1977 Geneva Protocol I prohibited, *inter alia*, any reservation relating to the prohibition of the use of weapons causing superfluous injury.[200] It was dropped by the Conference because of opposition from Western and socialist States who wanted the question of reservations to remain subject to the general rules on the Law of Treaties. The draft text nevertheless reflects the importance of the prohibition in the eyes of the ICRC, and it is possible to conclude that a humanitarian prohibition which cannot be subject to a reservation also cannot be overridden in the name of a reprisal. In any case, to the extent that the general rules relating to reservations prohibit reservations incompatible with the object and purpose of the treaty (where the treaty is silent, 1969 Vienna Convention, Art 19(c)), reservations relating to use of nuclear weapons are evidently incompatible with the object and purpose of rules to protect victims of war from the exceptionally harmful effects of these weapons, as well as the fact that their use violates many fundamental rules of humanitarian law.

In practice, the very nature of nuclear weapons (excluding virtually any possibility of limiting their effects to military targets and avoiding a total war) means that recourse to nuclear reprisals would necessarily violate prohibitions for which these reprisals are explicitly prohibited — for example the prohibition on attacking civilian populations or their property (*supra* para. 3.47). This is why such reprisals must necessarily be illegal.[201]

(iii) Necessity does not justify the use of nuclear weapons

3.89 Compromised between military necessities and humanitarian requirements, the law of armed conflicts does not accept the state of necessity except in those circumstances where it is expressly provided for. As stated by the International Law Commission about its Draft Article 33 on the state of necessity as a situation precluding illegality as a result of a violation of international law, this exception does not authorise a State to ignore the prescriptions of humanitarian law:

> "It would be absurd to invoke the idea of military necessity or necessity of war in order to evade the duty to comply with obligations designed, precisely, to prevent the necessities of war from causing suffering which it was desired to prescribe once and for all."[202]

If humanitarian law takes account of military necessities:

> "these are provisions which apply only to the cases expressly provided for. Apart from these cases,

---

[200] ICRC, Draft Additional Protocol to the Geneva Conventions of 12th August 1949, commentary, Geneva, 1973 pp.106-08.

[201] *Cf.* von der Heydte and Andrassy, in *Ann.I.D.I.*, Session of Nice, 1967, Vol. 52, Pt. II, p. 45; I. Brownlie, "Some Legal Aspects of the Use of Nuclear Weapons" *ICLQ* 1965, p.445.

[202] *Ybk.ILC*, 1980, II, Part 2, p.46, para. 28.

> it follows implicitly from the text of the conventions that they do not admit the possibility of invoking military necessity as a justification for State conduct not in conformity with the obligations they impose."[203]

The jurisprudence of course takes the same approach. Thus, in *Van Lewinski (alias Von Manstein)* case:

> "Once the usages of war have assumed the status of laws, they cannot be overridden by necessity, except in those special cases where the law itself makes provision for that eventuality."[204]

The rule is absolute:

> "[...] the rules of international law must be followed even if it results in the loss of a battle or even a war. Expediency or necessity cannot warrant their violation [...]"[205]

The rule applies equally in relation to nuclear weapons.[206] In the *Shimoda* case the Tokyo District Court, in response to the argument that all means to force the enemy to surrender are good, said:

> "[...] it is wrong to say that the distinction between military objective and non-military objective has gone out of existence because of total war".[207]

(D) The relevant rules of international law prohibiting the use of nuclear weapons apply to all States

3.90 The rules of the law of armed conflict and the law governing friendly relations which prohibit the use of nuclear weapons are, notably, those which establish:

- the limitation on the choice of means of attacking the enemy (*supra* paras. 3.47-3.80);
- the permanent obligation to distinguish between combatants and non- combatants (*supra* paras. 3.47, 3.59, 3.80);
- the prohibition against attacking civilian targets (*supra* paras. 3.47-3.48, 3.80);
- the prohibition against attacking health services (*supra* para. 3.62);

---

203 *Id.*

204 Hamburg, 19 December 1949, 16 *ILR* 512; see also *Examen* (Part 2), *loc.cit.* p.38 n.97.

205 US.Mil.Trib., Nuremberg, 19th February 1948, List, *et al.*, *Trials of War Criminals Before the Nuremberg Military Tribunals*, ed. by Sprecher and Fried, Washington, US G.P.O. 1951-1953, IX, p.1272; also, *id.*, Nuremberg, 30th June 1948, *Krupp*, *ILR* 15 p.628.

206 A. Andries, *loc.cit.* p.64.

207 *Jap.Ann.I.L.*, 1964, p.240.

- the prohibition against the use of chemical weapons or poisons or weapons which have indiscriminate effects (*supra* paras. 3.61, 3.73-3.74);
- the prohibition against the use of weapons which render death inevitable or cause unnecessary suffering (*supra* paras. 3.53-3.74);
- the prohibition against violating the territorial integrity of third States (*supra* paras. 3.67, 3.77);
- the prohibition against causing widespread, long-term and severe damage to the environment (*supra*, paras. 3.78-3.79);
- the obligation to respect the principles of proportionality and humanity (*supra* para. 3.80); and
- the prohibition against genocide or crimes against humanity (*supra* para. 3.49).

Most of these rules are set out in the classical instruments governing *jus in bello* - the 1868 St Petersburg Declaration, the 1874 Brussels Declaration, 1899 Hague Declaration IV, Regulation annexed to 1907 Hague Convention IV, 1925 Geneva Protocol, 1948 Genocide Convention, 1949 Geneva Conventions - which are generally considered to reflect customary law in practice,[208] jurisprudence,[209] and the writings of jurists.[210] Some of the applicable rules are found in the UN Charter and the law arising thereunder. Almost all of those which arise under the law of armed conflict come within the "general principles of humanitarian law" invoked by the International Court in the case concerning *Military and Paramilitary Activities in and against Nicaragua*.[211]

3.91 Now, whether in relation to customary law, or to the 1948 and 1949 Conventions, or to United Nations law on general principles of humanitarian law, these rules bind all States or virtually all States — as custom, general principles, or ratified treaties. The question is, do they bind, as between themselves or between themselves and third

208 See res.827 of 25th May 1993, para. 2., where the Security Council approves the Secretary General's report on the Statute of the International War Tribunal for crimes committed in the former Yugoslavia, where the Secretary General lists the conventions which, according to him, form part of international customary law: the 1907 Hague, Statute of the Nuremberg International Military Tribunal, 1948, Genocide Convention, 1945, 1949 G.C.; in doc. UN S/25704, 3rd May 1993, p.11, para.35.

209 For the customary character of the Hague Regulation, see Judgment of 30th September - 1st October 1946, *Procès des grands criminels de guerre devant le T.M.I.*, Doc.Off., Nuremberg, 1947, vol.1 p.267; see also the Intern. Mil. Trib. for the Orient, Tokyo, 12th November 1948 in *Ann.Dig.* 1948 Vol.15, pp.365-66; C. Rousseau, *Le droit des conflits armés*, Paris, Pédone, 1983, p.24 and the references; Germany Reichsgericht in criminal matters, 4th April 1922, *Ann.Dig.* 1 p.433, Nur., US.Mil.Trib., 28th October 1948, *Von Leeb et al.*, (German High Command Trial), *A.D.* 1948, 384 etc.

210 See, for example, A. Roberts and R. Guelff, Documents on the Laws of War, Oxford, Clarendon Press, 1989, pp.30, 35, 44, 138-39.

211 *ICJ Rep.* 1986 p.114, para. 220; see also p.112, para. 215 and p.113, para. 218.

States, those States which believe that the use of nuclear weapons is legal?

3.92 The opposition of certain States to a formal expression of the illegality of the use of nuclear weapons first occurred during the negotiation and adoption of the UN General Assembly resolutions condemning their use, and continued during the negotiations of Geneva Protocol I. It is accordingly by reference to their activities in those contexts that one must judge whether these States have been able to establish, for themselves, special rules relating to the use of nuclear weapons, i.e. rules excluding the application of the general obligations of the law of armed conflict.

During the adoption of the UN General Assembly resolutions condemning the use of nuclear weapons (*supra* para. 3.36), a certain number of States had voted against these resolutions or they abstained. To the extent that these resolutions represent positive law, abstentions are not to be considered as a negative vote. Since international law prohibits the use of nuclear weapons, this law certainly applies to States who always abstain during the affirmation of this rule of law. To prevent the application of this rule by creating another, its expression must be clearly stated; an abstention does not provide a clear expression in these terms, and is insufficient to allow a new rule to emerge for the abstaining States. Moreover, even if an abstention were to be considered as equivalent to a negative vote the act of abstention would not, as set out below, create a new rule.

3.93 To justify the modification of the law prohibiting the use of nuclear weapons, States favouring a modification of a pre-existing rule prohibiting their use are likely to invoke the fact that dissuasion through nuclear power has been around for fifty years without it being roundly condemned by the entire international community. The question referred to the Court relates to the legality of the use of nuclear weapons and threatened use. However, it is important to point out that the general approach to dissuasion practised by a small number of States does not constitute the threat of use of force and that accordingly the practice of dissuasion does not bear one way or the other on the legality of the use or threat of use of nuclear weapons.

3.94 This practice of dissuasion cannot therefore modify the pre-existing rules of international law which prohibit the use of nuclear weapons. Even as between the proponents of this practice and other States, the use of nuclear weapons remains illegal. This reasoning applies also in respect of States which vote against UN General Assembly resolutions condemning their use: opponents of these resolutions cannot impose their will on States who support them, since these States are re-stating existing law. All States therefore remain linked by common legal obligations: if not by the resolutions themselves, then through the law they enunciate according to the principle *prior in tempore potior in jus*. To recall, Art. 41 the 1969 Vienna Convention on the Law of Treaties states that:

> "1.Two or more of the parties to a multilateral treaty may conclude an agreement to modify the treaty as between themselves alone if:

(a) the possibility of such a modification is **provided for** by the treaty; or

(b) the modification in question is not prohibited by the treaty **and**:

(i) does not affect the enjoyment by the other parties of their rights under the treaty or the performance of their obligations;

(ii) does not relate to a provision, derogation from which is incompatible with the effective execution of the object and purpose of the treaty as a whole [...]" (emphasis added)

In this case, States to which this rule applies, and who would like to modify it, can do so under certain circumstances, but this new agreement — supposing it applies, *quod non* to nuclear weapons (see below) — applies only to these States and not to others (see Art. 34 of the 1969 Vienna Convention). The principle of the relative effect of treaties applies equally to other forms of international legal obligation, including customary obligations and those arising by operation of general principles.

3.95 If the States which argue in favour of the legality of the use of nuclear weapons can thus take advantage of a rule which would link them **only** in their relations as between themselves, it is still necessary that such an agreement should satisfy the obligation reflected in Art. 41 of the 1969 Vienna Convention, and notably to those conditions providing that the modification, by these States, of treaties normally applicable to nuclear weapons does not compromise:

(i) either the object or purpose of these treaties taken as a whole (Vienna Convention, Art 41(1)(b)(ii);

(ii) or the particular rights and obligations that other States parties to these treaties may rely upon or are subject to (1969 Vienna Convention, Art 41(1)(b)(i)).

3.96 It is doubtful whether the use of nuclear weapons could be compatible with the effective realisation of the object and purpose of treaties with humanitarian objectives, since their object and purpose is:

- in general, to reduce the suffering of people exposed to the direct or indirect effects of wars and to protect the victims of such conflicts;

- more specifically, to fulfil the particular objectives identified above (*supra* para. 3.90).

It has been seen that the use of nuclear weapons not only increases the suffering of victims, but necessarily contravenes the provisions of numerous treaties. Consequently, any agreement which they might have made would necessarily be contrary to the object and purpose of the above-mentioned instruments even as concerns relations between States advocating the legality of the use of nuclear weapons.

A fortiori, this is the only proper conclusion which can be drawn for legal obligations which are based upon the protection of victims and not the interests of States, and are beyond the scope of the application of the principle of reciprocity.

3.97 In the event that applicable treaties — those whose provisions have the effect of rendering illegal the use of nuclear weapons — establish laws which all State parties must respect, it is inconceivable that contracting parties should be able to conclude an agreement on the legality of the use of nuclear weapons without *ipso facto* violating the rights which other contracting parties have under those treaties (1969 Vienna Convention, Art 41(1)(b)(i)). In the event of a large-scale use of nuclear weapons **all** States would, directly or indirectly, be subject to the damaging consequences (by uncontrollable radiation, contamination and pollution). Accordingly, their enjoyment of their conventional rights would be affected and violated.

3.98 Finally, given that the applicable treaties establish humanitarian rules which by virtue of their importance are part of *jus cogens*,[212] any agreement contrary to these rules are necessarily null and void by virtue of Art. 53 of the 1969 Vienna Convention.

3.99 The question remains whether the efforts by certain States during the elaboration and adoption of 1977 Geneva Protocol I to "set apart" nuclear weapons by adopting declarations (*supra*, paras. 3.28 *et seq.*) precludes the application of that instrument to nuclear weapons in respect of treaty relations as between those States, and as between themselves and third States Parties to the Protocol. Several reasons lead to the conclusion that Protocol I does govern the use by those States of nuclear weapons.

(1) According to the way in which they have been characterised by their drafters, they are only "declarations"; *stricto sensu* they are not reservations within the meaning of Article 2 of the 1969 Vienna Convention on the Law of Treaties,[213] and accordingly other Parties do not have to enter objections to them since according to Article 2(d) only reservations can have the effect of modifying obligations under a treaty. These "declarations" therefore have no legal effects as against third States.

(2) Supposing, however, that these "declarations" did amount to reservations, they would still only be effective and admissible if they were compatible with the object and purpose of the Protocol (1969 Vienna Convention, Art. 19(c)).

---

212 *Id.*, 1980, Vol. 2, 2nd part, pp. 45 & 49; see also *Barcelona Traction*, 5th February 1970, *ICJ Rep.* 1970, p.32; *Principes*, *op cit.*, pp. 85-93.

213 Art.2(d): "'reservations' means a unilateral statement, however phrased or named, made by a State, when signing, ratifying, accepting, approving or acceding to a treaty, whereby it purports to exclude or to modify the legal effect of certain provisions of the treaty in their application to that State".

Moreover, as previously noted, nuclear weapons have effects on human health and the environment which are contrary to the classical rules of international humanitarian law. Their use would negate the entire Protocol since any use of nuclear weapons would allow a Party to circumvent its obligations under the Protocol with respect to conflict. In other words, it would not just be "certain provisions" of the Protocol which would cease to apply, but the totality of that instrument. It is doubtful whether such an approach could be compatible with the object and purpose of the Protocol.

(3) Having regard to the extraordinary effects of nuclear weapons, saying that it is possible to be a Party to Protocol I while reserving to oneself the right to use nuclear weapons nullifies the objective of the Protocol. It essentially allows a State to unilaterally decide whether it will apply the Protocol. Such a conditional application is entirely without validity in international law since it would allow a State to disengage itself from a treaty obligation whenever it wished, and avoid its obligation to carry out its treaty obligations in good faith (see 1969 Vienna Convention, Art. 26).

(4) If the "declarations" do amount to reservations, the fact that other Parties to the Protocol have not objected to them could imply that they have accepted these reservations (1969 Vienna Convention, Art. 20(5)) and their compatibility with the object and purpose of the Protocol. The silence of the Parties to the Protocol does not imply acceptance of these reservations, however, in the context of the annual support given by these States to the General Assembly resolutions declaring the illegality of nuclear weapons (*supra* para. 3.36).

(5) Maintaining the hypothesis that these "declarations" were reservations, they would permit their authors to use nuclear weapons without violating the Protocol. However, the use of these weapons necessarily violates the rules of international humanitarian law, which have been recognised by the whole of the international community as imperative. The reservations would, in effect, be void of content or effect (Vienna Convention, Art. 53).

3.100 Some may suggest that the relevant rules of international law are not *jus cogens* because some States claim that certain uses of nuclear weapons might be lawful and that consequently any illegality *per se* of the use of nuclear weapons under these rules is not accepted by the whole of the international community of States. This seems to be an inverted form of reasoning: if all States have accepted the imperative character of a rule, it is not possible for a handful of States, acting subsequently, to say that the rule is not imperative because the required quasi-unanimity is no longer evident as a result of their lack of support. It is at the moment of adoption and of the characterisation of the rule that it is necessary to determine whether the requisite quasi-unanimity of views is apparent.

(E) Conclusions

3.101 In summary, it has been shown in this Section that the use of nuclear weapons is subject to international law. It does not follow that just because nuclear weapons have different characteristics from other types of weapons that international law does not apply to them: practice (including that of the nuclear power States), jurisprudence and the writings of jurists are clear on this point (*supra* paras. 3.14-3.21).

3.102 The 1977 Geneva Protocol I applies to the use of nuclear weapons even if it does not expressly say so. The silence of the Protocol about nuclear weapons proves nothing, since the Protocol is silent about other forms of weapons. Their use is no less subject to the general rules of behaviour which are required by the Protocol. *A fortiori*, the specific prohibition in the 1977 Protocols against attacking nuclear power plants reflects the great concern of States about the release into the environment of radioactive material and supports the view that Protocol I does apply to nuclear weapons. As to the expressed desire of certain States not to apply Protocol I to nuclear weapons, it comes up against the strongly opposing views of the great majority of other States; practice consecutive to the adoption of the Protocol confirms that there was no agreement that the Protocol did not apply to nuclear weapons (*supra* paras. 3.22-3.35).

If the classical instruments governing the law of armed conflict do not expressly address nuclear weapons, the General Assembly of the United Nations has adopted a large number of resolutions solemnly condemning the use of nuclear weapons in any circumstances. These resolutions do not create new law, seeking only to recall that the use of nuclear weapons is governed by pre-existing rules (*supra* paras. 3.36-3.42).

3.103 It is the devastating effects of nuclear weapons which condemns their use: their power leads ineluctably to the death of many people within a certain radius; with strategic weapons the effect persists although it diminishes in scale. In any event, the use of even the smallest nuclear weapon has the potential to unleash a full-scale nuclear war with incalculable consequences; even the use of a strategic nuclear weapon would lead to greater losses amongst civilians than military personnel. By reason of these quantitative effects alone, the use of nuclear weapons violates the rules prohibiting the infliction of necessary death for adversaries, of causing indiscriminate effects, and encouraging the general rules of international humanitarian law (*supra* paras. 3.43-3.63).

The qualitative effects of nuclear weapons, characterised by the initial nuclear radiation and nuclear fallout and the consequences of these effects, brings nuclear weapons within the scope of rules prohibiting the use of poisonous and chemical weapons. Since these effects become cumulatively greater with the power of nuclear weapons, they lead to a greater certainty of killing their victims, thereby violating the prohibition against the use of weapons which render death inevitable. Health and rescue services having been destroyed or badly damaged, the use of nuclear weapons violates the immunity of medical corps and the rights of victims to have access to medical assistance. Moreover, since these effects may affect people outside the scope of the conflict, both in time and geographically, the use of nuclear weapons violates the prohibition on the use of weapons which cause unnecessary suffering, cause harm to civilians, and have indiscriminate effects. The principles of proportionality and humanity are obviously violated. And nuclear weapons are incapable of respecting the obligation not to cause widespread, severe and long-term damage to the natural environment, or violating the rights of third States under the laws of neutrality or general international law (*supra* paras. 3.64-3.77).

These violations are independent of the context in which they occur - international or non-international armed conflict - and they cannot be justified by reason of arguments relating to legitimate defence, reprisals or state of necessity since the law of armed conflict is independent of the *jus contra bellum*, which prohibits reprisals, excludes any possibility of reciprocity, and already takes account of the state of necessity (*supra* paras. 3.78-3.87).

3.104 The rules identified above are reflected in customary law and treaties binding all States, including those proponents of the legality of the use of nuclear weapons. These States have not even managed to create *inter se* different norms than those which they are bound to respect in their relations with third States. Such norms would be incompatible with the object and purpose of the general rules applicable to nuclear weapons and would violate the rights of third States and of victims. In any event, since these rules may be considered to be *jus cogens*, any agreement in violation of them would be *ipso facto* without effect (*supra* paras. 3.88-3.98)

SECTION B

The use of nuclear weapons violates applicable rules of international law for the protection of human health, the environment and fundamental human rights

(A) The use of nuclear weapons is subject to international law for the protection of human health and the environment and fundamental human rights

4.1 The use of nuclear weapons must also be considered by reference to those rules of international law which do not relate directly to armed conflict. As set out in Section A, the use of nuclear weapons can cause damage to human health and the environment in the territory of the State which uses a nuclear weapon, the target State or territory, third countries, and other areas beyond national jurisdiction. It can also violate fundamental human rights, including in particular the right to life.

4.2 The pernicious effects of radiation on human health and the environment were graphically illustrated by the accident which occurred at the Chernobyl nuclear power plant on 26 April 1986. The accident made clear that radiation does not respect national boundaries, that it can be carried for thousands of kilometres, and that wherever it is deposited it will cause harm to human health and the environment, with consequential adverse effects on agriculture, tourism and other industrial activities. For a small island State, the consequences of any such exposure would be catastrophic.

On 27 April 1986, Sweden, and then Denmark, Finland and Poland, detected significant increases in radioactivity levels.[214] Increased radiation levels were subsequently observed, *inter alia*, in Austria, German Democratic Republic, Hungary, Italy, Norway, Yugoslavia (29 April); Federal Republic of Germany, Switzerland, Turkey (30 April); France (1 May); Belgium, Greece, Netherlands, United Kingdom (2 May); and Iceland (7 May). Low-level increases were also detected in Japan and the United States. Significant increases of particular danger to human health were observed in the levels of Iodine-131, Caesium-134 and Caesium-137 immediately after the accident.[215] The scale of the disaster became clearer when the world learnt that in the 36 hours after the accident more than 100,000 people had been evacuated from a radius of some 20 miles around the reactor. The full effects of the accident

---

[214] See Salo, "Information Exchange After Chernobyl", 28 *IAEA Bulletin*, No. 3, p.18 (1986); see generally P. Sands, *Chernobyl: Law and Communication: Transboundary Nuclear Air Pollution — The Legal Materials* (1988).

[215] See Summary Report of 22 July 1986 of the Working Group on Assessment of Radiation Dose Commitment in Europe due to the Chernobyl Accident, noted in 28 *IAEA Bulletin*, No. 3, at p.27 (1986).

on people, property and the environment are still difficult to assess. In the USSR thirty-one people died as a direct result within a few weeks and a further three during 1987 as a result of on-site exposure.[216] The United Kingdom National Radiation Protection Board has estimated that in the EEC countries 1,000 people will die and 3,000 will contract non-fatal cancers because of the accident.[217] Many States, as well as the EEC, situated thousands of kilometres from the accident, took measures to minimize the effects, measures sometimes costly in themselves (as, for example, the protective medication undertaken in Poland) but which also caused losses to dairy and agricultural farmers, fish and meat producers and the tourist industries.[218] The effects in the Federal Republic of Germany were described as follows:

> "The widespread radioactive contamination of the air, water and soil entailed direct damage to spring vegetables; milk-producing cattle had to be kept from grazing; the consumption of milk and other foodstuffs had to be supervised; import restrictions became necessary; the fixing of state intervention levels led to a change in consumers' eating and buying habits; travel agencies and transport undertakings specialising in Eastern Europe business lost their clientele; and finally, seasonal workers in agriculture lost their jobs."[219]

4.3 The legality of the use of any nuclear weapon is subject to those rules of international law arising by operation of treaty, custom or act of international organisation which are intended to protect human health and the environment from pollution and to protect fundamental human rights. That body of rules is now extensive. Moreover, these rules are of "essential importance for the safeguarding and preservation of the human environment" within the meaning of Article 19(3)(d) of the ILC's draft Articles on State Responsibility, the serious breach of which may give rise to the commission of an international crime.[220] Just as the laws of armed conflicts prohibit "widespread, long-term and severe damage" to the natural environment (*supra*, paras. 3.78 and 3.79), so general international law now seeks to protect the environment and prevent damage to human health. The fundamental importance of rules protecting human health and the environment, and their interdependence with the maintenance of peace and security, has been recognised by all States participating at the UN Conference on Environment and Development in June 1992. The Security Council, meeting at the level of head of government or head of State, has declared that "non-military sources of instability in the ecological field

---

216 *The Financial Times*, 5 December 1987.

217 See NRPB, *A Preliminary Assessment of the Chernobyl Reactor Accident on the Population of the European Community* (1987).

218 See *The Financial Times*, 11 July 1986, at p.36; 22 May 1987, at p.3; 15 May 1986, at p.2; *The Economist*, 16 August 1986, at p.28.

219 38 *NLB* 21 (1986).

220 1980 *Ybk ILC*, Vol. II (Part 2), p. 30.

have become threats to international peace and security".[221] Earlier, in April 1991, the Security Council had reaffirmed in resolution 687/1991 that Iraq was "liable under international law for any direct loss, damage, including environmental damage and the depletion of natural resources, or injury to foreign [...] nationals" which occurred as a result of its unlawful invasion and occupation of Kuwait.[222] The protection of human health and the environment from damage, including that resulting from the use of nuclear weapons, is a fundamental objective of the international legal order as reflected in these recent developments. They serve to emphasise the context in which the legality of the use of nuclear weapons must be judged.

4.4 The practice of States reflects that the dual objectives of human health protection and environmental protection are interdependent and are treated in an integrated manner. Interdependence is evident from Agenda 21 (which recognises the "interdependence among the factors of health, environment and development"),[223] and from the Rio Declaration on Environment and Development (Principle 21 of which declares that human beings "are entitled to a healthy and productive life in harmony with nature").[224] The interdependence of human health and environmental protection objectives is also evident from the provisions of treaties expressly intended to prevent damage and adverse effects to human health and the environment from pollution,[225] other treaties having more general objectives,[226] and from decisions of relevant international bodies.[227]

4.5 In the context of nuclear weapons use there is no basis for distinguishing between

---

221 Note by President of the Security Council, 31 January 1992, UN Doc. S/23500, p.2 (1992).

222 3 April 1991.

223 *Agenda 21*, Chapter 6, para. 6.39, (A/CONF. 151/26 (1992)) citing recent analysis by the World Health Organisation.

224 A/CONF. 151/26 (1992), Vol. I.

225 Convention on Long-Range Transboundary Air Pollution, 13 November 1979, 18 *ILM* 1442 (1979) (1979 LRTAP Convention) Art. 1(a); UN Convention on the Law of the Sea, 10 December 1982, 21 *ILM* 1261 (1982); Art. 1(4) (1982 UNCLOS); 1992 UN Framework Convention Climate Change Convention, 9 May 1992, 31 *ILM* 849 (1992) Art. 1(1) (1992 Climate Change Convention).

226 See e.g. EC Treaty, requiring Community environment policy to pursue the objectives of "Preserving, protecting and improving the quality of the environment" and "protecting human health": EC Treaty, as amended by the Treaty on European Union, Art. 130r1, OJ No C 191, 29.7.92, pp. 27-8.

227 See e.g. UN Human Rights Commission declaration that the movement and dumping of toxic and dangerous products endanger basic human rights such as 'the right to the highest standard of health, including its environmental aspects, 'Resolution 1990/43, U.N. Doc. E/CN.4/1990/94 at 104, 6 March 1990.

human health protection and environmental protection. The fundamental rules of international law which are primarily intended to protect human health also bring environmental benefits and impose environmental obligations; rules primarily intended to protect the environment (often defined as including human health, as well as flora, fauna, soil, air, water, climate, landscape and historical monuments or physical structures, and the interrelationship among these elements).[228]

4.6 The international community has long recognised the inherent dangers posed by radioactive material for human health and the environment, as reflected in the large body of treaties which seek to minimize the risks. Regional and global instruments have been adopted to, *inter alia*:

- ban nuclear testing in the atmosphere, ocean or other space;[229]
- protect workers and the public from exposure;[230]
- limit the proliferation of nuclear weapons;[231]
- regulate transport in nuclear material;[232]
- regulate or ban transport of nuclear waste;[233]
- prohibit the emplacement of nuclear weapons in certain areas;[234] and
- create nuclear-free zones (and prohibit the use of nuclear weapons).[235]

4.7 It is clear from these international legislative efforts, as well as those cited in the preceding sections, that the international community has acted to limit releases of radioactive substances and to use all available methods to prevent any massive increases which would cause damage to human health and the environment. Accordingly, there can be no doubt that the use of nuclear weapons is subject to these

---

228 See e.g. Convention on Environmental Impact Assessment in a Transboundary Context, Espoo, 25 February 1991, 30 *ILM* 802 (1991), Art. 1(vii); Convention on the Transboundary Effects of Industrial Accidents, Helsinki, 17 March 1992, 31 *ILM* 1330 (1992), Art. 1(2).

229 Treaty Banning Nuclear Weapons Tests in the Atmosphere, in Outer Space and Under Water, 5 August 1963, 480 *UNTS* 43.

230 ILO Convention (No. 115) Concerning the Protection of Workers against Ionizing Radiation, 22 June 1960, 431 *UNTS* 41.

231 Treaty on the Non-Proliferation of Nuclear Weapons, 1 July 1968, 729 *UNTS* 161.

232 Convention on the Ban of Import into Africa and the Control of Transboundary Movement and Management of Hazardous Wastes within Africa, 29 January 1991, 30 *ILM* 775 (1991).

233 Treaty for the Prohibition of Nuclear Weapons in Latin America, and Additional Protocols I and II, 14 February 1967, 634 *UNTS* 326.

234 South Pacific Nuclear Free Zone Treaty, 6 August 1985, 24 *ILM* 1142 (1985).

235 Convention on the Physical Protection of Nuclear Material, 3 March 1980, 18 *ILM* 1419 (1980).

relevant rules of international law, which aim to prevent any increase in the level of ionising radiation in the environment.

(B) **The use of nuclear weapons violates international law for the protection of human health and the environment**

4.8 This rule arises from: (a) the obligation under general international law for every State to respect the sovereignty and territorial integrity of other States; (b) the obligation under general international law of every State not to cause damage to human health or the environment outside its own territory; and (c) obligations imposed under international law (particularly treaties, acts of international organisations, and custom) requiring States not to cause damage to human health and the environment in its own territory, in the territory of other States, and in areas beyond national jurisdiction.

(a) *Sovereignty and territorial integrity*

4.9 It is a well-established principle of international law that every State must respect the territorial sovereignty and inviolability of every other State. This is reflected in numerous judicial decisions and arbitral awards, as well as treaties and other international acts. An early example is the Award of Max Huber in the *Island of Palmas Case*, which holds that:

> "Territorial sovereignty ... involves the exclusive right to display the activities of a State. This right has as corollary a duty: the obligation to protect within the territory the rights of other States, in particular their right to integrity and inviolability in peace and in war, together with the rights which each State may claim for its nationals in foreign territory."[236]

4.10 The International Court itself has recognised the principle of "every State's obligation not to allow knowingly its territory to be used for acts contrary to the rights of other States".[237] This principle applies to any activity carried out or authorised by a State, including *a fortiori* the use of a nuclear weapon, and is applicable equally in times of war or other armed conflict.

4.11 The obligation to respect the sovereignty and territory of other States is a fundamental principle of international law. It is embodied in the principle of good-neighbourliness as set forth in Article 74 of the United Nations Charter. This provision reflects the agreement of the members of the international community that their policy and activities in their own metropolitan areas must take account of "the interests and well-being of the rest of the world, in social, economic and commercial matters."

---

236 Permanent Court of Arbitration (*Netherlands v. US*), 2 *R.I.A.A.* 829, 839.

237 *Corfu Channel* case (*UK v. Albania*), Judgement of 9 April 1949, *ICJ Rep.* 1949 pp. 4, 22.

4.12 The obligation to respect sovereignty and territory is clearly applicable to radioactive contamination. Any increase of levels of radiation in the territory of a State or of an area beyond national jurisdiction resulting from any activity of a State violates this principle of international law. The principle was cited by Australia and New Zealand in the Nuclear Tests Cases brought by them against France.[238] Australia claimed that the carrying out of atmospheric nuclear tests by France was in violation of Australia's rights on three counts: Australia's sovereignty over its territory; the right of Australia that nuclear tests should not be conducted in the atmosphere and, in particular, not in such a way as to lead to radioactive fall-out upon Australian territory; and the rights of Australia to the unrestricted use, **at all times**, of the high seas and superjacent air-space for navigation, fishery and other purposes, free of physical interference and risk of radiation pollution.[239] When asked by the President of the International Court of Justice, Sir Humphrey Waldock, whether it took the view that 'every transmission by natural causes of chemical or other matter from one state into another state's territory, air space or territorial sea automatically created a legal cause of action in international law without the need to establish anything more?', Australia responded, *inter alia*, that:

> "where, as a result of a normal and natural use by one state of its territory, a deposit occurs in the territory of another, the latter has no cause of complaint unless it suffers more than merely nominal harm or damage. The use by a state of its territory for the conduct of atmospheric nuclear tests is not a formal or natural use of its territory. The Australian Government also contends that the radioactive deposit from the French tests gives rise to more than merely nominal harm or damage to Australia.
>
> ...
>
> By way of elaborating .... the basic principle is that intrusion of any sort into foreign territory is an infringement of sovereignty. Needless to say, the Government of Australia does not deny that the practice of states has modified the application of this principle in respect of the interdependence of territories. It has already referred to the instance of smoke drifting across national boundaries. It concedes that there may be no illegality in respect of certain types of chemical fumes in the absence of special types of harm. What it does emphasise is that the legality thus sanctioned by the practice of states is the outcome of the toleration extended to certain activities which produce these emissions, which activities are generally regarded as natural uses of territory in modern industrial society and are tolerated because, while perhaps producing some inconvenience, they have a community benefit."[240]

4.13 Increased levels of radiation in the environment from any source, including the use of nuclear weapons, is not and cannot be tolerated by State practice. The preamble to the 1963 Treaty Banning Nuclear Weapon Tests in the Atmosphere, in Outer Space

---

238 See *Nuclear Tests* (Australia v. France), Interim Protection, Order 22 June 1973, *ICJ Rep.* 1973, p.99; *Nuclear Tests* (New Zealand v. France), Interim Protection, Order, 22 June 1973, *ICJ Rep.* 1973, p.135.

239 *Nuclear Tests* Case, (Australia v. France) Pleadings, Vol. I. p.522.

240 *Id.*, 525-26.

and Under Water affirms the desire "to put an end to the contamination of man's environment by radioactive substances", and the Treaty requires each party

> "to prohibit, to prevent, and not to carry out any nuclear weapon test explosion, **or any other nuclear explosion,** at any place under its jurisdiction or control:
>
> (a) in the atmosphere; beyond its limits, including outer space; or underwater, including territorial waters or high seas; or
>
> (b) in any other environment if such explosion causes radioactive debris to be present outside the territorial limits of the State under whose jurisdiction or control such explosion is conducted."[241]

The use of nuclear weapons cannot in any circumstances be considered a "natural use of territory in modern industrial society". And the use of nuclear weapons cannot in any circumstances be considered to provide a community benefit at "some inconvenience". In this regard, the community must include any third State not involved in a conflict which may suffer in human health or environmental terms, directly or indirectly, the consequences of radioactive contamination.

4.14 Moreover, every State is further restrained in the activities which it may carry out or permit by virtue of the prohibition on the abuse by a State of a right it enjoys under international law. Such an abuse will occur when a State avails itself of its rights in an arbitrary manner in such a way as to inflict upon another State an injury which cannot be justified by a legitimate consideration of its own advantage.[242] Any use of a nuclear weapon, whether or not it had consequences in a third State or in areas beyond national jurisdiction, would constitute an abuse of right.

4.15 The use of nuclear weapons by a State in war or other armed conflict is subject to the general obligation under international law to respect territorial sovereignty. Accordingly, any use of a nuclear weapon, alternatively any use which had consequences in a third State or in areas beyond national jurisdiction, would violate the general obligation.

(b) The general obligation of each State not to cause damage to human health or the environment outside its territory or other areas subject to its jurisdiction or control

4.16 Flowing directly from the fundamental primary obligation described in paragraphs 4.9-4.12 is the obligation of every State not to cause damage to human health or the environment outside its national territory. The general obligation under international

241 Art. I(1).

242 R. Jennings and A. Watts (eds.), *Oppenheim's International Law* (9th ed., 1992), Vol. I, p. 407; see also 1982 UNCLOS, Art. 300.

law to avoid transboundary injury to human health and the environment is reflected in the award of the Arbitral Tribunal in the *Trail Smelter* arbitration, which held that:

> "Under the principles of international law ... no state has the right to use or permit the use of its territory in such a manner as to cause injury by fumes in or to the territory of another of the properties or persons therein, when the case is of serious consequence and the injury is established by clear and convincing evidence".[243]

4.17 The formulation of this obligation is now codified in Principle 21 of the Stockholm Declaration and Principle 2 of the Rio Declaration, both of which provide, in relevant part, that:

> "States have, in accordance with the Charter of the United Nations and the principles of international law, the ... responsibility to ensure that activities within their jurisdiction or control do not cause damage to the environment of other States or of areas beyond the limits of national jurisdiction".[244]

In this regard, the use of the word "control" indicates that the obligation extends to activities carried out by States through, for example, submarines, vessels or aircraft which might launch a nuclear weapon from an area beyond its national jurisdiction.

4.18 This formulation has been accepted by all States and reflects a rule of customary law. The rule set forth in Principle 21 has been described by the UN General Assembly as one of the 'basic rules' governing the international responsibility of states in regard to protection of human health and the environment.[245] It has been endorsed or incorporated in its entirety into the Preamble of many treaties;[246] described as having the status of a "generally accepted principle of international law";[247] reaffirmed on numerous occasions in international soft law.[248] Most recently,

---

243 *United States v. Canada*, 3 *RIAA* p. 1907 (1941); citing Eagleton, *Responsibility of States*, 1928, p.80.

244 11 *ILM* 1416 (1972); 31 *ILM* 851 (1992).

245 UN General Assembly resolution 2996 (1972), 27 *UN GAOR* (Supp. No. 30) 42.

246 See e.g. Convention for the Prevention of Marine Pollution by Dumping of Wastes and other Matter, 29 December 1972, 1046 *UNTS* 120; 1979 LRTAP Convention; 1985 Convention for the Protection of the Ozone Layer, 26 *ILM* 1529 (1987); 1992 Climate Change Convention.

247 1985 Association for South East Asian Nations Agreement on the Conservation of Nature and Natural Resources, Art. 20.

248 See e.g. Charter of Economic Rights and Duties of States, Art. 30, UN General Assembly resolution 3281 (XXIX), 12 December 1974, *Ybk UN* 1974 at 402; Final Act, Conference on Security and Cooperation in Europe, Helsinki, 1 August 1975 ('each of the participating States, in accordance with the principles of international law, ought to ensure, in a spirit of co-operation, that activities carried out on its territory do not cause degradation of the environment in another

Principle 21 was fully incorporated as Article 3 of the 1992 Biodiversity Convention.[249] The substantive rule set forth in Principle 21 has been endorsed in a number of other treaties applicable to particular regions.[250] Article 194(2) of the 1982 UNCLOS, which enters into force later this year, and in any case reflects customary law, establishes a similar obligation specifically to protect the marine environment.

4.19 Principle 21 has been cited with apparent approval by at least one judge of the International Court[251] and is considered by many jurists to reflect a customary obligation.[252] Specifically in relation to ionizing radiation, UN General Assembly resolution 1629 (XVI), adopted in 1961, declares that:

> The fundamental principles of international law impose a responsibility on all states concerning actions which might have harmful biological consequences for the existing and future generation of peoples of other states, by increasing the levels of radioactive fallout.[253]

State or in areas lying beyond the limits of national jurisdiction' in I. Brownlie, *Basic Documents on Human Rights* (3rd. ed, 1992), p.417).

249 5 June 1992, 31 *ILM* 822 (1992); the Convention was signed by more than 150 States at UNCED, and entered into force on 29 December 1993. It now has more than fifty Parties.

250 See e.g. Treaty for Amazonian Co-Operation, 3 July 1978, 17 *ILM* 1045 (1978), Art. IV ('the exclusive use and utilization of natural resources within their respective territories is a right inherent in the sovereignty of each state and that the exercise of this right shall not be subject to any restrictions other than those arising from International Law'); 1981 Convention for the Protection of the Marine Environment and Coastal Area of the South-East Pacific, 12 November 1981, *IELMT* 981:85; Art. 3(5) (activities must be conducted so that 'they do not cause damage by pollution to others or to their environment, and that pollution arising from incidents or activities under their jurisdiction or control does not, as far as possible, spread beyond the areas where [they] exercise sovereignty and jurisdiction'); 1982 UNCLOS, Art. 193 ('States have the sovereign right to exploit their natural resources pursuant to their environmental policies and in accordance with their duty to protect and preserve the marine environment').

251 See Judge de Castro, dissenting, in the *Nuclear Tests* case, (*Australia v. France*), 1974 *ICJ Rep.* pp. 253, 389: 'If it is admitted as a general rule that there is a right to demand prohibition of the emission by neighbouring properties of noxious fumes, the consequences must be drawn, by an obvious analogy, that the Applicant is entitled to ask the Court to uphold its claim that France should put an end to the deposit of radio-active fall-out on its territory'.

252 See ILA, Report of the Committee on Legal Aspects of the Environment, *60th Conference Report*, p. 157 at 163; L. Goldie, "A General View of International Environmental Law - A Survey of Capabilities, Trends and Limits", in *Colloque La Haye*, pp. 66-9 (1973); A.C. Kiss, "La lutte contre la pollution de l'air sur le plan international", *Colloque La Haye*, pp. 169-174 (1973).

253 United Nations General Assembly resolution 1629 (XVI) (1961), 16 *UN GAOR* (1043 Plenary Meeting) at 505-07, UN Doc. A/PV.1043 (1961).

4.20 In using a nuclear weapon in war or other armed conflict, a State is subject to the specific obligation under international law to ensure that no damage is caused to human health or the environment of other States, or to human health and the environment in areas beyond the limits of national jurisdiction. Accordingly, any use of a nuclear weapon, alternatively any use which has consequences in a third State or in areas beyond national jurisdiction, would violate this general and fundamental obligation of international law.

(c) The specific obligations not to cause damage to human health and the environment

4.21 The primary and general obligations described in paragraphs 4.9 and 4.17 have been further elaborated into specific and detailed norms. These too would be violated by any use of nuclear weapons. They are developed by States through the adoption of a large number of treaties and other acts establishing more specific objectives for the protection of human health and the environment, including in particular the protection of air quality, freshwater resources, oceans and seas, biodiversity, and historical monuments or physical structures of significant cultural value.

4.22 A great number of treaties and multilateral acts at the global and regional level have been adopted to protect human health and the environment. They have received widespread support from States, and many now also reflect rules of customary law establishing specific obligations to protect human health and the environment, and to prevent significant damage thereto. In many instances these rules establish international obligations which are undoubtedly of "essential importance for the safeguarding and preservation of the human environment".[254]

4.23 Human exposure to ionizing radiation always causes some damage to **human health**, the protection of which is envisaged by many international agreements and those treaty and customary obligations which establish specific obligations. The Preamble to the WHO Constitution provides that "the enjoyment of the highest attainable standard of health is one of the fundamental rights of every human being without distinction of race, religion, political belief, economic or social condition". The WHO Constitution commits all members to achieving the objectives of the Organization, including "the attainment by all peoples of the highest possible level of health" (Article 1) and the improvement of "environmental hygiene" (Article 2(i)). To that end, the World Health Assembly adopted International Health Regulations in 1969. The Organization has also endorsed the 1990 Recommendations establishing specific levels of protection from ionizing radiation adopted by the International Commission on Radiological Protection (ICRP), which establish annual effective dose equivalent limits for members of the public of 5 MsV (0.5 rem).[255] Any increase above that

[254] *Supra.* note 220.

[255] ICRP Publication 60 (1991); Table S-4.

limit is deemed "unacceptable" on health grounds. The 1990 Recommendations replace earlier ICRP Recommendations[256] which provided the basis for the 1982 Basic Safety Standards for Radiation Protection adopted and published jointly by the IAEA, WHO, ILO and the Nuclear Energy Agency of the OECD.[257] The Standards, whose objectives include the provision of "guidance for the protection of man from undue risks of the harmful effects of ionizing radiation", set a limit for the annual effective dose equivalent for members of the public of 5 MsV (0.5 rem).[258] The same level of protection, reflecting the earlier ICRP recommendations, is applied in mandatory form under the law of the European Union.[259]

4.24 International law requires States to prevent damage to **air quality** from pollution, including that resulting from the use of nuclear weapons. Relevant international obligations are set forth in, *inter alia*, the 1979 LRTAP Convention[260] the 1982 UNCLOS,[261] and various regional marine environment protection treaties, including UNEP Regional Seas Conventions.[262] To the extent that the use of a nuclear weapon causes damage to the ozone layer and the climate system violations would also occur of the 1985 Convention for the Protection of the Ozone Layer (and related Protocol)[263] and the 1992 UN Climate Change Convention which commits all Parties to "protect the climate system for the benefit of present and future generations".[264]

---

256 ICRP Publication No. 26.

257 Basic Standards for Radiation Protection, 1982 Edition, IAEA, Vienna.

258 *Id.*, paras. 101 and 418.

259 Directive 84/467/Euratom, OJ No L 265, 5.10.1984.

260 *Supra*, note 225; see Article 2, reflecting the determination of the Parties "to protect man and his environment against air pollution" and to "endeavour to limit and, as far as possible, gradually reduce and prevent air pollution including long-range transboundary air pollution".

261 *Supra*, note 225; Article 212, requiring all States to adopt laws and regulations to 'prevent, reduce and control pollution of the marine environment, from or through the atmosphere, applicable to the air space under their sovereignty and to vessels flying their flag or vessels or aircraft of their registry'.

262 1974 Convention for the Prevention of Marine Pollution from Land-Based Sources, 4 June 1974, 13 *ILM* 352 (1974), Art. 3(c)(iv) (as amended); 1974 Convention on the Protection of the Marine Environment of the Baltic Sea Area, 22 March 1974, 13 *ILM* 546 (1974), Art. 2(2); 1983 Protocol for the Protection of the South-East Pacific Against Pollution from Land-Based Sources, 22 July 1983, *IELMT*, 983:54, Art. II(c).

263 22 March 1985, 26 *ILM* 1529 (1987); Montreal Protocol on Substances that Deplete the Ozone Layer, 16 September 1987, 26 *ILM* 1540 (1987).

264 *Supra* note 225; Art. 3(1).

4.20 In using a nuclear weapon in war or other armed conflict, a State is subject to the specific obligation under international law to ensure that no damage is caused to human health or the environment of other States, or to human health and the environment in areas beyond the limits of national jurisdiction. Accordingly, any use of a nuclear weapon, alternatively any use which has consequences in a third State or in areas beyond national jurisdiction, would violate this general and fundamental obligation of international law.

(c) The specific obligations not to cause damage to human health and the environment

4.21 The primary and general obligations described in paragraphs 4.9 and 4.17 have been further elaborated into specific and detailed norms. These too would be violated by any use of nuclear weapons. They are developed by States through the adoption of a large number of treaties and other acts establishing more specific objectives for the protection of human health and the environment, including in particular the protection of air quality, freshwater resources, oceans and seas, biodiversity, and historical monuments or physical structures of significant cultural value.

4.22 A great number of treaties and multilateral acts at the global and regional level have been adopted to protect human health and the environment. They have received widespread support from States, and many now also reflect rules of customary law establishing specific obligations to protect human health and the environment, and to prevent significant damage thereto. In many instances these rules establish international obligations which are undoubtedly of "essential importance for the safeguarding and preservation of the human environment".[254]

4.23 Human exposure to ionizing radiation always causes some damage to **human health**, the protection of which is envisaged by many international agreements and those treaty and customary obligations which establish specific obligations. The Preamble to the WHO Constitution provides that "the enjoyment of the highest attainable standard of health is one of the fundamental rights of every human being without distinction of race, religion, political belief, economic or social condition". The WHO Constitution commits all members to achieving the objectives of the Organization, including "the attainment by all peoples of the highest possible level of health" (Article 1) and the improvement of "environmental hygiene" (Article 2(i)). To that end, the World Health Assembly adopted International Health Regulations in 1969. The Organization has also endorsed the 1990 Recommendations establishing specific levels of protection from ionizing radiation adopted by the International Commission on Radiological Protection (ICRP), which establish annual effective dose equivalent limits for members of the public of 5 MsV (0.5 rem).[255] Any increase above that

---

254 *Supra*. note 220.

255 ICRP Publication 60 (1991); Table S-4.

limit is deemed "unacceptable" on health grounds. The 1990 Recommendations replace earlier ICRP Recommendations[256] which provided the basis for the 1982 Basic Safety Standards for Radiation Protection adopted and published jointly by the IAEA, WHO, ILO and the Nuclear Energy Agency of the OECD.[257] The Standards, whose objectives include the provision of "guidance for the protection of man from undue risks of the harmful effects of ionizing radiation", set a limit for the annual effective dose equivalent for members of the public of 5 MsV (0.5 rem).[258] The same level of protection, reflecting the earlier ICRP recommendations, is applied in mandatory form under the law of the European Union.[259]

4.24 International law requires States to prevent damage to **air quality** from pollution, including that resulting from the use of nuclear weapons. Relevant international obligations are set forth in, *inter alia*, the 1979 LRTAP Convention[260] the 1982 UNCLOS,[261] and various regional marine environment protection treaties, including UNEP Regional Seas Conventions.[262] To the extent that the use of a nuclear weapon causes damage to the ozone layer and the climate system violations would also occur of the 1985 Convention for the Protection of the Ozone Layer (and related Protocol)[263] and the 1992 UN Climate Change Convention which commits all Parties to "protect the climate system for the benefit of present and future generations".[264]

256 ICRP Publication No. 26.

257 Basic Standards for Radiation Protection, 1982 Edition, IAEA, Vienna.

258 *Id.*, paras. 101 and 418.

259 Directive 84/467/Euratom, OJ No L 265, 5.10.1984.

260 *Supra*, note 225; see Article 2, reflecting the determination of the Parties "to protect man and his environment against air pollution" and to "endeavour to limit and, as far as possible, gradually reduce and prevent air pollution including long-range transboundary air pollution".

261 *Supra*, note 225; Article 212, requiring all States to adopt laws and regulations to 'prevent, reduce and control pollution of the marine environment, from or through the atmosphere, applicable to the air space under their sovereignty and to vessels flying their flag or vessels or aircraft of their registry'.

262 1974 Convention for the Prevention of Marine Pollution from Land-Based Sources, 4 June 1974, 13 *ILM* 352 (1974), Art. 3(c)(iv) (as amended); 1974 Convention on the Protection of the Marine Environment of the Baltic Sea Area, 22 March 1974, 13 *ILM* 546 (1974), Art. 2(2); 1983 Protocol for the Protection of the South-East Pacific Against Pollution from Land-Based Sources, 22 July 1983, *IELMT*, 983:54, Art. II(c).

263 22 March 1985, 26 *ILM* 1529 (1987); Montreal Protocol on Substances that Deplete the Ozone Layer, 16 September 1987, 26 *ILM* 1540 (1987).

264 *Supra* note 225; Art. 3(1).

4.25 International law requires States to prevent damage to **biodiversity** (flora and fauna) from pollution, including that resulting from the use of nuclear weapons. International law for the protection of biodiversity is particularly well-established at the regional and global level. The Biodiversity Convention, which commits Parties to "promote the protection of ecosystems, natural habitats and the maintenance of viable populations of species in natural surroundings",[265] supplements other global agreements which have received widespread support. Of particular note is the 1971 Convention on Wetlands of International Importance, Especially as Waterfowl Habitat. Regional conservation agreements have been adopted for Africa;[266] the Americas;[267] East Africa;[268] South East Asia,[269] Europe, including the EC;[270] the South Pacific;[271] and the Caribbean.[272] Special protection is provided for many endangered species who would be destroyed by increases in radiation, including migratory species.[273]

4.26 International law requires States to prevent damage to **freshwater resources** (including vital groundwater resources) from pollution, including that resulting from the use of nuclear weapons. Increased levels of ionizing radiation in freshwater resources (rivers, lakes, groundwaters *etc.*) is prohibited by general international law, treaties and other international acts. Apart from the special regimes intended to protect individual rivers and river systems (e.g. the Rhine, Zambezi, River Plate),

---

265 1992 Biodiversity Convention, *supra* note 249, Article 8(d)

266 African Convention on the Conservation of Nature and Natural Resources, Algiers, 15 September 1968, 1001 *UNTS* 4.

267 Convention on Nature Protection and Wildlife Preservation in the Western Hemisphere, 12 October 1940, 161 *UNTS* 193.

268 1985 Nairobi Protocol concerning Protected Areas and Wild Fauna and Flora in the Eastern African Region, 21 June 1985, *IELMT* 985:47.

269 1985 ASEAN Agreement, *supra* note 247.

270 Institut de Droit International, Resolution on International Regulations regarding the use of International Watercourses for Purposes other than Navigation, Madrid, 19 April 1911, 11 *IPE* 5702. Council Directive 79/409/EEC of 2 April 1979 on the conservation of wild birds, *OJ* L 103, 25.4.1979, p.1; Council Directive 92/43/EEC of 21 May 1992 on the conservation of natural habitats and of wild flora and fauna, *OJ* L 206, 22.7.1992, p.7 (French).

271 Convention for the Protection of the Natural Resources and Environment of the South Pacific Region, Noumea, 24 November 1986, 26 *ILM* 38 (1987).

272 Protocol Concerning Specially Protected Areas and Wildlife in the Wider Caribbean Region, Kingston, 18 January 1990, 1 *YIEL* 441 (1990).

273 Convention on the Conservation of Migratory Species of Wild Animals, 23 June 1979, 19 *ILM* 15 (1980).

regional and global rules also exist. The International Law Commission's Draft Articles on the Non-navigational Uses of International Watercourse, which draws upon resolutions of the International Law Association and the Institut de Droit International,[274] provides that watercourse States "shall, individually or jointly, protect and preserve the ecosystems of international watercourses" and prevent "any detrimental alteration in the composition or quality of the waters of an international watercourse which results directly or indirectly from human conduct ... that may cause appreciable harm to other watercourses".[275] This general rule, which reflects customary law, is also reflected in regional treaties.[276]

4.27 International law requires States to prevent damage to the **marine environment** from pollution, including that resulting from the use of nuclear weapons. These norms are particularly well-developed, and are closely related to the obligation of all States to respect the high seas freedoms of all other States, which would be violated by radioactive pollution on the high seas. Specific global treaty obligations, many of which now reflect customary law, are set forth in, *inter alia*, the 1958 Geneva Convention on the High Seas[277] and the 1982 UNCLOS.[278] Equivalent treaty obligations are set forth in the various UNEP Regional Seas conventions, which have attracted such extensive support that they must, in their relevant parts, be considered to reflect customary law.[279]

4.28 International law requires States to prevent damage to **cultural and natural heritage** from pollution, including that resulting from the use of nuclear weapons. Under the 1972 World Heritage Convention, which has received widespread support across the globe, each Party undertakes "not to take any deliberate measures which might

---

274 See e.g. Institut de Droit International, Resolution on International Regulations Regarding the Use of International Watercourses for Purposes Other than Navigation, Madrid, 19 April 1911, 11 *IPE* 5702; ILA, Helsinki Rules on the Uses of the Waters of International Rivers, 52 *ILA* 484 (1967); ILA Rules on Water Pollution in an International Drainage Basin, 60 *ILA* 535 (1983); ILA Rules on International Groundwaters, 62 *ILA* 251 (187).

275 2 *YIEL* 764 (1991), Arts. 20 and 21(1).

276 See e.g. Convention on the Protection and Use of Transboundary Watercourses and International Lakes, 17 March 1992, 31 *ILM* 1312 (1992) Art. 1(2) and 2(1).

277 450 *UNTS* 82; Art. 25(2), providing that all States must "co-operate with competent international organizations in taking measures for the prevention of pollution of the seas or air space above, resulting from any activities with radio-active materials".

278 *Supra* note 225, especially Arts. 192 and 194(2).

279 See also the Convention for the Protection of the Marine Environment of the North-East Atlantic, 22 September 1992, LDC 15/INF.11, recognising the 'vital importance to all nations' of the marine environment and the flora and fauna it supports and the 'inherent worth' of the marine environment of the North-East Atlantic, and recalling the relevant provisions of customary law reflected in Part XII of 1982 UNCLOS, and in particular Article 197.

damage directly or indirectly the cultural or natural heritage ... situated on the territory" of other Parties."[280]

(d) The obligation not to cause massive damage to human health or the environment anywhere

4.29 The specific obligations described in paragraphs 4.24-4.28 are applicable to prohibit damage from an activity carried out or authorised by a State having consequences anywhere: in a State's own territory; in the territory of another State; or in areas beyond national jurisdiction.

4.30 In addition to the obligations to protect human health and particular environmental resources, international law requires States to prevent damage from radiation to certain geographic areas which are subject to special rules of protection. By general international law reflected in treaties and custom, States are specifically prohibited from causing damage to human health and the environment in areas outside the territory and exclusive jurisdiction of any State, including the high seas and its seabed and subsoil,[281] the moon and outer space,[282] and the Antarctic.[283] Regional agreements prohibiting any nuclear explosion whatsoever have been adopted in Latin America[284] and the South Pacific.[285]

(e) Conclusion

4.31 By way of summary, general international law prohibits a State from carrying out or authorizing activities which damage human health and the environment. In using a nuclear weapon in war or other armed conflict a State is subject to the specific obligations established by the rules of general international law reflected in treaty and custom. Any use of a nuclear weapon, alternatively any use which has consequences in a third State or in areas beyond national jurisdiction, would violate these rules of general international law. The use of a nuclear weapon which caused massive

---

280 Convention for the Protection of the World Cultural and Natural Heritage, 16 November 1972, 11 *ILM* 1358 (1972) Art. 6(3).

281 1982 UNCLOS, Art. 194.

282 Treaty on Principles Governing the Activities of States in the Exploration and Use of Outer Space, Including the Moon and Other Celestial Bodies, 27 January 1967, 610 UNTS 205 (especially Art. IV); Agreement Governing the Activities of States on the Moon and Other Celestial Bodies, 5 December 1979, 18 *ILM* 1434 (1979) (especially Art.7).

283 Antarctic Treaty, 1 December 1959, 402 *UNTS* 71 (especially Art. V, prohibiting nuclear explosions).

284 *Supra* note 233.

285 *Supra* note 234.

environmental pollution or damage to human health and so violates these essential rules would constitute an international crime (*supra* para. 4.3).

(C) The use of nuclear weapons violates international law for the protection of fundamental human rights

4.32 Human exposure to ionizing radiation will also violate basic **human rights** and fundamental freedoms. Any use of nuclear weapons is also subject to, and must comply with, relevant norms established under general and specific international human rights law. International law has long recognised that the quality of the human environment must be maintained to ensure the full enjoyment of basic human rights.[286] This approach is reflected in Principle 1 of the 1972 Stockholm Declaration,[287] Principle 1 of the Rio Declaration on Environment and Development,[288] and has been endorsed by the UN General Assembly, which has resolved that 'all individuals are entitled to live in an environment adequate for their health and well-being'.[289]

4.33 Pollution by radiation which damages human health and the environment violates international human rights standards, as reflected in treaty and customary law, including the right to a standard of living adequate for health and well-being[290] and the right to the highest attainable standard of health (including improvement of all aspects of environmental and industrial hygiene).[291] Similar rights are reflected in the 1981 African Charter ('all peoples shall have the right to a general satisfactory

---

286 UN GA res. 2398(XXIII) (3 December 1968); UN Commission on Human Rights, Resolution 1990/41, 6 March 1990.

287 "Man has the fundamental right to freedom, equality and adequate conditions of life, in an environment of a quality that permits a life of dignity and well-being, and he bears a solemn responsibility to protect and improve the environment for present and future generations."

288 "Human beings are at the centre of concerns for sustainable development. They are entitled to a healthy and productive life in harmony with nature."

289 Resolution 45/94, 14 December 1990; see also the Declaration of the Hague on the Environment, recognizing 'the fundamental duty to preserve the ecosystem' and 'the right to live in dignity in a viable and global environment, and the consequent duty of the community of nations vis-à-vis present and future generations to do all that can be done to preserve the quality of the atmosphere': 11 March 1989, 28 *ILM* 1308 (1989).

290 Universal Declaration of Human Rights, UN GA resolution 217 (III) of 10 December 1948, Art. 25; International Covenant on Economic, Social and Cultural Rights (1966 ICESCR), Annex to GA Res. 2200 (XXI) of 16 December 1966, 6 *ILM* 360 (1967), Art. 11(1).

291 1966 ICESCR, Art. 12(1) and (2)(b); European Social Charter, 18 October 1961, 529 UNTS 89, Art. 11; African Charter on Human and People's Rights (1981 ACHPR), 28 June 1981, 21 *ILM* 59 (1982) Art. 16(1).

environment favourable to their development'),[292] the 1989 San Salvador Protocol to the 1969 American Convention on Human Rights,[293] and the 1989 Convention Concerning Indigenous and Tribal Peoples in Independent Countries.[294]

4.34 In this regard Solomon Islands notes the views of the Human Rights Committee as set forth in a General Comment it adopted in 1984 on the Right to Life and Nuclear Weapons.[295] The Committee associated itself with the growing concern of the international community at "the development and proliferation of increasingly awesome weapons of mass destruction, which not only threaten human life but also absorb resources that could otherwise be used for vital economic and social purposes, particularly for the benefit of developing countries, and thereby for promoting and securing the enjoyment of human rights for all."[296]

4.35 The General Comment was adopted by consensus and states, in unambiguous terms, that the

> "use of nuclear weapons should be prohibited and recognized as crimes against humanity".[297]

Solomon Islands shares and fully endorses this view.

(D) International obligations for the protection of human health, the environment and human rights apply during armed conflict

4.36 Since the use of nuclear weapons must, *prima facie*, occur during a war or other armed conflict, it is necessary to consider whether, and if so to what extent, the customary and treaty obligations identified above apply during war or armed conflict. In this regard it is necessary to determine whether such obligations apply as between belligerents, and as between a belligerent State and third States not involved in the conflict.

---

292 1981 ACHPR Art. 24.

293 See Art. 11:
"1. Everyone shall have the right to live in a healthy environment and to have access to basic public services.
2. The State Parties shall promote the protection, preservation and improvement of the environment".

294 Geneva, 27 June 1989, 28 *ILM* 1382 (1989), Arts. 2, 3, 4(1), 7(4) and 15(1).

295 GenC 14/23, reproduced in M. Nowak *UN Covenant on Civil and Political Rights* (1993), p.861.

296 *Id.*, para. 4.

297 *Id.*, para. 6.

(a) The operation of treaties during armed conflict

4.37 Notwithstanding Article 73 of the 1969 Vienna Convention on the Law of Treaties, which provides that 'the present Convention shall not prejudge any question that may arise in regard to a treaty from ... the outbreak of hostilities between States, it is now generally accepted that the outbreak of an armed conflict "does not *ipso facto* terminate or suspend the operation of treaties in force between the parties to the armed conflict".[298] Moreover, a state of armed conflict "does not entitle a party unilaterally to terminate or to suspend the operation of treaty provisions relating to the protection of the human person, unless the treaty provides otherwise,"[299] and, as regards the outbreak of an armed conflict between some of the parties to a multilateral treaty, "does not *ipso facto* terminate or suspend the operation of that treaty between other contracting States or between them and the States parties to the armed conflict."[300] Treaties establishing international organisations are considered not to be affected by the existence of an armed conflict between any of its parties.[301] Accordingly, Principle 24 of the 1992 Rio Declaration, which provides that

> "Warfare is inherently destructive of sustainable development. States shall therefore respect international law providing protection for the environment in time of armed conflict and cooperate in its further development, as necessary"[302],

must be interpreted as requiring States to respect those rules of international law which provide protection for the environment in times of armed conflict (as well as in times of peace). This approach is consistent with the rules of environmental protection provided by Articles 35 and 55 of 1977 Geneva Protocol I. The support for the view that international obligations for the protection of human health and the environment survive the outbreak of hostilities is further reflected by the relevant provisions of Agenda 21, which called on the international community to consider measures in accordance with international law "to address, in times of armed conflict, large-scale destruction of the environment that cannot be justified under international

---

298 Institut de Droit International, Resolution of the Helsinki Session (1985), "The effects of armed conflicts on treaties", Art. 2, in *Tableau des Resolutions adoptées (1957-1991)*, (1992), pp. 174-75.

299 *Id.*, Art. 4.

300 *Id.*, Art. 5.

301 *Id.*, Art. 6.

302 See also Principle 26 of the 1972 Stockholm Declaration ("Man and his environment must be spared the effects of nuclear weapons and all other means of mass destruction"); 1982 World Charter for Nature ("Nature shall be secured against degradation caused by warfare or other hostile activities", and "military activities damaging to nature shall be avoided").

law."[303] Both the UNCED texts imply that treaties protecting the environment should, as a general principle, continue to apply in times of war and other armed conflict. This conclusion can also be drawn from UN General Assembly resolution 47/37, which stressed that the destruction of the environment, not justified by military necessity and carried out wantonly, was "clearly contrary to international law".[304] The General Assembly further urged States to "take all measures to ensure compliance with the existing international law applicable to the protection of the environment in times of armed conflict."

4.38 In the absence of a clear general rule it is nevertheless appropriate to consider the provisions of individual treaties. A review indicates that the vast majority of treaties which aim to protect human health and the environment are silent on the question of their effect during war and other armed conflict. A small minority of such treaties provide exceptions to the general rule of silence on the point, and even in respect of these treaties practice is not uniform.

4.39 Some treaties (such as those establishing rules on civil liability for damage) include provisions excluding the operation of their provisions to damage occurring as a result of war and armed conflict.[305] Other treaties include provisions permitting their total or partial suspension at the instigation of one of the Parties.[306] Still other treaties would appear not to apply during military hostilities since their provisions do not apply to certain military operations in peacetime operations.[307] In the other direction, however, are treaties which are specifically applicable to certain activities

303 *Agenda 21*, Chapter 39, para. 39.6(a), A/CONF.151/ L.3.add.39, 11 June 1992.

304 GA Res. 47/37 on Protection of the Environment in Times of Armed Conflict, 25 November 1992.

305 Convention on Third Party Liability in the Field of Nuclear Energy, 29 July 1960, 956 *UNTS* 251; Art. 9; Convention on Civil Liability for Nuclear Damage, 29 May 1963, 1063 *UNTS* 265; Art. IV(3)(a); International Convention on Civil Liability for Oil Pollution Damage, 29 November 1969, 973 *UNTS* 3; Art. III(2)(a); International Convention on the Establishment of an International Fund for Compensation for Oil Pollution Damage, 18 December 1971, 11 *ILM* 284 (1972); Art. 4(2)(a) (which also does not apply to oil from warships used on non-commercial service); 1977 Civil Liability Convention Art. 3(3); Convention on the Regulation of Antarctic Mineral Resource Activities, 2 June 1988, 27 *ILM* 868 (1988); Art. 8(4)(b) (if no reasonable precautionary measures could have been taken); and ILC Draft Articles on International Liability for Injurious Consequences Arising Out of Acts not Prohibited by International Law Art. 26(1)(a).

306 International Convention for the Prevention of Pollution of the Sea by Oil, 12 May 1954, 327 *UNTS* 3. Art. XIX(1), allowing parties to suspend operation of whole or part of Convention in case of war or other hostilities if they consider themselves affected as a belligerent or as a neutral, upon notification to the Convention's Bureau.

307 1972 London Convention, *supra* note 245, Art. VII(4) (non-applicability of Convention to vessels and aircraft entitled to sovereign immunity under international law).

which may be associated with hostilities,[308] or which implicitly apply during hostilities.[309] These limited examples (which cover nuclear accidents, oil pollution, etc) may be considered to create exceptional rules which expressly deviate from the general rule identified above, according to which treaty (and customary) obligations to protect human health and the environment apply in peace and in war.

4.40 The silence of the great majority of treaties intended to protect human health and the environment allows the conclusion that they are designed to ensure environmental protection at all times, in peace and in war, unless expressly excluded.[310] This conclusion is justified also by the fact that these treaties, by their terms and overall purpose, establish international obligations which are of "essential importance" for the safeguarding and preservation of human health and the environment (*supra* para. 4.3).

4.41 In considering the legal effect of human health and environmental protection treaties when an armed conflict occurs, it is also appropriate to distinguish between two types of conflict: those of an international character, and those of a non-international character. In the case of the former, it is further necessary to distinguish between the legal situation as between belligerents, and the legal situation between belligerents and States which are not involved in the international armed conflict.

(i) Non-international armed conflict

4.42 A State may not invoke a non-international armed conflict to terminate or suspend the application of a treaty. War or armed conflict are not identified by the 1969 Vienna Convention on the Law of Treaties as grounds for suspending or terminating a treaty. Accordingly, the use of a nuclear weapon in a civil war which had adverse consequences on human health and the environment would continue to be subject to the obligations of relevant treaties, including those indicated above which specifically address the protection of human health and the environment.

4.43 Moreover, international practice has tended to adopt a restrictive approach in applying the principle of *rebus sic stantibus* (see Article 62 of the 1969 Vienna Convention),

---

308 Protocol for the Prevention of Pollution of the Mediterranean Sea by Dumping from Ships and Aircraft, 16 February 1976, which generally prohibits dumping of materials produced for biological and chemical warfare (Annex 1, Section A, para. 9); and Protocol for the Prevention of Pollution of the South Pacific Region by Dumping, 25 November 1986, *IELMT* 986:87A; which prohibits special dumping permits from being granted in respect of materials produced for biological and chemical warfare (Art. 10(1) and (2) and Annex I, Section A, para. 6).

309 International Convention for the High Seas Fisheries of the North Pacific Ocean, 9 May 1952, 205 *UNTS* 65, which provides that Commission decisions should make allowance for, *inter alia*, wars which may introduce temporary declines in fish stocks (Art. IV(2)).

310 1959 Antarctic Treaty *supra* note 283, (Art. I(1)); 1988 CRAMRA, (Art. 2).

which should not be invoked in the case of a civil war involving the use of weapons which violate treaties for the protection of human health and the environment. This is appropriate given the nature of the international obligation in question (the protection of human health and the environment), which establishes rules of protection for the benefit of individual states as well as the international community as a whole. It is difficult to justify the invoking of the clause in the case of a non-international armed conflict, other than in the exceptional circumstances provided by Article 62 of the 1969 Vienna Convention.

(ii) International armed conflict

4.44 The 1969 Vienna Convention is also silent about the status and legal effect of treaties when an international armed conflict occurs. Traditionally, the view had been taken that as regards legal relations between belligerent parties their respective obligations under bilateral and multilateral treaties in force at the outbreak of hostilities were suspended, unless they had been adopted in consideration of that conflict. Recently, however, there has been growing support for the view that certain categories of treaty obligations, even as between belligerents, are not suspended during war or armed conflict.[311] This rule is confirmed by the writings of jurists.[312] The Institut de Droit International adopted a Resolution expressing the view that a treaty will continue to apply unless it limits military objectives:

> "Les traités restés en vigueur et dont l'exécution demeure, malgré les hostilités, pratiquement possible, doivent être observés comme par le passé. Les Etats belligérants ne peuvent s'en dispenser que dans la mesure et pour le temps commandés par les nécessités de la guerres"[313]

4.45 As regards treaty obligations between parties to a conflict and third States, the obligations arising from bilateral treaties are not affected by the state of war or armed conflict, unless performance of the obligations thereunder is rendered impossible. This general rule is subject to the exceptions expressly provided by a particular treaty, including those allowing for a right of unilateral denunciation and the application of clauses relating to *rebus sic stantibus* or *non adimpleti contractus*. Moreover, it is submitted the validity of treaties for the protection of human health and the environment governing relations between belligerent States and third States which are not parties to an armed conflict will not be affected by the conflict.

---

311 *Supra*. para. 4.37.

312 L. Oppenheim, *International Law*, Vol. II, 7th ed, H. Lauterpacht, ed., (1952), 304; A.D. McNair, *Law of Treaties* (1961), 705; C.B. Hurst, 'The Effect of War on Treaties', 2 *BYIL* (1924), 37 at 41.

313 Art 4, 6 *Ann.I.D.I.* 587; see also Arts. 7-11; cited in R. Tarasofsky, "Legal Protection of the Environment During International Armed Conflict", XXIV *NYIL* 17 (1993), at 63.

4.46 This approach is not affected by application of the law of neutrality (*supra* para. 3.67), which does not preclude the possibility that other obligations of the international law of peace continue to apply. Damage to human health or the environment of a neutral State, even if it results from an act of war committed by a belligerent State, is regulated by obligations of international law for the protection of human health and the environment. As confirmed by the general rules of international law governing State responsibility which do not allow exonerations for armed conflict (*infra* paras. 5.1-5.4), no exceptions apply to military activities of belligerent States.

4.47 As a general matter, therefore, the outbreak of war or other armed conflict should not be considered to automatically suspend or terminate those treaties between the parties to a conflict which are intended to protect human health and the environment and which do not exclude their application in time of war. Such treaties continue to apply where they are in force between one or more parties to a conflict and third States.

(b) Customary law

4.48 There are no reasons to justify a different conclusion in respect of obligations arising under customary law or by acts of international organisations (*supra* paras. 4.17-4.20 and 4.23-4.28) Certainly as regards relations between belligerent States and third States the existence of a war or armed conflict will not limit or otherwise affect the obligations imposed by customary norms protecting human health and the environment. Accordingly, the customary obligation reflected in Principle 21/Principle 2 would be violated should the adverse consequences for human health and the environment resulting from the use of a nuclear weapon be felt in a third state or in an area beyond national jurisdiction.

(c) Conclusion

4.49 It therefore follows that, as a general matter, the use of a nuclear weapon by a State in war or other armed conflict must comply with treaty and other obligations under international law which are intended to protect human health and the environment and fundamental human rights. Where an obligation is of "essential importance" for the safeguarding and preservation of human health, the environment and fundamental human rights the application of this rule becomes even more strict.

SECTION C

Any violation by a State of these obligations under international law gives rise to its international responsibility and liability

5.1 The use of a nuclear weapon by a State in violation of an international legal obligation for the protection of human health or the environment gives rise to the international responsibility of that State.[314] The principle that a breach of an international legal obligation under treaty or customary law, or perhaps even general principles of law, creates a further obligation, or a liability,[315] to make reparation is also well established. As the PCIJ stated in the *Chorzow Factory* case:

> it is a principle of international law, and even a general conception of law, that any breach of an engagement involves an obligation to make reparation. In judgment no. 8 (1927) (PCIJ, Ser. A,, No. 9, p.21) ... the Court had already said that reparation was the indispensable complement of a failure to apply a convention, and there is no necessity for this to be stated in the convention itself.[316]

5.2 A State which uses a nuclear weapon in violation of its international legal obligation to protect human health and the environment will be under an obligation to make reparation for the consequences of the violation. This arises from a principle of general application, and there is no reason why violations relating to human health and environmental obligations should be subject to a different approach. The general principle is clearly expressed in the judgment of the *Chorzow Factory (Indemnity)* case, where the PCIJ stated that

> The essential principle contained in the actual notion of an illegal act - a principle which seems to be established by international practice and in particular by the decisions of arbitral tribunals - is that reparation must, as far as possible, wipe out all the consequences of the illegal act and reestablish the situation which would, in all probability, have existed if that act had not been committed. Restitution in kind, or, if this is not possible payment of a sum corresponding to the value which a restitution in kind would bear; the award if need be, of damages for loss sustained which would not be covered by restitution in kind or payment in place of it - such are the principles which should serve to determine the amount of compensation due for an act contrary to international law.[317]

---

314 ILC Draft Articles on State Responsibility, Art. 1, 1977 II *Ybk ILC* (UN Doc. A/CN.4/302).

315 See also UNCLOS Article 139, and UNCLOS Article 235 which provides that States are "responsible for the fulfilment of their international obligations concerning the protection and preservation of the marine environment. They shall be liable in accordance with international law."

316 1927 PCIJ, *Series A*, No. 17, at p. 47.

317 *Id.*

5.3 In the event that the use of a nuclear weapon should cause damage to human health and the environment, especially in a third State not involved in the conflict, financial reparation should cover the costs associated with material damage to environmental resources (pure environmental damage) and consequential damage to people and property (consequential environmental damage), including restoration or reinstatement. This approach has been confirmed by Security Council resolution 687/1991, which reaffirmed that Iraq was liable under international law for, *inter alia*, 'environmental damage and the depletion of natural resources' resulting from the unlawful invasion and occupation of Kuwait.[318] Violations of international law arising from the use of a nuclear weapon would also give rise to the responsibility of the concerned State, together with the obligation to make reparation. In the case of an armed conflict resulting from the use of one or more nuclear weapons it will be virtually impossible to provide adequate financial reparation, providing a further compelling reason for concluding that any use of a nuclear weapon must, by virtue of its effects on human health and the environment, be illegal under international law.

5.4 International responsibility may also trigger the criminal liability of a State (and any person associated with a decision to use a nuclear weapon should be on notice that he or she will also be subject to criminal liability). According to the ILC "a serious breach of an international obligation of essential importance for the safeguarding and preservation of the human environment, such as those prohibiting massive pollution of the atmosphere or of the seas" should be categorized as an international crime, or delict.[319] The use of a nuclear weapon causing massive damage to human health or the environment *anywhere* would, it is submitted, constitute an international crime, and any member of the international community would have standing to challenge the act, since it would injure the rights of all States and members of the international community irrespective of where the damage to human health or the environment was actually felt.[320]

318 Security Council Res. 687/1991 of 3 April 1991, 30 *ILM* 847 (1991).

319 *Supra*. note 220.

320 See also ILC Draft Code of Crimes Against the Peace and Security of Mankind, Report of the ILC on its 43rd session, 30 *ILM* 1584 (1991), especially Draft Article 26 (stated to apply in times of peace as well as during armed conflict) provides that an individual who 'wilfully causes or orders the causing of widespread, long term and severe damage to the natural environment' would be guilty of a crime. Draft Article 22 provides that an individual who employs methods or means of warfare 'which are intended or may be expected to cause widespread, long-term and severe damage to the natural environment' would be guilty of an exceptionally serious war crime.

PART III

SUMMARY OF CONCLUSIONS

6.1 For the reasons sets out in these Written Observations, it is submitted that:

(I) **The General Assembly is competent to request an Advisory Opinion from the Court on the question and the Court is competent to and should give its Opinion on the question.**

(A) The General Assembly's request for an Opinion fulfils the conditions of Article 96(1) of the UN Charter.

(B) The General Assembly is acting in accordance with its obligations and rights under the United Nations Charter.

(C) The General Assembly's practice confirms its competence over matters relating to the effects on human health and the environment of ionising radiation resulting from the use of nuclear weapons:

(a) it has frequently addressed the legality of the use of nuclear weapons and related issues;

(b) it has addressed nuclear weapons under the aegis of disarmament;

(c) it has requested studies on the effects of the use of nuclear weapons.

(D) The Court should give the Advisory Opinion requested by the General Assembly.

(II) **Any threat or use of a nuclear weapon violates international law of armed conflicts.**

(A) Any threat or use of a nuclear weapon is subject to international law, including the rules relating to armed conflicts:

(a) any threat or use of a nuclear weapon is subject to general international law;

(b) any threat or use of a nuclear weapon is subject to the international law of armed conflicts;

(c) any threat or use of a nuclear weapon is subject to the 1977 Geneva Protocol I;

(d) nuclear weapons are subject to rules of international law specifically prohibiting their threat or use.

(B) Any threat or use of a nuclear weapon violates the international law of armed conflicts:

(a) any use of a nuclear weapon violates international law by reason of its quantitative and qualitative effects, which violate the relevant rules of international law that:

(i) limit the means of attacking the enemy;

(ii) prohibit direct or indirect attacks on civilian targets;

(iii) establish a permanent obligation to distinguish between combatants and non-combatants;

(iv) prohibit indirect or direct attacks against health services;

(v) prohibit the use of chemical or poisonous weapons or weapons which have indiscriminate effects;

(vi) prohibit the use of weapons which render death inevitable or cause unnecessary suffering;

(vii) prohibit violations of the territorial sovereignty of third States;

(viii) prohibit causing "widespread, long-term and severe damage to the environment";

(ix) require respect for the principles of proportionality and humanity; and

(x) prohibit crimes against humanity or genocide.

(c) The threat or use of nuclear weapons violates international law irrespective of the circumstances in which they are used.

(d) The threat or use of nuclear weapons cannot be justified by international law in any circumstances, in particular by reason of self-defence, reprisal, or state of necessity.

(C) The relevant rules of international law prohibiting the threat or use of nuclear weapons apply to all States.

(III) Any threat or use of nuclear weapons violates international law for the protection of human health and the environment and the protection of human rights.

(A) The threat or use of nuclear weapons is subject to international law for the protection of human health and the environment, and protection of fundamental human rights.

(B) The threat or use of nuclear weapons violates international law for the protection of human health and the environment, and fundamental human rights, by increasing levels of radiation in the environment which:

(a) do not respect national boundaries and violate the sovereignty and territorial integrity of third States;

(b) violate the general obligation not to cause damage to human health and the environment outside its territory or other areas subject to its jurisdiction or control;

(c) violate specific obligations not to cause significant damage to human health and the environment anywhere, including in particular air quality, biodiversity, freshwater resources; the marine environment, and cultural and natural heritage; and

(d) violate fundamental human rights.

(C) International law for the protection of human health and the environment and for the protection of human rights is applicable during armed conflict.

(IV) **Any use of nuclear weapons by a State entails its responsibility under international law and its liability to make reparation.**

6.2 Accordingly, and for the reasons set out in these Written Observations it is submitted that the International Court of Justice should give an Advisory Opinion which states:

(A) that the General Assembly is competent to request an Advisory Opinion from the International Court of Justice on this question, and that the Court is competent to and should give an Advisory Opinion on the question submitted;

(B) that any use of a nuclear weapon by a State would violate its obligations under international law as reflected in the rules of international law concerning methods and mean of warfare (*jus in bello*) and neutrality, ALTERNATIVELY that any use of nuclear weapons must not violate applicable rules of international law concerning methods and mean of warfare (*jus in bello*) and neutrality;

(C) that any use of a nuclear weapon by a State would violate its obligations under international law as reflected in the rules of international law for the protection of human health and the environment and fundamental human rights, ALTERNATIVELY that the use of nuclear weapons must not violate

applicable rules of international law for the protection of human health and the environment and fundamental human rights;

(D) that any use of a nuclear weapon by a State would constitute a crime against humanity, ALTERNATIVELY that the use of nuclear weapons in violation of international law constitutes a crime against humanity; and

(E) that any use by a State of a nuclear weapon gives rise to its international responsibility, ALTERNATIVELY that the violation by a State of its obligations under international law relating to the use of nuclear weapons gives rise to its international responsibility; and

(F) that any threat of use by a State of a nuclear weapon would, by consequence of the illegality of actual use, be prohibited under international law.

NOTE VERBALE DATED 19 JUNE 1995
FROM THE EMBASSY OF ITALY,
TOGETHER WITH WRITTEN STATEMENT
OF THE GOVERNMENT OF ITALY

AMBASCIATA D'ITALIA

L'AJA

-2252

VERBAL NOTE

The Embassy of Italy presents its compliments to the International Court of Justice and with reference to its letter 95588 of 8 February 1995 regarding the request for advisory opinion transmitted to the Court under the United Nations General Assembly Resolution 49/75K of 15 December 1994 concerning the legality of the threat or use of nuclear weapons, has the honour to enclose the written statement of the Italian Government.

The Italian Embassy avails itself of this opportunity to renew to the International Court of Justice the expression of its highest consideration.

The Hague, 19 June 1995

TO THE INTERNATIONAL COURT OF JUSTICE
THE HAGUE

Ministero degli Affari Esteri

SERVIZIO DEL CONTENZIOSO DIPLOMATICO
Ufficio dell'Agente del Governo italiano

THE ITALIAN GOVERNMENT,

Considering resolution 45/75 K, adopted by the United Nations General Assembly on December 15, 1994, whereby the Assembly addressed the Court of Justice a request for an advisory opinion on the following matter:

"is the threat or use of nuclear weapons in any circumstance permitted under international law?";

Considering the Court Order of February 1, 1995, establishing the deadline of June 20, 1995, for the presentation to the Court of written observations, in compliance with Article 66, paragraph 2, of its Statute;

[Texte illisible non reproduit]

1. First of all, the absence should be underlined of international general rules, and customary laws in particular, governing the use or the threat to use nuclear weapons.

The fact that numerous UN General Assembly resolutions have been adopted on this subject (1653/XVI, 2398/22, 2444/22, 2936/27, 2996/27, 3314/29, 33/71B, 34/58, 35/152D, 36/92, 36/100, 37/78J, 37/100C, 38/73G, 38/75, 38/183B, 39/63H, 39/148P, 40/151F, 41/60F, 42/39C, 42/42D, 43/78F, 44/117C, 45/59B, 45/94, 47/37, 47/53C, 48/72B) is at the same time an evidence and a consequence of this situation, and this is even more clearly demonstrated by the circumstance that the above UN resolutions were all adopted with a majority vote. It should hardly be noted that only if resolutions limiting the use or the threat to use nuclear weapons had been adopted by *consensus*, it would have been possible to speak about the beginning of a process of international prohibitive or limitative customary rules, compared to which those resolutions should be considered as *opinio juris*, already well defined and capable of originating the material repetition of similar attitudes (*diuturnitas*).

Moreover, one cannot construe that limitative factors, or even an actual prohibition can derive from conventional provisions envisaged by collective Treaties.

[Texte illisible non reproduit]

In the light of the above, it is impossible to consider the above-mentioned provisions as the source of juridical limitations on the subject of the threat to use or the use of nuclear weapons.

2. The opinion of those who consider that the provisions of the conventional war law on the limitations to the use of conventional weapons can by analogy be applied to the use of nuclear weapons, rests on even less sound foundations.

An argument against this use of analogy is the evident impossibility to concede that the provisions conceived to regulate the use of weapons having an at least relatively reduced destructive scope do have a so wide *ratio legis* that their application to the resort to and the use of nuclear weapons is functionally correct and adequate. The validity of this opinion is specifically and positively confirmed by the slow, but relentless building of a specific *corpus* of rules bound to be applied not only and not so much to the manufacturing and use of mass destruction weapons, but also and above all to the manufacturing and use of objects having those characteristics, and thus of rules pursueing the complex and delicate objective of disarmament.

It is first of all to be noted that some of these conventional provisions can be applied without distinction to all types of mass destruction weapons.

[Texte illisible non reproduit]

Moreover, conventions have been concluded which can specifically be applied to the manufacturing and detention of individual *species* of weapons that can be defined as mass destruction weapons, aiming at establishing international controls on their compliance (such as the Protocol on the Prohibition to Use Chemical Weapons of 1925, the Convention on their Ban of 1993, as well as the Convention on Biological and Bacteriological Weapons of 1972).

The above situation clearly shows that a process of gradual development of international rules on disarmament is underway, aiming at working out collective conventions tackling and solving - with no forced interpretations - the whole set of problems linked to the manufacturing, testing, detention and use of those weapons. Thus, adequate solutions are taking shape, which take into account the specific nature of each individual category of weapon, even from the point of view of their control.

It is therefore absolutely evident that any attempt to separately regulate the use of nuclear weapons in the absence of the simultaneous availability of adequate mechanisms of international control on the manufacturing and detention of these weapons would produce distortions, and could rather slow down the solution of the afore-mentioned problems.

[Texte illisible non reproduit]

It should also be underlined that the subject of the threat to use nuclear weapons gives rise to delicate questions, affecting - in particular - national defense and international policy strategies which can only be affected by *ad hoc* rules, to be conventionally defined. Therefore, it is the international community as a whole which should proceed in the direction of a global discipline of the whole subject, within the context of nuclear disarmament negotiations - which, on the other hand, were already launched a long time ago.

The above observations lead to the unavoidable conclusion that - within the limitations imposed by the NPT - the manufacturing and detention of nuclear weapons by certain States should be considered, for the time being, as legitimate, because they are not prohibited. The validity of this conclusion cannot be effectively questioned, also considering that such a stance should not hinder or slow down the process leading to nuclear disarmament, whose rapid and positive conclusion is strongly advocated by the international community as a whole.

This conclusion does not clash with the existence of some general prohibitions on the matter, whose objective is to avoid or limit resorting to armed violence.

[Texte illisible non reproduit]

Mention should finally be made of the principle of the respect for civil populations, generally defined by the IV Geneva Convention of August 12, 1949, and by Article 23, point e, of the Hague rules of 1989, according to which - on the basis of the principle of proportionality - the exercise of armed violence should be carried out so as not to bring about unnecessary, and thus superfluous or useless sufferings.

For the Italian Government
Prof. Umberto Leanza

NOTE VERBALE DATED 19 JUNE 1995 FROM THE EMBASSY OF MEXICO, TOGETHER WITH WRITTEN STATEMENT OF THE GOVERNMENT OF MEXICO

EMBAJADA DE MÉXICO

PBA-413

The Embassy of Mexico presents its compliments to the President of the International Court of Justice and has the honour to forward the written statement by the Government of Mexico on the request for an advisory opinion submitted to the Court by the Forty-Ninth United Nations General Assembly, through its resolution 49/75 K.

The above-mentioned written statement has been formulated by the Government of Mexico in accordance with the order issued by the Court on February 1, 1995, and in conformity with article 66 of the Statute of the Court.

The Embassy of Mexico avails itself of this opportunity to renew to the President of the International Court of Justice the assurances of its highest consideration.

The Hague, June 19, 1995.

President of the International
Court of Justice
The Hague

EMBAJADA DE MEXICO

WRITTEN STATEMENT BY THE GOVERNMENT OF MEXICO ON THE REQUEST FOR AN ADVISORY OPINION SUBMITTED TO THE INTERNATIONAL COURT OF JUSTICE BY THE FORTY-NINTH UNITED NATIONS GENERAL ASSEMBLY (RESOLUTION 49/75K)

CONTENTS

I Summary

II Introduction

III Expediency of the advisory opinion

IV Concept of nuclear weapons

V Possession of nuclear weapons

VI Prohibition on the threat or use of force in international law

VII Prohibition on the threat or use of nuclear weapons under any circumstance

First use
The threat of first use
Enforcement measures authorized by the Security Council
Individual or collective self-defense

VIII Prohibition on the use of certain weapons under international law

IX International humanitarian law

X Conclusions

WRITTEN STATEMENT BY THE GOVERNMENT OF MEXICO ON THE REQUEST FOR AN ADVISORY OPINION SUBMITTED TO THE INTERNATIONAL COURT OF JUSTICE BY THE FORTY-NINTH UNITED NATIONS GENERAL ASSEMBLY (RESOLUTION 49/75K)

SUMMARY

1. In accordance with the order issued by the International Court of Justice on 1 February 1995, and in keeping with the provisions of Article 66 of its Statute, the Government of Mexico hereby submits to the Court the following written statement in reply to the request for an advisory opinion, formulated by the Forty-Ninth United Nations General Assembly in resolution 49/ 75K, in regard to the following question:

"Is the threat or use of nuclear weapons in any circumstance permitted under international law?"

2. This written statement will answer the question presented to the Court in the negative. It will demonstrate that, by contravening the norms of international law currently applicable to the maintenance of international peace and security and international humanitarian law, the use or the threat of use of nuclear weapons is under no circumstance permitted by international law.

3. In this regard, it should be noted that on 9 June 1994 the Government of Mexico submitted a written statement to the International Court of Justice regarding the request for an advisory opinion formulated by the World Health Organization in resolution WHA 46.40, on the following question: "In view of the health and environmental effects, would the use of nuclear weapons by a State in war or other armed conflict be a breach of its obligations under international law including the WHO Constitution?" Although the aforementioned written statement focused on the content of the norms applicable to armed conflicts (*jus in bello*), the question formulated to the Court in United Nations General Assembly resolution 49/75K merits scrupulous analysis of the law on the maintenance of international peace and security.

4. In this written statement, the Government of Mexico will place emphasis on the norms of international law currently applicable to the maintenance of international peace and security, as well as of the law of armed conflicts. These norms are mainly contained in the Charter of the United Nations, in multilateral treaties and in declarations and resolutions adopted by the principal organs of the United Nations. With regard to the latter, the Government of Mexico recognizes the declarations and resolutions quoted in this written statement as norms of general international law, due to the fact that they either reproduce existing customary norms or have contributed to their consolidation.

INTRODUCTION

5. No threat is more imminent to the maintenance of international peace and security and to the survival of mankind itself than the very existence of nuclear weapons. The warlike nature of this type of weapons, their destructive capacity and their effects on all forms of life on earth, are more than enough to justify their disappearance from the world scene.

6. Aware of those dangers, the States have been addressing the issue of nuclear disarmament for several decades. At present, therefore, total elimination of nuclear weapons is one of the international community's priority commitments.1

7. Despite the fact that international law has been addressing the issue of nuclear weapons for some time, the establishment of an express prohibition on the use of such weapons has yet to meet with success. As will be demonstrated throughout this document, the absence of an express prohibition has proved irrelevant and, consequently, turn out to be insufficient to generate any presumption of the legality of the use or threat of the use of nuclear weapons. The norms applicable to armed conflicts and to the maintenance of international peace and security, which are of a legally binding nature for all the States (*jus cogens*), are more than sufficient to state without question that the use or threat of the use of nuclear weapons is under no circumstance permitted by international law.

EXPEDIENCY OF THE REQUEST FOR AN ADVISORY OPINION

8. By its very nature, the international system frequently faces situations in which the extent of the legal norms applicable to relations between States is not altogether clear. In such situations, delimiting the content of international law becomes an especially important task in which the International Court of Justice makes a highly significant contribution.

9. The need to specify the scope of the norms of international law is particularly evident in the case of nuclear weapons. The increasingly destructive capacity of this type of weapon poses an exceptional threat to international peace and security and also, evidently, to the fulfillment of the Principles and Purposes of the Charter of the United Nations. It therefore comes as no surprise that since the UN initiated its efforts, it has placed special emphasis on promoting disarmament and on seeking the elimination of nuclear weapons and weapons of mass destruction from national arsenals.2

10. Nuclear weapons, however, are regulated by international law in several manners. Rules have been established on prohibiting the use of nuclear weapons in certain regions,3 prohibiting nuclear proliferation,4 partially banning nuclear testing,5 etc., and it is precisely such wide-ranging regulations that have led States to uphold different positions with regard to the use or threat of the use of nuclear weapons.

11. Bearing in mind the importance to the international community of this topic and the differences in the approach taken towards it, the opinion of a judicial organ as important as the International Court of Justice would provide the States with an authoritative answer to a question of international import, and, evidently, with a more effective basis for progress in international co-operation towards nuclear disarmament.

12. It is not hard to perceive the political aspect of the topic submitted to the consideration of the Court. Nevertheless, the essentially legal nature of the question formulated makes the International Court of Justice the competent body in which to elucidate the issue. This is not the first time requests for advisory opinions having a significant amount of political opposition have been submitted to the principal judicial organ of the United Nations,6 yet the Court has in every case fulfilled the international community's expectations.

13. The Government of Mexico considers that the Court has been presented with an invaluable opportunity to support other organs of the United Nations in carrying out their duties,7 while at the same time contributing to further clarifying the norms

of international law. We are sure that the Court will take the best possible advantage of this opportunity.

THE CONCEPT OF NUCLEAR WEAPONS

14. The question formulated to the Court calls for a definition of the meaning of the term "nuclear weapon." To that end, we may refer to some of the definitions used in the international sphere:

15. Article 5 of the Treaty for the Prohibition of Nuclear Weapons in Latin America and the Caribbean (Treaty of Tlatelolco) defines nuclear weapons as "...any device which is capable of releasing nuclear energy in an uncontrolled manner and which has a group of characteristics that are appropriate for use for warlike purposes."

16. The Treaty on a Nuclear-Weapon-Free Zone in the South Pacific (Treaty of Rarotonga) defines as an "explosive nuclear device" any nuclear weapon or other explosive device capable of releasing nuclear energy, irrespective of the objective for which such a weapon may be used.

17. The term is also used in a generic sense in reference to atomic or hydrogen weapons of all types and to their delivery systems.8

18. As may be appreciated, although the definitions differ as to terminology, all focus on artifacts of mass destruction which function on the basis of nuclear energy, including their delivery systems. The aim of this document is to analyze the use or threat of the use of such instruments.

POSSESSION OF NUCLEAR WEAPONS

19. Before embarking on the analysis of the illegality of the threat or use of nuclear weapons, it is fundamental to dismiss at the outset that the possession of nuclear weapons by Nuclear Weapons States (NWSՈs) permits such States to threat or use such weapons against other States.

20. Certain States have sought to legitimize the use or the threat of use of nuclear weapons on the grounds that the Treaty on the Non-Proliferation of Nuclear Weapons (NPT) permits the five declared NWSՈs to possess such weapons. As will be demonstrated below, possession of nuclear weapons is solely temporary and initial, and does not legitimize the threat or the use of such weapons.[9]

21. Although the NPT is generally perceived as an instrument vital to international security, it led to the establishment of a discriminatory regime among the States parties by permitting the five declared nuclear powers to possess nuclear weapons while prohibiting the remainder to possess them.

22. In order to eliminate this discriminatory regime and attain a balance between the rights and the obligations of the Parties, the States undertook to pursue negotiations in good faith on effective measures relating to the cessation of the nuclear arms race at an early date and to nuclear disarmament, and on a Treaty for general and complete disarmament under strict and effective international control (Article VI). Furthermore, the Preamble to NPT calls for the liquidation of all their existing stockpiles and the elimination from national arsenals of all nuclear weapons and their means of delivery.

23. Accordingly, possession of nuclear weapons and, hence, the discriminatory regime of NPT, can only be interpreted as being temporary, until the ultimate goal of

complete elimination of such weapons is attained. On the other hand, possession of nuclear weapons by the five declared NWS had to be tolerated, but never accepted, as an initial step to start therefrom the efforts to achieve the ultimate goal of the Treaty, general and complete disarmament.

24. In this regard, the Decision adopted without a vote at the recent 1995 Review and Extension Conference of the Parties to the NPT,[10] whereby the Parties decided that the Treaty will continue in force indefinitely, could never be taken to mean legitimizing possession of nuclear weapons in an indefinite manner. Mexico's statement at the time of adoption of the decisions adopted by consensus reiterated that an indefinite extension of NPT did not mean the perpetuation of the dichotomy between Nuclear-Weapon States and Non-Nuclear-Weapon States, since the Conference had reaffirmed in that context that the ultimate goal of NPT is the total elimination of all nuclear weapons.[11] Thus, by reiterating that goal, the existence of nuclear weapons is clearly not legitimized by the international community and the use or threat of the use of such weapons would be contrary to international law.

25. In point of fact, the programme of action embodied in the Decision on the principles and objectives for nuclear non-proliferation and disarmament[12] contemplates the determined pursuit by the Nuclear-Weapon States of systematic and progressive efforts to reduce nuclear weapons globally, with the ultimate goal of eliminating those weapons, and by all States of general and complete disarmament under strict and effective international control.[13]

26. In this regard, the nuclear disarmament obligations contained in the Treaty have equally taken on indefinite force until they are fully complied with, and the organized international community will continue to work in favour of the abolition of nuclear weapons.

27. The Court may also wish to consider the Final Document of the Tenth Special Session of the General Assembly Devoted to Disarmament of 1978, in whose preamble it was stated:

"The General Assembly,

"Alarmed by the threat to the very survival of mankind posed by the existence of nuclear weapons and the continuing arms race, and recalling the devastation inflicted by all wars..."

Further below, the first operative paragraph of the Final Document declared that:

"...the accumulation of weapons, particularly nuclear weapons, today constitutes much more a threat than a protection for the future of mankind..."

28. Necessarily, once the international community has determined the threat nuclear weapons represent to the survival of mankind, it can be sustained an argument leading to deny that international law permits the possesion of such weapons. It is worth mentioning that the Final Document was adopted unanimously and it is so far an obliged reference of the multilateral negotiations taking place in the Conference on Disarmament.

29. The threat posed to the survival of mankind by the existence of nuclear weapons grants to the international community as a whole the right to pronounce itself on the illegality of such weapons and to act accordingly above any sovereign right that a State may claim to acquire any means it deems appropriate to guarantee its defense. Certainly, Nuclear-Weapon States cannot claim that this question belongs to its internal jurisdiction. The Charter of the United Nations undoubtedly

established as its principal purpose the maintenance of international peace and security. The mere possesion of nuclear weapons runs contrary to the security of mankind.

PROHIBITION ON THE THREAT OR THE USE OF FORCE IN INTERNATIONAL LAW

30. One of the basic norms for the fulfillment of the Principles and Purposes of the Charter of the United Nations may be found in the proscription of the threat or use of force against the territorial integrity or political independence of any State, or in any other manner inconsistent with the Purposes of the United Nations, as contained in paragraph 4 of Article 2 of the above-mentioned instrument.

31. The fundamental obligation of the States is to refrain from using force and to settle their disputes by peaceful means. As may be inferred from the paragraph quoted, the aforementioned prohibition is not only limited to the use of force, but also to the threat, and not only to the territorial integrity or political independence of any State, but also to any other means incompatible with the United Nations. Since those aims include the maintenance of peace and the development of friendly relations among States, the possibility of resorting to the threat or the use of force is practically forbidden. The threat or use of nuclear weapons is necessarily included within the bounds of that prohibition, and its actualization would therefore be contrary to international law.

32. The prohibition on the threat or use of force contained in the Charter has been reaffirmed by numerous resolutions and declarations adopted within the framework of the United Nations. The following are among the most prominent:

a. The Declaration on the principles of international law concerning friendly relations and co-operation among States in accordance with the Charter of the United Nations (resolution 2625 (XXV), annex), reiterates the language of Article 2 (4) of the Charter, and adds:

"Such a threat or use of force constitutes a violation of international law and of the Charter of the United Nations and shall never be employed as a means of settling international issues."

"A war of aggression constitutes a crime against the peace, for which there is responsibility under international law."[14]

b. The Declaration of Manila on the peaceful settlement of international disputes (resolution 37/10, annex) establishes that: "Every States shall settle its international disputes exclusively by peaceful means in such a manner as to ensure that international peace and security, and justice, are not endangered."[15]

c. The Declaration on the enhancement of the effectiveness of the principle of refraining from the threat or use of force in international relations (resolution 42/22, annex), in addition to reiterating the content of Article 2 (4) of the Charter, adds that such a principle is universal in character and is binding regardless of each State's political, economic, social or cultural system or relations of alliance.[16] Furthermore, it establishes that no consideration of whatever nature may be invoked to warrant resorting to the threat or use of force in violation of the Charter of the United Nations.[17]

33. As stated earlier, proscription of the threat or use of force in international relations is a generic prohibition that necessarily includes nuclear weapons. Additionally, the United Nations General Assembly has adopted various resolutions

which expressly state the prohibition on the threat or use of nuclear weapons. The following are among the most important:

a. By virtue of the Declaration on the prohibition of the use of nuclear and thermonuclear weapons (resolution 1653 (XVI)), the General Assembly declared that the use of nuclear and thermonuclear weapons constitutes a violation of the Charter, as acting contrary to the laws of humanity and as committing a crime against humanity and civilization. That condemnation was reaffirmed by means of resolutions 33/71 B, 34/83 G, 35/122 D, 36/92 I, 45/69 B and 46/37 D.

b. The Declaration on international co-operation for disarmament (resolution 34/88) called upon all the States not to use their military power for aggressive purposes, especially by applying force or threatening to apply it against the sovereignty, territorial integrity or political independence of any State.[18]

34. The Charter of the United Nations and the aforementioned resolutions make no distinction between the legal status of the threat of use of force and the use of force itself. Both situations are prohibited equally. In practice, however, greater emphasis has been placed on prohibiting the use of force. In cases in which the threat is actualized by the use of force, the attention will necessarily focus on the latter aspect. In any event, proscription of the threat of force will apply even if such a threat has not led to the use of force.

35. One way of explaining the difficulty involved in determining the existence of a threat of use of force may be found in the mechanism which establishes the existence of a threat to international peace and security, as contained in the Charter. In accordance with Article 39, the Security Council is responsible for determining the existence of any threat to peace, breach of the peace or act of aggression. The right to veto held by the five permanent members of the Council (which at the same time are the five declared nuclear powers), would procedurally hinder determining the existence of a threat, should one of those powers be involved. The impossibility for the Council to determine the existence of a threat of use of force due to the interposition of a veto, does not reduce, however, the legal force of the prohibition on any threat.

36. The Secretary-General of the United Nations, for his part, has indicated that the threat of use of force occurs when a State, in order to impose its will on another State, threatens to use force against that State. He has also specified that such a threat does not necessarily have to be made openly, but that on certain occasions veiled threats could be most effective, yet difficult to prove.[19]

37. The International Law Commission has considered the "threat of aggression"[20] a crime against the peace and security of mankind and has included it as an article separate from "aggression" within the draft Code of Crimes the Commission is currently working on.[21] Article 16 of the Code establishes the following:

"1. An individual who as leader or organizer commits or orders the commission of a threat of aggression shall, on conviction thereof, be sentenced.[22]

"2. The threat of aggression consists in declarations, communications, demonstrations of force or any other measures which would give good reason to the Government of a State to believe that aggression is being seriously contemplated against that State."[23]

38. Characterization of the threat of aggression as a crime against the peace and security of mankind by the International Law Commission reflects the status that the

concept has attained in international law, and is considered by experts to be the codification of a rule of international customary law.

39. Although both the threat of use of force and the use of force itself are prohibited under international law, the legal effects produced by either situation will have implications on the concept of self-defense. The International Law Commission has specified that the "threat of aggression" does not give rise to individual or collective self-defense under Article 51 of the Charter,[24] in contrast to aggression itself.

PROHIBITION ON THE THREAT OR USE OF NUCLEAR WEAPONS UNDER ANY CIRCUMSTANCE

40. The concepts set forth above lead to the definitive conclusion that there exists a rule of international law prohibiting the threat or use of force, including by means of nuclear weapons. Nevertheless, the threat or use of force by means of nuclear weapons may arise under various circumstances, which, once reviewed, would make it possible to prove that ***the threat or use of nuclear weapons is not permitted in any circumstance under international law.***

First use

41. As a direct consequence of the general prohibition on the threat or use of force, a first nuclear attack would violate the terms of Article 2 (4) of the Charter and would also, therefore, be contrary to international law, whether carried out against another Nuclear-Weapon State (NWS) or a Non-Nuclear-Weapon State (NNWS). The Declaration of the General Assembly on the prevention of nuclear catastrophe (resolution 36/100) sets forth that "States and statesmen that resort first to the use of nuclear weapons will be committing the gravest crime against humanity."[25] So far, the People's Republic of China is the only State that has adopted an official no-first use policy.[26]

42. The hypothesis of a nuclear attack against a NNWS would not only violate the rule contained in Article 2 (4) of the Charter, but also merit stronger sanctions under international law by constituting a breach of the underlying principle of *proportionality* established by the law on armed conflicts.[27]

43. Security Council resolution 984 (1995) and the declarations of NWSՌs setting forth positive and negative security assurances,[28] represented a step forward towards providing NNWSՌs with assurances against the use and threat of the use of nuclear weapons. Those security assurances have nevertheless proved insufficient, since they were not granted in a certain, unrestrictive, unconditional and non-discriminatory form.

44. Accordingly, the Decision on principles and objectives for nuclear non-proliferation and disarmament,[29] adopted without a vote by the 1995 Review and Extension Conference of the Parties to the Treaty on the Non-Proliferation of Nuclear Weapons (NPT), noting resolution 984 (1995) as well as the declarations of NWSՌs on positive and negative security assurances, indicated that further steps should be considered to assure NNWSՌs party to the Treaty against the use or threat of the use of nuclear weapons, which could take the form of an internationally legally binding instrument.

45. Although to date the Conference on Disarmament has been unable to negotiate a legally binding instrument containing assurances of universal scope to NNWSՌs against the use or threat of the use of nuclear weapons, the purpose of resolution 984 (1995) and the intent of the States parties to the NPT contained in the

Decision mentioned in the above paragraph, implicitly recognize the illegality of the threat or the use of nuclear weapons against a NNWS. Obviously, were the threat or the use of nuclear weapons a legal act, negative security assurances to protect NNWSѕs would have been unnecessary.

46. Despite the absence of a legally binding instrument on negative security assurances of universal scope, it should be borne in mind that in Additional Protocol II of the Treaty of Tlatelolco, the five declared NWSѕs undertook not to use or threaten to use nuclear weapons against the Contracting Parties to the Treaty.[30]

The threat of first use

47. A threat of first use could arise in a conflict, either by threatening a preemptive nuclear strike against a perceived threat of nuclear attack, or by threatening a nuclear strike against a possible attack by conventional weapons or by threatening a response to an actual conventional attack.

48. The threat of first use is a violation of the prohibition on the threat of use of force contained in Article 2 (4) of the Charter. The threat of first use is intrinsically a threat against the political independence or territorial integrity of another State. Any State either in current or potential conflict with a nuclear State advocating a policy of first use recognizes the threat posed by nuclear weapons and the possibility of their being used against it. Due to the unique nature of nuclear weapons, as weapons of mass destruction, they represent a threat of unequaled intimidation which would undermine the political independence of the threatened State.

49. The only exceptions established by international law to the general prohibition on the threat or use of force in relations between States are to be found in Chapter VII of the Charter. These exceptions are the enforcement measures authorized by the Security Council, and individual or collective self-defense.

Enforcement measures authorized by the Security Council

50. For the mechanism of collective security to enter into effect there must be a threat to peace, a breach of the peace or an act of aggression.[31] In any such case, the Security Council will be responsible for deciding and following up on the measures to be adopted to restore international peace and security.

51. Once the mechanism of collective security had been activated, it would be impossible for the Security Council to authorize the use of nuclear weapons against a State. Two arguments reinforce the above statement: first, the Security Council, being the organ that holds the primary responsibility for the maintenance of international peace and security, could not contemplate --even theoretically-- authorizing the use of weapons of mass destruction whose destructive effects on all forms of life on the planet have been scientifically determined.[32]

52. Secondly, the General Assembly has adopted a number of resolutions declaring that the use of nuclear weapons constitute a violation of the Charter of the United Nations and a crime against mankind (see paragraph 33 a. *supra*). Clearly, if the General Assembly has condemned the use of nuclear weapons, the Security Council is precluded from authorizing their use.

53. Therefore, Security Council resolutions 255 (1967) and 984 (1995), which provide that aggression or the threat of aggression with nuclear weapons against a NNWS would require the Security Council, and above all its permanent members, to act immediately in accordance with their obligations under the Charter, would necessarily have to be applied totally outside the realm of resorting to the threat or use of nuclear weapons.

Individual or collective self-defense

54. Article 51 of the Charter states: "Nothing in the present Charter shall impair the inherent right of individual or collective self-defense if an armed attack occurs against a Member of the United Nations, until the Security Council has taken measures necessary to maintain international peace and security..."

55. The intent of the above-mentioned provision is clear: any State has a legitimate right to make use of force to defend itself when it becomes the victim of an armed attack,[33] and other States may join in assisting the victim while the Security Council acts to fulfill the duties entrusted to it under the Charter.

56. Individual or collective self-defense is conceived as a means of preserving essential rights against irreparable damage when no other means of protection exist, and its exercise is therefore not absolute. Observance of the restrictions international law has imposed on self-defense is indispensable in maintaining its use within a framework of legality.

57. The right of self-defense is actualized only when the need for defense is immediate and overwhelming, and is considered legal when proportional to the armed attack that gave rise to such defense.

58. The International Law Commission has defined proportionality by stating that the size of the measures adopted by an injured State should be comparable to the graveness of the internationally illegal act it is facing and to its effects.[34] This means that self- defense cannot be excessive.

59. Necessity is the justification for an action involving the use of force. This means that unless certain measures are adopted against a State that has committed an act of aggression, essential rights of the aggrieved would be destroyed. Nevertheless, justification does not allow discretionality, and only such measures as are strictly necessary to put an end to the attack could be adopted under the title of self-defense.

60. As may be appreciated, the requirements of proportionality and necessity are concurrent. Necessity justifies the action, but that action cannot exceed the limits of proportionality and should cease as soon as no longer necessary. The legitimacy of the actions adopted under the concept of self-defense depends on the observance of the principles mentioned above.

61. The use of nuclear weapons in case of self-defense is not permitted under international law, owing to the fact that such use contravenes the principles of proportionality and necessity on which the legal nature of the aforementioned concept is based. In this regard, and to reaffirm the above, a distinction should be made between two situations in which the use of nuclear weapons could take place under this title: as a result of an act of aggression using conventional weapons or as a reaction against a nuclear strike.

62. In the first case, there is no doubt that a reaction using nuclear weapons to an attack perpetrated with conventional weapons violates the principle of proportionality, which by definition is incompatible with mass destruction.[35]

63. In the second case, the illegality of the nuclear response would violate other fundamental principles of international law, among the most prominent of which are those applicable to armed conflicts (see paragraphs, 77 and 78 *infra*). Although in theory the use of nuclear weapons could be justified by the provisions of Article 51 of the Charter of the United Nations and by applying the rules of international law

established by *The Carolina Case*[36] (any action of self-defense should fulfill the following conditions: an instant and overwhelming necessity for self-defense, leaving no moment for deliberation and no choice of means, and be proportional), such a justification would be highly questionable. Even by actualizing the requirement of absence of deliberation or choice of means, the condition of proportionality would not be respected, since in the case of a nuclear attack **the proportionality of a nuclear response would be uncontrollable and would endanger the security of mankind as a whole.**

64. Clearly, moreover, there is no possibility of resorting to self-defense to justify a first-use nuclear attack in cases of threat of the use of nuclear or conventional weapons, since, as stated earlier, there is no legal possibility of resorting to self-defense in cases of threats.

65. It should be borne in mind that the principal purpose of the United Nations, according to the Preamble of the Charter, is "to save succeeding generations from the scourge of war, which twice in our lifetime has brought untold sorrow to mankind." This purpose would clearly be frustrated if a State which had been subjected to nuclear attack were to retaliate in kind, since the likely outcome of such an exchange would be the massive destruction of life in both States, on the population of neighbouring States and excessively harmful effects on health and the environment in the rest of the world. Therefore, the second use of nuclear weapons is not permissible, whether in retaliation or self-defense, since defensive military actions is subject to the law of armed conflicts to the same extent as offensive actions.

66. With regard to the use of nuclear weapons as a means for reprisals, self-help, countermeasure, or, broadly speaking, in response to a violation by a State of an obligation stipulated in international law, it is possible to state that such use runs counter to international law and is inconsistent with the Principles and Purposes of the Charter of the United Nations.

67. The Security Council has stated on a number of occasions[37] that reprisals involving the use of force are prohibited under international law. Furthermore, the Declaration on the principles of international law concerning friendly relations and co-operation among States in accordance with the Charter of the United Nations (resolution 2625(XXV), annex), indicates that States have a duty to refrain from acts of reprisal involving the use of force.

68. The International Law Commission, for its part, has provided that contemporary international law does not permits neither reasonably armed reprisals, nor forms of self-help involving the use of force, nor armed intervention based on necessity.[38]

69. Finally, the International Court of Justice rejected arguments of self-help or self-protection in the Case of the Corfu Channel,[39] considering them contrary to international law.

70. There being no further need to enlarge on the subject, suffice it to say that save for the exceptions to the prohibition on the use of force contained in the Charter of the United Nations (see paragraphs 50 to 65 *supra*), any unilateral action, regardless of its nature, involving the use of force, is prohibited by international law.

PROHIBITION ON THE USE OF CERTAIN WEAPONS IN INTERNATIONAL LAW

71. The notion of expressly prohibiting the use of certain weapons first arose in the Declaration of Saint Petersburg of 1868. That document stated that the

progress of civilization should have the effect of mitigating the calamities of war as much as possible, and prohibited the use of any projectile weighing less than 400 grammes or loaded by means of fulminating or inflammable substances.

72. The Declaration of Saint Petersburg was followed by a series of international instruments in which the idea of preventing unnecessary suffering and superfluous damage to the enemy led to a prohibition on the use of certain weapons. Such instruments included The Hague Conventions of 1899 and 1907, which prohibited the use of poisoned or poisonous weapons and of arms, projectiles or materials causing unnecessary suffering; the Protocol of 1925 for the prohibition of the use in war of asphyxiating, poisonous or other gases, and of bacteriological methods of warfare (The Geneva Gas Protocol); and the Convention on the prohibition of the development, production and stockpiling of bacteriological (biological) and toxin weapons and on their destruction of 10 April 1972, etc.

73. All the above-mentioned instruments have made it clear that the right of the parties in an armed conflict to choose the means of harming the enemy is not unlimited and is, in fact, subject to restrictions. In this regard, it is worth highlighting Article 35 of the Protocol Additional I of 1977 to the Geneva Conventions of 12 August 1949, and relating to the Protection of Victims of International Armed Conflicts, which reaffirms that the right of the Parties to an armed conflict to choose methods or means of warfare is not unlimited and that it is prohibited to employ weapons, projectiles and material and methods of warfare of a nature to cause superfluous injury or unnecessary suffering. It also adds a prohibition against the employment of methods or means of warfare causing widespread, long-term and severe damage to the natural environment.

74. Certain States consider that the provisions of Protocol Additional I exclude nuclear weapons from their scope of application. It is held, however, that such an affirmation is unfounded. In the first place, because such an exclusion does not follow from the text of the said instrument, and even if it did, international humanitarian law has evolved in such a manner since the adoption of Protocol Additional I that it is impossible to affirm that its provisions merely extend to conventional weapons. In the second place, even if a reservation in relation to nuclear weapons did exist, it would be incompatible with the object and purpose of the instrument.[40]

75. The international community considers that certain types of armaments should be prohibited on account of their inhumane effects on individuals. However, none of the effects produced by the weapons expressly prohibited by international law can compare with those stemming from the use of nuclear weapons. Clearly, if weapons with lesser effects than those of nuclear weapons have been banned, all the more reason to extend such a ban to nuclear armaments.

76. To consider that the absence of a prohibition in international law directed specifically at nuclear weapons means that their use might be lawful, is not only unacceptable, but also queries the credibility of the international legal system.[41]

INTERNATIONAL HUMANITARIAN LAW

77. It is also important to analyze the rules of international humanitarian law in order to confirm the illegality of the threat or the use of nuclear weapons. Clearly, if we accept the principle by which the use of any weapon is legitimate only as far as it is employed to defeat the enemy, whether or not in self-defense, we could not even think that international law permits the possibility to defeat the whole of mankind. The nature of the effects stemming from the use of any kind of nuclear weapon stands as one of the strongest arguments to support on the illegality of the threat or

the use of nuclear weapons. International humanitarian law has elaborated on the principles mentioned below, all of which will lead to the conclusion that the threat or the use of nuclear weapons is not permitted in any circumstance in international law, including in case of an armed conflict.

a. *The principle of moderation.* According to this principle the right of belligerents to adopt means of injuring the enemy is not unlimited. This principle is contained in Article 22 of the Regulations annexed to the The Hague Convention IV of 1907 and Article 35 of Protocol Additional I of 1977 to the Geneva Conventions of 12 August 1949.

b. *The principle of humanity (De Martens Clause).* By virtue of the De Martens Clause[42] the provisions of the Protocol Additional I and the Geneva Conventions are applicable in any circumstance regardless of the unfavorable nature or origin of the armed conflict or in the causes invoked by the Parties to a conflict. Therefore, the first use of nuclear weapons would be encompassed under the scope of the above mentioned instruments in accordance with the Clause.

On the other hand, the principle of humanity, contained in the Preamble of The Hague Convention IV of 1907 and in Article 1.2 of the Protocol Additional I, establishes that in those cases not expressly foreseen in such instruments, civilians and belligerents are under the protection of the law of nations stemming from the usages, the principles of the humanity and the dictates of public conscience. Therefore, the illegality of nuclear weapons depends on the principle of humanity. There are sacred rules that cannot be violated, even if the enemy has breached them previously. Thus, Pictet when speaking of the prohibition on all reprisals against protected persons by the Geneva Conventions says: *"L'interdiction des represailles ainsi établie a un caractère absolu. Elle vaut même si la violation á laquelle on prétendre répondre s'est produite dans le champ des Conventions de Genève".*[43]

c. *The principle by which it is forbidden the use of weapons, projectiles, material and methods of warfare of a nature to cause superfluous injury or unnecessary suffering.* It is worth highlighting that regardless of the degree of improvement of nuclear weapons, due to the suffering infringed upon the belligerents and the civilian population, these weapons will always cause excessive damages and will have indiscriminate effects, even in sites far from the scene of operations (See Article 23 of the Regulations annexed to The Hague Convention IV of 1907 and Article 35 of Protocol Additional I of 1977).

It is also relevant the fact that the Protocol of 1925 for the prohibition of the use in war of asphyxiating, poisonous or other gases, and of bacteriological methods of warfare (The Geneva Gas Protocol) is applicable to nuclear weapons even if it was adopted before those weapons were created. George Schwarzenberger points out: "If it could be established that the use of all nuclear weapons involved necessarily the discharge of gases ennumerated in the Protocol, it would settle matters conclusively bettween the Parties to the Protocol. Even if the words "all analogous liquids, materials or devices" are so comprehensively phrased as to include any weapons of analogous character, irrespective of whether they were known or induced at the time of the signature of the Protocol. If the radiation and fall-out effects of nuclear weapons can be likened to poison,all the more can they be likened to poison gas which is but an even more closely analogous species of the genus poison".[44]

d. *The principle by which the civilian population enjoys general protection and the prohibition to carry out indiscriminate attacks.* In accordance to international humanitarian law, indiscriminate attacks are those that can reach both military targets and civilians. Nuclear weapons are essentially weapons of indiscriminate effects, irrespective of the concrete circumstances of its use (Article 51 of Protocol Additional I of 1977).

78. In light of the aforementioned considerations, in the opinion of the Government of Mexico the general principles codified in the Regulations annexed to The Hague Convention IV, the Protocol Additional I of 1977 to the Geneva Conventions of 1949 and in the Preamble of the Convention on prohibition or restriction on the use of certain conventional weapons which may be deemed to be excessively injurious or to have indiscriminate effects of 1980, are peremptory norms of general international law (*jus cogens*) as established by the Vienna Convention on the Law of Treaties of 1969.

CONCLUSIONS

79. The above paragraphs lead to the conclusion that in accordance with international law relating to the maintenance of international peace and security, to armed conflicts and to other obligations subscribed by the States on disarmament issues, the threat or use of nuclear weapons is not permitted by international law under any circumstances. The scope of the obligations that constitute the grounds for this conclusion make it evident that no circumstance whatsoever would justify the threat or use of nuclear weapons.

80. The body of international law on which such a prohibition is based is made up of conventional and customary norms, including peremptory norms of general international law by virtue of which the threat or the use of weapons of mass destruction could not be legitimized. On the contrary, the treaties and resolutions of United Nations organs, reinforced by the current status of applicability of norms on the maintenance of international peace and security, point to the ultimate goal of total elimination of all nuclear weapons.

NOTES AND QUOTATIONS

1. See, for example, the Preamble and Article VI of the Treaty on the Non-Proliferation of Nuclear Weapons (1 July 1968).

2. See, for example, Article 11 of the Charter of the United Nations and resolution 1(I) of the General Assembly, adopted unanimously on 24 January 1946.

3. Among them, the Treaty for the Prohibition of Nuclear Weapons in Latin America and the Caribbean (14 February 1967) and the Treaty on a Nuclear Weapon-Free Zone in the South Pacific (6 August 1985).

4. Treaty on the Non-Proliferation of Nuclear Weapons.

5. Treaty banning nuclear weapon tests in the atmosphere, in outer space and under Water (5 August 1963).

6. See Rossene Shabtai: *The World Court: What it is and how it works*, 1989, p. 106.

7. In particular, the First Committee of the General Assembly and the Conference on Disarmament.

8. United Nations. *Disarmament Topics: Towards a Nuclear Test Ban*, New York, July 1989, p. 22.

9. Therefore, it should be rejected the argument presented by some NWSՈs by which it is claimed that the possession of nuclear weapons may imply its use or threat of use. See the written statements presented by France and the United Kingdom regarding the request of an advisory opinion formulated by the WHO in resolution WHA 46.40 (International Court of Justice, *legality of the use by a State of nuclear weapons in armed conflict: written statements (originals)*, September 1994).

10. Decision adopted on 11 May 1995, document NPT/CONF.1995/L.6. The Conference was held in New York, N.Y., from 17 April to 12 May 1995.

11. Statement Mexico in document NPT/CONF.1995/PV.18, pp. 9-10.

12. Document NPT/CONF.1995/L.6 adopted without a vote by the Conference on 11 May 1995.

13 Paragraph 4 d).

14. Section I.

15. Paragraph 2.

16. Paragraph 2.

17. Paragraph 3.

18. Section II.

19. Report of the Secretary General on the question of defining agression (document A/2211 of 3 October 1952). cfr. in: Henkin, Louis et al. *International Law,* 1987. p. 681.

20. The definition of aggression is contained in General Assembly resolution 3314 (XXIX): "Aggression is the use of armed force by a State against the sovereignty, territorial integrity or political independence of another State, or in any other manner inconsistent with the Charter of the United Nations...". According to the above-mentioned resolution, not all forms of the use of force constitute an act of aggression, but aggression is the most serious and dangerous form of the illegal use of force (preambular paragraph 5 of the resolution).

21. Report of the International Law Commission on the work of its forty third session. Supplement No. 10 (A/46/10).

22. Although the draft Code places the responsibility on the individual, it has also provided that prosecution of the said individual for a crime against the peace and security of mankind should not exonerate the State in question from any responsibility, according to international law, for any act or omission attributed to it (Article 5).

23. The International Law Comission has indicated that the word "threat" means acts undertaken with a view to making a State believe that force will be used against it if certain demands are not met by that State. A threat may take the form of declarations (expressions made public in writing or orally), communications (messages sent by the authorities of one Government to the authorities of another Government, by no matter what means of transmission) and shows of force (e.g. concentrations of troops near the frontier). See: Yearbook of the International Law Commission, Vol. 2, Part 2, p.68, document A/CN.4/SER.A/1989/Add.1.

24. See development of the concept of individual and collective self-defense in paragraphs 54-65 *infra*.

25. Paragraph 1.

26. See declaration formulated by China on 5 April 1995, document S/1995/265.

27. See paragraph 63 *infra*.

28. The declarations of the five nuclear powers formulated on 5 and 6 April 1995 are contained in documents S/1995/261, S/1995/262, S/1995/263, S/1995/264 and S/1995/265.

29. Ibid. note 11 *supra*.

30. Article 3 of Additional Protocol II.

31. Article 39 of the Charter of the United Nations.

32. *Effects of nuclear war on health and health services*, Geneva, World health Organization, 1987; International Physicians for the Prevention of Nuclear War, *Radioactive heaven and earth*, Apex Press, 1991; Institute of Medicine, National Academy of Sciences, *The medical implications of nuclear war*, Washington D.C., 1986, among many other scientific studies.

33. The International Court of Justice has indicated that self-defense is limited only to a case of armed attack (*Military and paramilitary activities in Nicaragua and against Nicaragua,*26 November 1984).

34. See article 13 of the draft on responsibility of States being prepared by the International Law Commission in the report of the Commission on the work of its forty-fourth session. Supplement No. 10 (A/47/10), pp. 75-78.

35. H. Meyrowitz, *Le statut des armes nucléaires en droit international,* Y.I.L. 219, 1982.

36. The Carolina Case, in Moore, *Digest of International Law,* Vol. 2, p.409.

37. Resolutions 56 (1948), 188 (1964) and 228 (1966), among others.

38. Report of the International Law Commission on the work of its forty-fourth session. Supplement No. 10 (A/48/10), p.82.

39. Judgement of 9 April 1949.

40. In this regard, it could not be accepted the argument presented by the Government of the Russian Federation regarding the request of an advisory opinion formulated by the World Health Organization in resolution 46.40, by which it mentioned that reservations to Protocol Additional I show that the question of legitimacy or non-legitimacy of the use of nuclear weapons is not regulated by international law. (International Court of Justice, *legality of the use by a State of nuclear weapons in armed conflict: written statements (originals),* September 1994).

41. Therefore, the Government of Mexico cannot agree with the conclusion contained in the written statements of the Governments of the United Kingdom and the United States of America regarding the request of an advisory opinion formulated by the WHO, by which it has affirmed that there is no rule contained in either customary international law or treaty which expressly prohiibits all use of nuclear weapons (International Court of Justice, *op. cit.*)

42. The De Martens Clause establishes that the inhabitants and the belligerents remain under the protection of the rule of the principles of the law of nations, as they result from the usages established among civilized peoples from the laws of humanity and the dictates of the public conscience, until a more complete code of the laws of war has been issued.

43. Jean Pictet, cfr. in: Sandoz, Yves, *Des armes interdites en droit de la guerre,* Université de Neuchatel, 1975, p. 69.

44. Cfr. in Yves Sandoz, ibid., p. 64-65.

LETTER DATED 19 JUNE 1995
FROM THE AMBASSADOR OF THE RUSSIAN FEDERATION,
TOGETHER WITH WRITTEN COMMENTS
OF THE GOVERNMENT OF THE RUSSIAN FEDERATION

ПОСОЛ
РОССИЙСКОЙ ФЕДЕРАЦИИ

To the Registrar
of the International Court of Justice
Mr. E.Valencia-Ospina
Peace Palace

The Hague

The Hague, 19 June 1995

Dear Mr.Valencia-Ospina,

Please find enclosed "WRITTEN STATEMENT AND COMMENTS OF THE RUSSIAN FEDERATION ON THE ISSUE OF THE LEGALITY OF THE THREAT OR USE OF NUCLEAR WEAPONS".

Enclosure: as above mentioned, 20 pages

Sincerely

L.Skotnikov,
Ambassador of the Russian Federation

WRITTEN STATEMENT AND COMMENTS OF THE RUSSIAN FEDERATION ON THE ISSUE OF THE LEGALITY OF THE THREAT OR USE OF NUCLEAR WEAPONS

Moscow, 16 June 1995

1. The World Health Organization, by its resolution WHA 46/40 dated 14 May 1993, requested the International Court of Justice to give an advisory opinion on the following question: "In view of the health and environmental effects, would the use of nuclear weapons by a State in war or other armed conflict be a breach of its obligations under international law, including the WHO Constitution?"

2. The Russian Federation, being a UN member, is *ipso facto* a party to the Statute of the International Court of Justice under the provision of Article 93, paragraph 1 of the UN Charter and correspondingly is entitled to appear before the Court.

3. Having received an appropriate notification about the WHO's request and also about the readiness of the Court to accept, within the time-limit fixed by it, written statements of the states which are entitled to appear before the Court with respect to the question, the Russian Federation in accordance with Article 66, paragraph 2 of the Statute of the International Court has presented an appropriate written statement to the Court on 7 June, 1994.

4. Taking into account the above, as well as the fact that the similar statements have been presented to the Court by other states the Russian Federation, in accordance with Article 66, paragraph 4 of the Statute of the International Court and following the decision of the President of the Court of 20 June, 1994, hereby presents comments on the other relevant written statements pertaining to the issue.

5. The General Assembly, by its resolution 49/75K dated December 15, 1994, decided to request the International Court to give an advisory opinion on the following question: "Is the threat or use of nuclear weapons in any circumstances permitted under international law?"

6. The Russian Federation, proceeding from what was set forth in paragraph 2 above and having received an appropriate notification about the UN General Assembly request, in accordance with Article 66, paragraph 2 of the Statute of the International Court and in accordance with the decision of the Court dated February 1, 1995, hereby presents a written statement on the question, formulated by the UN General Assembly.

7. It is the opinion of the Russian Federation that questions formulated by the WHO and the UN General Assembly are essentially very similar and in this connection it thinks it possible and expedient to dwell on both of them in a single document which is being enclosed.

A study of written statements of other states even more firmly strengthened our opinion expressed in the Statement of June 7, 1994: the Court should not give an advisory opinion on the WHO's request.

1. In accordance with Article 96, paragraph 1 of the UN Charter the General Assembly or the Security Council may request the International Court of Justice to give an advisory opinion "on any legal question".

In accordance with paragraph 2 of the same Article, specialized agencies which may at any time be so authorized by the General Assembly may also request advisory opinions of the Court "on legal questions arising within the scope of their activities".

As applied to WHO, this general rule relating to all specialized agencies is specified in Article X, paragraph 2 of the Agreement between the UN and the WHO of 1948 and in Article 76 of the WHO Constitution.

According to Article X, paragraph 2 of the Agreement of 1948 the UN General Assembly entitles the WHO to make request to the International Court of Justice to give an advisory opinion on legal questions arising in the sphere of the competence of the Organization and others than those concerning relations between the WHO and the UN or others specialized agencies.

Under Article 76 of the WHO Constitution, Organization may request the Court to give an advisory opinion on any legal question arising within the scope of the Organization's competence.

Consequently, as distinct from the General Assembly and the Security Council, the WHO being a specialized agency, may request the Court to give an advisory opinion not on any legal question, but only on a legal question arising within the scope of the Organization's competence.

The WHO's competence is defined first of all in its Constitution. It is quite apparent that this document does not contain a provision, which would confirm *expressis verbis* that the WHO is competent to consider the matter of legality of use by a State not only of nuclear weapons but of any kind of weapons at all in an armed conflict.

The attempts to refer to an "implied" or "inherent" WHO's competence have no prospects either. This is proved by the 45- year practice of the WHO, which until the WHA resolution 46/40 of 14.05.93 has never appealed to the subject of legality of the use of nuclear weapons.

Accordingly, there is also no evidence that the WHO's practice or its resolutions have somehow developed the WHO's Constitution, so as to endow it with such a competence. In this respect, an analysis of WHO's activities, contained in Chapter I of the written statement presented to the Court by the UK Government in connection with the WHO's request, seems to be strongly convincing.

It is well-known that while interpreting a treaty any subsequent practice of its application which establishes the agreement between the parties regarding interpretation of the treaty (Article 31, paragraph 3.b of Vienna Convention of the Law of International Treaties, 1969) shall be taken into account. This rule is also applicable to the treaties setting up international organizations.

For us it's clear that WHA resolution 46/40 of 14.05.93, which was adopted with 73 votes "for", 40 - "against" and 10 "abstaining", does not establish such an agreement.

Thus, so far as the question of legality of the use of nuclear weapons does not fall within the competence of WHO and cannot emerge within this competence under Article 96, paragraph 2 of the UN Charter, Article 76 of WHO's Constitution and Article X, paragraph 2 of the Agreement between

between the UN and the WHO, the Organization had no right to request the Court to give an advisory opinion on such a question. So, the WHO Assembly's resolution and the question contained in it are the WHO's actions *ultra vires*.

2. In accordance with Article 65, paragraph 1 of the Statute of the International Court, the Court "may give an advisory opinion on any legal question at the request of whatever body may be authorized by or in accordance with the Charter of the United Nations to make such a request".

The verb "may", used in this wording, in our opinion, has two meanings.

First, the Court may give opinions exclusively upon the request of the body authorized to make such a request by the UN Charter or in accordance with it.

Taking into account what was said above in paragraph 1, it's difficult to consider the WHO as the organization authorized by the UN Charter or in accordance with it to make such a request in this particular case. Correspondingly, in our view in this case the Court hardly at all may, i.e. hardly has the right to give an advisory opinion upon such WHO's request.

However, naturally, the Court itself solves the question of its competence. And in this connection we would like once again to draw attention to the second meaning of the word "may".

As it was mentioned in our statement dated June 7, 1994 and in the statements of some other States, the Court may, but is not obliged to give advisory opinions i.e. it has a discrete competence in this respect.

In this context we would like to note those consequences for international law in general and for the law of international organizations in particular, which will arise as a result of the realization by the Court of its right to give advisory opinion upon WHO's request, whatever this opinion might be.

We would like to emphasize that we are putting aside political aspects and are talking about purely legal consequences which shall be of primary importance for the International Court while solving the question whether to give or not to give an advisory opinion.

In this sense it is important that in this case taking a decision to exercise its right and to give an advisory opinion, the Court, in a way would establish a precedent of encouraging international organization activities *ultra vires*, would lend to such illegal acts legal consequences which they were called upon to achieve (we stress once again: irrespective of what this advisory opinion might be).

In our view, such an action by the Court would be harmful for the development of international law in general and the law of international organizations in particular.

II

Despite the differences in the wording, questions put before the Court by the WHO and UN General Assembly are very similar. In our opinion, the question, contained in General Assembly resolution 49/75K dated 15 December 1994 is formulated in a more general manner and somehow covers the question put before the Court by the WHO. That's why, and also with due regard to considerations set forth in Section I above, in this Section we intend to concentrate mainly on the UN General Assembly question: "Are the threat or use of nuclear weapons in any circumstance permitted under international law?"

1. The very wording of the UN General Assembly question gives rise to questions.

First of all, in virtue of the principle of sovereignty, we treat as generally admitted the presumption that the state may accomplish any acts, which are not prohibited under international law. Basically, international law is a system of limitations, rather than permissions. In this connection, the question, whether international law permits the use of nuclear weapons or not is not likely to be correct. If we ask the question of this kind, we should ask whether international law prohibits the use of nuclear weapons. Anyway, the essence of the question is in the question whether international law contains the ban of the use of nuclear weapons or not.

At the same time, an extremely broad wording of the question formulated by the General Assembly, as well as by WHO, strikes one's eye.

It seems that the initiators of both requests didn't want to draw a distinction between the use of nuclear weapons by the aggressor and the use of such weapons in self-defence, for instance in the retaliation for the use of nuclear or some other mass destruction weapons, as well as a distinction in connection with the consequences of the use of nuclear weapons.

Meanwhile, in our opinion, these distinctions are very significant.

2. In our view, international law contains no general prohibition of use of nuclear weapons *per se*.

A study of main sources of international law - international treaties and international customs - proves our opinion. We don't consider here general principles of law, because we believe that they are reflected in international treaties or customs.

1) International treaties - general, as well as special - don't contain rules stipulating a complete ban on nuclear weapons *per se*.

A study of international treaties, especially those dedicated to the problems of nuclear weapons leads us to the following conclusions.

First of all, those treaties admit the existence of nuclear weapons and the possession of nuclear weapons by some states. At the same time these treaties envisage different limitations with respect to nuclear weapons, in particular:

- their proliferation (Treaty on the Non-Proliferation of Nuclear Weapons, 1968)[1/];

- their testing (Treaty on Banning Nuclear Weapon Tests in the Atmosphere, in Outer Space and Under Water, 1963; Treaty between the USSR and the USA on the Limitation of Underground Nuclear Weapons Tests 1974);

- their deployment in certain territories (Treaty on the Prohibition of the Emplacement of Nuclear Weapons and Other Weapons of Mass Destruction on the Sea-Bed and the Ocean Floor and the Subsoil Thereof, 1971; Treaty on the Prohibition of Nuclear Weapons in Latin America (Treaty of Tlatelolco), 1967; South Pacific Nuclear Free Zone Treaty (Treaty of Raratonga), 1985);

- certain types of nuclear arms, down to the elimination of certain types thereof, even if the word "nuclear" is not mentioned in the text. (Interim Agreement between the USSR and the USA on Certain Measures with respect to the Limitation of Strategic Offensive Arms, 1972; Treaty between the USSR and the USA on the Limitation of Strategic Offensive Arms, 1979, which though it has not entered into force so far, has been observed for several years; Treaty between the USSR and the USA on the Reduction and Limitation of Strategic Offensive Arms, 1991, to which, Russia, Belorussia, Kazakhstan, Ukraine and the USA have become parties after they have signed the 1992 Protocol to the Treaty; Treaty between

---

1/ The Russian Federation is continuing to exercise the rights and responsibilities of the former USSR under the international treaties.

Russia and the USA on Further Reduction and Limitation of Strategic Offensive Arms, 1993, which has not yet entered into force; Treaty between the USSR and the USA on the Elimination of Their Intermediate-range and Shorter-range Missiles, 1987).

Thus, treaties, devoted exclusively to nuclear weapons provide for significant number of restrictions in this regard, but there is no special treaty which would put a general ban on the use of nuclear weapons as such.

We think that there are no real prerequisites for concluding such a treaty at present as yet. No necessary and sufficient conditions exist. That is why the appeals of the General Assembly (General Assembly resolutions 45/59 A of 1990 and 46/370 of 1991) to the Conference on Disarmament proposing to begin on a priority basis talks aimed at the conclusion of a convention prohibiting the employment of nuclear weapons in any circumstances, have not been implemented. The very fact that there are projects of such a convention in General Assembly resolutions proves that presently no treaty provision in this regard exists.

Furthermore, it is apparent that while concluding numerous special treaties in this sphere, states have based their positions on the assumption that international law does not prohibit the employment of nuclear weapons as such. That is why treaties were signed with an aim either to lessen the possibility of its employment (for example, USSR-USA Treaty on the Prevention of Nuclear War of 1973; analogous treaties between the USSR and the UK (1978), the USSR and France (1976); the USSR-USA Agreement for the Creation of Nuclear Risk Reduction Centers (1987) or to pledge the non-employment of such weapons against specific countries, in specific regions or specific circumstances (the USSR, the USA, the UK and France have all signed Additional Protocol II of the Tlatelolko Treaty, in accordance with article 3 whereof they pledge not to use and not to threaten to use nuclear weapons against the State-parties to the Tlatelolko Treaty; the USSR and China have also signed a similar Protocol to the Raratonga Treaty).

There does not exist a provision containing a general prohibition of the employment of nuclear weapons as such also in international treaties, which are not specially devoted to the subject of nuclear weapons.

It is well known that the UN Charter (Article 2, paragraph 4) obliges the Organization members to refrain in their international relations from the threat or use of force against the territorial integrity or political independence of any state, or in any other manner inconsistent with the purposes of the United Nations.

In this sense, as the threat or use of force in general, the threat or use of nuclear weapons by a state is prohibited, as are the threat or use of any other kind of weapons.

At the same time the Charter does not impair in any sense the inherent right of individual or collective self-defence if an armed attack occurs against a Member of the United Nations (Article 51). Accordingly, in this sense the Charter admits the use of nuclear or other weapons *per se* by a state.

We do not consider the provisions of a number of the UN General Assembly resolutions, which stipulate that the use of nuclear weapons as such is a violation of the UN Charter (UN GA Res.1653 (XVI), UN GA Res.33/71/B, UN GA Res.35/152D, UN GA Res.36/923 and some others), as an authentic and binding interpretation of the UN Charter. Such General Assembly resolutions and declarations, regardless of how they were adopted, are not binding and do not create by themselves obligations for UN members. Any other, opposite view of the role of such General Assembly resolutions has no basis in the UN Charter.

A number of international treaties, not specifically devoted to the problem of nuclear weapons, contain certain restrictions in this regard (the Treaty on Principles Governing the Activities of States in the Exploration and Use of Outer Space, Including the Moon and other Celestial Bodies of 1967; the Antarctic Treaty of 1959). Nevertheless, there does not exist any general prohibition on the use of nuclear weapons in any such treaty.

Sometimes, to substantiate the point of view according to which international law prohibits the use of nuclear weapons, the reference is made to international human rights treaties and, in particular, to the Convention on the Prevention and Punishment of the Crime of Genocide of 1948.

We presume, however, that it clearly follows from the Convention that it is not the mere use of nuclear or any other type of weapons that constitutes genocide but respective act "committed with intent to destroy, in whole or in part, a national ethnical, racial or religious group, as such" (Article II of the Convention). Therefore, to qualify certain actions as genocide and as a violation of international law, one should take into account their aim and intent but not the weapons, means used to implement those actions.

Neither do we find correct the arguments that the use of nuclear weapons is not admissible under international law, because it violates the human right to life laid down, in particular, in the Universal Declaration of Human Rights of 1948 (Article 3) and the International Covenant on Civil and Political Rights of 1966 (Article 6).

The existence of the right to life does not mean that it is not possible to deprive a person of his life through legitimate use of force. This is confirmed, for instance, in Article 2, paragraph 2 of the European Convention on the Protection of Human Rights and Fundamental

Freedoms, which reads: "Deprivation of life shall not be regarded as inflicted in contravention of this article when it results from the use of force which... is absolutely necessary... in defence of any person from unlawful violence...". In this sense the use of nuclear weapons in self-defence does not constitute a violation of the right to life.

Besides, those putting forward arguments that the use of nuclear weapons is not admissible under international law, also appeal to international treaties codifying rules applicable to armed conflicts.

Restrictions set by the rules applicable to armed conflicts in respect of means and methods of warfare also extend to nuclear weapons. However, we are convinced that there is no general prohibition on the use of nuclear weapons as such in treaties codifying those rules.

The most recent rules applicable to an armed conflict are contained in Additional Protocols of 1977 to the Geneva Conventions of 1949. Restrictions on the methods and means of warfare are contained, in particular, in parts III and IV of the Additional Protocol I. However, as Frits Kalshoven reasonably observes, "the Diplomatic Conference" which adopted the Protocols, "was virtually unanimous in its view that it had not been convoked to bring the problems connected with the existence and possible use of nuclear weapons to a solution"1/. The drafting history of Protocol I shows that "any new rules and principles, embodied in the Protocol, were not written with a view to the potential use of nuclear weapons"2/. This is

---

1/ Frits Kalshoven. Constraints on the Waging of War, ICRC, Geneve, 1987, p.82.

2/ Ibid., p.104. In the introduction to the draft Protocols the ICRC had stated that: "Problems relating to atomic, bacteriological and chemical warfare are subjects of international agreements or negotiations by governments, and in submitting there draft Additional Protocols the ICRC does not intend to broach those problems". See: Commentary on the Additional Protocols of 8 June 1977 to the Geneva Conventions of 12 August 1949. Ed. by Y.Sandoz, Chr.Swinarski, Br.Zimmermann, Martinis Nijhoff Publ., Geneva, 1987, p.590.

reflected in the Protocols themselves in which there is neither reference to nuclear weapons nor mentioning of any other specific type of weapons, as well as in the declarations made by a number of countries (the USSR, France, the USA, Spain, the United Kingdom, the Netherlands, Belgium, the FRG and Italy) during the Conference, signing or ratification of the Protocol.

As is known, the 1949 Geneva Conventions contain no regulations concerning nuclear weapons.

Thus, the principal humanitarian law instruments adopted in the nuclear age do not prescribe any general ban on the use of nuclear weapons.

It is probably in this context that the advocates of illegality of the use of nuclear weapons substantiate their position by referring to earlier instruments - the Hague Conventions of 1899-1907 and even the Declaration to the Effect of Prohibiting the Use of Certain Projectiles in Wartime(St.Petersburg Declaration) of 1868.

In particular, they state that under the Declaration the only legitimate object which states should endeavor to accomplish during war is to weaken the military forces of the enemy; for this purpose it is sufficient to disable the greatest possible number of men, this object would be exceeded by the employment of arms which uselessly by aggravate the suffering of disabled men, or render their death inevitable; the employment of such arms would therefore be contrary to the laws of humanity.

Along with that, a reference is made to the "Martens clause" - a blanket formula contained in the Preambles to the Convention Respecting the Laws and Customs of War on Land of 1899 and to the Convention Concerning the Laws and Customs of War on Land of 1907 ("Until a more complete code of the laws of war has been issued, the... Parties deem it expedient to declare that, in cases not included in the Regulations adopted by them, the inhabitants and the belligerents remain under the protection and the rule of the principles of the law of nations, as they result from the usages established among civilized peoples, from the laws of humanity and the dictates of the public conscience"), as well as to Article 22 ("the right of belligerents to adopt means of injuring the enemy is not unlimited"), Article 23b) ("it is forbidden... to employ arms, projectiles, or material calculated to cause unnecessary suffering"), Article 25 ("it is forbidden to attack or bomb in any way whatsoever unprotected cities, towns, houses or premises") of the Regulations annexed to the Convention of 1907.

As far as the regulations are concerned, the rules laid down in Articles 22 and 25 contain restrictions which refer to the use of any types of weapons, including nuclear ones. However, these articles do not prohibit the use of any particular type of weapons.

As to the attempts to justify the illigimacy of the use of nuclear weapons by references that they cause "unnecessary sufferings while injuring, uselessly aggravate the sufferings of disabled men, or render their death inevitable", they are also hardly reasonable. The report of the ICRC experts entitled "Weapons that May Cause Unnecessary Suffering or Have Indiscriminate Effects" stated: "What suffering must be deemed "unnecessary" is not easy to define. Clearly the authors of the ban on dum-dum bullets1/ felt that the hit of a ordinary rifle bullet was enough to put a man out of action and that infliction of a more severe wound by a bullet which flattened would be to cause "unnecessary suffering"... The circumstance that a more severe wound is likely to put a soldier out of action for a longer period was evidently not considered a justification for permitting the use of bullets achieving such results. The concepts discussed

1/ The authors of the Hague Declaration Concerning the Prohibition of Using Bullets which Expand or Flatten Easily in the Human Body of 1899.

must be taken to cover all weapons that do not offer greater military advantages than other available weapons while causing greater suffering... In addition the concept of "unnecessary suffering" would seem to call for weighing the military advantages of any given weapon against humanitarian considerations"2/.

These reasonable comments of the ICRC experts confirm two considerations. First, the principle of not causing "unnecessary suffering" is not in itself a general ban on the use of nuclear weapons as such. Second, attempts to apply blanket norms formulated in the second half of the 19th century - beginning of the 20th century to new types of weapons do not seem to be convincing.

As to nuclear weapons the "Martens clause" is not working at all. A "more complete code of the laws of war" mentioned there as a temporary limit was "issued" in 1949-1977 in the form of Geneva Conventions and Protocols thereto, and today the "Martens clause" may formally be considered inapplicable.

But it is not all. Protocol I of 1977 reproduces, with slight changes (Art.35), the above-mentioned provisions of the Articles of the 1907 Convention, but they, being treaty norms, are not applied to nuclear weapons (see pp.10,11 above).

The view that the said blanket formulas are not considered by the international community as a whole as a general ban on the use of specific types of weapons, including nuclear weapons as such, is supported by the fact that international law did choose the option of special ban of particular types of weapons and their use. That is how the 1925 Protocol on the Prohibition of the Use in War of Suffocating, Poisonous and other Similar

2/ ICRC: Weapons that may Cause Unnecessary Suffering or have Indiscriminate Effects. Report on the work of experts. Geneva, 1973, p.13

Gases and Bacteriological Means; the 1980 Convention on Prohibitions or Restrictions on the Use of Certain Conventional Weapons, which May Be Deemed to Be Excessively Injurious or to Have Indiscriminate Effects, together with Protocols thereto; the 1972 Convention on the Prohibition of the Development, Production and Stockpiling of Bacteriological (Biological) and Toxic Weapons and on their Destruction; 1993 Convention on the Prohibition of Development, Production, Stockpiling and Use of Chemical Weapons and on their Destruction appeared.

It is probable that in some time a treaty will appear on the ban of the use of nuclear weapons and of nuclear weapons themselves. But today such a treaty does not exist.

2) Constraints on the use of nuclear weapons are provided not by a treaty law, but by customary general international law. However, we are quite sure that there is no customary rule of international law, prohibiting the use of nuclear weapons in general.

To respond in substance to the request of the General Assembly the Court in accordance with Article 38, paragraph 1(b) of its Statute, shall apply "international custom as evidence of a general practice accepted as law". As it was stated above, it is not a permissive rule, but the rule prohibiting the use of nuclear weapons *per se*.

Our study shows that there is no general practice accepted as law, that provides for such a prohibition.

For the purpose of this statement we do not intend to distinguish between the evidences of existence or, which is more accurate, of absence of relevant practice and *opinio juris*.

As it is shown above, the treaty practice, the treaty form of coordination the wills of States demonstrates not only the absence of a general prohibition of the use of nuclear weapons *per se*, but also the presence of presumption that in principle the use of nuclear weapons is admissible. This is testified by the treaty acts by which States voluntarily refuse to use nuclear weapons in certain circumstances or agree to adopt measures to reduce the risk of a nuclear war (Protocols to the Treaties of Tlatelolko and Raratonga, agreements between nuclear Powers, see above, pp.7,8).

There are also other international agreements of non-treaty nature which contain similar provisions about the voluntary refusal of nuclear states to use nuclear weapons (Memoranda on the security guarantees in connection with Belorussia', Republic of Kazakhstan' and Ukraine's adhesion to the NPT, signed by those states respectively and Russia, UK and USA in December 1994).

The unilateral will of states, their unilateral acts do not support the general practice and/or *opinio juris* on the matter under consideration either, quite on the contrary, what they do prove, is the lack of such practice and *opinio juris* and the presence of major contradictions in views.

While some states claim that any use of nuclear weapons would be contrary to international law, others officially proclaim the doctrine of nuclear containment and stick to it in practice, thus expressly emphasizing the admissibility of the use of nuclear weapons. At the same time the nuclear states made unilateral statements (see: UN Documents S/1995/261, S/1995/262, S/1995/263, S/1995/264, S/1995/265) in which, while granting to non-nuclear state-parties to the NPT the security guarantees against an aggression with the use of nuclear weapons, voluntarily gave up their right to use nuclear weapons in certain circumstances.

The reports themselves, submitted to the Court and thus containing the official point of view, testify that no uniform opinion exists among the states on this question.

It is noteworthy that the lack of a general prohibition of the use of nuclear weapons as such in international law is not signalled by nuclear states alone (see, for instance, the reports submitted by the governments of Germany and the Netherlands).

Some nuclear states have, at different times, made statements of the non-use of nuclear weapons first (the former USSR, China) which also signifies that, in their opinion, the use of nuclear weapons has not been banned in principle.

The advocates of the existence of such a ban in international law refer to a number of General Assembly resolutions (1653(XVI), 1961; 33/71B, 1978; 34/83B, 1979; 35/125D, 1980; 36/92I, 1981; 45/59B, 1990; 46/37D, 1991), where it is stated that the use of nuclear weapons would be a violation of the UN Charter and a crime against humanity.

As it has been already mentioned above (see page 8), such General Assembly resolutions do not create by themselves any obligations for states which are UN Members. They are not, in our opinion, an expression of *opinio juris* of the world community either. It is not even a question of the voting results on those resolutions (not one of them was adopted either by consensus, or by acclamation, or by a vast majority of UN Members). Many states vote for these resolutions, or abstain from voting, not voting against, having in mind that, according to the Charter, they do not create new law and do not signify the recognition of any rules as such, but are only of recommendatory nature.

This does not mean that these resolutions do not reflect the *opinio juris* of some states with a different point of view. Nevertheless, they do not represent a form of coordination of wills of all UN Members in relation to acceptance of these provisions as international law.

The same thing can be said about the question of in what capacity these GA resolutions form the other element of a customary provision - universal practice.

Furthermore, it is worth noting that the acts of international organizations even in their contents give proof to the fact that different opinions exist on the question at hand. Thus, in the resolution of the WHA 46/40 it is noted that "over the last 48 years marked differences of opinion have been expressed by Member States about the lawfulness of the use of nuclear weapons". The UN Security Council resolution 984 of 11 April 1995 (S/Res./984(1995) is also exemplary in this sense, because, according to it, the body charged with the main responsibility for the maintenance of international peace and security "takes note with appreciation" of the above-mentioned statements of nuclear states on the assurances to the non-nuclear Parties to the Nuclear Non-Proliferation Treaty (while these statements testify to a definite approach of their authors to the legality of nuclear weapons use). Furthermore, it is stated in this Security Council Resolution that, according to the relevant provisions of the UN Charter, "any aggression with the use of nuclear weapons would endanger international peace and security". Thus, it is clear from what is stated in the Security Council Resolution that not just any use of nuclear weapons per se would constitute a violation of the UN Charter but an aggression with the use of nuclear weapons.

In our opinion, the facts stated here prove conclusively that presently there is no universal practice nor a universal *opinio juris* on the unlawfulness of nuclear weapons' use. And if so no customary international law provision exists which would envisage a general ban on the use of nuclear weapons *per se*.

3. Naturally, all that has been said above does not mean that the use of nuclear weapons is not limited at all. Even if the use of nuclear weapons is in principle justifiable - in individual or collective self-defence - that use shall be made within the framework of limitations imposed by humanitarian law with respect to means and methods of conducting military activities. It is important to note that with respect to nuclear weapons those limitations are limitations under customary rather than treaty law.

The issue of legality of the use of nuclear weapons shall be dealt with on a case-by-case basis from a viewpoint of the correspondence of such use to criteria of self-defence and the above limitations.

As Hans Blix said, "it is certainly correct to say that the legality of the use of most weapons depends upon the manner in which they are employed. A rifle may be lawfully aimed at the enemy or it may be employed indiscriminately against civilians and soldiers alike. Bombs may be aimed at specific military targets or thrown at random. The indiscriminate use of the weapon will be prohibited, not the weapon as such"[1/]. We should add that it is a duly qualified use rather than the use of weapons as such at large that will be regarded as illegal.

1/ Hans Blix. Means and Methods of Combat. In: International Dimensions of Humanitarian Law. Publ. by UNESCO, Martinis Nijhoff Publ., 1988, p.144-145.

NOTE VERBALE DATED 19 JUNE 1995 FROM THE PERMANENT MISSION OF THE BURUNDI TO THE UNITED NATIONS

REPUBLIQUE DU BURUNDI

REPUBLIKA Y'UBURUNDI

MISSION PERMANENTE
DE LA REPUBLIQUE DU BURUNDI
AUPRES DES NATIONS UNIES
336 EAST 45th STREET
12th FLOOR
NEW YORK, N.Y. 10017
Tel: (212) 687-1180

Notre Réf: 204.09.15/393/RE/NY/95

La Mission Permanente de la République du Burundi auprès de l'Organisation des Nations Unies présente ses compliments à la Cour Internationale de Justice et, se référant à la lettre No. 95588 du 8 février 1995, a l'honneur de lui communiquer la position du Gouvernement du Burundi.

"Par ses résolutions 1653 (XVI) du 24 novembre 1961, 33/71B du 14 décembre 1978, 34/83G du 11 décembre 1979, 35/152D du 12 décembre 1980, 36/92 I du 9 décembre 1981, 45/59B du 4 décembre 1990 et 46/37D du 6 décembre 1991, l'Assemblée Générale déclarait que l'emploi d'armes nucléaires constituerait une violation de la Charte des Nations Unies et un crime contre l'humanité.

La République du Burundi, préoccupée par la menace ou l'emploi des armes nucléaires, a voté en faveur de la résolution de l'Assemblée Générale 49/75K du 15 décembre 1994 demandant un avis consultatif sur cette question.

La République du Burundi considère que cette résolution et les résolutions antérieures de l'Assemblée Générale rappelées ci-haut expriment à suffisance sa position sur cette question cruciale et réaffirme son entière adhésion aux susdites résolutions.

La République du Burundi est résolument opposée à la menace ou à l'usage des armes nucléaires, car cela violerait l'Article 2 (4) de la Charte des Nations Unies qui demande aux Etats Membres de s'abstenir, dans leurs relations internationales, de recourir à la menace ou à l'emploi de la force, sauf en cas de légitime défense comme le prescrit l'article 51 de la même Charte."

La Mission Permanente de la République du Burundi auprès de l'Organisation des Nations Unies saisit cette occasion pour renouveler à la Cour Internationale de Justice les assurances de sa très haute considération.

New York, le 19 ~~Juin~~ 1995

Cour Internationale de Justice
Peace Palace, 2517 KJ The Hague.

Mission Permanente aux Nations Unies

NOTE VERBALE DATED 20 JUNE 1995 FROM THE EMBASSY OF SWEDEN, TOGETHER WITH WRITTEN STATEMENT OF THE GOVERNMENT OF SWEDEN

EMBASSY OF SWEDEN
THE HAGUE

The Embassy of Sweden presents its compliments to the International Court of Justice and has the honour to submit the following information.

The Government of Sweden has been invited by the International Court of Justice to submit a written statement to the Court on the question raised in a request for an Advisory Opinion by the United Nations General Assembly (res 49/75 K) on the legality of the threat or use of nuclear weapons.

The Government of Sweden submitted on 10 June 1994 a written statement to the International Court of Justice as its answer to the Court to a similar question raised by the World Health Assembly. The Government of Sweden wishes to refer to that answer also in the present case.

For the sake of convenience the above mentioned statement of 10 June 1994 is annexed.

The Embassy of Sweden avails itself of this opportunity to renew to the International Court of Justice the assurances of its highest consideration.

The Hague, 20 June 1995

The International Court of Justice
THE HAGUE

Mailing address:
P.O. Box 90648
2509 LP The Hague
The Netherlands

Visiting address:
Neuhuyskade 40
2596 XL The Hague
The Netherlands

Telefon:
070 - 324 54 24

Telefax:
070 - 324 79 11

The Government of Sweden has been invited by the International Court of Justice to submit a statement on the question raised in a request for an advisory opinion submitted by the World Health Organization and referred to in the International Court's letter dated 14 September 1993.

Also the Swedish Parliament has taken an interest in the matter. On the initiative of a number of members, the Standing Committee on Foreign Affairs of the Parliament has made an analysis on International Law and Nuclear Arms, included in its Annual Report on Disarmament.

In the Report, which was approved by the Parliament on 2 June 1994, the Standing Committee concludes that the Government, in its reply to the International Court of Justice, should make it clear that the use of nuclear arms would not be in accordance with international law.

The Government of Sweden has taken due note of the decision of the Parliament and hereby submits to the International Court of Justice a translation of the relevant parts of the Report as its answer to the question put by the ICJ.

Unofficial Translation

Extracts from the Report of the Swedish Parliamentary Standing Committee on Foreign Affairs (1993/94:UU19)

Nuclear Weapons and International Law

As pointed out in several of the motions, attention was drawn to the question of the legality of the use of nuclear weapons when, at its meeting in May 1993, the WHO decided by a substantial majority, to request a statement by the International Court of Justice in the Hague as to whether the use of nuclear weapons was in compliance with international law. According to those who have presented these motions, the Swedish Government should make it clear in a statement to the International Court that the use of nuclear weapons does not comply with international law.

The Committee has discussed the question of nuclear weapons and international law before on several occasions. This was the case, for example in the most recent disarmament report (Report 1992/93:UU19) which was occasioned by a Social Democratic motion (1992/93:U404 (s*)) which requested i.a. that Sweden should present a proposal in the United Nations under which the use of nuclear weapons would be declared illegal.

A prohibition of the use of nuclear weapons and the closely linked question of non-first-use have been on the agenda of international disarmament forums (including the UN General Assembly) for a great many years, but no progress has been possible in matters of substance. Instead, in the nuclear disarmament process which has finally commenced, the major nuclear weapon powers have now decided on a method involving gradual reductions in their arsenals. The Committee considers it important that these efforts, which have resulted in tangible progress, receive support and encouragement.

Thus, the Committee considers that Motion U403 (s*), Petition 18, and Motion U409 (fp*), Petition 3, have been answered.

In his speech to the United Nations General Assembly on the occasion of the UN 40th Anniversary in 1985, the Prime Minister, Mr Palme, raised the question of the use of nuclear weapons. Amongst other things, he said that "We should consider the possibility to prohibit in international law the use of nuclear weapons, as part of a process leading to general and complete disarmament."

In an address to the Special Session of the United Nations General Assembly on Disarmament held in the summer of 1988, the Prime Minister, Mr Carlsson, once again raised the idea of the prohibition of the use of nuclear weapons previously proposed by Sweden. In this context, he recalled the restrictions which already apply under international law as regards the use of nuclear weapons. He also stated that the Swedish Government considered that the conclusion of an agreement prohibiting the use of nuclear weapons would be of considerable importance. At the same time, Ingvar Carlsson emphasized that an agreement of this nature must be supported by concrete disarmament measures in every area, including both nuclear and conventional weapons.

The Committee wishes to express, once again, its support for measures which may prevent the use of nuclear weapons. The question which the WHO posed to the International Court of Justice in the Hague concerns the content of current, applicable international law, but it will obviously have a political effect. Like other member states, Sweden has been given an opportunity to present its views in this question of law. The Committee presumes that the Government will take advantage of this opportunity.

The Committee notes that, as mentioned earlier, Sweden has unambiguously declared that restrictions exist under international law as regards the use of nuclear weapons.

A principle has existed in international law ever since the turn of the century, under which belligerents do not have an unrestricted right to choose weapons or methods of combat. In the Committee's opinion, the use of nuclear weapons would be restricted by the principles of distinction and proportionality under customary international law.

Under the principle of distinction, an attack on a civilian population or civilian property is prohibited. In the case of an attack on a military target, disproportionately substantial damage may not be inflicted on the civilian population or on civilian property.

The Committee notes that a principle of proportionality is embodied in the law of the UN Charter. Reprisals which are disproportionate in comparison with the provocation which preceded them are prohibited. It would be difficult to regard this principle as consistent with the use of nuclear weapons in retaliation against an attack using conventional weapons.

In the Committee's opinion, the Government should therefore make it clear in its reply to the International Court of Justice that the use of nuclear weapons does not comply with international law. This should be conveyed to the Government.

Hence, the Committee proposes that the Parliament, in view of Motion U403 (s*), Petition 17, and Motion U415 (s, fp, c, kds, v*), should inform the Government that it confirms the Committee's view.

The Committee notes that, in exercising its advisory functions, the International Court of Justice shall be guided by the provisions of its Statute in disputes in so far as it recognizes them to be applicable (Statute of the International Court of Justice, Chapter IV, Article 68). The provisions referred to appear in Chapter II, Article 38, Sub-section 1 of the Statute which reads as follows:

"The Court, whose function is to decide in accordance with international law such disputes as are submitted to it shall apply:

a. international conventions, whether general or particular, establishing rules expressly recognized by the contesting states;
b. international custom, as evidence of a general practice accepted as law;
c. the general principles of law recognized by civilized nations;
d. subject to the provisions of Article 59, judicial decisions and the teachings of the most highly qualified publicists of the various nations, as subsidiary means for the determination of rules of law."

(Article 59 states that the Court's decisions are only binding on the parties in dispute and as regards the case which has been adjudged.)

The Committee presumes that, in preparing its response to the International Court, the Government will scrupulously observe what can be adduced from the above guidelines presented in Article 38 of the Statute as regards why, in view of the medical and environmental effects of these weapons, the use of nuclear weapons in warfare or in other forms of armed conflict should constitute a breach of the obligations under international law, including the WHO Charter, of a state employing such weapons.

The Committee is aware that there are different opinions about what may constitute a basis under international law for a decision concerning the use of nuclear weapons. In this context, the Committee would like to draw the Government's attention to certain arguments - in addition to those already presented - which have been raised in the international debate by specialists in international law and which draw the conclusion that the use of nuclear weapons would be a breach of international law. These arguments primarily involve what may be characterized as general, fundamental legal principles, recognized by civilized nations.

* The Hague Conventions stipulate that the territories of neutral states are inviolable. Radioactive fallout, and other effects of the use of nuclear weapons in armed conflicts, do not stop at the frontiers of neutral states, however. As a result, in most cases the use of nuclear weapons would mean a breach of these conventions.

* The use of weapons which cause unnecessary suffering must be considered to be prohibited. The codification of the prohibition of dum-dum bullets was undertaken in accordance with this view, for example. The effects of radioactive radiation as a result of the use of nuclear weapons cause unnecessary suffering, not merely for third parties who are directly affected, but also future generations, for example as a result of genetic damage.

* In accordance with an established basic principle, expressed, for example, in the Declaration made by the 1972 UN Conference on the Human Environment, there are impediments to the use of weapons which cause extensive, long-term and serious damage to the environment. This is expressed in the Declaration as follows: "Man and his environment must be spared the effects of nuclear weapons."

* As far back as the 17th century, Hugo Grotius stressed that poisoning was not allowed under international law. In certain respects, the principle of the prohibition of toxic weapons has also been codified (chiefly as a result of the 1925 Geneva Convention). Certain residual products resulting from the use of nuclear weapons must undoubtedly be regarded as toxic.

The Committee assumes that these and other considerations which have been raised in the international legal debate, and also the content of existing comprehensive international agreements will be taken into account.

---

*) Letters in brackets refer to political parties: (c) Centre Party, (fp) Liberal Party, (kds) Christian Democratic Party, (s) Social Democratic Party and (v) Left Party.

NOTE VERBALE DATED 20 JUNE 1995 FROM THE EMBASSY OF NEW ZEALAND, TOGETHER WITH WRITTEN STATEMENT OF THE GOVERNMENT OF NEW ZEALAND

No.35/95

The Embassy of New Zealand presents its compliments to the International Court of Justice in The Hague and, with reference to the decision of the United Nations General Assembly, recorded in its resolution 49/75K, to seek an advisory opinion from the Court on the question: "Is the threat of nuclear weapons in any circumstance permitted under international law?", has the honour to refer to the Order of the Court dated 1 February 1995 inviting States entitled to appear before the Court to furnish information on the question in the form of written statements by 30 June 1995 in accordance with Article 66, paragraph 2 of the Statute of the Court.

Pursuant to this Order, the Government of New Zealand hereby submits the attached written statement on the question.

The Embassy of New Zealand takes this opportunity to renew to the International Court of Justice the assurances of its highest consideration.

NEW ZEALAND EMBASSY THE HAGUE

THE EMBASSY OF NEW ZEALAND
The Hague
20 June 1995

STATEMENT BY THE GOVERNMENT OF NEW ZEALAND

1. By resolution of 15 December 1994,[1] the United Nations General Assembly has requested an advisory opinion from the International Court of Justice pursuant to Article 96 of the Charter of the United Nations on the question: Is the threat or use of nuclear weapons in any circumstance permitted under international law?

2. This question was submitted to the Court on 19 December 1994. States entitled to appear before the Court and the United Nations have been invited by Order of the Court of 1 February 1995 to "furnish information" on the question in the form of written statements by 20 June 1995 in accordance with Article 66, paragraph 2 of the Statute of the Court.[2]

3. The request by the United Nations General Assembly follows an earlier request of the World Health Assembly, by resolution of 14 May 1993, for an advisory opinion from the Court on a similar but not identical question. New Zealand submitted a brief written statement in respect of that question on 8 June 1994.

4. New Zealand now wishes to furnish information to the Court with regard to the question presented in the request by the United Nations General Assembly. This statement furnishes information on New Zealand's position regarding nuclear weapons, and addresses the substantive legal considerations before the Court.

NEW ZEALAND'S POSITION REGARDING NUCLEAR WEAPONS

5. Although New Zealand is distant from major sources of international tension, its security, like that of other states, can be affected by events far beyond its immediate neighbourhood. The possession and use of weapons of mass destruction, including nuclear weapons, have implications for all states irrespective of their geographical location. The testing of nuclear weapons in the South Pacific region has also been, and remains, a special concern of New Zealand; it was in response to such testing that New Zealand and Australia brought a case against France before the International Court of Justice in 1973 concerning continued nuclear testing in the atmosphere in the region.[3] Measures to prevent proliferation of such weapons and towards nuclear disarmament have been national priorities for New Zealand for more than thirty years.

6. Central to New Zealand's approach are the objectives, shared with other States Parties, which are set out in Article VI of the Treaty on the Non-Proliferation of Nuclear Weapons (NPT) adopted on 1 July 1968, namely the pursuit of negotiations in good

---

[1] UNGA Resolution 49/75 K.

[2] New Zealand is a party to the Statute of the Court by virtue of Article 93 of the United Nations Charter.

[3] *Nuclear Tests (New Zealand v France)*, Judgment, I.C.J. Reports 1974, p.457.

faith on effective measures relating to cessation of the nuclear arms race at an early date and to nuclear disarmament, and on a treaty on general and complete disarmament under strict and effective international control. New Zealand has contributed towards these objectives at the national, regional and global levels, for example through the enactment of national legislation, the establishment of the South Pacific Nuclear Free Zone,[4] and involvement in multilateral disarmament negotiations and regimes, in particular efforts to secure a comprehensive nuclear test ban treaty.

7. In New Zealand's view, encouraging progress has been made towards the objectives set out in Article VI of the NPT during the last five years, with good prospects for further progress. The INF Treaty,[5] the START treaties[6] and the soon to be concluded comprehensive test ban treaty, together with developments in other areas of disarmament and arms control such as the 1993 Convention on the Prohibition of the Development, Production, Stockpiling and Use of Chemical Weapons and Their Destruction, are examples of the results which can be achieved through the negotiating process.

8. The NPT is a fundamental underpinning of further progress in nuclear disarmament and arms control. The continued importance of the Treaty is emphasised by the recent growth in States Parties to 178. Notably, they now include all five declared nuclear-weapon States as well as some states which were formerly in possession of nuclear weapons. The decision by the States Parties at their conference in May 1995 to extend the Treaty indefinitely further confirms its pivotal role in controlling nuclear weapons and in nuclear disarmament. The conference adopted unanimously a set of principles and objectives for nuclear non-proliferation and disarmament including the goal that negotiations on a universal and internationally and effectively verifiable Comprehensive Nuclear-Test-Ban Treaty be completed no later than 1996 and went on to state that, pending the entry into force of such a treaty, the nuclear-weapon States should exercise the utmost restraint.

9. Since 1972 New Zealand has taken a lead, with other States, in tabling a resolution each year at the United Nations General Assembly calling for a comprehensive test ban treaty to be negotiated. In 1993, for the first time, and again in 1994, the resolution was adopted by consensus. A comprehensive test ban treaty is now being negotiated in the Conference on Disarmament, with the active participation of the nuclear-weapon States. Such a treaty will make a significant contribution to halting the proliferation of nuclear weapons in all its forms, and hence have a major impact on the threat or use of nuclear weapons.

10. New Zealand strongly supports other recent multilateral steps towards nuclear disarmament that would further back up a comprehensive nuclear test ban. Such steps include the recent agreement by the Conference on Disarmament on a mandate for an ad hoc committee to begin negotiations on a treaty banning the production of fissile

[4] The South Pacific Nuclear Free Zone Treaty 1985, also known as the Treaty of Rarotonga.
[5] Treaty on the Elimination of Intermediate-Range and Short-Range Missiles, 1987.
[6] Treaty on the Reduction and Limitation of Strategic Arms, 1991 and 1993.

material for nuclear weapons purposes. New Zealand has also called for a negotiated and verifiable agreement to ban the future production of nuclear weapons.

11. Nuclear testing was a major factor in the establishment in 1986 of a South Pacific Nuclear Free Zone upon the entry into force of the Treaty of Rarotonga.[7] The Treaty reflects the collective will of South Pacific nations to renounce the possession of nuclear weapons, to ensure that nuclear weapons are neither tested nor stationed on national territory in the region, and to gain assurances of non-use of nuclear weapons from the nuclear-weapon States. Together with the areas covered by the adjacent Antarctic Treaty[8] and the Treaty of Tlatelolco,[9] the South Pacific Nuclear Free Zone contributes to an overall nuclear weapon free area which covers approximately 200 million square kilometres of the earth's surface.

12. In order to be fully effective, nuclear free zones require the support of all nuclear-weapon States. Nuclear-weapon States Parties to the Protocols to the Treaty of Rarotonga undertake not to use or threaten to use nuclear weapons against South Pacific states and not to test nuclear weapons in the region. The security of the states in the region, which have all renounced nuclear weapons, will be further enhanced when all nuclear-weapon States have accepted these obligations.

13. In 1987, soon after the entry into force of the Treaty of Rarotonga, the New Zealand Nuclear Free Zone, Disarmament and Arms Control Act was enacted by the Parliament of New Zealand. The Act creates a nuclear free zone within New Zealand and also gives effect at the national level to New Zealand's obligations under international disarmament and arms control treaties including the Treaty of Rarotonga, the Partial Test Ban Treaty[10] and the Biological Weapons Convention.[11] The Act makes it an offence for New Zealand citizens or persons ordinarily resident in New Zealand to manufacture, acquire or possess or have control over any nuclear explosive device or aid, abet or procure any person to do so within the New Zealand Nuclear Free Zone or, if they are servants or agents of the Crown, to commit such acts beyond the Zone. There are further prohibitions in the Act on the stationing or testing of nuclear explosive devices in the New Zealand Nuclear Free Zone, and on the entry into New Zealand internal waters of nuclear powered ships and nuclear weapons.

SOURCES OF LAW

14. The Court's jurisdiction to give advisory opinions arises from Article 65 of its Statute. The sources of law to be applied by the Court in considering questions submitted to it are as set out in Article 38(1) of the Statute, namely:

---

[7] *supra*, n.5.

[8] Antarctic Treaty 1959.

[9] Treaty for the Prohibition of Nuclear Weapons in Latin America (and Additional Protocols), 1967.

[10] Treaty Banning Nuclear Weapon Tests in the Atmosphere, in Outer Space and Under Water, 1963.

[11] Convention on the Prohibition of the Development, Production and Stockpiling of Bacteriological (Biological) and Toxin Weapons and on Their Destruction, 1972.

a) International conventions, whether general or particular, establishing rules expressly recognised by the contesting states;
b) International custom, as evidence of a general practice accepted as law;
c) The general principles of law recognised by civilised nations;
d) Subject to the provisions of Article 59 of the Statute, judicial decisions and the teachings of the most highly qualified publicists of the various nations, as subsidiary means for the determination of rules of law.

15. There is a considerable body of international law which is relevant to the issue of the threat or use of nuclear weapons. A number of treaties regulate nuclear weapons, and in various instances possession, testing, deployment, threats or use of nuclear weapons are expressly prohibited by them. Treaties to this end have been concluded in multilateral fora, and bilaterally between nuclear-weapon States. The nuclear-weapon States have also given unilateral commitments to non-nuclear-weapon States regarding the use of nuclear weapons.

16. There has, thus, been a progressive development of the international law relating to nuclear weapons since their inception. New Zealand regards this progressive development as reflecting an acknowledgment by all States that nuclear weapons, like other weapons of mass destruction, pose a particular risk to humanity, and that a special regime and special norms should apply to them.

17. Other more general international legal norms are also relevant to the threat or use of nuclear weapons, even though they may not expressly be stated to apply to them. Some of these pre-date the inception of nuclear weapons, and others are subsequent to them. This category includes international law regarding resort to force, the humanitarian laws of armed conflict, and environmental law, all of which, together with humanitarian principles, may be considered in relation to the question before the Court.

18. It is inevitable that requests for advisory opinions may touch upon issues that are at the vanishing point of international law. Advisory opinions are, by their very nature, seeking clarification. The formation of customary law rules at international law has been compared with the process by which paths are created over land: eventually the weight of footsteps stamps out a settled track. In the case of the legal regulation of nuclear weapons, the direction of this path and the ultimate goal have been set by a number of generally accepted multilateral treaties, including the cornerstone Treaty on the Non-Proliferation of Nuclear Weapons. The Court has now been asked to consider the extent of this development. In the words of Sir Garfield Barwick in his dissenting opinion in the *Nuclear Tests Case (Australia v. France)*:

> "It cannot be doubted that customary law is subject to growth and to accretion as international opinion changes and hardens into law. It should not be doubted that the

Court is called upon to play its part in the discernment of whether that growth has taken place to the requisite extent and that the stretch of customary law has been obtained."[12]

AGREEMENTS WHICH EXPRESSLY CONSTRAIN NUCLEAR WEAPONS

19. A large body of international law contained in arms control and disarmament agreements expressly constrains nuclear weapons in various respects. This includes prohibitions against the testing, deployment or use of nuclear weapons in Antarctica,[13] Latin America,[14] the South Pacific,[15] earth orbit, outer space, and on the moon and other celestial bodies,[16] and deployment on the seabed, ocean floor and subsoil thereof beyond the twelve-mile limit of national territorial seas.[17]

20. Several of these instruments express the goal in their preambles of the elimination of nuclear weapons.[18] The treaties establishing nuclear weapon free zones in Latin America and the South Pacific, together with the NPT, express in their preambles the view of the parties as to the threat which nuclear weapons present to life on earth.

21. Accordingly, arms control and disarmament agreements are important not only for the specific prohibitions and limitations they contain, but also as part of a notable body of developing international law that has as its objective comprehensive nuclear disarmament as a step towards more general and complete disarmament.

Multilateral Treaties

Treaty on the Non-Proliferation of Nuclear Weapons[19]

22. As already noted, the Non-Proliferation Treaty (NPT) is the most important international instrument regulating the possession of nuclear weapons and, *ipso facto*, their threat or use. Support for the NPT, together with the regional treaties concluded consistent with Article VII (the Treaty of Rarotonga in respect of the South Pacific and the Treaty of Tlatelolco in respect of Latin America), means that virtually all except a

[12] *Nuclear Tests (Australia v. France)*, Judgment, I.C.J. Reports 1974, p.253, at p.435. Sir Garfield Barwick's dissenting opinion applied equally to the Judgment in *Nuclear Tests (New Zealand v France)*, Judgment, I.C.J. Reports 1974, p.457, at p.525.

[13] Antarctic Treaty, 1959.

[14] Latin American Nuclear Free Zone Treaty 1967, also known as the Treaty of Tlatelolco.

[15] The South Pacific Nuclear Free Zone Treaty 1985, also known as the Treaty of Rarotonga.

[16] Treaty on Principles Governing the Activities of States in the Exploration and Use of Outer Space, Including the Moon and Other Celestial Bodies (Outer Space Treaty), 1967; Agreement Governing the Activities of States on the Moon and Other Celestial Bodies, 1979.

[17] Treaty on the Prohibition of the Emplacement of Nuclear Weapons and Other Weapons of Mass Destruction on the Seabed and the Ocean Floor and in the Subsoil Thereof, 1971.

[18] Treaty of Tlatelolco; NPT; Treaty of Rarotonga.

[19] Treaty on the Non-Proliferation of Nuclear Weapons, 1968.

handful of states (other than the five declared nuclear-weapon States) have undertaken not to manufacture or acquire nuclear weapons.

23. The specific obligations of the NPT are based around a number of objectives directed overall at minimising the danger of nuclear war:

a) the prevention of the spread of nuclear weapons;[20]
b) the assurance, through international safeguards, that the peaceful nuclear activities of states which have not developed nuclear weapons will not be diverted to making such weapons;[21]
c) the promotion, to the maximum extent consistent with the other purposes of the Treaty, of the peaceful uses of nuclear energy through cooperation and technology sharing;[22]
d) the undertaking by the parties to pursue further disarmament negotiations in good faith.[23]

24. The NPT does not refer to the threat or use of nuclear weapons. Nevertheless, in accordance with the United Nations General Assembly resolutions which led to the Treaty being drawn up, it embodies a balance of mutual responsibilities and obligations on the nuclear and non-nuclear Powers.[24]

Nuclear Weapon Free Zones

25. The development of regional nuclear weapon free zones, as contemplated by Article VII of the NPT, contributes further to the process of global nuclear disarmament and the strengthening of the international non-proliferation regime.

26. The Treaty of Tlatelolco,[25] concluded in 1967, prohibits parties from the testing, use, manufacture, production, acquisition, receipt, storage, installation, deployment and any form of possession of nuclear weapons in a zone encompassing the Latin American region, together with certain associated activities.[26]

27. The Treaty of Rarotonga of 1985[27] establishes the South Pacific Nuclear Free Zone in which states parties to the treaty agree not to manufacture or otherwise acquire, possess, have control over, station or test nuclear explosive devices. The parties also accept certain associated obligations and agree not to dump radioactive wastes and other radioactive matter at sea within the Zone.

28. Both treaties are accompanied by protocols to which the nuclear-weapon States may become party. The protocols contain specific prohibitions against, inter alia, using

[20] Articles I and II.
[21] Article III.
[22] Articles IV and V.
[23] Article VI.
[24] UN General Assembly Resolution 2028 (XX) of 23 November 1965, called for the conclusion of a Non-Proliferation Treaty based on five principles, including the principle that "the treaty should embody an acceptable balance of mutual responsibilities and obligations of the nuclear and non-nuclear Powers".
[25] Treaty for the Prohibition of Nuclear Weapons in Latin America (and Additional Protocols), 1967.
[26] Article 1(1)(a).
[27] South Pacific Nuclear Free Zone Treaty, 1985.

or threatening to use nuclear weapons against parties to the treaties.[28] All five nuclear-weapon States have given such an undertaking in respect of parties to the Treaty of Tlatelolco, albeit with qualifications in three cases in the event of an attack by a state party to the treaty in association with a nuclear-weapon State,[29] but only two nuclear-weapon States have thus far given such an undertaking in respect of parties to the Treaty of Rarotonga.

Partial Test Ban Treaty[30]

29. The community of nations has also agreed that the testing of nuclear weapons should be subject to a particular and much more restrictive set of rules than applies to conventional weapons. Significant legal regulation applies in this respect.[31]

30. The principal aim of the Partial Test Ban Treaty, as proclaimed in its preamble, is "the speediest possible achievement of an agreement on general and complete disarmament under strict international control" so as to "put an end to the armaments race and eliminate the incentive to the production and testing of all kinds of weapons, including nuclear weapons." The Preamble declares the further aim of the three Original Parties to the treaty as "the discontinuance of all test explosions of nuclear weapons for all time", and expresses their determination to continue negotiations to that end. The current negotiations in the Conference on Disarmament towards a comprehensive test ban are an earnest of the international community's intentions in this respect.

31. The parties to the Treaty undertake not to carry out any nuclear weapon test explosion, or any other nuclear explosion, in the atmosphere, under water, or in outer space,[32] or in any other environment if the explosion would cause radioactive debris to be present outside the borders of the state under whose jurisdiction or control the explosion is conducted.[33]

32. While the treaty does not specifically prohibit underground testing of nuclear weapons, such tests would be unlawful if the explosion from an underground test caused radioactive debris to spread beyond the borders of the state conducting the test.

[28] Article 3 of Additional Protocol II to the Latin American treaty; Article 1 of Protocol 2 to the South Pacific treaty.

[29] Their ratifications were accompanied by declarations outlining situations in which they would consider themselves not to be bound by the commitments of the treaty. Thus, the United Kingdom declared that "the Government of the United Kingdom would, in the event of any act of aggression by a Contracting Party to the Treaty in which that party was supported by a nuclear-weapon State, be free to reconsider the extent to which they could be regarded as committed by the provisions of Additional Protocol II."

[30] Treaty Banning Nuclear Weapon Tests in the Atmosphere, in Outer Space and Under Water, 1963.

[31] In addition to the Partial Test Ban Treaty, bilateral agreements restrict underground nuclear testing by some of the nuclear-weapon States (*infra*, paragraphs 43 and 44). Testing in certain parts of the world is also prohibited.

[32] Article I(1)(a).

[33] Article I(1)(b).

33. The moratoria on nuclear tests observed by four nuclear-weapon States in recent years further supports the view that nuclear testing should no longer be regarded as an option for any state.[34]

34. It can be argued that the Partial Test Ban Treaty forms the basis of a customary rule of international law that would prohibit the testing of nuclear weapons in the areas proscribed, and that such a rule would be binding on *all* states whether party to the treaty or not. In his dissenting opinion in the *Nuclear Tests Case (Australia v France)*, Judge *Ad hoc* Sir Garfield Barwick recognised this possibility:

> "It is said that there has been such a progression of general opinion amongst the nations, evidenced in treaty, resolution and expression of international opinion, that the stage has been reached where the prohibition of the testing of nuclear weapons is now part of customary international law...
>
> I think it must be considered that it is legally possible that at some stage the testing of nuclear weapons could become, or could have become, prohibited by customary international law. Treaties, resolutions, expressions of opinion and international practice, may all combine to produce the evidence of that customary law. The time when such a law emerges will not necessarily be deferred until all nations have acceded to a test ban treaty, or until opinion of the nations is universally held in the same sense. Customary law amongst the nations does not, in my opinion, depend on universal acceptance. Conventional law limited to the parties to the convention may become, in appropriate circumstances, customary law."[35]

The Antarctic Treaty[36]

35. The Antarctic Treaty provides, in Article 1, that Antarctica shall be used for peaceful purposes only. Any measures of a military nature, including the establishment of military bases, the carrying out of military manoeuvres, and the testing of any type of

---

[34] One of these nuclear-weapon States, France, announced on 13 June 1995 that it would resume a limited programme of nuclear testing between September 1995 and May 1996, prior to the conclusion of a comprehensive nuclear test ban treaty. The New Zealand Government has condemned this announcement of intention to break the moratoria, which runs counter to the unanimously agreed call on the nuclear-weapon States at the NPT Review and Extension Conference in May 1995 for "utmost restraint" by the nuclear-weapon States pending the entry into force of a Comprehensive Nuclear-Test-Ban Treaty and cuts across the on-going negotiations on that treaty as well as the wishes of countries in the South Pacific region expressed most clearly in the prohibitions on nuclear testing in the South Pacific Nuclear Free Zone Treaty, 1985. New Zealand has also condemned testing by the fifth nuclear-weapon State, China, which has stated, most recently at the plenary meeting of the Conference on Disarmament in Geneva on 1 June 1995, that it would abide by the Comprehensive Test Ban Treaty following its entry into force, and would stop testing. New Zealand would regard actions that may undermine the negotiations on a Comprehensive Nuclear-Test-Ban Treaty as contrary to principles of good faith on which treaty negotiations are founded.

[35] *Nuclear Tests (Australia v France)*, Judgment, I.C.J. Reports 1974, p.253, at p.435. Sir Garfield Barwick's dissenting opinion applied equally to the Judgment in *Nuclear Tests (New Zealand v France)*, Judgment, I.C.J. Reports 1974, p.457, at p.525.

[36] Adopted at Washington in 1959.

weapons, are prohibited.[37] The Treaty also prohibits any nuclear explosions in Antarctica and the disposal of radioactive waste there.

Outer Space Treaty[38]

36. The Outer Space Treaty is restrictive of nuclear weapons in two important respects. It prohibits placing nuclear weapons in orbit around Earth, installing them on the moon or any other celestial body, or otherwise stationing nuclear weapons in outer space. It also limits the use of the moon and other celestial bodies exclusively to peaceful purposes and expressly prohibits their use for, inter alia, testing weapons of any kind.[39]

Seabed Arms Control Treaty[40]

37. The Seabed Arms Control Treaty prohibits emplanting or emplacement on the seabed and the ocean floor and in the subsoil thereof of any nuclear weapons, or other weapons of mass destruction, as well as structures, launching installations or any other facilities specifically designed for storing, testing or using such weapons, beyond the outer limit of a twelve mile "seabed zone".[41] The same prohibition applies to the area *within* a seabed zone, except in relation to the coastal State concerned.

Major Bilateral Treaties Between the United States and the former Soviet Union/Russia

38. The two major nuclear weapon States, the United States and Russia, have also acknowledged the desirability of limiting nuclear arsenals and weaponry, by means of important bilateral agreements which have been developed in this respect.

Strategic Arms Limitation Talks

39. The Strategic Arms Limitation Talks (SALT) held between 1969 and 1972 produced a series of agreements concluded in Moscow in May 1972. The most important agreement in respect of limiting the size of the nuclear arsenals of the two countries was the Interim Agreement on Offensive Strategic Missiles,[42] which was

---

[37] Article I(1).

[38] Treaty on Principles Governing the Activities of States in the Exploration and Use of Outer Space, Including the Moon and other Celestial Bodies, 1967.

[39] The same prohibitions appear in the Agreement Governing the Activities of States on the Moon and Other Celestial Bodies, 1979.

[40] Treaty on the Prohibition of the Emplacement of Nuclear Weapons and Other Weapons of Mass Destruction on the Seabed and the Ocean Floor and in the Subsoil Thereof, 1971.

[41] In accordance with Article II of the treaty, the zone is measured in accordance with the provisions of the 1958 Convention on the Territorial Sea and Contiguous Zone.

[42] Interim Agreement on Certain Measures with Respect to the Limitation of Strategic Offensive Arms, 1972.

subsequently extended beyond its initial five-year period and provided for further negotiations toward a more comprehensive instrument.

Intermediate Nuclear Forces Treaty[43]

40. The Intermediate Nuclear Forces Treaty (INF), was concluded by the United States and the Soviet Union in December 1987, and entered into force in June 1988. It provided for the elimination, for the first time, of a whole class of nuclear weapons, that is, all United States and Soviet land-based missiles with ranges from 500 to 5500 kilometres.[44] The leaders of both countries publicly recognised the historical importance of this treaty in the disarmament process.

Strategic Arms Reduction Treaties

41. The two major nuclear powers have also taken steps to reduce their strategic nuclear arsenals though the Strategic Arms Reduction Treaties, START and START II.[45] START, signed by the United States and the Soviet Union in July 1991, aimed to reduce strategic arsenals by approximately one third. Belarus, Kazakhstan, Ukraine, and the Russian Federation assumed the obligations of the former Soviet Union under the treaty by means of a Protocol which was signed in May 1992 in Lisbon, and the Treaty entered into force on 5 December 1994.

42. START II was concluded between the United States and the Russian Federation in January 1993, to reduce the number of Russian and United States strategic weapons still further, and the condition precedent has now been met which would allow its entry into force.[46]

Testing of Nuclear Weapons

43. The Threshold Test Ban Treaty was concluded and signed by the United States and the Soviet Union in 1974[47] and ratified with a new verification protocol in 1990. The treaty establishes a nuclear weapons testing threshold, as between the parties, by prohibiting underground nuclear weapons tests having a yield exceeding 150 kilotons.[48] The treaty also enjoins the parties to minimise their underground nuclear weapons tests and to continue negotiations toward a cessation of all such tests.[49]

---

[43] Treaty on the Elimination of Intermediate-Range and Short-Range Missiles, 1987.

[44] By the definitions contained in Article II of the INF Treaty, an "intermediate-range missile" is a ground-launched ballistic missile (GLBM) or a ground-launched cruise missile (GLCM) having a range capability between 1000 and 5500km. A "shorter-range missile" is a GLBM or GLCM with range capability between 500 and 1000km.

[45] Treaty on the Reduction and Limitation of Strategic Arms, 1991 and 1993.

[46] The entry into force of START II was conditional on the prior entry into force of START I.

[47] Treaty between the United States of America and the Union of Soviet Socialist Republics on the Limitation of Underground Nuclear Weapon Tests, 1974 (and Protocol thereto).

[48] Article I(1).

[49] Article I(2) and I(3).

The Peaceful Nuclear Explosions Treaty

44. The Peaceful Nuclear Explosions Treaty, concluded and signed in 1976,[50] was also ratified with a new verification protocol in 1990. The treaty governs all nuclear explosions carried out by the parties at locations outside the weapons test sites specified under the Threshold Test Ban Treaty. The agreed statement accompanying the treaty specifies that a "peaceful application" of an underground nuclear explosion does not include the developmental testing of nuclear explosives.

COMMITMENTS BY THE NUCLEAR-WEAPON STATES NOT TO USE NUCLEAR WEAPONS

45. The five declared nuclear-weapon States have themselves placed restrictions on the possible threat or use of nuclear weapons through unilateral commitments they have given.

46. All five nuclear-weapon States have given unilateral assurances (referred to as "negative security assurances") about the circumstances in which they would *not* use nuclear weapons. Reliance on negative security assurances is the logical corollary to the obligations accepted by non-nuclear-weapon States in the NPT.

47. In 1995, the United States, the United Kingdom, France and Russia have harmonised their unilateral assurances to a large extent.[51] They have reaffirmed that they will not use nuclear weapons against non-nuclear-weapon States Parties to the NPT, except in the case of an invasion or any other attack on their territories, armed forces or other troops, their allies, or a state to which they have given a security commitment, carried out by such a non-nuclear-weapon State in association or alliance with a nuclear-weapon State.[52]

48. China's assurance is unconditional in that it is not limited to parties to the NPT but extends to all non-nuclear-weapon States. Its guarantee to non-nuclear-weapon States also applies "in all circumstances", and it has reaffirmed its undertaking not to be the first to use nuclear weapons at any time and under any circumstances.

49. The international community has been discussing for many years the possibility of incorporating negative security assurances into an international instrument. Most recently, the NPT Review and Extension Conference in May 1995 stated in the

---

[50] Treaty between the United States of America and the Union of Soviet Socialist Republics on Underground Nuclear Explosions for Peaceful Purposes, 1976 (and Protocol thereto).

[51] The five Nuclear Weapons States announced to the Conference on Disarmament Plenary of 6 April 1995, updated unilateral negative security assurances.

[52] In addition, in Resolution 984 (1995), adopted on 11 April 1995, the United Nations Security Council recognised "the legitimate interest of non-nuclear-weapon States Parties to the Treaty on the Non-Proliferation of Nuclear Weapons to receive assurances that the Security Council, and above all its nuclear-weapon State permanent members, will act immediately in accordance with the relevant provisions of the Charter of the United Nations, in the event that such States are the victim of an act of, or object of a threat of, aggression in which nuclear weapons are used".

Declaration of Principles it adopted without a vote that further steps, which could take the form of an internationally legally binding instrument, should be considered to assure non-nuclear-weapon States Parties to the Treaty against the use or threat of use of nuclear weapons. In New Zealand's view, this effort should not detract from the legal status that may be accorded to the present assurances given unilaterally. Such assurances, made in good faith, give rise to a legitimate expectation on the part of non-nuclear-weapon States that they will be complied with.

50. The Court, in its judgment in the *Nuclear Tests Case (New Zealand v France)*, stated that unilateral declarations by states may be binding at international law:

> "It is well recognized that declarations made by way of unilateral acts, concerning legal or factual situations, may have the effect of creating legal obligations. Declarations of this kind may be, and often are, very specific. When it is the intention of the State making the declaration that it should become bound by its terms, that intention confers on the declaration the character of a legal undertaking, the State being thenceforth legally required to follow a course of conduct consistent with the declaration. An undertaking of this kind, if given publicly, and with an intent to be bound, even though not made within the context of international negotiations, is binding. In these circumstances, nothing in the nature of a *quid pro quo*, nor any subsequent acceptance of the declaration, nor even any reply or reaction from other States, is required for the declaration to take effect, since such a requirement would be inconsistent with the strictly unilateral nature of the juridical act by which the pronouncement by the State was made.
>
> Of course, not all unilateral acts imply obligation: but a State may choose to take up a certain position in relation to a particular matter with the intention of being bound - the intention is to be ascertained by interpretation of the act. When States make statements by which their freedom of action is to be limited, a restrictive interpretation is called for.....
>
> One of the basic principles governing the creation and performance of legal obligations, whatever their source, is the principle of good faith. Trust and confidence are inherent in international co-operation, in particular in an age when this co-operation in many fields is becoming increasingly essential. Just as the very rule of *pacta sunt servanda* in the law of treaties is based on good faith, so also is the binding character of an international obligation assumed by unilateral declaration. Thus interested States may take cognizance of unilateral declarations and place confidence in them, and are entitled to require that the obligation created be respected."[53]

INTERNATIONAL LAW REGARDING RESORT TO FORCE

51. The threat or use of nuclear weapons has also to be considered with reference to the general rule in Article 2(4) of the United Nations Charter proscribing the threat or use of

[53] *Nuclear Tests (New Zealand v France)*, Judgment, I.C.J. Reports 1974, p.457, at pp.472-473.

force against the territorial integrity or political independence of any state, or in any other manner inconsistent with the purposes of the United Nations.

52. The Charter recognises only tightly prescribed exceptions to the general rule against the threat or use of force. Thus, the threat or use of force is lawful if made as part of Security Council enforcement action under Chapter VII of the Charter in the event of any threat to peace, breach of the peace or act of aggression, or if force is used in self defence as provided in Article 51 of the Charter.

53. Decisions by the Security Council under Chapter VII to take enforcement action in any particular case require the support of nine of the fifteen Council members, and are subject to veto by any of the permanent members of the Council. As the primary organ of the international community in respect of the maintenance of international peace and security, it can be expected that the Security Council will always be concerned to discharge its high responsibilities in full accordance with all applicable principles of international law.

54. The right of self defence is not open-ended. Under Article 51 of the Charter, the inherent right of individual or collective self defence in the event of an armed attack against a member of the United Nations is not impaired by the Charter "until the Security Council has taken measures necessary to maintain international peace and security". Members exercising this right are required to report immediately to the Security Council, and the measures that they have taken do not in any way affect the authority and responsibility of the Security Council under the Charter to take at any time such action as it deems necessary in order to maintain or restore international peace and security.

55. Moreover, the right of self defence cannot be exercised in isolation from other applicable rules and principles of international law. In particular, measures taken in self defence are subject, where relevant, to the laws of armed conflict generally. They must, for instance, be necessary and proportionate to the danger which they are designed to meet.[54]

56. Under customary international law, the right of self defence has included preventive measures taken in anticipation of an imminent threat, and not only upon the occurrence of an armed attack. While the relationship between this customary right of anticipatory self defence and Article 51 of the Charter has not been authoritatively established, at customary law the right appears to have been available only in cases of imminent and overwhelming danger.[55] It would also be subject to the same constraints of proportionality and other applicable rules of the law of armed conflict.

[54] The Court has held that the reliance on the right of (collective) self defence to support recourse to the threat or use of force in one case was not lawful because the canons of necessity and proportionality were not complied with: *Military and Paramilitary Activities in and against Nicaragua (Nicaragua v United States of America)*, Merits, Judgment, I.C.J. Reports 1986, p.14, at pp.122-123.

[55] The customary right of anticipatory self defence is generally acknowledged as having been implicitly recognised in the exchange of notes between the United States and Great Britain following the *Caroline* incident in 1837. The then United States Secretary of State, Webster, declared that a State is entitled to take forcible measures in self defence where it can demonstrate a:

57. The threat or use of nuclear weapons is also to be considered with reference to the doctrine of belligerent reprisals, by which an act that would normally be illegal is rendered lawful by a prior illegal act committed by the state against which the reprisal is directed where the objective of the state carrying out the reprisal is to compel a belligerent to abandon illegitimate acts of warfare.[56] Notwithstanding the reference to reprisals in the Geneva Conventions of 1949,[57] the continued application of this doctrine in view of the provisions of the United Nations Charter has, again, not been authoritatively established.

58. An international arbitral award in 1928 attached three conditions to the use of force in reprisal:

a) a previous act in violation of international law must have occurred;
b) an unsatisfied demand to cease the actions in question must have been made, since the use of force is only justified if absolutely necessary; and
c) the degree of force used in reprisal must not be disproportionate to the prior illegal act.[58]

59. Even in the case of belligerent reprisals, therefore, some constraints on the use of force would still be applicable.

INTERNATIONAL HUMANITARIAN LAW

60. The concept that the conduct of armed hostilities is governed by rules is well recognised in international law. Regardless of whether armed conflict is justified under the law concerning the resort to force, international humanitarian law applies to set limits on *how* any armed conflict may be carried out. The humanitarian laws of armed conflict set standards for the conduct of armed hostilities with the purpose of circumscribing the areas within which the savagery of war is permissible and limiting and reducing the suffering of individuals. In the words of the St Petersburg Declaration of 1868,[59] one of the earliest attempts to codify this area of customary law, international

---

> "necessity...instant, overwhelming, leaving no choice of means and no moment for deliberation....The act justified by the necessity of self defence must be limited by that necessity and kept clearly within it."

The Nuremburg Tribunal implicitly recognised the *Caroline* formula, and thereby the continued existence of the right to anticipatory self defence, in observing that:

> "...preventive action in foreign territory is justified only in case of an instant and overwhelming necessity for self defence, leaving no choice of means, and no moment for deliberation."

Quoted in Hearn, William R. *The International Legal Regime Regulating Nuclear Deterrence and Warfare*, LXI British Yearbook of International Law 1990, 199 at pp.211-212.

[56] *Oppenheim's International Law*, Vol.I (*Peace*), 9th edn, Sir Robert Jennings and Sir Arthur Watts (Eds), 1992, p.419 (n.12, and the works cited therein).

[57] *infra*, paragraph 70.

[58] *Naulilaa Incident Arbitration, Portugal v Germany* (1928) Reports of International Arbitral Awards, Vol. 2, p.1012.

[59] *infra*, n.74.

humanitarian law is designed to "conciliate the necessities of war with the laws of humanity".

61. One of the fundamental principles underlying this area of international law is the principle of humanity. In accordance with this principle, the use of force that causes suffering not necessary to obtain legitimate military objectives is barred.

62. While many rules of international humanitarian law are set out in international conventions, customary law remains very significant in this area. International conventions, in this area as others, are, however, contributing to the further development of customary law.

Application of international humanitarian law to nuclear weapons

63. In general, international humanitarian law bears on the threat or use of nuclear weapons as it does of other weapons.

64. International humanitarian law has evolved to meet contemporary circumstances, and is not limited in its application to weaponry of an earlier time. The fundamental principles of this law endure: to mitigate and circumscribe the cruelty of war for humanitarian reasons. The Nuremburg Tribunal put the matter in the following terms:

> The law of war is to be found not only in treaties, but in the customs and practices of States, which gradually obtained universal recognition, and from the general principles of justice applied by jurists and practised by military courts. The law is not static, but by continual adaptation follows the needs of a changing world."[60]

65. The "Martens Clause" included in the preamble of Hague Convention IV of 1907[61] pointed to the general applicability of international humanitarian law:

> "Until a more complete code of the laws of war has been issued, the High Contracting Parties deem it expedient to declare that, in cases not included in the Regulations adopted by them, the inhabitants and belligerents remain under the protection and the rule of principles of the law of nations, as they result from usages established amongst civilised peoples, from the laws of humanity, and from the dictates of public conscience".

66. The general application of international humanitarian law to the use of nuclear weapons has also been specifically acknowledged by nuclear-weapon States.[62]

[60] 22 *Trial of German Major War Criminals* 445 (1950). In the case of *Military and Paramilitary Activities in and against Nicaragua (Nicaragua v United States of America)*, Merits, Judgment, I.C.J. Reports 1986, p.14, at p.114, the Court said that the obligation to respect the Geneva Conventions 1949 "does not derive only from the Conventions themselves, but from the general principles of international humanitarian law to which the Conventions merely give specific expression".

[61] *infra*, n.75.

[62] Writers on the subject have pointed to military manuals on this point. For example, Hearn quotes a United Kingdom *Manual of Military Law*, as follows:

Customary Law Rules

67. The customary rules of international humanitarian law can be considered with reference to a number of interrelated propositions.

(1) The right to adopt means of injuring the enemy is not unlimited.

68. This general principle, first set out in the St Petersburg Declaration of 1868, has been reiterated in many international conventions since. The significance of this principle lies in the fact that combatants are not necessarily unrestricted in their use of weapons even in the absence of a specific prohibition relating to those weapons. This is in contrast to the general presumption of international law that actions by a state on the international plane are permitted unless there is a rule of law prohibiting them.[63]

(2) It is prohibited to use weapons or tactics that cause unnecessary or aggravated devastation and suffering.

69. While any armed conflict will inevitably cause suffering, this suffering must be limited to what is necessary to achieve the legitimate aims of the resort to force in accordance with the Charter of the United Nations. That is to say, any actions in armed conflict must be proportionate to the legitimate aims of the conflict. It is unlawful to cause suffering and devastation which is in excess of that required to achieve these legitimate aims. Application of this proposition requires a balancing of necessity and humanity.

(3) It is prohibited to effect reprisals that are disproportionate to their antecedent provocation or to legitimate military objectives, or disrespectful of persons, institutions and resources protected by the laws of armed conflict.

> "There is no rule of international law dealing specifically with the use of nuclear weapons. Their use, therefore, is governed by the general principles laid down in this chapter.... In the absence of any rule of international law dealing expressly with it, the use which may be made of a particular weapon will be governed by the ordinary rules and the question of the legality of its use in any particular case will, therefore, involve merely the application of the recognised principles of international law." Quoted in Hearn, William R, *The International Legal Regime Regulating Nuclear Deterrence and Warfare*, LXI British Yearbook of International Law 1990, 199, at p.223.

Likewise, Meyrowitz quotes United States military manuals, as follows:

> "In addition to analogy, the legality of new weapons or methods of warfare is determined by whether the weapon's effects violate the rule against unnecessary suffering or its effects are indiscriminate as to cause disproportionate civilian injury or damage to civilian objects." Quoted in Meyrowitz, Elliot: *"Prohibition of Nuclear Weapons: The Relevance of International Law"*, 1990, at p.31.

[63] This general presumption of law is derived from the case of *"Lotus", Judgment No. 9, 1927, P.C.I.J., Series* A No. 10.

70. Reprisals which are excessive in relation to provocation or which lack a reasonable connection to legitimate objectives are inconsistent with international law. In addition, reprisals must not be used against persons, institutions and resources protected by international humanitarian law: these include civilians and civilian populations,[64] civilian objects,[65] the natural environment,[66] the wounded, sick, shipwrecked, and prisoners of war,[67] and medical establishments and personnel.[68] At least some of these specific prohibitions may be regarded as forming part of customary law.

(4) It is prohibited to use indiscriminate methods and means of warfare which do not distinguish between combatants and civilians and other non-combatants.

71. Discrimination between combatants and those who are not directly involved in armed conflict is a fundamental principle of international humanitarian law. While it is prohibited to actually target civilians and civilian objects, there is no absolute protection from collateral damage. The application of the principle requires an assessment of whether the civilian casualties are out of proportion to the legitimate military advantage achieved and whether collateral damage is so widespread as to amount to an indiscriminate attack.

(5) It is prohibited to use asphyxiating, poisonous or other gases and all analogous materials

72. The use of poison and poisoned weapons has long been prohibited. The prohibition is set out in the 1925 Geneva Protocol[69] but also forms part of customary law.

(6) Methods and means of war should not cause widespread, long-term and severe damage to the environment

73. Long-standing international humanitarian law is relevant to this proposition.[70] A specific treaty prohibition is now contained in Protocol I of 1977.[71] Protection of the global environment is now a major concern of the international community, with widespread support for progressive development of international treaty law in this area.[72] The condemnation of the large-scale environmental damage wreaked upon

---

[64] Article 51(6) of 1977 Protocol I (*infra*, n.87).

[65] Article 52(1) of 1977 Protocol I.

[66] Article 55(2) of 1977 Protocol I.

[67] Geneva Conventions 1949 (*infra*, n.82): Article 46 of the First Convention, Article 47 of the Second Convention and Article 13 of the Third Convention.

[68] For example, Articles 19 and 24 of the First Geneva Convention 1949.

[69] *infra*, n.80.

[70] Damage to the environment in particular cases may, for example, not be justified by military necessity and be contrary to the laws of armed conflict accordingly.

[71] Articles 35(3) and 55(1) of the Protocol; also *infra*, paragraphs 94 and 97.

[72] In the last ten years, a number of major treaties for the protection of the global environment have been adopted: Vienna Convention for the Protection of the Ozone Layer, 1985; Montreal Protocol on Substances that Deplete the Ozone Layer, 1987; Basel Convention on the Control of Transboundary

Kuwait by Iraqi forces during the "Gulf War" in 1991 was in part a reflection of this concern. It would be a matter for consideration by the Court whether the avoidance of widespread, long-term and severe damage to the environment during war could yet be regarded as itself a rule of customary law.[73]

(7) Methods and means of warfare should not violate the neutrality of non-participating states

74. There are two key aspects to this rule. First, belligerents have no right to carry on hostilities in the territory of a non-involved state. Secondly, non-participating states have the right to exclude entry of belligerent forces. Consequently neutral states have the right to freedom from harm and injury arising from armed conflict with which they are not involved.

International Conventions

75. The main conventions in the area of international humanitarian law which remain in force and ought to be considered in the context of the threat or use of nuclear weapons are as follows:

St Petersburg Declaration 1868[74]

76. The Declaration sets forth two general principles which have remained the basic tenets of subsequent efforts in this area: that the right to injure the enemy is not unlimited and that means of warfare which cause unnecessary suffering are prohibited. The preamble to the Declaration sets out the following propositions:

> "Considering that the progress of civilisation should have the effect of alleviating as much as possible the calamities of war;
>
> That the only legitimate object which states should endeavour to accomplish during war is to weaken the military forces of the enemy;
>
> That for this purpose it is sufficient to disable the greatest possible number of men;
>
> That the object would be exceeded by the employment of arms which uselessly aggravate the suffering of disabled men or render their death inevitable;

Movements of Hazardous Wastes and their Disposal, 1989; Convention on Biological Diversity, 1992; United Nations Framework Convention on Climate Change, 1992. All of these treaties entered into force quickly and have wide international support.

[73] The relationship between customary international law and treaties was considered by the Court in the cases of *North Sea Continental Shelf*, Judgment, I.C.J. Reports 1969, p.3 and *Military and Paramilitary Activities in and against Nicaragua (Nicaragua v United States of America)*, Merits, Judgment, I.C.J. Reports 1986, p.14. In the former case, the Court noted that rules of customary international law may be crystallised or generated by treaties and bind states that never become party to them, and that such a process could in certain circumstances take place over only a short period of time. In the latter case, the Court reiterated that rules of customary international law embodied in treaties have an independent existence, and noted that instances of inconsistent state conduct do not affect the existence of a rule of customary international law where state practice has, in general, been consistent with it.

[74] 1868 St Petersburg Declaration Renouncing the Use, in Time of War, of Explosive Projectiles Under 400 grammes Weight.

> That the employment of such arms would, therefore, be contrary to the laws of humanity..."

77. The Declaration specifically prohibited the use of exploding bullets or bullets charged with fulminating or inflammable substances which weighed less than 400 grams.

The various conventions adopted at the Second Hague Peace Conference of 1907

78. The First Hague Peace Conference held in 1899 had adopted two conventions and two declarations relating to the laws of armed conflict. These embodied principles contained in the St Petersburg Declaration.

79. The Final Act of the First Conference proposed that a subsequent conference be held to consider matters on which no agreement was reached. Among the 13 conventions relating to armed conflict adopted at the Second Hague Peace Conference held accordingly in 1907, two may be argued to be of relevance to the question before the Court.

80. First, Convention IV (Convention respecting the laws and customs of war on land)[75] included the following provisions:

> "Article 22 The right of belligerents to adopt means of injuring the enemy is not unlimited.
>
> Article 23. In addition to the prohibition provided by special Conventions it is especially forbidden:
>
> a) To employ poison or poisoned weapons...
>
> b) To kill or wound treacherously individuals belonging to the hostile nation or army...
>
> e) To employ arms, projectiles, or material calculated to cause unnecessary suffering...
>
> Article 25 The attack or bombardment, by whatever means, of towns, villages, dwellings or buildings which are undefended is prohibited".

As already noted above,[76] the preamble of Convention IV of the 1907 Conference also included (as had the equivalent convention of 1899) the "Martens Clause". This clause was included because the drafters wanted to make it quite clear that "in the absence of a written undertaking, unforeseen cases should not be left to the arbitrary judgment of military commanders".[77] This clause, or something similar, has been reiterated in subsequent conventions.[78]

---

[75] 1907 Hague Convention (IV) Respecting the Laws and Customs of War on Land.

[76] *supra*, paragraph 65.

[77] Preamble to 1907 Hague Convention IV.

[78] For example, Articles 45 and 63 of the First Geneva Convention 1949, Articles 46 and 62 of the Second Convention, Article 142 of the Third Convention, and Article 158 of the Fourth Convention (*infra*, n.82); Article 1(2) of, and the Preamble to, respectively, Protocol I and Protocol II to the Geneva Conventions

81. Secondly, Convention V: the Hague Convention on Neutrality in Land War[79] declared that the territory of neutral powers was inviolable.

Geneva Protocol on the Use in War of Gases and Bacteriological Weapons[80]

82. This protocol embodied pre-existing customary law on the use in war of asphyxiating, poisonous or other gases and of all analogous liquids, materials or devices, declaring in specific terms that the prohibition shall be universally accepted as part of international law, and extended coverage to the use of bacteriological methods of warfare.

83. While it has been argued that this prohibition extends only to weapons whose prime effect is to injure by use of gas, analogous materials or bacteriological methods, it has also been argued that there is no basis for a distinction between the physical properties of poison gas and radiation, with the radiation-enhanced neutron bomb as an evident example.

The Genocide Convention[81]

84. This Convention, which applies in times of war or peace, restates existing customary law relating to acts of genocide. It prohibits a wide variety of acts but only where they are committed with intent to destroy national, ethnic, or religious groups.

85. Nevertheless, it has been argued that owing to their uniquely devastating effect the threat or use of nuclear weapons is likely to breach this convention, especially given the likelihood of escalation. Adherents of this view tend to claim that once the nuclear threshold is crossed escalation is extremely likely if not unavoidable, and that such escalation will lead to the inevitable annihilation of populations.

The 1949 Geneva Conventions

86. The four Conventions adopted by the 1949 Geneva Conference[82] are of broad application in cases of armed conflict. The Geneva Conventions are a comprehensive statement of international humanitarian law. They have very broad acceptance and may be considered declaratory of customary international law.

(*infra*, n.87); Preamble to the Convention on Prohibitions or Restrictions on the Use of Certain Conventional Weapons Which May be Deemed to Be Excessively Injurious or to Have Indiscriminate Effects, 1981.

[79] 1907 Hague Convention (V) Respecting the Rights and Duties of Neutral Powers and Persons in Case of War on Land.

[80] 1925 Geneva Protocol for the Prohibition of the Use in War of Asphyxiating, Poisonous or Other Gases, and of Bacteriological Methods of Warfare.

[81] United Nations Convention on the Prevention and Punishment of the Crime of Genocide, 1948.

[82] Geneva Convention for the Amelioration of the Condition of the Wounded and Sick in Armed Forces in the Field; Geneva Convention for the Amelioration of the Condition of Wounded, Sick, and Shipwrecked Members of Armed Forces at Sea; Geneva Convention relative to the Treatment of Prisoners of War; Geneva Convention relative to the Protection of Civilian Persons in Time of War.

87. While the first three conventions replaced earlier conventions on the same subject, the fourth, relating to the protection of civilians, dealt with matters not previously the subject of a specific convention. Together the four Geneva Conventions confirm the fundamental distinction between combatants and non-combatants and the prohibition against unnecessary and aggravated suffering. Each of the conventions contains a restatement of the "Martens Clause".[83]

Hague Cultural Property Convention[84]

88. International humanitarian law has long made some provision for the protection of cultural property during armed conflict. World War II demonstrated that the existing provisions were inadequate. This realisation led to the conclusion of the convention.

89. Cultural property to which the Convention applies is defined as movable or immovable property of great importance to the cultural heritage of every people, such as monuments of architecture, archaeological sites and works of art. Buildings, such as museums and large libraries which are designed to house movable property, are also covered by the definition. The Convention obliges parties to avoid action likely to expose such property to damage as the result of armed conflict.

90. The protections, however, are not absolute. They do not apply where cultural property is given a military purpose. In addition, the immunity of the property can be withdrawn in "exceptional cases of unavoidable military necessity".[85] This withdrawal of immunity endures only for so long as the unavoidable necessity continues and, whenever circumstances permit, advance notice must be given to the opposing party.

United Nations Convention on the Prohibition of Military Use of Environmental Modification Techniques[86]

91. This convention prohibits the hostile use of environmental modification techniques having widespread, long-lasting or severe effects. "Environmental modification techniques" refers to any technique for changing, through the deliberate manipulation of natural processes, the dynamics, composition or structure of the earth, including its biota, lithosphere, hydrosphere, and atmosphere, or of outer space.

---

[83] *supra*, n.78.

[84] Hague Convention for the Protection of Cultural Property in the Event of Armed Conflict, 1954.

[85] *ibid*, Article 11.

[86] United Nations Convention on the Prohibition of Military or Any Other Hostile Use of Environmental Modification Techniques, 1977.

1977 Protocols to the Geneva Conventions[87]

92. The two Protocols to the Geneva Conventions are, in part, declaratory of pre-existing customary international law and, in part, a further development of the law.

93. The Protocols again restate the basic principles that the right to choose methods of warfare is not unlimited and that weapons and methods of warfare which cause unnecessary suffering or superfluous injury are prohibited.

94. Protocol I also provides for the protection of the environment. It prohibits methods or means of warfare which are intended or may be expected to cause widespread, long-term and severe damage to the environment.[88]

95. The Protocols also contain important elaboration of the rules regarding the protection of civilians. The basic rule set out is in Article 48 of Protocol I:

> "In order to ensure respect for and protection of the civilian population and civilian objects, the Parties to the conflict shall at all times distinguish between the civilian population and combatants and between civilian objects and military objectives and accordingly shall direct their operations only against military objectives."

96. The Protocols set out a series of specific prohibitions for the protection of civilians. Acts or threats of violence, the primary purpose of which is to spread terror amongst the civilian population, are prohibited.[89] Indiscriminate attacks are defined and prohibited,[90] and precautionary measures are to be taken to spare the civilian population.[91] Attacks against civilian populations or objects by way of reprisal are prohibited.[92] Destruction of food sources required by civilian populations is prohibited,[93] as is the destruction of works or installations containing destructive forces such as dams.[94] Cultural objects and places of worship are protected from attack.[95]

97. In considering the application of the Protocols to the use of nuclear weapons, it is to be noted that two of the nuclear weapon States participated in the negotiations on the basis that new rules established by the Protocols would not be applicable to nuclear weapons. These reservations were repeated upon signature of the Protocols by the two states concerned and by a number of other states. The Protocols therefore clearly apply to the use of nuclear weapons only in so far as they set out general principles or rules of international humanitarian law that codify or represent customary international law.

[87] 1977 Protocol Additional to the Geneva Conventions of 12 August 1949, and relating to the Protection of Victims of International Armed Conflicts (Protocol I); 1977 Protocol Additional to the Geneva Conventions of 12 August 1949, and relating to the Protection of Victims of Non-International Armed Conflicts (Protocol II).

[88] *supra*, n.71.

[89] Article 51(2)of Protocol I; Article 13(2) of Protocol II.

[90] Article 51(4) and (5) of Protocol I.

[91] Articles 57 and 58 of Protocol I.

[92] Articles 51(6) and 52(1) of Protocol I.

[93] Article 54 of Protocol I; Article 14 of Protocol II.

[94] Article 56 of Protocol I; Article 15 of Protocol II.

[95] Article 53 of Protocol I; Article 16 of Protocol II.

Recent Developments

98. That international humanitarian law is continuing to develop, and retains its potency, is demonstrated by the statutes adopted in 1993 and 1994 by the United Nations Security Council to establish international tribunals in respect of serious violations of international humanitarian law in, respectively, the Former Yugoslavia and Rwanda and neighbouring countries.[96] The function of the tribunals is to call to account individuals responsible for such violations, which include, in the case of the Former Yugoslavia, violations of the laws or customs of war, specifically including employment of poisonous weapons or other weapons calculated to cause unnecessary suffering, wanton destruction of cities, towns or villages or devastation not justified by military necessity, and destruction done to institutions dedicated to religion, education, the arts and sciences, and historic monuments.[97]

Final Comments

99. New Zealand's position on nuclear weapons is clear. New Zealand strongly opposes the proliferation of nuclear weapons and supports measures for nuclear disarmament. It is also opposed to the testing of nuclear weapons, and is a strong supporter of a comprehensive nuclear test ban, which it has been calling for in the United Nations General Assembly since 1972. These have been priorities for New Zealand for many years.

100. As regards the legal question, it is the case that only in a limited (but nevertheless significant) number of cases do treaties prohibit in specific terms the use of whole classes of weapons: for example, biological weapons,[98] chemical weapons,[99] exploding bullets,[100] and certain booby traps and weapons based on non-detectable fragments.[101] It is also the case, however, that while nuclear weapons are the only "weapon of mass destruction" not expressly subject to general prohibition by treaty, there is a large body of international law, both treaty law and rules of customary international law, which circumscribes the threat or use of nuclear weapons. Treaties in the arms control and disarmament field circumscribe the threat or use in various respects, and other areas of

[96] UNSC Resolutions 827 (1993) and 955 (1994).

[97] Article 3 of the Statute of the International Tribunal for the Prosecution of Persons Responsible for Serious Violations of International Humanitarian Law Committed in the Territory of the Former Yugoslavia since 1991.

[98] Convention on the Prohibition of the Development, Production and Stockpiling of Bacteriological (Biological) and Toxin Weapons and on Their Destruction, 1972.

[99] Convention on the Prohibition of the Development, Production, Stockpiling and Use of Chemical Weapons and Their Destruction, 1993.

[100] 1868 St Petersburg Declaration Renouncing the Use, in Time of War, of Explosive Projectiles Under 400 grammes Weight.

[101] Protocols I and II to the 1981 Convention on Prohibitions or Restrictions on the Use of Certain Conventional Weapons Which May Be Deemed to Be Excessively Injurious or to Have Indiscriminate Effects (also known as the Inhumane Weapons Convention).

international law, particularly international humanitarian law, circumscribe other threats or uses of nuclear weapons, and bear on the question before the Court.

101. Moreover, international law and relevant state practice in this area has been steadily increasing and developing over the years. There have been developments at both the regional and the global levels and, in New Zealand's case, at the national level through the enactment of legislation. Emerging principles and developments in related areas of international law, such as protection of the environment,[102] can also be pointed to. All of this provides reinforcement for the view that various norms of international law have emerged in this area. Even if it may not yet be possible to say that, in every circumstance, international law proscribes the threat or use of nuclear weapons, there can be little doubt that the law has been moving in that direction. In New Zealand's view, the sooner that point is reached, through the progressive development of international law, including the negotiating process, the more secure the international community will be.

[102] *supra*, paragraph 73.

LETTER DATED 20 JUNE 1995 FROM THE AMBASSADOR OF INDIA, TOGETHER WITH WRITTEN STATEMENT OF THE GOVERNMENT OF INDIA

MOST URGENT

NO: HAG/POL/443/2/95 June 20, 1995

Your Excellency,

As you are aware, the UN General Assembly Resolution No. 49/75 K requested the International Court of Justice for an advisory opinion on the legality of the threat or use of nuclear weapons.

2. I am enclosing with this letter a 7-pages submission by India relating to this subject.

3. Furthermore, I also enclose herewith a counter-memorial on the WHO resolution relating to the request for an advisory opinion of the International Court of Justice on the legality of nuclear weapons.

4. I understand that the last date for the submission of these documents is 20th June 1995 and accordingly these are being sent to Your Excellency on a most urgent basis.

Please accept, Excellency, the assurances of my highest consideration.

With regards

Yours sincerely,

(I.P. Khosla)

H.E. Mr. Eduardo Valencia-Ospina
Registrar
International Court of Justice
Peace Palace
2517 KJ THE HAGUE

Status of Nuclear Weapons in International Law: Request for advisory opinion of the International Court of Justice.

The question whether nuclear weapons could be lawfully used in an armed conflict is regulated by international law, and in particular the law of armed conflicts and by principles of international humanitarian law. Under international law, use of force is prohibited in international relations. The prohibition contained in Article 2(4) of the UN Charter is so comprehensive and fundamental as to be regarded as a **jus cogens** or an obligation of an absolute character. On the basis of this principle it appears clear that any use of nuclear weapons as a measure of use of force to promote national policy objectives would be unlawful.

Most proponents of use of force, without denying the absolute character of the obligation contained in Article 2(4), contend that use of force by way of exercise of an inherent right of self-defence, which is preserved and protected under Article 51 of the UN Charter is admissible. However, the content and the circumstances under which the right of self-defence could be exercised is specified in the UN Charter itself and is related specifically only to an "armed attack" in the first instance. The same has to be reported soon thereafter to the Security Council and is subject to its right to take appropriate steps under Chapter VII upon a determination of the existence of a threat to peace, breach of peace, or an act of aggression.

It is further agreed that any use of force in self-defence has to be proportional to the means and ends involved or to the original wrongful use of force. Moreover, the right of self-defence is to be regarded as a provisional measure or a remedy and hence as soon as other means or measures became available, the resort to self-defence through use of force has to cease.

Even though an opinion is expressed that the reference to inherent right of self-defence in Article 51 provides the basis for States to undertake a preventive action in self-defence in the form of self-preservation this, according to a more prevalent view, is not supportable. According to the prevailing view that the qualification of the right of self-defence by the word "inherent" in Article 51 serves only to emphasise that the right is available to every State regardless of whether it is a UN member or not. Further, according to this view, the fundamental purpose of the UN Charter is to restrict the use of force by States to the utmost extent necessary, keeping in view Article 1(1) and Para

7 of the Preamble of the UN Charter. (**See Encyclopaedia of Public International Law, Max Planck Institute, Vol.4(N-2), North Holland Pub. Co., p.272.**).

It is even suggested that where one State preannounces an armed attack against another State, a hardly conceivable practice, preventive self-defence would be lawful!

In view of the above and given the strict limitations on the non-use of force and the right of self-defence, it is our view that use of nuclear weapons in any armed conflict as a first attack would be unlawful under international law.

The question then for consideration is whether the use of nuclear weapons would be lawful as a measure of reprisal or retaliation if the same is used by an adversary in the first instance. Reprisals or retaliation under international law are also governed by certain specific principles. First, reprisals to be valid and admissible could only be taken in response to a prior delict or wrongful act by a State. Second, such reprisals must remain within reasonable bounds of proportionality to the effect created by the original wrongful act. However, reprisals could not involve acts which are **malum in se** such as certain violations of human rights, certain breaches of the laws of war and rules in the nature of **jus cogens**, that is to say obligations of an absolute character compliance with which is not dependent on corresponding compliance by others but is requisite in all circumstances unless under stress of literal **vis major** (**see G. Fitzmaurice, General Principles of International Law, Volume 92 Hague Recueil Des Cours (1957-II), Pages 119-120**).

In other words, a nuclear weapon could not be used by way of reprisal against another State if that State did not commit any wrongful act or delict involving use of force. Second, when a State commits such a wrongful act or delict, the use of force by way of reprisal would have to be proportionate and as such if the wrongful act did not involve the use of a nuclear weapon, the reprisal could also not involve the use of a nuclear weapon. Third, even where a wrongful act involved the use of a nuclear weapon the reprisal action cannot involve use of a nuclear weapon without violating certain fundamental principles of humanitarian law. In this sense, prohibition of the use of a nuclear weapon in an armed conflict is an absolute one, compliance with which is not dependent on corresponding compliance by others but is a requisite in all circumstances.

In view of the above, use of nuclear weapons even by way

of reprisal or retaliation, appears to be unlawful.

In any case, if the wrongful use of force in the first instance did not involve the use of nuclear weapons, it is beyond doubt that even in response by way of retaliation States do not have the right to use nuclear weapons because of their special quality as weapons of mass destruction. It is also clear further that any wrongful act not involving use of force at all under international law could not be redressed or attempted to be met with any use of force with or without involving nuclear weapons.

This brings us to the question as to the legality of the use of nuclear weapons in an armed conflict on the ground that it is open as a measure of last resort under limited conditions as a matter of military necessity. A basic principle of the law of armed conflict and particularly the international humanitarian law, which is contained in Article 22 of the Hague Convention IV(1907) states that "the right of belligerents to adopt means of injuring the enemy is not unlimited". Their right in particular is conditioned by Article 23 of the Hague Regulations prohibiting the use of poison or poisoned weapons; the 1925 Geneva Protocol prohibiting projectiles, asphyxiating, poisonous and other gases which incidentally prohibits also the use of weapons which could cause genetic disorders and illness which is likely to prolong for a considerable amount of time; and by the basic principle enshrined in the Declaration of St. Petersburg of 1868 prohibiting any weapon "which uselessly aggravates the sufferings of disabled men or render their death inevitable".

Moreover, the very purpose of international humanitarian law is to forbid "indiscriminate attacks" and demand protection of civilians. 'Indiscriminate attacks' are generally defined as those that are not directed at any single military objective, those which employ methods or means of combat which cannot be directed at a specific military objective and those with effects which cannot be limited. In other words, indiscriminate attacks are those of a nature to strike a military object and civilians and civilian objects without distinction.

In addition to the above, the relationship between military advantage and the collateral damage involved also determines the legality of use of a weapon or a method of warfare employed. If the collateral damage is excessive in relation to the military advantage, the attack is forbidden.

Keeping the above considerations in view, it is easy to come to the conclusion that the use of nuclear weapons in an armed conflict is unlawful being contrary to the conventional as well as customary international law because such a use cannot distinguish between the combatants and non-combatants on the one hand and could cause excessive injuries to the combatants making their death inevitable and could even cause widespread and long-term damage which in some cases could even result in what is called as a "nuclear winter".

However an opposite view was expressed by some that the law of war or the humanitarian law could not be deemed to prohibit the use of nuclear weapons as that law grew up mostly only touching the old and more marginal weapons. They claimed that nuclear weapons being weapons of modern warfare are outside the scope of such a law. It is also their view that recent attempts to outlaw some newer method of warfare by implications did not outlaw the use of nuclear weapons in an armed conflict. Citing that almost all States are urging the conclusion of a convention to outlaw the use of nuclear weapons in an armed conflict, it is also argued that in the absence of any such convention their use is not prohibited. In the same connection the use of such nuclear weapons on Hiroshima and Nagasaki is also cited as an example of such legitimate use.

On the basis of above arguments, it is contended that international law does not provide for any blanket prohibition against the use of nuclear weapons and the legality of any specific use could however be apprised only in the total context of such specific use.

The above arguments in favour of the legality of use of nuclear weapons are convincingly contested. First it was pointed out that the development of humanitarian law and the specific principles indicated above which have the status of customary international law do not distinguish between major or minor methods of warfare or between major or marginal weapons. Second, some of the earlier opinions regarding the legality of nuclear weapons were not based on information and knowledge now available about the devastating effects of the use of nuclear weapons and their incompatibility with the fundamental norms of humanitarian law. Third, more recent efforts which reiterated the customary law developed on the basis of the earlier declarations or conventions also did not make any distinction between various weapons or methods of warfare. Fourth, the international community often engaged in further clarification, codification and progressive development of the law even when the principles involved in such an exercise are already regarded as well-established in international law. Examples of this kind of exercise are many and by way of illustration the 1982 UN Convention on the Law of the Sea, various declarations and treaties concluded reiterating the UN Charter principles and the international humanitarian law itself could be mentioned. Fifth, the use of nuclear weapons over Hiroshima and Nagasaki does not make that use lawful if their use is otherwise prohibited in law. On the contrary, the use of chemical weapons in World War I led to the negotiation of the Geneva Protocol outlawing their further use. The same should apply to nuclear weapons. Violations of international law like any law would only highlight the importance of complying with such law and do not make legal what is otherwise illegal.

The use of nuclear weapons in response to attack by a conventional weapon would patently violate the principle of proportionality but also a nuclear response to nuclear attack, would violate the principle of discrimination, humanity, environmental security and probably the principle of neutrality as such an attack would not distinguish between combatants and non-combatants- causing civilian casualties, ravaging the natural environment and contaminating the territory of neighboring and distant neutral countries. Nuclear deterrence had been considered to be abhorrent to human sentiment since it implies that a state if required to defend its own existence will act with pitiless disregard for the consequences to its own and adversary's people.

Another question which arises in relation to the theory of deterrence is whether the keeping of peace or the prevention of war is to be made dependent on the threat of horrific indiscriminate destruction which justifies the stockpiling of such weapons at an enormous expense, in the hope that they will merely act as a deterrent but will not infact be used. However those who do not have such weapons would all the time be racing to build them and those who already have nuclear weapons would continue to develop even more destructive weapons to maintain the superiority necessary for deterrence and this would keep humanity in the perpetual fear of total destruction. A better and saner way to secure everlasting peace would be to ensure that only are such weapons never used but also not made. The security of all nations would best be safeguarded by a nuclear weapon free world. If peace is the ultimate objective there can be no doubt that disarmament must be given priority and has to take precedence over deterrence.

The consideration of question of legality of use of

nuclear weapons is incomplete without consideration of the manufacture, production and stockpiling of nuclear weapons.

Since the production and manufacture of nuclear weapons can only be with the objective of their use, it must follow that if the use of such weapons itself is illegal under international law, then their production and manufacture cannot under any circumstances be considered as permitted. Besides, the manufacture and stockpiling of nuclear weapons would constitute as a threat of their eventual use.

In this connection, reference may be made to the Conventions on Biological Weapons and on Chemical Weapons which recognising the need to exclude completely the possibility of the use of such weapons, prohibit States parties to develop, produce, stockpile or otherwise acquire or retain the prohibited weapons. These Conventions clearly recognise and provide that the only effective way to prevent under any circumstances the use of a prohibited weapon is to ensure that no State undertakes the production or manufacture or retains such weapons. Accordingly, where States are in possession of chemical or biological weapons they are required to dismantle or destroy them under an elaborate procedure specified therein with built-in safeguards of international inspection. The need for these Conventions was felt because a number of States had made declarations/reservations to the 1925 Geneva Protocol to the effect that they could use, the prohibited gases, poisons etc in case they were subjected to an attack by such weapons.

The Chemical Weapons Convention and the Biological Weapons Convention by prohibiting the production, manufacture etc., of such weapons under any circumstances preclude their use even by way of retaliation in cases where they have been used by one party to a conflict.

Thus the use of nuclear weapons which is otherwise contrary to international law could only be effectively prevented by eliminating completely their production, manufacture and by ensuring the dismantling of existing nuclear weapons.

The production of weapons which have the capacity to destroy all mankind cannot in any manner be considered to be justified or permitted under international law.

It is also argued that declaring the threat or use of

nuclear weapons as illegal or unlawful would be a greater deterrent against any irresponsible use than treating such a use as legal; and further where such illegal use is still resorted to, the international community would at least have at its disposal the right to condemn the user and demand cessation of the wrongful act and attach such other legal consequences as are prescribed in the law of state responsibility.

In view of the above, it is submitted that the threat or use of nuclear weapons in any circumstance, whether as a means or method of warfare or otherwise, is illegal or unlawful under international law.

LETTER DATED 20 JUNE 1995
FROM THE ACTING LEGAL ADVISER
TO THE DEPARTMENT OF STATE,
TOGETHER WITH WRITTEN STATEMENT
OF THE GOVERNMENT OF THE UNITED STATES OF AMERICA

United States Department of State

Washington, D.C. 20520

June 20, 1995

Sir:

In accordance with the Court's order of February 1, 1995, and Article 66, paragraph 2, of the Statute of the Court, I have the honor to transmit to you the enclosed Written Statement of the Government of the United States of America concerning the Request of the United Nations General Assembly for an Advisory Opinion on the Legality of the Threat or Use of Nuclear Weapons.

Accept, sir, the assurances of my highest consideration.

Sincerely,

Michael J. Matheson
Acting Legal Adviser

Enclosure:

As stated.

Mr. Eduardo Valencia-Ospina,
Registrar,
International Court of Justice,
Peace Palace,
The Hague, The Netherlands

BEFORE THE

INTERNATIONAL COURT OF JUSTICE

The Hague

The Netherlands

Request by the United Nations General Assembly for an Advisory Opinion on the Legality of the Threat or Use of Nuclear Weapons

WRITTEN STATEMENT OF THE

GOVERNMENT OF THE UNITED STATES OF AMERICA

Conrad K. Harper
Legal Adviser

Michael J. Matheson
Deputy Legal Adviser

Bruce C. Rashkow
Assistant Legal Adviser

Office of the Legal Adviser
Department of State
Washington, D.C.

John H. McNeill
Senior Deputy General Counsel
Department of Defense
Washington, D.C.

June 20, 1995

TABLE OF CONTENTS

I. INTRODUCTION AND SUMMARY 1

II. IN THE EXERCISE OF ITS DISCRETION, THE COURT SHOULD DECLINE TO ISSUE AN OPINION 3

III. THE SUBSTANCE OF THE QUESTION POSED 7

A. Introduction 7

B. There is No General Prohibition on the Use of Nuclear Weapons 8
1. Customary Law 8
2. International Agreements 9
a. Use of Other Weapons 10
b. Agreements on Use of Nuclear Weapons 10
c. Agreements on Manufacture, Testing or Possession 11
d. Agreements on Accidental or Unauthorized Use 13
3. Conduct of States 14
4. Expressed Views of States 15

C. The Law of Armed Conflict Does Not Prohibit the Use of Nuclear Weapons 21
1. Attacking the Civilian Population 22
2. Indiscriminate Weapons 23
3. Proportionality 23
4. Poison Weapons 23
5. 1925 Geneva Protocol 24
6. 1977 Additional Protocol I 25
7. Unnecessary Suffering 28
8. Environmental Effects 29
9. Reprisals 30
10. Neutrality 31
11. Rendering death inevitable 32
12. Genocide 33

D. International Environmental Instruments Do Not Prohibit the Use of Nuclear Weapons 34
1. International Environmental Treaties 34
a. 1985 Convention for the Protection of the Ozone Layer 35
b. 1992 Convention on Climate Change 36
c. 1992 Biodiversity Convention 38
2. International Environmental Declarations 38
a. 1972 Stockholm Declaration on the Human Environment 38
b. 1992 Rio Declaration on Environment and Development 40

E. Human Rights Instruments Do Not Prohibit the Use of Nuclear Weapons 42

F. The Same Conclusions Apply to the Threat of Use of Nuclear Weapons 46

IV. CONCLUSION 48

I. INTRODUCTION AND SUMMARY

By resolution 49/75K of December 15, 1994, the United Nations General Assembly has requested an advisory opinion from the International Court of Justice on the following question:

> Is the threat or use of nuclear weapons in any circumstance permitted under international law?

Upon receiving this request, the Court fixed June 20, 1995 as the time limit within which written statements relating to the question might be submitted by States. The United States hereby submits its written statement.

This request is closely related to the request of the World Health Organization (WHO) for an advisory opinion on the legality of the use of nuclear weapons. The United States submitted an extensive written statement concerning that request on June 10, 1994, and is today submitting written comments on the submissions of other States in that case. In the present statement, the United States offers its views on important issues raised by the request of the General Assembly.

In particular, the United States believes that the Court, in the exercise of the discretion provided by Article 65, paragraph 1, of its Statute, should decline to provide an opinion. The question presented is vague and abstract, addressing complex issues which are the subject of consideration among interested States and within other bodies of the United Nations which have an express mandate to address these matters. An opinion by the Court in regard to the question presented would provide no practical assistance to the General Assembly in carrying out its functions under the Charter. Such an opinion has the potential of undermining progress already made or being made on this sensitive subject and, therefore, is contrary to the interests of the United Nations Organization.

Nonetheless, in view of the possibility that the Court may decide to provide an opinion, we offer views on the substance of the legal question presented by the request of the General Assembly. In the view of the United States, there is no general prohibition in conventional or customary international law on the threat or use of nuclear weapons. On the contrary, numerous agreements regulating the possession or use of nuclear weapons and other state practice demonstrate that their threat or use is not deemed to be generally unlawful.

Moreover, nothing in the body of international humanitarian law of armed conflict indicates that nuclear weapons are prohibited per se. As in the case of other weapons, the legality of use depends on the conformity of the particular use with the rules applicable to such weapons. This would, in turn, depend on factors that can only be guessed at, including the characteristics of the particular weapon used and its effects, the military requirements for the destruction of the target in question and the magnitude of the risk to civilians. Judicial speculation about hypothetical future circumstances on a matter of such fundamental importance would, in our view, be inappropriate.

In view of the importance of the legal question presented, the United States requests the opportunity to provide further comments or observations relating to the question should the Court determine to respond to the request.

II. IN THE EXERCISE OF ITS DISCRETION, THE COURT SHOULD DECLINE TO ISSUE AN OPINION

The United Nations General Assembly does, of course, have the authority under Article 96, paragraph 1, of the United Nations Charter to request the Court to give an advisory opinion on any legal question. It is nonetheless well established that, pursuant to Article 65 of its Statute, the Court has discretion whether to provide an advisory opinion even where it has jurisdiction to entertain the request.[1]

Where the proposed opinion would serve to assist another organ of the United Nations in understanding and carrying out its responsibilities, the Court has ordinarily been reluctant to refuse such a request.[2] However, in no case (other than the WHO

---

[1] Interpretation of Peace Treaties With Bulgaria, Hungary and Romania, Advisory Opinion, I.C.J. Reports 1950, p. 65 at p. 72; Reservations to the Convention on the Prevention and Punishment of the Crime of Genocide, Advisory Opinion, I.C.J. Reports 1951, p. 15 at p. 19; S. Rosenne, The Law and Practice of the International Court (2d ed. 1985), pp. 652, 658, 698.

[2] Interpretation of Peace Treaties With Bulgaria, Hungary and Romania, I.C.J. Reports 1950, p. 65 at pp. 71-72; Reservations to the Convention on the Prevention and Punishment of the Crime of Genocide, I.C.J. Reports 1951, p. 15 at p. 19; Rosenne, supra, p. 709. In other instances, the Court has indicated that only for compelling reasons should the Court decline to provide an opinion where it otherwise has jurisdiction. Judgments of the Administrative Tribunal of the International Labor Organization Upon Complaints Made Against the United Nations Educational, Scientific and Cultural Organization, Advisory Opinion, I.C.J. Reports 1956, p. 86. In that case, the Court concluded that:

(continued...)

request on nuclear weapons) has the Court been asked to provide an opinion on an abstract question, the answer to which could not reasonably be expected to provide practical guidance to the fulfillment of the functions of the requesting body. Unlike other requests for advisory opinions, the present request does not present a dispute or situation upon which specific legal advice can usefully be given. Rather, the request presents a very general and vague question that would of necessity involve complex legal, technical, political and practical considerations.

These matters cannot usefully be addressed in the abstract without reference to the specific circumstances under which any use of nuclear weapons would be contemplated. The Court should not, on a matter of such fundamental importance, engage in speculation about unknown future situations.

Where the issuance of an opinion will not provide any practical guidance to the requesting body, there is little reason for the Court to grant the request. This is particularly true where the requesting body is a specialized organ having limited

---

[2](...continued)

> Notwithstanding the permissive character of Article 65 of the Statute in the matter of advisory opinions, only compelling reasons could cause the Court to adopt in this matter a negative attitude which would imperil the working of the regime established by the Statute of the Administrative Tribunal for the judicial protection of officials.

Subsequently, the Court has reiterated the view that an opinion should be provided unless there are "compelling reasons to the contrary" without specifying the harm that a refusal to grant the request for the opinion would have to the United Nations system. Applicability of Article VI, Section 22, of the Convention on the Privileges and Immunities of the United Nations, Advisory Opinion, I.C.J. Reports 1989, p. 191.

functions (such as the World Health Organization). It is also true even where the requesting body is another principal organ of the Organization with more general responsiblities, such as the General Assembly. If the question posed is too vague and hypothetical to provide useful guidance to the requesting body, the Court should decline the request for an opinion.

Moreover, where providing an opinion might create difficulties for another part of the United Nations Organization in carrying out its responsibilities, or for States in conducting negotiations outside the United Nations, the Court may appropriately determine that the Organization is better served by the Court's declining a request.

An opinion on the complex and sensitive matter of the threat or use of nuclear weapons could complicate the work of States or other United Nations bodies, thereby undermining the progress already made in this area. Marked differences of opinion have been expressed by Member States about the lawfulness of the use of nuclear weapons.[3] The substantial progress made to date in controlling the possession and use of nuclear weapons has been possible because States have set aside their differences and concentrated on agreeing upon practical measures to reduce the danger of nuclear conflict. Pronouncements by the Court on the abstract question of the legality of the threat or use of nuclear

---

[3] This fact was expressly acknowledged in the resolution of the WHO Assembly ("WHA") that requested an advisory opinion on the lawfulness of the use of nuclear weapons. WHA Resolution 46.40 (1993), preamble.

weapons could well obstruct this progress and compel States to turn to a fruitless debate about the legal implications of the Court's pronouncements. To the extent that such pronouncements affected international instruments concerning environmental protection or human rights, there could be serious complications for international negotiation and cooperation in these fields as well.

Finally, an opinion by the Court offering advice on what is in many respects essentially a political matter could undermine its authority and effectiveness.

In exercising its discretion, the Court should, in the view of the United States, take into account the significant number of States that did not support this request. The proposal for this request was introduced in the First Committee of the General Assembly. While 77 States voted for the request, 33 States opposed it and 21 abstained.[4] The number of States that did not support the request was even greater when the matter subsequently came before the General Assembly. While 78 States voted for the resolution, 43 States opposed it and 38 abstained.[5] In short, there was very substantial disagreement within the international community as to whether such a request was appropriate.

---

[4] UN GAOR First Comm., 49th Sess., 24th Mtg., pp. 12-13; UN Doc. A/C.1/49/PV.24 (1994).

[5] UN GAOR, 49th Sess., 90th Plen. Mtg., pp. 35-36; UN Doc. A/49/PV.90 (1994).

For these various reasons, the United States believes the Court should, in the exercise of its discretion under Article 65 of its Statute, decline to provide a response to the request.

III. THE SUBSTANCE OF THE QUESTION POSED

A. Introduction.

Some States have by agreement undertaken not to possess or use nuclear weapons under any circumstances and others have undertaken not to use such weapons in certain defined geographical areas. Apart from this, there is no prohibition in conventional or customary international law on the threat or use of nuclear weapons. On the contrary, international law is replete with agreements that regulate the possession or use of nuclear weapons, providing compelling evidence that their use is not deemed to be generally unlawful. The practice of States, including the Permanent Members of the Security Council, all of which maintain stocks of nuclear weapons, further proves this point.

In addition, nothing in the body of the international humanitarian law of armed conflict indicates that nuclear weapons are prohibited *per se*. As in the case of other weapons, the legality of use depends on the conformity of the particular use with the rules applicable to such weapons. This would, in turn, depend on factors that can only be guessed at, including the characteristics of the particular weapon used and its effects, the military requirement for the destruction of the target in question and the magnitude of the risk to civilians. Judicial speculation on a matter of such fundamental importance would be inappropriate.

B. There is No General Prohibition on the Use of Nuclear Weapons.

It is a fundamental principle of international law that restrictions on States cannot be presumed but must be found in conventional law specifically accepted by them or in customary law generally accepted by the community of nations. There is no general prohibition on the use of nuclear weapons in any international agreement. There is likewise no such prohibition in customary international law. Such a customary prohibition could only result from a general and consistent practice of States followed by them from a sense of legal obligation. We submit, based on the following analysis of the agreements, conduct and expressed views of States, that there is no such practice.

1. Customary Law. Customary international law is created by a general and consistent practice of States followed by them from a sense of legal obligation.[6] Evidence of a customary norm requires indication of "extensive and virtually uniform" State practice, including States whose interests are

---

[6] See Restatement (Third) of the Foreign Relations Law of the United States § 102 (1987); Case Concerning the Continental Shelf (Libyan Arab Jamahariya v. Malta), I.C.J. Reports 1985, p. 13 at pp. 29-30.

"specially affected."[7] Among the actions of States that contribute to the development of customary international law are international agreements concluded by them, governmental acts, and official statements of what the law is considered to be. (However, mere hortatory declarations or acts not based on a perception of legal obligation would not suffice.)[8]

With respect to the use of nuclear weapons, customary law could not be created over the objection of the nuclear-weapon States, which are the States whose interests are most specially affected. Nor could customary law be created by abstaining from the use of nuclear weapons for humanitarian, political or military reasons, rather than from a belief that such abstention is required by law. Among the more important indicators of State practice in this area are the international agreements that regulate but do not prohibit nuclear weapons, the fact of the acquisition and deployment of nuclear weapons by the major military powers, and the official views expressed by States on this question.

2. International Agreements. We are aware of no international agreement -- and certainly none to which the United States is a Party -- that contains a general prohibition on the use of nuclear weapons. On the contrary, it is evident that

---

[7] North Continental Shelf Cases (Federal Republic of Germany v. Denmark; Federal Republic of Germany v. The Netherlands), I.C.J. Reports 1969, p. 3 at p. 43.

[8] See 7 R. Bernhardt, ed., Encyclopedia of Public International Law (1984), pp. 62-63.

existing agreements proceed from the assumption that there is no such general prohibition.

a. Use of Other Weapons. There are a number of prohibitions in international agreements on the use of other specific categories of weapons. These include: biological and chemical weapons (the 1925 Geneva Protocol);[9] the use of environmental modification techniques as weapons (the 1977 Environmental Modification Convention);[10] the use of exploding bullets (the 1868 Declaration of St. Petersburg);[11] and the use of weapons with non-detectable fragments (the 1981 Convention on Specific Conventional Weapons).[12] This pattern implies that there is no such general prohibition on the use of nuclear weapons, which would otherwise have found expression in a similar international agreement.

b. Agreements on Use of Nuclear Weapons. A few international agreements regulate the use of nuclear weapons, doing so in a way that indicates there is no general prohibition

---

[9] Protocol for the Prohibition of the Use in War of Asphyxiating, Poisonous or Other Gases, and of Bacteriological Methods of Warfare, 17 June 1925, 94 L.N.T.S. 65.

[10] Convention on the Prohibition of Military or any other Hostile Use of Environmental Modificiation Techniques, 18 May 1977, 1125 U.N.T.S. 3.

[11] Declaration Renouncing the Use, in Time of War, of Explosive Projectiles under 400 Grammes Weight, 11 December 1868, reprinted in A. Roberts & R. Guelff, Documents on the Laws of War (2nd ed. 1989), p. 63.

[12] Convention on Prohibitions or Restrictions on the Use of Certain Conventional Weapons Which May be Deemed to be Excessively Injurious or to Have Indiscriminate Effects, 10 April 1981, reprinted in Roberts & Guelff, supra note 11, p. 471.

on the use of such weapons. For example, there are agreements that prohibit the use of nuclear weapons in particular regions: Antarctica (the Antarctic Treaty);[13] Latin America (the 1967 Treaty of Tlatelolco);[14] and the South Pacific (the South Pacific Nuclear Free Zone Treaty).[15]

The Antarctic Treaty prohibits all nuclear explosions on the Antarctic continent. The Treaty of Tlatelolco prohibits the Latin American parties from using nuclear weapons under any circumstances; at the same time, two separate Additional Protocols, to which nuclear-weapon States are invited to adhere, obligate them to observe the same prohibition within a defined area in the Western Hemisphere. Similarly, Protocol 2 to the South Pacific Nuclear Free Zone Treaty (to which nuclear-weapon States are invited to adhere) prohibits Protocol Parties from using nuclear weapons against any Treaty Party. These provisions would make no sense if there were already a general prohibition on the use of nuclear weapons.

c. Agreements on Manufacture, Testing or Possession. A number of international arms control agreements prohibit or regulate the manufacture, testing or possession of nuclear weapons or systems for their delivery. These include the

---

13 Antarctic Treaty, 1 December 1959, 402 U.N.T.S. 71.

14 Treaty for the Prohibition of Nuclear Weapons in Latin America ("Tlatelolco Treaty"), 14 February 1967, 634 U.N.T.S. 281.

15 South Pacific Nuclear Free Zone Treaty, 6 August 1985.

1963 Limited Test Ban Treaty,[16] the 1967 Outer Space Treaty,[17] the 1968 Non-Proliferation Treaty,[18] the 1971 Seabed Arms Control Treaty,[19] the 1972 Anti-Ballistic Missile (ABM) Treaty,[20] the 1974 Threshold Test Ban Treaty,[21] the 1987 Intermediate-Range Nuclear Forces (INF) Treaty[22] and the 1991 Treaty on the Reduction and Limitation of Strategic Offensive Arms (START).[23] These treaties would be unnecessary if there were already a generally-accepted prohibition on the use of nuclear weapons.

Further, the terms of these treaties implicitly acknowledge in many ways that the continued possession and use of such weapons (within the confines of treaty limitations) are not

---

[16] Treaty Banning Nuclear Weapon Tests in the Atmosphere, in Outer Space and Under Water, 5 August 1963, 480 U.N.T.S. 43.

[17] Treaty on Principles Governing the Activities of States in the Exploration and Use of Outer Space, including the Moon and other Celestial Bodies, 27 January 1967, 610 U.N.T.S. 205.

[18] Treaty on the Non-proliferation of Nuclear Weapons, 1 July 1968, 729 U.N.T.S. 161.

[19] Treaty on the Prohibition of the Emplacement of Nuclear Weapons and Other Weapons of Mass Destruction on the Seabed and the Ocean Floor and in the Subsoil Thereof, 11 February 1971, 955 U.N.T.S. 115.

[20] Treaty on the Limitation of Anti-Ballistic Missile Systems, 26 May 1972, 944 U.N.T.S. 13.

[21] Treaty on the Limitation of Underground Nuclear Weapon Tests, 3 July 1974, 13 International Legal Materials ("ILM") (1974), p. 906.

[22] Treaty on the Elimination of Intermediate-range and Shorter-range Missiles, 8 December 1987, 27 ILM (1988), p. 84.

[23] Treaty on the Reduction and Limitation of Strategic Arms, 3 January 1993, 16 UN Disarmament Yearbook (1991), App. II, p. 450.

prohibited. For example, the Limited Test Ban Treaty (to which there are well over one hundred parties) permits underground nuclear weapons testing, while prohibiting testing elsewhere. This is a clear acknowledgment that the possession of such weapons by the nuclear-weapon States is lawful and implies that use in at least some circumstances would also be lawful, since possession and testing of such weapons would otherwise be purposeless. Likewise, the Non-Proliferation Treaty accepts the lawfulness of the development and possession of nuclear weapons by the nuclear-weapon States designated in the Treaty, which would be senseless if all uses of such weapons were unlawful.

The ABM and START Treaties go even further in that they sanction the need for deterrent nuclear-weapon forces, prohibit the creation of destabilizing defenses against them, and prohibit or restrict offensive forces that could destroy them. Furthermore, the START Treaty accepts the legality and propriety of limited deployments of nuclear-weapon systems that are deemed to contribute to a stable nuclear deterrent posture. This entire structure of obligations would be meaningless if the use of nuclear weapons were considered to be unlawful under all circumstances.

d. Agreements on Accidental or Unauthorized Use. International arms control agreements have been concluded which attempt in various ways to minimize the chance of accidental or unauthorized use of nuclear weapons. They include the 1963 "Hot

Line" Agreement,[24] the 1971 Accidents Measures Agreement,[25] the 1973 Prevention of Nuclear War Agreement[26] and the 1987 Nuclear Risk Reduction Agreement.[27] In addressing the need for arrangements to minimize the risk of unintended use of nuclear weapons, these agreements are additional evidence of the acceptance by States that the possession and use of such weapons are not generally prohibited.

3. Conduct of States. It is well known that the Permanent Members of the Security Council possess nuclear weapons and have developed and deployed systems for their use in armed conflict.[28] These States would not have borne the expense and effort of acquiring and maintaining these weapons and delivery systems if they believed that the use of nuclear weapons was generally prohibited. On the contrary, the possible use of these weapons is an important factor in the structure of their military establishments, the development of their security doctrines and strategy, and their efforts to prevent aggression and provide an essential element of the exercise of their right of self-defense.

---

[24] Memorandum of Understanding Regarding the Establishment of a Direct Communications ("Hot-Line") Link, 20 June 1963, 472 U.N.T.S. 163.

[25] Agreement on Measures to Reduce the Risk of Outbreak of Nuclear War, 30 September 1971, 807 U.N.T.S. 57.

[26] Agreement on the Prevention of Nuclear War, 22 June 1973, 24 U.N.T.S. 1478.

[27] Agreement on the Establishment of Nuclear Risk Reduction Centers, 15 September 1987.

[28] See Report of the U.N. Secretary-General on Nuclear Weapons, A/45/373, 18 September 1990, pp. 19-24.

(These deployments and doctrines are discussed in the 1990 Report of the Secretary-General on nuclear weapons.)[29] This pattern of conduct is inconsistent with the existence of any general legal prohibition on the use of nuclear weapons.

The fact that such weapons have actually been used in only one armed conflict does not suggest the contrary. Certainly nuclear-weapon States have preserved the option to use nuclear weapons if necessary, and (as is explained below) have not refrained from further use of these weapons because they believed such use to be unlawful -- which is an essential element in the development of customary international law.

4. Expressed Views of States. Various States have taken differing views on the legality of the use of nuclear weapons. As the United Nations Secretary-General has recently concluded, "no uniform view has emerged as yet on the legal aspects of the possession of nuclear weapons and their use as a means of warfare."[30] This is confirmed by the WHO resolution that requested an advisory opinion, which refers to the fact that "marked differences of opinion have been expressed by Member States about the lawfulness of the use of nuclear weapons."[31] The variety and disparity of views expressed by States demonstrates that there is no generally-accepted prohibition on the use of nuclear weapons. Under these circumstances, customary

---

[29] Id., pp. 61-71.

[30] Id., p. 130.

[31] WHA Resolution 46.40 (1993), preambular para. 9.

international law cannot be said to include such a general prohibition.

The position of the nuclear-weapon States is best illustrated by their official statements on nuclear-weapons use in the context of the Non-Proliferation Treaty and the Treaty of Tlatelolco. On April 5, 1995, Secretary of State Christopher announced that President Clinton had declared the following in the context of the Conference on the extension of the Non-Proliferation Treaty:

> The United States reaffirms that it will not use nuclear weapons against non-nuclear-weapon States Parties to the Treaty on the Non-Proliferation of Nuclear Weapons except in the case of an invasion or any other attack on the United States, its territories, its armed forces or other troops, its allies, or on a State towards which it has a security commitment, carried out or sustained by such a non-nuclear-weapon State in association or alliance with a nuclear-weapon State.[32]

Statements identical in substance were made at the same time by France,[33] Russia[34] and the United Kingdom.[35] The Security Council unanimously took note of these statements "with appreciation",[36] and no exception was taken to the reservation by these States of the right to use nuclear weapons in certain circumstances.

Likewise, at the time of its ratification of Additional Protocols I and II to the Tlatelolco Treaty, the United States

---

[32] U.N. Doc. A/50/153 (1995).

[33] U.N. Doc. A/50/154 (1995).

[34] U.N. Doc. A/50/151 (1995).

[35] U.N. Doc. A/50/152 (1995).

[36] UN Security Council Resolution 984 (1995), para. 1.

made a formal statement of understandings and declarations, including a statement that effectively reserved its right to use nuclear weapons against one of the Contracting Parties in the event of "an armed attack by a Contracting Party, in which it was assisted by a nuclear-weapon State . . . ."[37] Similar statements were made by the United Kingdom and the Soviet Union.[38] France stated that nothing in the Protocol could present an obstacle to "the full exercise of the right of self-defense confirmed by Article 51 of the United Nations Charter."[39]

Although these statements differ in some respects, they have certain important common features. In particular, none acknowledges any general prohibition on the use of nuclear weapons; on the contrary, each clearly reserves the right to use nuclear weapons in some circumstances. Further, limits are offered only with respect to certain States, thus indicating that there are no comparable constraints on the use of nuclear weapons against States generally.

Additional statements of nuclear-weapon States on the use of nuclear weapons are contained in Appendix I to the Secretary-General's 1990 Report.[40] In each case, the government

---

[37] 28 ILM 1423.

[38] Id. at 1418, 1422.

[39] Id. at 1415.

[40] Report of the U.N. Secretary-General on Nuclear Weapons, 18 September 1990, UN Doc. A/45/373 (1990), pp. 61-75; see also Statement of U.S. Defense Secretary Schlesinger of 1 July 1975, reprinted in 1975 Digest of U.S. Practice in International Law, pp. 800-01.

in question stated its resolve to act in such a manner as to avoid the necessity for the use of nuclear weapons, but in no case is there a recognition of any general prohibition on the use of nuclear weapons.

Beginning with Resolution 16/1653 in 1961, the U.N. General Assembly has adopted a series of resolutions declaring that the use of nuclear weapons is contrary to the U.N. Charter and international law generally.[41] It is well established, however, that aside from certain administrative matters, the General Assembly does not have the authority to "legislate" or create legally binding obligations on its members.[42] Further, such General Assembly resolutions could only be declarative of the existence of principles of customary international law to the extent that such principles had been recognized by the international community, including the States most directly affected.[43] In fact, there were a significant number of U.N.

---

[41] E.g., UN General Assembly Resolution 33/71 B (1978); UN General Assembly Resolution 35/152 D (1980); UN General Assembly Resolution 36/92 I (1981); UN General Assembly Resolution 46/37 D (1991); UN General Assembly Resolution 47/53 C (1992).

[42] See Charter of the United Nations, Article 11(1) ("The General Assembly may consider the general principles of cooperation in the maintenance of international peace and security, . . . and may make recommendations with regard to such principles . . . ."); Voting Procedure on Questions Relating to Reports and Petitions Concerning the Territory of South West Africa, Advisory Opinion, I.C.J. Reports 1955, pp. 90, 116 (separate opinion of Judge Lauterpacht) (". . . the General Assembly has no legal power to legislate or bind its Members by way of recommendations . . . .").

[43] See, e.g., S. Schwebel, 7 Forum Internationale (1985), pp. 11-12; Letter of U.S. State Department Deputy Legal Adviser (continued...)

Member States that did not accept these resolutions: in particular, these resolutions were not accepted by a majority of the nuclear-weapon States.

For example, Resolution 1653 was adopted by a vote of 55 to 20, with 26 abstentions, and each of the subsequent resolutions attracted at least 16 negative votes and a number of abstentions. In each case, the United States, the United Kingdom and France voted against the resolution. The representative of the United Kingdom, in explaining his Government's vote on Resolution 1653, stated that "so long as States possess nuclear weapons, they will use them in self-defense."[44] The representative of the United States stated that:

> . . . it is simply untrue to say that the use of nuclear weapons is contrary to the Charter and to international law . . . . Indeed, the very provisions of the Charter approve, and demand, the exercise of self-defense against armed attack. It is very clear that the Charter says nothing whatever about any particular weapon or method which may be used for self-defense.[45]

During the 1980s, the General Assembly adopted a series of resolutions urging the nuclear-weapon States to adopt a policy of refraining from the first use of nuclear weapons and to begin negotiations on a legally binding regime including the obligation

---

[43](...continued) Stephen Schwebel of 25 April 1975, 1975 Digest of U.S. Practice in International Law, p. 85; S. Schwebel, "Lawmaking in the United Nations," 4 Federal Law Review (1970), pp. 115, 118.

[44] 16 UN GAOR, 13th Sess., 1063rd Mtg., p. 803; UN Doc. A/13/PV.1063 (1961).

[45] Id. at 798.

not to be the first to use nuclear weapons.[46] Like the resolutions cited above, these resolutions on first use were not accepted by a significant number of U.N. Member States and in particular were not accepted by most nuclear-weapon States.[47] Further, the adoption of these resolutions implicitly indicates a general understanding that there is no existing prohibition on all uses of nuclear weapons, since there would be no need for first-use resolutions and agreements if all uses were already prohibited.

Taken together, these various expressions of the views of States demonstrate that there is no consensus on the question of the legality of the use of nuclear weapons. In particular, there is nothing approaching the degree of acceptance by States, and of acceptance by the States most specifically affected, that would be required to create obligations under customary international law.

Finally, there is nothing in the United Nations Charter, or in rules of customary international law embodied in it, that per se precludes the use of nuclear weapons. For example, States may use force when authorized by the Security Council under Chapter

---

[46] UN General Assembly Resolution 36/100 (1981); UN General Assembly Resolution 37/78 J (1982); UN General Assembly Resolution 38/183 B (1983); UN General Assembly Resolution 39/148 D (1984); UN General Assembly Resolution 40/152 A (1985); UN General Assembly Resolution 41/86 B (1986); UN General Assembly Resolution 42/42 A (1987); UN General Assembly Resolution 43/78 B (1988); UN General Assembly Resolution 44/119 B (1989).

[47] In each case, the United States, the United Kingdom and France voted against and each resolution attracted at least 17 negative votes and a number of abstentions.

VII or in the exercise of individual or collective self-defense. The exercise of self-defense is subject to the rules of necessity and proportionality, but the application of those rules to any use of nuclear weapons depends on the precise circumstances involved and cannot be judged in the abstract.

C. The Law of Armed Conflict Does Not Prohibit the Use of Nuclear Weapons.

The United States has long taken the position that various principles of the international law of armed conflict would apply to the use of nuclear weapons as well as to other means and methods of warfare.[48] This in no way means, however, that the use of nuclear weapons is precluded by the law of war. As the following will demonstrate, the issue of the legality depends on the precise circumstances involved in any particular use of a nuclear weapon.

It has been argued that the use of nuclear weapons is inherently precluded by the principles of international humanitarian law, regardless of the circumstances of their use. It seems to be assumed that any use of nuclear weapons would inevitably escalate into a massive strategic nuclear exchange, with the deliberate destruction of the population centers of the opposing sides.

Such assumptions are speculative in the extreme, and cannot be the basis for judgments by the Court on the legality of hypothetical uses of nuclear weapons that otherwise comply with

---

[48] See International Red Cross Conference Resolution XXVIII, 20th International Red Cross Conference (1965).

the principles of international humanitarian law. In fact, any serious analysis of the legality of a hypothetical use of nuclear weapons would of necessity have to consider the precise circumstances of that use. Such circumstances cannot be evaluated in the abstract, and any attempt by the Court to do so would, in our view, be inappropriate.

Various arguments have been advanced in support of the conclusion that the use of nuclear weapons is precluded by the law of armed conflict. In the following, we shall consider these arguments in turn and indicate why we believe each to be incorrect.

1. Attacking the Civilian Population. It has been argued that the use of nuclear weapons is unlawful in that it would constitute an attack on the civilian population. The law of armed conflict precludes making civilians the object of attack as such.[49] This, of course, does not mean that attacks on military objectives are prohibited simply because they may cause collateral civilian injury or damage -- as is often the case in armed conflict. This rule would not be violated by the use of nuclear weapons to attack targets that constitute legitimate military objectives, and in any event is subject to the right of reprisal (see below).

---

[49] See, e.g., U.S. Army Field Manual 27-10, Change No. 1, The Law of Land Warfare (1976) 4, para. 40(a) ("U.S. Army Field Manual").

2. Indiscriminate Weapons. It has been argued that nuclear weapons are unlawful because they cannot be directed at a military objective[50]. This argument ignores the ability of modern delivery systems to target specific military objectives with nuclear weapons, and the ability of modern weapon designers to tailor the effects of a nuclear weapon to deal with various types of military objectives. Since nuclear weapons can be directed at a military objective, they can be used in a discriminate manner and are not inherently indiscriminate.

3. Proportionality. It has been argued that the use of nuclear weapons would be unlawful because it would cause collateral injury or damage to civilians or civilian objects that would be excessive in relation to the military advantage anticipated from the attack[51]. Whether an attack with nuclear weapons would be disproportionate depends entirely on the circumstances, including the nature of the enemy threat, the importance of destroying the objective, the character, size and likely effects of the device, and the magnitude of the risk to civilians. Nuclear weapons are not inherently disproportionate.

4. Poison Weapons. It has been argued that the use of nuclear weapons would violate the prohibition in the 1907 Hague

---

[50] For a restatement of the general rule in this context, see, e.g., U.S. Army Field Manual, supra note 49, at 5, para. 40(b)(3) and (c).

[51] For a restatement of the general rule in this context, see, e.g., U.S. Army Field Manual, supra note 49, at 5, para. 41.

Convention on the use of poison weapons[52]. This prohibition was established with particular reference to projectiles that carry poison into the body of the victim. It was not intended to apply, and has not been applied, to weapons that are designed to injure or cause destruction by other means, even though they also may create toxic byproducts.

For example, the prohibition on poison weapons does not prohibit conventional explosives or incendiaries, even though they may produce dangerous fumes. By the same token, it does not prohibit nuclear weapons, which are designed to injure or cause destruction by means other than poisoning the victim, even though nuclear explosions may also create toxic radioactive byproducts.

5. 1925 Geneva Protocol. It has been argued that the use of nuclear weapons would violate the prohibition in the 1925 Geneva Protocol on the first use in war of asphyxiating, poisonous or other gases and analogous liquids, materials and devices[53]. This prohibition was intended to apply to weapons that are designed to kill or injure by the inhalation or other absorption into the body of poisonous gases or analogous substances.[54]

---

[52] Hague Convention (IV) Respecting the Laws and Customs of War on Land, Annex, Art. 23(a) reprinted in Roberts & Guelff, supra note 11, p. 53.

[53] Protocol for the Prohibition of the Use in War of Asphyxiating, Poisonous or Other Gases, and of Bacteriological Methods of Warfare, 17 June 1925, 94 L.N.T.S. 65.

[54] See F. Kalshoven, "Arms, Armaments and International Law", 191 Hague Academy of International Law (Recueil de Cours) (1985-II), pp. 283-84.

This prohibition was not intended to apply, and has not been applied, to weapons that are designed to kill or injure by other means, even though they may create asphyxiating or poisonous byproducts. Once again, the Protocol does not prohibit conventional explosives or incendiary weapons, even though they may produce asphyxiating or poisonous byproducts, and it likewise does not prohibit nuclear weapons.

6. 1977 Additional Protocol I. Additional Protocol I to the 1949 Geneva Conventions[55] contains a number of new rules on means and methods of warfare, which of course apply only to States that ratify Protocol I. (For example, the provisions on reprisals and the protection of the environment are new rules that have not been incorporated into customary law.)[56] It is, however, clear from the negotiating and ratification record of Protocol I that the new rules contained in the Protocol were not intended to apply to nuclear weapons.

At the outset of the negotiations that led to Protocol I, the International Committee of the Red Cross (ICRC) stated that:

> Prohibitions relating to atomic, bacteriological and chemical warfare are subjects of international agreements or negotiations by governments, and in submitting these draft

---

[55] Protocol Additional to the Geneva Conventions of 12 August 1949, and Relating to the Protection of Victims of International Armed Conflicts ("Protocol I"), 12 December 1977, 1125 U.N.T.S. 3.

[56] See M. Bothe, K. Partsch & W. Solf, New Rules for Victims of Armed Conflicts (1982), pp. 312, 317; International Committee of the Red Cross, Commentary on the Additional Protocols of 8 June 1977 (1987), p. 662.

> Additional Protocols the ICRC does not intend to broach these problems.[57]

Explicit statements to the same effect were made during the negotiations by various delegations, including France, the Soviet Union, the United Kingdom and the United States.[58]

Furthermore, in creating an ad hoc committee to consider specific restrictions on the use of conventional weapons thought to present special dangers to the civilian population, the Conference rejected a proposal to expand the scope of this study to nuclear weapons. The Committee concluded that the predominant view was acceptance of "the limitation of the work of this Conference to conventional weapons", noting in particular the important function of nuclear weapons in deterring the outbreak of armed conflict.[59]

Nevertheless, in light of the importance of this point, a number of States made clear formal statements upon signature or ratification emphasizing that the new rules adopted in the Protocol would not apply to nuclear weapons. For example, the signature of the United Kingdom was based on the formal understanding that:

---

[57] International Committee of the Red Cross, Commentary on the Additional Protocols of 8 June 1977 (1987), p. xxxii.

[58] E.g., Official Records of the Diplomatic Conference of Geneva, Vol. V, p. 134; Vol. VII, p. 193, 295; Vol. XVI, p. 188.

[59] Id., Vol. XVI, p. 454.

> . . . the new rules introduced by the Protocol are not intended to have any effect on and do not regulate or prohibit the use of nuclear weapons.[60]

Similar express formal statements have been made on signature or ratification by Belgium, Canada, Italy, Germany, the Netherlands, Spain and the United States.[61]

To our knowledge, no State made any comment or objection to any of these formal and clear statements and declarations, nor did any State express a contrary view in connection with its own signature or ratification of Protocol I. In short, the record of signature and ratification of the Protocol reflect a manifest understanding that nuclear weapons were not prohibited or restricted by the new rules established by the Protocol.

This conclusion is consistent with the analysis of those experts on international humanitarian law who are best informed on the Conference's work. For example, the Commentary of the ICRC concluded: that "there is no doubt that during the four sessions of the Conference agreement was reached not to discuss nuclear weapons"; that the principles reaffirmed in the Protocol "do not allow the conclusion that nuclear weapons are prohibited as such by international humanitarian law"; and that "the

---

[60] International Committee of the Red Cross, Public Information Division, CD-ROM on International Humanitarian Law (September 1993) (containing up-to-date list of signatures, ratifications, accessions and successions relating to international humanitarian law treaties, as well as the full text of reservations, declarations and objections thereto) (United Kingdom).

[61] Id. (Belgium, Canada, Italy, Germany, Netherlands, Spain, United States).

hypothesis that States acceding to the Protocol bind themselves without wishing to -- or even without knowing -- with regard to such an important question as the use of nuclear weapons, is not acceptable."[62] Likewise, the extensive commentary of Bothe, Partsch and Solf on the Protocols concludes that the negotiating record "shows a realization by the Conference that the scope of its work excluded the special problems of the use of nuclear weapons."[63]

7. Unnecessary Suffering. It has been argued that the use of nuclear weapons would violate the prohibition on the use of weapons that are of such a nature as to cause superfluous injury or unnecessary suffering.[64] This prohibition was intended to preclude weapons designed to increase the injury or suffering of the persons attacked beyond that necessary to accomplish the military objective.[65] It does not prohibit weapons that may cause great injury or suffering if the use of the weapon is necessary to accomplish the military mission. For example, it does not prohibit the use of anti-tank munitions which must penetrate armor by kinetic-energy or incendiary effects, even

---

[62] International Committee of the Red Cross, Commentary on the Additional Protocols of 8 June 1977 (1987), pp. 593-94.

[63] Bothe, Partsch & Solf, supra note 56, p. 191.

[64] See Convention (IV) Respecting the Laws and Customs of War on Land, 18 October 1907, 1 Bevans 631, Annex, Art. 23(e).

[65] The prohibition has been applied, for example, to lances with barbed tips and bullets that are irregularly shaped, scored or coated with a substance that would unnecessarily inflame a wound. U.S. Army Field Manual, supra note 49, p. 18, para. 34.

though this may well cause severe and painful burn injuries to the tank crew. By the same token, it does not prohibit the use of nuclear weapons, even though such weapons can produce severe and painful injuries.

8. Environmental Effects. Article I of the 1977 Environmental Modification Convention[66] prohibits "military or any other hostile use of environmental modification techniques having widespread, long-lasting or severe effects as the means of destruction, damage or injury to any other State Party." Article II defines the term "environmental modification techniques" as "any techniques for changing -- through the deliberate manipulation of natural processes -- the dynamics, composition or structure of the Earth, including its biota, lithosphere, hydrosphere and atmosphere, or of outer space."

Although one might imagine a hypothetical use of nuclear weapons to create an environmental modification technique (for example, to cause an earthquake or tidal wave), the Convention does not prohibit other uses of nuclear weapons (or any other weapon), even if they cause serious damage to the environment. Only the "deliberate manipulation" of environmental forces to cause destruction is covered.

Articles 35(3) and 55 of Additional Protocol I to the 1949 Geneva Conventions prohibit the use of "methods or means or warfare which are intended, or may be expected, to cause

---

[66] Convention on the Prohibition of Military or any other Hostile Use of Environmental Modificiation Techniques, 18 May 1977, 1125 U.N.T.S. 3.

widespread, long-term and severe damage to the natural environment." This is one of the new rules established by the Protocol that, as explained above, do not apply to nuclear weapons.

9. Reprisals. It has been argued that the use of nuclear weapons would not be consistent with the law of reprisals. For the purpose of the law of armed conflict, reprisals are lawful acts of retaliation in the form of conduct that would otherwise be unlawful, resorted to by one belligerent in response to violations of the law of war by another belligerent. Such reprisals would be lawful if conducted in accordance with the applicable principles governing belligerent reprisals. Specifically, the reprisals must be taken with the intent to cause the enemy to cease violations of the law of armed conflict, other means of securing compliance should be exhausted, and the reprisals must be proportionate to the violations.[67] As in the case of other requirements of the law of armed conflict, a judgment about compliance of any use of nuclear weapons with these requirements would have to be made on the basis of the actual circumstances in each case, and could not be made in advance or in the abstract. (Of course, as shown elsewhere in this submission, possible lawful use of nuclear weapons is not limited to reprisals.)

---

[67] U.S. Army Field Manual, supra note 49, p. 177, para. 497.

Various provisions of Additional Protocol I contain prohibitions on reprisals against specific types of persons or objects, including the civilian population or individual civilians (Article 51(6)), civilian objects (Article 52(1)), cultural objects and places or worship (Article 53(c)), objects indispensable to the survival of the civilian population (Article 54(4)), the natural environment (Article 55(2)), and works and installations containing dangerous forces (Article 56(4)). These are among the new rules established by the Protocol that, as explained above, do not apply to nuclear weapons.

10. Neutrality. It has been asserted that the rules of neutrality in the law of armed conflict apply to and prohibit the use of nuclear weapons. However, the principle of neutrality[68] is not a broad guarantee to neutral States of immunity from the effects of war, whether economic or environmental. Its purpose was to preclude military invasion or bombardment of neutral territory, and otherwise to define complementary rights and obligations of neutrals and belligerents.[69] We are aware of no case in which a belligerent has been held responsible for

---

[68] See Hague Convention V Respecting the Rights and Duties of Neutral Powers and Persons in Case of War on Land, 18 October 1907, reprinted in Roberts & Guelff, supra note 11, p. 63.

[69] See, e.g., Greenspan, The Modern Law of Land Warfare, p. 356 (1959); W. Bishop, Jr., International Law: Cases and Materials, pp. 1019-20 (1971).

collateral damage to neutral territory for lawful acts of war committed outside that territory.[70]

Further, the argument that the principle of neutrality prohibits the use of nuclear weapons is evidently based on the assertion that the use of such weapons would inevitably cause severe damage in the territory of neutral States. This assumption is incorrect and in any event highly speculative. The Court could not find that such damage would occur without knowing the precise circumstances of a particular use. Like any other weapon, nuclear weapons could be used to violate neutrality, but this in no way means that nuclear weapons are prohibited _per se_ by neutrality principles.

11. _Rendering death inevitable_. It has been argued that the use of nuclear weapons would violate the principle expressed in the 1868 St. Petersburg Declaration concerning weapons that "render death inevitable".[71] This assertion is evidently based on the argument that no nuclear weapon would leave those within the immediate vicinity of the explosion with any reasonable chance of survival.

This argument is based on a misconception of the St. Petersburg principle, which was directed at anti-personnel weapons that were deliberately designed to kill when that design

---

[70] _See_ G. Schwarzenberger, _International Law as Applied by International Courts and Tribunals_, Vol. II, pp. 582-591 (1968).

[71] Declaration Renouncing the Use, in Time of War, of Explosive Projectiles Under 400 Grammes Weight, 11 December 1868, _reprinted in_ Roberts & Guelff, _supra_ note 11, p. 29.

feature was not needed to disable enemy combatants.[72] This does not mean that it is unlawful to use a weapon that has a high probability of killing persons in its immediate vicinity if that design feature is required to fulfill a legitimate military mission.

For example, any large high-explosive or fragmentation weapon has a high probability of killing exposed persons within a certain distance of the detonation. An effective anti-submarine, anti-aircraft or anti-tank weapon has a high probability of killing the crews of these vehicles. This fact does not make these weapons unlawful, since these lethal effects are necessary for the effective accomplishment of their legitimate mission.

By the same token, a nuclear weapon is not prohibited per se by the St. Petersburg principle if its effects are required for a legitimate military mission. For example, the use of a nuclear weapon to destroy a naval vessel or an armored formation does not violate this principle, even though there would likely be a very high casualty rate among targeted combatants.

12. Genocide. It has been argued that any use of nuclear weapons which affects a large number of non-combatants could constitute genocide, and that the element of intent for genocide could be inferred from the mere failure of the person using the nuclear weapons to take account of its full effects. This is a

---

[72] The only specific weapons prohibited by the St. Petersburg Declaration are projectiles weighing less than 400 grams that are explosive or "charged with fulminating or inflammable substances." Id.

serious misstatement of the elements of the offense of genocide, which is only committed if violent acts are done "with intent to destroy, in whole or in part, a national, ethnical, racial or religious group, as such."[73] The deliberate killing of large numbers of people is not sufficient to establish this offense unless this genocidal intent is demonstrated (although such killing might, depending on the circumstances, constitute a violation of other rules of international humanitarian law). Like any other weapon from firearms to poison gas, nuclear weapons could be used to commit genocide, but this fact in no way renders their use illegal _per se_.

D. _International Environmental Instruments Do Not Prohibit the Use of Nuclear Weapons_.

No international environmental instrument is expressly applicable in armed conflict. No such instrument expressly prohibits or regulates the use of nuclear weapons. Consequently, such an international environmental instrument could be applicable only by inference. Such an inference is not warranted because none of these instruments was negotiated with the intention that it would be applicable in armed conflict or to any use of nuclear weapons. Further, such an implication is not warranted by the textual interpretation of these instruments.

1. _International Environmental Treaties_. It has been suggested that there is a "Principle of Environmental Security"

---

[73] Convention on the Prevention and Punishment of the Crime of Genocide, 9 December 1948, UN General Assembly Resolution 260 A(III), 78 UNTS 277, Art. II.

which supposedly forms part of the law of war. This principle is said to be evidenced by the provisions of a number of international environmental law treaties, including the 1985 Vienna Convention for the Protection of the Ozone Layer, the 1992 Framework Convention on Climate Change, and the 1992 Convention on Biological Diversity. However, none of the cited environmental treaties defines any "environmental security" principle, nor does any of them state or even suggest that there is such a principle.

None of these treaties was negotiated with any idea that it was to be applicable in armed conflict, much less to prohibit the use of nuclear weapons. None of them makes specific or veiled reference to armed conflict, and none of them relates in any concrete way to the use of nuclear weapons. The application of these treaties to nuclear weapons would be for a purpose wholly different from that which was contemplated by the negotiating States.

a. 1985 Convention for the Protection of the Ozone Layer. A review of the text of the Vienna Convention for the Protection of the Ozone Layer[74] reveals no intent, whether express or implied, to address the legality of the use of nuclear weapons or any other form of armed conflict. The only provision of the Convention that even purports to regulate the conduct of the Parties is a general statement in Article 2(1):

---

[74] Convention for the Protection of the Ozone Layer, 22 March 1985, 26 ILM (1987), p. 1529.

> The Parties shall take appropriate measures in accordance with the provisions of this Convention . . . to protect human health and the environment against adverse effects resulting or likely to result from human activities which modify or are likely to modify the ozone layer.

Article 2(1) does not contain any language which suggests that the Parties intended to prohibit any specific activities, and certainly none which suggests an intent to prohibit the use of any category of weapons.

Further, Annex I to the Convention sets forth an agenda for future research concerning substances and processes that may adversely affect the ozone layer. No reference is made, however, to research regarding the effects of the use of nuclear weapons, or to the effects of the use of any other weapons or means of warfare. The absence of any such reference further indicates that the Parties did not contemplate that the Convention would apply to such matters.

b. 1992 Convention on Climate Change. Nothing in the UN Framework Convention on Climate Change[75] addresses, expressly or by implication, the use of nuclear weapons or any other aspect of armed conflict. The objective of the Convention, as stated in Article 2, is to achieve "stabilization of greenhouse gas concentrations in the atmosphere . . . ." Similarly, the operative provisions of the Convention call on Parties to take various measures related to emissions of greenhouse gases. The Convention does not identify the use of

---

[75] United Nations Framework Convention on Climate Change, 9 May 1992, 31 ILM (1992), p. 849.

nuclear weapons as a source of greenhouse gases (although it identifies other such sources).

The record of the preparatory work for the Convention further establishes that the negotiating States did not intend to address the use of nuclear weapons. During preparatory work conducted by the United Nations Environment Programme (UNEP)/WHO Intergovernmental Panel on Climate Change that was tasked to develop possible elements of a convention, three proposals relating to armed conflict were suggested: one to refer to the 1977 Environmental Modification Convention,[76] a second suggesting a requirement that the climate be used only for "peaceful purposes", and a third suggesting that a linkage be established between nuclear stockpiles and climate change.[77] It appears, however, that none of these proposals (or anything similar) was put forward or discussed during the negotiations on the Convention that followed, nor were any such proposals included in the Convention text. The inescapable conclusion is that the States that negotiated the Convention did not intend to deal with such matters in that instrument.

---

[76] Convention on the Prohibition of Military or any other Hostile Use of Environmental Modificiation Techniques, 18 May 1977, 1125 U.N.T.S. 3.

[77] "Report on Legal Measures by the Topic Coordinators", Response Strategies Working Group, Intergovernmental Panel on Climate Change (1990).

c. 1992 Biodiversity Convention. Nothing in the text of the Convention on Biological Diversity[78] states or implies that it applies to the use of nuclear weapons or any other aspect of armed conflict. The only provision of even arguable relevance is Article 14, which requires that, in cases where an activity within a Party's jurisdiction poses an "imminent or grave danger" to biological diversity outside its jurisdiction, that Party shall "as far as possible and as appropriate" notify the States potentially affected and initiate action to "prevent or minimize" the danger. This provision is not designed to deal with armed conflict and in any event recognizes that there may be circumstances in which it is not possible or appropriate to prevent or minimize danger to biological diversity. Nothing in the negotiating record of which we are aware suggests that this general admonition was intended to regulate armed conflict, much less to prohibit nuclear weapons.

2. International Environmental Declarations. It has also been argued that the use of nuclear weapons would be contrary to a series of non-legally binding environmental instruments. As will be seen from an examination of those instruments, this conclusion is wholly unwarranted.

a. 1972 Stockholm Declaration on the Human Environment. The 1972 Stockholm Declaration of the United

---

[78] Convention on Biological Diversity, 5 June 1992, 31 ILM (1992), p. 822.

Nations Conference on the Human Environment[79] is not a legally binding instrument, but rather a political statement of aspirations. Nothing in the Declaration purports to ban the use of nuclear weapons in armed conflict. Indeed, the one principle (Principle 26) expressly addressing nuclear weapons merely states that:

> Man and his environment must be spared the effects of nuclear weapons and all other means of mass destruction. States must strive to reach prompt agreement, in the relevant international organs, on the elimination and complete destruction of such weapons.

At most, this is only a statement of a policy objective and is certainly not a statement of a legal prohibition on the use of nuclear weapons. All efforts at the Conference to prohibit the use of such weapons in armed conflict were rejected.[80]

Principle 21 of the Declaration provides:

> States have, in accordance with the Charter of the United Nations and the principles of international law, the sovereign right to exploit their own resources pursuant to their own environmental policies, and the responsibility to ensure that activities within their jurisdiction or control do not cause damage to the environment of other States or of areas beyond the limits of national jurisdiction.

It is clear, from a reading of the whole text of Principle 21, that it was designed to balance a statement of sovereign rights to exploit a State's own natural resources with a statement of the responsibility to ensure that the exercise of those rights

---

[79] Stockholm Declaration on the Human Environment (16 June 1972), section I of the Report of the United Nations Conference on the Human Environment, UN Doc. A/CONF.48/14 & Corr.1 (1972).

[80] *See* L. Sohn, "The Stockholm Declaration on the Human Environment", 14 *Harvard Int'l L.J.* (1973), p. 423 at pp. 508-11.

does not result in damage to others. It was obviously not drafted to apply to the conduct of armed conflict, much less to the use of nuclear weapons in foreign territory.

b. 1992 Rio Declaration on Environment and Development. The Rio Declaration on Environment and Development,[81] like the Stockholm Declaration, is a non-legally binding political statement of principles and goals, adopted by consensus at the 1992 United Nations Conference on Environment and Development (UNCED). It does not address, even by inference, the legality of the use of nuclear weapons in armed conflict.

Only one of the principles of the Rio Declaration addresses armed conflict. Principle 24 provides:

> Warfare is inherently destructive of sustainable development. States shall therefore respect international law providing protection for the environment in times of armed conflict and cooperate in its further development, as necessary.

Thus Principle 24 calls on States to respect the existing international law providing protection for the environment in times of armed conflict, but does not in any way identify the content of that law, or express an opinion on the adequacy of its content. Although some States at the Rio Conference sought a general principle condemning weapons of mass destruction, they failed in this effort.[82]

---

[81] Rio Declaration on Environment and Development (14 June 1992), United Nations Conference on Environment and Development, UN Doc. A/CONF.151/5/Rev.1 (1992).

[82] *See* J. Kovar, "A Short Guide to the Rio Declaration", 4 *Colorado J. of Int'l Environmental Law & Policy* (1993), p. 119 at p. 138.

Principles 1, 2 and 25 of the Rio Declaration have been cited for the proposition that the threat or use of nuclear weapons in an armed conflict would constitute a breach of generally accepted principles of international environmental law. However, none of these principles addresses armed confict or the use of nuclear weapons.

Principle 1 provides:

> Human beings are at the centre of concerns for sustainable development. They are entitled to a healthy and productive life in harmony with nature.

Principle 2 is a restatement of Principle 21 of the Stockholm Declaration. Principle 2 provides:

> States have, in accordance with the Charter of the United Nations and the principles of international law, the sovereign right to exploit their own resources pursuant to their own environmental and developmental policies, and the responsibility to ensure that activities within their jurisdiction or control do not cause damage to the environment of other States or of areas beyond the limits of national jurisdiction.

This text simply adds to Stockholm Principle 21 the words "and developmental" after the word "environmental" in the phrase "pursuant to their own environmental and developmental policies." It thus no more today supports the position that international law prohibits the use in armed conflict of nuclear weapons than it did twenty years ago.

Principle 25 provides that:

> Peace, development and environmental protection are interdependent and indivisible.

While this principle identifies peace as an essential prerequisite to sustainable development, it does not purport to outlaw war, or to make the use of nuclear weapons in armed conflict unlawful.

Neither the nuclear-weapon States nor those States that rely for their security on the nuclear-weapon capabilities of others would ever have accepted a prohibition on the use of nuclear weapons in the context of such an instrument. The attempt *ex post facto* to interpret these instruments as if such a prohibition had been accepted would be to stand these instruments on their collective head and reverse the clear intent of the States that negotiated them.

Further, to the extent that the Court were to decide that the use of nuclear weapons is prohibited or restricted by international environmental agreements or principles, very serious damage could be caused to international cooperation and the development of legal norms in this area. Any determination by the Court that these instruments prohibit or restrict the use of nuclear weapons would introduce a new and highly divisive element into international cooperation in this field.

E. Human Rights Instruments Do Not Prohibit the Use of Nuclear Weapons.

The argument has been made that the use of nuclear weapons violates the internationally guaranteed right to life, based on such international instruments as the Universal Declaration of Human Rights, the International Covenant of Civil and Political Rights, the American Convention on Human Rights and the European Convention on Human Rights. However, in the view of the United

States, the use of nuclear weapons in the exercise of legitimate self-defense would not be in any way inconsistent with such a right to life.

The human rights instruments which recognize a right to life do not by their terms prohibit the use of nuclear or any other weapons. For example, the Universal Declaration provides in Article 3 that "[e]veryone has the right to life, liberty and security of person."[83] Nowhere in the Universal Declaration is there any mention of a limitation or prohibition on the use of any form of weaponry. The formulation contained in the International Covenant on Civil and Political Rights differs only slightly, primarily by adding to this basic assertion that no one shall be "arbitrarily deprived" of life.[84]

None of these instruments prohibits, directly or indirectly, the taking of life for legitimate purposes, including in the exercise of the right to self-defense. That inherent right has long been understood and intended to comprehend the right to use lethal force, and it is inconceivable that the various human

---

[83] Universal Declaration of Human Rights, UNGA Res. 217A (III), UN Doc. A/811, adopted Dec. 10, 1948.

[84] Art. 6(1) of the 1966 International Covenant on Civil and Political Rights provides: "Every human being has the inherent right to life. This right shall be protected by law. No one shall be arbitrarily deprived of his life." See also the 1969 American Convention on Human Rights, Art. 4(1): "Every person has the right to have his life respected. This right shall be protected by law, and, in general, from the moment of conception. No one shall be arbitrarily deprived of his life." Article 4 of the 1981 African Charter on Human and Peoples' Rights states: "Human beings are inviolable. Every human being shall be entitled to respect for his life and the integrity of his person. No one may be arbitrarily deprived of this right."

rights instruments cited could have been intended to abridge that right so long as the rules of armed conflict and the limitations of the U.N. Charter are observed.

Thus, the prohibition in the International Covenant on Civil and Political Rights against arbitrarily depriving someone of his or her life was clearly understood by its drafters to exclude the lawful taking of human life. During the negotiation of the text which became Article 6, various delegations indicated a preference for including an explicit statement of the circumstances under which the taking of life would not be deemed a violation of the general obligation to protect life, including *inter alia* killings resulting from the use of force which is no more than absolutely necessary, or which occur in case of self-defense, or which are lawfully committed by the military in time of war.[85] Rather than attempt to identify all the possible circumstances under which the taking of life might be justified, the drafters agreed to a simple prohibition on the "arbitrary" deprivation of life. In any event, we know of no significant opposition to the proposition that the deprivation of life as a "lawful act of war" would not be violative of the protected right to life. The European Convention, which also guarantees the

---

[85] *See*, *e.g.*, Bossuyt and Humphrey, *Guide to the "Travaux Preparatoires" of the International Covenant on Civil and Political Rights* (1987), pp. 115-125.

right to life, specifically recognizes the right of States to deprive persons of their lives through lawful acts of war.[86]

It has been suggested that the Human Rights Committee, in General Comments issued in 1982 and 1984, has construed the Covenant on Civil and Political Rights as prohibiting the possession and use of nuclear weapons. That is not, however, what the Committee actually said, and those Comments are not in fact inconsistent with the view that the Covenant does not prohibit the taking of life for legitimate purposes, including the proper exercise of the right of self-defense.

The 1982 Comment, for example, notes that the U.N. Charter prohibits the threat or use of force by one State against another, but expressly recognizes the inherent right of self-defense.[87] The 1984 Comment, while recognizing that nuclear weapons are among the greatest threats to the right to life, does not purport to declare that possession or use of such weapons is

---

[86] Article 2 of the European Convention on Human Rights prohibits the intentional taking of life, save in the case of capital punishment, or following the use of force which is no more than absolutely necessary in quelling riots or insurrections, preventing the escape of a lawfully-held prisoner, effecting a lawful arrest or in self-defense. Article 15 prohibits derogations from Article 2 "except in respect of deaths resulting from lawful acts of war."

[87] See General Comment 6/16, July 27, 1982, at paragraph 2: "The Committee observes that war and other acts of mass violence continue to be a scourge of humanity and take the lives of thousands of innocent human beings every year. Under the Charter of the United Nations the threat or use of force by any State against another State, except in exercise of the inherent right of self-defence, is already prohibited. The Committee considers that States have the supreme duty to prevent wars, acts of genocide and other acts of mass violence causing arbitrary loss of life." HRI/GEN/1/Rev. 1 at p. 6 (1994).

prohibited *per se* by international law. Rather, it simply proclaims that the production, testing, possession, deployment and use of such weapons "should" be prohibited, thereby expressing an aspirational goal to be achieved and not a binding rule of international law.[88]

Accordingly, the citation of human rights instruments adds nothing to the analysis of the question whether the use of nuclear weapons is consistent with existing international law. The answer to that question is determined, as it must be, not by reference to human rights instruments but by application of the principles of international law governing the use of force and the conduct of armed conflict.

F. The Same Conclusions Apply to the Threat of Use of Nuclear Weapons.

The request of the General Assembly is somewhat broader than the request of the World Health Organization. Specifically, while the WHO request refers to "the use of nuclear weapons by a State in war or other armed conflict", the General Assembly request refers to "the threat or use of nuclear weapons in any circumstance". But even if this difference in the scope of the

---

[88] *See* General Comment 14/23, Nov. 2, 1984, paras. 4 and 6: "[T]he designing, testing, manufacture, possession and deployment of nuclear weapons are among the greatest threats to the right to life which confront mankind today. This threat is compounded by the danger that the actual use of such weapons may be brought about, not only in the event of war, but even through human or mechanical error or failure....The production, testing, possession, deployment and use of nuclear weapons should be prohibited and recognized as crimes against humanity." HRI/GEN/1/Rev. 1 at p. 6 (1994).

request was purposive, it does not lead to any different conclusion in substance.

In particular, if there is no prohibition *per se* on the use of a class of weapons, the "threat" to use such weapons is likewise not prohibited *per se*. States which maintain stocks of nuclear weapons for possible use in self-defense if the unfortunate necessity for such use should ever arise, and for the purpose of deterring aggression and hostile use of nuclear weapons by others, do not thereby violate international law if there is not an applicable prohibition on the possession or use of such weapons. (This is, of course, without prejudice to any specific obligation not to acquire, possess, deploy or use nuclear weapons that States may accept through such international agreements as the Non-Proliferation Treaty, the Tlatelolco Treaty, and the Outer Space Treaty.)

Indeed, many States rely for their security in large part on the nuclear capabilities of nuclear-weapon States, which have entered into mutual defense arrangements consistent with the collective self-defense principle recognized in Article 51 of the Charter. Nuclear deterrence has contributed significantly during the past 50 years to the enhancement of strategic stability, the avoidance of global conflict and the maintenance of international peace and security.

IV. CONCLUSION

The United States believes that the Court should, in the exercise of the discretion provided by Article 65, paragraph 1, of its Statute, decline to provide the opinion requested. In any event, there is no general prohibition in conventional or customary international law on the use of nuclear weapons, and there is no basis for speculation by the Court as to the manner in which the law of armed conflict might apply to the use of nuclear weapons in hypothetical future situations.

LETTER DATED 20 JUNE 1995
FROM THE MINISTER OF FOREIGN AFFAIRS
OF THE FRENCH REPUBLIC,
TOGETHER WITH WRITTEN STATEMENT
OF THE GOVERNMENT OF THE FRENCH REPUBLIC

MINISTÈRE
DES
AFFAIRES ÉTRANGÈRES

LE MINISTRE

RÉPUBLIQUE FRANÇAISE

PARIS, LE 20 JUIN 1995

Monsieur le Greffier,

Par ordonnance du 1er février 1995, la Cour internationale de justice a fixé au 20 juin 1995 la date à laquelle les Etats admis à ester devant la Cour pourraient présenter des exposés écrits sur une requête demandant un avis consultatif adressée à celle-ci par l'Assemblée générale des Nations Unies et portant sur la question suivante:

"Est-il permis en droit international de recourir à la menace ou à l'emploi d'armes nucléaires en toute circonstance?"

J'ai l'honneur de vous adresser ci-joint l'exposé écrit du gouvernement de la République française concernant cette requête.

Je saisis cette occasion pour vous faire savoir, en me référant à l'ordonnance de la Cour en date du 20 juin 1994, que le gouvernement de la République française, qui a examiné avec attention les exposés écrits présentés à la Cour à la suite de la demande d'avis consultatif présenté par l'Assemblée générale de l'Organisation mondiale de la Santé sur la licéité de l'utilisation des armes nucléaires par un Etat dans un conflit armé ne peut que confirmer entièrement les conclusions de son exposé écrit relatif à cette demande.

Le gouvernement de la République française estime que la demande de l'Organisation mondiale de la Santé est irrecevable.

En outre, pour les raisons développées tant dans l'exposé écrit relatif à cette demande que dans son exposé écrit relatif à la demande de l'Assemblée générale des Nations Unies, à laquelle il prie respectueusement la Cour de se reporter en tant que de besoin, ce gouvernement pense que la Cour devrait constater qu'une réponse serait inopportune; dans l'hypothèse où elle jugerait néanmoins appropriée une telle réponse, elle devrait constater qu'il n'existe, ni dans la constitution de l'Organisation mondiale de la Santé ni en droit international général, de prohibition d'emploi des armes nucléaires; certains signes montrent au contraire que le droit international général admet l'éventualité de cet emploi.

Je vous prie d'agréer, Monsieur le Greffier, l'assurance de ma haute considération.

Hervé de CHARETTE

LICEITE DE LA MENACE OU DE L'EMPLOI D'ARMES NUCLEAIRES

-REQUETE POUR AVIS CONSULTATIF-

EXPOSE ECRIT DU GOUVERNEMENT DE LA REPUBLIQUE FRANCAISE

JUIN 1995

Exposé écrit du gouvernement de la République française

Par ordonnance du 1er février 1995, la Cour internationale de Justice a décidé que les Etats admis à ester devant elle pourraient, dans un délai expirant le 20 juin 1995, lui adresser des exposés écrits sur une demande d'avis consultatif que l'Assemblée générale des Nations Unies lui a présentée par sa résolution 49/75 K du 15 décembre 1994.

La question posée à la Cour est la suivante:

"Est-il permis en droit international de recourir à la menace ou à l'emploi d'armes nucléaires en toute circonstance?"

La France estime nécessaire de faire connaître à la Cour, conformément à l'ordonnance susvisée, sa position sur la démarche des promoteurs de la résolution 49/75 K.

Avant d'exposer les observations qu'appelle de sa part, sur le plan du droit, la demande de l'Assemblée générale, la France rappelle, à titre liminaire et pour éclairer l'esprit dans lequel elle formule ses observations, que sa doctrine en matière de défense est fondée sur la dissuasion.

.../...

La France ne se connaît pas d'ennemi déclaré, et sa stratégie de dissuasion a un caractère strictement défensif: la France refuse la menace d'emploi et l'emploi de l'arme nucléaire, comme du reste de toute arme, à des fins agressives. Sa stratégie nucléaire est une stratégie destinée à empêcher la guerre et s'appuie, selon le principe de suffisance, sur des capacités limitées au strict nécessaire. Ces capacités s'inscrivent dans une stratégie purement dissuasive et non une stratégie d'emploi. Elles sont réservées à la dissuasion d'une agression contre les intérêts vitaux de la France, dont l'appréciation relève des plus hautes autorités de l'Etat.

L'arme nucléaire, réservée par définition à des situations conformes à l'article 51 de la Charte des Nations Unies, est pour la France une arme destinée à prévenir la guerre en la privant de toute rationalité.

La doctrine de dissuasion est la clef de voûte de la sécurité de la France.

En outre, nul ne peut ignorer que cette doctrine a, depuis près d'un demi-siècle, contribué au maintien de la stabilité et de la paix mondiales.

Il ne s'ensuit pas que le gouvernement français soit opposé aux efforts tendant à la réduction des armements nucléaires et, au-delà, à un désarmement général et complet sous un contrôle international efficace. Bien au contraire, son action internationale démontre qu'il entend exercer ses responsabilités à cet égard. Mais ces problèmes relèvent de négociations interétatiques et non d'une approche judiciaire. En outre la France s'élève avec force contre une tentative qui tend à mettre en cause, par une démarche dirigée contre les seules armes nucléaires et au risque d'ébranler un des éléments du système mondial actuel pour le maintien de la paix et de la sécurité

.../...

internationales, la politique des Etats dotés d'armes nucléaires et, au-delà, leur droit d'assurer leur défense par les moyens que leur permet le droit international en vigueur

Cela dit, l'objet du présent exposé est d'appeler l'attention de la Cour sur les points suivants:

1) Sur la recevabilité de la demande et l'opportunité d'une réponse: la question n'est pas de celles auxquelles la Cour peut répondre et la Cour devrait en tout état de cause constater l'inopportunité d'une telle réponse;

2) Sur le fond, et à titre purement subsidiaire: a) Il est évident que la menace ou l'emploi des armes nucléaires ne sont, pas plus que ceux des autres armes, permis en toute circonstance). b) Si la question posée dans la résolution 49/75 K était interprétée comme portant sur le point de savoir dans quelles circonstances la menace ou l'emploi des armes nucléaires seraient contraires au droit international, la Cour ne pourrait que constater que le droit international général ou coutumier ne comporte pas d'interdiction de l'emploi ou de la menace d'emploi des armes nucléaires. Certains instruments conventionnels ainsi que des résolutions du Conseil de sécurité montrent au contraire que le droit international général admet la licéité d'une telle menace ou d'un tel emploi.

.../...

I - Recevabilité de la question et opportunité d'une réponse

1 - Le gouvernement de la République française estime que la question posée n'est pas de celles auxquelles la Cour peut répondre dans le cadre de sa fonction consultative et qu'en tout état de cause la Cour sera conduite à constater qu'elle ne devrait pas y donner réponse.

2 - L'article 65 de son Statut laisse à la Cour toute liberté de déterminer la suite qu'elle estime devoir être donnée à une demande d'avis.

Dans son avis consultatif du 2O juillet 1962 relatif à "*Certaines dépenses des Nations unies*", la Cour a déclaré:

> "Si une question n'est pas juridique, la Cour n'a pas de pouvoir discrétionnaire en la matière: elle doit refuser de donner l'avis qui lui est demandé. Mais, même s'il s'agit d'une question juridique, à laquelle la Cour a indubitablement compétence de répondre, elle peut néanmoins refuser de le faire"(1).

Il s'agit là d'une jurisprudence constante, fermement maintenue par la Cour (2)

1 - *C.I.J.*, avis consultatif, 20 juillet 1962, *Certaines dépenses des Nations Unies, Rec.1962*, p.155

2 - *C.I.J.*, avis consultatif, 3O mars 1950, *Interprétation des traités de paix conclus avec la Bulgarie, la Hongrie et la Roumanie, Rec.1950*, p.72; v. aussi *C.I.J.*, avis consultatif, 28 mai 1951, *Réserves à la convention pour la prévention et la répression du crime de génocide, Rec.1951*, p.19; *C.I.J.*, avis consultatif, 20 juillet 1962, *Certaines dépenses des Nations Unies, Rec.1962*, p.155; *C.I.J.*, avis consultatif, 12 juillet 1973, *Demande de réformation du jugement n°158 du Tribunal administratif des Nations unies, Rec.1973*, p.175; *C.I.J.*, avis consultatif, 16 octobre 1975, *Sahara occidental, Rec.1975*, p.21; *C.I.J.*, avis consultatif, 15 décembre 1989, *Applicabilité de la section 22 de l'Article VI de la convention sur les privilèges et immunités des Nations Unies, Rec.1989*, p.191 etc....

.../...

La Cour considère également qu'en principe "la réponse à une demande d'avis consultatif ne doit pas être refusée" et "qu'il faudrait des raisons décisives pour déterminer la Cour à opposer un refus" à une telle demande.

Le gouvernement de la République française estime que, précisément, plusieurs "raisons décisives" existent en l'occurrence de ne pas répondre à la question posée par la résolution 49/75K.

3 - A cet égard, le gouvernement français croit qu'un rappel du contexte dans lequel la résolution 49/75 K a été adoptée et des conditions de cette adoption devrait faciliter l'appréciation de la nature et de la portée de la demande d'avis adressée à la Cour et de l'opportunité d'une réponse à la question posée.

Il semble superflu d'insister sur le fait que, comme le note l'ordonnance de la Cour du 1er février 1995, et comme le souligne la résolution 49/75 K elle-même, la demande présentée par celle-ci vient s'ajouter à la demande adressée le 14 mai 1993, sur le même sujet, dans le même but, par l'Assemblée de l'Organisation mondiale de la Santé. Qu'il s'agisse de pallier un échec probable, en raison de son irrecevabilité évidente, de la démarche tentée par le biais de l'OMS, ou plutôt de faire pression sur la Cour pour orienter sa réponse, il y a là une preuve flagrante du fait que la résolution ne répond pas à un besoin de l'Assemblée générale mais n'est qu'un élément d'une campagne politique orchestrée.

Le gouvernement français rappelle que l'Indonésie avait déjà présenté le 9 novembre 1993, au nom des membres du Mouvement des pays non-alignés, lors de la 48ème session de l'Assemblée générale des Nations unies, un projet de résolution

.../...

(A/C.1/48/L.25) qui aurait demandé à la Cour de répondre à la question: "Y a-t-il des circonstances dans lesquelles le droit international autorise la menace ou l'emploi de l'arme nucléaire?"(3)

Le 19 novembre, la délégation indonésienne déclarait(4) que "pour ne pas affaiblir l'impulsion donnée par les progrès en cours" dans le domaine du désarmement "les pays non alignés ont... décidé de ne pas insister pour qu'une décision définitive soit prise sur le projet de résolution A/C.1/48/L.25...". Ainsi, les promoteurs mêmes d'une demande d'avis consultatif sur les armes nucléaires reconnaissaient qu'une demande de cet ordre risquait d'avoir des effets négatifs sur des négociations en cours.

La résolution 49/75K a été adoptée par l'Assemblée générale le 15 décembre 1994 par 78 voix contre 43 (dont celles de quatre des Etats dotés d'armes nucléaires: France, Etats-Unis, Royaume-Uni et Russie, la Chine n'ayant pas pris part au vote) avec 38 abstentions (5). On ne peut que constater que, l'Organisation des Nations Unies comprenant 185 Etats membres, environ 4O°/° de ceux-ci seulement ont approuvé la résolution.

L'adoption de la résolution avait été précédée:

- d'un vote sur une motion d'ajournement, présentée par la France, et qui avait été repoussée par 68 voix contre 58 avec 26 abstentions (6),

- d'un vote sur une "motion de non-action" concernant un amendement oral, également présenté par la France, et tendant à la suppression, dans la demande adressée

---

3 - A/C.1/48/SR.23, p.9 et rapport de la Ière commission, A/48/676, p.10.

4 - A/C.1/48/SR 3O, p.2.

5 - A/49/PV.90, p.36

6 - *ibid.*, p.21

.../...

à la Cour, des mots "dans les meilleurs délais"; cette motion a été adoptée par 61 voix contre 56, avec 30 abstentions (7).

Auparavant, le 18 novembre, en 1ère commission, le projet avait fait l'objet d'une "motion de non-action" présentée par le Maroc et qui avait recueilli 45 voix contre 67 avec 15 abstentions (8). Il avait alors été voté par 77 voix contre 33, avec 21 abstentions (9).

Ces votes, et leur évolution entre l'examen de la question en 1ère commission et son examen en plénière, font apparaître les réserves de nombre de délégations à l'égard du renouvellement d'une démarche qui avait échoué l'année précédente en raison de son inopportunité.

Il ressort en effet des débats qui ont été consacrés à cette question tant en 1ère commission qu'en séance plénière que la présentation de la résolution en cause a été inspirée par des mobiles politiques étrangers aux préoccupations juridiques et à l'intérêt des travaux de l'Assemblée générale; elle avait pour but d'obtenir de la Cour une réponse déterminée, sans que les auteurs, malgré les avertissements qui leur ont été donnés à ce sujet, prennent en considération les dangers que pourrait présenter une réponse de la Cour à une demande par ailleurs sans objet réel.

La résolution 49/75K a en effet rencontré de vives oppositions, et ceci non seulement de la part d'Etats, comme la France, dotés d'armes nucléaires, mais aussi d'autres Etats, dont des Etats qui appartiennent au groupe même dont les instances politiques ont décidé sa présentation.

---

7 - *ibid.*, p.29

8 - A/C.1/49/PV.24, p.8

9 - *ibid.*, p.14

.../...

Lors de l'adoption de cette résolution, ses partisans n'ont nullement exprimé la préoccupation d'obtenir un avis juridique qui serait, en raison d'événements nouveaux survenus depuis la session précédente, devenu nécessaire à l'accomplissement des fonctions de l'Assemblée générale; ils n'ont, dans leur majorité, invoqué que la nécessité de mettre en oeuvre des décisions prises lors de réunions des ministres du Mouvement des Non-alignés. Il suffit à cet égard de citer l'intervention par laquelle le délégué de l'Indonésie (qui présentait le projet de résolution au nom des co-auteurs) s'est opposé, lors du débat en plénière, à la motion d'ajournement présentée par la délégation française:

> "... je voudrais, au nom de ma délégation, dire que nous apprécions la motion tendant à ne pas prendre de décision sur le projet de résolution, telle qu'elle a été proposée par la délégation française. Cependant, par principe, les pays non alignés appuient les décisions prises aux Réunions ministérielles qui ont eu lieu au Caire en juin 1994 et à New-York le 5 octobre 1994. A cet égard, compte tenu de la nécessité de mettre en oeuvre la décision prise aux réunions interministérielles du Mouvement des Non-alignés, je demande à tous les pays membres du Mouvement de s'opposer à cette motion tendant à ne pas prendre de décision";

ou encore, la déclaration par laquelle ce même délégué s'est opposé à l'amendement de la résolution, proposé par la France et tendant à la suppression, dans la demande d'avis, des mots "dans les meilleurs délais":

> "Pour les raisons que j'ai déjà évoquées, ma délégation voudrait déposer une motion de non-action concernant l'amendement proposé par la France, pour la simple raison que cette décision a été prise à deux réunions ministérielles du Mouvement des Non-alignés"(10).

---

10 - A/49/PV.9O, pp.27 et 28

.../...

On notera qu'ainsi que l'a souligné la délégation d'un des Etats membres de ce mouvement (11), le consensus sur ce sujet s'était érodé au sein des Non-alignés depuis l'adoption des décisions évoquées et qu'un nombre non négligeable de ses membres ont exprimé par leurs votes l'intention que toute décision sur la résolution soit ajournée ou même se sont prononcés contre cette résolution.

Lors des débats en 1ère commission et en plénière, peu de justifications de fond, sinon aucune, n'ont été données de la nécessité d'interroger la Cour. Lorsqu'elles l'ont été, aucune référence à l'accomplissement des fonctions de l'Assemblée générale n'a été faite. Une délégation (12) a exprimé l'opinion qu'un avis de la Cour serait de nature à faciliter, "notamment", des progrès vers le renforcement du Traité sur la non prolifération des armes nucléaires et d'un désarmement total; on peut mentionner aussi les propos, révélateurs du fait que la demande ne correspond qu'à la recherche de moyens à l'appui d'un objectif politique, d'une autre délégation (13) qui, pour justifier l'opportunité du vote du projet de résolution, a déclaré:

> "...nous pensons que les membres de la communauté internationale devraient être en mesure d'étudier tous les moyens permettant d'instaurer un monde exempt de la menace, de l'emploi ou du déploiement d'armes nucléaires et autres armes de destruction massive".

La plupart des intervenants, pourtant, dont l'argumentation, pour certains très développée, n'a reçu aucune réponse, ont souligné le caractère injustifié et l'inopportunité d'une demande d'avis à la Cour, et instamment demandé aux auteurs de ne pas insister sur leur proposition.

11 - Maroc, A/C.1/49/PV.24, p.6

12 - Papouasie-Nouvelle-Guinée, A/C.1/49/PV 24, p.3

13 - République islamique d'Iran, A/C/49/PV.90, p.29

.../...

Plusieurs délégations ont exprimé la crainte que le vote de la résolution apparaisse comme une tentative, préjudiciable au prestige autant de l'Assemblée générale que de la Cour, de faire pression sur cette dernière et d'orienter sa réponse au moment où elle était déjà saisie d'une demande de l'OMS relative à la licéité de l'emploi des armes nucléaires (14).

Il a été souligné que la question soulevée n'était pas d'une nature telle qu'elle puisse être soumise à un examen judiciaire (15), mais qu'elle était essentiellement politique, fort controversée, et qu'elle mettait en cause la politique et la doctrine de sécurité des Etats, et touchait aux droits souverains de ceux-ci (16).

On a aussi observé qu'il n'existait pas de motif d'adresser à la Cour une demande d'avis consultatif au moment précis où la fin de la guerre froide permettait que les négociations sur le désarmement prennent un nouvel élan (17).

On a fait valoir qu'un avis de la Cour ne pourrait avoir aucun effet pratique positif sur les négociations en cours dans le domaine du désarmement, ni, de façon générale, sur la paix et la sécurité internationales (18). Le délégué du Maroc à la 1ère commission déclarait à ce propos:

> "La délégation du Maroc pense qu'un avis consultatif sur une question essentiellement politique qui suscite de nombreuses controverses n'aurait en

---

14 - Maroc, Allemagne, Royaume-Uni, A/C.1/49/PV.24., pp.6, 7, 9.

15 - Australie, A/C.1/49/PV.24, p.15.

16 - Royaume-Uni, Benin, , A/C.1/49/PV.24, pp.9 et 11

17 - Benin, A/C.1/49/PV.24

18 - Royaume-Uni, A/C.1/49/PV.24

.../...

pratique que peu d'effet, les armes n'ayant jamais été limitées ou interdites que par la négociation d'un traité" (19).

et celui du Benin:

"Le Bénin est convaincu que la force et l'efficacité des mesures et accords de désarmement résident plus dans l'acceptation par les parties concernées des conclusions de leurs négociations que dans un quelconque avis juridique qui, en dernière analyse, ne se prononcera que sur un aspect d'un sujet de grande préoccupation pour la communauté internationale.

Le désarmement multilatéral s'inscrivant dans le cadre golbal des activités de l'Assemblée générale où les Etats exercent leur droit souverain, le recours à un avis, même consultatif, constitue un précédent préjudiciable à ce droit" (20).

En outre, a-t-on fait remarquer, un avis de la Cour sur la question posée pourrait avoir, sur les négociations en cours, un effet négatif. Quelle que soit en effet la réponse donnée, elle risquait de donner naissance à de nouvelles oppositions entre les Etats (21), d'introduire l'incertitude sur les bases sur lesquelles étaient entreprises les négociations et de durcir les positions(22). Ce sont du reste ces mêmes considérations qui avaient conduit au retrait en 1993 d'un projet de résolution sur ce sujet (23).

La crainte a été exprimée qu'une réponse de la Cour puisse porter atteinte à la confiance dans certains traités multilatéraux existants sur lesquels les Etats se reposent pour leur sécurité (24)

---

19 - Maroc, A/C.1/49/PV.24 , p.6.

20 - Bénin, A/C.1/49/PV.24, p.11

21 - Royaume-Uni, A/C.1/49/PV.24, p.9

22 - Royaume-Uni, A/C.1/49/PV.24, p.9

23 - Malte, A/C.1/49/PV.24., p.9

24 - Royaume-Uni, A/C.1/49/PV.24, p.9

.../...

Enfin, il a été souligné [25] qu'une telle réponse risquerait de détourner l'attention de l'accumulation d'armes conventionnelles et des programmes clandestins d'acquisition d'armes de destruction massive et de leurs vecteurs qui étaient en cours dans de nombreuses régions du monde.

4 - De l'avis du gouvernement français, la première "raison décisive" qui devrait conduire la Cour à ne pas répondre à la question posée par la résolution 49/75 K est que, sous un habillage juridique hâtif, cette question n'est pas de nature juridique.

Le gouvernement français n'insistera pas à cet égard sur le fait - qui ressort à l'évidence des circonstances de son adoption (v.*supra*, para.3) que la question est posée à des fins politiques. Il sait que les motivations politiques d'une demande d'avis consultatif ne constituent pas en elles-mêmes, d'après la jurisprudence de la Cour, un motif pour ne pas y répondre.

Mais il sait aussi que, conformément aux exigences des articles 96 de la Charte et 65 de son Statut, si la Cour décide de répondre à une question dont les motivations sont politiques, c'est à la condition que la question posée soit, elle-même, une "question juridique" et relève de l'exercice normal de ses fonctions judiciaires. "Si une question n'est pas juridique, la Cour n'a pas de pouvoir discrétionnaire en la matière: elle doit refuser de donner l'avis qui lui est demandé" [26].

---

25 - France, Royaume-Uni, A/C.1/49/PV.24., pp.9 et 10

26 - *C.I.J.*, avis consultatif, 20 juillet 1962, *Certaines dépenses des Nations Unies, Rec.1962*, p.155

.../...

Or la question posée dans la résolution 49/75 K est en soi de nature politique et non juridique, en ce sens qu'elle cherche à obtenir de la Cour que celle-ci, allant clairement au-delà de la volonté bien établie des Etats, se prononce sur des problèmes que ceux-ci n'ont pas traités. On le verra, les Etats ont délibérément évité d'aborder, directement ou indirectement, le problème des armes nucléaires sous l'angle de la licéité de leur emploi ou de la menace de leur emploi. La résolution 49/75 K tend à entraîner la Cour, en la faisant participer à un débat lui-même purement politique, dans un domaine qui ne relève pas de sa fonction judiciaire.

Ces considérations devraient, de l'avis de la France, conduire la Cour à constater que, toutes autres considérations mises à part, elle ne peut pas répondre à la demande d'avis présentée par la résolution 49/75 K.

5 - En outre, la question posée par cette résolution se caractérise par sa généralité et son caractère vague et imprécis, alors que, selon l'article 65 du Statut de la Cour, les demandes d'avis consultatif doivent être formulées "en termes précis".

Ici, il ne s'agit pas de l'interprétation d'un traité déterminé, ou de l'application d'une règle de droit international déterminée, ou même d'une branche déterminée du droit international. Il est demandé à la Cour de se prononcer sur la licéité de la menace ou de l'emploi des armes nucléaires au regard de règles non précisées de ce droit. Ni les règles juridiques qui pourraient éventuellement être en cause ni les éléments de fait qui pourraient éventuellement être pertinents n'ont été indiqués.

A n'en pas douter, cette imprécision est due au fait que les promoteurs de la question posée ne cherchent pas la réponse à un problème juridique réel dont la solution serait nécessaire, ou même simplement utile, à l'exercice des compétences de

.../...

d'orienter la réponse de la Cour, à obtenir de celle-ci qu'elle leur fournisse des éléments qui puissent venir à l'appui de leurs thèses politiques.

On est loin de la situation qui, par exemple, a conduit la Cour à répondre, malgré ses aspects politiques, à la demande d'avis relative aux conditions de l'admission d'un Etat comme membre des Nations unies, en déclarant:

> "Il a été... prétendu que la question posée doit être tenue pour politique et qu'elle échapperait à ce titre, à la compétence de la Cour. La Cour ne peut attribuer un caractère politique à une demande libellée en termes abstraits, qui, en lui déférant l'interprétation d'un texte conventionnel, l'invite à remplir une fonction essentiellement judiciaire"[27].

Dans le même avis, la Cour précisait encore la portée de l'expression "question juridique":

> "Fixer la portée d'un texte conventionnel, dans l'espèce déterminer le caractère (limitatif ou non limitatif) des conditions d'admission qui s'y trouvent énoncées, est un problème d'interprétation et, partant, une question juridique" [28].

Non seulement la question posée se caractérise par son imprécision, mais elle est aussi, comme l'ont souligné certains Etats lors du débat sur l'adoption en 1ère commission de la résolution 49/75K [29], purement abstraite et hypothétique.

---

27 - *C.I.J.* avis consultatif, *Conditions de l'admission d'un Etat comme membre des Nations Unies (art.4)*, *Rec.1947-1948*, p. 61

28 - *ibid*, p.61

29 - Maroc, A.C1/49/PV.24, p.6

.../...

6 - Certes, la Cour peut donner un avis juridique sur une question abstraite. Mais, dans la mesure où la question supposerait des spéculations sur les circonstances dans lesquelles la menace ou l'emploi des armes nucléaires seraient contraires au droit international, la Cour ne pourrait disposer des éléments concrets nécessaires pour y donner une réponse juridique.

Ainsi que la Cour l'a indiqué:

> "Pour être à même de se prononcer sur des questions juridiques, un tribunal doit avoir connaissance des faits correspondants, les prendre en considération et, le cas échéant, statuer à leur sujet"[(30)].

La fonction judiciaire implique l'application de règles juridiques à des situations spécifiques. Alors même qu'elle a à connaître de situations passées ou actuelles, donc dont les éléments factuels sont relativement bien définis ou faciles à établir, la Cour estime devoir faire preuve d'une prudence particulière pour la prise en compte des informations nécessaires à la formation de son jugement [(31)]. Ici, en revanche, une réponse à la question posée à la Cour pourrait entraîner celle-ci dans des spéculations sur les situations largement imprévisibles et très diverses dans lesquelles pourraient être employés différents types d'armes nucléaires, sur les conditions non moins hypothétiques dans lesquelles pourrait avoir lieu cet emploi ou sur les effets, très différenciés, de celui-ci, ou encore sur les circonstances dans lesquelles il pourrait y avoir recours à la menace d'un tel emploi.

---

30 - *C.I.J.*, avis consultatif, 21 juin 1971, *Conséquences juridiques pour les Etats de la présence continue de l'Afrique du Sud en Namibie (Sud-Ouest africain) nonobstant la résolution 276 (1970) du conseil de sécurité, Rec.1971*, p.27

31 - cf par exemple *CIJ*, arrêt du 27 juin 1986, *Affaire des activités militaires et paramilitaires au Nicaragua et contre celui-ci, Rec.1986*, **pp.39 et ss.**

.../...

Il est matériellement impossible que la Cour se livre à un tel examen systématique *a priori*, pour qualifier juridiquement les divers faits ou situations qu'elle aurait envisagés. Le lui demander est, de l'avis du gouvernement français, méconnaître sa fonction judiciaire. La Cour ne peut fonder une appréciation juridique sur des "circonstances" qu'elle devrait elle-même établir.

De plus, compte tenu notamment du fait que certains emplois massifs d'armes conventionnelles peuvent avoir des conséquences aussi graves, voire plus graves, que celles de l'emploi d'armes nucléaires, la Cour estimera sans doute qu'il ne lui appartient pas d'établir des distinctions là où le droit n'en établit pas, et que l'examen auquel on tente de la conduire est juridiquement inapproprié.

7 - En outre, si la Cour est en principe favorable à ce que réponse soit donnée aux demandes d'avis consultatif, c'est dans la mesure où sa réponse "constitue une participation de la Cour (...) à l'action de l'Organisation"[(32)].

Or une réponse donnée par la Cour, loin de constituer une contribution positive à l'accomplissement des fonctions de l'Assemblée générale, et des Nations Unies dans leur ensemble, ne pourrait avoir qu'une incidence négative sur les négociations en cours pour parvenir à un monde plus sûr.

8 - Non seulement la réponse à la question posée ne pourrait être établie qu'à partir d'éléments contestables, mais on voit mal en quoi cette réponse, quelle qu'elle soit, pourrait constituer une "participation de la Cour à l'action" de l'Assemblée générale et aurait "un effet pratique à l'heure actuelle" [(33)]. Ni la résolution 49/75 K ni les débats

32 - *C.I.J.*, avis consultatif, 30 mars 1950, *Interprétation des Traités de paix conclus avec la Bulgarie, la Hongrie et la Roumanie, Rec.1950*, p.71

33 - *CIJ*, avis consultatif, 16 octobre 1975, *Sahara occidental, Rec.1975*, p.37

.../...

qui ont précédé l'adoption de cette résolution ne contiennent la moindre justification de la nécessité ou de l'utilité d'une telle réponse pour l'action propre de l'Assemblée générale. Le motif en est simple: la réponse n'est ni nécessaire ni utile à l'Assemblée (ou à l'Organisation dans son ensemble [(34)]) pour l'accomplissement de ses fonctions.

Il résulte en effet de la Charte elle-même que les décisions de désarmement ainsi que la réglementation des armements relèvent des pouvoirs souverains des Etats. Aux termes du 1er paragraphe de l'article 11 de la Charte:

> "L'Assemblée générale peut étudier les principes généraux de coopération pour le maintien de la paix et de la sécurité internationales, y compris les principes régissant le désarmement et la réglementation des armements, et faire, sur ces principes, des recommandations soit aux Membres de l'Organisation, soit au Conseil de sécurité, soit aux Membres de l'Organisation et au Conseil de sécurité".

et selon l'article 26:

> "... le Conseil de sécurité est chargé... d'élaborer des plans qui seront soumis aux Membres de l'Organisation en vue d'établir un système de réglementation des armements".

---

34 - Il est caractéristique, à cet égard, que, lors de l'adoption par le Conseil de sécurité, le 11 avril 1995, de la résolution 984 (1995) relative aux assurances de sécurité récemment données par les cinq Etats dotés d'armes nucléaires (cf para.32 ci-dessous), aucun représentant n'ait fait mention de la demande d'avis consultatif adressée à la Cour. Bien plus, si les dangers présentés par les armes nucléaires ont été amplement évoqués, la question de leur licéité n'a été qu'effleurée, par un seul représentant, celui de la Malaisie, qui s'est borné à regretter que le paragraphe 9 de la résolution "écarte la question de la légalité de l'emploi d'armes nucléaires car il justifie l'emploi ou la menace de l'emploi d'armes nucléaires en cas de légitime défense". Cette remarque constitue une reconnaissance du fait que l'emploi des armes nucléaires est licite au regard du droit positif(S/PV.3514, p.16).

.../...

La réponse de la Cour, quelle qu'elle soit, n'aurait donc, s'agissant d'un avis consultatif, non obligatoire, et qui ne s'adresse pas aux Etats, juridiquement pas d'effet sur l'action de ceux-ci dans un domaine qui relève de l'exercice de leur souveraineté.

En revanche, l'absence d'un avis consultatif portant sur la licéité de l'emploi ou de la menace d'emploi de telle ou telle arme ne fait nullement obstacle à ce que l'Assemblée générale exerce dans ce domaine le pouvoir de recommandation qui est le sien. On ne peut du reste que constater, s'agissant des armes nucléaires, que cette absence n'a pas empêché jusqu'à présent l'Assemblée d'adopter des recommandations touchant ces armes.

9 - La France, qui est au nombre des Etats qui se sont opposés avec vigueur à l'adoption de la résolution 49/75K, espère que la Cour voudra bien tenir compte, dans son examen de l'opportunité de donner réponse à la demande d'avis qui lui a été adressée, des considérations qui précèdent.

Il ressort à l'évidence des débats qui ont précédé l'adoption de la résolution 49/75, et du texte même de cette résolution (35) que ses auteurs et les Etats qui ont voté en sa faveur n'ont pas recherché l'éclaircissement d'un point juridique, mais qu'ils ont eu pour seul but d'obtenir de la Cour l'affirmation de l'illicéité en toutes circonstances de l'emploi des armes nucléaires et de la menace d'un tel emploi. Il est non moins évident qu'à travers la contestation, sans le moindre fondement juridique, de la licéité de cet emploi, ou de la menace d'un tel emploi, c'est la possession même de ces armes qui est visée, et que la demande, malgré l'aspect général dont on a prétendu la revêtir, est en fait dirigée contre la politique de défense et de sécurité des Etats dotés d'armes nucléaires, dont la situation est pourtant consacrée par plusieurs traités, dont le Traité sur

35 - cf 1er, 3ème, 5ème et 6ème alineas du préambule.

.../...

la non-prolifération. Il est clair enfin que cette démarche n'a pas pour objectif de faciliter l'accomplissement des fonctions de l'Assemblée générale, mais n'est inspirée que par l'espoir de trouver dans une réponse de la Cour un appui à des politiques nationales tendant à un désarmement, non général et complet, mais qui s'appliquerait sélectivement aux seules armes nucléaires.

La France est convaincue qu'une telle utilisation de la procédure consultative n'est pas conforme aux fins pour lesquelles celle-ci a été instituée par la Charte. La procédure consultative est destinée à permettre à certains organes ou institutions de recueillir de la Cour un avis juridique qui les assiste dans l'accomplissement de leurs fonctions. Elle n'a pas pour objet de permettre à tout groupe d'Etats, pussent-ils recueillir au sein de ces organes ou institutions une majorité de votes, de faire interroger la Cour dans le seul but d'obtenir de celle-ci une réponse qui conforte leurs positions politiques nationales.

La France est en outre convaincue, et elle l'a souligné devant l'Assemblée générale, que les efforts déployés pour orienter les délibérations de la Cour ne sont pas respectueux de l'indépendance et du caractère judiciaire de celle-ci.

Enfin, la question posée, en demandant une déclaration de principe normative sur une question que les Etats ont délibérément évité d'aborder dans les instances de négociation où ils auraient pu, s'ils l'avaient estimé opportun, la traiter, tend à faire jouer à la Cour un rôle de législateur, qui n'est pas le sien et qui l'est d'autant moins que, malgré l'habillage juridique que l'on a donné à cette question, le problème soulevé devant la Cour est un problème exclusivement politique, et qui touche à la question essentielle du maintien de la paix.

.../...

La Cour ne peut ignorer, dans sa décision sur l'opportunité d'une réponse, qu'il est impossible d'examiner le problème des armes nucléaires indépendamment de leur objet réel, qui est d'éviter la guerre. Elle ne peut ignorer que, depuis des décennies, la politique de dissuasion a contribué à écarter le risque d'un nouveau conflit mondial.

Or il ne relève pas de la fonction judiciaire de la Cour de se prononcer sur la place de la politique de dissuasion dans le maintien de la paix mondiale, ou de porter directement ou indirectement une appréciation sur les équilibres stratégiques actuels ou sur la politique de défense de tel ou tel Etat, ou de tenter de règlementer, *de lege ferenda*, cette politique. En invitant la Cour à de telles démarches, on risque de compromettre ou discréditer son rôle judiciaire. La question du statut des armes nucléaires et de leur emploi ne peut pas faire, en l'état actuel du droit international, l'objet d'un avis consultatif.

Même si, directement, l'avis demandé ne peut avoir de conséquence juridique ou pratique, il ne serait pas indifférent que la Cour ait cru devoir prendre position sur une question éminemment politique. Quel que soit le sens de sa réponse, celle-ci ne pourrait, comme nombre d'Etats l'ont souligné, avoir que des conséquences négatives sur les négociations internationales en cours visant à assurer, par la maîtrise des armements, la paix et la sécurité du monde.

La France croit donc que la Cour ne devrait pas s'engager dans la voie où on veut l'entraîner, et qu'elle devrait juger inopportune une réponse à la demande qui lui a été adressée.

.../...

II FOND

10 - Bien qu'il espère qu'elles ne seront pas nécessaires, eu égard à ce qui précède, le gouvernement français croit devoir présenter, à titre subsidiaire, des observations sur le fond de la question posée à la Cour.

11 - Le premier problème qui se pose à propos de cette question est celui de son sens et de sa portée exacts.

On le rappelle, la question soumise à la Cour se lit:

"Est-il permis en droit international de recourir à la menace ou à l'emploi d'armes nucléaires en toute circonstance?"

La question, posée en ces termes, appelle une réponse simple et évidente: cette réponse est négative. La menace ou l'emploi des armes nucléaires ne sont pas permis en toute circonstance, puisqu'il est clair qu'ils sont interdits dans tous les cas où le droit international interdit de façon générale la menace ou l'emploi des armes, c'est-à-dire dans les circonstances où cette menace ou cet emploi seraient contraires au principe coutumier du non-recours à la force repris dans l'article 2 paragraphe 4 de la Charte des Nations Unies. Une telle réponse se suffit à elle-même: la question ne demande pas à la Cour d'aller au-delà, et la Cour s'est du reste déjà amplement prononcée dans d'autres aaffaires sur le principe du non-recours à la force et sur son corollaire, le droit de légitime défense.

.../...

Si en revanche, allant au-delà du texte et du sens naturel et ordinaire des termes de la question, on interprétait celle-ci comme invitant la Cour à rechercher s'il existe des circonstances, et lesquelles, où la menace ou l'emploi des armes nucléaires seraient interdits alors que la menace ou l'emploi d'autres armes ne le seraient pas, le gouvernement français démontrera dans la suite de cet exposé que la réponse, pour autant que la Cour s'estimerait en mesure de la donner, ne pourrait être que négative.

12 - Compte tenu du sujet, le gouvernement français doit toutefois apporter, à titre liminaire, quelques précisions sur le cadre de ses observations.

Tout d'abord, la question posée à la Cour : "Est-il permis en droit international de recourir à la menace ou à l'emploi d'armes nucléaires en toutes circonstances?" ne saurait être interprétée comme signifiant que la menace ou l'emploi des armes en cause ne serait admissible que si le droit international le permettait expressément.

Il convient en effet de rappeler le principe fondamental suivant lequel les limitations de souveraineté ne se présument pas [(36)]. Le droit des Etats de déterminer l'organisation de leur défense et de choisir librement, sauf règle prohibitive spéciale, les moyens de défense qui leur conviennent découle de la souveraineté et de l'indépendance des Etats. Ce principe a été consacré par la Cour elle-même lorsqu'elle a déclaré qu'"il n'existe pas en droit international de règles, autres que celles que l'Etat intéressé peut accepter, par traité ou autrement, imposant la limitation du niveau d'armement d'un Etat souverain, ce principe étant valable pour tous les Etats sans distinction[(37)]".

---

36 - *CPJI*, arrêt du 7 septembre 1927, affaire du *Lotus*, *série A, n°10*, p.18.

37 - *C.I.J.*, arrêt du 27 juin 1986, *Affaire des activités militaires et paramilitaires au Nicaragua et contre celui-ci, Rec.1986*, p.135

.../...

La liberté des Etats d'exercer leurs droits ne dépend pas de l'existence de règles permissives, de telles règles n'étant nécessaires que pour apporter des exceptions éventuelles à une règle prohibitive. En l'absence de règle de prohibition "en toute circonstance", l'emploi ou la menace d'emploi des armes nucléaires doivent être considérés comme autorisés, hors les circonstances particulières où ils seraient interdits.

D'autre part, la Cour, si elle décidait de traiter le problème qui lui est soumis, ne pourrait, compte tenu de sa fonction judiciaire, le faire qu'en termes juridiques, et non en termes stratégiques, politiques ou moraux. En particulier, on le répète, il n'est pas et il ne saurait être demandé à la Cour de se prononcer par voie consultative sur les politiques de défense souverainement arrêtées par les Etats. En outre, il n'appartiendrait pas à la Cour de "se lancer dans des appréciations d'ordre militaire" [(38)]

De plus, compte tenu du caractère abstrait de la demande, le gouvernement français comprend que la référence au "droit international" qui figure dans celle-ci ne peut concerner que les règles du droit international applicables à tous les Etats, c'est-à-dire du droit international coutumier. La question posée appelle en effet une réponse valable pour tous les Etats, indépendamment de leurs engagements conventionnels particuliers.

Enfin, le gouvernement français observe que l'appréciation des "circonstances" mentionnées dans la demande ne peut être faite que dans le respect d'une part des compétences souveraines des Etats et d'autre part des pouvoirs et attributions des organes compétents de l'Organisation des Nations Unies, en l'occurrence du Conseil de sécurité.

---

38 - *CIJ*, arrêt du 24 juin 1986, *Affaire des activités militaires et paramilitaires au Nicaragua et contre celui-ci, Rec.1986*, p. 28.

.../...

Les considérations qui suivent montrent, de l'avis du gouvernement français, que, si la Cour estimait pouvoir et devoir répondre à la question posée, elle ne pourrait que constater l'absence d'une interdiction de menace ou d'emploi portant sur les armes nucléaires.

A

13 - Le gouvernement français estime qu'il n'existe, dans le droit international général ou coutumier, aucune règle qui s'opposerait au principe même de l'emploi des armes nucléaires.

Les règles concernant le recours à la force dans les relations internationales n'impliquent aucune prohibition spécifique de la menace ou de l'emploi des armes nucléaires. Il n'existe aucun principe coutumier établissant une telle prohibition. On trouve bien au contraire dans le droit conventionnel des indications montrant que le droit international général admet l'emploi des armes nucléaires, comme le confirment certaines résolutions du conseil de sécurité.

°

° °

14 - En ce qui concerne tout d'abord la menace d'emploi des armes nucléaires, il est clair que, la seule catégorie de menace régie par le droit international général étant celle de recours à la force, interdite par la règle coutumière reprise dans le paragraphe 2 de l'article 4 de la Charte, c'est sous cet angle que la question doit être examinée.

.../...

15 - On notera tout d'abord que les auteurs de la question posée à la Cour n'ont pas défini ce que recouvrait, selon eux, la notion de menace d'emploi des armes nucléaires, ni au regard de quelles règles de ce droit la licéité de cette menace devrait être appréciée.

L'article 2 paragraphe 4 de la Charte ne contient pas de définition de la notion de "menace" en elle-même et la pratique n'a pas permis de dégager une telle définition. On peut cependant considérer que l'idée de "menace" au sens du principe du non-recours à la force implique celle de coercition pour amener un Etat à une conduite ou à des actes différents de ceux qu'il pouvait librement choisir.

Quoi qu'il en soit, le paragraphe 4 de l'article 2 de la Charte prohibe la menace de recours à la force "soit contre l'intégrité territoriale ou l'indépendance politique de tout Etat, soit de toute autre manière incompatible avec les buts des Nations Unies". Il est donc indispensable, pour apprécier la licéité d'un recours à la menace d'emploi de la force, de se référer aux objectifs de la menace et à la nature de l'action dans laquelle elle serait mise à exécution. Cette réglementation s'applique à la menace d'emploi des armes nucléaires comme à toute menace d'emploi des armes.

En particulier, l'annonce par un Etat que, s'il est l'objet d'une agression armée, il fera usage de ses armes, et notamment, le cas échéant, de ses armes nucléaires, ne saurait être considérée comme une "menace de recours à la force" interdite par le droit international. D'autre part, l'existence de systèmes militaires défensifs, qui est conforme au droit international et en particulier à la Charte des Nations Unies, et dont la licéité a expressément été reconnue par la Cour dans l'*affaire des activités militaires et paramilitaires au Nicaragua et contre celui-ci* (39), implique en elle-même une "menace",0 de nature dissuasive.

---

39 - cf *supra*, para.12

.../...

Considérer qu'il y a là une "menace" interdite par le principe du non-recours à la force serait jeter le doute sur toutes les armées du monde. S'agissant plus particulièrement des armes nucléaires, le fait que le protocole n°II au Traité de Tlatelolco pour l'interdiction des armes nucléaires en Amérique latine, en date du 14 février 1967, et le protocole 2 au Traité de Rarotonga sur la zone dénucléarisée du Pacifique Sud, en date du 6 août 1985 [(40)] demandent aux Puissances dotées d'armes nucléaires, en cette qualité [(41)], de ne pas recourir à la menace ou à l'emploi d'armes nucléaires contre les parties contractantes montre à l'évidence que la possession de ces armes pour les besoins de sa défense n'est pas en soi une "menace" interdite par le principe consacré par le paragraphe 4 de l'article 2 de la Charte.

En revanche, dès lors qu'une menace de recours à la force tend à un objectif contraire à l'article 2 paragraphe 4 - étant rappelé que celui-ci ne peut être lu qu'en relation avec son corollaire, l'article 51, et le chapitre VII de la Charte - cette menace est illicite, et ceci indépendamment des moyens qui seraient employés si la menace était mise à exécution.

On ne peut donc que constater que, dans certaines circonstances, la menace d'emploi des armes nucléaires pourrait, comme pour toute autre arme, être constitutive d'un acte contraire au droit international général. Il en serait ainsi si cette menace tombait sous le coup de l'interdiction coutumière de la menace de recours à la force armée reprise dans l'article 2 para.4 de la Charte. Mais cette illicéité tiendrait aux

40 - La France n'est pas partie à cet instrument.

41 - L'article 28 para.1 c) du Traité de Tlatelolco pose comme condition de l'entrée en vigueur de celui-ci la signature du protocole n°II "par toutes les Puissances qui possèdent des armes nucléaires"

.../...

circonstances et aux objectifs recherchés par la menace, non au fait que celle-ci impliquerait des armes nucléaires.

L'existence de traités (les protocoles au Traité de Tlatelolco et au Traité de Rarotonga, susmentionnés), dont la portée est limitée à la fois géographiquement et quant aux Etats pouvant s'en réclamer, qui interdisent expressément la menace d'emploi des armes nucléaires, confirment que cette menace n'est pas en soi juridiquement interdite.

16 - La même analyse vaut pour l'emploi des armes nucléaires. Il est clair que dans certaines circonstances l'emploi des armes, dont les armes nucléaires, pourrait être constitutif d'un acte d'agression.

Toutefois, la qualification même de l'attaque armée en tant qu'acte d'agression ne résulterait pas alors de l'arme employée mais des circonstances et des caractéristiques de cette attaque en elle-même.

On notera du reste que la résolution de l'Assemblée générale des Nations Unies n°3314 (XXIX) du 14 décembre 1974, "définition de l'agression", si elle cite le bombardement parmi les actes qui, sous réserve de l'appréciation du conseil de sécurité, remplissent les conditions d'un acte d'agression, ne propose aucune indication sur les armes avec lesquelles pourrait être effectué ce bombardement et, en conséquence, ne vise pas spécifiquement les armes nucléaires.

En tout état de cause, comme le reconnaît la résolution 3314 (XXIX), il appartient au Conseil de sécurité, en vertu de l'article 39 de la Charte, de constater un

.../...

acte d'agression, et cette constatation est effectuée compte tenu des "circonstances pertinentes", qui ne peuvent, par définition, être déterminées par avance.

17 - L'article 2 paragraphe 4 ne saurait, on l'a dit, être lu indépendamment de l'article 51 de la Charte qui réserve expressément l'exercice, "jusqu'à ce que le conseil de sécurité ait pris les mesures nécessaires pour maintenir la paix et la sécurité internationales", du "droit naturel de légitime défense individuelle ou collective" en cas d'agression armée, auquel "aucune disposition de la ... Charte ne porte atteinte".

On sait que les domaines réglementés par le droit coutumier de la légitime défense et l'article 51 de la Charte ne se recouvrent pas exactement, que les règles coutumières et la règle conventionnelle n'ont pas exactement le même contenu et que ces règles conservent une existence juridique distincte (42). Mais ni le droit coutumier applicable à la légitime défense individuelle et collective ni l'article 51 de la Charte ne règlementent ni ne limitent les moyens militaires par lesquels un Etat peut exercer son droit naturel de légitime défense.

Certains, pour étayer leurs thèses selon lesquelles l'emploi des armes nucléaires serait prohibé, croient pouvoir avancer que cet emploi ne pourrait être conforme à la règle coutumière selon laquelle la légitime défense "ne justifierait que des mesures proportionnées à l'agression armée subie, et nécessaires pour y riposter"(43).

Ces affirmations sont sans aucun fondement et constituent de simples pétitions de principe. L'évaluation de la nécessité et de la proportionnalité des mesures de riposte

---

42 - *CIJ*, arrêt du 27 juin 1986, *Affaire des activités militaires et paramilitaires au Nicaragua et contre celui-ci*, *Rec. 1986*, p.94 et ss

43 - *C.I.J.*, arrêt du 27 juin 1986, *Affaire des activités militaires et paramilitaires au Nicaragua et contre celui-ci, Rec.1986*, p.94)

.../...

à l'agression , généralement acceptées comme liées à la notion de légitime défense [44], est essentiellement tributaire des circonstances et ne peut relever d'interdictions spécifiques établies a priori. Elle dépend de la nature de l'agression, de son ampleur, du risque qu'elle fait courir et de l'adaptation de la réplique au but défensif recherché, c'est-à-dire de la capacité des moyens employés de faire échec à l'agression. Ce critère de proportionnalité ne permet pas en lui-même d'exclure par principe l'utilisation, que ce soit en riposte ou en premier emploi, de quelque arme déterminée que ce soit, et notamment de l'arme nucléaire, dès lors que cet emploi vise à faire face à une agression, et qu'il apparaît comme le moyen adéquat pour faire face à celle-ci. Toute autre conclusion viderait la notion même de légitime défense de son sens et de sa portée. L'établissement *a priori* d'une réglementation en ce domaine ne relèverait en tout cas pas d'une instance judiciaire.

La France appelle l'attention sur le fait que, comme pour l'agression, l'appréciation, dans chaque cas, des divers éléments d'une situation dont il est saisi en vertu de l'article 51 relève, aux termes mêmes de la Charte, de la compétence du Conseil de sécurité. Toutefois chaque Etat souverain, avant que le Conseil ait pris les mesures nécessaires pour maintenir la paix et la sécurité internationales, dispose également de sa propre liberté d'appréciation. Le Conseil de sécurité pourrait, s'il l'estimait nécessaire à l'exercice dans un cas particulier des compétences qui lui sont dévolues par la Charte et qu'il détient à l'exclusion de tout autre organe ou organisation, demander à la Cour un avis consultatif pour éclairer son action. Mais, pour les motifs déjà indiqués, la Cour pourrait, même dans une telle hypothèse, être conduite à estimer impossible de donner réponse à une telle question, si celle-ci lui était présentée en des termes aussi vagues et imprécis.

---

44 - même arrêt, *Rec.1986*, p.1O3

.../...

En tout état de cause, la France est convaincue que la Cour, si elle estimait devoir émettre un avis dans l'affaire présente, ne pourrait que constater qu'aucune règle de droit international général applicable à la légitime défense ne s'oppose à l'emploi des armes nucléaires dans le cadre de celle-ci et en conformité avec les règles générales qui la concernent.

°

° °

18 - Il est clair que le droit international général relatif à la menace et à l'emploi de la force dans les relations internationales n'implique aucune prohibition spécifique de l'emploi des armes nucléaires ou de la menace de cet emploi. On ne peut également que constater l'absence d'autre règle coutumière interdisant l'emploi des armes nucléaires.

19 - Il serait vain de tenter de déduire l'existence d'un principe de prohibition de l'emploi des armes nucléaires des traités qui peuvent concerner directement ou indirectement cet emploi ou des résolutions que l'Assemblée générale a adoptées sur ce sujet. Il serait non moins impossible de soutenir que ce principe pourrait avoir valeur coutumière.

20 - Les régimes conventionnels qui contiennent des dispositions relatives aux armes nucléaires n'obligent que les Etats qui sont parties aux traités les instituant et sont sans effet à l'égard des Etats tiers. Ils concernent l'installation, le placement, la détention, le transfert, la fabrication, les essais ou, dans certains cas, la destruction de ces armes. Ils ne traitent qu'exceptionnellement de l'emploi de celles-ci. Lorsqu'ils comportent, de la part des Etats dotés d'armes nucléaires qui y souscrivent, une

.../...

renonciation à cet emploi ou à la menace d'un tel emploi (45), ce n'est qu'à l'égard d'un cercle déterminé d'Etats, et sous des conditions précises. Ils ne contiennent aucune condamnation juridique des armes nucléaires.

Ces simples constatations suffisent à établir qu'ils ne correspondent pas à une règle de droit international général ou coutumier, préexistante ou en voie de formation, qui prohiberait l'emploi ou la menace d'emploi des armes nucléaires.

21 - Un éventuel principe coutumier d'illicéité de l'emploi des armes nucléaires ne saurait non plus être tiré d'un texte tel que le protocole n°I du 8 juin 1977 additionnel aux conventions de Genève de 1949.

Tout d'abord, en tant qu'instrument conventionnel, ce texte ne lie que les Etats qui y sont parties, sous les réserves dont ces Etats ont cru devoir assortir leur ratification ou adhésion, et il n'est pas opposable aux Etats qui ne l'ont pas accepté. Il n'est en particulier pas opposable à la France, qui non seulement ne l'a pas signé, mais même a indiqué, lors de son adoption par la conférence diplomatique sur la réaffirmation et le développement du droit international humanitaire, qui s'est tenue à Genève de 1974 à 1977, qu'elle ne s'opposerait pas à un consensus mais qu'en raison des réserves que lui inspirait le texte - indépendamment (cf ci-dessous) de tout problème d'applicabilité aux armes nucléaires - elle ne se considèrerait pas comme liée par ce consensus. Ce protocole ne saurait donc en tout état de cause être considéré comme reflètant en lui-même l'"*opinio juris*" de la France, qui est, en l'affaire présente, en sa qualité d'Etat doté

45 - Protocole n°II au Traité de Tlatelolco pour l'interdiction des armes nucléaires en Amérique latine, 14 février 1967; Protocole II au Traité de Rarotonga sur la zone dénucléarisée du Pacifique Sud, 6 août 1985, susvisés.

.../...

d'armes nucléaires, un des "Etats particulièrement intéressés" au sens de la jurisprudence de la Cour. (46)

En outre, les circonstances mêmes de la négociation de ce protocole excluent que l'on puisse rechercher dans les règles qu'il pose ou confirme une interdiction d'emploi de l'arme nucléaire. Dans sa note introductive aux projets de protocoles, le Comité international de la Croix-rouge avait en effet précisé que "les problèmes relatifs aux armes atomiques, bactériologiques et chimiques font l'objet d'accords internationaux ou de délibérations entre les gouvernements, et le CICR, en présentant ses projets de protocoles, n'entend donc pas les aborder". C'est sur ce principe que s'est déroulée la conférence, comme en font foi les déclarations de certains Etats, dont la France (47), au cours de la conférence.

Le fait que la conférence n'a pris en considération que les armes conventionnelles ressort également de la création en son sein d'une commission *ad hoc* sur "les armes conventionnelles". On notera que, deux délégations ayant proposé la suppression du mot "conventionnelle" dans le mandat de ladite commission, en vue d'étendre sa compétence aux armes nucléaires, bactériologiques et chimiques, cette proposition a été repoussée, le texte du mandat, avec le mot "conventionnelle" ayant été

---

46 - *C.I.J.*, arrêt du 20 février 1969, *Affaires du Plateau continental de la mer du Nord (République fédérale d'Allemagne/ Danemark; République fédérale d'Allemagne/Pays-Bas) Rec.1969*, p.43

47 - Lors de l'adoption du protocole, le 8 juin 1977, le représentant de la France a notamment déclaré: "La délégation française tient à préciser très nettement que son gouvernement ne saurait admettre en aucun cas que les dispositions du Protocole I puissent porter atteinte au "droit naturel de légitime défense" que la France entend exercer dans sa plénitude conformément à l'article 51 de la Charte des Nations unies, ni que les dispositions du Protocole puissent lui interdire l'emploi d'aucune arme spécifique qu'elle juge nécessaire à sa défense. Le Gouvernement français a pris acte dès 1973 de ce que le CICR n'avait pas inclus dans ses projets une réglementation des armes atomiques. En participant à l'élaboration des dispositions des Protocoles additionnels, le Gouvernement français n'a donc pris en considération que les conflits menés avec des armements conventionnels. Il tient par suite à marquer qu'il considère pour sa part que les règles desdits protocoles ne s'appliquent pas à l'emploi des armes nucléaires" (Actes VII, p.199, CDDH/SR.56, par 3).

.../...

adopté par 68 voix contre 0 avec 10 abstentions. De plus, par sa résolution 22, elle a recommandé la convocation d'une conférence "en vue d'aboutir a) à des accords portant interdiction ou limitation de l'emploi d'armes conventionnelles spécifiques, y compris celles qui peuvent être considérées comme excessivement nocives ou frappant sans discrimination compte tenu de considérations humanitaires et d'ordre militaire; et b) à un accord sur un mécanisme conçu pour réviser de tels accords et examiner les propositions d'accords nouveaux du même genre".

La France, lorsqu'elle a adhéré en 1984 au protocole n°II relatif à la protection des victimes des conflits armés non internationaux a néanmoins estimé ne pas pouvoir devenir partie au protocole n°I, notamment parce qu'elle n'avait pas discerné, lors de la conférence, un consensus suffisant sur la portée exacte des obligations qu'assumeraient en matière de dissuasion les Etats qui accepteraient d'être liés par cet instrument (48).

Elle ne peut cependant que constater que plusieurs Etats ont assorti leur signature ou leur ratification de déclarations d'où il ressort que les règles introduites par le protocole n'interdisent ni ne règlementent l'emploi des armes non conventionnelles, et en particulier des armes nucléaires. Ces déclarations n'ont, à sa connaissance fait l'objet d'aucune contestation.

Ainsi, le problème de l'emploi des armes nucléaires a été délibérément exclu du plus récent effort général de codification et de développement du droit humanitaire.

---

48 - Une explication de vote, écrite, par laquelle l'Inde a indiqué qu'elle s'était jointe au consensus sur l'actuel article 35 "étant entendu que les règles fondamentales contenues dans cet article s'appliqueront à toutes les catégories d'armes, à savoir les armes nucléaires, bactériologiques, chimiques, conventionnelles, ou toute autre catégorie d'armes (Actes VI/CCDH SR.39, p.114) et les commentaires doctrinaux ci-dessus évoqués lui paraissaient susceptibles de créer une ambiguïté sur un point essentiel.

.../...

On voit aussi que les Etats participant à la conférence ont estimé que les règles figurant dans le protocole ne pouvaient pas en elles-mêmes suffire à établir l'illicéité de l'emploi d'armes spécifiques, à quelque type qu'elles appartiennent.

22 - L'Assemblée générale des Nations unies a adopté certaines résolutions affirmant soit dans leur dispositif, soit plus souvent, au cours des dernières années, sous forme de "rappel" figurant dans leur préambule, l'illicéité de principe de l'emploi des armes nucléaires: cet emploi constituerait, affirment ces résolutions, une violation de la Charte des Nations unies, et un crime contre l'humanité [(49)].

On ne peut envisager que ces résolutions puissent en elles-mêmes être la source d'une règle juridique. En dehors du fait que les résolutions de l'Assemblée n'ont pas valeur juridique contraignante, les conditions d'adoption de celles-ci, par des votes comportant une très forte opposition minoritaire, dont celle des Etats les plus intéressés, avec une importante abstention, empêcheraient en tout état de cause de les considérer comme déclaratoires de règles juridiques préexistantes et même comme expression probante d'une *opinio juris*, fût-ce de la part des Etats qui les ont soutenues [(50)].

23 - On rappellera les conditions de formation de la coutume telles que définies par la jurisprudence de la Cour. Ainsi que l'a déclaré celle-ci:

> "La substance du droit international coutumier doit être recherchée en premier lieu dans la pratique effective et l'*opinio juris* des Etats, même si les

---

49 - Parmi ces résolutions, celles qui sont le plus souvent évoquées par les partisans d'une illicéité de principe de l'emploi des armes nucléaires sont la résolution 1653 (XVI) "déclaration sur l'interdiction de l'emploi des armes nucléaires et thermonucléaires" du 24 novembre 1961 et la résolution 2936 (XXVII) du 29 novembre 1972. Elles ont été suivies d'une série de résolutions (Rés.33/71 B, 35/152 D, 36/92 I, 45/59 B , 46/37 D, 47/53 C et 48/76 B) déclarant que l'emploi des armes nucléaires serait illicite et lançant aux Etats un appel en faveur de la conclusion d'une convention interdisant la menace et l'emploi de ces armes.

50 - cf para.29 ci-dessous

.../...

conventions multilatérales peuvent avoir un rôle important à jouer en enregistrant et définissant les règles dérivées de la coutume ou même en les développant"[(51)].

Le fait que la pratique soit générale a "un rôle essentiel" dans la formation de la coutume, et il est indispensable que les Etats "qui sont particulièrement intéressés" y participent [(52)]. En l'espèce présente, une "pratique" en la matière ne pourrait venir que des Etats auxquels le statut d'Etats dotés d'armes nucléaires a été reconnu.

Le gouvernement français entend montrer que la pratique et l'*opinio juris* de ces Etats et l'*opinio juris* des Etats qui ne disposent pas de ces armes attestent l'inexistence d'une règle coutumière d'interdiction de l'emploi des armes nucléaires. Bien plus, la pratique et l'*opinio juris* des uns et des autres vont dans le sens de l'inexistence d'une telle règle.

24 - S'agissant de la pratique des Etats dotés d'armes nucléaires, on constate, et l'on ne peut évidemment que s'en féliciter, qu'aucun d'entre eux n'a fait usage de ces armes depuis le dernier conflit mondial. On ne saurait cependant en déduire l'existence d'une pratique de "non-emploi" fondée sur la conviction de se conformer à une obligation juridique, et y voir le signe d'une coutume établie ou en voie de formation. Tout d'abord, pour que cette abstention puisse être ainsi considérée, il aurait fallu que les Etats en cause se trouvent confrontés à une situation réunissant les conditions qu'eux-mêmes mettent à l'emploi de leurs armes nucléaires; or ce cas ne s'est pas présenté, grâce, au moins en partie, aux effets de la politique de dissuasion.

---

51 - *C.I.J.*, arrêt du 3 juin 1985, *affaire du plateau continental (Jamahiriya arabe libyenne/Malte), Rec. 1985*, p.29-30, par.27; *C.I.J.*, *affaire des activités militaires au Nicaragua et contre celui-ci, Rec.1986*, p.97, par.183

52 - *C.I.J.*, arrêt du 20 février 1969, *Affaires du Plateau continental de la mer du Nord (République fédérale d'Allemagne/Danemark; République fédérale d'Allemagne/Pays-Bas), Rec.1969*, p.43

.../...

En tout état de cause, l'affirmation officielle et répétée de cette politique, de la part d'Etats qui sont manifestement "les plus intéressés" à la question, l'opposition desdits Etats aux résolutions susmentionnées de l'Assemblée générale ainsi qu'à la résolution 49/75 K elle-même, qui tend à mettre en doute la licéité de ces armes, et donc leur politique de défense et de sécurité, les précisions ou conditions dont ils ont assorti les engagements conventionnels de non-emploi qu'ils ont souscrits (53) montrent à l'évidence que leur pratique et leur *opinio juris* sont fondées sur la licéité de l'utilisation des armes en cause et de la menace de leur utilisation, dans les circonstances où le droit international admet le recours à la force et à la menace de la force, et donc qu'il n'existe pas de règle coutumière qui en établirait l'illicéité.

On verra (*infra*, para.29 et 30) que la pratique de nombre d'Etats non dotés d'armes nucléaires va également dans le sens de la licéité des armes nucléaires et de leur emploi éventuel.

25 - S'agissant de l'*opinio juris* des Etats, il est évident qu'il n'y a pas d'opinion générale selon laquelle l'emploi des armes nucléaires serait illicite ou devrait être spécifiquement rendu tel.

Comme le note l'"Etude d'ensemble des armes nucléaires" mise à jour en septembre 1990 à la suite de la résolution 43/75 N (1988) de l'Assemblée générale (54): "Bien qu'un vaste débat soit en cours, dans différentes enceintes, on ne note aucune convergence d'idées au sujet des aspects juridiques de la possession d'armes nucléaires et de leur utilisation en tant que moyens de guerre".

---

53 - La France a assorti sa signature du Protocole II du Traité de Tlatelolco d'une déclaration indiquant notamment: "Le Gouvernement français interprète l'engagement énoncé à l'article 3 du Protocole comme ne faisant pas obstacle au plein exercice du droit de légitime défense confirmé par l'article 51 de la Charte des Nations Unies".

54 - Document A/45/373 du 18 septembre 1990, para. 506.

.../...

26 - La France n'ignore pas l'existence de certaines thèses, développées jusqu'à présent essentiellement sur un plan purement doctrinal, souvent à l'appui d'objectifs politiques ou moraux d'organisations non gouvernementales ou associations nationales opposées à l'arme nucléaire et qui, ne pouvant trouver dans le droit international général de normes positives prohibant ces armes, cherchent à démontrer l'existence d'un principe juridique d'interdiction de leur emploi en bâtissant un raisonnement à partir de règles relevant de diverses branches spécialisées du droit international.

Selon ces thèses, qui ont trouvé leur expression dans certains des exposés soumis à la Cour à propos de la demande d'avis présentée par l'Organisation mondiale de la Santé, les règles dont on propose la prise en compte pourraient, sans mentionner directement les armes en cause, s'appliquer à elles par implication ou par extension.

L'idée est ainsi avancée que certaines règles concernant le droit humanitaire et le droit de la guerre, et même les droits de l'homme, ou le droit de l'environnement impliqueraient interdiction de l'emploi des armes nucléaires. S'agissant des droits de l'homme, l'emploi des armes nucléaires irait à l'encontre du droit à la vie, ou même à l'encontre du respect de la vie privée, inscrits dans certaines conventions relatives aux droits de l'homme. S'agissant de l'environnement, cet emploi irait à l'encontre d'un principe de protection de l'environnement déduit de diverses conventions, résolutions ou déclarations. S'agissant du "*jus in bello*", certaines règles du droit des conflits armés impliqueraient interdiction de cet emploi.

27 - Le gouvernement français ne croit pas qu'il soit nécessaire de discuter longuement des arguments avancés à l'appui des thèses selon lesquelles on pourrait

.../...

trouver dans les normes relatives à la protection des droits de l'homme ou dans le droit de l'environnement un fondement pour la reconnaissance d'une prohibition de principe de l'emploi des armes nucléaires. Il est en effet évident que ces arguments n'ont et ne peuvent avoir en l'espèce aucune pertinence.

Aucune prohibition d'emploi des armes nucléaires ne peut être déduite des principes relatifs aux droits de l'homme, et en particulier du droit à la vie. La situation de conflit armé entraîne nécessairement des atteintes à la vie, et les textes conventionnels qui consacrent le droit à la vie ne lui reconnaissent pas un caractère absolu. On mentionnera, à cet égard, le paragraphe 2 de l'article 15 de la convention européenne des droits de l'homme, du 4 novembre 1950, qui apporte, pour les actes licites de guerre, une exception explicite au principe du droit à la vie posé par l'article 2 de la convention. Ainsi que le montrent les travaux préparatoires, l'article 6 du Pacte des Nations Unies relatif aux droits civils et politiques doit être interprété dans le même sens.

Comme on le sait, l'idée de protection de l'environnement en tant que tel est en fait récente. Cette protection constitue un objectif politique et non un principe juridiquement établi. Elle s'organise peu à peu dans le cadre de conventions spécifiques.

Il serait pour le moins hasardeux de prétendre établir l'existence, à l'heure actuelle, de principes du droit international général ou coutumier, reconnus comme tels ou en voie de formation, concernant la protection de l'environnement en temps de conflit armé. On ne saurait en tout état de cause en déduire la prohibition d'emploi de certaines armes, quelles qu'elles soient.

Certains croient pouvoir trouver une base juridique adéquate à l'appui de leur théorie selon laquelle l'emploi des armes nucléaires serait illicite au regard du droit de l'environnement dans des textes comme la déclaration de Stockholm adoptée le 16 juin

.../...

1972 par la Conférence des Nations Unies sur l'environnement ou la déclaration de Rio de Janeiro adoptée le 14 juin 1992 par la Conférence des Nations Unies sur l'environnement et le développement.

Cette thèse n'est pas acceptable. Outre le fait que ces textes n'ont évidemment pas valeur juridique obligatoire, et n'ont pas davantage acquis une portée coutumière, ils ne concernent à aucun degré, même indirectement, la licéité de l'emploi des armes nucléaires.

Aucun indice de l'existence, en droit international général ou coutumier, d'une interdiction ou d'une limitation de l'emploi des armes nucléaires ne saurait non plus être recherché dans les conventions relatives au droit de l'environnement ou contenant des dispositions concernant l'environnement (55), qui ne concernent pas davantage la conduite des opérations militaires et la réglementation des armes. Outre le fait que le caractère conventionnel de ces textes les exclut du champ de la question posée à la Cour, il est bien évident que les Etats dotés d'armes nucléaires ou certains d'entre eux n'y seraient pas devenus parties s'ils avaient pu les considérer comme allant à l'encontre de leur politique déclarée dans un secteur touchant à leur sécurité même.

De façon générale, la France observe que la recherche systématique, et du reste vaine, d'éventuelles possibilités de mise en cause de la licéité de l'emploi des armes nucléaires dans tous les secteurs du droit qui pourraient, selon certains, avoir un rapport, si lointain soit-il, avec la question, non seulement est un signe du caractère partisan de l'entreprise, mais montre également que ses auteurs sont conscients de la fragilité de leurs thèses.

---

55 - Par exemple, la convention pour la protection de la couche d'ozone, Vienne, 22 mars 1985; ou la convention-cadre des Nations Unies sur les changements climatiques, New-York, 9 mai 1992; ou la convention sur la diversité biologique, Rio de Janeiro, 22 mai 1992; ou la convention de l'UNESCO pour la protection du patrimoine mondial culturel et naturel, 16 novembre 1972.

.../...

Or une telle entreprise, qui est faite à propos de l'emploi des armes nucléaires, mais qui pourrait l'être plus tard à propos de n'importe quel aspect de l'action des Etats, n'est pas sans danger, dans la mesure où elle tend à introduire de fâcheuses incertitudes dans des secteurs importants des relations internationales.

28 - Le gouvernement de la République française ne croit pas non plus nécessaire, dans le cadre des présentes observations, de discuter en détail de la thèse qui prétend trouver dans le droit relatif aux conflits armés des normes juridiques d'où serait susceptible d'être déduite une interdiction d'emploi des armes nucléaires.

Les tenants de cette thèse prennent en particulier appui à cet égard - sans se préoccuper du reste de déterminer lesquels ont un caractère coutumier et lesquels ont un caractère conventionnel - sur divers règles ou principes énoncés dans le protocole I du 8 juin 1977 additionnel aux conventions de Genève de 1977, et notamment "l'interdiction de l'emploi d'armes, projectiles et matières ainsi que des méthodes de guerre de nature à causer des maux superflus" (art.35, para.1 du protocole), ou l'interdiction d'emploi d'armes ou moyens de guerre susceptibles de causer "des dommages étendus, graves et durables à l'environnement naturel" (art.35, para.2), ou la nécessité d'établir une distinction entre les objectifs militaires, d'une part, et la population civile et ses biens de l'autre, ou l'interdiction des attaques sans discrimination, au sens de l'article 51 du protocole, ou le critère de proportionnalité posé par cet article.

Le gouvernement français récuse formellement le raisonnement ainsi proposé. Outre le fait que ce n'est pas selon cette procédure que sont traditionnellement établies les prohibitions d'emploi des armes, la méthode est aléatoire, et ne pourrait en tout cas pas aboutir au résultat souhaité par ses auteurs.

.../...

La thèse avancée suppose qu'il soit établi, selon les méthodes admises de détermination de la coutume, que les différentes règles évoquées correspondent bien toutes à des principes coutumiers reconnus comme tels et, dans l'affirmative, que soit défini le contenu exact de ces principes.

Or ce contenu, avec l'évolution de la conception même de la nature de la guerre internationale dans les conflits majeurs ou la survenance d'armements et de méthodes de combat nouvelles, comme le bombardement aérien, ainsi que les réalités des conflits, en particulier du second conflit mondial, a fait l'objet, et fait encore, l'objet de discussions doctrinales.

A cet égard, le gouvernement français doit souligner à nouveau que les principes du droit international coutumier applicables dans les conflits armés ne sauraient être recherchés dans le protocole I de 1977. Outre les motifs évoqués ci-dessus (*supra*, para.21), si on ne peut contester que certaines dispositions du protocole trouvent leur inspiration dans des principes du droit international coutumier, il est flagrant qu'elles en constituent à d'autres égards un développement. Le titre même de la conférence au cours de laquelle cet instrument a été élaboré: "conférence diplomatique sur la réaffirmation et le développement du droit international humanitaire applicable dans les conflits armés" en témoigne. Le caractère nouveau de certaines de ses dispositions est trop évident pour que l'on s'y attarde (il en est ainsi, par exemple, pour les dispositions des articles 35 et 55 relatives à la protection de l'environnement, et aussi de certaines interdictions de représailles). Mais même celles de ses dispositions qui sont fondées sur des principes généraux de base du droit existant assortissent ceux-ci de conditions et de modalités non prévues par ce dernier. En tout état de cause, le protocole ne saurait être considéré comme ayant "supplanté" le droit international coutumier ni comme la source de règles qui se seraient intégrées à l'ensemble du droit international général et seraient maintenant acceptées à ce titre par l'*opinio juris* des Etats.

.../...

Il faudrait ensuite, une fois dégagés et définis les principes coutumiers de base dont on considèrerait qu'ils peuvent être éventuellement pertinents, établir qu'ils seraient susceptibles d'être appliqués à l'emploi des armes en général et des armes nucléaires en particulier, et que les Etats, en les établissant, ont entendu qu'ils s'y appliquent.

Il faudrait enfin, une fois identifiées les règles par hypothèse applicables à ces armes, établir qu'il en ressort une règle d'interdiction de leur emploi, soit de façon générale, soit selon les circonstances.

Etant donné le caractère nécessairement abstrait et général des règles éventuellement formulées, et la diversité et l'imprévisibilité de l'objet auquel elles auraient été reconnues applicables, une conclusion relative à la licéité ou à l'illicéité de l'emploi des armes nucléaires impliquerait non une constatation, mais une construction du droit.

En outre, il n'existe pas, chez les Etats, une *opinio juris* selon laquelle une interdiction d'emploi des armes nucléaires découlerait des principes ou règles du droit international, quels qu'ils soient.

29 - S'il est évident que les Etats dotés d'armes nucléaires qui pratiquent la politique de dissuasion considèrent la menace ou l'emploi éventuel de ces armes comme permis par le droit en vigueur, il est non moins évident que, parmi les Etats qui ne disposent pas des armes en cause, il n'existe pas d'*opinio juris* générale selon laquelle un tel emploi serait illicite. Bien plus, on le verra (*infra*, para.31 et 32) la pratique de nombre d'entre eux va dans le sens de la licéité de ces armes et de leur emploi éventuel.

.../...

Certains invoquent cependant, comme prétendue preuve d'une *opinio juris* générale selon laquelle l'emploi des armes nucléaires serait illicite, les résolutions sus-évoquées dans lesquelles l'Assemblée générale a porté des condamnations contre cet emploi. En réalité, lesdites résolutions prouvent plutôt que ceux mêmes qui posent en principe que cette utilisation est interdite ont, pour le moins, des incertitudes sur l'existence de cette interdiction en tant que règle juridique s'imposant aux Etats. Le simple fait, du reste, qu'ils interrogent la Cour sur ce point invalide la prétention déclaratoire de ces résolutions.

Au surplus, tout en affirmant une règle d'interdiction de l'utilisation des armes nucléaires, ces résolutions ont pour objectif opérationnel l'ouverture de négociations pour l'établir. Ainsi, par exemple, la résolution 36/92 I du 9 décembre 1981 après avoir déclaré que "Le recours aux armes nucléaires constituerait une violation de la Charte des Nations unies et un crime contre l'humanité", déclarait que le recours ou la menace de recours aux armes nucléaires "devraient donc être interdits [ce qui implique qu'ils ne le sont pas] en attendant le désarmement nucléaire" et demandait que "l'on envisage... d'examiner la question d'une convention internationale sur le non-recours aux armes nucléaires et la prévention de la guerre nucléaire, ou de tout autre accord en la matière, compte dûment tenu des propositions et des vues des Etats à cet égard".

Cette résolution, comme toutes celles appelant, par des formules diverses, à des études sur la conclusion d'une convention concernant le non-recours aux armes nucléaires (résolutions 1653 (XVI) du 24 novembre 1961, 33/71 B du 14 décembre 1978, 35/152 D du 12 décembre 198O...) montre que, dans l'esprit même de ses auteurs, le principe évoqué n'est pas juridiquement consacré.

La même conclusion peut être tirée des propositions faites au cours des dernières années en vue de la conclusion d'un traité sur l'interdiction des armes nucléaires - qui

.../...

n'ont pas abouti. On peut rappeler, à titre d'exemples, la formule d'interdiction d'usage à l'encontre des puissances non dotées d'armes nucléaires réunissant certaines conditions, qui avait été présentée en 1990 lors de la conférence d'examen du TNP ou le projet de convention sur l'interdiction de l'utilisation des armes nucléaires présenté à l'Assemblée générale des Nations unies en 1991 et à nouveau en 1992 (56).

On notera aussi que nul ne conteste que les engagements unilatéraux pris par certaines puissances dotées d'armes nucléaires de ne pas utiliser en premier ces armes, ou les assurances de sécurité récemment données par les cinq membres permanents du conseil de sécurité de ne pas les utiliser contre des puissances non dotées d'armes nucléaires parties au TNP (57), l'ont été de façon discrétionnaire et non pas en vertu d'une obligation juridique. Or ces engagements, qui relèvent de la souveraineté des Etats, ont un contenu qui comporte des limites, en particulier le droit de légitime défense.

30 - Il ne saurait du reste en être autrement, car la pratique générale dans le domaine de l'interdiction ou de la règlementation des armements est de procéder par voie conventionnelle.

Toutes les interdictions partielles ou totales d'emploi d'armes déterminées ont été établies ainsi. Il suffit, à cet égard, de mentionner:

- la déclaration de Saint Pétersbourg du 29 novembre/11 décembre 1868 concernant l'usage de certains projectiles en temps de guerre,

---

56 - Résolution 46/37 D du 6 décembre 1991 et résolution 47/53 C de 1992, adoptée par 126 voix contre 26, dont la France, avec 21 abstentions.

57 - cf para.32 ci-dessous

.../...

- le protocole de Genève du 17 juin 1925 concernant la prohibition d'emploi à la guerre de gaz asphyxiants, toxiques ou similaires et de moyens bactériologiques,

- la convention du 10 avril 1972 sur l'interdiction de la mise au point, de la fabrication et du stockage des armes bactériologiques (biologiques) ou à toxine et sur leur destruction,

- la convention du 10 octobre 198O sur l'interdiction ou la limitation de l'emploi de certaines armes classiques qui peuvent être considérées comme produisant des effets traumatiques excessifs ou comme frappant sans discrimination,

- la convention du 13 janvier 1993 sur l'interdiction de la mise au point, de la fabrication, du stockage et de l'emploi des armes chimiques et sur leur destruction.

La règlementation de l'emploi d'une arme suppose en effet des règles précises qui ne peuvent être établies que par des conventions spéciales. Il ressort clairement de leur action diplomatique que les Etats qui souhaitent obtenir une interdiction spécifique d'emploi de l'arme nucléaire indépendamment d'un désarmement général et complet et avant celui-ci n'en estiment pas moins qu'une telle interdiction ne saurait résulter, comme pour toute autre arme, que de la négociation d'une convention spéciale à cet effet.

B

31 - On ne peut donc trouver dans le droit international général ou coutumier d'interdiction de l'emploi des armes nucléaires. En revanche, le droit conventionnel

.../...

fournit des indications témoignant de la licéité en droit international général de l'emploi de ces armes en certaines circonstances.

Il est rappelé que, de façon générale, le droit conventionnel concernant les armes nucléaires reconnaît la licéité de la détention de ces armes par les "Etats dotés d'armes nucléaires".

Les traités relatifs à la maîtrise des armements conclus entre Puissances dotées d'armes nucléaires reconnaissent évidemment la licéité de la détention de ces armes.

Mais c'est sur le Traité du 1er juillet 1968 sur la non prolifération des armes nucléaires que le gouvernement français doit appeler tout spécialement l'attention de la Cour. Alors que des instruments conventionnels concernant d'autres armes prohibent pour tous les Etats la possession [(58)] ou l'emploi [(59)] de ces armes, le traité sur la non prolifération reconnaît expressément le caractère d'"Etats dotés d'armes nucléaires" aux Etats "qui ont fabriqué et fait exploser une arme nucléaire ou un autre dispositif nucléaire explosif avant le 1er janvier 1967" (art. 9, para.3 du Traité). Le but même du Traité est certes d'éviter la prolifération nucléaire, et donc l'accroissement du nombre des Etats disposant d'armes nucléaires. Mais, en adhérant, dans l'exercice de leur souveraineté, au TNP, les 178 Etats qui y sont aujourd'hui parties ont expressément admis le statut que ce traité reconnaît, en leur assignant des responsabilités particulières, aux Etats dotés d'armes nucléaires au sens du paragraphe 3 de son article 9.

La Conférence de prorogation du TNP, qui vient de se tenir à New-York du 17 avril au 12 mai 1995 et à laquelle assistaient 175 des Etats parties, a décidé sans vote la

---

58 - convention du 10 avril 1972 sur l'interdiction de la mise au point, de la fabrication et du stockage des armes bactériologiques (biologiques) ou à toxine et sur leur destruction; convention susvisée du 13 janvier 1993 sur les armes chimiques.

59 - Protocole de Genève du 17 juin 1925 sur les gaz asphyxiants, susvisé

.../...

prorogation indéfinie du Traité. Aucune des décisions, déclarations ou recommandations adoptées lors de la Conférence ne fait état de la nécessité d'un avis consultatif sur la licéité de l'emploi ou la menace d'emploi des armes nucléaires. Ces événements confirment le statut des Etats dotés d'armes nucléaires et montrent en même temps que les problèmes relatifs à ces armes sont traités par les Etats indépendamment des problèmes juridiques éventuellement liés à celles-ci.

Sans qu'il soit besoin de discuter du point de savoir si et dans quelle mesure la licéité de la détention implique directement licéité de l'emploi, il ressort de plusieurs autres traités que le droit international laisse ouverte la possibilité d'un emploi des armes nucléaires.

Ainsi, le traité de 1967 sur l'espace extra-atmosphérique, de même que le traité sur la dénuclarisation du fond des mers et des océans, qui interdisent le placement d'armes nucléaires dans certains espaces déterminés, ou le Traité de 1959 sur l'Antarctique qui interdit les explosions nucléaires dans cette région, en vue d'empêcher l'utilisation des armes nucléaires dans les espaces que concernent ces traités, impliquent par là-même que la présence ou l'emploi, selon le cas, de ces armes seraient licites en l'absence de telles dispositions.

De même, en concluant le protocole additionnel n°II au traité de Tlatelolco visant l'interdiction des armes nucléaires en Amérique latine, qui prévoit la signature du protocole additionnel n°II audit traité par "toutes les puissances qui possèdent des armes nucléaires", les Etats qui sont parties à cet instrument ont non seulement reconnu le statut d'"Etat doté d'armes nucléaires", mais confirmé le fait qu'hors engagement conventionnel contraire, un emploi des armes nucléaires est en soi juridiquement possible.

.../...

Il convient de souligner que si elles avaient estimé qu'un principe de droit international général ou coutumier s'opposait à la reconnaissance du statut des Etats dotés d'armes nucléaires, les parties à ce traité n'auraient pas fait de la participation audit protocole des Etats possèdant des armes nucléaires une condition de l'entrée en vigueur du traité. A tout le moins auraient-elles pris soin de rédiger ce protocole de sorte que l'engagement qu'il contient apparaisse comme une simple confirmation d'un tel principe. Tel n'est pas le cas.

32 - Outre le droit conventionnel évoqué ci-dessus, des résolutions du Conseil de sécurité, et en particulier la résolution 984 tout récemment adoptée, le 11 avril 1995, viennent confirmer non seulement, comme le TNP, le statut d'Etat doté d'armes nucléaires et même - ce qu'une délégation, en le regrettant, mais sans apporter de contestation sur le plan juridique, a du reste expressément reconnu (60) - que l'éventualité de l'utilisation de ces armes dans l'exercice du droit naturel de légitime défense individuelle et collective conformément à la Charte n'est pas à écarter. Cette confirmation a d'autant plus de poids que la résolution 984 a été adoptée à l'unanimité des membres du Conseil de sécurité, auquel, on le sait, les Etats membres des Nations unies ont conféré la responsabilité principale du maintien de la paix et de la sécurité internationales, en reconnaissant qu'en s'acquittant des devoirs que lui impose cette responsabilité, le Conseil de sécurité agit "en leur nom".

La résolution 255 du 19 juin 1968, faisant suite à l'adoption par l'Assemblée générale du T.N.P, avait reconnu qu'une menace ou un acte d'agression nucléaire contre une puissance non dotée d'armes nucléaires "créerait une situation dans laquelle le Conseil de sécurité et, au premier chef, tous ses membres permanents dotés d'armes

60 - cf note 34 ci-dessus.

.../...

nucléaires, devraient agir immédiatement conformément à leurs obligations aux termes de la Charte des Nations unies".

Il est rappelé que, le 6 avril 1995, les cinq Etats dotés d'armes nucléaires ont, par des déclarations nationales, donné des assurances de sécurité aux Etats non dotés de ces armes parties au Traité sur la non prolifération. Pour la première fois de telles déclarations étaient faites par les cinq Etats dotés d'armes nucléaires, pour la première fois aussi elles comportaient à la fois des garanties positives et des garanties négatives de sécurité.

Commentant la déclaration française dans une communication à la commission des affaires étrangères, de la défense et des forces armées du Sénat, le ministre français des Affaires étrangères, M. Alain Juppé a indiqué qu'il s'agissait, pour les Puissances nucléaires, d'"apporter une contribution importante au renforcement du régime international de non-prolifération des armes nucléaires". Rappelant que la politique étrangère et de défense de la France est conduite dans le cadre des articles 2 para.4 et 51 de la Charte, il a indiqué qu'"Il ne fait pas de doute, dans ce contexte, que les assurances de sécurité sont compatibles avec notre stratégie de dissuasion". "Nos déclarations au titre des assurances de sécurité", a-t-il précisé, "n'affectent naturellement en rien notre droit inaliénable à la légitime défense tel que consacré par l'article 51 de la Charte des Nations Unies". "Au total ... notre décision touchant aux garanties positives et négatives de sécurité est conforme à notre politique de dissuasion; elle contribue à notre sécurité en contribuant aux renforcement des efforts contre la prolifération des armes nucléaires dans le monde; elle s'inscrit dans le cadre de nos responsabilités particulières en tant que membres permanents du conseil de sécurité".

Le 11 avril 1995, le Conseil de sécurité a adopté la résolution 984 (1995). Par cette résolution, le Conseil "prend acte avec satisfaction des déclarations faites par

.../...

chacun des Etats dotés de l'arme nucléaire (S/1995/261, S/1995/262, S/1995/263, S/1995/263, S/1995/264, S/1995/265), dans lesquelles ceux-ci ont donné aux Etats non dotés d'armes nucléaires qui sont parties au Traité sur la non-prolifération des armes nucléaires des garanties de sécurité contre l'emploi de telles armes" (dispositif, para.1) (61).

---

61 - Lors de la séance où le conseil de sécurité a adopté la résolution 984, le représentant permanent de la France a notamment déclaré:

"En adoptant la résolution 984 (1995) à quelques jours de l'ouverture de la Conférence d'examen et de prorogation du Traité sur la non-prolifération nucléaire, notre Conseil vient de procéder à un acte d'une importance particulière, dont la portée n'échappe à aucune de nos délégations. Ce texte traduit en effet la volonté commune des puissances nucléaires, membres permanents, de répondre aux aspirations de la Communauté internationale et de favoriser l'universalité et la prorogation indéfinie d'un Traité qui, aujourd'hui plus que jamais, demeure la pierre angulaire du régime de non-prolifération.

"La résolution qui vient d'être adoptée se veut en effet une réponse gobale, collective et concrète aux aspirations légitimes des Etats non-nucléaires dans le contexte de l'après-guerre froide.

"Il s'agit tout d'abord d'une réponse globale car, contrairement à la résolution 255 (1968), le texte que le Conseil vient d'adopter concerne aussi bien les assurances positives que les assurances négatives de sécurité.

"Il s'agit également d'une réponse collective, car pour la première fois, les cinq puissances reconnues comme telles par le TNP ont été en mesure, non seulement de co-parrainer une telle résolution, mais également d'harmoniser très largement leurs déclarations nationales. Les Cinq donnent à tous les Etats dotés d'armes nucléaires parties au TNP des assurances négatives harmonisées, renforçant ainsi leur sécurité.

"Il s'agit enfin d'une réponse concrète car, pour la première fois, une résolution du Conseil de sécurité précise les mesures que pourra prendre le Conseil en cas d'agression, dans les domaines du règlement des différends, de l'assistance humanitaire et des compensations aux victimes.

"La résolution qui vient d'être adoptée par le Conseil n'existerait pas sans les engagements pris à titre national par chacune des puissances nucléaires reconnues. L'importance fondamentale des déclarations conjointes prononcées le 6 avril dernier par les représentants permanents des Cinq à la Conférence du désarmement m'amène à en réitérer la teneur dans cette enceinte.

"S'agissant tout d'abord des assurances négatives, la France réaffirme

"qu'elle n'utilisera pas d'armes nucléaires contre les Etats non dotés de l'arme nucléaire parties au Traité sur la non-prolifération, sauf dans le cas d'une invasion ou de toute autre attaque menée ou soutenue par un tel Etat, en alliance ou en association avec un Etat doté de l'arme nucléaire, contre elle, son territoire, ses forces armées ou autres troupes, ou contre ses alliés ou un Etat envers lequel elle aurait un engagement de sécurité" (S/1995/264, annexe, p.2).

"La France précise donc au profit des Etats signataires du TNP les garanties qu'elle avait données en 1982.

"La déclaration faite le 6 avril à Genève constitue également une étape très importante dans la mesure où, pour la première fois, la France s'engage à donner des assurances positives à tous les pays non dotés de l'arme nucléaire parties au TNP, afin de marquer sa détermination à saisir le Conseil dans l'hypothèse où ceux-ci seraient attaqués ou menacés par des armes nucléaires.

"Au cours des nombreuses consultations menées dans le cadre de la préparation de ce projet, des voix se sont fait entendre pour exprimer le souci que les engagements

.../...

Il reconnaît le désir légitime des Etats non dotés d'armes nucléaires "d'obtenir l'assurance que le Conseil de sécurité, et en premier lieu tous ses membres permanents dotés de l'arme nucléaire, prendrait immédiatement des mesures, conformément aux mesures pertinentes de la Charte des Nations Unies, au cas où lesdits Etats seraient victimes d'un acte d'agression impliquant l'emploi d'armes nucléaires ou menacés d'une telle agression" (*ibid.*, para.2). Tout en reconnaissant que tout Etat peut attirer son attention en pareil cas, il "reconnaît également que les Etats dotés d'armes nucléaires qui sont membres permanents du Conseil de sécurité porteront immédiatement la question à l'attention du Conseil et s'emploieront à obtenir que celui-ci fournisse, conformément à la Charte, l'assistance nécessaire à l'Etat victime" (*ibid.*, para.3). Il rappelle les moyens dont il dispose pour aider un Etat non doté d'armes nucléaires se trouvant dans la

---

communs pris par les puissances nucléaires concernant les assurances dites positives puissent garantir la saisine effective du Conseil. Sur ce point, la déclaration faite par la France me paraît de nature à dissiper à la fois toute ambiguïté et toute appréhension. Je cite:

> "La France considère que toute agression accompagnée d'armes nucléaires menacerait la paix et la sécurité internationales... La France reconnaît qu'il est légitime que les pays non dotés de l'arme nucléaire parties au TNP soient assurés que la communauté internationale, et au premier chef le Conseil de sécurité des Nations unies, réagirait immédiatement conformément aux obligations de la Charte, dans l'hypothèse où ils seraient agressés ou menacés de l'être avec l'arme nucléaire".
>
> "Eu égard à ces considérations, la France déclare ce qui suit:
> "La France s'engage, en tant que membre permanent du Conseil de sécurité, en cas d'agression avec emploi d'armes nucléaires, ou de menace d'une telle agression à l'encontre d'un Etat non doté d'armes nucléaires partie au TNP, à saisir sans délai le Conseil de sécurité et à agir en son sein pour que celui-ci prenne des mesures immédiates en vue de fournir, conformément à la Charte, l'assistance nécessaire à l'Etat qui sera victime d'un acte ou d'une menace d'agression.
> "La France réaffirme, en particulier, le droit de légitime défense, individuelle ou collective, reconnu par l'article 51 de la Charte, dans le cas où un membre des Nations unies est l'objet d'une agression armée - y compris avec l'emploi d'armes nucléaires - jusqu'à ce que le Conseil de sécurité ait pris les mesures nécessaires pour maintenir la paix et la sécurité internationales" (ibid, p.3).

"Le fait que notre Conseil se soit prononcé de façon très claire sur cette résolution qui appelle à l'adhésion universelle au TNP et souligne la nécessité pour les Etats parties au Traité de respecter pleinement toutes leurs obligations, témoigne de la volonté des membres de la communauté internationale d'oeuvrer en faveur d'un renforcement du régime de non-prolifération".

.../...

situation considérée, invite les Etats membres à prendre, individuellement ou collectivement, les mesures appropriées en vue de répondre à une demande de l'Etat victime en matière d'assistance technique, médicale, scientifique et humanitaire et se déclare prêt à examiner les mesures qui devraient être prises à cet égard, et exprime son intention de recommander des mesures appropriées en vue de répondre à une demande de cet Etat concernant le versement d'une indemnité par l'agresseur, conformément au droit international, en réparation des pertes, dommages ou préjudices subis du fait de l'agression (*ibid.*, para. 4, 5 et 6). Il se félicite que "certains Etats" "aient exprimé l'intention de venir immédiatement en aide ou de prêter immédiatement un appui, conformément à la Charte, à tout Etat non doté d'armes nucléaires partie au Traité sur la non-prolifération d'armes nucléaires qui serait victime d'un acte d'agression avec emploi d'armes nucléaires ou serait menacé d'une telle agression" (*ibid.*, para.7). Il engage tous les Etats à poursuivre de bonne foi, comme le prévoit l'article VI du TNP, "des négociations sur des mesures efficaces relatives au désarmement nucléaire et sur un traité de désarmement général et complet sous un contrôle internaional strict et efficace, qui demeure un objectif universel". Enfin, il réaffirme (*ibid.*, para.9) le droit naturel de légitime défense individuelle ou collective tel que consacré à l'article 51 de la Charte des Nations unies.

Ainsi, loin de tendre à une prohibition des armes nucléaires, la résolution 984, après la résolution 255, confirme au contraire l'existence d'un ensemble d'Etats dotés d'armes nucléaires, comme le fait le TNP lui-même. Elle ne porte aucune condamnation *a priori* sur l'emploi des armes en cause. Elle envisage seulement l'hypothèse où cet emploi ou sa menace constitueraient une agression, ce qui renvoie aux règles générales de la Charte et ne permet pas de singulariser sur le plan du droit l'utilisation des armes nucléaires par rapport à d'autres moyens d'agression. En outre, comme la résolution 255, la résolution 984 ne concerne que les agressions ou les menaces dirigées contre une certaine catégorie d'Etats déterminés en fonction des obligations internationales qui les

.../...

lient (les Etats non dotés d'armes nucléaires parties au TNP), ce qui en tout état de cause, et même si elle avait énoncé une condamnation de l'emploi des armes nucléaires, aurait empêché que celle-ci puisse être considérée comme ayant une portée générale.

Enfin, au-delà de la reconnaissance du statut des Etats dotés d'armes nucléaires, le Conseil de sécurité, et à travers lui l'ensemble des Membres des Nations Unies, en reconnaissant le rôle positif spécifique que peuvent jouer ces Etats face à la situation envisagée paraît confirmer l'utilité, dans les circonstances actuelles, de la capacité dissuasive de ces Etats.

CONCLUSIONS

33 - En conclusion, le gouvernement français estime que le droit international général relatif à la menace et à l'emploi de la force dans les relations internationales n'implique aucune prohibition spécifique de l'emploi des armes nucléaires ou de la menace de cet emploi. Aucune autre règle coutumière n'interdit l'emploi de ces armes.

Une prohibition ou réglementation d'emploi d'une arme, ou d'un type d'armes particulier, ne peut provenir, comme le démontre la pratique internationale, que de conventions spéciales. Une telle prohibition ne saurait résulter que d'une règle spécifique, liant les Etats qui l'acceptent.

Les règles conventionnelles relatives à l'emploi des armes nucléaires demeurent d'une part exceptionnelles et d'autre part de portée limitée. Le fait que ces instruments ou bien consacrent la détention d'armes nucléaires par les Etats en cause, sans traiter de l'emploi de ces armes, ou bien contiennent sur ce point des engagements précis, qui au surplus demeurent limités, confirme l'absence d'une règle de droit international général les prohibant.

.../...

Le comportement même des Etats, que ceux-ci approuvent ou réprouvent l'éventualité de l'utilisation des armes nucléaires, manifeste du reste leur ferme conviction qu'il n'existe pas de règle l'interdisant et même qu'une telle utilisation pourrait être licite. Les recommandations émises, dans l'exercice de leurs fonctions, aussi bien par l'Assemblée générale (malgré les affirmations d'inspiration purement politique contraires figurant dans certaines de ses résolutions) que par le Conseil de sécurité montrent que l'un et l'autre partagent cette conviction.

Le gouvernement français croit donc qu'il est non seulement injustifié mais impossible de formuler sur la base de règles générales en vigueur, quelles qu'elles soient, un principe d'interdiction d'emploi des armes nucléaires qui en serait déduit, ou y serait implicitement contenu.

Le gouvernement français considère en outre qu'il n'est pas possible d'indiquer de façon abstraite et générale dans quelles circonstances cet emploi serait licite ou illicite en dehors du principe incontesté qui gouverne l'usage de la force dans les relations internationales: il ne pourrait y avoir recours à l'emploi des armes nucléaires que dans les circonstances où la Charte autorise le recours à la force.

Si cependant la Cour estimait devoir examiner l'ensemble des arguments sus-évoqués, cet examen ne pourrait, selon le gouvernement français, que confirmer que, comme la pratique et l'*opinio juris* des Etats le font clairement apparaître, aucune règle juridique, quelle que soit sa source, ne prohibe actuellement l'emploi des armes nucléaires.

Toute autre conclusion ne saurait, de l'avis du gouvernement français, être atteinte par la Cour que si celle-ci faisait oeuvre de législateur. Elle se substituerait, ce

.../...

faisant, aux Etats qui, dans l'état actuel du droit et de la situation internationale, n'ont pas cru devoir interdire l'utilisation de ces armes.

La Cour ne devrait pas se lancer dans cette voie, en se rappelant que, ainsi que le notent Jean Pictet et M. Pilloud dans l'introduction du commentaire du Titre IV du protocole I de 1977:

> "si les Etats n'ont pas voulu résoudre (le problème de "la licéité à la guerre de certains usages des armes nucléaires") dans le cadre de la CDDH" (conférence de Genève sur le droit humanitaire) c'est qu'il a des implications qui dépassent le droit international humanitaire, comme il est dit clairement dans le passage du rapport de la Commission *ad hoc*" (sur les armes conventionnelles) (62). Mais c'est peut-être aussi parce qu'ils savaient que le problème n'était pas soluble à court terme et qu'il aurait paralysé l'adoption des protocoles".

Il ressort des débats sus-évoqués de l'Assemblée générale sur la résolution 49/75K que ces préoccupations demeurent valables.

En conséquence, le gouvernement de la République française estime, à titre principal, que la question posée par l'Assemblée générale n'est pas de celles auxquelles la Cour peut répondre dans l'exercice de ses fonctions judiciaires et que, de toute manière, la Cour devrait exercer le pouvoir d'appréciation qu'elle tient de l'article 65 de son Statut et refuser de se prononcer sur la demande qui lui a été soumise.

---

62 - La commission ad hoc avait en effet reconnu que "les armes nucléaires en particulier ont une fonction spéciale, qui est de décourager le déclenchement d'un conflit armé de grande envergure entre certaines puissances nucléaires".

.../...

Si la Cour estimait toutefois approprié de donner réponse à la question posée, elle ne pourrait que constater que l'emploi des armes nucléaires, ou la menace de cet emploi ne sont certainement pas permis en toute circonstance. Ils ne le sont que dans les circonstances tout à fait exceptionnelles où le droit international général autorise le recours à la force, notamment dans le cas de l'exercice du droit de légitime défense.

Le gouvernement français souhaiterait avoir l'occasion de présenter de nouvelles observations sur la question posée si la Cour décidait d'y répondre./.

LETTER DATED 20 JUNE 1995 FROM THE AMBASSADOR OF THE FEDERAL REPUBLIC OF GERMANY, TOGETHER WITH WRITTEN STATEMENT OF THE GOVERNMENT OF THE FEDERAL REPUBLIC OF GERMANY

DER BOTSCHAFTER
DER BUNDESREPUBLIK DEUTSCHLAND

The Hague, 20 June 1995

To the
Registrar of the
International Court of Justice
Mr. Eduardo Valencia-Ospina
Peace Palace
Carnegieplein 2
2517 KJ The Hague

Dear Mr Valencia-Ospina,

referring to your letter of February 8, 1995 to the Foreign Minister of Germany respecting the General Assembly's request for an advisory opinion on the threat/use of nuclear weapons, I beg to pass on to you the enclosed statement of the Federal Republic of Germany. The original ist accompanied by a translation of courtesy in English.

Sincerely yours

Wilhelm Haas

June 1995

Statement by the Government of the Federal Republic of Germany

for the International Court of Justice

on the request made to it by the United Nations General Assembly for an advisory opinion

on the following question:

"Is the threat or use of nuclear weapons in any circumstance permitted under international law?"

I.

From the standpoint of the Federal Government there are compelling arguments against the International Court of Justice giving an advisory opinion on the above question.

1. The Federal Government recognizes the aspects which, following a *prima facie* examination of the request, might argue for a substantive reply: Article 96 (1) of the Charter of the United Nations authorizes the General Assembly to request an opinion from the International Court of Justice on "any legal question". The Court has made substantive replies to all previous requests from the General Assembly. It has up to now been rather cautious in interpreting its discretion under Article 65 (1) of its Statute for declining a request. The Court has repeatedly stated that a substantive reply to an organ of the United Nations authorized to make a request should "in principle" not be declined (*ICJ Reports* 1950, 71; 1956, 86; 1989, 189).

2. In this case, however, following a closer examination of the Court's jurisprudence, a different conclusion suggests itself.

a) The Court has unequivocally stated that it may only examine legal questions:

> "... the Court can give an advisory opinion only on a legal question. If a question is not a legal one, the Court has no discretion in the matter; it must decline to give the opinion requested" (*ICJ Reports* 1962, 155).

In the view of the Federal Government the question before the Court is basically a political one.
Although the Court has also repeatedly stated that legal questions often have political aspects and that this fact should not hinder it in its mainly judicial task of interpreting a treaty provision (*ICJ Reports* 1948, 61; 1962, 155; 1980, 87), this request by the General Assembly is a different matter. Just as the request formulates a legal question merely at first glance, the reply, too, can only be a seemingly legal one. In reality the Court is being asked to examine what is at heart a highly political issue.

Nuclear weapons are not only a means of warfare like other weapons. Their main purpose is political: they are meant to help prevent any kind of war. Their use cannot be assessed using the norms of international law without such an assessment turning from a judicial into a political one.

While the question by the General Assembly regarding the legality of the "threat or use of nuclear weapons" is formulated as if the eventuality of their use in wartime could be assessed separately from their main political purpose of preventing war, this assumption is misleading. The eventuality of the use of nuclear weapons in wartime has remained hypothetical for decades. This realization has influenced major security policy decisions by states and alliances and will continue to do so in future. It is a realization which can be counted among the basic conditions underlying the relative political stability in international relations.

Were the Court now, against this background, to assess in an abstract legal manner the hypothetical use of nuclear weapons, this advisory opinion could only seemingly be a purely judicial clarification of a legal question. The subject of the assessment would, in the final analysis, be key security policy elements of today's global order. Regardless of the conclusions such an advisory opinion were to reach on the matter, it would be perceived as a reply to a political question.

b) Should the Court nevertheless decide that it has before it an essentially legal question requiring clarification, it would still need to decide how to make use of the discretion allowed in Article 65 of its Statute:

> "But even if the question is a legal one, which the Court is undoubtedly competent to answer, it may nonetheless decline to do so" (*ICJ Reports* 1962, 155).

The Court has repeatedly emphasized its discretion:

> "Article 65 of the Statute is permissive. It gives the Court the power to examine whether the circumstances of the case are of such a character as should lead it to decline to answer the Request" (*ICJ Reports* 1950, 72; confirmed in, for example, *ICJ Reports* 1962, 155).

The Federal Government is aware of the fact that the Court has also emphasized that only "compelling reasons" could cause it to refuse to answer a legal question (*ICJ Reports* 1956, 86; 1989, 191). The Federal Government is of the opinion that such compelling reasons for refusal exist in this case. The "propriety" of judicial involvement with this question is more than doubtful for various reasons, if the Court's own criteria are used:

> "... the Court has always been guided by the principle that, as a judicial body, it is bound to remain faithful to the requirements of its judicial character even in giving advisory opinions" (*ICJ Reports* 1973, 175).

aa) The Court would be forced to overstep the bounds of its function as the "principal judicial organ of the United Nations" (Article 92 of the Charter). Because of its judicial function the Court is obliged to respect the law-making, in a sense "legislative" prerogative of the states.

Rather than giving an abstract answer to the abstract question of the legality of nuclear weapons, the international community has chosen an entirely different course to deal with the legal aspects of the nuclear risk. It has for decades made efforts to limit the specific risks of nuclear weapons by elaborating new international legal norms. In doing so it has chosen the option of continually developing a special international treaty law devoted to this purpose.

A general legal ban on nuclear weapons has never been on the agenda in any negotiating forum, even though various states have long demanded such a ban. There have been two main reasons for this: firstly, the recognition that no consensus can be reached on such an aim due to its politically controversial nature; secondly, fear of jeopardizing what is legally and politically possible, since a polarizing argument on an unachievable goal blocks the road to gradual success.

This process of gradually developing treaty law on nuclear disarmament and arms control has proved remarkably successful. One of the most important achievements, apart from the major bilateral disarmament treaties, was the conclusion of the 1968 Treaty on the Non-Proliferation of Nuclear Weapons (NPT) which now has 178 member states and which was recently indefinitely extended. This treaty by no means envisages a general ban on nuclear weapons but rather expressly presupposes the control over such weapons by five nuclear-weapon states, which are, however, pledged

> "to pursue negotiations in good faith on effective measures relating to cessation of the nuclear arms race at an early date and to nuclear disarmament, and on a treaty on general and complete disarmament under strict and effective international control" (Article VI of the NPT).

On the occasion of the indefinite extension of the NPT, over 170 States Parties confirmed these aims by consensus on 11 May 1995 and adopted the catalogue of measures entitled "Principles and Objectives for Nuclear Non-Proliferation and Disarmament" (Document NPT/CONF.1995/L.5 of 9 May 1995). This significant document underlines the above-mentioned gradual approach, i.e. to deal with the nuclear threat through treaties, and it contains important objectives for the further development of international treaty law, for example the completion of the negotiations on a Comprehensive Test Ban Treaty "no later than 1996".

In this context it becomes clear why we are concerned about jeopardizing what is legally possible. The indispensable focussing of all efforts onto the coming nuclear disarmament, arms-control and non-proliferation tasks, the significance of which can scarcely be overestimated, could lose its drive if the Court were to supply an advisory opinion on the abstract question of the legality of nuclear weapons. Whatever the Court's reply, it could not fail to have consequences for a sensitive, complex negotiating process which, for good reason, has never included the issue now before the Court.

bb) In addition, were the Court to reply to the request, it could in our view not avoid issuing a number of speculative statements going beyond its judicial function. It is true that one of the Court's tasks is to answer abstract legal questions (*ICJ Reports* 1948, 61; 1954, 51); it may also make findings as to factual issues (*ICJ Reports* 1971, 27). However, should the problems regarding fact-finding be obvious, this may lead the Court to refuse to give an opinion (*ICJ Reports* 1975, 28).

In answering the above request the Court would have to embark upon a host of speculative considerations in order to take account of the variety of differing situations in which the threat or use of nuclear weapons might be conceivable. The Court would be obliged to analyze different types of nuclear weapons and to assess different theories regarding the effects of their possible use. All this would require the Court to analyze a plethora of extremely complex and at the same time controversial hypotheses. This would no longer be judicial fact-finding but rather guesswork regarding hypothetical scenarios.

cc) The General Assembly's request also leads to the question of the Court's integrity, the significance of which is illustrated by the following quotation:

> "There are inherent limitations on the exercise of the judicial function which the Court, as a Court of justice, can never ignore... The Court itself, and not the parties, must be the guardian of the Court's judicial integrity" (*ICJ Reports* 1963, 29).

This question becomes particularly relevant in this case, since there is the danger of a pointless procedure. The Court has described its advisory function as follows:

> "The function of the Court is to give an opinion based on law, once it has come to the conclusion that the questions put to it are relevant and have a practical and contemporary effect and, consequently, are not devoid of object or purpose" (*ICJ Reports* 1975, 37).

In earlier requests made by the General Assembly, especially regarding constitutional aspects of the Charter, the "practical and contemporary effect" of the Court's advisory opinions was mostly not in doubt. However, the history of a number of General Assembly resolutions on the legality of nuclear weapons has shown that there are highly different but at the same time extremely hardened opinions on this matter and that there are numerical majorities in this conflict of opinions but no signs whatever of consensus.

In other words we are dealing with a legal issue with political implications which by its very nature must remain politically controversial, thus allowing for no common *opinio iuris* supporting a universally valid legal reply. Under such circumstances it is hard to see the purpose of an advisory opinion, since it could scarcely serve to overcome the difference of opinions within the General Assembly. Were an opinion nonetheless to be given, the perception of the Court's integrity might be affected.

3. In 2 a), 2 b) aa), bb) and cc) above the Federal Government has presented four major aspects, any one of which should in its opinion lead to rejection of the request. Should the Court fail to share this view, the Federal Government begs to suggest that in any case the sum total of the above reservations is so weighty that the Court would be well advised to exercise its discretion to reject the General Assembly's request.

II.

In case the Court enters into an examination of the substance of the General Assembly's request, the Federal Government makes reference to section II of its statement of June 1994 on the World Health Organization's question regarding the legality of the use of nuclear weapons. These comments also apply *mutatis mutandis* to the General Assembly's additional question on the legality of the threat of nuclear weapons. Such a "threat" can only be permissible in the exercise of the inherent right to individual or collective self-defence.

LETTER DATED 20 JUNE 1995
FROM THE PERMANENT REPRESENTATIVE OF LESOTHO
TO THE UNITED NATIONS

THE PERMANENT MISSION OF THE KINGDOM
TO THE UNITED NATIONS

REF LM/ICJ/1

CABLE ADDRESS
MACHABA

KHOTSONG
204 East 39th Street
New York, N.Y. 10016
Telephone (212) 661-1690
Facsimile (212) 682-4388

June 20th, 1995

Mr. Mohammed Bedjaoui
President of the International Court of Justice
Peace Palace
2517 KJ, The Hague
Netherlands

Your Excellency,

The Kingdom of Lesotho has the pleasure to submit the following in response to the invitation of the International Court of Justice to make statements on the question requested by the United Nations General Assembly:

"Is the threat of nuclear weapons in any circumstance permitted under international law?"

The Kingdom of Lesotho is concerned about the continuing threat of nuclear weapons and therefore supported the United Nations General Assembly Resolution requesting the advisory opinion on this issue.

The Kingdom of Lesotho is resolutely opposed to the threat or use of nuclear weapons, and will support the various international and regional initiatives for prohibiting nuclear weapons. These include the establishment of a nuclear weapons free Africa and United Nations resolutions calling for a convention on the threat or use of nuclear weapons.

The Kingdom of Lesotho believes that any threat or use of nuclear weapons violates Article 2(4) of the United Nations Charter, which prohibits the threat or use of force except in self defense as provided in Article 51.

/..

LETTER DATED 20 JUNE 1995 FROM THE GENERAL DIRECTOR FOR MULTILATERAL ORGANIZATIONS AT THE MINISTRY OF FOREIGN AFFAIRS OF ECUADOR

EMBAJADA DEL ECUADOR
EN LOS PAÍSES BAJOS

NON OFFICIAL TRANSLATION

Excellency:

With reference to the consultive opinion required to the International Court of Justice by the General Assembly of the United Nations, through resolution 49/75 K, with the purpose of getting the Court's opinion weather the international law will authorize, under any circumstances, the threat or use of nuclear weapons, the Government of Ecuador would like to transmit to his Excellency the following considerations:

A) The International Court of Justice is perfectly competent to pronounce her self weather the threat or use of nuclear weapons is legal or illegal;

B) The subject presented by the General Assembly of the United Nations offers different phases of juridical analysis, being necessary the opinion of the International Court of Justice in all of them.

C) The use or threat of use of nuclear weapons is out of question in zones that are geographically clean of nuclear weapons, as is the case of Latin America. Within this region, to which Ecuador is a part of, the Treaty of the Proscription of Nuclear Weapons (Treaty of Tlatelolco) of 1967 and its additional protocols, prohibit any practice, use or possession of any nuclear weapons;

D) Also should be analyzed weather the threat or use of nuclear weapons is legal or illegal, in relation with the principles of the International Humanitarian Law, particularly those consecrated in the Conventions of Geneva of 1945, and in the additional Protocol I of 1977;

His Excellency
Mohamed Bedjaoui,
President of the International Court of Justice
The Hague

EMBAJADA DEL ECUADOR
EN LOS PAÍSES BAJOS

It is clear that the use of nuclear weapons creates cruel and inhuman sufferings upon its victims, weather they are in combat or not, and that it leaves lethal effects on humans for many years. Having said this, the use of nuclear weapons contradicts the humanitarian dispositions against the use of warlike artifacts that provoke cruel and unnecessary sufferings to its victims.

Besides, the use of nuclear weapons does not discriminate by general norm the military objectives from civil objectives. This factor equally attends against a fundamental principle of the International Humanitarian Law: which takes care of the protection of innocent people during war times.

On the other hand, the effects of the use of nuclear weapons, in all cases, will cause devastating effects on the environment. In consequence, it opposes to the humanitarian conditions that prohibit the destruction of the environment, which is the only guarantee of the survival of the human species, and of the whole chain of life of the planet.

E) The analysis weather the threat or use of nuclear weapons is legal or illegal, should also be reflected on the legal perspectives from the principles of Nuremberg from 1945.

On one hand, the disproportions of a nuclear response, and the uncontrollable effects that a nuclear device has, can easily go against the law and the uses of the war (such as the attack to unarmed or wounded people, to minors, to people protected by non violent humanitarian or religious organizations, peace missionaries and journalists, or the destruction of cultural and civil property, etc.)

On the other hand, the use of nuclear weapons has the consequences that fit perfectly with the legal figure of war crimes against humankind: the assassination and extermination of entire populations and other inhuman acts committed against the civil population;

F) The effects of the use of nuclear weapons can also contradict other international norms, apart from the already mentioned, that refers to the use of inhuman warlike artifacts, such as those of The Hague Conventions of 1899 and 1907, and the Protocol of Geneva of 1925;

G) The threat or use of nuclear weapons has consequences that contradicts the legal international ordering that protects and guarantees the operation of Human Rights of the people.

The Republic of Ecuador considers that the pronouncement of the International Court of Justice about the illegality of nuclear weapons will help fortalice the arguments of the people and the

EMBAJADA DEL ECUADOR
EN LOS PAÍSES BAJOS

nations that with deeds instead of words, will support a genuine process of no proliferation and nuclear disarmament progressive and verifiable.

Considerations related with the effectiveness and applicability of international law should not prevent the pronouncement of the International Court of Justice over the question submitted by the General Assembly of the United Nations. It is true that the instruments of military power and political influences of certain states can not be counteract in an automatic way, arguing a simple legal principle. This is nothing new as it is of general knowledge that international law unfortunately does not have at this moment the power to impose their decisions on different matters, among them the ones related to nuclear disarmament. Nevertheless, seen from another point of view, a juridical pronouncement over the illegality of nuclear weapons would be a transcendental fact and highly estimable: it has been historically demonstrated that juridical stipulation, apparently utopian, in their own way and not with little trouble, have contributed in forging the human conscience of the nations and promote a universal spirit of solidarity, pacifist and cooperative.

Taking this opportunity to renew to Your Excellency the assurances of my highest consideration.

Rodrigo Yépez Enríquez
General Director of Multilateral Organizations
Ministry of Foreign Affairs

COMMUNICATION DATED 20 JUNE 1995 FROM THE AMBASSADOR OF EGYPT, TOGETHER WITH WRITTEN STATEMENT OF THE GOVERNMENT OF EGYPT

Embassy
of the
Arab Republic of Egypt

0/74

Mr. Eduardo Valencia-Ospina,

The Embassy of the Arab Republic of Egypt presents it compliments to the International Court of Justice and has the honour to inform the honourable Court that, with reference to its letter dated 8 February 1995 and in connection with the order of the International Court of Justice of 1 February 1995, the Embassy of the Arab Republic of Egypt has the honour to present, herewith enclosed, the written statement of the Arab Republic of Egypt on the Legality of the threat or use of Nuclear Weapons.

The Embassy of the Arab Republic of Egypt avails itself of this opportunity to renew to the International Court of Justice the assurances of its highest consideration.

E. Saad

Chargé d'affaires a.i
E. Saad El Sayed

The Hague, 20 June 1995

Mr. E. Valencia Ospina, Registrar of
The International Court of Justice
PEACE PALACE
2517 KJ THE HAGUE

LEGALITY OF THE THREAT OR USE OF NUCLEAR WEAPONS

(REQUEST FOR ADVISORY OPINION)

ORDER OF 1 FEBRUARY 1995

WRITTEN STATEMENT OF EGYPT

INTRODUCTION

I. Terms of the Request and Standing of Egypt

1. By resolution 49/75K of 15 December 1994, the General Assembly of the United Nations decided, pursuant to Article 96, paragraph 1, of the Charter of the United Nations, to request the International Court of Justice urgently to render its advisory opinion on the following question:

> "Is the threat or use of nuclear weapons in any circumstance permitted under international law?"

2. The Court, by its Order of 1 February 1995, fixed 20 June 1995 as the time-limit within which written statements relating to the question may be submitted to the Court by Member States who are entitled to appear before the Court, in accordance with Article 66, paragraph 2, of its Statute. That Order of the Court was notified to the Government of the Arab Republic of Egypt. Egypt, is an original Member of the United Nations, and by virtue of Article 93 of the United Nations Charter *ipso facto* a party to the Statute of the Court. It is in these circumstances a State to which the Court is open under Article 35 of the Statute of the Court and entitled to appear before the Court.

II. Egypt's Interest in the Question

3. Egypt is a non-nuclear State. Egypt has a definite interest in avoiding any use of nuclear weapons. As a peaceful and peace-loving State, Egypt has entered the Treaty on the Non-prolifera-

tion of Nuclear Weapons of 1968.[1] She has, also, acceded to the I.A.E.A. safeguard agreements. Furthermore, she is a leading country in the efforts for disarmament, and in particular nuclear disarmament, through regional and universal means. Egypt, *inter alia,* has launched a campaign in 1974 to establish a Nuclear Weapons Free Zone in the Middle East. Furthermore, she has made an initiative in 1990 to create an area free of weapons of mass destruction in the Middle East. Egypt believes that the most efficient way to eliminate the nuclear threat is by absolutely prohibiting and eliminating nuclear weapons.

Equally, Egypt is concerned by the threat or use of nuclear weapons for reasons of human rights and humanitarian considerations, as well as from the economic, social and environmental perspectives. Egypt entirely depends on river waters for irrigation and drinking. She also largely depends on sea waters for fishing as well as on wide areas of agricultural land for subsistence. The use of nuclear weapons is surely to cause long-term and severe damage to these resources making life almost impossible.

For these reasons, *inter alia,* Egypt has voted in favour of General Assembly resolution 49/75K, and has a special interest in the advisory opinion of the Court. From this perspective, Egypt is making its written statement.

4. This written statement is divided into two Parts. Part I ascertains the competence of the General Assembly to request an advisory opinion from the Court on the subject-matter of the request. It also establishes that the Court is competent to give, and should give, an advisory opinion on the question submitted. Part II demonstrates that the threat or use of nuclear weapons in any circumstance is illegal under international law.

---

[1] 7 *I.L.M.* 811 (1968).

PART I

COMPETENCE AND ADMISSIBILITY

III. The General Assembly of the United Nations is Competent to Request an Advisory Opinion on the Present Question

5. According to paragraph 1 of Article 96 of the Charter of the United Nations "[t]he General Assembly ... may request the International Court of Justice to give an advisory opinion *on any legal question*."[2] The General Assembly now requests an advisory opinion from the Court on a legal question. The advisory opinion requested relates to the legality of the threat or use of nuclear weapons in any circumstance under international law, which necessarily, and by definition, is a "legal question". It concerns the *international legal aspects* of nuclear weapons; *i.e.* whether the threat or use of nuclear weapons is compatible with the rules of international law. And, thus, if there would be a breach of obligations under international law when there is a threat or use of such weapons. This question involves the *interpretation* of international norms which might be applicable to the threat or use of nuclear weapons which is a legal process. Thence, the Assembly's request for an advisory opinion satisfies the conditions of Article 96(1) both *ratione personae* (it being authorized to make a request) and *ratione materiae* (the request being on a legal question). The General Assembly, therefore, is competent to request an advisory opinion on the present question, and has thus acted *intra vires*.

[2] Italics added.

6. The General Assembly has a special interest that the Court answer the question put to it in the affirmative. The question falls squarely within the ambit of the Assembly for it includes, as it does, both the *jus ad bellum* question of the threat or use of force (Articles 2(4), 10, 11, 12 and 14 of the Charter), as well as that of the *jus in bello* relating to certain weapons of mass destruction. Answering the request by the Court would enlighten the General Assembly on the legal aspects involved.

IV. The Court is Competent to Render its Advisory Opinion on the Present Question

7. Article 65 of the Statute of the Court stipulates that:

> "The Court may give an advisory opinion on any legal question at the request of whatever body may be authorized by or in accordance with the Charter of the United Nations to make such a request."

Accordingly, the Court, has the discretion to render advisory opinions on "legal questions" put to it by duly "authorized" organs of the United Nations or international organizations. In the present request the two conditions (*viz.* a legal question and an authorized body) are fulfilled. Although it is not duty-bound to give this legal advice, for the language of Article 65 is permissive rather than mandatory,[3] the Court has summarized its practice in the granting of advisory opinions as follows:

> "The Court has repeatedly stated that a reply to a request for an advisory opinion should not, in principle, be refused and that only

---

[3] *Interpretation of Peace Treaties (First Phase), Advisory Opinion of 30 March 1950 : I.C.J. Reports 1950*, p. 65 at pp. 71 f.; and *Western Sahara, Advisory opinion of 16 October 1975, I.C.J. Reports 1975*, p. 12, para. at p. 21.

> compelling reasons would justify such a refusal."[4]

In the present case there are no "compelling reasons" in the sense that the advisory opinion does not relate to a dispute in which one of the parties has not recognized the competence of the Court to decide its dispute which is referred to the Court in the guise of an advisory opinion.[5] As no compelling reasons for its refusal exist, there is no reason why the Court must not render its advisory opinion.

6. The mere fact that the question may have been politically motivated cannot prevent the Court from rendering its advisory opinion. It is the Court that has affirmed that:

> "in institutions in which political considerations are prominent it may be particularly necessary for an international organization to obtain an advisory opinion from the Court as to the legal principles applicable with respect to the matter under debate ..."[6]

Furthermore, the Court said that:

> "It has been argued that the question put to the Court is intertwined with political questions, and that for this reason the Court should refuse to give an opinion. It is true that most interpretations of the Charter of the United Nations will have political significance, great or small. In the nature of things it could not be otherwise. The Court, however, cannot attribute a political character to a request which invites it to undertake an essentially judicial task ..."[7]

---

[4] *Application for Review of Judgment No. 158 of the United Nations Administrative Tribunal, I.C.J. Reports 1973*, p. 166, para. 40 at p. 183.

[5] *I.C.J. Reports 1975*, p. 12, at p. 25.

[6] *Interpretation of the Agreement of 25 March 1951 between the WHO and Egypt, I.C.J. Reports 1980*, p. 73, para. 33 at p. 87.

[7] *Certain Expenses of the UN, Advisory opinion of 20 July 1962, I.C.J. Reports 1962*, p. 151 at p. 155.

9. The advisory opinion of the Court will be of great practical value. By virtue of the exercise of its advisory role, the Court contributes to the effective functioning of the United Nations. In fact, the Court has abundantly reiterated that its advisory function constitutes its participation in the activities of the United Nations of which it is the principal judicial organ.[8] The present request pertains to a question that lies within the core mandate of the United Nations and particularly the General Assembly, *viz.* the maintenance of international peace and security, and disarmament and arms control efforts. The advisory opinion of the Court is, also, very likely to contribute to a greater understanding and appreciation of the principles of humanitarian law. A statement by the Court on the legality of the threat or use of nuclear weapons under international law will surely have a positive effect on the long-standing negotiations in the United Nations and elsewhere, and would resolve any controversy over the issue. The Court itself has declared that:

> "The function of the Court is to give an opinion based on law, once it has come to the conclusion that the questions put to it are relevant and have a practical and contemporary effect and, consequently, are not devoid of object and purpose."[9]

In the light of its *dictum*, the Court should entertain the request made by the General Assembly for its advisory opinion because the question put to it in resolution 49/75K is relevant and has practical and contemporary effect.

---

[8] *Interpretation of Peace Treaties (first phase), Advisory Opinion, I.C.J. Reports 1950*, at p. 71.; and *Reservations to the Convention on the Prevention and Punishment of the Crime of Genocide, I.C.J. Reports 1951*, p. 15 at p. 19.

[9] *I.C.J. Reports 1975*, p. 12, para. 73 at p. 37.

CONCLUSION:

10. By virtue of Articles 96(1) of the Charter and 65 of the Statute the of Court and of their combined effect, and for the reasons set out above, it is submitted that the General Assembly of the United Nations is competent to request an advisory opinion from the Court on the subject-matter of the request; and that the Court is competent to give, and should give, its advisory opinion on the question addressed to it.

PART II

MERITS

11. Nuclear war has been "[r]esolutely, unconditionally and for all time condemn[ed] ... as being contrary to human conscience and reason, as the most monstrous crime against peoples and as a violation of the foremost human right - the right to life".[10] Nuclear weapons pose the greatest danger to mankind and to the survival of civilization.[11] General Assembly resolution no. 1653 (XVI) of 24 November, 1961 entitled "Declaration on the Prohibition of the Use of Nuclear and Thermo-nuclear Weapons" must be seen as a prohibition *de lege lata* of nuclear weapons.[12] It declared that the use of nuclear weapons would be

---

[10] General Assembly resolution no. 38/75 B of 15 December, 1983.

[11] Paragraph 47 of the Final Document of the First Special Session on Disarmament of the General Assembly of 1978.

[12] Its preamble states that:

contrary to the spirit, letter and aims of the United Nations and, as such, "a direct violation of the Charter of the United Nations". Besides being a violation of the Chartor of the United Nations, the resolution stated that it "would be contrary to the rules of international law and the laws of humanity and a crime against mankind and civilization."

12. Equally, resolution 2936 (XXVII) of 29 November, 1972 on the Non-Use of Force in International Relations and Permanent Prohibition of the Use of Nuclear Weapons, declared "the permanent prohibition of the use of nuclear weapons". By the inherent qualitative and quantitative characteristics of their effect, nuclear weapons necessarily have indiscriminate effects and are thus harmful to man and his environment. The international consensus on their illegality leaves no room for convictions to the contrary.

13. The abhorrence of nuclear weapons has driven the international community to take measures to eliminate them. The first General Assembly resolution[13] established the Atomic Energy Commission with the view to "control[ling] ... atomic energy to the extent necessary to ensure its use *only for peaceful purposes*".[14] Furthermore, the Treaty on Principles Governing the Activities of States in the Exploration and Use of Outer Space,

---

[12](...continued)
"the use of weapons of mass destruction, causing unnecessary human suffering, was in the past prohibited, as being contrary to the laws of humanity and to the principles of international law, by international declarations and binding agreements, such as the Declaration of St. Petersburg of 1868, the Declaration of the Brussels Conference of 1874, the Conventions of the Hague Peace Conferences of 1899 and 1907, and the Geneva Protocol of 1925, to which the majority of nations are still parties".

[13] Resolution no. 1(I) of 24 January, 1946.

[14] Italics added.

including the Moon and Other Celestial Bodies[15] prohibited the placing in orbit around the earth of any objects carrying nuclear weapons or any other kinds of weapons of mass destruction, the installation of such weapons on celestial bodies, or their stationing in outer space in any other manner.[16] Also, the preamble of the Treaty on the Non-proliferation of Nuclear Weapons of 1968[17] expressed the desire of the international community for the "cessation of the manufacture of nuclear weapons, the liquidation of all their existing stockpiles, and the elimination from national arsenals of nuclear weapons". Moreover, nuclear weapons have been banned from whole regions in the world. Nuclear Weapon Free Zones have been established in Latin America and the Caribbean and in the Southern Pacific. A similar free zone will soon be established in Africa. Egypt, as already mentioned, has taken two universally supported initiatives that would ban nuclear weapons in the Middle East.[18]

V. The Threat or Use of Nuclear Weapons Violates Humanitarian Law

A. The *jus ad bellum*:

14. Article 2(4) of the Charter of United Nations prohibits "the threat or use of force against the territorial integrity or political independence of any state, or in any other manner inconsistent with the purposes of the United Nations." Further-

[15] Signed at London, Moscow and Washington on 27 January, 1967.

[16] Article IV.

[17] 7 *I.L.M.* 811 (1968).

[18] *Supra*, para. 3.

more, paragraph 7 of the Preamble of the Charter states that "armed force shall not be used, save in the common interest". Thus, the threat or the "first use" of force, including nuclear weapons, is illegal. This being a principle of international law does not need any further argument.

15. As for the legality of the "second use" of nuclear weapons, it must be determined in the light of legal considerations of the exceptions to the principle of non-use of force taking into consideration the characteristics of such weapons. These exceptions are Security Council enforcement actions under Chapter VII of the Charter of the United Nations, and self-defence under Article 51 of the Charter. In both cases the use of nuclear weapons would be illegal. It is not imaginable that the Council would resort to the use of nuclear weapons with all their indiscriminate and immense disastrous effects which would surely upset, *and not maintain*, international peace and security. Furthermore, the use of nuclear weapons would not respect, in particular, the rule of proportionality which is an important condition for the exercise of the right of self-defence.

16. Consequently, the use of nuclear weapons, even when the use of force becomes permissible, is illegal because such use of force has to correspond to the requirements of the *jus in bello*.

B. The *jus in bello*:

17. *The prohibition of indiscriminate attack against civilians and their property:* As a rule of international law, "[t]he civilian population ... as well as individual civilians, shall

not be the object of attack."[19] It is especially forbidden "[t]o destroy ... the enemy's property, unless such destruction ... be imperatively demanded by the necessities of war".[20] The attack or bombardment, by whatever means, of towns, villages, dwellings, or buildings which are undefended is prohibited.[21] Equally, in "bombardments all necessary steps must be taken to spare ... buildings dedicated to religion, art, science, or charitable purposes, historic monuments, hospitals, and places where the sick and wounded are collected ..."[22] Furthermore, it is also prohibited to attack civilian hospitals, convoys of vehicles, hospital trains, specially provided vessels on sea, aircraft exclusively employed for the removal of wounded and sick civilians, the infirm and maternity cases, or the transport of medical personnel and equipment.[23] In order to ensure respect for and protection of the civilian population and civilian objects, it is required that the parties to the conflict at all times "distinguish between the civilian population and combatants and between civilian objects and military objectives and accordingly ... direct their operations only against military objectives."[24] Thus, indiscriminate attacks are prohibited.[25]

[19] Article 52(2) of the First Protocol Additional to the Geneva Conventions of 12 August 1949, and Relating to the protection of Victims of International Armed Conflicts of 1977.

[20] Article 23 (g) of the Hague Regulations Respecting the Laws of and Customs of War on Land annexed to Convention No. IV of 1907.

[21] *Ibid.*, Article 25.

[22] Article 27 of the First Protocol of 1977.

[23] Articles 18, 21 and 22 of the Geneva Convention Relative to the Protection of Civilian Persons in Time of War, of 12 August 1949. United Nations, *Treaty Series*, Vol. 75, p. 366. Also, Articles 12, 22 and 23 of the First Protocol of 1977.

[24] *Ibid.*, Articles 48 and 51(2).

Therefore, the law has provided that such protected objects shall be marked with a distinctive emblem to make them obvious for the enemy. Hence, the law does not leave room for the use of weapons which might have an incidental effect on civilian and protected targets.

18. Whereas, by the inherent qualitative and quantitative characteristics of their effect, nuclear weapons necessarily have cataclysmic and indiscriminate effects and cannot distinguish between combatants and non-combatants and between protected and unprotected objects, and are expected to cause incidental loss of civilian life, injury to civilians, damage to civilian objects, or a combination thereof, which would be excessive in relation to the concrete and direct military advantage anticipated, their use cannot at all be legal.

19. *The prohibition against the use of weapons which render death inevitable or cause unnecessary suffering:* "The right of belligerents to the conflict to adopt means of injuring the enemy

---

[25](...continued)

[25] *Ibid.*, Article 51. According to Article 51 indiscriminate attacks are:

"4. ...

c) those which employ a method or means of combat the effects of which cannot be limited as required by this Protocol;

and consequently ... are of a nature to strike military objectives and civilians or civilian objects without distinction.

5. Among others, the following types of attacks are to be considered as indiscriminate:

a) an attack by bombardment by any methods or means which treats as a single military objective a number of clearly separated and distinct military objectives located in a city, town, village or other area containing a similar concentration of civilians or civilian objects; and

b) an attack which may be expected to cause incidental loss of civilian life, injury to civilians, damage to civilian objects, or a combination thereof, which would be excessive in relation to the concrete and direct military advantage anticipated."

is not unlimited."[26] This rule imposes on the belligerents the obligation to refrain from cruel or treacherous behavior. As far as weapons are concerned, since the nineteenth century this humanitarian principle has been embodied in two rules: one forbids the use of poisons, while the other prohibits the use of weapons capable of causing superfluous injuries. Nuclear weapons fall in the latter category.

20. The Laws of the Hague[27] and Geneva[28] provide that it is especially forbidden to employ weapons, projectiles and material and methods of warfare of a nature to cause superfluous injury or unnecessary suffering. It goes without saying that the enormous blast waves, air blasts, fires, residual nuclear radiation or radioactive fallout, electromagnetic impulses and thermal radiation, which are primary effects of use of nuclear weapons, cause extensive "unnecessary suffering".[29]

21. *The obligations to respect principles of proportionality and humanity:* According to the First and Second Geneva Conventions of 1949, it is prohibited to attack establishments and mobile medical units of the Medical Service, hospital ships[30] military hospital ships and establishments ashore[31] in any circumstance.

---

[26] Article 22 of the Regulations of 1907; the preamble of the Declaration of St. Petersburg of 1868 expresses the same idea.

[27] Article 23 (e) of the Regulations of 1907.

[28] Article 35(2) of the First Protocol of 1977.

[29] Also *cf.* General Assembly resolution no. 1653 (XVI) of 24 November, 1961.

[30] Articles 19 and 20 of the Geneva Convention for the Amelioration of the Condition of the Wounded and Sick in Armed Forces in the Field, of 12 August 1949. United Nations, *Treaty Series*, Vol. 75, p. 62.

[31] Articles 22 and 23 of the Geneva Convention for the Amelioration of the Condition of Wounded, Sick and Shipwrecked Members of Armed Forces at Sea, of 12 August 1949. *Op. cit.*, Vol. 75, p. 116.

However, by reason of the inherent nature of the effects of nuclear weapons such protected objects will nevertheless be indiscriminately attacked.

22. *The prohibition against causing widespread, long-term and severe damage to the environment:* It is prohibited to use "methods or means of warfare which are intended or may be expected to cause damage to the natural environment". It is equally forbidden to carry out "[a]ttacks against the natural environment by way of reprisals".[32] This makes the use of nuclear weapons, even in reprisal, unlawful because its use, even if it were not used with the intent to attack the environment, it will definitely harm the environment.

23. *The obligation not to prejudice the health or survival of the population:* Belligerents are prohibited from the use of "methods or means of warfare" which may be expected to cause widespread, long-term and severe damage to the natural environment, and thereby prejudicing the health or survival of the population.[33] Since nuclear weapons are sure to cause such negative effects to the environment and the health or survival of human beings they are covered by that prohibition.

24. *The obligation to distinguish between combatants and non-combatants:* The distinction between combatants and non-combatants is one of the most important victories and accomplishments of international law since the early beginnings of the nineteenth century. Any authorization of nuclear weapons will definitely cause this principle to collapse.

---

[32] Article 55 of the First Protocol of 1877.

[33] *Loc. cit.*

25. The Declaration of St. Petersburg of 1868[34] stipulated that "the *only legitimate object* which States should endeavour to accomplish during war is to *weaken the military forces* of the enemy",[35] thus, ordering belligerents to always distinguish between combatants and non-combatants. By virtue of the customary rule contained in the Declaration, the use of nuclear weapons against civilians is illegal.

VI. The Threat or Use of Force Violates Modern International Law

A. The Law of Human Rights:

26. Modern international law has internationalized human rights on a full-blown scale. The well being and welfare of the human person, now considered the centre of the universe, is the main concern of most international organizations including the United Nations. International law has given great attention to the development of the individual and his rights. Human health, civil, political, economic, and social rights, etc., being the subject of many conventional as well as customary rules, form an integral part of modern international law. The threat or use of nuclear weapons, or even the least approval of them, would destroy the whole structure of this modern design of international law based on the respect for the human person, rendering that law devoid of cohesion.

27. *The right to life:* "Every human being has the inherent right

[34] Singed at St. Petersburg 29 November - 11 December 1868.

[35] Italics added.

to life."[35] Although it is expected that in times of war human beings, whether military or civilians, might perish, the killing of human beings should not exceed the limits of lawful acts of war. It should be recalled that Article 40 of the Fourth Geneva Convention stipulates that "[i]t is prohibited to order that there shall be no survivors". Although an order to use nuclear weapons does not have to state that "there shall be no survivors", it is an indirect order to do so by virtue of the immense devastating and killing capabilities of such weapons. It is submitted that the use of nuclear weapons necessarily cause wide-scale deaths, thus depriving human beings of the right to life.

28. *The right to enjoy the highest attainable standard of physical and mental health:* Everyone has a right to "the enjoyment of the highest attainable standard of physical and mental health."[37] It is needless to say that the adverse effects of nuclear explosions on the human health are immeasurable and irreparable. Two generations continue to suffer from the Hiroshima and Nagasaki bombs. It is noteworthy that existing modern nuclear weapons may be hundreds of times more powerful and damaging than those thrown over Japan in 1945. The use of nuclear weapons is an absolute impediment to the "enjoyment of the highest attainable standard of physical and mental health" by human beings.

B. The prohibition against genocide or crimes against humanity:

29. According to Article II of the Convention on the Prevention

---

[36] Article 6(1) of the International Covenant on Civil and Political Rights. United Nations, *Treaty Series*, Vol. 999, p. 171.

[37] Article 12 of the International Covenant on Economic, Social and Cultural Rights. *Ibid.*, p. 3.

and Punishment of the Crime of Genocide of 1948[38] any acts "committed with the intent to destroy, in whole or in part, a national, ethnical, racial or religious group" is considered genocide. Therefore, any use of nuclear weapons, which are capable of destroying large parts of a population, against civilian population would constitute a crime against humanity, and thus is illegal.

C. The International Law of Environment:

30. Every State has, in accordance with the Charter of the United Nations and the principles of international law, the responsibility to ensure that activities within their jurisdiction or control do not cause damage to the environment of other States.[39] More emphatically, Principle 26 of the Stockholm Declaration of 1972 declared, *inter alia*, that:

> "Man and his environment must be spared the effects of nuclear weapons and all other means of mass destruction."

31. Equally, Article I of the Convention on the Prohibition of Military or Any Other Hostile Use of Environmental Modification Techniques (ENMOD) of 1977[40] provides that it is prohibited "to engage in military or any other hostile use of environmental modification techniques having widespread, long-lasting or severe effects as the means of destruction, damage or injury to any other State Party." It also prohibits States from assisting, encouraging or inducing any State, group of States or interna-

[38] United Nations, *Treaty Series*, Vol. 78, p. 278.

[39] Principle 21 of the Stockholm Declaration of the United Nations Conference on the Human Environment of 1972, 11 *I.L.M.* 1416 (1972); and Principle 2 of the Rio Declaration, 31 *I.L.M.* 851 (1992).

[40] United Nations, *Treaty Series*, Vol. 1108, p. 151.

tional organization to engage in activities contrary to the provisions of paragraph 1 of Article I. Thus, the Convention prohibits the use of nuclear weapons which are weapons the use of which has "widespread, long-lasting or severe effects" on the environment.

D. Use of nuclear weapons violates territorial sovereignty:

32. States have, in accordance with the Charter of the United Nations and the principles of international law, the responsibility to ensure that activities within their jurisdiction or control do not cause damage to the environment of the *other States or of areas beyond the limits of national jurisdiction.*[41] However, electromagnetic impulses resulting from a nuclear explosion at an altitude of 100 k.m. may travel to up to 1100 k.m.[42] Radioactive contamination may also reach the neighbouring countries of the State in which the explosion occurred. This being so, the use of nuclear weapons violates the territorial sovereignty of other States which is a fundamental principle of international law and the principle good neighbourliness provided for in Article 74 of the Charter of the United Nations. In the Nuclear Tests Case, Australia maintained that by carrying out atmospheric nuclear tests France was, *inter alia,* in violation of the territorial sovereignty of Australia. It was claimed that "fall-out had been recorded on Australian territory".[43]

---

[41] Principle 21 of the Stockholm Declaration of 1972 and Principle 2 of the Rio Declaration of 1992.

[42] 1987 WHO Report, para. 13 at p. 11 (French).

[43] *Nuclear Tests Case (Australia* v. *France), Judgment of 20 December 1974, I.C.J. Reports 1974*, p. 253, para. 19 at p. 258.

VII. Submissions

A. Competence and admissibility:

33. It is submitted that:

- the General Assembly of the United Nations is competent to request an advisory opinion from the Court on the subject-matter of the request; and
- the Court is competent to give, and should give, its advisory opinion on the question addressed to it.

B. The illegality of the threat or use of nuclear weapons:

34. It is submitted that the threat or use of nuclear weapons undermine the whole design of disarmament measures directed at prohibiting their development, acquisition and use since 1945.

35. It is submitted that:

A. The threat or use of nuclear weapons is contrary to principles and rules of general international law, and constitutes a direct violation of the Charter of the United Nations. In particular it violates the following basic principles:

1. The prohibition of threat or use of force in international relations;
2. The obligation to respect the requirement of proportionality in cases of legitimate use of military force;
3. The prohibition against genocide or crimes against humanity;

4. The obligation to respect the territorial sovereignty of other States.

B. The use of nuclear weapons is contrary to principles and rules of the international law of armed conflicts. In particular it violates the following basic principles:

1. The prohibition to attack civilians;
2. The prohibition against disproportionate harm to civilian population;
3. The obligations to respect principles of proportionality and humanity;
4. The obligation to distinguish between combatants and noncombatants;
5. The prohibition against the use of weapons which render death inevitable or cause unnecessary suffering;
6. The prohibition against causing widespread, long-term and severe damage to the environment;
7. The obligation not to prejudice the health or survival of the population.

C. The use of nuclear weapons is contrary to principles and rules of the international law of human rights. In particular it violates the following basic principles:

1. The right to life;
2. The right to enjoy the highest attainable standard of physical and mental health;
3. The right to a clean and safe environment.

LETTER DATED 20 JUNE 1995 FROM THE AMBASSADOR OF QATAR, TOGETHER WITH WRITTEN STATEMENT OF THE GOVERNMENT OF QATAR

EMBASSY OF
THE STATE OF QATAR
LONDON
Ambassador's Office

سـفارة دولـة قطـر
لنـــدن

1 South Audley Street,
London W1Y 5DQ
071 493 2200

H.E. Dr. Eduardo Valencia-Ospina
Registrar
International Court of Justice
Peace Palace
2517 KJ The Hague
The Netherlands

London, 20 June 1995

Re: Legality of the threat or use of nuclear weapons (Request for Advisory Opinion)

Sir,

The Embassy of the State of Qatar presents its compliments to the International Court of Justice and, in pursuance of Article 66, paragraph 2, of its Statute and with reference to the Order of the Court dated 1 February 1995, has the honour to transmit to you herewith the Written Statement of the Government of the State of Qatar covering the points which it would like to submit for the consideration of the Court in the court's advisory proceedings on the "Legality of the threat or use of nuclear weapons" requested by Resolution 49-75K of the General Assembly of the United Nations dated 15 December 1994. The Written Statement is signed by Qatar's representative, H.E. Dr. Najeeb Al-Nauimi, Minister Legal Adviser.

Please accept, Sir, the assurance of my highest consideration.

Ali M. Jaidah

WRITTEN STATEMENT OF THE GOVERNMENT OF QATAR

20 June 1995

Legality of the Threat or Use of Nuclear Weapons (Request for Advisory Opinion)

1. The question upon which the advisory opinion of the Court has been requested was laid before the Court by a letter dated 19 December 1994 addressed by the Secretary-General of the United Nations to the Registrar. In that letter the Secretary-General informed the Court of Resolution 49/75K adopted by the General Assembly of the United Nations on 15 December 1994, in accordance with Article 96, paragraph 1, of the Charter of the United Nations, by which it had decided to submit one question to the Court for advisory opinion[1]. The text of that Resolution is as follows:

> "*The General Assembly*,
> *Conscious* that the continuing existence and development of nuclear weapons pose serious risks to humanity,
> *Mindful* that States have an obligation under the Charter of the United Nations to refrain from the threat or use of force against the territorial integrity or political independence of any State,
> *Recalling* its resolutions 1653 (XVI) of 24 November 1961, 33/71 B of 14 December 1978, 34/83 G of 11 December 1979, 35/152 D of 12 December 1980, 36/92 I of 9 December 1981, 45/59 B of 4 December 1990 and 46/37 D of 6 December 1991, in which it declared that the use of nuclear weapons would be a violation of the Charter and a crime against humanity,
> *Welcoming* the progress made on the prohibition and elimination of weapons of mass destruction, including the Convention on the Prohibition of the Development, Production and Stockpiling of Bacteriological (Biological) and Toxin Weapons and on Their Destruction and the Convention on the Prohibition of the Development, Production, Stockpiling and Use of Chemical Weapons and on Their Destruction,

[1] Resolution 49/75 was adopted by 78 votes to 43, with 38 abstentions.

> *Convinced* that the complete elimination of nuclear weapons is the only guarantee against the threat of nuclear war,
> *Noting* the concerns expressed in the Fourth Review Conference of the Parties to the Treaty on the Non-Proliferation of Nuclear Weapons, that insufficient progress had been made towards the complete elimination of nuclear weapons at the earliest possible time,
> *Recalling* that the General Assembly, convinced of the need to strengthen the rule of law in international relations, has declared the period 1990-1999 the United Nations Decade of International Law,
> *Noting* that Article 96, paragraph 1, of the Charter empowers the General Assembly to request the International Court of Justice to give an advisory opinion on any legal question,
> *Recalling* the recommendation of the Secretary-General, made in his report entitled "An Agenda for Peace", that United Nations organs that are authorised to take advantage of the advisory competence of the International Court of Justice turn to the Court more frequently for such opinions,
> *Welcoming* resolution 46/40 of 14 May 1993 of the Assembly of the World Health Organisation, in which the organisation requested the International Court of Justice to give an advisory opinion on whether the use of nuclear weapons by a State in war or other armed conflict would be a breach of its obligations under international law, including the Constitution of the World Health Organisation,
> *Decides*, pursuant to Article 96, paragraph 1, of the Charter of the United Nations, to request the International Court of Justice urgently to render its advisory opinion on the following question: 'Is the threat or use of nuclear weapons in any circumstance permitted under international law?'".

2. Article 65, paragraph 1, of the Statute of the Court is the basis of the jurisdiction of the Court in advisory proceedings. It provides as follows:

> "The Court may give an advisory opinion on any legal question at the request of whatever body may be authorised by or in accordance with the Charter of the United Nations to make such a request".

WRITTEN STATEMENT OF THE GOVERNMENT OF QATAR

Article 96, paragraph 1, of the Charter of the United Nations provides that:

> "The General Assembly or the Security Council may request the International Court of Justice to give an advisory opinion on any legal question".

By virtue of each of these provisions, the Court is competent to give advisory opinions "on any legal question". The question now before the Court is a legal one since the matter lies in the interpretation of the Charter of the United Nations. Also the question raises legal issues of profound importance concerning general international law, customary international law, and the law of the United Nations System.

The wording of Article 65 of the Statute - "The Court may give an advisory opinion" - does not impose upon the Court the duty to comply with a request, *i.e.* the Court has the discretionary power to give an advisory opinion[2]. But the Court has held that "the reply of the Court, itself an 'organ of the United Nations', represents its participation in the activities of the Organisation, and, in principle, should not be refused[3]". Furthermore, "[i]t is well settled in the Court's jurisprudence that... the Court should entertain the request and give its opinion unless there are 'compelling reasons' to the contrary[4]". The fact that some States have denied the Court's jurisdiction does not qualify as such a reason. As the Court has held, "As the opinions are intended for the guidance of the United Nations, the consent of States is not a condition precedent to the competence of the Court to give them[5]". The question before the Court is not a political matter[6] even though the present request for an advisory opinion has a political background. Furthermore it does not relate to the conduct and position of a number of States which own nuclear weapons and have not given their consent to the Court's jurisdiction[7]. When it examines the propriety of giving an opinion on the present subject,

---

[2] *Western Sahara, ICJ Reports* 1975, p. 21. *Application for Review of Judgment No. 333 of the United Nations Administrative Tribunal, ICJ Reports* 1987, p. 31.

[3] *Interpretation of Peace Treaty with Bulgaria, Hungary and Romania, First Phase, Advisory Opinion, ICJ Reports* 1950, p. 71.

[4] *Privileges and Immunities, ICJ Reports* 1989, p. 191.

[5] *Ibid.*, p. 188-189.

[6] See S. Rosenne, *The Law and Practice of the International Court*, Second Revised Edition, Martinus Nijhoff Publishers, 1985, No. 283, pp. 702-708.

[7] *Eastern Carelia*, 1923, *PCIJ Series B*, No. 5, pp. 27-28.

the Court will be unable to find any circumstance or compelling reason to refuse an advisory opinion.

Since the request of the General Assembly clearly falls within the advisory jurisdiction of the "principal judicial organ of the United Nations", the Court should give an opinion on the legal question submitted to it by the General Assembly. The present advisory proceedings appear "comme un instrument de 'diplomatie préventive', un moyen privilégié pour la Cour de désamorcer les tensions et de prévenir les conflits en disant le droit"[8].

Dr. Najeeb Ibn Mohammed Al-Nauimi
Minister Legal Adviser
Representative of the Government of the State of Qatar

---

[8] *Les ressources offertes par la fonction consultative de la Cour internationale de Justice. Bilan et perspectives*. Communication de M. Mohammed Bedjaoui, Président de la Cour internationale de Justice au Congrès des Nations Unies sur le droit international public, New York, 14 mars 1995.

LETTER DATED 22 JUNE 1995
FROM THE PERMANENT REPRESENTATIVE
OF THE MARSHALL ISLANDS TO THE UNITED NATIONS,
TOGETHER WITH WRITTEN STATEMENT
OF THE GOVERNMENT OF THE MARSHALL ISLANDS

Republic of the Marshall Islands

Permanent Mission to the United Nations

220 East 42nd Street, 31st Floor • New York, New York 10017
Tel. (212) 983-3040 • Fax. (212) 983-3202

22 June, 1995

Excellency,

I have the honor to submit the following statement for consideration in the advisory opinion requested in the United Nations General Assembly resolution 49-75 K on the question:

"Is the threat or use of nuclear weapons in an circumstance permitted under international law?"

It is with great regrets that this statement is submitted late and though this in no way indicates a lack of concern from the Marshall Islands on this very important and critical topic, I wish to convey my profuse apology, indeed, for this late submission and hope that Your Excellency will see fit in the consideration of the question confronting not only the Court but the international community as a whole as well.

I extend, Excellency, my personal and warmest regards.

Laurence N. Edwards
Permanent Representative

Mr. Mohammed Bedjaoui
President of the International Court of Justice
Peace Palace
2517 KJ, The Hague
Netherlands

International Court of Justice Advisory Opinion on the Threat or Use of Nuclear Weapons

1. Introduction

The Republic of the Marshall Islands is the easternmost group of islands in Micronesia, located approximately 1500 miles south southwest of the Hawaiian Islands in the Central Pacific between 4° and 14° N. latitude and 160° E. longitude. Though the 34 low-lying atolls and 1225 islands and islets totaled 70 sq. miles of land area, its ocean area spans some two (2) million square kilometers.

The history of the Marshall Islands is one that is marred by foreign domination. The first contact with European occurred between 1529 and 1568 when Spanish navigator Alvaro Saavedra sighted them. In 1878 Germany signed a commercial treaty with the Chiefs and in 1885 Marshall Islands were declared a German protectorate and remained so until 1914. In 1914 the Marshall Islands were seized by the Japanese and, in 1919, along with other islands in the region, the group became a League of Nations Mandate administered by Japan. The post World War II era ushered in a new "administration" when the Marshall Islands became a part of the United Nations Trust Territory of the Pacific Islands administered by the United States of America.

It was during the last administration that the two of the northwest most atolls in the Marshall Islands were used as a testing ground for at least sixty six nuclear bombs. The residents of these atolls were informed of this decision three months after it was made by the Joint Chiefs of Staff in Washington, DC. When objection was raised later on the decision by the American public and media, one of the US Presidential Advisors quipped: "There are only 90,000 people out there...Who gives a damn?"

Some of these explosions were up to a thousand times greater than the nuclear bombs detonated in Hiroshima and Nagasaki. In fact, one of the biggest hydrogen bomb ever tested in the world, code name Bravo, was detonated on March 1954. This testing had significant effects on the health and environment of the islands. As such, not only did this very issue catapult the islands into the international arena, but it gives the Marshallese people a special interest in the question of the legality of the threat or use of nuclear weapons.

2. The threat of nuclear weapons

The Republic of the Marshall Islands, as one having first hand experience of the devastating impacts of nuclear weapons, believes that the threat of use of nuclear weapons continues. Despite the end of the Cold War nuclear weapon States have yet to relinquish their policies of first use, use and threat of use of nuclear weapons. These issues are very central to not only the basis of Marshall Islands foreign policy, but are the very cornerstone by which the United Nations objective for World Peace can be achieved.

The Marshall Islands believes the international community must address this issue now.

3. Nuclear Testing

The devastating impact of nuclear testing in the Pacific from 1946 to 1992 has contaminated numerous islands and large areas of ocean with radiation. In the Marshall Islands alone, several islands were vaporized and others have been declared unihabitable for thousands of years. The United States Atomic Energy Commission has called the Marshall Islands "by far one of the most contaminated areas in the world." Health related problems, such as miscarriages, still births, cancers, birth deformities and other radiogenic diseases have increased by up to 10 times pre-testing levels in areas closest to the testing."

A description of some of these effects is given by Ms. Lijon Eknilang from Rongelap Atoll:

"I was seven years old at the time of the Bravo test on Bikini. I remember that it was early in the morning that I woke up with a bright light in my eyes. I thought someone was burning the house. Soon after we heard a big loud noise, just like thunder and the earth started to move...Then came the fallout. It was while and to us kids we thought it was white soap powder. The kids were playing in the powder and having fun, but later on everyone was sick and we couldn't do anything...My cousin died of tumor cancer in 1960. In 1972 I had another cousin die of leukemia. Two of my sisters have had thyroid surgery. I have had seven miscarriages and still births. There are eight other women on the island who have given birth to babies that look like blobs of jelly. Some of these things we carry for eight months, nine months. There are no legs, no arms, no head, no nothing. Other children are born who will never recognize this world or their own parents. They just lie there with crooked arms and legs and never speak. Already we have seven such children..."

When such problems were substantiated, the residents of the atolls believed to have been affected were relocated; these include Bikini, Enewetak, Rongelap and Utirik. The people of Bikini remain nomads to this very day residing several hundreds miles on a much smaller island than Bikini Atoll itself. Land is considered security in the Marshall Islands customs and mores; in fact, a common saying: "Without land a Marshallese is nobody–it is land that makes a person Marshallese" suggests the Bikinians and Ronglapese are nobody as long as their lands are un-inhabitable. The severity of this assertion can only be understood by the Bikinians particularly as several of their islands were vaporized during the tests.

With a total of only 170 square kilometers of land, Marshall Islands views this loss of lands as a severe renting of their cultural fabric. This will never be compensated for by those responsible for their destruction. Mindful of this land constraint of land for settlement, Ronglapese and Bikinians have been forced to reside in the two urban centers as well. This in turn has cause a major concern as Ebeye, on of these urban centers, a 66 acre island, housed a population of 9500. This is a major increase from its original population of 16 persons.

Other social problems associated with the overcrowding in the urban centers are major hurdles to overcome today.

4. Marshall Islands interest in nuclear disarmament

Given its extensive first hand experience with adverse impacts of nuclear weapons, Marshall Islands decision to ratify the Nuclear Non-Proliferation Treaty this year is understandable. This objective of the treaty of "the cessation of the manufacture of nuclear weapons, the liquidation of all their existing stockpiles, and the elimination from national arsenals of nuclear weapons" is wholly consistent with Marshall Islands' foreign policy of peaceful co-existence as well as with the overarching goal of the international community to achieve global peace.

5. The need for a Court Opinion

Given the legal and moral implications attached to the use or threat of use of nuclear weapons, and owing to the international community's goal for achieving global peace, this issue presses on the need to consider it in legal terms to achieve total consistency with other legally binding agreements which call on the international community to a common undertaking.

On this very issue, Marshall Islands is of the view that the use or threat of use of nuclear weapons is not permitted under international law. It has been clearly documented in the Marshall Islands and elsewhere where nuclear testing has been conducted that the severity such tests have on health and the environment are enormous.

prohibit the use of poisonous substances, the use of indiscriminate weapons, the causing of unnecessary or aggravated suffering, the causing of long-term damage to the environment and the violation of neutral territory.

The threat to use nuclear weapons is also prohibited under the United Nations Charter (Article 2 (4)) which prohibits the threa or use of force, and the Nuremberg Principles, which prohibit the planning and preparation of a war crime. Furthermore, there is a general principle of law that the threat to use unlawful force is itself unlawful. Any acts committed in contravention to these internationally legally binding conventions require equal legal corrective measures.

6. Conclusion

As a victim of nuclear weapons that Marshall Islands has witnessed first hand the unprecedented and awesome destructiveness of such weapons. The Marshall Islands kindly requests the Court to confirm the commonly held view that the threat and use of nuclear weapons is both inhumane and illegal.

WRITTEN COMMENTS
OF THE GOVERNMENT OF THE SOLOMON ISLANDS

Request by the United Nations General Assembly for an Advisory Opinion on the Legality of the Threat or Use of Nuclear Weapons

Further Written Observations Submitted by the Government of Solomon Islands to the International Court of Justice

Government of Solomon Islands

20 September 1995

INTRODUCTION

1. On 20 June 1995 Solomon Islands submitted Written Observations to the International Court of Justice pursuant to the request by the UN General Assembly for an Advisory Opinion on whether the threat or use of nuclear weapons was in any circumstances permitted under international law. These brief Further Written Observations are now submitted by Solomon Islands in response to the Court's Order of 1 February 1995 fixing 20 September 1995 as the time-limit within which States and organisations having presented written statements may submit written comments on the other written statements.

2. Solomon Islands welcomes the fact that 28 members of the United Nations have submitted Written Observations, reflecting the importance of the question posed by the General Assembly. Since this number includes seven States which did not submit observations in the WHO request, a total of forty-two States have now submitted written observations in the two requests. Of these, an overwhelming majority have made submissions arguing against the legality of the use of nuclear weapons in any circumstances.

3. Solomon Islands has carefully considered all of the Written Observations submitted in relation to the General Assembly's request. They do not generally raise new issues or arguments beyond those addressed by States in their Written Observations in the WHO request. Accordingly, Solomon Islands refers the Court to its Further Written Observations of 20 June 1995 in the WHO Request, which apply *mutatis mutandis* to the issues and arguments raised by proponents of the legality of the use or threatened use of nuclear weapons in their written statements in the request. Solomon Islands also refers the Court and other States submitting written statements to the Annexes to its Written Observations in the WHO request, filed with the Court on 20 September 1994, which include all relevant General Assembly resolutions and documents relating to scientific aspects of its arguments.

4. In these Further Written Observations Solomon Islands wishes only to respond briefly to selected points made by these States, and reserves its right to respond in greater detail to these and other points during the oral phase envisaged by the Court.

5. Solomon Islands re-emphasises three introductory points. First, nothing it has read in the written statements submitted in the General Assembly's request alters its views on the procedural and substantive aspects of the question asked by the General Assembly, or on the need for the Court to address the substantive issues raised by the question. Second, concerning the scope of the question posed by the General Assembly request it is important to emphasize that:-

(a) the Court is not being asked to act as a legislator or to advise on the type of actions the nuclear weapon States should or should not adopt in international disarmament negotiations, but only to record that the use or threatened use of nuclear weapons would be a breach of international law; and

(b) that the Court is not being asked to advise on the possession of nuclear weapons, or on the policy of dissuasion or deterrence, neither of which Solomon Islands considers amounts to a threatened use of nuclear weapons.

6. And third, Solomon Islands reaffirms its view that the Court has never before been so acutely in a position to make a major contribution to the affirmation of the rule of law in international relations, and to uphold the necessity of the principle of non-contradiction in the global system of international law.

COMPETENCE

7. The General Assembly is clearly competent to make the request. No State has objected to the competence of the General Assembly to make the request.

8. The suggestion by certain States that General Assembly resolution 49/75K was adopted by a small number of States[1] and in controversial circumstances which reflected its political sensitivities is wholly irrelevant to the issue of competence or propriety (see e.g. France, pp. 4-13; the United Kingdom, paras. 2.4-2.11). Equally irrelevant is the implication in the view of the United Kingdom that the involvement of non-governmental organisations in lobbying efforts might in some way taint the *bona fides* or legitimacy of resolution 49/75K (the United Kingdom, Written Observations, paras. 1.2 and 2.2-2.3). The resolution was adopted by a majority of the members of the United Nations which voted on the matter. As previously stated by Solomon Islands (WHO, Further Written Observations, para. 2.5), its support for the request, and its observations on these matters, are driven by interest in clarifying and confirming the rules of international law in relation to the use and threatened use of nuclear weapons has rather more to do with the past (and current) activities of certain nuclear weapons States in and around its territory. The efforts of responsible non-governmental organisations, including associations of professional physicians, in raising public awareness and contributing to the processes of international law are to be welcomed.

PROPRIETY

9. Only a small number of States have expressed the view that the Court should, for the

[1] France notes that only about 40% of the United Nations' 185 members supported resolution 49/75K; a similar statistical analysis, which Solomon Islands does not consider to be a particularly authoritative way of making arguments in international law, would reveal that only about 3% of the UN members would consider the use of nuclear weapons to be lawful in any circumstances: see *infra*. para. 18.

first time in its history, exercise its discretion and refuse to give the Advisory Opinion requested. An overwhelming majority of the 185 members of the United Nations have either expressed a clear preference in favour of the Court's giving the Advisory Opinion or have not opposed it on grounds of propriety or otherwise. These include not only *all* developing countries submitting Written Observations, but also a significant number of developed countries (Ireland, Japan, New Zealand, Sweden). At least one nuclear-weapon State (China) has not objected to the propriety of the Court's giving an opinion on the substance. Just seven States (Finland, France, Germany, the Netherlands, Russia, the United Kingdom, the United States) objected on the grounds of propriety. Two States which objected in relation to the WHO request (Australia and Italy) have not objected in relation to the General Assembly request. In this context the burden is again very much on these States to satisfy the Court with compelling reasons why an Advisory Opinion should not be given.

10. Solomon Islands has already set out its reply to the views of these States, indicating why there are no such "compelling reasons", and it refers to these here *mutatis mutandis* (WHO, Further Written Observations, paras. 3.3-3.27). The Court is competent to give and should give an Opinion on the legal question posed by the General Assembly. The following paragraphs restate Solomon Islands' position.

11. The Opinion requested is undoubtedly a "legal question".[2] It has been made to the Court as the principal judicial organ of the United Nations, and it invites the Court to contribute to the effective functioning of the United Nations system, and in particular that of the General Assembly within that system. The question posed by the General Assembly clearly falls within the objective and functions of the Charter of the United Nations, which embraces a broad range of activities relating to international peace and security, including the legality of the use or threatened use of force.

12. A substantial number of United Nations member States have voted in favour of Resolution 49/75 K requesting the Court to give an Advisory Opinion. No member of the UN has denied that the resolution was not validly adopted. Moreover, for the reasons set out below, contrary to the assertions by the United States (Written Statement, p.6) and France (Written Statement, pp.16-17), the request is appropriate and will help the General Assembly in its activities relating to international peace and security.

13. First, Solomon Islands reiterates the importance for the United Nations General Assembly to be advised by the Court on the legal status of the use of nuclear weapons. The Court, in accordance with its long standing and well-established practice, should give an Advisory Opinion on the question posed. As Egypt has

[2] Conditions of Admission of a State to Membership in the United Nations, Adv.Op., 28 May 1948, ICJ Reports 1947-1948, p. 61.

indicated, there are no compelling reasons which require the Court not to give an Advisory Opinion (Written Statement, p.5).

14. Second, the Opinion requested is of genuine importance for the General Assembly in the conduct of its activities related to the use of nuclear weapons. In line with the views expressed by Samoa (Written Statement, p.5) and Egypt (Written Statement, p.6), Solomon Islands considers that the Court's Opinion will, in concrete terms, enlighten the General Assembly in the conduct of its activities in promoting further negotiations on nuclear disarmament.[3] Contrary to the assertion of Finland (Written Statement, p.2), the Netherlands (Written Statement, p.4) and the United Kingdom (Written Statement, pp.19-20), the viability of existing achievements in the field of nuclear disarmament and non-proliferation would not be undermined by the Court giving an Opinion. In any event, the issues of legality of threat and use and disarmament are related but clearly distinguishable. The ascertainment of the legal status of the use of nuclear weapons would allow the General Assembly to ensure that its activities are carried out properly and in a manner which takes fully into account the priority needs of the international community.

15. Third, Solomon Islands recalls that the political character which the question might have does not prevent the Court from giving an Opinion. The question put by the General Assembly relates to the compatibility of the threat and the use of nuclear weapons with international law. The General Assembly is therefore inviting the Court to address a legal question and carry out a task clearly within its judicial function. In this context, contrary to the assertions of some States (see France, pp.19-20 and Germany, p.2), the fact that the question has political implications is not in itself an obstacle to the competence of the Court.[4] It should also be added that in giving the Opinion the Court would not go beyond its judicial function and embark upon a legislative or policy-making course, as some States have suggested (France, p.19, Finland, p.1).

16. Fourth, it is for the Court to decide if a request for an Opinion fulfils the conditions of Article 96(2) of the United Nations Charter. There are no criteria other than those set forth in this provision which should prevent the Court from giving an Opinion. In this respect, the United Kingdom has misunderstood or even misinterpreted the practice of the Court (Written Statement, pp.9-18). The Court has obvious competence to give an Opinion.

17. Finally, Solomon Islands points out that the answer cannot be detrimental to on-going disarmament negotiations (quite the contrary). This should be clear enough from the successful indefinite extension in May 1995 of the 1968 NPT after the WHO and

[3] Western Sahara, Adv.Op., 16 October 1975, ICJ Reps. 1975, p.37.

[4] See Certain Expenses of the UN, Adv.Op., 20 July 1962, ICJ Rep. 1962, p.155.

General Assembly requests had been made. Rather, it is actions such as France's decision of 13 June 1995 to resume nuclear testing in the Pacific region and its explosion of a nuclear device on 5 September 1995 which are far more likely to be detrimental to on-going disarmament negotiations than an Advisory Opinion which the Court might render. These actions are incompatible with France's commitment of May 1995 to exercise "utmost restraint" on the conduct of nuclear tests following the indefinite extension of the 1968 Treaty on the Non-Proliferation of Nuclear Weapons and before the adoption of a comprehensive test-ban treaty in 1996.[5] It is actions such as this which "pourrait avoir qu'une incidence négative sur les négotiations en cour pour parvenir à un monde plus sur." (France, p. 16, para. 7). If a State is able to act thus in time of peace, Solomon Islands feels all the more concerned about what might happen in time of war or armed conflict. Solomon Islands maintains its hope that no further tests will take place before or after the Court gives this Advisory Opinion.

SUBSTANTIVE LEGAL ARGUMENTS

18. Whilst a small number of States have been silent or ambiguous on the substantive aspects of the question posed by the General Assembly, the overwhelming majority have expressed the view that any use or threatened use would be contrary to international law. Of the twenty-eight States submitting Written Observations just six (France, Italy, the Netherlands, Russia, the United Kingdom, the United States) have been prepared to positively express the view (or suggest) that the use of nuclear weapons could *in any circumstances* be lawful.

19. The arguments put forward in favour of the legality of the use or threatened use of nuclear weapons in relation to the request for an Advisory Opinion by the General Assembly are essentially the same as those relied upon in arguments made pursuant to the WHO request. Solomon Islands has already responded to these arguments in some detail (see WHO, Further Written Observations to the WHO request, paras. 4.2-4.96). Since these Further Written Observations address most of the arguments made in favour of the legality of the use of nuclear weapons, these should be referred to and treated as applying *mutatis mutandis* to the arguments in favour of legality put forward by some States in responding to the General Assembly's request.

20. Not wishing to burden the Court with an unnecessary restatement of its earlier Written Observations, Solomon Islands recalls only its essential submissions:-

(a) international humanitarian law prohibits the use of nuclear weapons even if it does not do so expressly: UN General Assembly resolutions prohibiting their use provide evidence of this rule, and the opposition of certain States to these

[5] Principles and Objectives for Disarmament for Nuclear Non-Proliferation and Disarmament, para. 4(a), NPT/CONF.1995/L.5.

resolutions cannot limit a prohibition based upon customary obligations; with regard to the numerous agreements which regulate their possession, testing, dissemination or elimination, as well as the hitherto unsuccessful efforts to conclude an agreement prohibiting their use, they show that possession or elimination of nuclear weapons is beginning to be regulated but do not indicate that their use would be lawful (on these points see Solomon Islands' WHO Further Written Observations, paras. 4.25-4.42, 4.55-4.71);

(b) risks of general nuclear war,[6] effects on civilians, violations of the neutrality of third States, and of genocide similarly indicate a general prohibition on the use of nuclear weapons (on these points see *ibid.*, paras. 4.8-4.9, 4.11, 4.45-4.53, 4.71);

(c) international law prohibits the use of nuclear weapons by reason of their effects (as weapons causing inevitable death and unnecessary suffering, poisoning or asphyxiation) (see *ibid.*, paras. 4.5-4.7, 4.4.13-4.23); and

(d) the rules of the 1977 First Additional Protocol, as well as those relating to the protection of the environment and human rights, are applicable to any use of nuclear weapons; the rules on self-defence, reprisals or the protection of the environment do not justify their use (see *ibid.*, paras. 4.44, 4.73- 4.74, 4.81, 4.88-4.93).

20. Since one State - the United Kingdom - has referred extensively in its Written Observations to some of the arguments made by Solomon Islands in its WHO Written Observations, it is appropriate for Solomon Islands to respond briefly to some of those British arguments. Some of these are also taken up in the Written Observations of other States arguing in favour of the legality of the use or threatened use of nuclear weapons.

21. According to the United Kingdom, the American, British and French declarations on the inapplicability to nuclear weapons of the 1977 First Additional Protocol reflect a general agreement of all States participating in the Geneva Diplomatic Conference on the negotiation of the Protocol. The United Kingdom submits that Solomon Islands is wrong to affirm that there was no consensus in favour of the views expressed in the declarations of these three States.

[6] Solomon Islands' view that the use of tactical nuclear weapons would lead to wholesale nuclear war appears to be shared by President Francois Mitterrand of France: "On ne peut pas se servir des armes tactiques. S'en servir, c'est déclencher la guerre nucléaire ... [Les armes tactiques] ne peuvent pas être l'appendice d'un armement conventionnel, et donc d'une guerre classique" (16 October 1986, cited in J. Attali, Verbatim II (1986-1988), Fayard, 1995, at pp. 180 and 197).

22. Solomon Islands considers that the United Kingdom's interpretation is quite wrong and should not be relied upon or endorsed by the Court. No support has been put forward to challenge the fact that:

- at the time of the first session of the Conference, several States wanted the Conference to address nuclear weapons (*ibid.*, para. 3.48); and

- at the close of the Conference, India and Rumania stated their view that various provisions of the First Additional Protocol did apply to nuclear weapons (*ibid.*, para. 3.50).

23. The United Kingdom apparently considers that the declarations of these two countries were ambiguous. It is difficult to see why. Without entering into the precise details of the language used, Solomon Islands believes that these two declarations were enunciated in a clear manner and were not the subject of any greater or lesser discussion than the declarations of the United States, the United Kingdom and France. The Conference was equally silent about both sets of declarations. No greater weight or authority attaches to either set, each of which, in effect, neutralises the other, i.e. there was no consensus. If, as is claimed, a genuine consensus had existed as to the inapplicability of the First Additional Protocol to the use of nuclear weapons, the Court may well ask why France felt impelled to state and restate in its Written Observations to this request for an Advisory Opinion that

> "elle n'avait pas discerné, lors de la conférence, un consensus suffisant sur la portée exacte des obligations qu'assumeraient en matière de dissuasion les Etats qui accepteraient d'être liés par cet instrument." (France, Written Observations, p. 33)

24. Declarations on the inapplicability of the First Additional Protocol were made subsequently by certain members of NATO, at the time of their ratification of the Protocol, and these were not subject to objections by other parties to the Protocol. However, each of these were in the nature of "declarations": they were not "reservations". Since only reservations can modify the legal effect of a treaty (1969 Vienna Convention on the Law of Treaties, Arts. 2(d) and 21(1)), and only reservations have legal effects vis-a-vis States that do not object to them (*ibid.*, Art. 21(3)), these "declarations" cannot be considered as modifying in any way the nature or scope of the legal obligations set forth in the Protocol (on this point see Solomon Islands, Written Observations, para. 3.99).

25. Moreover, the United Kingdom (Written Observations, para. 3.55) and other nuclear weapon States accept that those provisions of the First Additional Protocol which reflect customary international law are applicable to the use of nuclear weapons. Without prejudice to Solomon Islands' other arguments, this important point should be reaffirmed by the Court. The Court should also take the opportunity to restate the relevance of the Martens Clause and its applicability to the use of nuclear weapons. Contrary to the views of at least one nuclear weapon State ("As to nuclear weapons

the 'Martens Clause' is not working at all ... today the 'Martens Clause' may formally be considered inapplicable", Russia, p. 13), Solomon Islands shares the views of the International Law Commission that the Martens Clause

> "now has the status of general international law. In essence, it provides that even in cases not covered by specific international agreements, civilians and combatants remain under the protection and authority of the principles of international law derived from established custom, from the principles of humanity and from the dictates of public conscience."[7]

26. The Court might also wish to consider the scope and effect of the rule set forth in the 1868 Declaration. The United Kingdom (Written Observations, para. 3.65) considers that it is wrong to argue for the illegality of the use of nuclear weapons on the basis of the prohibition on weaponry which renders death inevitable (as envisaged by the 1868 St Petersburg Declaration). The United Kingdom's view is that the Declaration was only intended to prohibit the use of explosive bullets directed against individuals. It was not, it is claimed, intended to protect persons who find themselves close to the explosion from incidental injury or fatality, and it is not applicable to explosive artillery shells.

27. Solomon Islands does not share this narrow interpretation of the Declaration, and has already explained why the principles underlying it are applicable to nuclear weapons (Written Observations, para. 4.5). The rule in the St Petersburg Declaration, enunciated in an abstract and non-specific manner, is to be interpreted more broadly. The humanitarian basis of the Declaration of St Petersburg requires that the prohibition on the use of weapons which render death inevitable is entirely separate and independent from the particular rule enunciated *in concreto* on the prohibition of the use of explosive bullets. The principles of the Declaration, as set forth in its preamble, apply to all types of weapons, including nuclear weapons.

28. The St Petersburg Declaration recognises the necessities of warfare whilst safeguarding certain fundamental principles of humanity. In this perspective, an explosive bullet prohibited by the Declaration is to a non-explosive bullet what a nuclear weapon is to a conventional weapon. A bullet is aimed at a single combatant. A shell is aimed at a group of combatants. That which is prohibited for an "individual" projectile (the explosive bullet) need not necessarily be prohibited for a "collective" projectile (bombs or shells), if the latter does not have the same effects as the explosive bullet. If, however, a nuclear weapon (or an explosive shell) has on a group of combatants the same effect as that produced by an explosive bullet on a single combatant, it will, it is submitted, be prohibited as contrary to the principle and rule set forth in the St Petersburg Declaration.

29. The United Kingdom (Written Observations paras. 3.68, 3.70 and 3.73) further

---

7 United Nations, Report of the International Law Commission on the work of its forty-sixth session, 2 May - 22 July 1994, GAOR A/49/10, p. 317.

challenges Solomon Islands' view that the use of nuclear weapons will necessarily entail indiscriminate effects and heavy losses in the civilian population, leading to a possible genocide. Solomon Islands has sufficiently responded to this argument in its Written Observations (Paras. 4.8-4.11, 4.45-4.48) and does not feel the need to develop its arguments further.

30. With regard to the applicability and effect of human rights and environmental instruments to the use of nuclear weapons, Solomon Islands is pleased to note that most of the nuclear weapons States have now seen fit to address the relevance of these rules which impose fundamental norms of international law. The fact that the views of States do differ widely does present the Court with an opportunity to address an issue of fundamental importance.

31. As to the effect of international human rights instruments, a number of States have sought to challenge the arguments of Solomon Islands and others as to the applicability of such instruments to the use of nuclear weapons. Discussion has in particular focused on the right to life (see the United Kingdom, paras. 3.99-3.108; the Netherlands, para. 27; the United States, pp. 42-46). Solomon Islands agrees that the right to life is not to be construed in these instruments as absolute, and has never suggested otherwise. Two points need to be made. First, the Netherlands, the United Kingdom etc now appear to accept the relevance and applicability of human rights instruments to the use of nuclear weapons. They do not deny that these instruments apply in times of war as in times of peace, at least insofar as the right to life is concerned. Second, they appear to agree that death from an *unlawful* use of a nuclear weapon would also violate Article 6 of the 1966 ICCPR (and similar provisions in regional instruments).

32. Since, in Solomon Islands' view, it is difficult to conceive of any situation in which the use of nuclear weapons could be lawful under international law (i.e. because it had no radioactive effect likely to endanger civilian health or third States, would not be detrimental to the environment, and would conform to all rules of international humanitarian law) it follows that the use of nuclear weapons will also violate the right to life. The inevitability and extent of, and risks relating to, such a violation justifies the view that any use of a nuclear weapons would constitute "a crime against humanity" (on this point see Written Observations, paras. 3.36 and 3.42).

33. As to the effect of international environmental agreements, it is clear that most States share Solomon Islands' views on the interpretation and applicability of the *jus in bello* rules concerning the protection of the environment, as well as the applicability of general international environmental law to the use of nuclear weapons.

34. Some states have sought to show that environmental agreements are not relevant to this issue because they have not "in terms" addressed the use or threat of use of nuclear weapons (the United Kingdom, para. 3.111), or because an implicit conclusion to that effect would lead to absurd results (the United Kingdom, para.

3.112 allowing, for example, the 1987 European Convention for the Protection of Pet Animals to be construed as prohibiting the use of nuclear weapons) or because they are not expressly or impliedly applicable in armed conflict or to nuclear weapons per se (the United States, p.34). These arguments miss the point. As with human rights, the unlawful use of nuclear weapons which causes environmental damage beyond that which is permitted by international environmental agreements or customary law would also violate those instruments or rules (in particular those relating to the protection of resources whose use would be significantly impaired as a result of contamination by radioactive material, i.e. biodiversity, watercourses, the marine environment). Moreover no response has been given by these States to the view of Solomon Islands and others that international environmental agreements and customary law in the field apply in times of war as in times of peace, unless their provisions direct otherwise (Written Observations, paras. 4.37-4.41) and that accordingly contamination arising out of any use of a nuclear weapon would violate the provisions of applicable treaties. This view has been applied in express terms by the International Law Commission in respect of its own 1994 Draft Articles on the Law of Non-Navigational Uses of International Watercourses: in the Commentary, but not in the Articles themselves, it is stated that "the present articles themselves remain in effect even in time of armed conflict" (*ibid.*, p. 316, para. 3). (Report of the ILC on the work of its forty-sixth session, 2 May - 22 July 1994, GAOR, 49th session, Supplement No. 10). The Court should, in respect of environmental agreements, apply the same presumption in favour of applicability where an instrument is silent.

SUBMISSIONS

35. Accordingly, and for the reasons set out in its earlier Written Observations and in these Further Written Observations it is submitted that the International Court of Justice should give an Advisory Opinion which states:

(A) that the General Assembly is competent to request an Advisory Opinion from the International Court of Justice on this question, and that the Court is competent to and should give an Advisory Opinion on the question submitted;

(B) that any use of a nuclear weapon by a State would violate its obligations under international law as reflected in the rules of international law concerning methods and means of warfare (*jus in bello*) and neutrality, ALTERNATIVELY that any use of nuclear weapons must not violate applicable rules of international law concerning methods and means of warfare (*jus in bello*) and neutrality;

(C) that any use of a nuclear weapon by a State would violate its obligations under international law as reflected in the rules of international law for the protection of human health and the environment and fundamental human rights, ALTERNATIVELY that the use of nuclear weapons must not violate applicable rules of international law for the protection of human health and the environment and fundamental human rights;

(D) that any use of a nuclear weapon by a State would constitute a crime against humanity, ALTERNATIVELY that the use of nuclear weapons in violation of international law constitutes a crime against humanity; and

(E) that any use by a State of a nuclear weapon gives rise to its international responsibility, ALTERNATIVELY that the violation by a State of its obligations under international law relating to the use of nuclear weapons gives rise to its international responsibility; and

(F) that any threat of use by a State of a nuclear weapon would, by consequence of the illegality of actual use, be prohibited under international law.